Jakob Böhme

Jacob Behmen's theosophick philosophy unfolded:

In divers considerations and demonstrations

Jakob Böhme

Jacob Behmen's theosophick philosophy unfolded:
In divers considerations and demonstrations

ISBN/EAN: 9783337775490

Printed in Europe, USA, Canada, Australia, Japan

Cover: Foto ©ninafisch / pixelio.de

More available books at **www.hansebooks.com**

Jacob Behmen's
𝕿𝖍𝖊𝖔𝖘𝖔𝖕𝖍𝖎𝖈𝖐 𝕻𝖍𝖎𝖑𝖔𝖘𝖔𝖕𝖍𝖞
UNFOLDED;
IN DIVERS
Confiderations and Demonftrations,

SHEWING

The Verity and Utility of the feveral Doctrines or Propofitions contained in the Writings of that Divinely Inftructed AUTHOR.

ALSO,

The Principal Treatifes of the faid Author Abridged.

And *Anfwers* given to the Remainder of the 177 *Theofophick Queftions*, Propounded by the faid *JACOB BEHMEN*, which were left unanfwered by him at the time of his Death.

As a help towards the better Underftanding the *Old* and *New Teftament.* Alfo what Man is with refpect to Time and Eternity.

Being an Open Gate to the Greateft Myfteries.

By *EDWARD TAYLOR.*

With a fhort Account of the LIFE of *JACOB BEHMEN.*

LONDON, Printed for *Tho. Salusbury* at the Sign of the *Temple,* next the *Inner-Temple Gate* in *Fleetftreet.* 1691.

THE
Publishers Preface
TO THE
READER.

WE do with all Respects and Candidness, present you with the Works of one who was a true and faithful Labourer in his Day; his Pains hath been bestowed, in watering and cultivating, what was sown by another Hand. And having imployed his Time and Talent well, is entered into his Lord's rest; enjoying that Peace which must necessarily result from a faithful Performance of a Trust given by our great Lord.

We can give but a very short account of the Author, but hope this Publication may produce a fuller, from some of his Personal Acquaintance. As we are informed, it was one Mr. Edward Taylor an English Gentleman, the latter part of his time he lived at Dublin, in much Privacy and Retirement, where he made this his Work and Business. He died at Dublin about the Year 1684 His Manuscripts were preserved by the Care of a Friend, and brought over hither, where they have lain some time in Private; But considering how much we are beholding to our Predecessors for their great Pains taken to inform us, their Writings Published being a Testimony of their good Will to Posterity : And also considering the Labour taken by this good Man for a Publick Benefit, we could not in Justice to the Author deceased, nor with the respect we owe to all Mankind as our Brethren, suffer so Good and Profitable a Work, to Perish under our Custody; without incurring the guilt of Ingratitude, if not of Inhumanity. We have hereby indeavoured to set this Light in Publick View, and that it may prove of use to direct the Course of any, in this dark and dismal Passage, towards the Haven of Rest, is what we earnestly desire and seek. He was a Devout Christian, a Sincere Protestant, living in the Commu-

(a 2) nion

The Publishers Preface to the Reader.

nion *of the Church of England, and earnest he was in vindicating the Truth, abhorring a bare outside Formality, which only hath the Name and Profession, but wants the Nature, Life and Power of Religion.*

He was not for making Rents and Divisions amongst Men, by setting up a new Sect, or having a People called after his Name, thereby to gain Applause, or to make himself great. But made it his Business to Learn and Improve, in the Knowledge and Understanding of the Divine and Natural Mysteries.

We are very apt to regret the loss of worthy Instruments, such as have been raised up in an Extraordinary Manner, and Eminently Qualified above their Brethren, hoping that if we had enjoyed their good Converse, we might have greatly benefited and improved thereby: without doubt they have a great Happiness that injoy such a Benefit and improve it.

But we must consider that they are but Men, and are indeed but Instruments or Vehicles, and it is very rare but that the Purity and Excellency of Truth conveyed by them, receives some Shadow or Soil from the Medium. Their chief work hath been to direct us to the Fountain of Wisdom, which is open at all times to all Persons, ready to inform all that truly seek Wisdom there: And from this Universal Fountain every one receives according to their Capacities.

And accordingly it is required, that every one should Communicate or Prophecy according to their proportion of Faith received; now Faith is every particular Man's Evidence, and not another's.: Thus, although one may have a larger Measure, or more Mysterious, yet there is no disharmony, but all tends to the Benefit of the whole. And teaching all Wisdom, that every one may be presented perfect in Christ.

Although we cannot Comprehend all Truth, let us remain humble sincere Searchers, and in due time we shall be rewarded with her Treasures; when the Captious, Disdaining, Mocking Spirits, shall reap their Reward, that is to be perfected in that Principle they have given themselves up to as Servants.

The Writings of the Divinely inspired Jacob Behmen, *called the Teutonick Philosopher, have been by many received with great Satisfaction, and have contributed towards the Extricating their Minds out of those Labyrinths and Difficulties, wherein Evil Practice and Opinions (kept up by Custom) had involved them.*

The greatest Objection raised against the said Writings have been their Abstruseness, and Uncouth Expressions, making them almost impossible to be understood; which now is answered and removed; Here being a Person raised up to bear Testimony to their Truth, who by delivering his Sense in more usual and familiar words, it is hoped may have render'd them clear.

In

The Publishers Preface to the Reader.

In his *Considerations on the Subject*, *Matter and Scope of the Writings of* Jacob Behmen, He doth (*from the Types*, *Figures and Sacrifices under the Law*, *from things we are most conversant with through the whole Creation*, *from Heaven and Earth*, *and from Man himself*) *Demonstrate the Truth of his Doctrine to be well-grounded*, *upon the uncontroulable Maxims of Confessed Theology and Philosophy*.

The 177 *Theosophick Questions which were propounded by* J. Behmen, *of which he lived to Answer but* 13, *and part of the* 15*th*, *the rest of them lying unanswered*, *till this Good Man being spirited thereto*, *took up the task*, *and hath performed it as an able Workman*, *Answering the Remainder*, *and hath given us some Meditations on part of the said Questions and Answers*: *All treating of the highest Mysteries*, *and yet what we (in Duty) ought to be most conversant about*.

His Extracts of several of the Works of Jacob Behmen *were intended for the use of those that had not*, *or could not procure the said Writings*, *and also to give a Summary Account of the whole*: *which may be as an Introduction*, *opening the Gates to us*, *and promote a further Communication of these great and most useful Truths*.

The Apostle Paul *preached to the* Athenians *the Knowledge of that God whom they ignorantly adored*: *Even so these Writings serve or tend to teach us by plain Demonstration what we*, *like the* Athenians, *are too Ignorant of*. *It is written* God is one, *which certainly is as true as where it is said*, *There are three that bear Record in Heaven*.

It is written, Our God is a confuming Fire. *And yet said to be*, Heb. 12. 29. *Light*, *and Love*, *and in him is no Darkness at all*, *that he is meek*, *merciful*, *of everlasting kindness*, *and that fury is not in him*.

It is also written, God fware by two Immutable things, in which it Heb. 6. 18. was impoffible for God to lye. *And because he could Swear by no greater*, *he Sware by himself*, *That Blessing he would Bless* Abraham : *And Curse him that Cursed* Abraham. *Here are two Principles clearly express'd*, *and* Gen. 12. 3. *both called Immutable* : *The one* Wrath and Fury, *and a* confuming Fire; *The other* Love, Meekness *and* Light *ineffable*.

Had Man stood in his Primitive State totally resigned to the Divine Love, *he had not known the Principle of Wrath*, *but it had remained more hidden than the bitterness of the Root is in the most pleasant Fruit*. *But when Man was fallen into the state of Evil and Good*, *the Infinite Love of God descends in order to restore him*, *and then sets before him Blessings on the one hand*, *and Cursings on the other*. *These great Truths are at large treated of and explained*, *and by them we are Taught what Use and Improvement to make thereof*.

How can we tell what God's Mercy is, *till we come to know him that*

(b) *is*

The Publishers Preface to the Reader.

is Merciful; And what Chrift's Merits are, till we know Chrift in us and him Crucified? For if we content our felves with an Hiftorical Knowledge, it is to be feared it will be attended with an Hypocritical Obedience. The Law that all true Chriftians ought to fquare their Actions by, is the New Commandment; elfe they are not known to be Chrift's Difciples.

All thofe worthy Inftruments that have Taught or Writ from the Holy Aointing, directed their Hearers or Readers, to him that is the true Teacher, that they might receive their Knowledge from the fame Root with themfelves. And then unto fuch they wanted no Epiftle of Recommendation, they being their Epiftle written with the Spirit of the Living God, not in Tables of Stone, but in the fleshly Tables of the Heart, known and read of all Men.

To fuch the Language of the Scriptures comes to be more clear, and can difcern the Correction, Inftruction and Comfort held forth in them, and how they are able to furnifh the Man of God to every good Work. Alfo why there is no Ability in them to furnifh any man elfe, but as they Convert, and become new Men.

The great Affair of Man's Happinefs depending upon the Converfion of his Will; for as the firft Man by turning his Will from God into this World from the Unity and Harmony he at firft was placed in (and fo was truly Honourable) into Multiplicity, Selfhood, Luft and Enmity: thereby became an abominate to God's Holinefs, attracting a Beftial Body, and a Mind darkned, Ignorant and Eftranged from God.

It is real Refignation that brings a Death upon Self-hood, and that muft continually be performed, that the Enmity being mortified, the refigned Will may become an Inftrument in God's Hand, to be agitated thereby; for his Servants we are whom we yield Obedience unto.

Here arifeth the ftrife and warfare in Man, The Corrupt Will in Selfhood accounts it folly and madnefs to fubmit to Death, when the Pleafures and Voluptuoufnefs of this VVorld might be lived in and injoyed. But the refigned fees, that as at firft it precipitated Man from that Happy ftate in which he was placed; fo the tendency and end thereof is to fill us with Eternal forrow and mifery. Thus it is to become Fools that we may be made VVife, and Poor that we may be made Rich; as having Nothing, yet poffeffing all things;

" This is the State which Reafon's fplendid Schools,
" Do nominate the Paradife of Fools.

Whatever fpecious Pretences to Religion may be made by any, though very fair and beautiful to fhew, where this corrupt Will in Self-hood is unmortified; and the Path of Refignation not trod, that Religion is vain, deceitful

The Publishers Preface to the Reader.

ful and destructive. As the Prophet Isaiah declared in the Name of the Lord; For as much as this people draw near me with their Mouth, and with their Lips do honour me, but have removed their Heart far from me, and their fear towards me is taught by the Precepts of Men: Therefore the Wisdom of their Wisemen shall perish, and the Understanding of their Prudent Men shall be hid. Our Saviour reciting this place of the Prophet saith, But in vain do they Worship me, teaching for Doctrines the Commandments of Men. The Wisdom of this World which is Foolishness with God, existing in the perverted Will of Man, which hath broken it self off from God, and stands upon its own bottom; by this Wisdom the World neither can know or worship God. The Wisdom of God in his Servants stands in an humble Resignation of themselves to the Divine Love, in order to a Regeneration of their Wills, which is not effected but by slaying this opposite Will in which stands the Enmity in order to know a new Life generated; and as long as Truth and Error, Light and Darkness are in this World, so long must and will this Warfare be continued; happy is he that goes off a Conqueror, for his Garland or Crown is sure to him. And as the World by Wisdom knew not God, so hath it fared likewise in respect to the inquiries made concerning Nature. From hence it is the Apostle Paul gives a caution, To beware lest any Man should spoil them through Philosophy and vain Deceit, after the Tradition of Men, after the Rudiments of this World, and not after Christ.

An empty and vain Philosophy hath been introduced and kept up in the World, by Men of corrupt minds estranged from God, and therefore ignorant of Nature: For it is as impossible truely to know Nature, separate and removed from God, as it is to know God in the Wisdom of this World, or truely to worship him, with a Heart removed far from him.

What hopes was left after the miserable Fall of Man, when God cursed the Earth for Mans sake, but only the Descent of God, or the Incarnation of Jesus Christ; that inspoken Word of Life, in order to a happy Restoration and Renovation? For as all things were made by this Eternal Word, so all things are upheld by it: This is the Healer of our Wounds, and Repairer of our Breaches. This Word is declared by Moses, and by the Apostle Paul to be near us, even in our Hearts and in our Mouths, that we need not say, Who shall ascend into Heaven, or descend into the Deep to fetch it? This was the Rock in the Wilderness. This is the Stone of Fire in Ezekiel. The Stone with seven Eyes upon it in Zechariah. The White Stone with the New Name, in the Revelation. This is the Salt which we ought to have in our selves. This is the Water and Spirit whereof we must be Born again.

King Solomon was indued with great Wisdom, and may properly be said

Isa. ch. 29. 13, 14.

Mat. ch. 15. v. 29.

1 Cor. ch. 3. v. 9.

Deut. 30. 14. Rom. 10. 8.
1 Cor. 10. 4.

The Publishers Preface to the Reader.

to have been an Eminent Philosopher; take his Description of Wisdom, and where it is to be found.

Wisdom ch. 7. She is the Breath of the Power of God, and a pure influence flowing from the Glory of the Almighty : Therefore can no defiled thing fall into her. And being but one she can do all things : And remaining in her self she maketh all things new : And in all Ages entring into holy Souls, she maketh them Friends of God and Prophets. All good things together came to me with her, and innumerable Riches in her hands. And a greater than Solomon saith, Seek ye first the Kingdom of God, and his Righteousness, and all these things shall be added to you.

This Certainly is not only our Duty, but the great Affair most worthy our Enquiry and Industry. That Work which Man alone is capacitated for, by reason of his noble Extract, and that which is alone a suitable reward to render him truely happy.

It is this Work and Wisdom, that the Writings of Jacob Behmen, and these following, are conversant about; laying the Foundation deep, firm and solid ; and thereupon raising a regular and noble Building.

Here is described at large our Malady and Remedy, both with respect to Time and Eternity; for the Instruction and Teaching of those he calls his School-fellows, and to the perusal of the said Writings, we recommend the Candid Reader. And shall conclude with a Testimony concerning the Writings of Jacob Behmen *from an Ingenious and Learned Hand.* "Whatso-
" ever the thrice great Hermes delivered as Oracles from his Prophetical
" Tripos; or Pythagoras *spake by Authority*; or Socrates debated ; or A-
" ristotle affirmed ; yea whatever Divine Plato Prophesied, or Plotinus
" proved ; this and all this, or a far higher and profounder Philosophy is
" (I think) contained in the Teutonicks Writings. And if there be any
" friendly Medium which can possibly reconcile those Ancient Differences
" between the Nobler Wisdom, which hath fixt her Palace in Holy Writ,
" and her stubborn Handmaid, Natural Reason, this happy Marriage of
" the Spirit and the Soul, this wonderful consent of Discords in one Har-
" mony we owe in great measure to Teutonicus *his Skill.*

" Only let not the Non or Misunderstanding of the most rational Reader
" (if not a little sublimed above the Sphere of common Reason) be im-
" puted as a fault to this Elevated Philosopher, no more than 'twas to the
" Divine Plotine, whose highest Notions many, even of his own School, after
" much Study were not able to reach.

The way to profit in reading these Writings is to be possest with patience, our Minds standing in singleness and simplicity, and in this frame of Mind, to seek diligently, pray earnestly, and to resign up our Wills intirely to the

Guidance

The Publishers Preface to the Reader.

Guidance and *Conduct of the Divine Love.* *Importunity and Industry often prevails to the obtaining the desired End, when Sloth and Negligence meets with Disappointments and Shame.* Let us humble our selves under the sense of our Misery, and submit to the mortifying our corrupt Wills, and proceed on to Experience a Separation or cleansing from all filthiness of the Flesh, and more secret defilements of the Spirit, through the Power and Energy of the Heavenly Fire, the Divine Life, the Breath or Word of God: That knowing a Death unto Sin, we may also know a Life unto Righteousness, which in the true Heavenly Process being offered up to God as an acceptable Sacrifice, a permanent, fixed and immortal State may be manifest, where there shall be no more going forth for ever. If these following Sheets contribute in some measure towards the directing and assisting of any, especially the honest Industrious Searcher, it will greatly rejoice the Persons concerned; it being their end and design in the present Publication.

Rev. 3. 12.

Farewel.

Some

Some Words used by Jacob Behmen *explained near to his deep Sense.*

A*byss*, is an Infinity peculiar only to each of the Three Principles.

Amass, is a Spirit or Will bringing it self into substance, compaction or manifestation.

Anguish, is the third Form of the seven Properties of the Eternal Nature, made of the two first Forms, and making the Sulphurous Spirit.

Centrum or *Centre*, is the Flash standing in every Will to make an opening. Three Principles, *Ch.* 14. *v.* 67.

Christ, by the word Christ is meant the inward new Man in the Spirit of Christ, understood inwardly.

Element, call'd the one or holy Element, is of or according to the second Principle generated-Eternally out of the Eternal Nature or great Mystery, which are according to the first, but where-ever they generate the holy Element there is Paradise.

Ens, the proper or peculiar Being or Essence, (Good, or be it Evil) of a thing.

Eternal Nature, is of the first Principle, and is that in which standeth two Kingdoms; one, the pure Virgin Wisdom of God, the one holy Element, the cause of the four Elements and Stars: The other, the severe fierce wrath: According to which God calleth himself a consuming Fire. It is therefore the great Mystery.

Expressed word comprizeth all Creatures Visible and Invisible.

Fiat, the Eternal speaking Word or Creating Power proceeding from the Freewill of the Abyss. Also the desire of the Soul taking the power of the holy Love Tincture, and makes it Essential.

Flagrat, or sudden fright, terror, shriek, flash, the severing the two Principles of Light and Darkness; resembling that in Thunder and Lightning, Gunpowder, *&c.* The pregnant Eccho of the sound of Eternity, speaking (by Magical Firebreath) Love or Anger; Life, in the Light; Death, in the Darkness. Which is called the Salnitral Flagrat.

Idea, is the *Ens*, which with Man first is, and then known: But we wrong God unless we say, it is, because God seeth it.

Incensive, a Divine Sparkle, captiv'd so as can only glimmer, not shine forth.

Magia, there are two *Magia*'s, one of the Unity, the other of the Multiplicity, or Astral Powers. And two *Magi* in Man, the Spirit of God, and Reason, into the latter the Devil easily insinuates.

Majesty, the Light of the Glorious Son of God, the second Principle, according to which only God is called God, for according to the first, *viz.* the Fathers Property, he is not called God, but a consuming Fire.

Lubet, a Longing Delight or *Beneplacitum*. In God, it is the free pregnant will to Manifestation in Nature and Creature; without which all had been an Eternal stilness. The *Lubet* in Man, is the moving will to Good or Evil.

Mysterium Magnum, that out of which all Visible and Invisible Concreates proceeded; it is of the first Principle. *Vide* Eternal Nature.

Out-birth, the visible, palpable, mortal part of this World call'd the Anger-fire.

Salniter,

Salniter, is that which in the Sulphur is awakened by the heat arising into a Flagrat out of the Brimstony, Watry and Earthy Properties, whereby the Properties are Explicated.

Satban, is meant the Spirit of Error, and not always a Creaturely Devil, but the Property of such an Erroneous Spirit.

Salitter, (call'd) Divine *Salitter*; represented by the Earth, but like the pure Heaven; in it are moving, springing Powers, producing all manner of Divine Trees, Plants, &c. with Heavenly Colours, Smells, Tasts, whereof this Worlds Trees, Gold, Silver, precious Stones, &c. are hard, dead, dark shadows. But this *Salitter* and *Mercurius*, (i.e.) Divine *Mercurius*, is the Food of Angels and Holy Souls.

Sophia, the true noble precious Image of Christ, viz. the Wisdom of God, the Tincture of the Light.

Source, the original quality or essential property to Love and Anger, Light and Darkness, both according to time and Eternity.

Ternarius, or number three in the Language of Nature the Divine Birth in the six Forms of Nature, which are the six Seals of God.

Ternary (call'd) *Ternarium Sanctum*, holy Flesh or holy Substance, or Corporizing of Angels and holy Souls.

Tincture, is in Angels and Glorified Saints the Virgin Love-fire. In Man that which *Adam's* Fall caused almost wholly to disappear. In Vegetables, Animals and Minerals their Vertue, Vitality, or Life, Spirit and Power.

Turba, is taken for a fierce Wrath-fire, which destroyeth a corruptible Body. Sometimes for horrid Tempests or Hellish Blasts, general Contagions, awakened by common Sins, call'd *Turba Magna*. Sometimes for the Eternal Wrath-fire, which swalloweth up an Evil Spirit without a Body; and may be called *Turba Maxima*.

I. *The seven Spirits of God, or powers of Nature, as they shew and manifest themselves in Love and Anger, both in the Heavenly and Hellish Kingdom, and also in the Kingdom of this World; not Extracted out of the* Mysterium Magnum, *but Transcribed page 22.*

Anger		Hellish		World		Earthly Kingdom	
	1. Astringent, Desire.		Hardness, Cold, Covetousness.		Cold, Hardness, Bone, Salt.		
	2. Attraction or Compunction of Sense.		Compunction, Envy.		Poyson, Life, Growth, Sences.		
	3. Anguish or Mind.		Enmity.		Sulphur, Perceivance, Pain.		
Love	4. Fire or Spirit.	Heavenly	Pride, Anger. Love-fire, Meekness.		Spirit, Reason, Desire. Venus-sport, Lifes, Light.		
	5. Light or Love desire.		Divine Joy.		Speaking, Crying, Distinguishing.		
	6. Sound or Understanding.		Heaven.		Body, Wood, Stone, Earth, Metal, Herb.		
	7. Body or Essence.						

This was received from the Author *Jacob Behmen* in such a Form by *Abraham Van Someerveldt*.

II. *The Ten Forms of Fire.* *Extracted out of the Answer of the First of the Forty Questions of the Soul.*

Form 1. THE Eternal Liberty (having, and) being in it self, the Will. Signified by *Sem*.
Form 2. The being Desirous. Signified by *Arphaxad*.
Form 3. The sharp drawing, causing the Opposite Will. Signified by *Salah*.
Form 4. The Flash of Lightning, caused by the Liberty, and causing the Anguish. By *Eber*.
Form 5. The Eternal Nature, or great Mystery, whence the two Kingdoms proceed. Signified by *Peleg*.
Form 6. The two Principles, of Fire and Light. *Regu*.
Form 7. The *Magia*, making its own Looking glass, as Life, is of Fire and Water. By *Serug*.
Form 8. The *Turba*, that breaketh the outward Life, Strength and Omnipotence. *Nahor*.
Form 9. The Virgin Tincture, Love-fire, Life of Angels and Holy Souls. Signified by *Terah*.
Form 10. The Entrance into the Holy * *Ternary:* Corporifing of Angels and Holy Souls.

* Which is the holy Earth, or holy Flesh. Signified by Abram.

III. *The Three Principles are,*

Principle 1. THE Spring or Fountain of Darkness.
Principle 2. The Vertue [or Power] of Light.
Principle 3. The Outbirth [generated] out of the Darkness by the Power of the Light.

Represented by Similitudes, viz.

1. Man's Soul, giving Reason and Thoughts, signifieth the Father.
2. The Light shewing the Power of the Soul, and how to direct it, representeth the Son.
3. The Mind resulting from this Light, and governing the Body, resembleth the Holy Ghost.

1. The Darkness in us, which longeth after the Light, is the First Principle.
2. The Vertue of the Light, whereby we see Intellectually, is the Second Principle.
3. The longing Power proceeding from the Mind, and that attracteth or impregnateth it self, whence groweth the Material Body, is the Third Principle.

There is an inclosure, knot or stop between each Principle.
See Chap. 7. of the Book call'd, *The Three Principles,* Vers. 21, 22, 23.

A Preface to the Book of Extracts,

AND

The following Confiderations by way of Enquiry into part of the Scope of the Writings of *Jacob Behmen.*

THE Extracts of the Aurora was intended for the particular ufe of one only, without his purpofe of proceeding farther in the other Books, or imparting that, as can hardly efcape any ones obfervation.

And tho' more be done than was at firft defigned, yet o o little is done, and with too many defects.

The proceedings in it, like as of a Traveller through a fpacious Territory, hath been to comprehend and report the varieties there, according to the degree of ability, intentnefs and capacity of the paffenger.

Or as one admitted into exquifite Gardens, deckt with plenty of all curious flowers, &c. fills his hand with a few of thofe he beft knows, or moft admires, according to what skill he hath.

Or as one at a Royal Feaft, feeds only on what his appetite moft relifheth.

Where the Writer hath contracted below the fublimity of the fubject, the Reader may with fome eafe fupply that defect by recourfe to, and confulting the bleffed Authors Books themfelves.

A   *To*

The Preface.

To make them truly conspicuous were the work of a divinely irradiated Expositor, not of an abridgement: And thereto to adapt the minds of (but) the Sons of Wisdom is the Prerogative of the God of Wisdom; for it would bring down Paradise as near us, as mortals could bear so sweet a neighbourhood.

Prayer might help us to power, to see (as it were) the voice of the Author J. B. *or rather of God in him; for that voice leads us thro' the creatures to the creating Word, convincingly demonstrating not only that God is, but what he is, what he is not, and what of him may be seen in every creature good, bad and mixt, angelical, rational, animal, vegetative, mineral, and the dark earth. Also in all Kingdoms paradisical, astral, elementary, and the dark abyss. And how he may be found in all things good, bad and mixt, in love and wrath. Also whence man fell, what and how low his fall, and how to be restored by Jesus Christ.*

And all this not a new Doctrine, but that which is substantial, orderly, firmly and naturally founded on the immovable principles, and uncontroulable maxims of confessed Theology and Philosophy, both sacred and natural.

Conside-

Confiderations by way of Inquiry and Search
INTO THE
Subject Matter and Scope of the Writings of the Divinely inftructed *JACOB BEHMEN*.

Section or Chapter I.

Of the two Principles Darkneſs and Light, whence are come evil and good, fiercenefs and meekneſs, anger and love.

1. TO begin with things neareft our outward fenfes, Palpable bodies, as Darkneſs, Cold, &c. They condenfe, croud, throng and fubftantiate; contrariwife Light and Heat rarifie, attenuate, make thin or fubtle, and actuate bodies adapted thereunto.

2. Both (whilft in due proportion) equally good and amicable, but in what time or place foever, either be extreamly prevalent and tyrannous, they become inftantly inimicitious and deftructive.

3. The confideration whereof, and confequences deducible thence, might caufe *J. A. Comenius* to be offended with *Campanella* for founding all productions on the conteft of two contrary Principles. Backing his difguft on *Grotius*'s Argument againft the Manichees; that of two contraries; deftruction might follow, but no augmentation.

4. But without ftrife, fprings no production; and without contraries, is no ftrife.

5. The two Principles of Light and Darkneſs cannot be faid to have beginning, but are coeternal; yet one (the Light) fwalloweth up the other as the day doth the night. — *What the two Principles unfevered are.*

6. The flagrat or operation of the darkneſs is God's anger; and the flagrat or manifeftation of the light is his principle of Love. Thefe two not fevered, make one triumphant Kingdom, wreftling to exalt the fublime joy of the holy, fweet, divine free will of God. — *An infinite perfect good.*

7. But after fevering, become two Worlds; viz. one the dark, cold, fierce, harfh, bitter, ftinging fire World. The other the delightful, loving, fweet, joyful, ravifhing, holy World; yet the holy World hath the Potence of the other, as its perfectly perpetual root or fountain. As the natural heat in mans body is of fuch abfolute neceffity and ufe, while moderated by due proportion of cold, for That is the food of the heat; but if either heat or cold domineer, it becomes rapacioufly ruinous. — *Root of evil.*

8. Now whereas it is faid above, that Darkneſs and Light are without beginning and

Considerations on the Scope of Jacob Behmen.

and coeternal. And it being true, that Angels as well as all other creatures had a beginning; it may be asked, how can it be true, and in what sense understood, that darkness should be without beginning, seeing the Holy Ghost saith, *God is light, and in him is no darkness at all* ? Also *what communion hath light with darkness* ?

1 *Joh.* 1. 5.
2 *Cor.* 6.14.

9. This, tho' it be cleared in the following part of this discourse, yet a little to open the way as we go, that the inquirer may not be offended, nor he that seeks occasion think he finds it; it is answered by way of explanation.

What the eternal darkness is not.

10. That it is not meant a Nescience, Defect or Ignorance, much less an evil in it self.

11. But by it is understood an Adumbration, like a dark crudity. An eternal original to substance; Might, potence, and essence. A center or root (austere and earnest) like a hot and cold fire, which principle is understood to be the Fathers property or first principle; according to which he is called a jealous or zealous God, and a consuming fire. A Power-world in its own property, secret, hidden in, and by the second principle of glorious Light and gracious Love; as the night by the day, or the wiek of a Candle by splendor of the light; but is manifested and awakened by severation of the second principle from it, in, or upon any separate unclean spirit or creature.

What is meant by eternal or original darkness.

12. For tho' it was from eternity, yet was in the highest harmony, and so is in God in eternity, undividable and inseparable from the most holy, spiritual Light-world and Love principle, yet in its own Abyss, and distinct property, it is as is above described.

13. This after severing from the Love-principle, is as the glowing fire, the flame whereof is extinct, in which principle the dark life burneth.

14. And must needs be called the first; because from it (as from an eternal root of living fire) the majestick splendor of glorious light is eternally generated, which so, is the second Eternal Principle.

15. Thus these two principles, in perfect unity (as in Eternity they are in God) are the One Only Highest, absolute Compleat Good; but where-ever-the Light is withdrawn, There is found a wrathful, fierce, evil spirit, creature, thing or world.

16. For further explanation we may observe, That the Holy Ghost, who saith (as above) *God is light, and in him is no darkness at all,* saith also, *a Fury is not in me.* And That yet (besides in many other places of the same and other Prophets) saith, b *For behold the Lord will come forth with fire, and with his Chariots like a whirlwind, and render his anger with fury, and his rebukes with flames of fire.* Again, c *When I shall execute Judgments in thee in anger and in fury, and in furious rebukes.*

a *Isa.* 27. 4.
b *Ch.* 66. 15.
c *Ezek.* 5. 15.
d *Micah* 1. 3.

17. But God's so doing, is called His d coming forth of His Place, and His strange work.

18. Thus is found, that the Astringent and Attracting Powers, by their contrariety, produce Anguish, That Anguish, a stinging, raging, pricking sense, not by Agent and Patient, but by violence and impatience: This Raging Spirit cannot deliver it self from the strong bands of the Astringency; whence by strugling, Heat is excited, the extremity whereof is fire.

19. The food of the fire is cold, as hath been said, or for want of it the heat and fire would fall into anguish; but Infinity hath no deficiency; therefore the fire by rarefaction breaths the Sullen Cold into the Liberty called Air, That again by condensation (being imposed upon by its father, the Cold) falls to water, which again by the inkindled Element is lickt up as its nutrition. Thus by an immutable Law and Chain of Causes, the Separators wisdom useth This great Machin to effect the parcels into an intire harmony.

CHAP.

Considerations on the Scope of Jacob Behmen.

CHAP. II. *A Description of the seven Fountain Spirits.*

1. BUT before we consider the three Worlds existing on the Foundation of the above two Principles, let the seven Fountain Spirits in the Divine Power of the Father be known; represented by the seven Lamps before the Throne. In the outward World by the seven Planets: Among us by the six days of the Creation, and One, the seventh of Rest; also by the seven simple Metals appropriated to the seven Planets; the seven Stars in the Revelation, with many the like important, and more than speaking demonstrations.

2. A method to be profitably used on this weighty Subject may be, First, To name, define and describe them severally and distinctly; Secondly, To demonstrate them in some measure to the Reason of Mankind, yea to the eye and senses; thereby to give assurance that the blessed Author *J. B.* in his discovery of them, was not beating the Air, but building on a Rock not to be shaken.

3. Definitions of the seven Fountain Spirits in the Divine Power of God the Father.

4. The Astringent, binding, piercing, compacting, knitting Power, secret and hidden in the Divine Power of the Fathers Salitter. A sharp power like Salt, whence existeth (in the evil and mortal part) a power locking up, as are the outward earth and stones. 1. *Astringent.*

5. An Attraction vanquishing the harsh Astringency, which is both sweet, mild, meek, and also bitter, the stirring of the desire and cause of life, whence also water originateth. Out of these two Fountain Spirits is the heart or Son of God generated, from Eternity in Eternity. Also of them (with the rest of the seven Spirits) is the Son of God, the Heart, by Eternal generation to all Eternity; as saith the Lord, *My Father worketh hitherto, and I work.* 2. *Attraction.*

6. The Bitter or Anguish Fountain-Spirit (a cause of the mind, senses and thoughts, a triumphing exalting of Joy to the highest degree to trembling in its own quality, it) forms all sorts of red colours in its own quality, in the sweet quality white and blew; in the astringent, green, dusky and mixt colours. But if it be moved too much, it kindleth the sweet and astringent, and all becomes a raging, tearing, stinging, burning poison; like the torment of a plague-sore: When enkindled in the Hellish Property, it extinguisheth the Light; perverteth the sweet quality into loathsom stink; the Astringent into sharp, dark, coldness, also sour, rank, bitter fierceness to all Eternity; when enkindled in the Heavenly power, it is the Spirit of the jealous, zealous, unquenchable wrath of God, as is in *Lucifer* and his Legions. 3. *Anguish.*

7. Heat, the true beginner of life, and of the true spirit of life, It kindleth all the qualities, generating the Light in them; whence exist the senses and thoughts. For when the bitter spirit (with the heat) passeth thorow the astringent; and the Sweet, mildly yielding passage; the two open gates (the eyes) are made. 4. *Heat producing light.*

8. The Holy Gracious Love kindled by the heat in the Sweet Quality. Here is all pleasant, ravishing sweetness, light and glorious, the fountain of eternal free, immense brightness of love. Here all Tongues stammer, Hands shake, Pens blot, and Hearts flame, that Taste, See, Hear and Feel it; even so *Amen.* 5. *Light producing love.*

9. The Tone or Sound of the Divine Word, whence is speech and language, also the singing of Angels, and opening the Divine Kingdom of Joy. Here all Colours, Beauty and Ornament is seen. This Tone or Mercurius, originateth in the 6. *Sound or noise.*

hard

Considerations on the Scope of Jacob Behmen.

hard Aſtringency as the Father, and the whole Salitter is the Mother; for if the Aſtringency were both Father and Mother, a *Stone* would found.

7. 10. The Body generated out of the ſix other Spirits, and in which they dwell as their *Sabboth*; wherein all heavenly figures, (joy, *&c*) ſubſiſt, image and form the ſpirit of Nature, wherein Heaven it ſelf and Angels are formed. the manſion or body in which the ſix do reſt (as the kingdom of divine Glory.)

11. Now we may ſee that all the Spirits together are God the Father.

What the three are in Trinity. 12. The life generated by them all, and generating the life in them all in triumph, is the true Son of God, the ſecond Perſon in the Holy Trinity.

13. And the power of the ſeven Spirits proceeding continually in the ſplendor of the life forming all things in the ſeventh Nature-Spirit, is the true Holy Ghoſt, the third Perſon in the Deity.

CHAP. III. *Demonſtrations of One, or the firſt Spirit.*

HAving deſcribed the ſeven fountain Spirits, now to proſecute the Method propounded in the laſt precedent Section, here *follow* the Demonſtrations of the ſeven in order.

Demonſtrations of the firſt fountain Spirit. The Aſtringency. (*Viz.*)

1. It is not to be ſaid This or That is Firſt or Laſt, being All from Eternity, and One in Another; but that the Aſtringency which is call'd the firſt, is truly what it is above defined and deſcribed to be, is what will be demonſtrated.

2. The outward Senſes of us all, inform themſelves, that there are cold, crude, tough, impenetrable Bodies; or a power tending to impenetrability: and our Reaſon conſenteth that there muſt be a Root, and This Root cannot but be called the Binding or Aſtringency.

1. As That which cauſeth Cold to condenſe Air to Water, and Water to Ice.

2. That purſues condenſed feces of Matter (with the help of the bitter quality) to Earth or Sand, and That agen onward to Stone.

3. That alſo compacteth fluid parts to ſtalks, ſtems of corn, *&c.* the Boles skin and bark of Trees.

4. That alſo incloſeth the tender Brains and Marrow in Skulls and concave Bones.

5. That contracteth and obdurates the ſubtle parts of Metals to a continuity, and reſtrains or confines their allected vertues, even to Unity & Identity by continuity. By Theſe and a thouſand more doth the Aſtringent Spirit demonſtrate it ſelf to be One Fountain, whoſe outward Agent is (confeſt by Antient and Modern Philoſophy to be) *Saturn.*

(2.) CHAP. IV. *Demonſtrations of the ſecond fountain Spirit, the* Attraction.

1. WE find ſomthing Breaking the *Bonds*, elſe would the Aſtringency hold all as in a dark, dry, hard Priſon, all would be ſtone, bone, or the like dead concrets; no Production, no Creation: And the ſtronger this Attractive Power is, the ſtronger the other bindeth; alſo the more Tough and Ponderous the Aſtringency,

the

Considerations on the Scope of Jacob Behmen.

the more actively vigorous is This. As the more you compress Air, or Water, the greater violence hath the so suppressed body to resist; as Wind causing Earthquakes, or Gunpowder Pent.

2. We find a contrariety of Sweetness and Bitterness, which we cannot but see comes from the cold Astringency ; That Property being one, and to every one the same: But This it is That in the Good Part, being its Native Original, is a *Sweetness* ; but in the crude undigested part a *Bitterness*.

3. We find inclinations put into things different from themselves ; for by *This*, Man's eager harshness is (by due ingredients interposing) taught and composed to affable Mildness ; the *New Temper* becomes (in time) *Connatural*, and a Habit: like as a bitter Apple is matured to a sweet Temperature.

4. We find This gives continual opposition and interruption to the piercing Astringency by its own bitter harshness, and such fire as is in a Stone ; and by the penetrating violence is excited, and so is a cause of life. The outward instrument is *Mercury* in conjunction with *Jupiter*.

CHAP. V. *Demonstrations of the third fountain Spirit, the* Anguish. (3.)

1. THis is like (and no more but like) a dying Astringent Torment, like that of dying Creatures, which our Senses often tast some forerunings of; So as the second is a cause of Life; This is a cause of Sense, feeling, perceiving, and consequently of the Mind and Senses in all subjects; which the Separator hath fitted and exalted thereunto, as Angels and Men; and in some degree in inferior sensitive Creatures.

2. We find there is something that lifteth up the mind to *Great Joy*, even to the excess of gladness ; This cannot be the first, for That depresseth ; nor the second, for That only enliveneth, it is therefore This ; for This is an Elevator to the highest joy and triumph, helping on to excess of *Laughter*.

3. We may find it, not only in its mean as above, but in its extream ; for in every body wherein it is too much enkindled it is a *Raging Poison*, resulting as well from its own Nature as from the Extremities of the two first Fountains, introducing desperation and hellish rage in the Creatures like to the Gall in the body, very good in causing and exalting life, also a very evil incendiary in disordering the whole frame of Nature. The outward instrument of This fountain Spirit is *Mars* conjunct with *Mercury*.

CHAP. VI. *Demonstrations of the Spirit producing Heat.* (4.)

THe whole Creation is acted by this Spirit as the great Engine of Omnipotence.

1. Hence is it that the Celestial fire emitteth its beams to the joy of the Universe : so that every leaf and pile of grass hath a tongue to tell it us.

2. The Subterranean fire, which (like the heart in the body of Animals) doth officiate in the Work-house of This Ball is applied by the Separator (the Father of Nature) to generate Metals, medicinal Earths, efflux of Fountains, hot and sanative Baths, &c.

3. Lastly, It is demonstrated by every Man and other living Creature from Youth to giving up the Ghost, as also by Vegetables, Minerals, &c. from their

dwelling

Considerations on the Scope of Jacob Behmen.

dwelling in the Sperm or Seed, to their maturity and declining: who all by the due temper, violent extream or fading of This Spirit, have the proportion of increase or declination to *Nullity*; for This as a Weather glass or Index, shews their degrees of vigour or languishing.

4. But let it suffice no longer to hold a Candle to the Sun, which in conjunction with *Mars*, is in the out-birth the great instrument which doth abundantly demonstrate and figure This 4th Spirit, and on the 4th day was the Sun created or enkindled.

The 4 first Spirits thus distinctly known, open us among many others, the Scriptures following.

John 3. 19.   5. *This is the Condemnation, that light, &c. and men love darkness, &c. because their deeds are evil*; that is, they are comprised in the first four forms, refusing to be enkindled by the light of the 5th form, but remain by the Astringency immeasurably covetous, by the attraction uncontroleably proud, by the property of the anguish, repleat and swoln with envy, and by (That of the fire) have fierce furious anger.

Jam. 4. 1.   —— Our *lusts warring in our Members, the cause of Wars*, which remain such till the light of God or second Principle enkindles it, and so compose Peace.

Psal. 49. 12.   —— Man is become *like the Beast that perisheth*; Like the Wolf and Swine by the astringent covetousness. The Lion, Horse, Cock by the proud elevating, attracting will. Like the Toad, Torpedo, *&c.* by the anguish. Like Dogs, Tigers, *&c.* by the furious fiery property.

Thus the Soul like the Traveller fell among Thieves, where he perisheth till the good Samaritan takes pity.

6. In these 4 *Adam* was dead till God inspoke the Word promising life; the way of reviving is by enkindling light, and in the light the Divine Love clearly typified by the Law of Sacrifices; for as the Sacrifice gave it self up in a flame (as of love) to ascend, leaving only its ashes, which were *His* (till then) Impediments, so is this.

Rom. 2. 8.   *Indignation and wrath, tribulation and anguish on every Soul of Man that doth Evil*; These are the 4 murthering Spirits. But *glory, honour and peace to every one that worketh righteousness.* &c. Here are the three last Spirits of the seven, *viz.* The 5th, the Light or Love-fire, signified by Glory. The 6th the sound or spirit enabling to heavenly Songs of Praise, signified by honour. And the 7th the Body or Sabbath in which all the other six spirits being by the 5th and 6th brought into harmony, do inhabit, rest and dwell, signified by Peace.

(5.)   CHAP. VII. *Demonstrations of the Spirit producing Light and the Love fire.*

1. THis demonstrates it self in every thing more or less on this side the hellish Principle, but the first four (excluding Addition,) are in, and (in a sort) compose, comprehend and include the dark World, and That is the harsh Astringency, strong Attraction, raging Anguish, and hungry Fire: These limit the first or hellish Principle which can never comprehend the Light; for That never proceeds to enkindle it, for it wants oil and must ever want it; because their perpetual Enmity doth ever more dry it up.

2. Now that which composeth Peace is, where the fire proceedeth to the blowing up of Light, the Meekness whereof satiateth the hungry Fire, and becomes food for the other three Spirits, who before (like Milstones without Corn) grind and impetuously rub and grate each other.   3. This

Considerations on the Scope of Jacob Behmen.

3. This did *Lucifer* and his Legions till the gracious *Jehovah* not being pleas'd that so great a space of the Salitter as that now included by the Stars, should remain under the Darkness which then cover'd that Deep, call'd for Light, which was this 5th Spirit, and its appearing caus'd each of the other four to kiss and sweetly strengthen the other, and draw all one way, and not prey one on another.

4. The Scripture saith, *Perfect love casts out fear*, for fear hath torment, which it doth by taking away the enmity, and harmonizing the first four forms of the discording Spirits. Love is the fulfilling of the Law; for it doth all, suffers all, and that always; but until the 4th Spirit (the Fire) attains the Light and Love Spirit, the first four neither do, nor can fulfil the Law, but undo all by their Dissonancy.

The three first years the fruits in *Canaan* were to be accompted as uncircum- *Livit.* 19. 23, cised. The 4th year to be of Praise to the Lord, but not to be eaten till the 5th 24. year. The three first years signifie the three first Forms of the eternal Nature, *viz.* Binding, Attracting and Anguish, which (before enkindling of the other four Forms) are enemicitious and the foundation of the hellish Principle. But the 4th year was the fruit to be of Praise to the Lord more nearly than the other; because out of it is enkindled the light and love-flame. Yet the Tribes of God were not to eat it till the 5th year; for then it became good nourishment by the enkindled Light and principle of Love, and not before.

The sweet Perfume was only of four Heterogeneous Ingredients, *viz. Stacte Exod.* 30. 35. or *Stacus*, a bitter tasted Arabian flower, and *Onyca* a sweet spice, *of each a like quantity*, signifying the two first Forms, which are both alike strong, or alike weak every where. The third is *Galbanum* very stinking, signifying the third Form, the Anguish. The fourth is *pure Frankincense*, a Gum of sweet Odour to feed the Fire, which Fire is the fourth Form.

Obj. Will any say, How are we concern'd to penetrate into the distinct Forms and Properties of Nature call'd fountain Spirits? Is not this the tree of Know- ledge of Good and Evil which *Adam* fell by searching, sounding and feeling after, with neglect of the tree of Life?

Answ. It is true, he should not have known this experimentally; for his know- ing the third Principle separated from the second, was as fatal (had not infinite Mercy interposed) as the knowledge of this (which is the first Principle) had been to *Lucifer* and his Angels.

But Man being fallen, it is as highly profitable to him to have the distinct un- derstanding of this, as it was hurtful to our first Parents; for as the Phyfitian and Chyrurgeon ought to find the spring of disorders in the Sick, or the depth of the Wound, even so here, our knowing this is as the spreading the snare in the sight of a Bird.

Thus appears it that the Lord is the *All* in all things, *with the froward he will shew himself froward*, &c.

These four Fountains are the indissoluble band, the root of all things visible and invisible, the immediate cause and strong might of all eternal things, and (with the interposition of second causes may be truly said to be) the cause of transitory Beings; for these are the root of their roots, the cause of their causes, the in- strumental first Mover of their Motion, and Parent of their immediate Parents.

Daniel's vision of four Monarchies figureth the four first Forms, all which *Dan.* 7. (excluding the 5th, (*viz.*) the enkindling the Light) are called four great Beasts.

1. The first like a Lion, (*viz.*) the Astringent, Binding, mighty Power, the *v.* 4. lofty *Babilon*.

2. The second like a Bear, (*viz.*) the strong, cruel Attraction, the inflexible, *v.* 5. unalterable, inexorable Empire of the Medes and Persians.   B   3. The

8 . *Considerations on the Scope of* Jacob Behmen.

v. 6. 3. The third like a Leopard; for anguish is compos'd of several ingredients, like as are the colours of the spotted Leopard, as is also the belly of a Toad. And the Greek Empire is said to have consisted of about a Hundred and forty sorts of People or Nations

v. 7. 4. The fourth Beast was dreadful and terrible, not likened to any Beast, but
v. 13. (being as fire) is said to devour and break in pieces; such were the Romans. But
v. 14. one like the Son of Man came, and to him was given dominion and glory, an ever-
Chap. 2. 47. lasting kingdom: here is the 5th form, *viz.* the enkindling of the light signified.
ch. 7. 2. 6. Represented also by the 4 Winds of Heaven; 4 wings of a Fowl, and 4 heads.
Job. 11. 17. Thus *Lazarus* having lain in the Grave four days the true light raised him.
Zech. 6. 2, 3. They are figur'd by four Chariots, but Horses in three of them of differing colours one from the other; but the 4th was of Horses of differing colours among
v. 5. themselves, (*viz.*) Grizled and Bay expounded by the Angel to be four Spirits of
the Heavens, which go forth from standing before the God of the whole Earth.
2 *Kings* 13. Will any think it to be without a mystery, that *Elisha* was wroth with *Joash* King
19. of *Israel*, for smiting on the Ground but three times, saying, *Thou shouldst have smote five or six times, then hadst thou smote the Syrians till thou hadst consumed them;* for the Prophet had promised he should consume them.

v. 17. But *Joash* being held by his wickedness in the first four forms smote but thrice; for had he (as the Prophet saith) smote five times, he had enkindled the Light of the Liberty in his forms, & as an addition, had he smote six times, he had brought the illustrated forms into Harmony of Love, whereby his Enemies, the oppressing Assyrian (*viz.*) the Enmity had been consumed.

Amos 1. 3, 6, Will any think it was without a Mystery, that the Prophet *Amos* eight times
9, 11, 13. reciteth, *For three Transgressions* of *Damascus*, of *Gaza, Tirus, Edom, Amon, Moab*,
ch. 2. 1, 4, 6. *Judah, Israel, and for four, I will not turn away the Punishment thereof.* For 'tis apparent, that the three or four first forms comprise all Sin.

But if the vigorous true Light be enkindled, it flameth to a Love of God, and is Death to Sin by discovering it, awakening it and working it out, cleansing the Conscience, destroying the Enmity of the first four forms, and so creating Peace to them that were far off, making them nigh.

But it may be granted, there is an Ingredient of Light admitted into, and retained by the first four Forms; but it is as that the Apostle *Paul* saith, Science falsly so call'd: Such is this, it is an insinuation of a faint, false, delusory Light, comprehending the Craft, Subtlety, Sophistry, Serpentine wisdom to abuse the Senses, and mis-imploy the out-born Natural Powers to jugling Deceits, uniting Earthiness and Sensuality to devilish Designs. Of this Wisdom the Lord saith, *If the Light that is in thee be Darkness, how great is that Darkness?*

Very apt and pertinent to this Discourse is it to consider, That though the Per-
Exod. 30. 23, fume ascending from us was compounded of very unlike Parts, some of them
24, 25. also very Unpleasant, yet the Holy Oyl descending on us was compounded of five
v. 34. Kinds, all excellent Good, Delightful and Pleasant; for we understand that the 5th form enkindles the Light, which makes the four first from the Discords to be a Harmony and a rich Concord: Such are all Gods approaches to us; as *Joseph's*
Gen. 41. 34. Law in *Egypt* was, That four Parts should be the Peoples, and but the 5th Part to be *Pharoah's*, figuring this 5th form's being taken as the Lord's Part only, who is meant by *Pharoah*.

Divine Love hath its Root in the Centre of the Essence of the first four Spirits; but most immediately in the Light, and that from the Fire. And the Activity of the four first Spirits, as a perpetual Rotation, causeth that Love can never Cool. Thus is it strong as Death; for Love is that Name which the God of Life is known to us by: whom thus to know, *is Life Eternal*. The Instrument in the Outbirth of this Spirit is *Verum*. CHAP.

Confiderations on the Scope of Jacob Behmen.

CHAP. VIII. *Demonftration, being of the Sound, Tone, Noife or Voice.* (6.)

Shall there be need to demonftrate this which Heaven and Earth Ring of? And Hell (after its capacity) hath alfo fome impreffions of? It may fuffice briefly to fhew This to be a diftinct Fountain; for that it is the Refult only of the United Operation of the five precedent Spirits meeting in the feventh, is no Argument, why This alfo fhould not be one; for any one could not be without every one.

The Aftringency had not what to bind, but that the matter is produced by the other properties; and fo of the reft.

1. As the light is the opening of the darknefs thro' the fourth Fountain the fire, fo is the voice of the firft four Fountains thro' the opening of the light revealing the Kingdom of Joy with its Beauty, Colours and Ornament wherever it is treafur'd.

2. As we fee fire fleeping in a Flint awakened by a ftroke; fo doth the tone or found ftart up and difperfe it felf fo far as its vigour conquereth the refiftance of contrary motions or folids, and then expireth.

3. As the life lies in a fwound in vegetables till revived by the return of the Spring, or as odours lie couch't in dead earth till midwif'd by the Sun thro' the ftalks of flowers: So the varieties of Infinity remain fecret and dumb as in the myftery till this Oratory publifheth, till this Herald proclaim it, who by its continual motion fpeaks all and fhews all. The Reprefenter of this fixth Fountain Spirit is in the out-birth *Mercurius*.

CHAP. IX. *Demonftration of the Body generated out of the other fix Fountains.* (7.)

1. IF a mighty Prince fhould in regulating a world of laborious Subjects directed by a Council of men experienced in exquifite Art, wanting neither time or other requifite to accomplifh fome ftupendious ftructure, or vaft piece of magnificence, fhould after all be able to accomplifh only trifles, were ftrange. Or rather what could not mens higheft prudence, ferved with the confluence of abundance of willing agents, fufficient helps, and competent time, atchieve, acquire, and bring to effect.

2. And fee we not what the fix overflowing Fountain Spirits (ranged by omnipotence, conducted by infinite Wifdom, exercifing from eternity their irrefiftible Powers) have conceived, travell'd with, brought forth and improved, as the Holy One hath willed.

3. And can any doubt they who have ferved to found and lay the Top-ftone of infinite numbers of Fabricks in the Aftral, Elementary and Terreftrial Worlds, fhould be unfurnifhed with a Royal Palace for themfelves.

4. This feventh Fountain Spirit is their Body, Manfion and Sabbath, the eternal Reft eternally generated. In This they work their hallowed wonders, in this they planted a feed or fperm, whereon the Holy Ghoft brooded, and in fix days hatcht the generation of the Heavens and Earth, with their Hofts, Thrones and Royalties: Hence were founded the Ant and Elephant, the Infects as well as Leviathan: And but for this, God would have been wholly an unfearchable God, nor could any Creature, Angel or other have been made.

5. We

Considerations on the Scope of Jacob Behmen.

4.   5. We say in things of our little Horoscope the end of Motion is Rest; and shall the Originals, whence all things exist want a Rest, for themselves? Must our six days toil end in one of rest; and shall these supream Agents reach no Sabbath wherein to triumph in, with, and for the delight of the Lord of the Sabbath?
 This seventh Spirit is therefore the quiet receptacle of them all.
 6. Out of which, according to the harmony of the Divine Unity, they never for one moment can possibly depart. And over the Threshold of which, according to the separate Property, whereby they are rent from the glorious Unity, they never put a foot, or can for ever enter.
 7. Will therefore the Human Off-spring, whose departure is as written by the Sun Beams, reunite and do its first works, those whereunto he was created, and the pure works of the second *Adam* whereunto he was regenerated
 8. Be it said, forasmuch as by his departure he is so far degenerated, that his Soul by a willing captivity is under the rage of the first four Spirits, from whom the light is withdrawn. His Spirit that was a meek divine Ruler, hath lost its dominion to so great a degree of fierceness, that the Astral rule all. His Body which was formed out of the one pure Element, out of which Element came also the four, and to have been a perpetual figure of the holy third Principle, as his Soul and Spirit were of the first and second. And which body of his should have eaten Paradisical food, is now a captive under the four Elements in so great rigour and vileness, that Nature shames at its Beastiality, till thus it travels thro' sorrow, pain and shame to the dust.
 But the Soul and Spirit may here be baptized and regenerated.
 9. And because the fruit cannot be brought back to the Tree; but the Apple must first perish, and the seed in it first die as doth the grain of Corn before it increase; therefore the Soul and Spirit must also die the mystical death (that is) to its strange will, to secure them against the second death, or before they are capable of the first Resurrection.
 10. From the same ground is it that the Body also must die and lose its new gotten bestial Image, before it can put on immortality, and the Image of the heavenly, whereunto Jesus came to conduct it.
 11. But we may know these things are not the work of faint wishes, but call for striving, watching praying, fighting, contending, running, working, searching, knocking, that fruit may be produced by patience; for Heaven may not be ascended by earthy wings, therefore let the Earth beware of resisting when Heaven stoops, descends and enters it.
 12. To subject mad Mankind to this its only good, the gracious *Jehovah* on *Adams* departure, left his Soul should be a Devil, his Body a Beast, and the Woman generate a Race of Monsters in the out-birth, and of totally proud hellish spirits in the inward; reimplanted the Word of Eternal Life as a seed, or as a light shining in a dark place, to which they (only) do well, who take heed so as to obey, such shall by the Divine Guide lose their All, and be as a Fool or Child as to self-wisdom, but proceeding that way under the Cross possess all things.
 13. For as there is no salvation in any other; so is there no other way of entring there into.
Deut. 27. 12. The six names of the Tribes on Mount *Gerizim* to bless, represent the six active Fountain Spirits according to the second principle, and *Gerizim* the seventh or heavenly body where they rest.
 And the other six on Mount *Gebal* to curse, exhibit the same six Fountains according to the first principle or dark world.

The

The seven Pillars on which Wisdom built her house, points out the seven Foundation Spirits. *Prov. 9. 1.*

The six Steps to *Solomons* Throne hath the same signification, and the Throne it self the seventh, whither they led and ascended, was the Sabbath or Rest. *1 King. 10. 18, 19.*

So the seven Seals, seven Trumpets, and seven Vials, signifie the same seven Fountains, yet all hidden and according to the Darkness, where neither can the Book be read, till first the Seals be gradually opened; the mind and voice of the Trumpets be distinguished, till they be orderly sounded ; nor the things contained in the Vials discerned, till severally effused by the Lamb and his successive Angels. *Rev. 5. ch. 8. ch. 15.*

But the seven Golden Candlesticks are the seven according to the second Principle or Light-World, seen all manifestly at once. The same also are the seven Stars at once giving their splendor. Again, we read there were seven Lamps of fire burning before the Throne, which the Text faith are the seven Spirits of God. *Rev. 1. 13, 16, 20. ch. 4.*

We find, and 'tis observable, the Revelation gives the Vision treble to each ; (*viz.*) To the dark impression, by Seals, Trumpets and Vials.
To the Light impression, by Candlesticks, Stars and Lamps.
So the seven lean Kine and blasted Ears, signifies what we have, the seven Properties : The seven fat and good, what God made the seven Properties to be.

CHAP. X. *Of the Three Principles of the Divine Essence.*

1. BY a Principle is meant a chief beginning power, a self-subsisting Life, an original root, foundation, or in some sense a mystery or genus, whence other Spirits, Bodies, Species or things originate, as from a Supream Power.
And thus is God the only one Principle.

2. And this one Principle is also three Eternal Births or Principles, ever without ceasing, begetting, being begotten, and proceeding by, in and from each other, of which all Worlds are conjunctly or severally an Image, but very different according to the inscription, stamp, figure and degrees they attain, or are capable of.

3. And tho' the three Principles are by an indissoluble band ever inseparably one in God, yet are they distinguishable.

4. But in the Creatures in the separate Properties are terribly manifest, which tho' *Adam* was not to have known in himself, yet is it what we ought to know.

5. God said, *Let us make Man in our Image, after our likeness,* but faith not so of the other Creatures ; Man in his first make being most perfectly his figure and off-spring.

6. Yet every of the other Creatures, the Astral, Elementary, Vegetative, Sensitive and the Dark World, do all in their various kinds (more or less perfectly) represent him; *for the invisible things of him from the Creation of the World are clearly seen, being understood by the things that are made, his eternal Power and Godhead.*

And as there are the united three bearing record in Heaven ; so are here an agreeing three, bearing record on Earth; (*viz.*) Spirit, Water and Blood.

CHAP. XI. *Concerning the first Principle*, in four Demonstrations.

1. THE Abyss of the Father distinct from the second and third, is understood to be an eternal indissoluble band and Original to Potence, a center or root of substance; an earnest longing to the birth of the majestick Light or Lustre; an austere vigour like an eternal infinite hot and cold fire.

That this is so, and (in some measure) what it is, may be shewed to the very Senses.

1.
Inanimate Creatures shew the first Principle.
1. *The Elements.*
3. *The Astral World.*

2. *Demonstration.* The insensitive Creatures witness it. The Rock where grows the Diamond, the Oar whence proceeds the Gold, the shell in which is fed the Pearl, the Earth whence issue forth the plants, do all figure their root, the darkness or first Principle their substantial root, center, basis, or immovable foundation.
3. Again, the Elements have the cold and heat to be founded on, representing this Principle called the Eternal Darkness; for from the degrees of cold and hot fire, proceed not the Earth and Stones only, but Air and Water.
4. Lastly, The Astral World, whence spring the Elementa' figures the same darkness, as is most evidently seen in some of the Royal Stars called Planets, *Saturns* condensing, strong binding contraction impresseth in Lead, Stone &c. a dry, hard and hardly to be penetrated weight; so doth *Mars* confer on Iron, &c. both are substantial figures of the same Eternal Principle.

2.
4. Evil Sensitive Creatures.
5. Good Sensitive Creatures.

5 *Demonstration of the first Principle*, is in the Sensitive Creatures both evil and good. The evil, whose hurtful properties of venom, stings, poisonous, fierce and cruel qualities shew they originate from the dark Principle, and some of them especially love darkness, some of them are outwardly dark, as that dangerous reptile called in some parts the Blind-worm, &c.
6. It is seen also in good Sensitive Creatures, either as they partake of the hurtful property by being soon moved to choler, and then mischievous and vindictive, or else as the dark Principle takes hold of them, clogging them with sluggish inactivity, and depressed limbs; dark bodies, rough hides, &c.

3.
6. *Angels.*

7 *Demonstration.* It is evident in Intelligent Creatures; for into this Principle of Might and Potence the Pride of the Devils cast them, in which their light being extinct, they are shut up for ever.

4.

8 *Demonstration.* It is evident in Rational Creatures; viz. Man, whose sad fall brought his human Soul which originated out of this Eternal Principle, yet illustrated by the second to so great a degree into this, that such men as shall continue Rebels to the Light of the Son of God (which on Man's fall was in-spoken again) do remain a plain and terrible figure of this first Principle in the dark impression on their Souls; for they being hardened and fixt in disobedience, are as sealed up in utter enmity against the Divine Kingdom of Love and Purity.
9 And such mens bodies are the drudges of their darker minds, being as truly a figure of the Eternal Darkness, as are those bodies of the hurtful Animals.
10. But (which is also to be bewailed) the Children of the day have in the unmortified part of their Souls, too lively Characters of this first Principle;

and

Confiderations on the Scope of Jacob Behmen.

and their Bodies are made like thofe of the Elementary Creatures, fubject to vanity, travelling in pain and diftempers, till (as the effect of all) comes the anguifh of death; for they are fallen under the Regiment of the Aftral evil influences till their mortal fhall put on immortality, by the grace of the fecond Principle, the free mercy of God in Jefus Chrift.

11. As for the difobedient that climb up into the firft Principle, or fall into the third Principle, fhutting their Eyes againft the fecond, they muft ever bear the Image they here conformed their minds to, and grow up in; for man having his root in the Power that is without beginning can find no end. *Oh therefore that we were wife, that we underftood this, that we would confider our Letter end.* Deut. 32. 29.

12. The out-birth into which *Adams* fall hath caft our mortal bodies is fignified by the Earthen Veffels, which having toucht fome legally unclean thing, could not be made clean and purified, but muft be broken; fuch is the mortal body of all the Children of *Adam.*

13. But thofe Veffels which were of Brafs or other metal, being wafht, &c. were become clean; for Metals are one ftep higher, more noble, deriving from the Aftral Powers more immediately, and with a purer tincture, more fimple, lefs volatile than our flefhly Tabernacles.

CHAP. XII. *Of the Second Principle,* in four Demonftrations.

1. THE Divine Wifdom, and that of this World, are on terms of hoftility; hence was it that when the Lord himfelf in the flefh preacht Salvation, his Divine Wifdom explicated by the moft familiar Parables, higheft Evidence, and more than Angelical Skill, was derided and blafphemed by many, not of the lower ruder fort only, but by the Rabbies, men skill'd in the Law of God according to the letter, men of parts, zealous and outwardly holy, the Guides of the multitude, men according to the Law blamelefs. But the Doctrine of the Lord Jefus was underftood very well by all fuch (tho' otherwife weak) in whom the love of it wrought obedience to it, and who by the Spirit of Holinefs were taught to refufe the pleafures of fin: To them no Yoke fo eafie as Chrift's. nor any Load fo unfupportable as that of fin: Thefe knew what it was to be born again, without, and not of the will of the flefh: And Chrift's Life and Doctrine was plain, and fo is ftill, to fuch, and none but fuch.

2. If any fuch fhall perufe thefe Lines (their inward fenfes being unlockt) they, if they prefs after this Principle with earneftnefs, may find it informing, enlightning and affifting them.

3. But to the full thefe are fulfom and offenfive; to the wife they are folly; for this Principle divefts them of their own felf-will, before it inducts them into the univerfal holy will. And if Divine Difcourfes lead not to cleanfe the heart, it cumbreth the head, and cloys the appetite; and fo Men do with Truths as Children with Birds, either they crufh them, or let them fly away.

4. But tho' the glory of the fecond Principle be fo much above fallen Man's reach, yet fuch efficacy hath it on the whole Creation as is demonftrable to any rational Creature; for God hath not left himfelf without witnefs by giving Rain, &c. *The Ubiquity and Abyfs of the fecond Principle.*

5. To difcourfe this where may we not begin? for it is every where infinite. It is the glory in the Infinite Abyfs of the Father. It gave Glory, Purity, and the Vertue of the Angelical World. It alfo gave the third Principle in this out-birth,
all

Confiderations on the Scope of Jacob Behmen.

all the Excellency and Beauty it hath in it; only the hellish Principle hath shut it self up from it, and is dead to it.

1. 6 *Demonstration.* That tho' no Language can exprefs it, yet every one that is regenerated doth in fuch meafure as he hath attained the Regeneration, know this, for he liveth in it. The more or lefs fuch are fick of Sacred Love; fo more or lefs feel they this. And the more we die to our immoderate Lufts after the Dominion of the whole third Principle; the more doth this Principle evidence it felf in us. And in fuch proportion as we enlighten our firft Principle, or Souls Original ftanding in the firft four forms of Nature proceeding by Divine Power to enkindle the true Light in them, in the fame meafure is our Root tranfplanted to grow in this Paradifical Field or Principle.

2. 7 *Demonstration.* But we are to know by way of Explanation, This to be a paffing into Death, and thro Death into Life, of which the Holy Scripture is plentiful.
Nor may even *Plato*'s defcription of Love be counted difcordant to this, who defines Love to be one's dying to his own Body, and living to the Body beloved.
8. For the living to the Divine Light and Love of the fecond Principle, (which is the property of the Son of God) is a dying to us and ours; that is, to our whole depraved Image, much like as the Day is the Death of the Night.

3. 9 *Demonstration.* The fecond Principle is fhewed by the Sacrifices which were confumed by the Holy Fire, whereby they died to their firft Form, and lived to a new one; that is, were tranfmuted into the holy Flame.
10. And as what part of the Sacrifice would not enkindle into the holy Flame figuring This Principle, fell to Afhes as into the perifhing third Principle: Even fo fee we much of the Regenerate Man ftay below, and be uncapable of the New Image, but be as Afhes.
11. Now we fee that Afhes may be heated, but Flame not: Such is the Earthy Man and Senfual part; yet we fee after the procedure of a fecond work, Men do tranfmute common Afhes into a Lucid and Tranfparent Body.
12. So may our vile Bodies by the procedure of the fecond work, (the Refurrection) be tranflated into a clarified Chriftalline Temple, for our immenfe glorified Souls, and they both be the Hallowed Habitation of our refigned, humble, divinely irradiated Spirits.
13. And our illuftrated Afhes, glorified Souls, and meek human Spirits (being firft clothed with the Robe of Chrift's Righteoufnefs, and heavenly Humanity, the Virgin of God's Wifdom) will be both fuitable guefts for the New *Jerufalem*, as a Bride adorned for her Husband, and alfo be Eternal Temples for the Holy Ghoft.
14. Thus hath been given a glimpfe what the fecond Principle is in it felf, and what its Operations are in us as to our firft Principle. It now refts to fearch what it is in the third Principle in us, and in the whole Creation.
15. In us it is our Principle of Divine Underftanding, directing to know our Creator, the End of our Creation; and wherein lies our true good. The Eye thus enlightned, informs the Affections, that from the Reafon offered, they fhould,
16. On the Principles of Juftice pay the Debt we owe for our Being, and the Means wrought for our Reftauration to Well-being, and of ingenuity willingly and thankfully to adore him as the only Fountain of Good, and to efteem every thing in that degree as they partake of that Fulnefs to figure and refemble him. 17. And

Considerations on the Scope of Jacob Behmen.

17. And on the Principles of Self interest, to prevent eternal loss, or be eternal gainers, as our choice or rejecting shall render us capable or otherwise.

18. These Notions and Beams of Light when the Understanding receiveth from the second Principle, it offereth to the Judgment to consider of.

19. The Judgment hath the Senses to consult, who are grown so dim-sighted, having from their youth been habituated to the Good or Evil of the third Principle, that they cannot see beyond it, but judge as the Beasts do of Pleasure or Pain; nor can they see the least cause to deny themselves of any one thing they lust after, whereof (if denied) they allarm the Passions which have their Root in the first Principle.

20. The Passions are as furious, violent, impetuous Storms, which often obscure and impose on the Eye of the Mind, and sometimes immerse the Ship of the whole Man, setting on fire and extremity the whole frame of Nature, so that the Judgment wants power to get the Will right.

21. Here the New Man, as Child of the holy second Principle, hath need enough to pray always fervently; to knock, wait, use much abstinence, with highest diligence to watch, to stand on its guard, to use much violence and severity, and, that often, to fight the faithful Combate till he kill the Murtherers; to die from day to day, thereby to be pluckt as a brand out of the fire. He shall find great necessity of help from Heaven to bind the Strong Man.

22. But most especially in some persons, whose originals having been strongly rooted in the first four Forms of the first Principle conveyed by Generation, and perhaps also reinforced by their Constellation, so that they have much of the Serpent in them. In such Souls the work of Resignation to the Divine Conduct goes very hardly, slowly, sadly on, with many recoils, notable resistance and reluctance, that they resemble the Child possessed with that kind that goeth not out but by prayer and fasting.

23. Others having so deep Root, their Wills being lapsed and wedded to the third Principle, either having so great possessions, as seem rather to be possessed with them, than to possess them; or having long enjoyment, their Evils plead Prescription and Custom. Some by their Constitution incline to delicacy, or by their Constellation and Complexion to airiness; many such find the Cross too heavy; do look back; the Pearl in their Account is too dear.

24. Others Good Intentions are covered with so much rubbish, that they will not be at the pains of removing it; for indulgence to their ease, and perhaps ensnaring reputation with men, foils and pinions them.

Many of the above strive to enter, but are never able; therefore withdraw from the Yoke; their Goodness is only as the morning dew.

25. But the Judgment rightly informed sees all things as they are, things present as if past, things to come as if present; it sees the Out-birth brave with a borrowed Goodness only entrusted to it, to shadow the Grace and Glory of the true Fountain of Goodness. It sees the World on fire, the Heavens rolled up, the Lord sitting on his Judgment-Throne; sees the triumphs of the humble, and tremblings of the proud.

26. As for things visible, the Glory of the visible Heavens figuring that of the true Heavens, the Earth that of the Divine Salitter. 'Tis true, in this dead Earth the surviving relicks of Good strive to produce perfect Bodies of several kinds, but the Curse hindereth. It would have Paradice bud and bear fruit, holy and pure productions every where, but it cannot, for Death is entred at the door opened by the first *Adam*.

27. Had indeed Life been received as offered by the second *Adam*, Paradice might well have blossomed in the Out-birth, and his Kingdom have come with
power

power in every place as it did at his Transfiguration. His Kingdom might have come on Earth as it is in Heaven, where Paradice might have flourished.

4. 28 *Demonstration*, is Natures labour after Perfection, and the tincture in it, shewing some faint impulses, and producing precious Stones, Gold and other Metals, Medicinal Earths, Spices, excellent Fruits, &c. And in the Seas, Pearl, Amber, &c. all which are but shadows and reflected figures, wherewith the third Principle representeth the Glories of the second.

29. Therefore the enlightned Judgment guides the Will not to regard these things for themselves, but for the infinite Excellency of that represented by them.

30. If it be true that I love not the part I see or touch of my worthy honoured Friend, but for that part of him which I see not, nor touch outwardly; for that is indeed the Excellency and the True Man, much less then do I regard his meer shadow.

CHAP. XIII. *Of the Third Principle*, in four Demonstrations.

1. IF the Greek Christians think the Holy Ghost proceeds only from the Father, and not from the Son, they must probably have some other meaning than is known to some of us; for the Holy Ghost proceedeth from the Father and the Son.

2. The four Anguishes of the first Principle generate the Light of the second, and from the infinite Might and Strength of the first, and the infinite Lustre of the second, is generated the infinite Glory and Love of the third, which third Principle is the Property of the Third Person in the Trinity.

3. Hence is it, that the third Principle is not only the growing Vertue of Paradice, but also of the Out-birth the Astral, Elementary and Visible Material World also.

1. *Demonstration.* For as the Air is produced by Fire and Light, yet being produced, is not only a Self-subsisting body, but the food of the Fire, and consequently of the Light; so is the third Person to the first and second.

  1. The Out-birth is not the first; for it cannot be a Root, but a Fruit; not a Foundation, but a Superstructure; not a Creator, but a Creation; composed of Darkness or substantial matter, like a Chaos arising from the first, and the Light arising from the second.

  2. Neither is it the second, as is apparent; being a distinct Life in a sort inanimate without understanding an Image of the inward spiritual World in the various Figures and Properties thereof, representing all as in a Mirrour. As we see the outward glorious Sun figures the infinite inward second Principle, but is not a seeing, but a seen Light or Power.

  3. What then if it be neither the first nor second, can it be but the third? And tho' the third it only be, yet it hath in every part of it the vigour of the first Principle, and vertue of the second in some measure or other; for if in any part were nothing of the first, there could be no Being but a Nullity; and if in any part were nothing of the second, there were only Death and Hell manifest.

7. Now forasmuch as in some places and things the first swalloweth up the second, the Wrath and Curse seems only to be there, and in other parts or things the second or sweet Property of the Life is prevalent, there riseth a Life, for his Light is the Life of Men.

2 *Demon-*

Confiderations on the Scope of Jacob Behmen.

8 *Demonftration.* But in fome alfo the Love in the Light fwalloweth up the firft Principle : And there is a twofold Birth, an Inward and an Outward. The Inward is Divine, Heavenly, Holy in an Eternal Excellency, as in the new Birth or Regeneration; but it extendeth not to Tincture the Outward Man, becaufe the Curfe fubjected it to Wrath and Corruption.

2.

9. The Lord Jefus Chrift brake the Bands; for it was not poffible he fhould be holden of them, though the weight of the whole World lay on him.

10. Becaufe his Heavenly Humanity did not only unite it felf to the Mortal Flefh of the Virgin *Mary*; which Heavenly Humanity, was the Holy Thing begotten by the Holy Ghoft, the pure Virgin Image of Modefty, Virgin *Sophia*, the Firft-born of every Creature, the Heir of all Things, the Lamb flain from the Foundation of the World, the Word that was made Flefh. But the fame Divine Man, which both came from Heaven into, or in the Virgins Womb; but alfo then was, and is in Heaven, this very fame Word united it felf to the fecond Perfon, the Almighty Son of the Almighty God. Thus was it that this Saviour and Mediator our Immanuel, is the Mighty One on whom Help was laid; for in Him the Three Principles fhew themfelves in their feveral Incomprehenfible Fountains.

What the Heavenly Humanity is, and doth; And how he doth it.

11 *Demonftration.* The Love in the Light can alfo Tincture the Outward Man in the third Principle; and the Outward Man may, by the preffing of the Inward into, and through it with Power, put off its Old Garment of Sicknefs and Infirmity, and be cloathed with the New Robe. A glimpfe whereof is feen in the Faces of *Mofes* and *Stephen*, and more fully in the Tranflation of *Enoch* and *Eliah*; but above all in the Lord's Transfiguration, and Converfe after his Refurrection. But it is a very hard great Work; becaufe the Third whole Principle in us is eftranged and dead to it, by the very heavy Fall.

3.

12 *Demonftration.* It may alfo be obferved, that the Love in the Light hath its outward Figures, and impreffeth it felf in this Third Principle to the outward Senfes.

4.

1. As in the Aftral Kingdom, principally in the *Sun*, *Jupiter* and *Venus*. (2.) In the Air in the Concord of the Elements, giving delightful fweet Weather. (3.) In the Senfitive Creatures, as Doves, Lambs, &c. (4.) In Harmony of Mufical Sounds and Voices of Birds. 5. In Vegetables by moft Sanative, odoriferous, excellent Fruits, Roots and Seeds. 6. In curious Colours of Flowers, in the fhadows of degrees of Light in Clouds. 7. In Minerals, as in Gold, Silver, Copper, and by the Tincture giving luftre and vertue to Pretious Stones and Gems. 8. In the Seas, in Pearl, Amber, Coral, &c. So if the outward Heaven fhew the Glory of the Lord, the Earth fhews his Handy-work.

CHAP. XIV. *How the Sacrifices fhew the Three Principles.*

1. The three grand Sacrifices were, 1. The Burnt-offering. 2. The Peace-offering. 3. The Trefpafs-offering or Sin-offering, unfolding the Three-fold Myftery.

2. The firft grand Order of Sacrifices was the Burnt Sacrifices, which confifted of four Kinds. Either, 1. Of the Herd. 2. Of the Flock. 3. Of Fowls. 4. Of the Meat-offering : Even fo doth the firft Principle fhew it felf in four, and but four forms. But agen, the Burnt-offering differed from the other two Sacrifices in three things. 1. That thefe muft be only a Male, the other might as well be

(1.) *Levit.* 2.14. *Lev.* 2. 1.

Confiderations on the Scope of Jacob Behmen.

be a Female. 2. That it muft be all cut in Pieces, whereas the other muft be only divided, not cut in Pieces, and the Fat of the Inwards offered to the Lord. 3. The Burnt-Offering was after only wafhing wholly offered, no Part with-held fhewing two Figures.

1.   3. The firft Principle or Fathers Property as one entire Effence, without dividing the Tinctures of Female from the Male, which, though cut in pieces (whence all Multiplicity exifts) yet is ftill one not to be divided from it felf, as was the Burnt Sacrifice, the only whole Offering without referve.

2.   4. It figureth the Man before he had trod any fteps towards his Fall; for he was of the entire one, though confifting of many Parts, yet able wholly to go up to the Lord, as the whole Burnt-offering did.

(2.) 5. The fecond grand Sacrifice was the Peace-offering, which differed from the Burnt, as was noted; 1. In being as well of Female. 2. Reftrained only to the Herd and Flock; whereas both Burnt and Sin-offerings might be alfo of Fowl and Meat-offering. 3. It differed from the other two, in that its Fat and Inward part was the Lords, and the reft the Priefts; but not to be eaten by any legally unclean Perfon. The Peace-offering had alfo a double Figure.

  1. It reprefented the fecond Perfon of the Glorious Trinity. 1. In that in him the two Natures were united. 2. In whom the two Tinctures, Male and Female, were refumed into one Perfon; which we fee in that the Sacrifices were of two, and only of two Kinds. Agen, They were fevered into two parts; the Fat of the Inwards from the reft that was the Lords, the reft the Priefts; but was Holy, and not to be eaten by any legally unclean Perfon.

  2. 6. The Peace-offering was the Figure of the New Man, in whom, the difappeared Image which the firft *Adam* loft is revived; by which re-union, the fallen Man is become new; which renewed Man is fanctified to be the Priefts part, but the other, *viz.* The renewing Image is Gods part; So in the Revelation it's faid. *And hath made us Kings and Priefts,* (viz.) *according to thefe two Images.* 1. The Image of God, or renewing Power. 2. The renewed part the Confort, Affociate and Servant, ever refigning it felf to the Will of that Image of God, or Renewer: So that the Servant becomes alfo Holy, and may not be toucht by any unclean Perfon, Will or Spirit.

(3.) 7. The third grand Sacrifice was the Sin or Trefpafs-offering, which differed from the two former: 1. In the General, It was to be only a Bullock. 2. In Particular, to the feveral forts of Sinners and Occafions, were appropriated feveral forts of Sacrifices. 3. In the Place where it was to be Sacrificed, (*viz.*) The Fat at the Altar for Burnt-offerings, but the Carcafs, Hide, and Dung in a clean place without the Camp. This figureth the third Principle, as it comprehends the fallen Apoftatized Man. The Bullock figures the fallen ,Humanity, the Fat the Heavenly Humanity, or Reftoring Tincture which was only the Lords and it alone worthy to be offered at the Altar. But the Carcafs, Hide and Dung, the fenfual, impure, finful Man was carried out of the Camp, yet it muft be to a clean place; where it muft be burnt, not faid to be offered, for it was too vile. But the Burnt-offering is call'd the *continual Burnt-off ring.*

  8. A Monk of the fame Monaftery and time with *Luther,* having compleated the time enjoyn'd them for Prayer: added, afking, Whether he had not now done what was fully fufficient? Had an audible Anfwer in thefe words, (*viz.*) *Redde mihi medium Lunam, folem & canis iram*; Give me the Half-Moon, the Sun, and the Anger of the Dog.

  9. The words import to my underftanding as follows, by the Three Things required, his whole three Principles or whole Man, his Soul, Spirit and Body; for by the Anger of the Dog, the firft Principle is charactered, which excluding the

Light,

Considerations on the Scope of Jacob Behmen.

Light, is comprifed in the firſt four Forms, extendeth no higher than to fiery Rage, and is the ſtate or place called in the Revelations *without*, where are Dogs.
2. The Sun, which was required to be given, evidently ſignifieth the ſecond Principle, which the outward Sun repreſenteth. 3. The Half-Moon meaneth his third Principle, which corporifeth the Elementary Concrets, and influenceth their Mutations by her own Regular Laws in Conceptions, Progreſſions, Maturations, and Tranſmutations, Reſolvings and Declenſions of Terreſtials, and in the fluxes of the Tides.
10. But if to another Man my Conſtructions ſquare not, be it left as that on which is hanged no ſtreſs, but a great probability.

The three Principles of *Sal, Sulphur* and *Mercury*, compoſe every thing that hath a created Being, from the top of Heaven to the bottom of Hell (as I may phraſe it) in the Dark, light and mixt Worlds or Out-birth.

CHAP. XV. *Of* Jehovah, *and the Creation.*

1. LET us now, after a View of the Three Principles, come to a ſummary diſquiſition (how brief ſoever) yet that may ſome way aſſiſt the willing Mind, how, through the Creatures to diſcover ſome glimpſe of the Omnipotent Majeſty, whoſe Offspring we are; or rather, whoſe Offspring we were; really retaining in our depravity only ſome faint Reflections, and nigh worn out Impreſſions of that dear beauteous Image we had.

2. A glance of the Moſt High in the Face of his only Son is (without Compariſon) (infinitely preferrable to all the moſt ſublime Speculation and Wiſdom of Man; for it is That we loſt by the Fall, and the knowledge of That, is That we are taught to hope for in our Reſtoration by Jeſus Chriſt.

3. And though it be hard, yet poſſible, to all in whom the Light hath ſo en-kindled Love, as they ſearch for it as for hidden Treaſure.

And becauſe we are as one Purblind, not able to ſee afar off, we are to ſeek by things within our Ken; and thence is it the Apoſtle faith, *The inviſible things of him* Rom. 1. 20. *from the Creation of the World, are clearly ſeen, being underſtood by the things that are made his Eternal Power and Godhead.*

4. By his Eternal Power, is underſtood according to the firſt Principle, the in-diſſoluble Band, the Father's Property, according to which he is a conſuming Fire, and that Work call'd his ſtrange Work, and his coming forth to that, his coming out of his place.

5. But by his Godhead is underſtood, according to the ſecond Principle or Son's Property, in which he is *Jehovah*, Gracious and Merciful, long-ſuffering, and abundant in Mercy and Truth; Mercy it ſelf, forgiving Iniquity, Tranſgreſſion and Sin.

6. Now to know God really and truly in any meaſure, is to know the Son of *Transforming* God, who is the Regenerator, by the Co-operation of the Holy Ghoſt, in ſome *Knowledge of* meaſure cleanſing the Heart of every thing that may be call'd Self, and ſubjecting *God.* it to the Obedience of the Holy Univerſal Will; making it run with Delight and Joy in that Way which to the unmortified part is grievous.

7. For his firſt four Forms, having by the Grace of God generated the fifth, the Love in the Light, the Soul thus divinely irradiated falls very ſick of Love, and nothing can give Eaſe and Content longer, than while he is following his Beloved, either by patient waiting for him, or doing or ſuffering what he willeth him to obey and ſuffer.

8. Now

Considerations on the Scope of Jacob Behmen.

A Glance of the Contemplative and distinct knowledge of God.

8. Now we are to know that from Eternity is the first, second, and third Principles according to the Fathers, Sons, and Holy Ghosts Properties, the One living in the Other, having all One holy free Omnipotent Will. And that the Infinite Abyss, wherein Eternally dwell the seven Spirits, and in every the least imaginable Circle whereof dwells the whole Holy Trinity, Abyss or immeasurable heighth, depth, length and breadth, which Men and Angels can reach no number of, nor conceive its immensity, is as the Holy Body of God, who is its Soveraign Creator, Owner, and as a Soul and Spirit to it.

9. But this pure Abyss is Holy, and as one Holy Element the Seventh (the Laboratory of the other Six) hath in it all Powers and Vertues, out of which Heaven, Angels, and all Inferior Productions come; for in it is the Divine Salitter and all Qualities in indissoluble Amity and perfect Harmony, due Equality most dearly embracing each other; being the Mystery of all the various Powers.

10. And from the two first Principles therein by the *Exit* of the Holy Ghost, were Throne Angels created, according to the several Properties of the seven Fountains Spirits, with their Hosts respectively, having the great Might of the first Principle, Glorified with the Majestick light of the second, the Son of God.

11. But *Lucifer* and his Angels extinguish'd in themselves the glorious Sweetness of the second, by giving up their Will into the first four Forms, which without the second, are at Eternal Enmity.

12. Also out of the Holy Element were created the two active Elements of Fire after the Property of the Father, and Air (wherein is Light) after the Property of the Son. Out of which two, after dividing of the Properties in the Dark Deep (the effect of the Fall of the Angels) came the Mortal Water and Dead Earth, in both which, by the prevalence of the Astringency, came Rocks and Stones.

Whence the two Active Elements sprung.

13. To cease that immoderate Coagulation the Word commanded Light, expelling *Lucifer*, at which the Holy Angels rejoyced; *Where wast thou when the Morning Stars sang together, and all the Sons of God shouted for joy*; for then was the Out-birth or third Principle founded by the *Exit* of the Holy Ghost.

Some stop begun to the breach by Fall of the Angels by the Creation.

14. Then also out of the Holy Element, and the divided Properties, which *Lucifer* had brought into a confused Chaos or Dark Deep, the Word spake the Astral Heavens, the Seven Planets after the Properties of the Seven Fountains, and all the other Stars and the Terrestial Ball, after the infinite variety of the Properties.

The Creation.

15. Also out of the Holy Element and the Astral Birth, came the four Elements, and out of the Elements the Transitory Creatures. Some bare the Figure of the first four Forms separated from the Light as venomous Creatures, Toads, Torpedo's, &c. from the Anguish: Scorpions, Spiders, Basilisks, &c. from the Fire; for every Property would be Creaturely. Some also figur'd the second Principle in Innocency, Meekness, and Love; as Lambs, Doves, &c.

Man created Gods Image, and what that was.

16. Then in the Throne of secluded *Lucifer* and his Angels, the Word spake Man, such an Image of God, as might not only be the second Race of Intellectuals; but a compleat Image of all the three Principles. That is, his Soul out of the first Principle or Dark Power-World; his Spirit out of the second, the Holy-Light World; his Body out of the one Holy Element, the Root of the four Elements; so that he might by his Divine Holy Principle of Love and Meekness illustrate, and sweetly use his first, as the fallen Angels should have done: He was also furnished with the third Principle, which the Angels were not; and in that respect a more compleat Image of God than they: over which third Principle he might also bear Rule by the Power of the Divine second Principle.

17. And by his third (in subordination to the second) might Rule over the Astral Birth and Elementary, not only as He was the Natural Lord in that Principle,

Considerations on the Scope of Jacob Behmen.

ciple, but ennobled also with the Light or Angelical Principle, and therefore able and adapted to Rule over the Creation knowing what they were, whence they sprung, and whither they tended; for all Properties were open in him; therefore *Adam* could name them knowing their Parentage and Use.

Thus the manifold Wisdom of God appeareth in every thing, and summarily to be observed in these following.

18. First from the first Principle glorified with the second, according to the seven Fountains, were created the Throne Angels, Arch-Angels and their Hosts.   1. *Angels.*

19. The Creatures that derive immediately from the One Holy Element as the Paradisical Body of *Adam*, that was more pure than seven times refined Gold, and to have remained eternally.   2. *Man's Body.*

20. The Astral Birth of the Visible Heavens, and their Invisible Powers: Of Alliance, Dependance and Affinity, with which is Man's Astral Spirit called his Prophetick Evester; which ordinarily predicts by Dreams, a kind of Intuitive Impulses of approaching Good or Evil; small, also important natural Events, &c.   3. *Astral and Visible Heavens.*

21. Out of the Astral seem to be born Those Mortal (yet to the outward Eye mostly invisible) Creatures, in all the four Elements called Aerial Spirits, prodigious Predicters of Wars by Armies in the Clouds: Others also of the Fire: Some Aquastrish, and Those of our Horoscope Terrestrial and Subterranean, that are about Minerals, of which This Discourse is not sollicitous.

22. Out of the Holy Element proceeded the two Elements; and consequently the four; more Pure and Paradisical than after the Curse.   4.

23. Henceby the steddy Conduct of the Separator or Father of Nature (substituted by the Great Creators word) and by the Spirit of the Tincture, have sprung the Animal, Vegetative and Mineral Kingdoms, to the composition of every of which Naturalists find the Principles of *Sal, Sulphur* and *Mercury*, more or less pure, according to the Body which it composeth, and the Tincture wherewith it is more or less sublimed and ennobled.

24. But *Lucifer* by his renting from the total Unity, thereby making the Properties separate, prophane and unclean, there proceeded out of the first four Forms hellish, immortal, fierce, horrible, poisonous Creatures, to whom Death and Darkness (the fierceness of the Properties) is no woe or torment; for it is their Life. But Hell is therefore an intolerable Hell to Angels and Men, because they were created to another State, in another Principle, for another End.

25. From all the three Principles, with the Potence of the first, Love fire of the second, and moving Life of the third, was Man created. And as such with the Light of God, which is not quite extinguished in him; for when once awakened by Divine stirring and his hungry desire, let none think it impossible he should see into the several Principles that are truly in him; for the Child knoweth his Parents better and better as himself groweth to be a Man. A breath of Air is like the whole Element, a drop like the whole Ocean, a spark like the whole Origin, a clod like the whole Ball.   5.

CHAP. XVI. *Man's Estate before his Fall.*

1. MAN being ranged a little lower than the Angels, yet with one Principle more, hath a Spirit penetrating as theirs; if brought into an earnest hunger to search and knock. Let none forbid so doing; for God delights to be sought and known; by such can he be most loved and admired that most discover of him.

2. And

Considerations on the Scope of Jacob Behmen.

2. And those his Children who know most clearly what they fell from, will strive most to be recovered; and those that penetrate deepest into that dismal plight whereinto they have plunged themselves, must needs be most profoundly Humbled; and Those that find the prosecuting of their own Wills to be a Fighting against God their Restorer; will be easiest prevailed with to lay down their Arms; Die to their Wills; Resign themselves to His Conduct; Repair to His School; Bear His Yoke: at any price Buy the Pearl; Fight the Battle of Faith; that they may lay hold of Eternal Life. *Wisdom calls*; *They only are the Sons of Wisdom who will bear.*

I come now to the following most Important Points and Enquiries.
1. What Man was before his Fall.
2. By what degrees he fell.
3. What Fallen Mans Estate was, and is.
4. What may be his Recovery.

1. Concerning *Man's Estate before his Fall.*

3. God made Man, in, or after His Image (as hath been shewn) how he was God's Image; *viz.* an *Extract* out of all the *Three Principles*: The Ignorance whereof befel *Audeus*, in the fourth Century after the Incarnation; who said God had Hands and Feet.

(1.) 4. But God's Image was to express in *Adam*, that He had in *Harmony His whole First Principle*, and all things subordinate to It; so that the four Forms did mightily establish him; and This Harmony stood by the *Love-Fire and Holy Light of the Second Principle*; by which also he could Rule over his Third Principle.

(2.) 5. He was so perfectly God's Image, as that he was capable of Eternity, without any necessity in his own constitution to make him obnoxious to *Mortality*. Else how is his Death denounced the Penalty of his Disobedience?

(3.) 6. Nor could he be clogg'd before he fell, with a *Dark Body*, stuft with the Elements, and built upon Bones to bear it up, as may appear by four Evidences.

Evidence 1. The Elemental Fruits are Mortal; therefore are proper Food to support the Transitory Creatures that feed on them.

Evidence 2. Bones proceed as Stones also do, from the too hard coagulation of the *Astringency*, producing (in the Saline Element) the *Principle of Mortal Salt*.

Evidence 3. The food from the four Elements requires a gross Elementary Carcass to digest, and draught to evacuate their *Earthy Part*; both inconsistent with the *Purity and Eternity of Paradise*.

Evidence 4. The Elements themselves pass into their Ethers, and cease as to their present Existence, when the Mystery shall be fulfilled, and the End hath found the Beginning.

(4.) 7. *Adam* was a Virgin of Purity, with both *Masculine and Feminine Tinctures*, as is evident; for 'tis said (when *Adam* only was made) *Male and Female* created he them, so compleat was He as able to *Increase and Multiply*, and *Blessed thereunto*, v. 28. By both Tinctures; not by two Persons; for *Eve*'s being made, is not recorded till *Gen.* 2. 21.

Obj. 8. Will any say *Adam* and *Eve* were made at once? *Gen.* 1. 27. *Gen.* 2. 28. but only the Order more at large given.

Answ. 9. It is answered by the *Holy Ghost*; where, the Apostle convinceth by One Argument the reasonableness of the *Woman's Subjection*; because of the *Priority* of Man's Creation.

10. This must also be noted, the *Woman* was not given him, as were the Females to other Creatures.

Also that before her being made, God said all was *Very Good*; Rested from his *Creating* work; Blessed a Sabbath; Planted *Eden*, Watered it; caused it to Grow; and

Considerations on the Scope of Jacob Behmen.

and the Sacred Records name the Rivers, and several quarters whitherward their Effluxes directed themselves; what Lands they washed, &c.

11. But farther, that the Propagation of *Adam*'s Race should have been by *Adam* alone, is demonstrable (among many other produceable) by the following Arguments.

12. There was no Rending of the body to have been; for Rending is inconsistent with the Happy, Perfect Eternal State of Union; dividing the Properties caus'd Enmity, as in Heat, Cold, &c. *Argument 1.*

13. The hanging on him the Bestial Genitals is, That whereof Nature it self (as depraved as now it is) is Ashamed of, and Blusheth at: The Soul hideth it self all it can from This Monstrous filthy Brutish Deformity, which it would not do, had it been it self of no higher Extraction. This the very Fallen Man well sees, to be a New Strange Hateful Image, whereto therefore It would not be subjected by the Creation. *Argum. 2.*

14. The Law of Circumcision on That Member, shews God's displeasure at That New-gotten way, like the Bestial Propagation. *Argum. 3.*

15. The Lord Jesus His preferring the Chaste Virgin Life, tho' (of pity to our Impotence and Infirmity) restraining them, only to it, to whom power is extended thereunto, signifieth (as himself said in another case not very forreign to this) that in the beginning it was not so. *Argum. 4.*

16. The sad and astonishing Effect as the first fruit of Copulation after dividing of the Tinctures was, when *Eve* brought forth *Cain*, she said, *I have got a Man from the Lord*, more truly rendred, I have got a Man The Lord; intimating that she thought That Son was the Seed promised should break the Serpent's Head. But he prov'd (as the Seed of the Serpent) the Murtherer of him who bare the Image of the promised Seed which was so great a consternation, that she conceived no more till after 70 years. *Argum. 5.*

17. The disregard God sheweth towards That Divided Image, * who also in the Transgression shewed a disregard towards the Inhibition of the Most High God; which disregard for Humbling That Sex, appears, *Argum. 6.* * Viz. The *Woman.*

1. By enjoyning Their Subjection, and she to have power on her Head, because of the Angels (that is to say) Those flaming glorious Virgins in whom the Tinctures are in inseparable Union, are God's immediate Vicegerents, and would not that the separate Tincture should forget its Declension, and forgo or surmount its Station; but be Modest, Submissive. and Humble.

2. By not admitting them any Token of Resumption into the Covenant under the Law, whereas the Males had That of Circumcision.

3. By admitting and enjoyning only the Males to Worship at *Jerusalem* thrice every year; and when the Women came, they came only into a Court in the Lord's House more remotely scituate than the place for the Males.

4. By the little mention of the bringing forth any Woman before the Floud, and without Record of the Age of any Woman in the whole Old and New Testament, *Sarah* only excepted.

18. The Law of Uncleanness after Child-bearing shews how impure This way of Propagation is; for the Woman having brought forth a Man-child, was unclean seven days, and to continue without touching any hallowed thing, or approaching the Sanctuary 33 days. But if she had a Maid-child, her Legal Uncleanness was for fourteen days, and not to be purified till sixty six days.

Whereas seven days sufficed for cleansing a Leper, or one who had an Issue; Those on the eighth day might come into the Tabernacle of the Congregation as before. *Argum. 7.* *Lev.1. 2,4,5.*

19. All which evinceth the Human Birth by the Woman to have much more

D   in

Considerations on the Scope of Jacob Behmen.

in it than bodily Pollution, since separating the Tinctures. For the Leprosie was a bodily Pollution in a high degree; but the cleansing the Woman being near Five times as much for a Man-child, and near Ten times as much for a Maid-child, is a too pregnant Testimony that the Impurity of. This Propagation is exceeding great, which moved *David's* Confession; *I was Born in Iniquity, and in Sin did my Mother Conceive me.*

Argum. 8.   20. Man's Propagation after Separating the Tinctures is defiled with much Immodesty and Lust; so that it derives Filth, Sin and Shame (as by a Torrent down a Precipice) from one Dark Soul to another: For abating the Impetuousness of which, *Isaac* the Son of the Promise was not only of *Abraham*, when Old, but of Aged *Sarah*, with whom it was ceased to be after the manner of Women; and Lust was withered, and the eminent *Joseph*, *Samuel*, and other choice Servants of God were of great Modesty, and obtained by Prayer.

21. But at once fully to convince us of our Impure Descent from *Adam* and *Eve*, the Lord Jesus was of the Virgin.

CHAP. XVII. *Of a Virgin-Propagation.*

Q. 1. WILL any ask, *Could a Virgin-Propagation possibly have been?*
A. The Lord speaketh nothing in vain, and He it was that said, *God is able of these Stones to raise Children unto* Abraham. But,

2. It is answered, That tho' the above Arguments may challenge the force of Demonstration to enlightened Reason; yet, because the Senses often make Mutinous Resistance to solid Reason, the Senses shall be (by what follows) gratified, as far as the Sublimity of the Subject may expose it self to the view and touch.

Demonstrations to the Senses of a Virgin-Propagation.

Demonst. 1.   3. Light (with little loss) penetrateth Glass, so plentifully, as can improve Generation by contraction of its Central and Original Property thro' Burning-glasses, by which also it can destroy; as 'tis said *Archimedes* did the Roman Navy at *Syracusa*; and we see Light, not only walking thro' Christal, but Multiplying by the Motion.

4. And can any think *Adam's* Pure Body (whilst capable of Eternity) had not Less in it obstructive to his Magical Will, for Divine Imployment; or rather More Assisting Power, than Condensed Ponderous Glass or Christal have of opposition or furtherance of the Solar Raies?

Was not His whole Man fortified by Harmony for Vigorous Operations?

Demonst. 2.   5. See we not the subtle Atoms of Fire, insinuate thro' the Pores of Gross Iron Pots, to the evaporating of Liquor, with the ascending Breath whereof, the subtle fiery Atoms cloath themselves and take wing, till only Dregs uncapable of Light be captiv'd in the Pot, and finally the Iron become Lustrous, as if it also wished no longer to be Iron, but Fire and Light.

See we not Fiery Atoms, as calmly enter the finer Pores of Silver Vessels, and with like facility make passage through the most exquisite Pores of Golden Vessels.

6. And should not That Glorious Creatures Body (a glimpse whereof was *Moses* Shining Face and Wondrous Works) have been more Potent to work His Creators Will, in His Own Principle, than these Dead Instances?

Consider we also the Healing Emanations from the Bodies of the Disciples, as the Power of Raising the Dead, *&c.*

7. See

Confiderations on the Scope of Jacob Behmen. 25

7. See we not the due affection of the Blood, drawn out of the Veins, with That *Demonſt.* 3. remaining in the Veins. And if That which iſſued out at one Orifice be kindly treated abroad, how it difpatcheth quick Meſſengers to impart the Vertue thereof, not only to that Wound whence it iſſued, but to as many other as the Body hath ſuffered by.

8. And ſhall we abridge the Magical-Child, of the kind Aſſiſting Intercourſe of Its natural Parent, of what the Abient Man, and Cold Blood is privileged with.

9. A Woman, Great with Child, doth often Impreſs Magically on the Fruit of *Demonſt.* 4. her Womb Cherries, Strawberries, *&c.* things She Longed Earneſtly for, as well as other tokens of Ill, Created by her Paſſions of Fear; others do Mortally Wound by their Anguiſh, Defpair. *&c.* Others Exalt to expreſſions of Joy, by the raiſed Serenity of the Mother's Spirit; as the Babe, in the Womb of *Eliʒabeth*, leapt at the Salutation of the Virgin *Mary*.

10. If therefore ſuch Vigour remain as the Relique of Languiſhing Magick-Power, in ſo great a degree Dead, and almoſt forgotten; and that in the weaker Sex of the divided Tincture of Mortal Man, when Rowſed; ſhall any doubt but That ſufficient Virtue and Majeſty Sate enthroned in *Adam*, whilſt perfectly Enriched and Ennobled with both the Tinctures? Who was a Spark of God's Omnipotence, Divinely to effect what His Creator bleſſed him to, (*viʒ.*) to Multiply the New Race, bearing God's compleat Image, inſtead of the Apoſtate Angels, who by extinguiſhing the Kingdom of Love (implanted in their Creation) had let looſe, awakened, and introduced into themſelves, the Wrath of the firſt Principle, and ſo perverted God's Holy Work, by the Wrath of the firſt four Spirits.

11. We ſee an Ability of Propagation in the Univerſal Sperm iſſuing at the Con- *Demonſt.* 5. duct Pipes of the three Principles. The Eye obſerves it in Shell-fiſh, Trees, Flowers, Herbs, having their various Kinds in their reſpective Seeds with their Tinctures of Male and Female united, or Fire and Light in one. And though theſe laſt, the Vegetative Tribe be more remote than the Senſitive; yet every one gives Pregnant Teſtimony to illuſtrate and lead to the moſt Noble.

12. And ſhall any think, Man, whoſe Original exempted him (had he perſever'd) and fixt and ſet him on high, far above the reach of any the leaſt approach of Mortality; as Sorrow, Wearineſs, Sickneſs, Sleep, could admit the Defect of any thing that might tend to impeach his Perfection? Should not he be fully able to perform all the Parts of what might concern the perpetuating his Race, by communicating his Heat and Light as the Sun doth his,in pure Modeſty, and higheſt humble Love, that his Divine Offspring might have aſſiſted in that holy Paradiſical Imployment.

13. It ſeemed needful to be thus Large, to be a High and Powerful Incitement to all the Sons of Wiſdom, to fix their Souls on noble Divine Objects, by the Example of the Sons of Princes, who level at Kingdoms.

14. Let therefore the Sons of God pity and pray for, and never envy gods of clay, who covet Crowns of glittering Earth, ſtuft with Thorns, waſht with Tears and Blood of oppreſſed Innocents, often ſupported by Fraud, and not ſeldom blown off by the breath of Curſes juſtly caus'd.

15. At beſt the centre of Cares, ſurrounded by ravennous hungry Vultures.

I ſay, Let not the Children of the Day caſt their Eyes on theſe, nor ſuffer themſelves to be encircled and enchanted with ſuch Mockeries; but ſet their whole Hearts on the Everlaſting Inheritance forfeited by *Adam* and *Eve*, but redeemed by the Promiſed Seed, the Humble Son of the Eternal Virginity, the Glorious Lord Jeſus.

16. This hath alſo been the larger infiſted on to keep us in conſtant Self-abaſement, that every of us hath ſo Prodigally waſted our Heavenly Portion, and fed among

Confiderations on the Scope of Jacob Behmen:
among Swine; Abandoned our dear pretious Virgin Image of Purity and Modefty, and become Shamelefs and Filthy with the Deformity of the Luftful Beafts that have no Law.

Alfo to facilitate, explicate and introduce what follows; which is to Enquire according to the Method propofed.

CHAP. XVIII. *Of fome Steps by which* Adam *declined towards his heavy* Fall.

1. THAT Man having both Tinctures was perfect Male and Female, and fo was very good, hath been fhewed from Scripture, and proved to the enlightned Reafon, and demonftrated to the very Senfes, though now they are fo dull.

2. Alfo. That Man fhould have have Exerted his Holy Ability of Will, and United it to his Excellent Power, is plain: But he did it not, is as plain; by neglect whereof, it was faid, *It is not good that Man fhould be alone, but a Meet-help fhould be made him.* Then God caft *Adam* into a deep fleep, took from him a Rib, of That made a Woman. What a ftrange change fee we, fo vaft, fo fudden an Alteration!

3. Was *Adam* good, perfectly fo, to walk with God like a God, in a Heavenly or Paradifical ftate for ever ? Wants he a Help, by Subftraction to receive Addition ?

4. Will any one penetrate into this, to them, or him be it faid. Seeing *Adam* would not ftir up both the Tinctures, which in great Might were United in him, but would in this alfo be an Angel, to remain barren as they. Whereas he as a Centre or Fountain, fhould have ftreamed out a new Race; therefore the Gracious Creator let him fleep as one in a Swoun, then divided from him the Female Tincture and the leffer part of his Effence or Strength, fignified by a Rib, which is part of the out-guard of the Internal Organs of Life, and therewith built a She-Man.

5. Both were Holy, but Danger of Tranfgreffing was near; hence came the fevere Penal Law, That they fhould not Eat of the Forbidden Fruit, (*viz.*) That of the third Principle, wherein were the Properties of Good and Evil, both of the Aftral and Elementary World. And the knowledge of both the Properties was in the Fruit; for he was to Rule over, and not receive into himfelf the third Principle; the Properties in it were divided by reafon of the diforder caufed by the Fall of *Lucifer*; and therefore meat only for the Tranfitory Creatures.

Now come we to the Degrees by which Man declined.

1. 6. Step, muft be his not Exerting, Executing and Exercifing the Power his gracious Creator invefted him with.

2. 7. Step, was his Sleep. Sleep or Swouning is Death's Elder Brother, a Debility to the Motion of Senfitive Creatures; an Inability in a great meafure to Action, every Inclination to it is Hoftility againft an Eternal perfect ftate; *Noah*'s fleep fhew'd the Figure of *Adam*'s fhameful Sleep: And *Lot*'s Sleep figur'd fomewhat worfe than Shame, as the Confequence of *Adam* s fleep; yet both effected by their declining in the third Principle, in oppofition to which, *Daniel* calls the Angels *Watchers.*

3. 8. Step, was his being divided Dividing by diffection or difcontinuance of Parts is Diminution, and fo Diametrically oppofite to entirenefs, warring againft Union. For, if the leaft divifible Part be fevered or cut off from any Body, wanting the

leaft

Considerations on the Scope of Jacob Behmen.

least degree of Infinity, that whence it is dissected, how immense soever, is made less, till the Section do as really and locally Re-unite, as before it separated.

9. But *Eve* being taken from *Adam*, made her a Numerical Self, was a Local severing, as truly distinct as the Female from the Male of other Creatures; nor could the Tinctures re-unite to be as before in pure Virgin Modesty, but she became no Restorer, but a Help to prevent a worse state; but how a Help may be demonstrated thus.

10. The strugling of the three first Forms generateth the fourth, as the contest *Demonst.* 1. of the two first begets the third; so the discord of the fourth doth wrestle till it produce the fifth; and so of the rest. This while they were in sweet Harmony in one only individual *Adam*, he might, like the Sun, irresistibly have diffused and shed his potent Influence; but after one rending, must follow a farther rending of the Body. But a bare incision to divide without Separation(or any part) of discontinuance of Parts, may be only such as may stir up to Action, though not without thwarting, reluctance or regret, which may farther appear.

11. A Tree partly by its secure situation, from shaking, jogging, stormy pushes *Demonst.* 2. or rugged touches may have its Mercurial Vertue slumbering, as Fire in Ashes, the Sulphur in it be num'd, and the whole in a Lethargy: when by cleaving the Root with a wooden Wedge, that part is awakened, and the contrary qualities of its Composition, mutually and gradually excite and call one another, till like a Clock-work they conspire and joyn Hands to bring on their great End. But if the Plant voluntarily consent wholly to give up its Will to breathing out its Odour and Fruit, what need concussion, or slashing, or any cleaving or dividing at all.

12. And though this dividing of *Adam* was as the Lancet of a merciful Chirurgeon; yet every Wound of a Friend supposeth Necessity, and consequently incongruous with the perfection of entire Peace and Union.

Though also these Demonstrations speak plainest after *Eves* Transgression; yet may we scrutiny by the Effect into what occasioneth it.

13. Step, was *Adam's* Lusting after *Eve*; for when he took her in his Lust, where 4. was then his Modesty, Divine Virginity and Purity? The heavenly Virgin withdraws from every the least appearance of Unchastity or Inconstancy.

14. Step, was the Tree of Temptation; *Adam* having a little declined from his 5. Primary Perfection, which brought the Necessity of dividing him; yet reigning as a Mighty Powerful Son of the Almighty God in all the three Principles and being subject only to God, what wonder was the sprouting of that Plant in Obedience of his Royal Magical desire? which was so Potent in all the three Principles, as to any thing in them irresistible. What could hinder, seeing he had divided himself from himself; but that a Plant with divided Properties of Good and Evil should put forth its Fruit in the third Principle, and offer it self to the touch and taste of him, who was immediate Lord both in Right and Possession, in and over the same third Principle.

15. Step, was *Eve*, who being less than the half of the new Enthroned Prince, 6. and curiously Eying the air Form and charm'd by the Serpent's subtle Rhetorick Took and Eat of it, as also then did *Adam*, seeing that she fell not instantly Dead, which introduced such an Ample Fall, as at which the Heavens blush, the Earth quakes, the Dark World domineers.

16. For *Adam's* first Principle consisting of the four first Forms, by the Departure of the Lustre of the second Principle of Love and Meekress, Peace and Joy; became Dreadful, and full of Anguish. And his third Principle became Dark and Opake; his Strength became Bones, his Tincture in part extinguish'd, the rest of it became Beastial, Mortal, and the Properties of it became Enemicitious, then must

must he have Gutts, and a Draught to eject the Putrifying Elemental Food. The Astral World also drew and inclined him as their various wrestling got predominance.

17. The Tree and Fruit, was no better nor worse than what we have, but alike unsuitable to him, as Hot or Cold Poison is to us: Their Fallen State as sadly alter'd, as if a Man who should Rule over the Beasts, should (as *Nebuchadnezzar*) have a Beast's Heart and Organs given him; for they regarded not, that from Talking of it, God's severe earnest Command had inhibited and forewarned them.

18. For the Food ordained for them had the Properties in Perfect Harmony; no Curse, Mortality, Sickness, Sorrow, Care, Pain, not the least appearance of Evil, but of the One Holy Element purely Paradisical, and whereof They might be able to live eternally. It was the Quintessence and Divine Word substantiated, such as feeds the Blessed in the Resurrection.

They were not to have known Evil and Good in the Root of them, divided as hath been said. Yet tho' the Experimental Knowing it were destructive to them, it is destructive to us to be ignorant of it.

19. As a Traveller, observing the Disaster of another (who contemning warning) lost his way and himself, unwarily inducted and strayed with him, is Now highly concerned to know the Aberrations, which his Ill Leader should not have known, that he may extricate and disentangle himself, retrieve the Miscarriage, and shun the Precipices and Perils so fatal to his forerunner.

CHAP. XIX. *What Fallen Man's Estate was by the Fall.*

1. THE second Principle being the Majestick, Sweet, Divine Love, Meek Light, and the Chast Virgin of God's Wisdom, was withdrawn, and he left dead as to it.

1. His Soul, tho' it had lost the Divine Life of Pure Angelical Modest Love, yet being out of the Fountain Spirits, was incapable of Dissolution, but must ever remain its own stinging Fire, and its own Anguish, without possibility of enkindling the Light.

2. For Now had he the Introduced Enmity there, and the four Original Fountains of Binding, Attracting, Anguish and Fire, whereof his Soul (as to its first Principle) was originated and made, stood in irreconcileable Enmity as to any Power remaining in *Adam* to compose them; These Contrarieties (like Murtherers) might well be Those of whom *Cain* was after afraid.

3. His Body (like That of the other Creatures in the third Principle of which it was) became subjected to the Astral Evil Influences, and to the Divided Properties of the Elements, which had power to impose the Necessity of Pain, Sickness, Want, continual Danger, transitory Mutations, Mortality and Putrifaction, till Man should return to the Dust which he was come to be: And that every part, the Astral and Elementary, were fallen back or receded, and Those parts resumed into its own several Æther, Principle or Receptacle, like other Beasts.

4. And while he was Toiling under his Evil Influences, loads of Sin and the Curse, he might (like the tame Beasts) feed on the Food they did eat, of Roots, Herbs and Fruits, wherein were the Evil and Good Properties; and he might (like the wild Destroying and Ravenous Beasts, Fowls and Fishes of Prey) kill and feed on the tame, and live in Fear and hostile Enmity with his fellow destroyers, who bear the Image of the Dark World.

5. He might also (till his Astral Revolution, or other Evil had given extream Date

Considerations on the Scope of Jacob Behmen.

Date and Period, to his Accursed Dying Life) have, (like other Beasts) generated his Children, having Now the Members (Monuments of Sin and Shame) hung on him for Propagation. And Those his Off-spring should inwardly have been Devils, and outwardly Beasts, according to the third Principle. Yea and what could have hindred but Their Bodies should have been conformed to the Image of the several Beasts here, whereof Their Minds had the Nature, Affections and Qualities, as of Dogs, Goats, Foxes, Swine; Bears, Wolves, Tygers, Vipers, Serpents, Toads, Lions, &c. And to have had no other Resurrection than those mischievous odious Animals, by Their monstrous Idea's to bear the Image of the Dark World's Properties.

6. Whither Fallen Man was hurrying, may farther appear, by some notorious consequences of our Defection.

1. The Americans, in many parts (like Beasts of Prey) devour Raw Flesh; some yet worse, eat the Flesh of Serpents, and other unclean Creatures; some elsewhere said to be Canibals.

2. It is by Geographers ob'erved the Tartars to be so far Dogs and Cats, that They are born blind, and till five days cannot see plainly.

3. The Dark World, or first Principle, hath arrested the Africans, conforming their very out-side by a black hue to their Evil Natures.

7. So did the Astringency ratifying the Covetous Will of *Lots* Wife, prevail to a terrible extream, so as to fix her a Pillar of Salt.

As did the same Principle of Bitterness, Anguish and Fire consume *Sodom*.

8. It is observed by uncontrollable Authors, That the Devil, (tho' so crude and unsuitable, direful a Companion) hath (by Infernal Sophistry) used some unhappy Elementary Compounds, wherewith he hath dismally and fatally cohabited with lustful, beastly, filthy People of both Sexes, whose Sensuality coupled to their Sinful Desires, had deformed into his Image; so that he hath carnally cooperated to the sateing their obscene decrepid Lusts.

9. Not only Thus as above, but we had a concurrence to Generate a Race of Human Forms. Incarnate Devils. Children They are said to be (no doubt) of Darkness, and literally of Their Father the Devil.

10. Such was That call'd a *Succubi* Wife to a Gentleman in *Germany*; concerning whom *John Frederick* (then Prince Elector of *Saxony*) desired *Luther's* Opinion, who judged it a Devil; desiring the Prince to note heedfully what That Off-spring would demonstrate themselves. *Mart. Luther: Colloquies. Chap.* 35.

11. Perhaps the Old Enemy (who once used the Serpent) might in the above Story, (to prevent the horror of his own Approach, and effect his uncouth Machinations) imploy some Terrestrial, Aerial or Aquastrish Creature, wherein to unite himself to one whose Sins had depraved and subjected to so base, perilous and prodigious a Consortship.

12. There were in *Luther's* time some Abject Productions in *Saxony* call'd *Kilcrops* or *Suppositii* (with us Changelings) One of Them *Luther* saw at *Dessaw*; it did eat as much as two Threshers, another suckt six Nurses dry; if any thing Ill happened in the house, would laugh and be joyful, but while all went Well would cry and be very sad.

13. Such was the Transformation of *Nebuchadnezzar*, that his Hairs were as Birds Feathers, and his Nails as Claws.

14. Such a Subjection hath our Elementary Structure lapsed into by the Fall, that it may as really be Transformed as an unburnt Earthen Vessel may: And that tho' usually by consent of the Will, as in Witches.

15. Yet may it also be sometimes without consent, and by the Arch Enemy be imposed on, as was the Woman at *Isenach*, who in a Conflict of fifteen or sixteen hours

hours was Transformed into That of a Calf, her Hands and Feet bent, and like Horns or Hoofs; her Tongue rough and dry; her Body cold and swoln, yet her Soul found to be safe, and her Body by Prayer Restored to its Human Form.

16. Man became vain in his Imagination, and his foolish Heart was darkened. They were Worshippers of Angels, of the Host of Heaven, of Devils, of Brute Creatures of Garlick as in *Egypt*, of Stocks, Things almost incredible to us: That Rational Creature should make Their Hope and Confidence to be in Irrational, till we reflect on all Nations in This Age pretending Improved Skill and Knowledge, yet still do place Their Confidence in Money.

CHAP. XX *Of Mans Recovery; how he was he'ped again by Christ; and by what wonderful way and method Redemption was & is wrought.*

1. WHO is sufficient to tell This. what Vessel may carry This Treasure? It was studied by the Holy Angels, is the Ornament of Heaven, will be the Song in Eternity. It is the sum of what the Spirit of God hath been dictating to the Prophets, pointing at by the Law and Ceremonies proclaiming by the Apostles and Saints in His Word in the Mouth of all his Servants thro' all Generations.

2. Now, tho' none can say how high the eighth Sphere is, much less the Infinity beyond or without it; yet every one can measure his own heighth, being really part of it. So, as far as can be reached by So vile a Nothing, some particle of the Abyss of Grace may in Childish Simplicity be stammer'd out, and haply some Assistance given to Such Inquirer, whose Inward Senses shall be opened in any degree of aptness to the Sublimity of the Matter, and whose Spirit shall be Humbled and held back to the lowly manner of exhibiting the same.

3. All Knowledge not leading us Humbly towards Jesus Christ is Ignorance, and compared with the Light set up in us by Him, is Blackness; with the Vertue of it, is Dung; with the Holiness and Purity of it, is Filthiness; with the Order of it, is Confusion and Amusement of Spirit; with the Utility of it, is meer Loss of precious Time.

4. We have in the precedent Discourse beheld the direful shameful State *Adam* declined into by the Loss of the Divine Virgin of God's Wisdom, with whom he should alwaies have lived in Purity, Modesty, and Perfection of Love: Who whilst he stood, his Soul was of the Might of Eternity, his Spirit of the Pure Majestick Divine Light, his Body out of the One Holy Element more Noble than seven times Refined Gold, as the Shining Sun, and capable to endure in Eternity.

5. But Sin marr'd all, his Holy Body degenerated as from Celestial Christal to Putrifying Carrion, which must know Dissolution, and for any Power remaining in him, must have returned to the Divided Elements, without hope of Recollection and Resurrection. Which might cause some of the Antients, who (better knew what the body is come to be, and what Principles and Elements compounded of, than what at first it was, much less what the Merciful Creator was about for Restoring his Lost Image: It might strongly sway some Wise Men in several Ages) to laugh at the Novelty of the Resurrection, as did the Athenians.

6. The Gracious and Merciful Creator pitying His Undone Creature of Love, to His Own Precious disappeared Virgin Image, having no motive from any want in Him of His Creature, nor any worth in the Creature, nor any ability remaining in His Creature to help Himself, but of His Own Only Meer, Free Grace and Goodness, His Tender Bowels of Infinite Love wherewith His Compassions were enkindled, did set Infinite Power and Wisdom on work to supplant the Serpent

in

Considerations on the Scope of Jacob Behmen.

in Man, by reimplanting again the Dear Bride of Purity and Modesty to whom *Adam* was at first Married, but had adulterously, causlesly and foolishly left, having treacherously abandoned himself, and betaken to the Divided Properties.

7. God in-spake again the Ingrafted Word, saying, *The Seed of the Woman shall break the Serpent's Head*; which Word so reimplanted was like a spark of Fire falling into Tinder; or like Seed sown; or like Leven hid in three measures of Meal; for it was a Living Power, a Speaking Witness. It was call'd the Lamb slain from the Foundation of the World, the Powerful Love of Jesus Christ the second Person of the Trinity, who by That Power of Love filleth all places in the Heavens and Earth in His Own Holy Principle, and This Love is Jesus Christ Himself.

8. The second *Adam* and Holy Seed did not only come in the Fulness of Time into, or in the Womb of the Virgin *Mary* when He took Flesh, but then at the instant of *Adam*'s Fall at the Father's in-speaking did implant himself to overthrow the work of the Devil.

9. And stood at the Door of *Adam* and *Eve*, and alwaies standeth at the Door of every Child of Theirs ever since, none excepted in the Light of Their Life, Preaching Salvation, and with the Mighty Power of the Holy Ghost reproveth Sin, convinceth of Righteousness, judgeth Disobedience, and warneth all, more or less, of the Judgment to come.

10. This Living Word, or Word of Life, hath call'd it self by several names, for all names are in it. It is the Refiners Fire, a Light shining in a Dark place, *Emmanuel*, The Saviour, The Hope of *Israel*, The Rock of Ages, The Redeemer, Love, Wisdom, Righteousness, The Holy Thing. Life Eternal, where-ever, and in whomsoever Obedience is yielded. It is of invincible Strength, will any lay hold on it? brings irresistible Arguments, will any lay them up in their Hearts; uninterrupted Peace, will any sit still under its Counsels? His Weapons can neither be warded nor blunted; His Defensives are impenetrable.

11. The Word replanted in *Adam* and *Eve* after Their Disobedience, is call'd an Ingrafted Word, tho' it was carried downward chiefly, or most visibly in the direct Line thro' *Seth* to *Enoch*, who was in the Sabbath as the Seventh Day, of whom came *Methusalah*, who (as the longest Liver recorded) figured Eternity, yet was the same in Them as a Priesthood to be Leaders and Stars to Their Brethren; The same Principle being (with less Brightness) in others also; for neither is the Sun visible, but to Them who have a Receiving Power: So nor were the rest of Mankind wholly Blind, but had Their Talents entrusted to Them. And this Line of the Holy Seed were as the Lord's Candlesticks and Lamps, whereat others were to enkindle their weaker Lights.

12. It may be noted that the Heathen have all of Them the Gospel more or less obscurely Preached in them. For as they without the Written Law do the things contained in the Law; so do they without the Written Gospel partake of the Mercy published by the Gospel.

13. That is, being conscious to themselves of their Faults, yet find (by the Smiles of the Heavens in the Fruitful Seasons, and in the suitable Productions of the Earth) that they receive Good for Evil, which is the Vertue of the second Principle or Gospel written on the whole Creation. Notwithstanding all which, if they harden their Hearts they become Sinners against Law and Gospel, the Law written in their Hearts, and the Gospel shining in the Light of their Understandings, so conspicuously, that tho' some of Them Laughed at the news of the Resurrection, we hear Them serious at the tydings of the Judgment to come, having every one of Them a Self-condemning Judge in his bosom.

14. Love is strong as Death, but This Love is much stronger, only Sin and finally Impenitent Men, Hell and Devils judge themselves unworthy of it. But

E   This

Considerations on the Scope of Jacob Behmen.

This hath knockt at the Door of every Sinners Heart, and cryes, *How long, ye simple Ones, will ye Love Folly and Scorning, and Hate your own Mercies?*

15. *Abel* and *Seth* had the Hearing Ear; in that Line it most eminently descended by a continued Succession thro' all Generations, yet sometimes thro' very dirty Channels; for tho' all were such till This Seed took Root in some, and bare Paradisical Fruit, and made them fit for the Masters Table; yet some were much more foul than others.

2. He enters into Foul Hearts, tho' himself be so High born, and Purity it self, that passing into Foul places cannot be defiled, but as a Refiners Fire not comprehended by the Dross, which yet it purgeth away. A work only possible to Omnipotence.

A few Considerations of that which shall be the Wonder of Eternity follow.

CHAP. XXI. *Of the Incarnation of the Lord Jesus Christ.*

1. 1. IT ought Attentively to be pondered, that when the Fulness of Time, or Limit of the Covenant was come, Jesus took Man's whole Nature of the Virgin *Mary*; but inasmuch as she was the Daughter of *Joachim*, and *Anna*, and of *Eve*, she could not be totally a Virgin of Purity: *Who can bring a clean thing out of an unclean? not one.*

2. 2. That Jesus Christ neither came into a Clean Vessel, nor took a Pure Nature on Him, but made the Vessel Clean, and the Polluted Nature to become Pure. The misunderstanding of which caused the *Colliridiani* to render to the Virgin *Mary* Divine Worship.

3. 3. We must know, that when our Redeemer took our Nature on him, He took it out of all the Virgin *Mary*'s Essences; as well those of her Soul given her out of the first Principle, and those of her Spirit given her out of the second, as those of her Body out of the third Principle. All which, Soul, Body and Spirit, were propagated by her immediate Parents, *Joachim* and *Anna*.

4. 4. We are to know, the Lord destroyed not Those Essences; for He came not to destroy, but took them as they were. And by the Divine New Man which He brought with Him, and which Himself was, Refined and Sanctified them, in them to work Their and Our Eternal Salvation.

5. 5. We cannot say there was no Evil in the Root of the Essences He took from the Virgin *Mary*, as was mentioned above. But his Divine Conception Exempting Him from any the least Impression, Stain or Spot, did illustrate and clarifie them. As Fire doth Iron, the Tincture doth Metals, or the Sun Transmutes the Harsh, Sour, and Ill Properties of Fruits.

6. 6. We are not to doubt whether the Lord took a Human Soul from the Virgin or no, about which many have erred; for how else had the Essences of Our poor Captivated Souls been rescued; had not the second *Adam* as truly assumed a Human Soul, as that whereof the first *Adam* consisted? It was Our Souls that had Sin and Death, and were to be Redeemed; so Our Gracious Lord made His Soul, which was also a True Human Soul, the Offering for Sin.

7. 7. Nor need we fear that the Lord took not Our Mortal Flesh and Blood on Him, but brought Heavenly Flesh in His Conception, and only Heavenly Flesh; for He took also Our True Body of Flesh and Blood on Him from the Virgin *Mary*; He took our Weak Infirm Body subjected to Passions of Hunger, Sleep, *&c.* wherein lay Wrath and the Curse, all which He bare with the Sufferings incident thereunto, as Temptations, Scourgings, Reproaches, Piercings, Crucifying, Anguish,

Death,

Considerations on the Scope of Jacob Behmen. 33

Death, Burial. And raised the Self-same Body which gives us assurance of our Resurrection, and opens a Door for the Body (though now Mortal) to partake with the Soul, Eternal Life.

8. We are to know, that our new Bodies, will be the same very true real Bodies we now have, and not other Bodies; though not consisting of Accidents, not palpable, yet substantial, as is manifest by what follows.

9. The Mutations in Nature are no destruction of Bodies; as a Grain of Wheat being sown, passeth several Mutations, yet is still the same. For whereas at first it dies, it is only by the Separator resolved into the divers Kinds of its own Composition, that it may be capable of Commixture, and Unite assimilated Bodies to it, and so Collect encrease of *Mater*, which it admits in no greater Proportion than to be the Father and Mother of all it self, and augment and multiply it self by; yet still is Wheat, though hath the Increase of Quantity of many Grains of Wheat; as an Oak is but an Accorn improved.

10. Nature in orderly Motion goes forward, and will not return into its Mystery by the Steps it went out, till it hath compleated its Circulation. You may as well return the Sun Eastward over us, as make a Fruit become a Tree; but in its orderly Motion; first into a Fruit and Seed, then is the new one the old renewed, rather than another. So is the new Body (though Glorious) not existent, but by the dying of the old.

11. As *Adam*'s Fall made him not another Man, but was still the Self-same, in another, a Monstrous Image, as we also are deformed by that direful Fall: So the Lord Jesus raising up his own Dead Body, and cloathing it with Glory and Immortality, and thereby giving us a Resurrection to be like him, doth not make us to be other Men than now we are, with loss of our Monstrosity and Access, and recovery of the Glory we were created in, and is by Him graciously purchased for us.

12. We are to know, That the Lord Jesus Christ when he assumed Flesh and Blood in the Virgins Womb, was then not only there, but then also sate and reigned in the whole infinite Abyss of the Father.

13. We are also to know, That after the Divine Nature or Infinite Godhead of Jesus Christ had assumed the Humane Nature, He remained the self-same unmixed Glorious second Person as before. And yet that by taking the Humanity from the Virgin *Mary*, He really became what he was not before; (*viz.*) a real Son of Man, with a true Humane Soul, Body and Spirit, as we are, and capable to Suffer and Die.

14. We are to know, the Humane Nature or Creature in the Ascention and Glorification, was not swallowed up by the Divine Nature, as a flame of a Candle is by the Sun extinguish'd; But the Humane Nature now Glorified, remains for ever a Glorified Body; being, the same true individual Humane Nature or Man, which was Crucified, Dead, Buried and raised up by his Almighty Power, as the first Fruit, Original, and Author of the General Resurrection.

15. That the Lord Jesus Christ, who in the Womb of the Virgin, became as truly a Man as we are, who have our Souls, Spirits and Bodies propagated by our immediate Parents. Yet that besides the infinite Dignity of his Almightiness, as the second Person and Son of God by Eternal Generation, which united Himself to His created Humane Soul, Spirit and Body. I say, besides all this, He was the true created Son of God, and so was a true Heavenly Man, and a Virgin of Holiness, Purity and Modesty; And so begotten by the Holy Ghost.

16. In which respect He was no Son of Man (even as neither was the first *Adam*) but as truly the Son of God by Creation, as with respect to His Godhead, He was by Eternal Generation. And though the words, *Thou art my Son, this day I have begotten*

Demonst. 1.

Demonst. 2.

Demonst. 3.

9.

10.

11.

12.

Psal. 2. 7.
Hebr. 1. 5.

E 2

Considerations on the Scope of Jacob Behmen.

begotten thee may be underſtood of the Eternal Generation; for the Father ceaſeth not to beget His Eternal Son from Eternity and in Eternity; yet the words may well be applicable to this Heavenly Humanity, whereof both *David* and *Paul* ſpeak

17 But becauſe this 12th Note laſt aſſerted, is hard to be underſtood ſince Man's Fall; partly, becauſe it is of ſo Noble Extraction, and ſeeming to be of ſo rare mention in the Holy Scriptures, ſo remote from Senſe, and Man's dull Apprehenſion, of ſo excellent Nature, and ſo highly profitable and advantageous to be known. Alſo that the penetrating into the Knowledge of it, requires Divine Wiſdom, enlightned Underſtanding, it calleth for higheſt Attention, as that plainly teacheth the Way God took and ſtill taketh for recovery of loſt Mankind. It is farther clear'd by what follows; more eſpecially by the following *Pag.* 32. in *Chap.* 22.

13.   18. We ought to know that the Divine Subſtance which United to it the Eſſences of the Humane Soul in *Mary*, came not thither deſcending from the higheſt Heaven, or great Local Diſtance. But the Word which God inſpake again in Paradice, imaging it Self in the Light of Man's Life, and waiting in all the Holy Men, being the Word of Divine Wiſdom, out of the Tincture of the Holy Element, which is every where, and pure before God; that Word, took to it for an Eternal Propriety the Eſſences of Man's Soul, in and of *Maries* Virgin Matrix Not entring in, but unlocking, ingenerating and unſhutting what *Adam* had bolted up in Death.

14.   19. That though this Word were not the Almighty, ſecond Perſon of the Trinity; yet was it the Word of Wiſdom which *Adam* turned from, and in diſobeying it, he and we all, rebel againſt God more immediately than if we ſhou'd ſtubbornly reject the Command of an Angel of God. This Word of Divine Wiſdom is a Virgin of Purity, and here became the Bride to the Humane Soul; for as the Soul had the Tincture of the Fire, This brought the Tincture of the Light, and the Uniting of the Heavenly Image of Purity, to the Image that was Impure, did Tincture the Fire-Soul, and both became one Self-ſubſiſting Eternal Man.

15.   20. We are alſo to know, That foraſmuch as the two Tinctures were (at the inſtant of the Virgin *Maries* ſaying, *Be it unto me,* &c) United, and were become One Man the Image the firſt Man did bear; yet ſeeing the Fire-Soul did once treacherouſly chooſe an Earthy Luſt, inſtead of Divine Love;

21. To the end it might be now powerfully Tinctured no more to recede, and that the whole Humane Nature might be led through Death into Eternal Life; therefore did the Lord (mighty to ſave) take the whole Man, by being Bridegroom to the Virgin *Sophia*, and for that the Man (or Creature) ſtood in the Holy Element, which is pure, and every where, yet is the ſame Element, Inferior to Omnipotence; it was needful Grace and Love ſhould Unite the Creature to the Deity, which raiſed it above all it loſt in the firſt *Adam*.

22. For the Lord became as a Servant, to advance and ſecure his Servant, both the Image it once had, and add to it more : which will be the ſtupendious Contemplation of Eternity; but all this by the Lord's Incarnation was brought to paſs.

23. So that here was One, and that One conſiſted of the true Almighty Son of God, and the Holy Virgin of Wiſdom the Tincture of the Light. (*viz*.) His Heavenly Fleſh and Blood; Alſo of the Eſſences of Man's Eternal Soul, the Temporary Aſtral Soul and Elementary Body. So that not only the Eternal Fire Soul is meekened, nouriſhed and fed to live Eternally, but the outward Soul and Elementary Body are ſecured of a Reſurrection, by the raiſing of the Holy Aſtral and Elementary Body of the Lord Jeſus Chriſt, the firſt Fruits of them that ſlept, leaving nothing unraiſed, but the Linnen Cloaths in the Sepulchre. CHAP.

Considerations on the Scope of Jacob Behmen.   35

CHAP. XXII: *Of the Heavenly New Man, or Divine Humanity of Jesus Christ; what it is, where it is, and how to be participated of by us.*

IT is written, That ye put off, *&c.* the Old Man, *v.* 23. and be renewed, *&c.* and *v.* 24. that ye put on the New Man; which (after God) is created in Righteousness and true Holiness.   *Eph.*4. 22,23; 24.

Q. What is This New Man which we are to put on?
A. It is Jesus Christ; as it is written, put on the Lord Jesus Christ, *&c.* so are we said to be cloathed upon with our House which is from Heaven; call'd a Building of God.   *Rom.* 13. 14. 2 *Cor.* 5. 1,2.

1. So we find cloathed with Humility, cloathed with Honour, cloathed with Shame, intended not as a Covering, but as *Transmutation* of Us, from one contrary to another; as the Woman cloathed with the Sun, her Divine Light instead of her Darkness.   *Psal.* 104.1. *Psal.* 109.29. *Rev.* 12. 1.

Q. What of Christ may we put on, and be cloathed with, and wherewith to be cloathed upon?

2. Not His Almightiness; for that His Omnipotence is, what no Creature can behold and reach; so is the Brightness of his Fathers Glory, upholding all things by the Word of his Power.   *Negat. A.* 1.

Nor the *Body, Soul,* and *Spirit,* He received from the Virgin *Mary*; That was Earthy, a Soul, Body and Spirit descending from *Eve*; That being born of the flesh was flesh. As such (which he humbled himself to take) he was the Son of Man, and our Brother; so also we put him not on. As such he remains; for That Humanity of Christ which he had from the Virgin, remains a Creature, not so mixt, as to be confounded and swallowed up by the Deity.   *Negat. A.* 2. *Acts* 1.11,11.

3. The two Men in White, testified he should so Descend as they had seen him Ascend; as is also asserted in the 11th Particular of the Incarnation.

4. But the New Man, is the Heavenly New Man, or Heavenly Humanity of Jesus Christ, being the *humble pure Virgin of Wisdom* which *Adam* lost, and as it were died to him, disappeared, retiring into its own *Ether.*   *A.* 3. *Affirmatively*

The first *Adam* had (as it were) repudiated This Chast Holy Image; This is by the second *Adam* (the Lord from Heaven) restored and married to His, and in His to our) Earthly Humanity. It was His, at the instant, when the Holy Ghost overshadowed the Virgin *Mary.* It is Ours, when, by the Holy Ghost we are begotten again, and That Divine Image is awakened and stirred up in us.

5. Of This, let none marvel that my weak hand, begs Strength, and delights to speak; for *This is That dear pretious Image of Virginity, Purity and Modesty*; whose Eternal, Perfect. Sweet Love, was (by Apostate *Adam*) exchanged for the Lust of a Woman, which soon sway'd him to Mortality.

6. This (as the Sun to the outward World) would have been Man's Guide, being her self out of the Abyss of Infinite Wisdom. This (the Promised Seed bringing with him) still sweetly and convincingly woo's at the Door of every Man's Heart.

7. But in regard she is Heavenly, she can have no acquaintance with one that is resolved to be Earthy, she will be Married only to That Soul, that It regenerateth, which *Nicodemus* understood not at first, and none ever can, who like not to be divorced from the Old Man, and die daily.

To

Considerations on the Scope of Jacob Behmen.

To others, these Writings are Sounds, not Substances; for This Tree of Life may not be toucht by them who love That of Good and Evil.

8. This Heavenly Humanity (that disappear'd, when *Adam* fell) yields the Water of Life, which becomes a Well, springing up to Eternal Life. This is the Childrens Bread; It fills Paradise; feeds the Angels, and all the Blessed for ever.

9. This is the Quintessence of Things; the Holy Element; whence streamed out the four Elements. It is the Life and Vertue of the Eternal Nature, or great Mystery. It is That Pearl, which whoso finds and buys, is a cheap Bargain, whatever it costs.

The Lord's Supper. 10. This is Christ's Heavenly Flesh and Blood, wherewith he feeds His, in the Sacramental Feast. But being come now to That, which men make occasion of Controversie, it may be profitable to discourse it.

John 6. from 47. *v.* to 59. *v.* And again, in 63. *v.* it is said, I am the living Bread that came down from Heaven, *v.* 53. Except ye eat his Flesh, and drink his Blood, ye have no Life in you.

11. The Jews understanding This (as many still do) to be meant of his outward Flesh and Blood, said, (and that rightly) How can This Man give us his Flesh to eat? for That had been (so understood) not intended by him; and Canibal-like to them.

12. But the Lord interprets himself, first, Negatively in 63. *v.* not his outward Flesh (as they thought to be meant) profiteth nothing. But Affirmatively, *v.* 50. and 58. the Lord himself is express; That the Flesh he meant was also Bread, and that Bread was the Bread which came down from Heaven, *viz.* the Word of God. Hence arise Two controversial Points different from each other, and both from the Truth

First Error, about the Lord's Supper. 13. One Party say, they eat the outward flesh, which being eaten, they swallow into their Beastial Carkass. This, the other Party opposeth, saying, That flesh (though now glorified) remains a *Circumscriptive Creature*; therefore may not be eaten every where at once; and that it is not Many, but One; therefore may not be eaten at all.

Second Error. This last Party (in opposition to the former) yet farther say, they eat That Flesh, and drink That Blood only by Faith or Imagination, but know nothing of the Heavenly Flesh or Humanity; but still understand only the outward Flesh. Though the Lord is express in This, that it is the Spirit that quickneth; the Flesh profiteth nothing, and that his words are Spirit and Life; and that it is That Bread which came, or cometh down from Heaven.

14. The Mouth, and Eating of the Soul, are real and substantial, though not Palpable, yet not Imaginary.

What is not, and what is received in the Lord's Supper. 15. It was not the outward Flesh and Blood they did eat and drink; for He sate with them when they did eat and drink.

Shewing plainly, that the Sacramental Flesh and Blood, is the Divine Flesh and Blood that came down from Heaven.

16. In This *Enoch* walked with God; and fed so heartily on *This Food*, that the Food of the third Principle would no longer down with him; This New Wine made the Bottle New; This (like the Tincture that transmuteth Metals) Enflamed and Translated his whole Man; so that his very third Principle was swallowed up, by the Divine second Principle.

By This, all the Holy Men before Christ's Incarnation were nourished in their Pilgrimage on Earth; and by This, were carried home to their Native Country.

17. This was the Rock that followed them in the Wilderness; for they did all eat the same spiritual meat, and drink the same spiritual drink, and That Rock was Christ.

18. This

Considerations on the Scope of Jacob Behmen.

18. This is the Tree of Life, which is Angels Food; and had never returned to be the Food of the Fallen Posterity of *Adam*, had not the second *Adam* opened a door in our hearts thro' which to enter, and given as a mouth to eat it, and receive Life and Vigour from it.

This First-Born of every Creature was Heir of all things. *Who the Heir*

19. But This is not the *Only begotten Son*; for so, He is the true second Person of *of all things* the Trinity, and Lord of all things; but This is the *Created Son or Word*, who is *is, and who he* the Heir of all things; This is the *New Man*; it is not said, This is the *Omnipotent is not?* *God*; but That *Holy Heavenly Image of God*, wherein the first *Adam* was Created, and which (on his Disobedience) disappeared, as to him; and as to him, was *Dead*; and said to be the *Lamb slain*.

20. This did the *Only begotten Son of God* bring with *Him*; He, who was the True Second Person of the Trinity did Reunite This in himself to the Fallen, and (so by Him) Restored Human Nature; and having made Men Priests, made them also Kings. reigning over the first and third Principles in Man; irradiating and divinely governing the first, and sacrificing the Wills-Lusts, and misplaced Love to the third Principle.

21. *This Holy Thing* was begotten by the *Holy Ghost*, as the *Pure Heavenly Humanity* united to the Earthly or Fallen Humane Nature comprising the Essences of the Virgin *Mary*, as a Daughter of *Eve*.

22. The Lord saith, *He that eateth my flesh and drinketh my blood, hath Eternal Life*; He saith not, He that eateth and drinketh it worthily, hath Eternal Life, but he that eateth and drinketh. For none can be said to eat That Flesh and drink That Blood, that eat and drink unworthily; they eat and drink, what is common to those that have not Eternal Life; and but eat and drink the Elements only, or (what more is at most) but Imagination, grounded on, and extended no farther than on the History: Never the more enabled to enter into the Sufferings, Dying, and New Life of Christ.

CHAP. XXIII. *Man's mistaken way towards a supposed Happiness.*

1. THE State of the Children of *Adam* is the same with Those; a *Behold I will* a Hos. 2. 6. *hedge up thy ways with Thorns, and wall a Wall, that she shall not find her* b v. 27. *paths*; b *and she shall follow after her Lovers, but she shall not overtake them*; *and she shall* God's graci-*seek them, but she shall not find them:* Then *shall she say, I will go and return to my first* ous method to *Husband*; *for then it was better with me than now*. And God proceeds against the *recall men.* Apostate Adulteress to the end of v. 13. but in v. 14. and to the end of the Chapter returns her to him, &c.

2. Wise men in every Generation, have sought in the Treasures of the Creation *Worldly Wis-* for *Real Happiness and Rest*: And after they have div'd into the deep; ransackt the *dom's vain* many Mysteries obvious to Artists; collected the scattered parcels of Felicity, *attempts.* (dispersed in the Earth;) pierced the Bowels of Nature (as well Astral as Elementary;) Anatomised the Creatures, and sum'd up their *Totals*: Yet still could not overtake their Lovers, but their way was wall'd up, and some of them found theirs hedged up (perhaps with Thorns.) Many have sought the Living among the Dead; every Creature eath told them it is not in Me. So their quest resulted in Dissatisfaction.

3. Wise men's increase of *Wisdom*, hath been the increase of *Sorrow*; in which *The effect of* they lay down in the Grave, forgetting and being forgotten their Thoughts pe- *Man's Wis-* rishing, they left *sad Memento's of the Vanity of every thing*. *dom.*

Those

Those of them only have been truly Wise, whom God hath led beyond their own, into his School of the Love of Purity and Holiness, as *Job's* three Friends, *Hermes* and others such, seem to be.

4. For since the World, by Wisdom knew not God, those only were *Truly Wise*, and still are, who ceasing from things Visible, are guided to things Eternal.

The way to true Wisdom.
5. Our Lesson is, (as to the Wisdom of This World) to become Fools; and as such, to crucifie our Wills to the Lusts of the Eye, Lusts of the Flesh, and Pride of Life; and as little children who Will nothing, but the supply of Necessities, and do (without contract, Bargain or Regret) what the Father bids; His Will is their Pleasure, and as a reward of their Resigned Obedience, they know no perplexing Cares; foreca[st]ing Fears; crafty Excuses, Dissimulation, Malice,&c. but have a mild Serene Face; a Peaceable contented Mind, a cheerful Innocent Behaviour; while awake, and when they lie down, fall sweetly asleep.

CHAP. XXIV. *The Lord's way home for Man to follow.*

1. BUT Man hath travelled with the Prodigal from *This White State.* To him straying; will he suffer one (that heartily wisheth the good of Souls) to say, Stand still and consider if a Good End be better than a Bad; a Good Way must be better than an Evil; for the Evil Way tends to a Bad End.

1. Disswasives from Death.
2. And to shew whether his way be not bad, let him look narrowly, heedfully and impartially into his own Heart and Inclination; where he shall find a Body of *Self-Love*, coveting to get All, which comes from the first Form (the Astringency.)

2. 3. Next, He shall find an eager Desire to be Exalted, and Great above others; which Pride cometh from the second Form of Nature, the Attraction or Constringency.

3. 4. Next, He shall perceive a contemning, despising and envying of others, That he thinks he exceeds in Worth, and they him in Fortune, or the like; which he frettethat. This proceeds from the third Form of Nature, the Anguish.

4. 5. And then he shall find violent Anger, Rage and Fury, when crost or curb'd by any one which cometh of the fourth Form of Nature, the Fire.

6. And under these four Heads, Troops of Sins Appendixes to these; which well consider'd, may make him much rather than blessed *Paul*, cry out, *Oh wretched man that I am, who shall deliver me from the Body of this Death?* He may now see how Evil in themselves these Disorders and hellish Principles are, and how Evil to him, how Dangerous to erect a Government in his private particular Soul, opposite to the One entire, gracious, universal omnipotent Will, and Government.

7. When thus the Light of Jesus Christ ariseth, it both sheweth the Malady and the Cure: And this Light is not under a Bushel, but as universal (yet not seen by the wilfully Blind) as the outward Sun to all Mens outward Senses.

The voice of Wisdom calls at every Mans Heart, and where they listen it teacheth.

1. Perswasives to Life.
7. To dye to the tyranny of their own Wills and so be like Children; for Mens own Wills compass them about with sparks of their own kindling, viz. Common Fire (not that of the Altar) which leads them in the Dark to lye down in Sorrow; for as far as *Atom* did and we still do introduce our Wills into the third Principle, we are like sad Eclipses in Hostility against the Heavenly out-goings.

2. 8. The true Divine Light of Jesus Christ where it is followed, generateth a warm, chearing dear Love to the New Man growing out of the Old: as in a balance the New is lift up in that degree of Swiftness, as the Old sinketh down. It springeth

out

Confiderations on the Scope of Jacob Behmen. 39

out of the Old as a fair Flower out of the dark Earth, as it were out of the Grave of the Old.

9. This Light of Jefus Chrift alfo, fo winneth on the Soul, that it is refigned to the Guidance of true Wifdom, being that of the Univerfal Holy Will. For finding their own to be deceiving and deceived, they become to it as Fools for Chrift's fake; not only content, but habitually longing to know, nor do, nor be any thing but what their crucifyed Lord willeth in them.   3.

10. This Light having kill'd the perverted Will, wrought Divine Love and Refignation, doth betroth the Soul to the Virgin of Modefty and Purity again, from whom *Adam* departed, whom the Lord from Heaven, the fecond *Adam*, brought with him; by him fhe was re-efpoufed to the Humane Nature, no more to be Divorced. For Man having Travelled by Art into Nature by his own Wifdom (like a dark Head) fteered his own Will to the Defigns of a Corrupt Heart,and laboured all Night catching nothing; wherewith being weary, learns to Obey and be as a little Child, and then finds reft, yet in fuch degree and proportion, as his continuance in Child-like Obedience is more or lefs Univerfal and Stedfaft.   4.

11. *Adam* loft, and we lofe the Heavenly Virgin of Purity and Modefty, by finding and living to the Luft of the third Principle, (*viz*.) The feeming Wifdom guiding to obtain the miftaken fatiety of Pleafure, Profit and Honour by the Elementary, palpable Tranfitory and Aftral World.

12. When Man makes thefe idolatroufly the object of his Love, Hope, Delight and Confidence, as the rich Man in the Gofpel did, which fhould be ufed only as a Picture or Glafs. through which, to Contemplate (by Divine Skill) the Eternal Powers reprefented by them: He catcheth at a Shadow, worfhips the Afs on which he was to Ride.

13. It is evident his thus Living to his third Principle,was his, and is our Dying to, and Lofs of the fecond Principle, and 'tis as clear the Dying to the Third, that is, only giving it leave to hang to us as an old loofe Garment, or looking through it as through a Cloud or Medium on the Sun, or regarding it as a Letter much blotted, for the Efteem we bear to the Hand whence it came; or as a much faded imperfect Portraicture of an Abfent Friend. or as a Perlpective-Glafs. Thus only to ufe it, is rightly to Live to it, which is really to Die to it : and fo to Die to it, is really to Live to the fecond Principle, and to reunite to the Eternal, Chaft, Holy, Modeft, pure Virgin, which difappeared on *Adam*'s difobedient Lufting; for the Lufting awakeneth the Knowledge of Evil and Good, which the Virgin abhorreth, and left Man fhould be quite ftranged.   *What that Death is that gives true Life.*

14. Therefore, to Extricate us of this miferable Toil, came the Son of the Virgin, whofe Doctrine teacheth us, That it is a greater Bleffednefs to give than to receive; for that the Holy Life World confifting in the Might and Vertue of the fecond Principle, cannot be fupported and receive Nourifhment from the divided Properties of the third, which confifteth of Tranfitory mutable Powers; becaufe what is of Good in thofe outflown Powers,is the free Gift out of the Abyfs of the true and greateft Bleffednefs, the fecond Principle.

15. All therefore who Die not to the Leffer, cannot Live to the Greater Bleffednefs; if we Die not to all things but Chrift, we are unworthy of Him. Whatever is divided from Him is Dead, for He only is Life : and God is called God, according to His infinite Abyfs of Light, Love, Life, Goodnefs and fecond Principle; for according to the firft is a confuming Fire.

16. Man living to the Cheating Pleafure of the third Principle is Dead, as the Widow is faid to be, who liveth in Pleafure.

We ftartle at being Adulterers, Idolaters, *&c.* yet fo we are, while we Live (that is) till we Die with Chrift. Till we pafs through Death (that is) truly and
F   really

really Die to the Wrath, fierceness and Dark Anguish of the first Principle; the Root of the Soul as to the Father's Property. And until we Die to the Deceitful, Volatil, Bewitching Pampering Lust of the third Principle, whereinto Man's outward Body (like those of the Beasts) is fallen; wherein also lodgeth the Curse: till This be, we are Dead as to God. But being indeed mortified to both these, we are in the same degree raised again to live the Life of Jesus Christ, a Life of Love, Humility, Patience, chearful Submission and Obedience, as our Progress to the Death of both these extends and ascends or amounts unto.

17. For the Death to these two Principles as to their Prevalence, is such an emptying us of our selves, as enables (without Reluctance) to Pray the Lord to exercise his whole Will in us, and on us; regarding in nothing its Greatness or Contemptibleness, its Sweetness, or Bitterness, its Gratefulness or grating Temper; but only esteeming every thing without Reflection or Sticking, ever equally acceptable, that the Divine Will shall direct and allot us to do or submit to.

18. And this Life of Sacrifice hath a thankful Reverence in it, and is as whole as the Burnt ones were, without the least reserve. This Life is no longer ours; for we are first Dead; But is the Life of Christ the meek Child like Life, taught us by the Cross of Christ, the Footsteps of the Lord are plain and conspicuous in this good Path.

19. It is both in Word and in Power, but neither is the Word or Power ours, but 'tis the Holy Word and Power whence *Adam* departed as the fallen Angels had done before, and in which Word and Power the Blessed Angels converse and are Established: In which *Adam* might have lived Gloriously (without knowing the Cross, as do the Angels.)

20. But the restored Image grows not but under the Cross; Thus did *Abel* under the Hate of *Cain*: *Enoch* and *Noah*, under the Pressures of the highly wicked old World: *Lot* under the filthy *Sodomites*: And infinitely above all, thus did our Almighty Saviour: whom, if we will follow, it must be in Deepest Humility bearing his Cross, which must be also ours, divesting our selves of all Self-pleasing, and whatsoever fallen Man calls and thinks to be his; for this is the Holy Soul's weaning time; when as Heirs of the Faith of *Abraham*, they also keep a great Feast as he did at weaning *Isaac*.

21. This Feast is a real feeding on the Heavenly Flesh and Blood of Christ, a Drinking of the Water that becomes a Spring of Water in us to Eternal Life. It is a Life hid with Christ in God, a walking with God, and a putting on the Lord Jesus Christ, the Marriage Supper and Wedding Garment, a Peace passing the understanding of all, except the Children who are regenerated, and to them only known in such measure ordinarily, as they have made Progress in Mortification, and so grow in the new pure Image of God, restored us by Jesus Christ.

22. For a close, let all be warn'd not to contemn if they understand not some things, and so judge themselves unworthy of this Childrens Bread.

The Reason why so few understand the Holy Scriptures (which yet many often read) is, because few give up their Wills to Obey, and Regeneration is the Necessary Qualification to attain true Wisdom.

Hence is it that from a Corrupt Mind (though refinedly Penetrating) the Writings of the Blessed *Jacob Behmen* are Seal'd up, and as if Dumb; from such were the very Sermons of the Lord himself (who so spake as never Man spake) hidden. *And none of the wicked shall understand, but the wise shall understand.*

Dan. 12.
v. 10.

Here endeth the Considerations, &c.

The 177 Theoſophick Queſtions of the bleſſed *Jacob Behmen* divide themſelves into Ten grand Diſtributions or Kinds, being of ſo many various Aſpects; (viz.)

THE firſt four *Queſtions are moſt immediately concerning God in his Infinite Abyſs.*   I.

The ten following concern *Angels good and bad, from the fifth Incluſive to the fifteenth Excluſive.*   II.

The 23 next ſucceeding are of the *Creation in general, ranged into three diſtinct Eminencies, deduced from the 3 Principles, making in all 37. viz.*   III.
  1. That out of the firſt *Principle or dark Abyſs in the 15th, 16th, and 17th Queſtions.*
  2. That out of the ſecond *Principle the Angelical holy World, in the 18th, and 19th Queſtions.*
  3. That out of the third *Principle the Viſible Creation and contrariety in it, from the 20th Queſtion incluſive to the 38 excluſive.*

The one and forty ſubſequent *Queſtions concern the Creation of Man, and that whereunto* Adam *had relation whilſt he ſtood, and when he fell, from the 38 Queſtion incluſive to the 78 excluſive.*   IV.

The ſixteen next *Queſtions are of* Adam's *Off-ſpring down to* Moſes, *from the 78 Queſtion incluſive to the 94 Queſtion excluſive.*   V.

The eight following are of the *Figures and Sacrifices in* Moſes *and the Prophets, from the 94 Queſtion incluſive to the 102 excluſive.*   VI.

The forty next *Queſtions concern Chriſt, his Birth, Life, Sufferings Death, Deſcending, Reſurrection, Appearing, Converſing with his Diſciples, and Aſcenſion, from 102 incluſive to 142 excluſive.*   VII.

The eighteen ſubjoyned *Queſtions concern the Diſciples, their Pentecoſt, the ſpeaking with all Tongues; what that Language was; the Teſtaments; what that Fleſh and Blood is; the power of Remiſſion, or the Keys, from 143 incluſive to the 160 excluſive.*   VIII.

The next four *Queſtions are concerning a true Chriſtian and Antichriſt,* Babel, *the Beaſt and the Whore, from 160 incluſive to the 165 excluſive.*   IX.

The laſt 13 *Queſtions concern the ſlaying of the Beaſt; what is the dying of, and what dieth in a true Chriſtian. Alſo what is the dying of the wicked call'd an Eternal dying. The Souls ſeparation from them both; their ſeveral different Eſtates, the Reſurrection and final Judgment; this Worlds Diſſolution. The Eternal Habitation and Joy of the Saints, and the Eternal Priſon of the accurſed. And whether they ſhall admit any alteration from the 165 Queſtion incluſive to the end, being the 177.*   X.

Extracts

Extracts of the Answers of the first Fourteen, and part of the Fifteenth of the 177 Theosophick Questions.

The First whereof is, *Viz.*

Q. 1. *What God is Distinct from Nature and Creature?*

Ans. 1. ALL Goodness in Nature manifesteth what God is in his Eternal Love, Joy, Mercy and Glory of Heaven. And all Contrariety, Misery, and Evil in Nature; shews his Eternal Wrath, Fury and consuming Fire of Hell, God by the Eternal Unity, perfection of Clearness and Purity: Eternally, equally alike. and at once through and through all, every where, whose immensity is Abyssal; yet his Manifestation distinguishable; but whatever hath Limits of number and measure, is imagible.

Rom. 1. 19, 20.

2. And wheresoever the Good moveth in his sweet Love, there is God's flowing forth in the Idea or Object of the Eternal Desiring, where the Love findeth it self, as in Angels and Blessed Souls.

Q. 2. *What is the Abyss of all Things where is no Creature, the Unsearchable Nothing?*

A. 1. The Abyss of all things is an habitation of God's Unity. The Will is the Eternal Father of the Byss; a meer Love-longing. The finding Power of Love, the Son, generated by the Will. The out-going Power of the desirous Love, the Holy Ghost (*viz.*) the Spirit of Divine Life. That which is gone out from the Will, Love and Life, is the Wisdom, (*viz.*) Contemplation of the Unity which by Love brings it self into Powers, Colours and Vertues.

2. In the Unity rest all the six Powers, being the Eternal Sabbath: which Unity is call'd the Nothing, because it is God himself, being incomprehensible and inexpressible or ineffable.

Q. 3. *What is God's Love and Anger? How may it be only one thing?*

A. 1. All things consist in Yea and Nay, be it Divine, Diabolical or Earthy. The One (*viz.*) the Yea, or Affirmation is meer Power, Life, Truth or God Himself. The Nay, or Negation, manifesteth the Yea by its contrary. They have two Centres, as Day and Night, Heat and Cold. The No is a reflex Image of the Yea. The Yea uncloseth, and the Nay incloseth. The Yea or Unity, is an outflowing Exit or Emanation of the Nothing, which yet is the Ground of all Beings: The Nay is an indrawing own-hood, or a something making a Byss or Ground, whence come Forms or Properties.

2. As

The 177 Theosophick Questions Answered.

2. As, 1. Sharpness, causing Density and Cold, the Cause of Temporal and Eternal Darkness. (1.)
2. Attraction, the Cause of all Separation and Motion. 3. Perception, the Cause of finding it self like a great Anguish. 4. Fire from the Motion in the Darkness. But in the Unity of God, is a clear, soft gentleness; from these two Contraries, originate this Worlds Fire and Water. (2, 3.) (4.)

And from the enkindling of the outflown Will, is the 5th, (*viz.*) The great Love-fire in the Light. For if the Unity stood not in the Fires might, it would not be Operative, but without Moving or Joy. Whereas in it, is the Holy Ghost himself. (5.)

3. Hence comes the Eternal Nature's Fire, whence are Angels and the Souls of Men; but the clear Deity becomes not creaturely: being an Eternal Unity, yet dwelleth through Nature, as Fire shineth through Iron. Here we understand the the Potentiality of Angels and Souls, who by loosing the Love-fire, enter into Self-desire, and the Anger fire.

4. Out of this holiest Love fire, is flown out a beam of the perceptible Unity, the High Name Jesus, who assuming the Humanity, in the central Anger-fire, gave it self into the Soul, and by kindling again the Love-fire United it to God.

The 6th Property is the Sound or Distinctions, in both Fires alike at once. In the Devils and Damned, who have no Understanding, but sharp Wit to try the Foundation, and abuse the Powers of Nature by Deceit and Voluptuousness. In this Property stand the Holy Powers and Names, and the wonder-doing Word, which the Evil Spirits by Transmutation misuse. (6.)

5. Here is the whole *Cabal* or *Magia*, where the imperceptible worketh in the perceptible. Before this Door stands the Law of *Moses*, Exod. 20. 2, 3, 7. not to misuse it on Pain of Eternal Punishment. The 7th Property is substantiality, whence existeth the Visible World. In which is both the central Fires, according to Love and Anger. But the Holy Fire lyeth hidden by the curse with Sin, as is to be seen by the Tincture: yet if God will, there is a possible Entrance. (7.)

6. The outflown Holy fire is the Paradise, which Man cannot find, unless first it be found in himself. Thus is the perceptible Unity or Love-fire, and the Anger-fire, or Root of the Eternal Nature, which in its Centre is Eternal Darkness, and Torment, both from Eternity in Eternity; yet with two Eternal Beginnings, as is to be apprehended in the Fire and Light.

Q. 4. *What was before Angels and the Creation were?*

A. 1. Then was God, with the two central Fires which were one Substance, but distinguished as Fire and Light: in them lay the one Element, and the infinite Powers of generating Wonders, Colours and Vertues; in them lay the Idea of all inward Angelical Kingdoms, and Souls, and of all Creatures of this World, in perfect Harmony.

2. But when the central Fire, with Self-desire moved, to visible formation, and stirred the Eternal Will of God in both Fires, then the Idea to the Praise of God, became Image like.

3. In this the hellish Foundation also brake forth, which God rejecting out of his Work, shut up in-Darkness, remaining to this day, as hungry Jaws longing to be creaturely.

4. Into this Anger-fire, *Lucifer* lusting powerfully to domineer over the Meek Love of God, lost the Throne of the central Love-fire, possessing only that, where hot and cold are in strife. Being a Centre of the Visible World.

Q. 5. *What was it of which the Angels were made? What in the Word of God became Creaturely?*

A. 1. The Substance of the Good Angels, is out of the two central Fires of Fire and Light, but their Idea, Spirit or Powers, are out of the Out-flowing, Infinite, Mighty, Holy Names of God.

2. They are many, and every Throne Angel according to the Peculiar, of the various Names and Offices himself and his Legions are illustrated with.

3. The Prince-Angels are as the Spirits of the Letters, and the other as the joyning of Words and Sentences. And as our Alphabet, hath our whole understanding of all Substances: So is God's Word of all things, and the Angels are his Letters, in the Divine Alphabet. 4. And did not the Curse, to prevent our abuse, hinder? Man having shut up himself in the NO: So great is the Authority in what his Mouth carries, that he might triumphantly do wonders as the Angels, *Deut.* 30. 14. *Rom.* 10. 8.

Math. 17. 20.

5. If the Creatural Life stood not in an own Will, in the Property to the Fire, Lucifer could not have separated himself from the Good.

6. The Angels are within and without this World, yet in another Principle or World (*viz.*) in the One Element, whereout came and still cometh the Four Elements, and are Princes of the Constellations: But some are of a more outward Chaos or Kind in the Four Elements, call'd Starry Spirits, (*viz.*) Ascendants.

Q. 6. *What do Angels, and why doth God's Power become Image-like?*

A. 1. Out of the Mind come Thoughts, and from them Imaginations, whence Longing and Delight exist; and we rule all things by the distinction of words: So God (*viz.*) the Eternal *Mind, by His out-flowing Powers, brought out the Angelical Idea, and the Holy Angels are as God's Thoughts, revealing His Mind as his Work Instruments to manifest the Eternal Powers, they are as Strings in the great Harmony, as our articulate Words, so are they distinct Parts of the Love-sport.

* *Trismigistus in his Poimander.*

2. And their great Joy and Knowledge of the Eternal Wisdom humbleth them before such Highness, left they lose that honour. Their feeding is an indrawing of the Unity, which is the Balsam, that their Central Fire awake not the Wrath; for the Devil's Fall is their Looking-glass.

3. The most gross Compaction of the Outward World, is the out-flown Inward World, in the two Central Fires. The most Outward is the four Elements, the next Inward is the Astral; the third the Quintessence; the fourth the Tincture; the fifth the Clear God. The more inwardly we reach, the nearer God. And were we awake from *Adam's* Earthy Love, we might very well see Heaven.

(1. 2. 3. 4. 5.)

Q. 7. *What moved Lucifer to depart from God?*

A. 1. The Potence of Forming standing in the Transmutation, *viz.* His Receiving Power; therefore the out-flown Will in the Central Fire of the Eternal Nature, made him elevate himself to despise the Resignation, but would try the Properties of the Eternal Nature, and so misused the Holy Name in himself, and willed to domineer over the Thrones, and brake himself off from the Unity. Then instantly the Properties were manifest, as hard, sharp, sour, bitter, stinging, and the tormenting, cold and hot fires.

Q. 8. *How*

The 177 Philosophick Questions Answered.

Q. 8. *How could an Angel become a Devil? What is a Devil?*

A. 1. He would not be under the speaking of the Unity; which was Balsam to his Fire-Life, but be his own speaking, so his Fire could conceive no glance, but the Holy Name and Central Love Fire withdrew.

2. If he would be an Angel again, his Fire Life must be killed with Love, but this the Hellish Foundation neither will nor can do, as Fire cannot endure Water.

3. Their whole Life is a Despair, Venom, Dying, Stink, Sorrow, Shame and Torment, that he hath trifled away the Divine Express, Reflex Image, and got the Form of Poisonous, Venomous Beasts and Worms, according to their various Properties of Pride, Covetousness, Envy, &c. all contrary to Wisdom, Truth, Love, &c. Thus good men have turned evil, and fallen into Perdition.

Q. 9. *Why did not the Omnipotent God prevent the Fall of Lucifer?*

A. 1. Whilst Fire and Water are in a Vegetable, they lovingly embrace each other, but once sundred, do never more desire each other, but as Mortal Foes, whenever they encounter, the one dies.

2. So Love and Anger (where in Harmony) bring the first, Sweet Delight, the other Life and Strength, and are two Eternal Principles, having each an Eternal Will, Foundation and Centre of its own: Therefore if the Anger will sever, the Love doth not hinder with force: Nor could the Love work otherwise, than like it self; else God would be at odds in himself. But if the Created Image the No or Anger give its Will to the Yea or Love, it would be chang'd into a Love-Fire.

3. And tho' the Anger be an Eternal Principle, and part of God's Omnipotence, the fault was the Creatures; for in the unimaged Power, the Love doth ever burn. And God's hardening is not sending a strange fierce Wrath into any, but it is left to its own fierceness, on which Judgment passeth.

The Anger is Love's manifestation; and the Fallen Angels are the Looking-glass of the Good Angels.

Q. 10. *What did the Devil desire for which he left God?*

A. ' He would be an Artist; their Joy still is in Transmutation of themselves into Forms. Subjection in Humility pleased him not, but would be a God to himself and his Legions. The Magick ground of Omnipotency pleas'd him, which made him elevate himself above the Efflux of the Unity; and prove the Properties, but he knew not how it would be with him when the Light should extinguish; for then came Darkness, and the cold sharpness of the Fierceness, and he instantly at utter Enmity against God, and all Angelical Hosts.

Q. 11. *What was the Strife between Michael and the Dragon, and what are they?*

A. 1. Michael is the Figure of the Divine Power, not as a Creature, but as the opening and moving of the Eternity, which name after, in Jesus, was ordained for Man.

2. The Dragon is Hell manifested, the Will of the Anger, and the Wrath of the Properties, as Heat, Cold, Woe, the first Principle, a Hunger and Thirst, a Dying Quality. Satan is the Will to Contradiction and Lies. *Belial* the Lust to Uncleanness. *Belzebub* a Source of Idol Gods. *Asmodeus* a Spirit of Fury and Madness. *Lucifer* of Pride and stately climbing up.

3. Their

3. Their Strife was, as of the firſt and ſecond Principles, as was That of Jeſus in his forty days Temptation, and of *Iſrael* while *Moſes* was in the Mount. In This Strife the Dragon is driven out of the Holy Name; in This Strife Chriſt brought the Will of Man through Death and Hell to ſubſiſt in God, unpaſſive, that it may ſubſiſt in the Fire, unapprehended by the Fire; or as the Sun kindleth it ſelf in the Elements, yet keepeth its Light to its ſelf; or as Fire blazeth through Iron, yet is not Iron. So clear muſt be the Will which God's Unity is to poſſeſs; till the Will be thus, the Dragon exiſteth in it.

4. Thus may Love and Anger be ſo unſevered, as to be One only thing; as Fire and Light. The Power of the Anger cauſ'd the Fire Kingdom to form it ſelf into a Den of Dragons, which God permitted that he might not further diſturb the Creation.

Q. 12. *How can Man poſſibly know the Deep Unity?*

A. 1. Reaſon imagineth God conſulted with Himſelf about the Predeſtination. But the out-flowing Names of the Powers, is the Counſel of God. The wonder-doing Word it ſelf, in the Figures or Reflections of the Holy Names, which Figures are cal'd the Idea.

2. The Eternal Nature imageth it ſelf according to the Forms to Fire as hard, ſharp, fierce, *&c.* in the No or Anger; yet illuſtrated by the Yea or Light, and they wreſtle as a Love ſport, which brings the Imaging into Triumph, and overcometh the Dragon.

3. In This Strife Jeſus ſunk himſelf into the Humanity, Redeeming Man, and Ruleth till his Enemies be his Footſtool.

4. To ſhew the poſſibility for the Spirit to ſearch the Depth of the Deity. Know, Man is an Image of God, according to Love and Anger.

Firſt, The Soul is of the Eternal Central Fire, whence all Creatures come, but not out of the Pure God.

Secondly, The Spirit of the Soul out of the Central Fire, and Idea of the Light, ſprung from the Power of God, is the Temple of the Holy Ghoſt, in which Chriſt feedeth the Soul with His Fleſh and Blood, with Divine and Human Balſam.

5. The outward Body is out of the four Elements and Aſtrum which Rule the Outward Life, after which *Adam* luſted and broke himſelf from the Unity of God, and the Will was captivated, the true Spirit diſappeared, and the Idea inoperative, which Right Spirit Jeſus in-drew again, and reſtor'd with the Balſam of Love in the Light. In This Light, may the Soul ſearch out all things operatively in the Underſtanding, as did the Prophets of Old, tho' incomprehenſible to Outward Reaſon.

Q. 13. *How and whither was the Dragon, &c. thruſt, ſeeing God fills all things? &c.*

A. 1. His Thruſting out was Effected by the name of the Holy Powers of the Throne which *Lucifer* had, is ſevered from God's Holineſs, dwelleth under the Firmament, and in all Quarters of the Earth, betwixt Time and Eternity. Alſo in the out-flown fierce Wrath of the four Elements, but cannot touch the Good Power of the Elements.

2. Tho' there are ſome Good Powers, in which is wholly the Fire of the Light, yet in Man is Good and Evil; the Evil being captivated by the Good, unleſs by Man's Will, or by *Turba Magna* the Evil exceedeth the Good.

3. The Expulſed Dragon is not the Central Fire of the Eternal Nature, but an Efflux from it, reſembling Smoke. The Helliſh Den preſents it ſelf ſometimes

in the Upper Region, where from great Heat and great Cold break Thunder-bolts. Also in great Wildernesses, and in great Clefts and Concaves in the Earth, where the Highly Damned Spirits and Souls of Men are horribly terrified. But the Sun and Water hold them hidden as yet.

4. God is to Hell as a Nothing; as Light to Night; as Life to Death. The great Shame, Reproach, Anguish and Torment of the Devil is, that he is so near God, yet cannot possibly attain him.

Q. 15. *Had Hell a Beginning, and may it have an End?*
A. 1. God's Anger hath been from Eternity, but not as Anger ; but as Fire hidden in Wood or a Stone.

2. The enkindling was in the Fall of Lucifer. And having an Eternal Foundation, it can never cease, unless the Creation totally be annihilated, and that the receptibility of the Eternal Nature should extinguish, and the Kingdom of Joy and Triumph cease.

There must be two Eternal Beginnings one in another, the one to manifest the other.

Thus far the Extracts of the Answers of *Jacob Behmen* given to the first Thirteenth, and part of the Fifteenth Question.

Here follow orderly the Answers of all such of the 177 Questions of *Jacob Behmen* which were left, as far as yet appears, unresolved by the blessed Author himself, beginning at the 14th of those Questions.

Q. 14. *What is Lucifer's Office in Hell with his Legions?*

A. 1 *a* What God's working in Hell is, will be shewn in the 17 of these Answers. *b* as also what and where Hell is. What is the Dragon, is resolved by the blessed *Jacob Behmen* in the 11th Answer. *c* What the Dominion of Good Angels is, will fall under the 19th; all which may contribute much to the present Inquiry. *a Answer 17. b From v. 3. to the 15. c From v. 16.*

2. The Dark World existeth of six of the seven separate Properties, because *to the end.* the seventh is the rest of the other ; therefore not properly to be understood of *c Answer 19.* That World, where no Rest shall be for ever ; for *Lucifer* and his Angels, as they *from v. 16. to* are Creatures, tho' revolted and in rebellion against the God of Love and Good- *the end.* ness ; yet are Subjects in His Kingdom of Wrath, and ready Servants to the Active Fierceness thereof. For tho' the Principle (wherein they are Instruments) be without beginning, and as it is in God for ever unmanifested, yet as it is in the Creatures (the Secluded Angels) it is a Fire of their own kindling, wherein (as being their Life) they are more or less exu'reamly active and skilful, according as their Tincture rooted in their Forms of ife is more or less fortified, and excelling that in others for Puissance and Exquisiteness.

3. Consider we that God's working in Hell must needs be in all the seven Properties of the Dark Abyss, in the first four whereof the Apostate Angels are like ready Actives, having no other Will, or have they fitted themselves for any other work or use, but to Image the Abyss of the first Principle ; some of them most strongly bear the Astringent impressed Powers, others the restless Conftringent Attraction, others the Cruel Self gnawing Worm of Anguish, others the Raging Hot Fire, that is severally one sort under the prevailing Tyranny of the one, others of the other : Tho' the whole four unite in every one in the Eternal Band, as in some horrid Creatures here, the Anguish of Cold Venom is prevalent; yet in this Elementary Fabrick there is an allay of some contrary Property in some weak proportion, else were the Creatures here, as the horrid ones there. But thus the Office of the Black Spirits is in all their Forms wholly extream, tho' in
G one

one only is the Extremity in the higheft degree their Natures are capable of, as is feen in Difeafed Bodies, that one of the Humours is predominant.

4. From thefe things is difcernable what *Lucifer's* Office is in Hell, which is to be the moft copious, ample, compleat Image of the Jealoufie, Zeal, Indignation, Fierce Wrath, or Devouring Fire proceeding from the Breath of the Almighty Father. And the Will and Life of This Prince (the Mafter piece of Horrour, and ftupendious Epitome of the Dark Centre) doth therein fubfift, ever enkindling in his own Body, and every Member of it (being the whole Dominion of the Dark Troops) one entire fupply as out of a Fountain of Fury, Rage and Fiercene's, as naturally as do iffue Contagious Emanations from a Plague Sore, or the Mortal Fumes from the Dead Sea (affecting the Birds attempting to flie over it) as is reported.

5. And this He doth really, as the Sun doth the glorious bright Beams, or the Ocean fweileth the Veins of Springs which empty back into it; or as Fogs afcend from corrupt Lakes; and in This God's Infinite Abyfs of the firft Principle (is as the bottomlefs Deep to a fragment of a thin Superficies, or the Heat of the Sun to an Object through the Burning-glafs) affording an unfearchable immediate fupply of the Treafure of Wrath, with an hungry defire thereunto. Thus doth the Breath of the Lord (like a River of Brimftone) enkindle that Lake where they have made themfelves as Fuel fully ready dry.

6. And as a good Graft or Branch inoculated into a Crab-ftock produceth fruits of its own property, tho' it be fed by the four Stock, haply delightful, warm, fpicy, grateful, quite other than the Crab it felf; fo contrariwife doth *Lucifer* and his Hellifh Legions appropriate to themfelves only That out of the Abyffal Principle wherein themfelves inhabit, whereof they fubfift, and whereby they are fhut up and comprehended, which their depraved Bodies can only affimilate, that is the fix working Properties enraged to extremity by the withdrawing of the Divine Holy Principle.

7. And as *Lucifer* and his Angels did (in the time of this World) abufe all the Holy Names and Powers they could reach, profaning them to effect their filthy Impoftures; fo fhall they defire ever to do; but the Aftral Influences (which like Gold and Poifonous Mercury commixed yielding matter for their fallacious Jugling) being once withdrawn) then can they only in their Black Magick exceffively and infatiably hunger to repeat (as before) their Blafphemies, but remain impotent, and no more feife on it than a man can on a fhadow, nor reach it, than Dogs the Moon they bark at becaufe all the good Intermixing Powers are for ever withdrawn into their feveral peculiar Ethers.

8. Alfo as the Evil Legions do according to their various Orders and Properties more exceed, fome in one, fome in another of the four Central Forms of the Dark Abyfs: So *Lucifer* (as the Centre of them all) abounds at once in every one, in the moft capacious degree of a Creature. Thus we fee fome Fifh found on one Coaft, Arm or Channel; fome other forts on another quarter, latitude or bofom, yet in the Sea are all forts at once: So That once, Brighteft of Angels, and now Blackeft of the Deformed Furies, is the Comprehender of the various Anguifhes, and all in the extreameft degree a Creature poffibly may, and in that refpect (according to the Dark Impreffion) imageth moft exactly the Infinite firft Principle.

9. And tho' *Lucifer* and his numerous Legions (who are as much his, and have a Will as fixedly dependant on; and with his as the Leaves do on the Will of the Tree) have refufed, and been unworthy the Honour and Bleffednefs of retaining the Image, and ferving the Glory of the Holy dear Principle of Love and Goodnefs, but by forming themfelves according to Enmity, Filthinefs and

Deceit,

The 177 *Theosophick Questions Answered.*

Deceit, would break their Order, stray and think to free themselves from the Bands of the Almighty, be their own Lords, exercise a peculiar Tyranny; by which Exorbitant Lust they willed to quit the Duty they owed the Universal Soveraign, and sought a Happiness beyond the limit thereof; he would be a Mock-God, assume Rule, Authority and Self-Soveraignty: Yet did as one who would put out his own Eyes that himself might be invisible.

10. Wherefore now, if he will no longer be a Child of the Day, he must be a Captive in the Darkness; if he will not serve his God in the fulness of all things, he must serve the Forms of Enmity in the want of all things & if he will shut himself up from the golden State of Purity wherein he lived for the delight of his God, he must be an Anguish Fountain, as Rusty Iron which yet is of use among other parts of the Creation, and his own Rigour is his clog, as bitter Astringency curbs the corroding Anguish of *Mars*. The Magistrate hath Executioners for Capital Crimes, who have not a contrary Will to the Justice of their Lord, though adverse to his Clemency. The Prince hath Armed Troops, whose will is the same with his Imperial Commands to prosecute his Enemies with Fire and Sword, and whose life like that of Beasts and Birds of Prey, is to proper in the Destruction of others.

11. Here may the Apostles words be applied, Behold the goodness and severity of God, to them that fell severity, but to thee goodness if thou continue in his goodness. Let it not be thought that by the Rebellion of *Lucifer* God hath lost the least part of His infinite Glory; for as *Lucifer* and his Legions are gone into a Will, Desire and Hunger opposite or adverse to the delighted or well-pleasing Will of the Goodness and loving Kindness of God in his Son the Lord Jesus Christ, the Image of whom they bare; yet are they gone no farther but to be comprehended in and made one Will. Desire and Hunger in and with the fierce Wrath and Vengeance of the Almighty Father in His first Principle, without generating His Delight his Son the Lord Jesus Christ, the least doubt whereof is derogatory to the Glory of God's Omnipotence; nor can they possibly have any other Will but that of Enmity and Wrath, being departed from that of Love; for Love is the Cement, Chain or Ligament, the want whereof renders every Property at utter Hatred and loathing of any other Property. Now though in the Holy World are all the Powers, yet without the least Dissonance, because Love fills them all.

Object. 12. But the Mind of some may Judge, that to say that *Lucifer* and his Angels have one Will with the Property and Wrath of the Father, seems absurd; for God having no greater fixt Enemy than the Devil, That Enemy cannot have one Will with God: And that to say there is something in God which is not God; is to say, there is something in God which is not himself; which were rather Madness than Folly, rather Blasphemy than Error; for it divides the Infinite One from the Infinite One.

A. 1. By way of Concession. 1. *Lucifer* and his Legions are at Enmity against God. 2. There is nothing in God, but what is God. 3. That God cannot be divided from or against Himself, for an Infinite cannot be divided against an Infinite.

13. 2. It is answered by way of Solution; 1. That though *Lucifer* and his Angels are at Enmity against God; yet it follows nor but they may be subservient to his Omnipotence; as we see Darts and Poison used against some noxious Creatures, and some hurtful Beasts against other hurtful Beasts; also Fire many ways, how wrathful soever it is of its own Nature. And shall any thing render it self so Perverse, Vain or Evil, that the Infinite God cannot Extract his own Glorious Ends out of it? Fire, Thunder, Hail-stones, *&c.* are treasured against the day of Battel, a Lion to kill the deceived Prophet, a Bear them that reproached *Elisha*, he

(1.)

he calls for the Sword, Pestilence, Famine, Caterpillars, Barrenness; and is there Evil in the City, and the Lord hath not done it? And as this World is the Image of the Eternal, so the Evils here are the lively Figures of those; and as many Mens Sins (like so many filthy Exhalations, generating Toads in the lower Region, as over the Isle of *Jersey* is said to be done) conspire into a General Contagion of Sweeping Plagues whereby the Transgressors (excluding themselves the Kingdom of Purity and Love) are Instruments of their own Misery; so in that Abyss they act continually the Tragedy of their own desperate Horror, and yet therein do the Will of the Almighty God who comprehends the dark Abyss, and are one Will with his Wrath, devouring Fire and fierce Indignation.

(2.) 14. Though there is nothing in God but what is God, it must be understood of Powers as they are in God; so his Principle of Infinite Potence and Wrath, as it is in God generating the Glorious Love delight His Son, and being Eternally undividable from His Goodness and Grace, it is God; but as God makes Himself Creaturely, that is spoke forth the Creation out of Himself, and as the Creature perverteth his own Way, misimployeth his entrusted Talent, then are the Properties which are only distinguishable as they are in God, but separate, Divided and Evil as they are in the Creatures; yet those Evil Properties have one will. bent, hunger and fierce or rapid Inclination with the Principle of the Wrath, Zeal and Jealousie of God: which is most righteous and just in God, but most cruel, ferine, inimicitious, wicked and unclean in the Evil Angels and Reprobate Souls.

(3.) 15. That God cannot be divided from God; for it were to be divided from Himself, as impossible as to feign two Infinites, which were brutish, weak and vile to think, and which nothing above spoken can be construed to imply; yet that all Powers come from Him, shews uncontroulably they are all distinctly in Him, but not divisibly as they are in him; for in the Infinite God all is infinitely Good: The Evil is only as the Properties are separated in the Creatures who extinguish in themselves the Vital Spirit of them, the pure Universal Life, which kept sweet Order and Harmony by the Bonds of Love, but once dissolved, Antipathy and Death domineers in the Dark Wrath; yet God according to the first Principle gives, or is the Essence and Immortality thereof. For as in Him we live, move, and have our Being, *viz.* our Eternal Blessedness and Transitory Being of Good and Evil; so by Him and in Him (according to the Property of the first Principle) hath the whole Dark World theirs: as well their Being or Existence as their Tincture, Immutability or Perpetuity.

16. And this is plainly demonstrable in the Creatures, both in the cruel, fierce wild one's, and in the gentle tame Beasts; but especially in Man. See we an impious, injurious, implacable, malicious Man (causelesly yet) sollicitously hunting, pursuing ensnaring and tormenting his Neighbour, with how great Delight and Pleasure he sees his unrighteous Projects succeed? Wherein hath a grinning kind of satisfaction, one Property being proud of the other, which makes him insult like those that shall kill the Witnesses, Rejoyce, Feast and send Gifts one to another. For their first Principle enthroned, ruling over, is at rest in their third, but when their Designs prove Abortive, an Evil Spirit from God troubles them, and do as *Saul*, want *David*'s Harp to blunt the Point and Edge of their Forms of Life, which now sharpen, grow fierce, grate, rub and torture one the other, turning (as in *Haman*) the confluence of all other good into Gaul and Wormwood, because their first Principle cannot generate the second, being Strangers to the Life of God through the Ignorance that is in them, on loosing the Charms of the third, do like a Mill wanting Corn, grind themselves, and the Powers do all form themselves into Hostility, immediately entring into an irreconcileable Conflict.

17. See we also an upright perfect Man, though he entirely wisheth the Good of
all

The 177 Theosophick Questions Answered.

all Men; yet when he seeth a vile Person hatching and perpetrating his Outrages on the Lamb-like Innocents, and that also he sees the Righteous God, either by His own immediate propitious Hand, or by spiriting the oppressed, or any other to defend or avenge Him: What kind of solace and thankful frame appears in this Pious Observer? Exalting Him to a real Delight and Joy, for there being the self-same Forms of Life, composing the Holy Soul as the other (though not the Holiness of the Soul, for that is a Divine awakening as a Flame out of a dark Fire) the sweetness such a one shareth (by seeing the Peaceable delivered, or Vengeance taken on the fixed Enemy, whose desperate Resolutions pusht him on to destroy) is much more than it can be of content to the Blood-thirsty when their Plots prolper; as it is written, *Rejoyce over her my People, and ye holy Apostles and Prophets.*

18. Thus see we Revenge to be so sweet, that often it requires sowre Sauce, our first Principle being so strong, that it is obnoxious to catch as Tinder, while it is as a burning Coal to the Hand of him that carries it; and though we sadly Experiment it, yet how propense are all Men as Men to rush on those Pikes, to sat our Hunger after it, which erroneously deem a real Felicity to be in it. And thus to the penetrating Mind is God obscurely, yet distinctly, imaged in bad Men, but evidently in good Men; but *Lucifer* is obscurely, yet distinctly shewn in good Men, expresly character'd in bad Men. See the Answer of *Jacob Behmen* to the 8th of these Questions.

Here begins the Third Grand Distribution, which compriseth the 23 next following Questions.

Q. 15. *Hath the Foundation of Hell taken a Temporary Beginning, or hath it been from Eternity? or how may it subsist Eternally, or not?*

A. That part of Answer to this weighty Question, which the God of Wisdom vouchsafed to make by his Eminent Servant the Author in the four Verses beginning the Answer, is full and clear to such of his Children who are Proficients in the rest of his Precious Writings; but for the sake of other sincere, faithful Enquirers, who are less conversant in them, it may be requisite to add something more.

5. Now It is granted, That neither Men nor Angels should have known it, had not their depravity awakened it; thus it is a dear bought Knowledge, and what Men buy dear, it is fit they should have. Yet though Hell hath opened a terrible Everlasting Abyss of Wrath, it is the Artifice of the Deceiver to suggest to besotted Men the Non-Entity, That there is no such; endeavouring to make Atheists in Judgment, that such may be more Obdurate and Blasphemous as well as more Blind than the Devils themselves who both believe and tremble. And to the Atheists in Practice is suggested the Mutability of it to embolden them in Lewdness.

6. But to take away the Pillow from under both their Heads, it will be found that an Atheist in Judgment (if there be really any such) is both a Scorn to the Evil Angels, and by putting out the Eye of his Reason (which distinguisheth him from the Beast that perisheth) is transformed thereinto, and the Atheist in Practice is his own Condemner and striveth in vain to put out the Eye of his own Intellect, gleaning (as it were) Stubble, *&c.* wherewith to burn himself; thus is it the Complaint, *My people Perish for want of Knowledge.*

7. We are to know, that though Hell began when the evil Angels did put out their own Eyes; yet their so doing was a Deprivation of one Principle, not a Creation of another; but the revealing the Principle of Wrath till then hiden, as it is still hidden in God and the Heavenly Holy World. Nor is it less demonstrable than the Natural outward Night, for the absence of the Sun is the presence of the

the Night, and the first Principle is figured thereby; for the invisible things of Him from the Creation of the World are clearly seen, being understood by the things that are made, &c. Let it be considered, that though there are no Places on or in the Earth, where there is Day, but there succeslively also is Night; but there are many Places in Caverns under the Earth, where day never approacheth. And though beyond the acute Angle, or Cone of the shadow of our Globe in the Deep, made by the more exceeding over proportion of the length of the Sun's Diameter to that of ours, there can be no Night; yet in the Opake Orbs of the Moon and Stars, it must be alike demonstrable as with us.

8. And to proceed one step farther in Answer of the Question, whether the Foundation of Hell be Temporary. It must be confessed, that as every thing hath a Root, and that nothing can live longer than its Root; therefore, Eternal things must proceed out of the Eternal Root; and that Hell hath a Perpetuity must be believed by all who credit the Testimony of the Prophets, and Christ himself, and the Darkness there to be the blackness of Darkness, where the Worm is Immortal, and the fire not extinguishable. What room then is left for the least doubt that Hell or the Stream of Wrath is issued out of an infinite Eternal Fountain. Also that as the scorching heat of the outward Sun not only consisteth, but naturally Uniteth with the cheering Splendor thereof; So doth the Abyss of Wrath consubstantiate, and is one Essence in the Almighty Trinity, with the infinite gracious Goodness and Holiness of the Divine Principle of Love and Delight.

9. They who will not understand but Cavil at this, will yet acknowledge the same in unwarrantable words; viz. Those who are for particular Reprobation of an indefinite Number of Men who are (say they) Decreed of God from Eternity to be for ever the Objects of His Displeasure; in speaking so hardly of the gracious God are yet forced to own the Principle of Zeal, Anger or Wrath to be from Eternity in God; but to bring it into act so early as to determine an immutable Law for such Persons by Name and Number irreparably to be for Everlasting Burnings, is much more than is here asserted; for they make the Wrath of God divisible. even in Him before the moving to Form any Eternal Images of Himself Humane or Angelical: for their boldness herein themselves must be accomptable; but here 'tis only said, it is in God from Eternity, yet only distinguishable, but not divisible, and that in the Creatures, and in them only the Wrath became separate, manifest and divisible. But more of this will fall under the Answer of the Seventeenth Question.

Q. 16. *Why hath God poured forth such fierce wrath wherein an Eternal Perdition will be ?*

A. 1. To the right resolving this must be shewn, 1. What God's Wrath is? 2. How it may remain Eternally? 3. Why hath God poured forth this Eternal Wrath?

1 *Q.* 2. For the first, we are to know that Wrath as it is in God is an unsearchable Abyss; for as God is Infinite, so is his Anger, and all else as it is in him.

3. For his Wrath may not be understood from Eternity and in Eternity to be so awakened as we see it in the Creatures; but is one entire Harmonious Triumphant Perfection in and with himself, of which the Heat in the Light of the outward Sun is a Shadow.

Jude 14. 15. 4. A little Similitude of which was the Zeal of *Enoch*, also in the Angel when
Exod. 14. 24, looking through the Fire and Cloud, he troubled the Egyptians; in *Moses*, when
25. he brake the Tables and commanded the Slaughter; in *Phineas*, whose Javelin
Exod. 32. 19, staid the Plague; in *Elijah*, who burnt the two Captains with their Fifties, and kill'd
27. the

The 177 Theosophick Questions Answered. 53

the 400 of *Baal*'s Priests; in *David*, *Elihu*, &c.; But above all in the meek Saviour, Numb. 7. 8. who yet denounced many Woes like Claps of Thunder against *Corazin*, the Scribes 11. the Rich, the Blind Guides, &c. in *Matthew* and those in *Luke* part of that Wrath of the Lamb, from which the Mighty Men invoke the Rocks to hide them. Rev. 6. 16.

5. Yet that Evil Angels and Evil Men fall finally, having fitted themselves for Destruction, works no Wrath to make Alteration in the Almighty God; even as we see the outward Sun is still the same, though by Burning glasses its beams are contracted to fierceness, till it becomes intolerable to Sensitives, and destructive to combustible Opposites and Objects.

6. And if Men extinguish in themselves the Holy gracious Light and dear Love Principle, their Precipitance extendeth only to themselves, blowing up in them the dark Fire, fierce Centre, or Matrix and Anguish of the first Principle, and the four Forms whereof it is constituted. As blow out a Candle, there remains only the dark, burning, stinking Snuff.

7. *How may and must this Wrath have Eternity?*   2 Q.

A. Though the Holy Writings which we call the Bible, often assert and inculcate this Perdition to be Everlasting; yet some (no mean Men) have otherwise understood it, as *Origen*, &c. haply being replenish'd and swallow'd up with infinite Love and Grace of the Holy second Principle, they could not penetrate the extent of this, nor should *Adam* nor his Offspring have so done.

8. But we having kindled so much of it in us, are to know it, not to distract or distress us, but to warn us, as *Paul* saith, knowing the Terrors of the Lord, we perswade, &c. This Wrath is of Eternal Duration; for it is of Eternal uncreated Extraction as to its Original. It is always Morning with it, bearing equal date with God's other Attributes, and so with God himself.

9. God being infinitely all that he is, is also infinitely Just, and Almighty, True and Faithful; we can no more say his Grace and Love to have Priority, than the Light of a Candle can precede the firing the wiek, or than Man's Intellect could precede the enkindling his Humane Soul, or than the Fruit can prevent the Tree, or That the Root.

10. Can we well conceive the Eternal Permanence of God's Goodness, and why not his Infinite Power and Justice, is there room to doubt that to be a part of him?

11. Must the Fruit and Flower live, and not the Root? must the Eye see, if the Man die? or the Candle shine, when the Wiek is cold? Then may the Principle of Sweetness, Meekness, Grace and Love, survive the Principle of Strength, Might, Potence and Wrath.

The last Branch of the Question is, *Why hath God poured forth Eternal Wrath?*   3 Q.

12. God according to the first Principle is not called God, but a consuming Fire; nor is he called God according to the out-birth or third outward Principle; for the Devil is called the God of this World, though Divine Omnipotence guides and restrains in all Occurrences; for no place or space excludes him, for God is in it, or more properly it in Him, comprehended by Him, yet God's infinite Abyss of Love and Goodness is His Heaven, That his Throne.

13. When God created Angels (the first race of Intellectuals known to us) they were made out of Himself; of his Abyss of Might and His Abyss of Goodness, or of His first and second Principles, Darkness and Light, in such Excellency as are the Angels who so continue.

14. When also God created Man (His second race of Intellectuals) it was out of the two former Principles in Conjunction with the third, yet in such sweet order as we know little of, a glimpse whereof is seen in the resigned, humble, regenerate Soul, who lives in God, and hath there His Possessions and Reversions; about

that

that is employ'd His Fear, Care, Grief; also His only Delight and Satisfaction both for time, and for ever; yet all this is but a glimpse of what we were at first, and shall be at last.

15. These things being premised, give us a prospect what good, beautiful excellent Creatures, Angels and Men were, and should all have continued to be.

16. For if God had willed the one to be Devils, the other to be inwardly so, and outwardly Beasts? How is it they were all created Divine and perfectly Good?

17. But they directly against the confessed Will of the gracious Creator (who never did nor ever can will any thing sinfully Evil, but Good and only Good) both the fallen Angels, and *Adam* formed in themselves a Will perverse to the Sovereign Will, shutting up their whole selves from the only true Guide, and Eternal Light and Wisdom, and so became Dark, and such Fools for whose back is the rod, and being Estranged, snuffed at Reproof, grew into Scorning, Enmity and Diametrical contrariety and hatred of Holy things.

18. Their own private will became their God, for having broken the sweet Bands of Love, they made a League with Hell and Death; for the Divine Light withdrawing, or rather, they declining its Councels, the dark fierce fire became their very Essence and Life, under the domineering Power, whereof the fallen Angels, by their departure from the sweet Kingdom of Love and Peace have forever subjected themselves. into which obstinate hardened Men also throw themselves. And this is so contrary to God, that his Spirit loatheth them and withdraweth, and his so withdrawing is God's pouring out Eternal Wrath, and the way how, and cause why it is the Eternal Perdition.

Q. 17. *Whereas God is and remaineth Eternally undivided, what then is his working in the Place of Hell? Is there indeed a certain Place of Hell, or not?*

A. 1. Here on a Position premised, is a Question proposed, and a second Question occasionally put. It seems fit to strengthen the Concession by explaining it.

2 That, although every part of the Creation consisteth of various Heterogeneous and contrary Properties, all which is not only derived from God, but their Life, Motion and Being is in Him; yet is He from Eternity in Eternity, the same undivided One.

3. For if an Infinite were divided into Parts the Parts must also be Infinite, and then must be more than one Infinite which were a Contradiction as equally vain, as to say, that Almightiness doth divide it self against Almightiness.

4. But that the Infinite Almighty comprehendeth all Properties in perfect Supream Excellency is clear, and that Himself remaining still in Himself, can yet make Himself creaturely in Infinite Multiplicity, is as clear and visible.

5. The outward Sun, consisting of Light and Heat, can by its Beams help Generation of Infinite Productions Good and Bad, even poisonous, perilous Images of the dark World, and this principally by His Heat; but by His Light can attenuate, penetrate and change gross dark Bodies; yet Himself (as the outward Agent of Omnipotence) remain untouch'd, unaltered, unaffected, unsubjected in any degree whatsoever, by his so doing to the things wrought.

6. For, alluding to the instance in the Answer to the last preceding Question. If Sin, like a Burning-glass contract the hot Beams, it may be intolerable to the Sinner or Object opposed to it; yet is the glorious Sun still the unaltered same.

7. The Gardner Roots up, dryes and burns the Weeds. The Sovereign Power guards the Peaceable, and curbs the implacable. But if the good Plant would wear out the strength of the Weed, by extracting and transfusing into it self part of its

Nutri-

The 177 *Theosophick Questions Answered.*   55

Nutritive Property; the good Plant may degenerate into a Wild one, or Weed Also if a private Person shall unauthorized make himself a Judge or Publick Arbitrator, he may fall into a Crime on the other hand; for these things are the Gardener's Work to whom Vengeance belongeth, Mens own Vindictive Desire is touching pitch.

8. Now to Answer directly what *God's Working in Hell is?* It is answered,   1 Q.
That his working there is only according to the first Principle, according to   A.
which, he is not called God, but a consuming Fire.

9. God's working in Hell convinceth Atheism to be an Error. The Devils be-   1.
lieve so as to make them tremble; Men were loth to believe God made the World
and Them, though so evident as to leave them inexcusable, this they are now
assured of, by His destroying both It and Them.

10. God's working in Hell openeth every Book of Conscience; *Dives* extenu-   2.
ates not his Crimes; but roars out his Torments. That Place of Darkness affords
Light enough to read Guilt by, and thereby give Immortality to that Worm.

11. God's working there, restores the Memory; *Dives* had not forgotten his   3.
former calling of *Abraham* Father, as if That would have Privileged him: nor had
he forgotten his Brethren, who perhaps had run Parallel with him in his Sin.

12. God's working there, confirms perpetual Existence to all there, where every   4.
black Machination ever stands in its own Substance, not barely a Shadow, but permanent without Vizard or Varnish, in Horrid real Forms.

13. There God receives the Glory of His Truth in all His Threatnings. There   5.
the Voice of the infinitely precious Blood of the Lord Jesus Christ the Eternal Son
of God, which had been trampled on, as if it had been an Unholy Thing, hath
due Audience and exact punctual Answers. Also the Cry of all the Blood and
Tears of all His murthered and oppressed Members, from *Abel* to the last Man,
hath ample satisfactory Answers.

14. There God receives the Debt due to His abused Patience, and due to the   6.
Holy Ghost, who had been continually striving, and as long rejected, grieved,
scorned, and his sweet Councils, gracious and safe Motions, reproached and blas-
phemed.

15. There God reigns in all the Seven Forms of Nature, according to the Dark   7.
Impression; for the wicked Impenitent Will whereunto the very Gospel of Jesus
Christ hath been a savour of Death unto Death, this very Obstinate Will is here a
sweet savour to the Divine (and here immutable) Justice; for the Righteous Lord
loveth Righteousness.

16. *Is there indeed a Place of Hell, or not?*   2 Q.
That there is a Hell, Atheists only deny; and what Hell is, the Children of the   A.
Day know little of; nor should *Adam* or his Children have known it, for it was
not prepared for them; but as it is written, Prepared for the Devil and his
Angels.

17. Man grew up into that Principle as it were by Accident; yet are like to
have no small share of it. 'Tis true, *Lucifer* and his Legions were Sinners of elder
Date, and fell from a higher Seat, as it were down a greater Precipice. But Man
hath sinn'd against means incomparably fit, of invaluable Price, and freely and
frequently tendered to restore him.

18. Oh that Men were wise that they knew This, that they would consider
their latter End. Consider this, you that forget God, lest he tear you in pieces and
there be none to deliver. Knowing the Terrors of the Lord, we perswade Men.
Will Men employ no serious Thoughts on this, but treasure up wrath against the
day of wrath? &c.

19. Now whether Hell be a Place; It's answered, Hell is a Principle consisting
H of

The 177 *Theosophick Questions Answered.*

of fixt Enmity against God's gracious Nature, against all the Holiness, Truth, Love and Goodness; and all this as it consists of the Evil of Evils, that is to say, Sin. Hell also is a fixt Hatred against all God's out-goings; in His Mercy and Bounty, giving Beauty and Order to all his Creation Celestial, and Out-birth, and this Hell is, as by the Evil of Deprivation. And as Hell is an Evil of Sence and Torment, it takes in all the Horrors generated in the Womb of the fierce part of the whole Seven Fountain Spirits, as far as the Bounds of the first Principle.

20. We are farther to know, that a Principle cannot want Place, but dwells in its self, for Place cannot contain or comprehend a Principle.

21. An Explanatory Similitude or Instance is found in Man. What part of him is the Place or Receptacle of Wickedness ? It's answer'd, no part of a hardened impenitent Sinner refuseth to be its Dwelling-place, his whole Soul, Spirit and Body, and it, like a Contagion, invadeth all Places and Persons, fitted to receive it, that either by Word, Work, Writing, President, Wish, or otherwise he can extend himself unto.

22. But in a Man wherein the Divine Word is awakened and is prevalent, the Darkness or hellish Principle can encroach no farther than its own unsanctified, unhallowed part. And if any Man follow the Lord fully, he is fenced (as the Cherubim doth Paradise) so that the Dark Powers are shut out of that Man.

23. Shortly then, as much of the Infinite Abyss as shall not be ennobled and enriched by the sweet Vertue, Purity and Splendor of the Holy Powers, shall be the place of the Everlasting Hell, or Lake of Fire.

Q. 18. *Where is the Place of Heaven where the Angels dwell ? How is the same distinguished from Hell ? Is the same also a certain (circumscribed) Place ? How is it to be understood ?*

A. 1. If I am understood by a very few, what wonder; seeing the Lord Jesus saith, *Except a Man be born again, he cannot see the Kingdom of God ?* The Question where Heaven is, presupposeth the Knowledge of what it is ; but to speak what it is, will be met with when God shall excite and instruct any one to answer the following Questions. It seems therefore fit to restrain my self here to the Limit of this Question, and observing that Boundary ; It's answered,

2. Heaven being a Principle cannot be circumscribed, even as God is not comprehended, but comprehends the whole infinite Abyss. So neither is Heaven excluded out of any place, nor included in any place, but possesseth the infinite Liberty; for it both contains and is contained in all the three Principles. Yet is so in them as not to touch nor be touched by the first Principle in its fierceness; but in its Might and Potence : Nor the third in its divided Out-birth, but in its Quintessence, as it stands in the Holy Element, and that in the Wisdom, and as it is purely the out-spoken Word.

3. And all this in the entire Concordance with the Majesty and Divine Omnipotence of the second Principle, which in all the Seven Fountain Spirits hath Eternal Dominion. So that where ever the Love and Goodness of God manifesteth it self, there is Heaven, yet dwelling in it self, in its own Divine Principle, streaming through the activity of some or all of the Seven Fountain Spirits, as they severally move themselves, in some places or things more brightly, in others more obscurely, as is seen in the mixt World.

4. But the Illustrious Principle, whereof the Spirits of Just Men made perfect, are capable, is most Triumphant in the uninterrupted, unveiled, paradifical Part or World ; for there the Fire of the first Principle and the effluenced spoken Matter of the third are irradiated, sublimed and crowned, by the Splendor of the second :

The 177 Philosophick Questions Answered.

second: In this place or part of the Principle, stands the Eternal weight of Glory for the General Assembly and Church of the First-born.

5. Now seeing our gracious Creator made us at first Heavenly, though we became Earthy, and Heaven being the Country whence we sprung; also that it is so near us, it being said it is not excluded out of any place: And that it was on our first Departure re-implanted or inspoken again into us. It may be demanded, how is it we are commanded to *strive to enter in at the strait Gate*, &c. Also, *Many shall strive to enter in, and shall not be able*. Again, *Work out your Salvation with fear and trembling*. Again, *We are Strangers to the Covenant of Promise, having no hope, and without God in the World*, with many the like sad Characters of us.

6. The Reason of all which, is thus to be understood; *Adam* our Root, introduced Bitterness, and the Fruit hath that Rellish: And tho we were engrafted into the Noble Vine, yet do we suffer our selves to degenerate into a Wild one, producing Grapes of *Sodom*. *Adam* as our Fountain, flowed out unwholsom Water, causing Barrenness, though Christ as *Elisha* would have heal'd it with his Salt; we go on to Poison our selves yet more; the Man naturally Blind or Deaf, is not so extreamly such as the resolvedly Blind and Deaf.

7. Heaven is near us, so is it to Hell; yet at sufficient distance till the Will be turned to seek it. Heaven is in us (Thanks for ever be to God in Jesus Christ the Restorer, and Heaven Restored) yet still in its own Principle, not in our Beastial Part, but in the Light of our Life, wherein the Candle of the Lord is put as a Tincture. Wo to that Soul who rebelliously refuseth to be guided, favour'd and tinctured by it. To enter in at the straight Gate, it is required that we die to the Old perverted Man, and something more.

8. *Enoch* and *Eliah*, whil'ft in the Body of the four Elements, were so far tinctured as to be truly in Heaven; yet in regard *Adam* had so far divided himself, as to lose the Unity of the one pure Element: when they were again become United in the One Holy Element, they could not but disappear as to the Four Elements.

Q. 19. *What are the Dominions or Thrones, and Principalities of Angels, Evil and Good in the Invisible World? How is the Spiritual World of Eternity to be understood in the Visible World? Are they also severed by Place and Abode? Or what is the inward Foundation?*

A. 1. To make an orderly Answer hereunto must first be shewn (as an inward Foundation) the Spiritual World of Eternity with what clearness may be, and that it is in the Visible World: and thence the Inhabitants of the Spiritual World may be the more satisfactorily discovered.

2. To do which, beginning below in the Out-birth, Stone and Earth have the Commixture of the other Parts of the Creation to their Composition, though named from one prevailing Property, they have the occult sence of Sympathy and Antipathy; as the Loadstone, Bloodstone, &c. Stones have Water, Fire, Oyl, Sulphur, Mercury with the Salt, as the Artist sees.

3. And the Earth and Waters have the other two Elements in them, and (tho' captiv'd by the Curse) have the Vertue of whole Paradise founded by the second Principle exerted by the good Astral Powers, producing all Gems, Gold, Medicinal Earths, and in the Fruits all Tasts, Odours, Sanative Herbs, Nourishing and Cordial; the inward Vertues of all which, are real Heaven and Paradise, labouring to deliver themselves (under the Ashes and Curse) from the oppressing hellish Properties.

The 177 Theosophick Questions Answered.

4. In the same, who seeth not the Spiritual Evil World manifest in Dark Properties and Figures? So that both the Spiritual Worlds are uncontroversibly in them.

5. In the Outward Heavens this Truth is convinced by benign and malevolent Aspects, powerfully influencing to, the conception and propagation of a Good or Evil Will, in every of the Creatures (not Man excepted) since his sad Fall.

6. But Man, whose Immortal Soul is of the first Principle of Might and Potence, his Spirit of the second Principle of Love and Meekness his Outward Man consisting of the Mortal Soul that exerciseth the Outward Sensual Will, five Senses, &c. out of the Astral Heavens, and his fleshly part out of the Elements (whereinto it is miserably fallen) Man thus hath the most strict Alliance, most express Characters, and most Catholick Conformity to the total God, as he hath made himself creaturely in the Eternal Nature, and Eternal Spiritual Worlds of Darkness and Light, and in his Out-birth of both kinds: So that he penetrateth Hell and Heaven, into either of which he putteth the Hunger of his Will, in that he is at home.

7. If he resisteth the Holy Ghost, he is one with the Devil in his Hellish Wrath, who would be his own Law-giver, making War against God and all the Holy Angels, but by enkindling the Light of Christ, Self-will dies, a new one becomes natural, which warreth against the Evil Angels, subjecting it self to the Scepter of Christ the Captain of our Salvation, having communion with the whole Holy Spiritual World.

8. The Discording Will in the seven Properties make the Evil Spiritual World, but where they are in perfect Harmony; (viz.) having One, and but One Universal Will, united as are the three first Principles through the Infinite Abyss makes the Holy Spiritual World.

9. Now as the Out-birth, which is the Off-spring of the inward, hath Fountains and Streams; and as the Natural Body hath Head and Members, the Body Politick Magistracy and governed, and in the Outward Heavens one Star differeth from another in glory: Even so is it in the Holy Spiritual World; *Michael* is call'd the Arch-Angel, and that *Michael* and his Angels fought against the Dragon, &c.

10. Thus the Throne or Arch Angel is to his Kingdom or Legions as the Tree to the Branches, as was *Adam* to his Human Race, or as is the Liver to the Veins.

11. In that distinct sense the Apostle saith, *Whether they be Thrones, or Dominions, or Principalities, or Powers*, &c. some are Cherubims, viz. Images and Seraphims, (viz.) Flames.

12. All which the inspired *Jacob Behmen* rangeth under three Hiarchies each more peculiarly to one of the three distinct Principles, having the Propriety of three Worlds like Nests of Spheres. This from Stars to Stars was *Lucifers*, the other two without and beyond it containing such part of the Infinite Abyss as exeeds all Human number. In each of which (as the Sun to the Stars) is a Soveraign, and under each of the Angelical Kings numerous (rather innumerable, almost infinite) Hosts, and all those severally excelling, some according to one, some more especially according to another of the seven Properties.

13. In all which the Son of God and Sacred Trinity Reigns, neither near to, nor far from every the least imaginable point, filling and comprehending all, supporting all, and delighting to behold it self in all.

14. Nor can the Angelical Worlds be excluded out of place, or included in any thing but Principles, but (as it is in the Spiritual World) may be resembled to the Mind and Thoughts of Man, which is limited in the Evil Man to the Dark Principle, and in the Holy Man to the Heavenly Principle.

15. As the outward Sun is not bounded by any part of its own deep in which

it

it is King, but only by the Darknefs. Thus the Holy Angels are with us (as God's excellent Engines) to protect and guard us, knowing us as far as we are enriched with their Principle.

16. They have the Supream Creature Authority under the Son of God over Kingdoms, as is faid, *Michael* your Prince, (viz. of the Jews) helped the Angel, who, coming to *Daniel*, had been hindred by the Kings of *Perfia* 21 days.

17. How mighty their Strength, and tranfcendent their Nature, and perfect foever to behold the Moft High, yet their fweet humble modeft Love (notwithftanding their fublime Purity) is fuch, that they difdain not to ferve and dandle fuch vile wretched Creatures as Man; fuch is the flaming Love they abound with to Chrift, that they vouchfafe to do for us what finful abjects even fcorn to do for their poor Brethren, by conftant watching, care, &c. As they did for the Child loft in a Wood (for a time) in *Franconia*, whom (a Snow falling) they fed and guided at laft homeward.

The Innocency, Chaftity and Modefty of Children, is that, why Angels delight them; and no marvel, feeing the Lord of Angels gave a little Child as a Pattern of Humility to his Apoftles; for Children (fome more eminently) have Angelical Sparkles of Paradice in them, and before knowing Evil, have lively Figures of the Children of the Refurrection.

18. And feeing there never was, nor can be more than three Univerfal Principles, out of fome or all of them muft all things originate, immediately or mediately.

19. Whence 'tis plain, that Angels and Man's Spirit are of one fubftance; even as the Fire in the luminous Globes, is the fame with that which being funk down by the Separator, is confined in the Bowels of the Earth for generating of Metals, &c.

20. The Angels are fo near of kin to us, that they appear in Human Form. And tho' they are not Almighty, but depend for Eternal Subfiftence and Food from God's Infinite Store, yet are they far above all Human Might and Power.

21. 1. Becaufe they are not at all detained from action by their own Bodies.

22. 2. Becaufe they can have no Refiftance from any Elementary Bodies fimple or compound, in exercife of any of their proper Powers and Offices. The Terreftrial Globe hinders not their feeing a Pin's point (were it) in the Centre of it.

23. 3. Becaufe they dwelling in Eternity, need not time; whence it is that tho' they are but in one place at once, yet can inftantly be in another, not fo flowly as Light or Lightening; for that needs fome time to pafs from Eaft to Weft; for altho' perhaps it hath no detention from its own gravity, yet is fubjected to fome refiftance by interpofing Atoms, and fpace or diftance.

24. Their Expedition is otherwife than our Thoughts; for our Thoughts being repofed, require time to diffipate obftructions, immuring them, and collect Requifites, having firft been informed by the Affections or Senfes; but thefe fublime Agents, being above all fuch inferior Laws, can inftantly effect what time muft meafure it felf out to us to think.

25. Thus was it, an Angel flew in one night 185000 of *Sennacherib's* Army, as before all the firft-born of all the Land of *Egypt*, paffing by all where the Blood was on the Lintel.

26. 4. Becaufe of their Noble Tranfcendent Nature perfectly fixt in them: Their Saturnine Property is not their burthen, but their moft ftrong Compaction, and fo of the other Properties: Yet how perfectly foever they are honoured with the Majeftick Names, they admit more (as by adventitious occurrents, not unfitly call'd Improved and Acquired Experience) of the works of Infinite Grace, Mercy and Bounty of God to Apoftate, Penitent Converts, at which they rejoyce.

27. Angels

27. Angels have the Senses of Seeing, Touching, Hearing, &c. yet without Organs; whence they are affected with Delight and Dislike; Earnest Desire, Joy, Grief, Pleasure and Pain.

Their Understanding is vast and perfect, for they penetrate all Creatures of their Principle Simple or Compound, as far (at least) as their Principle is an Ingredient, which yet is bounded by the adverse Principle; for the Holy Angels are as Children to the Sinful Tricks of the impure separate World, as are the Evil ones to them. The infinite God only comprehends all Things as one, and all Time and Eternity as present.

But the Good Angels see not things above them in their own very Principle; for they desire to look or pry into the Mystery of the Incarnation; by which lost Mankind are found.

Q. 20. *Out of what is the Visible World Created, seeing the Scripture saith, God made all things by his Word? how is the same to be understood?*

A. 1. First, By way of Simile. A Wheat Corn is sowed, there is produced a Blade, Ear, Husk or Chaff; The Ear, Straw and Chaff as an Appurtenance to the Corn; or an Accident is likened to the Visible World, the Grain of Corn to the fixed Harmony produced into Existence by the Power of the Seven Fountain Spirits. The Spirit of the Grain to the Quintessence, and the Quintessence is the one Element, having in it the Mystery and vertue of the Four Elements, and the Power of the Holy World, and God himself, is likened to the Husbandman.

2. Thus as the Son is the Infinite Majesty, Light and Speaking Word, Express Image of the Father; and as the Holy Ghost is the Infinite Breath of Father and Son: So is the Holy Spiritual World the Image of the Father, Son and Holy Ghost in the Heavenly Powers, Vertues, Colours, and infinite Variety and Harmony of it. And as the Paradisical Principle is the Image of God's Holiness, and the dark Abyss the Image of God's Potence; so is the Out-birth the Image of the two Spiritual Worlds, in the Good and Evil Properties whereof it is Composed. And the Varieties therein Image the Varieties of the Eternal Mansions, and these Creatures all those Eternal Creatures of all Kinds.

3. Another Simile may be the enkindling of a common Fire, the hunger whereof attracts the Circumambient Air for Nourishment; yet the Fire remains an hungry fierceness still; the Air (by way of Supplement to the vacuity endeavoured by the Fire) becomes it self enkindled into a Radiant Flame, the operation whereof is various; first, at nearest distance are hot active Productions, also luminous active Productions. Secondly, At greater remove are other less fiery and luminous, yet excellent Productions of both Kinds, (viz.) with the Temperament of Fire and Light. 3. At the most remote Extream, bounding the stream of the Fires spherical activity, are produced sluggish, dark, cold, glutinous (Passive rather than Active) Bodies.

4. The first Production of the Fire shews us the two Spiritual Worlds of Fire and Light. The second the Angelical World, in which are the Souls and Spirits of Mankind.

5. The third the Out-birth consisting of the visible Heavens, and this poor sorry Ball of Earth and Waters.

6. Over this Out-birth of the third Principle, Man should have continued Ruler, and have subsisted in his Divine Principle; but falling into it, became (much a Bruit) into the sluggish, cold, passive Principle as to his Body, and entred into the dark Principle with his Soul and Spirit.

7. Out

The 177 *Theosophick Questions Answered.*

7. Out of which, the infinite Grace of the Almighty Saviour, by dying Himself to the third Principle taught us so to do, redeemed the Body, and by bringing in the Righteousness of Perfect Obedience, teacheth us to die to the separate Self-Will and Lust, Unites us to the Universal Will, which is call'd most truly, a New Birth, or a being Born again.

8. Thus may be seen, that the self-same Word, which out of the seven Properties created the vast Imperial Spiritual World, in the first and second Principles created also the Visible World, four Elements and Stars, and the (in a great degree) dead Earth and Waters, to be the Image of the Image of the Omnipotent Trinity, having something of all Powers in it. And affording a suitable Medium to Cloath the Good and Evil Angels, when needful, for the Execution of their several contrary Offices.

Q. 21. *Whereas God and his Word is only Good, whence proceeded the Evil in the Essence of this World? for there are Poisonous Worms, Beasts, Herbs or Weeds and Trees, also Venom in the Earth, and other things?*

A. 1. To such as are meer Strangers to the Writings of *Jacob Behmen*, the Answer here intended will seem obscure and brief; but repetition of things spoken before, and the laying open of Foundations, may not be expected.

2. We know not God in His Infinite Abyss, (that is) in the Will to the Anguish; but we may know Him as He manifesteth Himself in the seven Properties of the Eternal Nature; wherein are four Anguishes.

3. 1. Binding; to which are referr'd all Astringent Bodies, as resisting to be moderated by penetrating Compounds. Thus the Barks of some Trees, some Fruits and some Waters, by their Excess of Compacting or Ligation are so obstinately Crude as to Petrifie some Bodies, and impose intolerable Laws on others, as the Barks of Oaks, the Asian Gauls, *&c.* are Poison to Vegetation.

4. 2. Constringency or Violence of Attraction; to which Head must be referr'd in Minerals, some Vegetables, *&c.* Mercurial Poisons.

5. 3. Anguish, Properly so call'd; whereto is referr'd all akeing, cold, tormenting Venom, as of Toads, and in many Vegetables, being a cold Fire.

6. 4. Fire; to which is referr'd all the fierce, raging Poisons in the Basilisk, Scorpions, Spiders *&c.* and in many Martial Vegetables, and Corrosive Minerals.

7. Now all these Properties in the Creation not proceeding to the enkindling of the Light, and in the Light the Love, and which would produce the Harmony of Sound, must be comprised in the Evil Principle, shut up and sealed therein.

8. As we see all those Sensitive Animals are either Mutes, or that they have only a murmuring, harsh, discordant, hissing, croaking, or other hideous Voice.

9. Thus is it, That though the infinitely Glorious Creator be Perfection of Superlative Goodness, from Eternity in Eternity: yet these separate pieces of the Creation, including and shutting up themselves in the Wrath of the first Principle, must needs be Unclean, Inimicitious, Evil, Venomous and Poisonous; remaining as a *Caput Mortuum* to the rest of the Creation.

Q. 22. *Why must there be Strife or Contrariety in Nature?*

A. 1. The Answer of the last foregoing Question opens this also; for the Contrariety in Nature causeth Strife, and the Strife Production of the same contended for. And this is as Natural as for a Tree to have a Root, or a Torch to have Matter whereon the fire may live to elevate the blaze.

2. And if by striving it can reach no higher than the first four Forms, there it produceth

produceth bitter, stinking, harsh, four, inimicitious Properties in Transitories; and in Eternals Tormenting Woe, Anguish, sharpened Rage, Despair, &c. But if their Strife attain the Liberty; if their Contrariety proceed to the Unity, and enkindle the meek, pleasant Light, wherewith it is nourished, fed and satisfied, by which also is generated sweet delight, and dear, chast Love, the Strife there is highly profitable. And then the greater the Strife, the more noble and exalted is the Rapture of Sublime Joy.

3. For, without contrariety (that is) contrary Properties, is no strife, and without strife is no production, and without production all would be a stilness, inactivity and unknown to it self.

4. Thus the Properties, which (when separate) are Authors of a Hellish Kingdom, are also (when they operate harmoniously) the exalters of the Divine Blessed Kingdom of Love: Whereby is apparent that the worst is in its due place as good, and as liberally contributeth to the perfect harmony and happiness as the best, both in the Out birth or World, and in the Spiritual World, whereof this is a shadow and representation.

Q. 23. *What is the ground of the four Elements? How is the Division effected, that out of one four are come to be?*

A. 1. An Element is no Compound but one Simple Body, of the greatest extent of any in the Outward World. They are four. Fire, Air, Water, Earth.

2. The Fire preys upon the Water and Air: The Air is breathed out of the Water by the incitement of the Fire. The Water is the contraction of Air by the vicinity of the astringent cold Earth, but the Earth is one Body of no great intimacy with either of the other, only a Sediment resulting from the separating power of the other three Elements.

3. Nor yet may it be wondred that the four were once one, and proceeded from one; seeing they are still one, differing only in the degrees of Rarity and Density; for as the Earth drives up the Water, so doth the Water raise up the Air, and the Fire being violently active, surmounts all.

4. Come we now to consider how the one was separated into four; to make which plain, it was necessary when the Omnipotent God willed to make himself creaturely, that the seven Properties should every one of them form their respective Powers into so many various Existencies; And then there came out of the one pure Element (which is the Mystery of all things) an Heavenly Earth of Paradisical Salt, or Divine Spiritual Salin Spirit or Property, or Pure Holy Salitter. An Humble Meek Spirit, which was the Living Water. A pure exalted Breath, bringing the unconceiveable Joy, Life, and serene Tranquillity into the Divine Spiritual World.

5. And lastly; An holy, cheering, active Fire, according to the Property of the second Principle, without Rage, Fierceness, Curse or Wrath at all, but generating the Light and Flame of Love.

6. But when *Lucifer* and his Legions (not keeping the sweet Order in which the Creator had enthron'd him, and gloriously inflated them) would be Gods to themselves, found resistance and a soveraign check at the Bounds of the Principle, the total God had allotted them, they grew displeased, and gradually their Holy Love-fire disappeared, instead of which came a Raging Dark Fire, whose fierceness dried up their Humble, Sweet, Meek Water, and their Smoke became a Blackness, suffocating the Serene Air. And their Royal Angelical Christalline Bodies became gross, contracted, crude, rough, deformed, harsh, bitter, hot, cold poisonous, stinking, prophane, inimicitious, filthy, wrathful, dark, blasphemous Existencies.

7. And

The 177 Theosophick Questions Answered.

7. And thus were the four Elements polluted, and wretchedly confounded into a dark diforderly commixture, which the Antients call'd a *Chaos*.

The farther procefs from This Evil State of things, will fall under the Anfwers of the 33, 34, 35, 36 and 37th Queftions, by whomfoever they fhall (by Divine Affiftance) be refolved.

Q. 24. *Wherefore, and to what ufe and benefit are the Stars created?*

Anf. 1. This of the Stars includes the Sun and Moon; for they alfo are two of the Royal Stars. To the better difcourfing, which it may be orderly, 1. To fay what they are. 2. What they figure and reprefent. 3. What they are Inftruments to do.

2. They are in the Out-birth vigorous Engines of Omnipotence, that by occult (1.) and Spiritual Powers can infenfibly influence and act irrefiftible applications for the concreting or generating, improving & diffolving of all the various Bodies within the Sphere of their Activity or Principle, being of the Outward World or Third Principle.

3. Thus by fimilitude the Angels are call'd Stars: As doth the Lord of Angels humble himfelf to be call'd a Star feveral times in the Sacred Records.

4. What they reprefent and figure? The four Forms or Anguifhes of binding (2.) attracting Anguifh and Fire, reprefent the firft whole Principle, and do form *Saturn, Jupiter, Mercury* and *Mars*. The two Forms of Majeftick Light and dear Love, figure the whole fecond Principle, and do form *Sol* and *Venus*. And the feventh Form of habitation, a feeming change or inconftancy, a feeming alteration of increafe, and diminution of Effence, being the Scale and Method of the third Principle formeth the Moon with her Changes and Eclipfes.

5. The feven Royal Stars are like vowels or fpirits of Letters, and the innumerable others are like confonants forming infinite variety of fyllables and words; for as words are the opening of the fecret lockt up Mind, fo are the Stars the opening of the Dark Myftery or Chaos fhut up in the Anguifh Chambers. And as the various Properties of the feveral Principles are couched in, and expreffed by the vowels and fpirits of the Letters peculiar to them; fo the feven Royal Stars are fuited in, and qualified by the three Principles, and the feven Properties of the Eternal Nature.

6. Thus the Stars figure God in his Almightinefs, Infinity and Eternity, according to the firft Principle. In His Majeftick Triumphant Kingdom of Light, according to the fecond, and in His Gracious Kingdom of Love, according to the third Principle. And are in the very third Principle the exprefs word of what the Devils are in the Dark Abyfs, and of what the Holy Angels are in the Heavenly World. In all which they are an Image of the Image of God fo expreffly, that the Throne or Angelical Kings (according to each of the feven Fountain Spirits) are imaged by the feven Kingly Stars. The Hofts and Legions of the feven Angelical Kings, by the reft of the innumerable Conftellations and leffer Glories.

7. What they do inftrumentally? *Mofes* faith, they were for figns, feafons, (3.) days, months and years. *Deborah* makes them Warriors; The Stars in their courfes fought againft *Sifera*. The wife men found one of them a Harbinger to tell them of Chrift's Incarnation.

8. The wife Antients penetrated fo far into their Properties, Virtues and Orderly Applications in Human and all Terrene Bodies, Affairs, Governments, that by true Natural Magick they could demonftrate their occult Energies by fenfible Influences. And the Egyptian *Magi* imitating *Mofes*, may not be concluded

I meerly

meerly Impoftors, tho' their Acquired Operations (how really natural foever) muft humble themfelves before the ftupendious *Fiat* of the God of Nature. The *Babylionian Magi* (whereof *Daniel* and his Companions were) could interpret and difclofe Secrets. And the wife men find the King of the Jews by clear Induétions and Conclufions of Natural Operations; as are found Real Caufes by Natural Confequents.

9. But fome Modern Pretenders to Wifdom, little more than gaze on the Stars, and take up with names and numbers; and where they fee more, will entitle Satan to the honour of God's great excellent Works amongft his Creatures.

10. Having thus made way, be it known, Man hath an Aftral Spirit call'd by Some an *Evefter*, by others otherwife, which laies hold on him at the enkindling of his Life, when his *Embrio* in the Conception is ennobled by a Living Soul; and that Aftral Spirit fublimeth or debafeth his Intelleét, decorateth or incurvateth his Mind towards Good or Evil. This (as the Separators Inftrument) doth model and diftinguifh into Sexes, difpenfeth fuch Peculiar Properties as their fucceffive afcending Regiments, by prevalence or precedency, fhall imprefs then and at the Birth, the Internal Faculties more or lefs capacious, &c. The whole compofure of Body, the Eye, Feature, Stature, Lineaments, Voice, Seal of the Palm, Tinéture of the Parts, caft of the Hair, &c.

11. The Stars are fuch Aibitrary Lords, fince *Adam's* heavy Fall fubjeéted him thereunto, that they can well proportion the Elementary Body of one, a Mind well compofed, Atchievements fuccefsful, his courfe renowned. Another they load with an incumbring Body of Ill Symmetry, perverfe Humours, and unprofperous, and finifh him with a Tragical *Exit*.

12. The Aftral Vertue is woven into all the variety of Minerals; diftributing weight to one, making Lead from *Saturn*, fo *Mars* harfhnefs makes Iron, *Venus* Copper; thofe with the work of the power of *Sol* produceth Gold, and fo of the reft.

13. Their Vertue is alfo as apparent in the other parts of the Creation, as in Vegetables from the Cedar to the Hyffop or pile of Grafs. In Infeéts, that there is infufed both utmoft diligence and providence, which is obferved in the Ant. What is the Spur of the delicate curious Bee, the crafty induftrious Spider, the profitable Contexture of the Silk-worm with its Tranfmigration; all proceeding from the ftrife of the Properties?

14. In Senfitives and Animals are there Infcriptions, fome fitted by the firft four Forms, or fome of the four for prey and hoftility, others by conjunétion of more benevolent Afpeéts are mild, fome very docible. So in the general Body of Nature (by fome call'd the Soul of the World) are Sympathies and Antipathies, &c. In all which no caufe is left to doubt, but their Vertue is exprefly eminent in the feveral Elementary Worlds. Who fees not that all things bear their Impreffions? Some according to the Darknefs, and others the Light, and fome after the mixt Powers, from their peeping up into Propriety till their being refumed by their feveral Ethers and firft Principles.

15. As the Stars are over, under and incircle us; fo their Energies and Powers are in us and on us; we are ftrong in their ftrength; they are not ours more properly than that they are us, even a very great part of us. They are the Pilot of the Elementary part, and the Chariot of our Eternal Soul. And (to our fhame and forrow it muft be acknowledged) they are (in very many) Lords paramount, even over the High-born, Noble, Eternal Soul; very many give up their Will to their Conduét; for, never laying hold of the Grace provided for them in the true *Jubilee*, are voluntary Ear-boar'd Slaves.

16. But all thofe whofe Immortal Souls (derived them from Human Generation)

The 177 Theosophick Questions Answered.

tion) are Enlightned by Jesus Christ, he stirs up and makes to grow the seed hidden in them; shewing them how to dye to the Old Man, the Will of the four Forms or Properties, and are New Born by the blowing up of the Light, Meek, Holy Powers, all such are established in Divine willing, working, and persevering. And in all such Persons the starry Spirits are serviceable Agents, kept under due Order and Discipline; and being kept so, are of excellent Profit and Advantage to the helping on the Soul like a Ship to her Haven.

17. The Starry Spirit is in this Man like the Waters which sometimes have cross Currents; the Elementary Body is the Ship, the Soul the Merchandize, the Word or Lord Jesus the Helms-man, the Spirit of Grace the Gale: Now though the Starry Properties are often cross Tides, oppposite Streams to the hindrance of the Voyage, so violent as carry with them all untackl'd Ships, who like dead Fishes are precipitated with the Stream; yet the regenerated will, finds such a steady Pilot for his Guide, and such vigorous Gales from above, that the Ship (against its own Nature) wafteth the Merchandize through, over and against the thwarting Streams to its longed for Haven. By all which, we see to what Profit the Stars were Created, the thing proposed.

Q. 25. *What is the Ground of the Temporal Nature-Light, and of the Darkness; from whence doth the same arise? or out of what did they Exist?*

A. 1. The Temporal Light and Darkness are the manifest Figures of the Eternal second and first Principles. As the desire of Rest moves Men to Motion: So the longing after the Light agitates the Eternal Matrix of the first Principle to a constant employing the four Properties of it, that they may enter into the Light, whereby they become known; which else would be an Eternal stilness.

2. Thus a violent suffocating, rubbing or breaking, causeth an extending in some Bodies, an impressing in others, a discontinuance of Parts in others, and extracts Heat, Fire, and the vertue of Light out of cold, moist and compacted Bodies; to this is referred the vertue of the Usnea on the Skulls of stranzled Persons.

3. For the Contracting Property interrupted by the Attracting, depresseth to Anguish, and those three sharpen themselves into a fourth (*viz*. Fire;) yet not one, nor all of these are known to themselves, but remain Captive in gross Darkness, till the Light be enkindled in them. As a Man having all the Properties, Proportions and Forms of other Men, is still unknown to himself, if he hath no Understanding; for wanting the Light and Knowledge, he is below the Wit, Craft, Memory and Docility of many Beasts, Birds, &c.

4. And yet is worse if at rest in that dark State. Whereas the noble Faculties irradiated by the Light makes Man (though naked) rule over the Bruits, whom Nature hath arm'd with defensive Hides, Scales, Hoofs; also, offensive Horns, Teeth, Tallons, &c.

5. Now whence the Temporal Light ariseth is evident to come from the Eternal Light; as the Temporal dark Matrix deriveth from the Eternal dark Matrix. Yet though in the Temporal Matrix, Mystery or Chaos was potentially all Properties, but without Ability of stirring up it self into a flaming Lustre, till the Divine Power *or fiat* call'd up the Light, as Jesus did *Lazarus*; for till then, it was lock'd up as fire in a Flint, green Sticks, or wet Hay, not touching each other.

6. Nor could the Light till severed from the Darkness, officiate to attenuate and form the crude Matter to be fruitful; but was as Fire under Ashes, inoperative, unactive. Wherefore the Light was severed, that it might (as force United is) be most Powerful. Yet when it was severed and collected by enkindling the place of the Sun, and Orbs of the Stars, it was no otherwise withdrawn, than as a

Conquering

Conquering Prince, having added some Province to his Empire, on his retiring leaves such part of his Army as may cause continually due Execution of his Pleasure.

7. So the Sun and Stars have no other entire Separation than consisteth with the leaving a competent Portion of their Vertue every where to effect by Conjunction all needful Operations. It is left in every of the Elements as we see. also the Elements have among themselves a mutual Commixture of each others Property, and all (as hath been said) of them, some Proportion of the Vertue of the Light: the Hellish Part and Principle only excepted.

Q. 26. *What is the Heaven created out of the midst of the Water? And what is the Separation of the Water above the Firmament from the Water underneath the Firmament?*

A. To answer this, it is necessary to distinguish what is meant by the Above, the Midst, and Underneath; for a Firmament is fixt in the midst between the Waters Above, and those Underneath.

If Above, were meant above the Middle Region, or Stars; then Beneath, may be on, or in the Earth, and the Midst must be a space or local distance.

1. But, First, God is every where, Heaven is also in the World, though this World be not in Heaven; the Above and Beneath therefore must be otherwise understood than locally.

2. Where an Hour-glass is measuring of Time, Eternity is also in every Minute of it; yet is so Above, as Incomprehensible to Time.

3. The New Man is Above; yet so, with and in the Old, as to Rule and Act it, and so divided from the Old, as to be Incomprehensible to it.

4. We find a Water call'd, Living Water, which who Drinks, it shall be in him a Well of Water springing up to Eternal Life. This is also the Water of Regeneration, *Except ye be born of Water,* &c. These Waters (none doubts) are those Above, yet must be Drunk where the Divine Life is, being the true Eternal Life, and of such as shall be cleansed.

5. There is a Divine Love, and there is an outward Love or Lust; They are one from Above, the other Beneath, yet not sever'd by place, but by a fixt Firmamament, Gulph or Principle. And if they were as like each other as true and false Light, or as Tin and Silver; yet coming of different Properties are uncompoundable as Silver and Tin incorporate, and Sowder not.

6. Thus the Waters which are Above the Firmament are Holy, Pure, Heavenly; those Underneath are our Mortal Waters wherein is the Wrath, yet wherein also may the Holy Waters (which are Above) penetrate; as Heaven doth this World; for the outward Water cannot Subsist and Unite with it, or Comprehend it; as neither can this World be in, Unite with or Comprehend the Holy Heaven. Therefore how near soever the inward or outward Waters are one to the other, they are immoveably sundered, till the Judgment of God burn off the Curse at the time of the Separation.

8. And the Holy Heaven may as well be said to be Created, and Creating out of those Living Waters, as the outward Heaven to have been Created out of these Waters, on whose Face dwelt the Darkness, when first the Spirit of God began to move thereon.

Q. 27. *What is the Ground of the Male and Female Kind in the Essence of this World? Whence is the Conjunction and Desire arisen? Could not the same be effected in one only Ground without dividing?*

A. The

The 177 Theosophick Questions Answered.

A. The Question having three Branches requires a distinct Answer to each part;

1. To the first it must be said, The Male and Female Essence of this World have (1.) their Root in the very Properties whereof the World it self consisteth. And tho' the same Tinctures be an Image of the two Spiritual Worlds, and of the Principles, yet the dividing of the Tinctures are not in the Divine World; for though they are there, yet are United and so are not two, but one Potent glorious Power.

2. Will any say, Why differs the Copy from the Original? It's answer'd, The four Elements though divided, are a Figure of the inward World; yet the inward World consisteth in one undivided Element, whence the four proceeded.

3. Now this is a manifest dividing of the Tincture of the Fire from that of the Light, which the Elementary Creatures bear in two distinct Bodies, divided each from other; for as the four several Properties of the first Principle longed to be Creaturely, and attained their Images in the several Transitory Creatures; so the two Tinctures longed and obtained their Images in the two distinct Sexes of the Transitory Creatures.

4. To the second Part, whence the Conjunction and Desire is arisen? which is (2.) for that they come from one only Root, and are there really one only Tincture; therefore being divided, do they so exceedingly desire one the other, as is seen among the many Kinds of Birds and Beasts: Also in the Properties of the Minerals; for we may see how *Mars* naturally incorporated and digested with, and made tough by *Venus*, and then brought into an Hunger, and fed by *Sol*; transmuteth into the desired Metal, or Solar Body. This Desire Nature sheweth in Mulberry-Trees, and that of the Vine and Elm, &c. And not only in Minerals, Vegetatives and Animals,

5. But in the Sympathies of the outward Universe is this apparent; as in every Element and part of Element; who all retire to their several Centres as soon as they get dismist from their Obligations to other different Elements. Also in the Union of Will between the Loadstone and Needle; more especially in Man, the bare Instances whereof would be a Volume; one whereof may be:

6. We see how exceedingly every Man is affected with the Good or Ill Opinion others have of him, drawing a kind of Life or Death from their Affections or Ill Humours; shewing the Souls of all Men to have but one only Root, Body or Fountain, and the Severals to be but Drils or Twigs.

7. To the third Part, Whether it could not have been otherwise, &c:? 'Tis answer'd, The Male and Female Tinctures are originally one glorious Power-World, in which all Properties are United; but when that one Element or Divine Eternal Nature was moved to give out the Astral Heavens and four Elements in their divided Properties: Those Beasts, Birds and Fishes which were distinguished into Male and Female Sexes, and did propagate themselves by Commixture, were the most apt Expressions of the Astral Spirit and Powers, and plainest Characters of the inward distinct Wills; For granting that World (whereof this is an Image) the longing Desire it had to be Imaged, it could not possibly be otherwise. For though the Female and Male Properties are shewn obscurely in the Spawn and Melt of Fishes; but not so conspicuous as in those greater Kinds of Fishes which bring forth young, large full-formed Fishes: Also not so plainly in Insects, as in more mature Sensitives, nor in Immoveables, as in Insects; yet perceptible it is in every of them.

8. But all this relates to Temporary Creatures, Extracts of the Stars and Elements, having no Original Right, but Usurping Dominion over Man's pure, holy Humane Body; for that being out of the Quintessence was capable of Eternity; therefore not out of the Stars which shall fall into their Ether: nor out of the four Elements, which shall dissolve and be Melted by their Central Fire

9. The

The 177 Theosophick Questions Answered.

9. The dividing of the Tincture into two diftinct Sexes in Man was no otherwife needful, but as a Chirurgeon impreffeth an Incifion to fave a maimed Limb from a Gangrene. To man thus it became alfo of abfolute neceffity, becaufe he was fallen headlong from his Magiftracy over both the Aftral and Elementary Powers to be a poor Captive under their Domination.

Q. 28. *What are the Principles of the Spirit of this World, of the Superior or Inferior Being?*

A. 1. A Principle is a New Birth, or New Life. The Eternal Deity is the only One Principle wherein is Eternal Life, the Creation of Angels and Men are its manifeftation, yet is there another Principle (rightly call'd the firft) which is alfo Eternal, but not of Life Eternal, but of Death ; where-ever the Divine Principle is not manifeft.

2. Into which, when *Lucifer* and his Legions had thrown themfelves, Man was created to fupply that place. And left when he fhould fall, he might become a Devil alfo, the third Principle was created to help him,

And were it not out of the Queftion, and that perhaps it may fall under another Queftion to be anfwered by a more enlighten'd hand, it fhould be here fhewn how the Man's concern in This Created World was, what adequated and priviledged him (tho' fallen) to a poffibility of being recovered, which here (not without fome reluctancy) I muft be content to omit in this place.

3. Now (reftraining my felf to the limits of the Queftion) with all brevity, 'tis anfwered, That the moft or innermoft Principle of This Worlds Spirit is the Powers of the Stars in all the Creation. The Light of the Sun and the Aftral World is out of the fecond Principle. And were not fome Wrath in the Sun fhewn by the intolerable Heat, it might unite with the Light of the Eternal Spiritual World; but as it is, the Tincture in it is the moft noble of all Vifibles, as a God in Nature, not only wholly ufelefs to Evil Angels, but a check to many of their works; for they (like Adulterers) love the Twy-light.

4. The next Birth or Principle downward in the Spirit of this World inferior to the Aftral, is the Elementary; which is not fo remote from the wrathful or firft Principle as is the former, but are another or fecond Birth, the Stars being reckoned the firft. Whence it is that Man's Elementary part (fince the Fall) is tranfitory, grofs and fluggifh; like as the Bodies of Beafts, for the Spirit of this World doth in this Birth boil up the half dead Salitter, grofs Sulphur, and infected Mercury: So that the Body were a lump, did not the Sun's luftre or glance give him Eyes, and it, with the other powers of the Stars in the Properties of the firft Principle, enkindle the other Senfes, making it thereby a poor Cottage, but badly furnifhed to ferve the Noble Eternal Soul, and fweet penetrating intelligent Spirit.

5. But the Sun, &c. is a Principle deeper, fhewn (among other ways) by their fecret irrefiftible Agitations, and vigorous Influences on all adapted Subjects, as alfo by their unaltered fteadinefs.

6. The laft and loweft Principle in the Spirit of this World is, the wrathful, mortal, tranfient, mutable Birth. This is one fad confequence of Man's departure from, and prophaning of the Holy Powers, and of the Evil Angels introducing the dark fiercenefs of the Properties of the firft Principle, into the Myftery or Chaos, out of which the *Fiat* by the Separator produced This whole Outward World.

For the Evil had planted it felf in the deep of this Out-birth probably bounded by the *Primum Mobile*; and was call'd by *Mofes* a darknefs on the face of the deep.

7. And

The 177 Theosophick Questions Answered.

7. And this fierceness is part of the heavy Load, thorny Cross, severe School, and rigorous trying Fire of the Regenerate Sons of God. The same is also part of the Over-load, Plague and Torment of the Rebellious, who in their Anguish curse and look upward. And the same is also the vanity and misery the Creatures groan and travel in pain under, who shall be delivered from it.

But the Spirit of This cannot look into the Divine World; and if it endeavours to snatch the Virgin Image, it is but as a Thief.

Q. 29. *What is the Sperm or Seed of the Generation of all things?*

A. 1. By Sperm is meant a Seed, Root or *Ens* yielding matter or substance out of which Form is produced. And by all things meant in the Question is understood all the Out-world, consisting of Stars, Elements and their Concretes. *What is meant by the Sperm*

To which (thus understood) it is answered.

2. That there is an Immediate Cause of all things, that may be call'd a Root, Seed or Sperm; for, to believe the Visible World to be its own Cause, were Heathenism.

3. The Answer is brancht. 1. Negatively, That this Immediate Cause or Sperm cannot be one of the Principles; for in one Principle all Varieties and Properties are not found, but in This World is a commixture of all Varieties and Properties: Not an Herb or Flower purely a simple, but a composition made up of many Properties. *What the Sperm is not?*

4. Nor can This Sperm be all the three Principles themselves; for so is nothing below Infinity; no, not the Divine World, but the Omnipotent is the alone Possessor of all the three Principles, in him only they all subsist.

5. Nor, infinitely less can it be God, a thought of which were derogatory to the Purity and unapproachable Light and Holiness of His Nature and Essence.

6. If therefore the Sperm be not one Principle, having but part of the Properties, nor all three united; because they are inseparably in the One God, and that all Properties owe their Fountains to them. This Sperm can but only be a product from the same Principle, according to, and after all the Properties.

It is therefore not a beginner of Existence, but a begun Existence; not a beginner of Life, but a begun Life.

7. Now for an Affirmative Answer, The Sperm of all Visible things is a Spiritual, and (to our outward Eyes) Invisible *Ens*, consisting of, and containing all the Powers, Properties, Vertues, Varieties, and every distinct Genus and Species potentially, which the Visible World hath in its multiform, express, divided parcels. *What the Sperm is?*

8. It must be confessed to be the great Mystery; great, because in its womb lie all things: A Mystery, because all is wrapt up in it, and spring from it.

9. It is also the Eternal Nature; Nature being generated by the Principle, and furnished with the Native Birth of all the Properties: Eternal, as it is the Root of the Temporary Creation, and its Centre, Retreat and Æther.

10. It may also be call'd a Quintessence; as it contains in Union all the four Elements and Astral Birth.

It is the Image and Imager, the impresser and bringer into Forms of the whole three Principles, and seven Fountain Spirits, the Mirrour of all Forms and Powers.

Is it objected, God's Creating all things by His Word, is a giving Being where none was, exclusive of all Intermediate Causes, and the Out-birth was a substance from a Nullity or Vacuum? *Obj.*

11. It is answered; It is no derogation of Omnipotence, having out of himself spoken an excellent Image of himself, a Power-world or other Creature, that the same generateth more even to Infinity. The Trees, Fowl, Fish, Man as well *Anf.*

as

The 177 Theosophick Questions Answered.

as Elements, had all seed in themselves. Thus a Carpenter makes Tools, and with them makes more.

12. The Apostle saith, That by Faith we understand that the Worlds were framed by the Word of God, so that the things that are seen were not made of things that do appear; he saith not, they were made of no pre-existent matter, but not of things that do appear.

13. And *Moses* recording the Generation of Heaven and Earth, saith, And the Earth was without Form, and void, and darkness was on the face of the deep. And again, The Spirit of God moved on the face of the Waters. Loe here is something call'd Earth, something call'd Water, and some space call'd deep, before so much as Light was call'd for. But how the Earth, Water and Space prove this great Mystery, Eternal Nature or Quintessence, to have priority of Existence, and what that Matter and Space import, will fall under the Questions yet behind more properly than here; whomsoever God shall enlighten to make Answers to them.

Q. 30. *What is the distinction or difference of the Sperm or Seed betwixt Metals, Stones and Vegetables, viz. Herbs, Trees, and Earthy things, or Mineral Earths?*

A. 1. *David* saith, *With the pure thou wilt shew thy self pure, and with the froward thou wilt shew thy self froward.* The Light and Heat of the Sun exciterh the Mercury and Sulphur to germinate in the Saline Property, and so prosper all Vegetations in quite contrary Qualities with equal vigour.

2 Sam. 22. 27.

2. For as we may not multiply Principles nor Properties; so neither may we Sperms; all of which may be distinguished, rather than divided.

3. Their known number and distributions are fully sufficient to methodize innumerable Concretes, not admitting the least disorder or confusion, but yet abounding with infinite variety, and every individual duly ranged into an exact order and subjection, as of all the seven, so especially of some one who hath peculiar Superiority.

4. Hence is it that the Roots, Herbs, Fruits and Seeds sort themselves after the seven Properties, and in them the Sperm is various; either as the Spirit of the World, or Astral Spirit impresseth the Infusing Matter or Sperm in some according to the Evil Dark Impression, and such have much malignity, some especially are mortally vitiated.

5. Others in which the Astral Spirit impresseth on the infused Sperm a vertue according to the Light Divine Kingdom, subliming those Vegetatives to be cordial, sanative and restorative. All as the Spirit of the World dispenseth the general universal Sperm according to the Dark Light, or Mixt Impressions.

Saturn, Mercury, Jupiter, Mars, Sol, Venus, Luna.

6. No otherwise are the Metals; their kinds are seven, Lead, Quick-silver, Tin, Iron, Copper, Gold, Silver. The Tincture of *Sol* and *Venus* is yellow and rosie, or redish, and of the other five either earthy, darkish, pale or white.

Thus is the order in precious Stones, of them are also seven distributions, besides those of Coral and Amber, which are Vegetatives and Chrystal, a figure of the pure Water, and besides those in Animals, Shell-fish, &c.

7. And of the seven Orders of precious Stones, two are of a bright burning Lustre, as the two sorts of Metals, one and the other of a yellow glory answering to Gold and Copper in Metals; They are, 1. Black as the Morion. 2. Red or Purple, as the Ruby and Granat, for the Onyx is more pale. 3. Green, as the Emerald. 4. Changeable, as the Jasper and Chrisophras. 5. Sky-colour, as the Saphire and Amethist. 6. Yellow, as the Jacinth. 7. Bright and burning, as the Carbuncle, Chrisolite and Calcedon.

8. The

The 177 Theosophick Questions Answered. 71

8. The Properties handed by the Astral Influences are so various, that Herbs are much exalted, others much debased by Evil Constellations: But Metals are less casual, their Sperm being better fixt or coagulated, precious Stones least of all (if at all) being in good measure free from the Curse.

9. Thus Vegetables are produced by their Sperm, in their Properties, thro' the Elements, according to the several Principles sorted by the distinguishing Stars.

Metals are Vegetables transplanted, passing a second fermentation and sublimation from the Internal as well as the External Fire, whose Spirits have a new fixation.

10. Precious Stones are Metals transplanted passing a third coagulation; they attain the Love Principle in the Light, as far as Visibles are capable, and are the Triumphs of the Starry Powers in their exalted Perfection; yet is of the same Original Sperm with the more inferior part of the Creation.

Q. 31. *How is the Copulation and Conjunction of Female and Male Nature effected, whence their Seed and Growth ariseth?*

A. The six first Verses of the Answer of the 27th Question, gives great Light to the first part of this; for there is shewn the Cause why the desire of Male and Female is to each other: And that not in Animals only, but in Vegetatives and Minerals; leaving only that here be signified how that is effected, whence their feed and growth ariseth, which may be understood by what follows.

1. The Male-power consisteth in the Properties of harsh Astringency, bitter Attraction and Fire. The Female Power is of the Properties of the four part of the Harshness, the anxious part of the Bitterness and the Light Spirit. Both make up one Indissoluble Band and Immortal Worm, having one and the same only Root; therefore must incline to each other.

2. As part of a growing Tree clave off from the rest, yet fast in the same Root bent off, inclines of its own Nature up again towards the Trunk whence it was rent, and in the Root whereof it is a sharer and lives, whereunto being reunited, concurs to bear fruit.

3. Also, as the Fiery Property longs after That of the Liquid, whereby Vegetation issueth; so longs the Male for the Female Property: And being united, have One only Will in their various Properties, contributing each the Powers by Natural Instinct which they earnestly thirst after, to obtain such increase as suits their Magick seeking. To which united desire the Astral and Elementary Spirits assist, and in a sort intrude themselves, wrestling for predominancy.

4. In which strife the prevailing power denominates the Sex, and the most genuine Ascendant Planets impress the Properties as Supream Agents of the Principles. The Elements also entitle themselves to be Nurses and immediate Parents. Thus thrives the Seed, and in this order, under these Laws, and by these necessary consequences from real Causes, is growth of all the Species in every genus where is Male and Female.

5. And by consent of all Powers giving into one all their Wills, the food is so concocted and digested, that (the tartarous part being separated) it becomes an assimilating Vapour, and That spirated Vapour is enriched with all the Properties, in which are generated (according to the four E ements) the four Complexions, as Blood, Melancholy, Flegm and Choler; and of their and the other Properties, Nerves, Membranes, Gristles, Bones, also Veins, Flesh, Fat, Urine, Spittle. And from the fierce Earthy Vapour, the Gravel and Stone In this sense also may it be said, What is your Life, it is but a Vapour? And from a second force are all the Pores bored, so numerous in the Skin, thro' which the Hairs excresce and are vapoured.   K   Q. 32.

The 177 Philosophick Questions Answered.

Q. 32. *What is the Tincture in the Spermatick kind or species whence the Growth and Lustre ariseth?*

A. What the Sperm is not, and what it is, the Answer of the 29th Question telleth us. This Answer only addeth what the Tincture in the Spermatick Nature is, producing Growth and Lustre.

1. The Tincture is a Potent Will, the pleasant House and Propriety of the Soul, very pure and subtle of its own Nature, yet flexible and mutable; for it is Divine in the Holy Principle, dark in the fierce Principle, and deceitful in the Out-birth. As the Air suits it self to every Creature, also to all sorts of Pipes, yet very differently. Thus the Tincture is insinuated into all Intellectual, Rational, Animal, Vegetative, Mineral and Infernal Existencies, yet hath no Life of its own.

2. The same is thus understood; The Elementary Essences compose a Body, the Astral Spirit adds Life to the Body, the Tincture brings Light to the Living Body, such Light as the Senses move by.

3. Thus far are the meer Animals associates with Man. Then to Man is not only all That, but their Tincture exceedingly higher, to which was also a Soul out of the first Principle, and the Virgin of Divine Wisdom having Life in it self, and giving Divine Understanding, in which respect Man is an associate with the Angels.

4. The Tincture is the sweet Odour, Beauty, and cheering Verture; Taft and Vigour found in Vegetatives. The Vertue and Lustre in Minerals, as far as the Properties assist, or at least impede not, and transmuteth and sublimeth them: It is also the sparkling glory and transparency in precious Stones, with the eminent various Excellencies.

5. Yet, to shew it not to be holy in it self, and to have Divine Understanding, as is and hath the Virgin, it is Evil in the Evil; for the Evil Angels have a Tincture, tho' a defiled one; even as the Air of it self Pure, may be made Pestilential and nauseous.

6. And seeing the Tincture is so eminently Noble, Excellent and Eternal; therefore the prophanation and perverting it, render Angels and Men obnoxious to the Eternal Vengeance of the Offended Majesty of the Almighty God.

Q. 33. *Out of what are all the Creatures of the Mortal Life sprung forth and created?*

A. 1. The Creatures of the Mortal Life are sprung out of the four Elements animated by the Astral Powers and Properties, all which proceeded from the one Element, and seven Fountain Spirits, concerning which the Answers of the 23, 24, and 25 Questions particularly discoursed.

2. The Mortal transitory Creatures have their Root in the Dark Out-birth, yet some more out of one Element and Property, and some especially out of other Elements and Properties, of which much might be said, as also of the permanence of their Ideas or Figures, but that the Answers of the other subsequent Questions will meet with those things if God shall vouchsafe Light to any to answer them.

3. Briefly now, the transitory Creatures bear the Figures (and but the Figures) or shadows of every Principle, every Property, and every Element, and consequently of all Worlds. That the Lord God Almighty may be adored, admired and known in proportion, and according to the capacity of us His Creatures, by some more intimately, by others with a more remote, less perfect, and less distinct Knowledge, as the Image they are entrusted to contemplate, is more or less express improved, and kept bright and serene by our viewing Divinity in them.

4. They

The 177 *Theosophick Questions Answered.*

4. They also bear all Figures, that the Lord may behold Himself in those His Wonders Imaged in, by and through all things; for all things are in Him, from Him and for Him, for whom waits all Honour, Love, Subjection and Obedience for ever.

Q. 34. *What was the Archeus or Separator of their Kind or Species and Property which formed them, and still to this day formeth them?*

A. The Answer of the last Question derives their Original from the four Elements, and this must tell what Architect contriveth their Structure. 'Tis true, the Elements and their Products are the Matter whereof they are; but what divides the Matter into Portions, and those Parts into Method and exact order with different Sexes, Colours and Qualities Good, Evil and Mixt?

1. Are they made of the Earth? Why eat they not Earth? For every Creature subsisteth of its own Root or Mother, but they subsist by the Astral Productions in the Elements, and must do so, or of meer Earth: The Earth, and the other outward Elements would be still Barren, were they not pusht on and moved by their immediate Causes.

2. Hence 'tis clear, the Transitory Creatures proceeded from the Aquastrish Womb of the Elements; which may be well call'd their Mother, or Female Matrix, and the fiery Part or Masculine Limbus is their immediate Father; but the animating Vertue of the Stars is their Quintessence or Tincture; the which Astral Spirit is their Separator, and gives them various Colours, Properties, active or sluggish Fabricks, of nimble Wings or unweldy Bulks. As doth the same Tincture also cause those great varieties of Colours of the many Thousands of different Flowers, Herbs and Vegetatives.

3. This is not barely like a Refiner's Fire which segregates Metals, and thrusts and divides to each in the Crucible all its own; Gold to Gold, or Copper to Copper; for that Mechanick Skill tortures and mortifies the Matter rather than exalts or improves it.

4. But he that is enabled from above, prosperously to Transmute, Augment and Tincture Metals; must remove Obstructions of Mortal Heterogeneous Parts, and then knows how to animate, fortifie and fructifie the United Homogeneous Parts. And do all with such a Fire as that wherewith the Astral Powers generate Minerals, produce Animals, and feed and cause their so great growth; which is done by satiating and converting their constant Anguish and Hunger (which Anguish and Hunger is not radicated at all, but transmuted) into constant Joy, Love and Victory; and the Light World awakened therein.

Q. 35. *What are the six Days Work of the Creation and the Sabbath?*

A. The six Days Work of the Creation and the Sabbath, being severally and at large treated of in the 12, 13, 14, 15, and 16th Chapters of the *Mysterium Magnum*, may not be toucht here.

Q. 36. *What is the Difference or Distinction of the Mortal Creatures? And what is their Chaos wherein each Kind liveth, and wherein are they distinct and severed one from another?*

A. None can call this Question too curious; for God who made nothing in Vain, made not all Creatures but to be of high Consideration, and the Lord sending us to learn Providence and Industry of the Ant, doth much more establish his

K 2   almost

The 177 *Theosophick Questions Answered.*

almost Infinite Number of Creatures, to be for vast Uses, grand Speculation and Importance.

It having been shewn whence they were produced, and by what Power divided, it must now be shewn what their Differences and distinct Kinds are.

1. *Moses* teaching the order of the Creation, saith, *Let them* (meaning the Creatures of the Out-birth) *come forth every one after their Kind.* By which word [Kind] is understood their several Properties, and of the Properties are seven and no more, which Patronize all Creatures: and every of the seven is as clearly distinguish'd in the Animals; as in Minerals, and Pretious Stones.

2. And though they are all in, and of one Principle; yet in them may all the three Principles be evidently distinguished, according to the Order engraved on them, by the Sacred Hand of the Creator, in Conformity to all His other more Divine and Illustrious Works; for His Words are His Works.

1. 2. As First, The Dark Matrix, like a Fountain, issued those of the first four Forms, *viz.* The Cold, Astringent, Tenacious, greedy Animals, which are a numerous Family; some more, some less vigorous; as Wolves, Swine, *&c.*

2. 4. Next, the Attractive constringent restless Quality or Kind; as Foxes, Serpents, *&c.*

3. 5. Another of the despairing anguishing Property; as Dogs, some Venomous Creatures, *&c.* Therefore is a Mad Dog so Contagious.

4. 6. The Fourth is of a fiery, rapacious, ravenous, voracious, haughty Tribe; as Lions, Vultures, Eagles *&c.*

5. 7. The Fifth Sort or Kind, are of a merry, airy Inclination; some more thus; as Birds, others more according to the Spirit of the World, as some other Birds, Apes, *&c.* And of the same Kind (more especially principl'd with Love) as far as the Out-birth is capable of it; as Lambs, Turtle-Doves, some more laxe or rather lustful, as wanton Creatures.

6. 8. The Sixth is the Property of the Sound in harmonious, sweet Singing-birds, Chirping their Musical Notes to the Praise of the glorious Creator.

7. 9. The last are great, bulky, unweldy, huge, lumpish Beasts; and the Chaos of them is part of themselves: or that whereof their various Properties shew them to be part; for the Will of every of them willeth its Property; and thereby willeth it self, and would be much more so, yet knoweth not what it self is.

Q. 37. *To what End, or wherefore were the Mortal Creatures created?*

A. 1. The more Perfect of them are composed (together with the Internal Organs) of Flesh, Blood, Bones, Scales, Skin, Hair, Feathers (of which I may be excused from Curiosity, not being on Natural History or Dissection) Thus is Man of Flesh, *&c.* his Nails resembling the Scales, *&c.* They have also Craft, Wrath, Love, every of the Five Senses, Invention, Providence, Memory, *&c.*

2. To call them moving Plants is too low, but only that it leadeth the Mind to view the Harmony of all the Creatures; how they variously, some more clearly, others more obscurely, Image and Shadow every of the three Principles, and the seven Properties of the Eternal World.

3. Whence they sprung, appears by several Answers of the foregoing Questions; particularly in that of the 33th.

4. And now among the many Glorious Ends of their Creation, the following brief hints are some. They are, at fourth Degree, from the Principles and Properties created; 1. To Figure the Dark Abyss. 2. The Light World, though very obscurely. 3. The Out-birth or outward World of the Stars and Elements, with the almost infinitely various Tendencies, Inclinations and Impulses of them: By every

The 177 Theosophick Questions Answered.

every of which the Almighty Creator uncovereth his veiled Omnipotence, infinite Grace and Wisdom.

5. The Contemplation of them, is both a pleasant and a perplexing Laboratory, or serious Book for Man's Study, and as it were a Play-Book for the Angels; whose piercing understandings read the Effects by the Causes, while declined Man groweth by the Information of the Senses at a piece-meal guess of the Causes, from Experience of the Effects.

6. It must be confest that *Adam* (being as to his Body or third Principle in his first and pure state, Lord of the Mystery whence they proceeded) could more sensibly discover and Epitomize them than the Angels: as the Lord Jesus had a feeling of our Infirmities, by His gracious humbling Himself to be as one of us. But *Adam*'s bright Eyes were darkened by the dismal lapse.

7. Men may see themselves in the brute Creatures. 1. All Unregenerate Men (1.) are figured either by the greedy ones. 2. Or by the haughty proud Beasts. 3. Or by the envious Reptils, where (by the way) may be observed that Envy is found among the Poorer sort; for the venomous Creatures are rather creeping than going. 4 Or by the cruel wrathful ones. And all these are of the first Principle without proceeding to enkindle the Light of the second Principle, and are call'd by the Names of those Creatures in the Sacred Records.

8. Other Creatures there are that figure the Light World or second Principle, (2.) by their Innocence, Love, Usefulness and Loveliness; in which they glorifie the Creator, and like a dark Shadow pourtray the same.

9. There are other Creatures, more especially of the Out-world or World's (3.) Spirit, as those that have Lunary Bodies produced, improved and transacted by her Mutations; which extends very far also to the whole Creation.

10. My last Consideration (restraining my self to brevity) is somewhat abstracted, which is, That their Root is not so ignoble and Vile, but their Forms and Idea's (for the sake of their Tincture) have a prospect into Perpetuity, each into their natural Æthers; as is signified by the Apostle, that the Creatures Travel in pain, groaning under forced (and as to them) causeless Vassalage, shall be deli- Rom. 8. ver'd into the glorious Liberty of the Children of God, where the Drunkard's Horse shall, like *Balaam*'s Ass, convince mens Madness, and cruel Excess. The abused toil of the Laborious Ox, the innocent life of the Patient Lambs, both employed to nourish filthy Lusts; the cruel Delight of Hunting to the heart-breaking of the Deer and Hare, &c. shall at last be material Witnesses of Man's aggravated Guilt, perpetuated Apostasy, and lawless Irregularities.

Q 38. *Whence was Man Created as to his Body?* The Fourth grand Distribution.

A. 1. Not of the Earth; for the brute Animals are more nobly descended, not of the four Elements which are the Matrix of the Earth; for of that Matter are the Brutes form'd, and the Elements are Transient, and must melt or resolve into their first Principles.

Not of the Astral Out-birth, for the Stars shall fall; that is, cease their present Order, and pay the Debt of their various Properties to the Æther, whence they were separated.

2. But because *Adam*'s Body was of Eternal Duration, had he not sinned, it could not derive from a fading Root; as Eternity is not founded on Mortality: which forceth our search to ascend a step higher.

3. It shall therefore be to the Divine Salitter, which also hath the Water-spirit in it, from both which the Stars were breathed. And this Divine Salitter as it hath in it all the Powers of the Properties, together with the Divine
Sulphur

Sulphur and Mercury, is call'd the great Myftery, Eternal Nature, or Quint-effence.

4. Out of this was Created *Adam's* Holy, pure Paradifical Body, capable of Eternal Life. This Divine Saliter *J. B.* calls the Holy Ternary, that is a Celeftial Paradifical pure Earth; whence grows Heavenly holy Fruits, and near unto it no Curfe ever can enter or approach; for thereinto cometh nothing that defileth. Of this Duft or this Ground *Mofes* fpake, that God formed Man. But they who fuppofe it to be our dead Duft, wherein is the Wrath and Fiercenefs, do not only err by means of the Veil before *Mofes's* Face, but alfo by reafon of the Veil on their own Hearts and Eyes.

Gen. 2, 7.

Obj. 5. The Apoftle faith, The firft Man is of the Earth earthy; The fecond is the Lord from Heaven.

A. 6. That it could not be this, nor the Elements, nor the Aftral Birth is clear; but therefore that it muft be the Heavenly Earth, is of forcible Confequence. The Apoftle faith not what *Adam* was, or was extracted from; but what he is, or is come to be; but if he had fo faid, yet the Proportion betwixt the fecond and firft admits no Comparifon.

7. Between a Mote in the Sun and the whole Glorious Sun, is fome Proportion; for the leaft of Quantities taken from the greateft of Bodies below Infinity, hath Proportion to that whence it was; for it leaves the other really leffened, but all created Worlds, bear no Proportion with the Infinite Son of God; for all breathed out from an Infinite leaves ftill an Infinite, and the Infinite is not leffened by it.

8. The Apoftle therefore in this place, either doth not fpeak of *Adam's* firft ftate, or doth not leffen his Extraction, but adoreth the Glory of the fecond *Adam*, as the Work-mafter excelleth the Work made; for when of the Angels it is written, *And hath made them all miniftring Spirits:* Of the Son it is faid, *Let all the Angels of God worfhip him.* Alfo, *Thy Throne, O God, is for ever and ever,* &c.

Q. 39. *What was the Infpiration or Breathing in, whereby Man became a living Soul?*

A. 1. The Infpiration of Man's Soul was out of the firft Principle the Father's Property: which confifteth of the firft four Forms of Nature, of this Living Root, fprung his Immortal Living Soul.

2. Yet fo is it, that wherever, or in whomfoever the fecond Principle is fhut out, that Exclufion is truly call'd the Death of the Soul; for the Living Soul by that Deprivation enters or remaineth in Death, which though improperly may be called an Immortal Death, being a Death to the Glorious fecond Holy light Principle.

3. The Soul is taken fometimes for the two firft Principles. *I faw the Souls of them who had been flain,* &c. for here the third Principle was afleep. Sometimes it's taken for the whole Man. *If thou wilt make thy Soul an Offering for Sin,* &c. The Lord Jefus offered up all the three Principles meant here by his Soul, and as was fhadow'd by the whole burnt Sacrifice: But in this Queftion, Soul is reftrained only to the firft Principle; becaufe other Queftions particularly reach the other two.

Rev.

The above brief Anfwer may here fuffice; becaufe *Jacob Behmen* fo largely refolveth it in the Anfwer of the firft of the Forty Queftions of the Soul.

Q. 40. *What is the Immortal Life in Man,* (viz.) *the Soul, and what is the outward Life in him?*

A. 1. The

The 177 Theosophick Questions Answered.

A. 1. The Principle of Man's Immortal Life is, what the Answer of the last foregoing Question renders it; that is, a Life sprung from the wrestling of the first four Forms of the first Principle. They generate a strong, stern, eager sting, prickle; poison Life, or bitter Root; which (as doth the Gall in living) Bodies strikes up or enkindles Life.

2. This being rooted in the Eternal Beginning, or from the Eternal Abyss of the Father's Property, can never find End, or limit of Race: But Either, is according to the Fountain and Essence of its own Nature, dark, raging and fierce for ever, or in the Holy Principle of Love in the Light World, happy for ever.

3. It must now be told what the outward Life of this World in Man is, and must be sadly acknowledged to be Earthy and Sensual; here is the Lust of the Eye, the Lust of the Flesh, and Pride of Life: So that it may be said, Shut the five Windows, that our House may be truly Light within.

4. The Beasts live as Man doth, having all the five Senses, as he, in some of them more sharp; also some of them extend the Thread of their time to greater Measure: are generally more exempt from Sickness, wholly Privileged from careful Perturbations; in good Measure, without fear of future Events or Sorrow, &c.

5. So that Mans outward Life, or third Principle, as now it is from first to last, renders him of all Creatures the most Miserable. And his restless striving to satiate the Lusts of this Worlds Spirit by Wealth, Greatness, &c. is an additional Sorrow and Vexation, which some of the Ancients skilfully mitigated by wise Moderation and Contentation.

6. Who sees not how much more grievous this Pilgrimage and Travel is to Man, than to any other Creature? Because his Creator made him for the Excellent, Holy, Sweet Paradifical Life: Even as Hell is most intolerable to Evil Angels and lost Men, who were created to be Inhabitants of Heaven; whereas it is no Wo to those horrible Creatures that figure the fierceness of the Properties; for that is their Life.

7. Yet it is true, the poor Brute Animals groan under the Curse Man subjected them to; for they should have been harmless Figures of the Astral and Elementary Powers.

8. To conclude the Answer of this Question, let it be seriously considered, That if Man will think to feed his Immortal Principle with Mortal Food, (viz.) his Soul, with this third Principle, he doth as a cruel Murtheress, who to still her unhappy Nurse-Child. instead of Food, amuses its Eyes with Objects, and its Ears with Sounds, and answers its hungry Laments with louder Noises, till she hath forced it to sleep, who so pines and destroys it.

9. But the Love of God in Jesus Christ is the true real Food of the Soul; it is true, not like Shews and Sounds which are delusive; also real and substantial, not a Shadow, which every thing here else is, as to the Soul. This Love, as Food, generateth its like in the Soul and strengthens it; This Love, as Physick, Purgeth out all other Love, and it reigneth and remaineth for ever.

Q. 41. *What is the Idea, or exact express reflex Image of God in Man, wherein God worketh and dwelleth?*

A. If a Volume were written to Answer this Question (as well might be, by reason of the Excellency and Importance of the Subject) yet still it would be as under Locks and Seals from the fallen *Adam*, until he enter into the Knowledge at the right Door of that he lost by his Fall.

1. The Doctrine of the Resurrection was call'd Babling, by the studious Athenians;

nians; for Man is dead to the Holy Divine Image: and in all who so abide, the outward Astral Spirit and Elementary Body, is the only Bridle of Suspension and Mitigation of the hellish Image, or dark Principle.

2. But had Man no more, he were in no better state than the brute Beasts; for in the Astral and Elementary they are in common with Man; and in the dark Principle he is one with the Evil Angels.

3. Yet so exceeding Great and Adorable was God's Grace, Love and Pity, that the same Grace was like a Seed inspoken into him at the Fall; which in all by whom Obedience is yielded, beareth Fruit to Eternal Life; but it lyes as Dead in such who bury it under the Dominion of the Astral Spirit, or that choak it under the Thorns of the Elementary Body.

4. And all Impenitent Rejecters of God's regenerating Grace, how subtle and studiously penetrating soever, have no part nor lot in this Matter; but are absolute Strangers, guided by an unreasonable Model of Humane Reason, resulting from the Information of the Sences, twisted with the Maxims of Serpentine Wisdom.

5. Nevertheless, the Poor in Spirit that dyeth to its own Will and Lusts, hath lively Characters of the Idea of the Divine Image and Birth; for such a dying enters the Soul into the first Resurrection.

6. God's Image is not in the Earthquakes of the first Principle, nor in the Lightning and Thunders of the third Principle; but most nearly in the small still voice of the Proclaiming his Gracious, Merciful, Long-suffering Name; for that is the second Holy Principle.

7. And this speaking Almighty Word cannot be more than stammer'd by words; no more than Omnipotence can be comprehended by Concrets. With what Eye can a Sinner behold the unexpressible loveliness of That ravishing Face, where dwells That Majesty which is the Express Image of the Father, and before whom the Angels cover their Faces?

I must say, when a drop of that Ocean of Love and Mercy blesseth my Soul, I melt, I stammer, I am astonished. Lord what is Man?

8. God's exact Image consisteth of all the three Principles; The first and third in perfect Order being thorowly illustrated by the second. The mighty longing of the first, like a Hunger, produceth or begetteth the meek Will, and glorious Majestick Principle of Light, according to which, God is cal'ed God. And of the longing and will proceedeth the desiring, which is a Love-spirit, producing Millions and Miriads to Infinity of Variety, wherein the three behold themselves in parcels.

9. But in Man behold themselves in one entire Image; yet not in fallen Man, but in the man Christ Jesus, by whom and for whom, are all things.

10. The Idea and perfect Image of God is only in Christ, yet not as He is the Second Person of the Three; for so He is the inaccessible Light and the Original which is Imaged; but He is the perfect Image of God, as He is the Divine Humanity or Heavenly Man the First-born of every Creature

This Virgin-Image was in *Adam* before he lusted, whereby he was in Christ God's exact Image, having all the three Principles in due Harmony, being the true Character, Idea and Figure of the Glorious Trinity.

11. This is also in an obscure and less conspicuous way, in every one who is Begotten again by the Holy Ghost. The mortified, humble resigned Will, entreth into the way of the Cross quietly, patiently; Love makes it sweet, this is a putting on Christ; for here the Lord is Born, is Formed, sways the Righteous Scepter, Transforming that Soul into the Virgin Image in some degree; but the glance of this stops my Hand, extracts a Groan, swallows me up; I flame, am almost devoured. My Lord, what is this Earthen House? Q. 42.

The 177 *Theosophick Questions Answered.*

Q. 42. *What was Paradise wherein God Created Man? Is the same Alterable or Changeable, and a Creature, or doth it stand in the Eternal Ground?*

A. It hath been reported that a Painter would have Drawn the Lineaments of the Lord when in Flesh; which by reason of His Majestick Face, he could not perform,
 The like Fond attempt were it to Survey Paradise by Humane Art or Instruments; which if it were a place cannot be found, and if it prove a State or Principle, cannot be comprehended.
 1. The Answer may first be Negatively; that it is not a Place or Locality. (1.)
  1. Because then as the most worthy the Garden of *Eden* should not have been the place named for *Adam*'s Seat, whence proceeded the four Rivers; but Paradise is not called the Garden, nor is the Garden stiled Paradise.
  2. Nor is it changeable; for though it disappeared as to the first *Adam*; yet the second *Adam* granted it to the Thief.
  3. Positively; Paradise is the one, holy, pure Element, having its Eternal Fountain from the second Principle, and every of the seven Properties are in it, in great Purity, and Splendor. So that had any created Angel the Task, perfectly to Epitomize it, he could do it but according to his excellent measure, yet not fully: Nor to Human Apprehension; for as Paradise is the heavenly Body of Christ, so is it the Womb of Angelical Conception, comprehending them, but cannot be fully comprehended by them; as neither can the Sun's lustre be by us comprehended
  4. Heaven is Paradise, and the Paradifical Principle is Heaven; and when they are Contemplated, their Glory swallows up all created Angels as well as Men. It is an Over-match to penetrate the Holiness, Purity, Immensity or rather Infinity, Transparency, Simplicity, Variety, Succeffive Formations; with all Powers, Colours, Vertues, Sounds, Odours, Substantials; the Quinteffence and Elixir of the outward Quinteffence and Elixir; the Harmony, Peace, Gravity and Eternity; its ample Commensuration and Redundancy to the most noble, expatiated, sublime and exalted Capacities.
  5. So that proceed they never so far in this ravishing Traverse and Quest, there is still a prospect of more and other; they must say, in our Father's House are many Mansions, at whose right hand are Pleasures for evermore; such as Eye hath not seen, nor Ear heard, nor hath entred into the Heart of Man to conceive.
  6. A faint Similitude may be a fresh springing flowry Meadow, where stand Thousands of fragrant Flowers, some more Beautiful than other, all shewing their peculiar Beauties without grudging, and how the Divine Vertue in the third Principle, is become Material : the taft whereof, causeth the Creation to be in Anguish and Travel to be delivered from the Vanity, and Groan after freedom from their Bondage.
  7. And though Paradise be not excluded this World, yet a great Gulph interposeth betwixt it and the World; the Mind, when inflamed with Divine Love, feels what the stammering Tongue cannot tell to others.
  8. The Corporeity of Paradise is not palpable, that Salitter is Holy and Pure, like that of the Angels, (*viz.*) a bright, transparent, visible Substance.
  9. It's Birth or Productions are in all things, and therefore immeasurable and innumerable; which is thus to be discovered and understood. Let the Divine Light and Vertue be likened to the Mind of Man : The Paradifical Fruits to the Thoughts, eacht Thought hath a Centre whence other Thoughts spring; so also do those Heavenly Fruits proceed from, and in unwavering Eternal Love.

L   10. The

The 177 *Theosophick Questions Answered.*

10. The Fire there, is God the Father; the Light, God the Son; the Air, God the Holy Ghost; It's Profundity and Extent are not bounded.

11. The Idea or Figure of the Creatures here are there, but not their Spirit, much less their Substance; for, for that End they were Created.

12. All Holy Works stand there in their Figure, and all Words spoken by the Human Tongue from a Divine Root; as the wicked Works and Words do in Hell.

13. I compare the Arabian Odours, Oriental Gems, Palms of *Asia*, Wine of Pomegranates, the American Pine-Apple, and what else is most desirable, in comparison of the Paradifical Productions, to the obscure Vitality surviving in Mens Dead Bodies; generating some as it were Fibres of Gold amongst the decaying Teeth, and the Usnea on the Skulls of Persons Strangled. And all things of less Excellency in this World in comparison of Paradise, to the Excrementitious growth of Hair and Nails in their Dormitories.

14. I compare Man's outward Astral and Elementary Life, to that in Paradise, to idle deceitful Dreams, some disquiet ones, some wrathful, some frightful, some wicked and obscene; many, many ways Evil. And our Translation hence I compare to the Morning awakening time, terrifying some as Slaves to their grievous Chains and hateful Drudgery: and others as great Conquerors are usher'd in State to the Princely Triumphant Chariots.

Q. 15. Say any, say not all (retaining the least degree above perfect Madness) if Paradise be thus infinitely Good, what shall I receive in exchange for it? And how shall I search the Path leading to it? What Key opens the Door of it?

A. 16. The Lord Himself tells us, *Except a Man be born again, he cannot enter into the Kingdom of God*; And by way of Explanation addeth, *that which is born of the Spirit is Spirit.* And again, *Except ye eat the Flesh of the Son of Man and drink his Blood, ye have no life in you*; and by way of Explanation addeth, *It is the Spirit that quickneth the Flesh profiteth nothing; my Words are Spirit, and they are Life.*

17. Where we see the New Birth and Eating Christ's Flesh are the same. Also that to be spirited by the Spirit of Christ, and to feed on the Word of Christ, are the very same: Whence it is that true Spiritual Life is revived, or stirred up in us.

18. The New Man regenerated out of the Earthy Man being a Virgin may Sup with the Eternal Virgin; and as the Lord while in our Flesh had the heavenly Flesh and Blood, which swallowed up the other: So we in His Meek, pure Spirit, carry it also in our Earthy Body, and if we live in the New heavenly Flesh and Blood in the Body, Power and Vertue of Jesus Christ; that is, in the Son by the Holy Ghost to the Father: Then, when the old one falls off, we live in the New heavenly Flesh and Blood, and our Works are no longer ours, nor our Words ours, but God doth all in us.

19. To this Man, every with-drawing Thought from an entire Subjection, is his Cross; for to him Honour and Contempt, Sweet and Bitter, Penury and Plenty, Heavy and Light, are no more any of these; for he loves not the one, nor flyes from the other; but the Divine Will is his Joy and Content, the thing sought, and his full satisfaction.

Q. 43. *Why did God Create in the Beginning but one Man, and not forthwith a Man and a Woman together, as He did the other Kinds of Creatures? or other Species?*

A. 1. God created the other Creatures to manifest his various divided Powers, that in them he might severally Image every of them; by those wrathful fierce ones in the dark World, the loving Innocent ones of the Light World's Property, and others of the meer Elementary World; and that the seeming contrary and

discording

The 177 Theosophick Questions Answered. 81

discording Properties might in distinct Forms and Creatures, one excite the other to a general Harmony, whereunto they still serve.

2. But Man He created to a higher and more excellent Sphere; for he was in one only Person, to comprise as in an Epitomy, the Image of the total God, having his Root in the Eternal dark World, or that of Fire: His Life, Glory Vertue, and Fruit in the Eternal Light-world or second Principle of Love and Holiness: and the third Principle being that of the purest Astral and Elementary World, was but to Hang to him, over which he was to bear rule.

3. Nor could he have been God's compleat Image, had not the Tincture of the Fire, and also of the Light been incorporated in him, (that is) both the Male and Female Properties.

4. Therefore was it that he was but One Undivided, to Image God, who is distinguished into Three; yet is One, and Eternally the same Infinite, and in Himself the Undividable One.

5. And as the One God remaining but One, diffuseth Himself into Multiplicity; so should *Adam*, had he remained an Undivided one, Magically have propagated a Blessed, Holy, Numerous Progeny in perfect Modesty and Purity; yet bearing in them all, every Power of the Principles and every Property in great Harmony, as are found in the Angelical World, as well as in the Astral and Elementary.

6. But when once *Adam* had his *Eve* rent from him, we see what Misery, Distraction, Laceration and Wo soon follow'd, by disappearing of the pure Virgin Modesty.

Q: 44. *Was the first Man in such a habit of Condition created to Eternal Life, or to Change and Alteration?*

A. 1. When Men search the wretchedness of fallen Man's present Estate, it may seem incredible that ever he was a glorious and compleat Image of God, and of all Worlds.

2. As one seeing the Ruins of a Royal City, which Sword and Fire hath laid in Ashes, heap'd into Rubbish. Desolation plead Prescription, and Years have cloathed the Hillocks in Green, especially if some Earthquake had razed the Situation; the Beholder of these Remains, though credibly inform'd, can scarce credit that ever it deserved half, what perhaps Fame (too sparingly) reported it to be.

3. Thus Men looking on their own feeble, sickly, filthy, short-liv'd Bodies, can see little more than a Bestial Image. But farther penetrating the Deformities of the Soul, at Hostility against even God Himself, and torn by Civil War within it self, and by means of God's withdrawing abused Grace, it is invaded by gross Darkness: Little more can be seen but what is devillish.

4 But G'ory be to God in the highest, that Jesus took this fallen Image and led it through Death into Eternal Life. The sad Prospect of what Man is, joyned with the Ignorance of what he was, raiseth the blind Conceit that he was created to Alteration

5. But to shew how Excellent Man was by Creation, and that he was not subject to Alteration; yet that I may shun Repetition, do return my self to the Answers of the 38, 39, 40, and 41st Questions. Only let it be remembred, that God denounceth as the Wages of Disobedience, Alteration, Death and Deprivation of the Paradisical Glory.

6. And that the Alteration was Translation to a better Place, must needs be an Error springing from our Ignorance, of what Paradise is, and what that state is; I return my self to the Answer of the 42 Question.

L 2 Q: 45.

Q. 45. *What manner of Image was* Adam *before his* Eve ? *In what Form and Condition was he, when he was neither Husband nor Wife, but both ?*

A. 1. He was so made, as to possess the Throne of expulsed *Lucifer*; he was therefore an Image of God's Power, as well as his Holiness, which made him the Object of *Lucifer's* Malice.

2. And forasmuch as *Lucifer* affected to lift up himself in that part of God's Image entrusted to him, consisting of Potence and Mightiness to such excess as eclipsed his holy, pure lustre.

Therefore to prevent it in *Adam*, there was added to him the third Principle; for it was Matter for some humble Contemplation: But *Lucifer* (not balanced therewith) Imaged in himself a desire of Rule above the End or Limit of Creature Nature.

3. *Adam* was also lower than *Lucifer*; because the Subjects of this Monarchy were only potentially or virtually existent, not actually produced. And it is found that gradual access to exercise of Authority, is less obnoxious to inordinate Practices, than instantaneous Entrance upon Soveraignty. His gracious Creator saw it safer for him to be raising of Fruit, than at once to enjoy a reaped Crop.

4. But he was Privileged above the Angelical Hierarchy that had left their Habitation, being a more compleat Image of God than they, having one Principle more intrusted to him.

5. His Fall was into that third Principle; which though the Holy World should be withdrawn from him, yet was not that Principle sinfully Evil in it self; but the first Principle (excluding thence the Holy World) is Evil in it self, into which the Angels fell.

6. The third Principle God annexed to *Adam* (for knowing he would not remain faithful in the Virgin State) that into it infinite Love and Goodness might enter to help him again, which *Jehovah* Christ did, by re-uniting the Eternal Divine Virginity to the Sick infected Humanity.

7. And thus Tinctured the Humanity, enkindling in it a true Heavenly spark of holy Fire, which when our Humanity in Christ yields it self up into, it is a Sacrifice turned into a Love-flame. Like as the right Tincture transmuteth Metals, and the Elixir Tinctures Mans sickly Body.

8. Now to say what was the Image, Likeness, Form and Fashion of *Adam* when he was neither Husband nor Wife, and yet Both.

He was, as to his first Principle or Eternal Soul, Potent and Mighty, resembling him to the Father, and to the Angels who are Mighty in Power. In his second Principle or Divine Spirit, he was as a God in Holiness, Love, Purity and Brightness; which illustrated his first Principle, joyning the Dove and Lamb to the Lyon. In his third Principle, he was Prince over the Astral Heavens; a remainder whereof was in *Joshuah*, who stopt the Sun and Moon. And under his God, Soveraign over the Elementary Worlds, a remainder whereof is seen in *Moses* over the Waters, and *Elias* over it, and the fire.

9. His Body was as those in the Resurrection, with this difference, that having both Tinctures, he could have been Magically fruitful; whereas they and the Angels are in that respect Barren; and was all this in great Modesty, Simplicity, Wisdom, Unity, dear Love, Holiness, and immaculate Purity.

Q. 46. *Had* Adam *before his* Eve, *Masculine Members, and such Bones, Stomach, Guts, Entrails, Teeth, and also such things as we now have ?*

A. 1. *Adam's*

The 177 Theosophick Questions Answered.

A. 1. *Adam's* Holy Virgin state exempted him from those impure, deformed, bestial Members for Propagation, which yet (pitying our Wo and Necessity is bore with by Divine Patience; but the Filthiness of it, is signified by the Circumsicion, and is that whereof Nature it self (as depraved as it is) blusheth and is ashamed.

2. And Bones were Strengths; for the Saturnine Compaction could not petrefie to that excess till his Body, which was derived from the Astral Root (or one Element, whence they were also breathed out) became subjected to those Astral Powers; which were to have continued his Servants and Subjects.

3. The Teeth, Stomach, Gutts, evacuating Vessels, &c. which we now have, could not befal him while he remained in his Holy State; for his food was holy, pure, heavenly, such as might stand in Eternity; for such was he, not as yet confined under the Horoscope of Time.

4. He stuft not himself with the Elements, nor to speak strictly, doth he so yet, no nor do the Animals; for the Elements feed the Plants, and the Animal Creatures feed on the Plants produced by the Elements, but Man on the Animal Creatures like a Wolf, and on the Plants like an Animal.

But *Adam's* Food was Holy, Paradisical, Angelical, Eternal, needing no evacuation; eaten only in the mouth, not tartarous; which the Law commanding the Israelites to carry out a Paddle to cover theirs without the Camp, signifieth. And that other Law prohibiting and strictly nominating unclean and clean Creatures pointeth at.

Q. 47. *If Adam also had been thus, as we are now, how was it possible he should in such a condition have been able to stand without suffering and corruption?*

If *Paracelsus* thought by feeding on that whereof the Stars subsisted to extend his Thread of Life to what length he would, it was a thing might soon be purposed.

1. 'Tis true the Elixir, if duly and naturally collected, epitomising the Universe, must be granted to do much in tincturing the Vital, Natural and Animal Spirits; whereby the Astral and Elementary Man may be strongly fortified, the Natural Balsam restored radically, dregs obstructing the quick interiours of the Powers separated, highly conducing to health.

And the long Lives before the Flood, as well as many since, seem to be referred to their happy Knowledge of this almost Paradisical Secret, as an immediate eminent Second Cause.

2. Yet must it not be denied, that besides the Supream Law for abridging Man's Race, the Astral Revolutions summon us to a period, and the Volatile Nature of the Elementary Fabrick, loosen the connexions of our Outward Man, from Affinity to the fixed Inward Man, in so manifest a degree, that we bring from the Womb the Seeds of our Mortality, our Bones are senseless, dead, and (as to themselves) dry already; our need of frequent sleep pourtrays death; our food is corruptible; those few that attain the Winter of Age, then fall to Ashes by their Cold Fire, others fall to Ashes by the Hot Fire, as it is written, *Your Fathers, where are they?* Also like as it is said, *If there had been a Law that could have given Life, verily Righteousness had come by the Law*; so had there been an happy Eternity attainable out of the Reliques of *Adam*, we had been thence raised to Immortality, but not by dying,

3. But seeing there was no such, therefore the Second *Adam* breaks through death into Eternity; because *Adam* having subjected himself and us to the Stars and Elements, therefore that part of us under that Rule must change as they, who by wrestling vary their Powers; nor are the Stars nor Elements themselves on a surer Basis, but that the one must one day fall, the other melt.

Q. 48.

The 177 Theofophick Questions Anfwered.

Q. 48. *Should Adam's eating and drinking have been after a Paradifical manner, without care, diftrefs and forrow, if he had flood out the Trial r Proha ?*

A. 1. It is written, *The Kingdom of God is not Meat and Drink, but Righteoufnefs, Peace and Joy in the Holy Ghoft*: Yet the Lord faith, *I will drink no more of the fruit of the Vine, till I drink it new in my Fathers Kingdom.* The Manna alfo by allufion is call'd Angels food.

2. *Adam's* eating without care, diftrefs and forrow, was without diftruft of want, therefore without care; without fubtlety and difappointments; therefore without diftrefs; without forrow, being ever a gainer, having fupp'y out of the Ocean, needing only to abound in humble gratitude.

Adams aradifical food is fometimes fignified by Bread of Life, Water of Life, a Tree of Life, Manna, New Wine. &c.

3. Thofe fruits are real and fubftantial; more Divine than to be palpable of true Power and Vertue to nourifh to Eternal Life; therefore muft be incorruptible, having the forms of the fruits in this World; for this is the reprefenation of That, tho' but as a dead, dark fhadow, as the hufk; This hath the Curfe in it, but the fruits there have the purity, realnefs or effence exifting in, and deriving from the Omnipotence and Luftre of the Second Principle.

4. The dead fruits here which (mold and perifh figure) thofe heavenly ones: The faded ftains of things here, point at thofe living, bright, glorious colours, the variety of thefe, the infinity of thofe; thefe Trees as it were pourtray thofe; this very dead Earth, in a fort, figureth the Divine Salitter, our Mortal Dead Water, the Pure River of the Living Water; our Air their Air, which is of the Holy Ghoft; our mufical Sounds hint at their ravifhing, living, fpeaking Airs; our plucking and eating our fruits, figure their fo doing; the ftre gth we receive and retain thereby, figureth the fame in them; our feemingly delightful Objects, figure their tranfcendent glorious Objects.

5. But all in fo vaft difproportion, as a dead Corps to a flourifhing, lively, noble beautiful, exquifite perfon, or as a contemptible, fottifh natural Ideot to the moft acute, accomplifht, profound contemplative, experienced Philofopher, or as a leprous, deformed, loathfom Body, to the moft rare, perfect, healthy one; or as a maimed, impotent, treacherous Slave, chained for term of Life in a ftinking Dungeon, to a profperous renowned Captain at the Head of a mighty Victorious Army.

For how much a glorious, pure, bleffed State exceeds a vile, wretched, perifhing State, fo much doth the Food *Adam* had tranfcend ours; That was the quinteffence, life, and one holy Element, this is the excrefcence of the four Elements travelling and clogg'd by the Curfe.

Q. 49. *Should Adam in Paradife have eaten fuch fruit as the heavenly eating fhall be after this time ? or whereinto fhould he have eaten? where fhould the fame have continued, feeing all the Beings of this World are earthy and tranfitory, and he only was an Eternal Heavenly Image, and needed not the Vanity ?*

A. 1. Chrift in His beginning of Miracles, gave His beft Wine at laft, which is applicable to us (by way of allufion) who are ftrayed, when at laft we return to our Native Paradifical Country.

2. This Queftion leads me not to fay what *Adam's* food was to have been; for that falls under the 52 Queftion; therefore reftraining my felf to the prefent enquiry, which is, whether his eating had been the fame which fhall be? and where

it

it should have been, seeing he only needed not the Vanity, and that this World hath nothing in it but what is transitory. To which I answer.

3. Paradice is the similitude, manifestation and revealed Image of the incomprehensible God, and is such a similitude as is in its infinite extent, variety, purity and eternity incomprehensible; being, in all such places and for ever, more or less visible, where God is more or less manifest in his Grace and Love; for it is God's opened Book to Angels and the Blessed.

So that it cannot be said to have a Beginning, End, or Limit of Extent.

4. In this blessed state or place was *Adam's* whole Man, whose Third Principle as well as his First, shone throughly and gloriously in the Lustre of the Divine Second Principle, yet did his First and Third remain really such, as they shall also continue to be in the Blessed after the Resurrection.

5. *Adam* was in the Garden of *Eden*, but was also in Paradice, or the Heavenly State; nor needed he, nor should he have tasted the fruit of the Third Principle; for that was poison to him. Thus may be seen where his food lay; and that tho' he were in the Garden of *Eden*, he was of a higher Principle as far above it.

Q. 50. *Whether did the four Elements also Rule in* Adam *in his Innocency, or but one only in the equality of likeness of the four Elements? Did he also before he fell feel heat and cold?*

A. 1. *Adam's* Body was not made of the four Elements; if he had, they had Ruled there

2. For first, every Concrete is subject to the Powers whence it originateth, but the very Beasts derive from a more noble Ruler, (*viz.*) the Astral Spirit also. (1.)

3. Because, contrary Properties in Principles must produce contrary Qualities in Bodies compounded of them, unless their contraries accord in a harmonious Cement; now the divided Elements remain ever in irreconcileable equal distance. (2.)

4. Because, tho' Time is in Eternity comprehensibly and Eternity in Time incomprehensibly, yet a transitory Root may not found an Eternal Tree; thus from the transitory Elements some Vegetatives, &c. but such was not *Adam's* Body; for it was capable of Eternity, not measurable by Time. (3.)

5. For these Reasons the four Elements were not Rulers in him, but one in the likeness of the four, but that one was holy, consisting of all Powers in the perfection of Temperature, whence were breathed the Astral Worlds, and four Elements.

6. But the Elements divided according to the four Anguishes of the Eternal dark Abyss or first Principle; one into raging fierceness of Cold, another in a clogging Body, another into Evaporating; and the other into scorching consuming Heat, which it still is, and over which and the Astral World was *Adam* put, as over the rest of the Lords Handy-work, far above the Extremities of the four Elements and precipitant driving of the Stars.

Q. 51. *Should any thing have been able to Kill or Destroy* Adam?

A. 1. That which hath a Temporary Root, must from the Necessity of its own Structure, suffer Mutation, not that any *Ens* may properly be said to be annihilated; but the Fabrick must separate, and the Parts be returned into their proper Æthers, or first Principles.

2. But so was not *Adam*; therefore could not Perish from the Ruin of his own Foundation; yet leaving the Place and Order wherewith his Gracious Creator had vested him, he transform'd himself from the precious Image he had into

such

such Deformity; that for the Virgin to continue his Yoke-fellow longer, was as impossible, as it is for a Living Man to put off his Body, and dwell in the Body of a Dead Man.

3. This was *Adam's* being kill'd; who, as the Rebel Angels by imaging in themselves the Forms and Puissance of the first Principle, withdrew them from the Meekness and Love of the second. So *Adam* by imaging in his Will the Vanity of the Out-birth or third Principle, the Powers of the first became severally enraged, his second Holy Principle obscured, and his glorious Body (otherwise Eternal) became dark, gross and bestial.

4. For the Magical Soul and evil Spirit impressed on it the Image it had it self been infected with. Thus the Immortal Man died, (that is) Sin transmuted him into a degenerate, deformed, impure state.

Q. 52. *What should have been* Adam's *Condition and Estate upon Earth? What should he have done, if he had continued in Paradise?*

A. 1. When Good Angels humble themselves to become visible to the outward Eye, they come as Strangers, and when Evil ones intrude, they borrow wherewith to hide their horrid Form; but *Adam* was by his third Principle, natural Proprietor, and at Home.

2. Yet as the Lord Jesus saith, speaking of Children, *Their Angels always behold the Face of my Father which is in Heaven*; so at once they behold the Face of God, and carefully Nurse the Children committed to them. Thus also was *Adam* in the Garden of *Eden*, as a Prince and Natural Lord (by Donation) of the Creation, and then also walking with God in Paradise or Heaven, and an Image of the Almighty Three, beholding the Son of God, who is as the Delight, Heart or Face of the Father.

3. As to what *Adam's* Food should have been 'tis answered, 1. Negatively, Not the Earthy Meat or Mortal Water, not that of the Elements, nor Stars or Astral Spirit; for all those have their Periods and are Transitory.

4. But his Food was Bread and Water of Life, Paradifical Food, Immortal Fruits; Angelical, Pure and Eternally Substantial, wherein no Vanity could insinuate.

5. Will you say what is that? I answer, the Divine Flesh and Blood of Christ, his heavenly Body, the one holy Element, the Quintessence in the Eternal World.

6. Will you ask what is that? I answer again, What is it that feeds the Soul in the Sacrament of the Lord's Supper? What is it transforms the starving fallen Man into an Angelical Divine Will, enables him (till then a Stranger) to live the Life of Christ in Love, Meekness, Resignation, thankful Obedience, cheerful Suffering: having one Spirit, one Will, one Life with Christ? Is not this the Old Wine whereof whoso drinketh, desireth not the New; for he saith the Old is better.

7. This Flesh and Blood is Meat and Drink indeed : Oh my Soul, taste and see how good the Lord is. 'Tis so sweet, that this World's bitter Cup rellished with this Tincture is Acceptable, and this World's sweetest Products to him that hath tasted this, are unpleasant, and in comparison of this is Vanity.

8. But more particularly, *Adam's* Eating must have been suitable to the several Desires he had, and those Desires are according to the several Spirits and Capacities, and those Spirits answer to, and are modell'd by the several Principles, whereof he was founded.

9. Those Principles are Three, as to avoid tediousness (which I studiously shun) do refer my self to the 8th Verse of the Answer of the 45th Question; where the Principles are explicated, and something in fallen Man may be produced to Demonstrate this great Truth. 10. It

The 177 Theosophick Questions Answered.

10. It is undeniable that in us Men are three Spirits. The Animal or Soulish Spirit, the Vital Spirit, and the Nutritive Spirit; these also are to be found (in a very obscure Figure) in the Beasts, but in Man they grow from three Eternal Roots; The Animal Spirits live in the first Principle, whence also (as a Figure) were breathed the four Forms in the Astral Spirit : The Vital Spirit is in the second Principle : The Nutritive Spirit in the third.

11. *Adam's* Soul did Eat of the Meek, Heavenly, Holy Flesh and Blood , or Life and Love of the Almighty Son of God, or second Principle; it could not be fed by Spirit, for it Self was Spirit. In this Divine Light and Meekness dwelt *Adam's* Vital Spirit as a twig on a Vine; and his Nutritive Spirit was fed by the Holy part of the third Principle.

12. In this Principle of Holy Paradifical Excellency, flourish all Eternal, pure Fruits, whose unexpressibly Exquisite and Incomprehensible Varieties, real Entities or Substances are no more but shadowed (and that darkly) under the Curse by this World's Excellencies.

13. Those Divine Productions are the Quintessence Eternally fixed in the Temperature, consisting of all the seven Properties of the Eternal Nature in Triumphant Harmony, and these were the Fruits on which *Adam* should, and Blessed Men shall, live Eternally.

Q. 53. *What was the Earth with its Fruits before the Curse, when it was call'd Paradise?*

A. What Paradise is, was shewn in the Answer of the 42 Question. And the Trees in Paradice are, will be met with in the 56 Question. And that This Worlds fruits were not those of Paradice is plain in the Answer of the 4 Question.

1. The thing here enquired is, what the Earth and its fruits were before the Curse; therefore that if the fruits of the Earth before the Curse were call'd Paradice, it was not properly, but figuratively, as representing Paradice, which it did, tho' very imperfectly in many parts.

2. For if we understand by the fruits the Plants, it must be acknowledged that seeing the Fall of the Angels stirred up disorders in the great Mystery which introduced a Darkness in the Deep ; whereby the Properties being separate from the Harmony, were unclean, and every Property willed to be creaturely.

Thence came out Evil Plants, whose extremities shewed them degenerated from the Temperature, also evil Beasts, *&c.*

3. 'Tis true, the second Principle so influenced the whole Creation and blessed it, that the Evil part was subjected under the Good ; the Evil was thus very good, to shew the various Powers of the incomprehensible World, the Earth also, and all its fruits, might then well be called good ; because the Divine part had the Dominion, and from it the whole was denominated.

4. For the Good Powers were so far exempted from the Evil, that they could not be affected or impaired by them, unless they first laid off their own Good Property voluntarily ; which *Adam* did, introducing not only Pollution into himself and posterity, but Enmity into all the contrary Qualities in the Creatures ; who, tho' contrary in their Qualities and proper Constitutions, were as harmless each to other before, as the Wormwood is to the Liquorice Root, which extracting the bitter Quality, leave the other the more easie attraction of the sweet nourishment, yet was the one as really bitter as the other was sweet.

5. Yet all those contraries, tho' not in the perfect Harmony and Temperature, by the Divine Blessing, were very good, and thus was every thing before the Curse good.

The 177 Philosophick Questions Answered.

Q. 54. *Should the Propagation possibly have been without Man and Wife, seeing in the Resurrection of the dead they shall not be Man nor Wife, but like the Angels of God in Heaven?*

A. 1. That Propagation was to have been, is clear; because all mankind was not made at once: But that it was not to have been by Husband and Wife distinct, as are the Male and Female of other Creatures, appears; in that when the Man was made, he was expresly said to be Male and Female, after which the Creator said all was very good.

1. 2. 2. 1. Then it followed that the Creation was blessed. 2. The Creatures di-
3. 4. stinguished by sundry names. 3. The scituation of *Eden*, described. 4. The Geographical courses of the four Rivers, assigned, to which point of Heaven they
5.   inclined. 5. The Countries of their Travels and Peregrination particularized.
6.   6. The proper Treasures of *Pison*, the first of them noted.

3. All which we may not think but the Holy Ghost apparently to signifie a Mystery of intervening, thus all orderly recorded. The Jewish Rabbins can note intermission of time by an accent or little addition to an Hebrew Letter, and a prolongation by protraction of the spirits of their characters; and an abrupt cutting off by a small dash, and shall we see nothing by interposing a Volume of six branches between *Adam's* Creation and that of *Eve*.

Forty or di- 4. So that much time (why not * forty years? *viz.* a year for a day, tho' he
vers years. was not in time, but in eternity) may be proportioned, in which was his probation, and in which all these things are stated passing after the Creation of *Adam*, the Male and Female Man, before the extracting and building of the Woman out of, and distinct from him.

5. And tho' the time be not in plain words in *Moses*, yet is signified year for year by the Israelites forty years Trial in the Wilderness, in which they liv'd like *Adam* on Paradisical Manna; and again like him, who should have been confirmed, but missed by unstedfastness; so they who should have entred *Canaan*, kindled Wrath against themselves, by the Lust of the Midianitish Women.

But why it was that Man was only one, and not two, like other Beasts, is referred to the review of the Answer of the 43 Question.

Q. 55. *How could it have been possible that a Man and Wife should have continued eternally? Would God change his Creature Man, seeing in the Life Eternal they shall be like the Angels? Was Adam also in the beginning created in the same Angelical Form or Imaging, or in another, then he shall arise again and live for ever?*

A. 1. The Question intends an Eternal Well-being or Blessedness, which must concern those who bear the Divine Image.

What That is, how born in them, is explained in the 41st Answer, also in the 45th and 46th; and that in the Form gotten by Man's Disobedience he could not continue without suffering and corruption, is cleared in the 47th Answer; so that the preceding Answers being heedfully digested, will make repetitions needless; for they are with great care to be avoided, if real advantage be designed, little therefore remains to be answered.

John 3. 13. 2. Let it be considered that the Lord saith, *No man hath ascended into Heaven, but he that came down from Heaven, the Son of Man which is in Heaven*; the Son of Man, or Heavenly Man, or Divine Humanity.

3. The Divine Virgin was ever in Heaven, and cannot come from Heaven so far as to quit that Tenure. But when Man had exchanged that Love for the Lust

of

The 177 *Theofophick Queſtions Anſwered.*

of a Woman, it was the Almighty Son of God, and Son of the Virgin, reſtored the Virgin or Heavenly Man to Fallen Man.

4. The Reſtoring of this Virginity is the Forming of Chriſt; and as it grows, the Man comes to be a Man in him; thus puts he on Chriſt and the divided Tinctures of Man and Woman (gotten as to the dividing of them by the inactivity of him who had the Virgin Energy) put on him, that diviſion muſt ceaſe and terminate, and the diſtinct Properties unite in the Heavenly Man.

5. And thus it may be ſaid, There is neither Male nor Female, but Chriſt is all in all; for neither Male nor Female is or can be ſuch; for the Virgin Energy comprehendeth both. *Gal.* 3. 28.

6. And Chriſt alone hath aſcended into Heaven. As when men ſpeak of a Tree, they mean every twig and ſprout; ſo Chriſt conſiſteth of every ingrafted Branch, and the flouriſhing of them is the flouriſhing of the Tree.

7. Thus the Lord ſaith; *The works that I do, ſhall ye do, and more alſo*; for as the fruit ſhews it ſelf by the Branches, tho' their Vertue derive from the Tree or Vine, ſo is it here.

Q. 56. *What were the Trees in Paradice which were amiable or pleaſant to behold, and good to be eaten of?*

A. 1. Tho' no Language of the Fallen Man can tell us men intelligibly what they are; yet I ſhall branch my Anſwer into four parts. 1. To ſay what they are not. 2. What they reſemble. 3. Whereunto they ſerve. 4. Whence they proceed.

2. What they are not. 1. They are not Figures, for the production of the Aſtral and Elementary Worlds and Powers, do figure, or are figures of them. 2. They are not only Spirit, but are Subſtance; for the Trees and Productions of the Out-birth, tho' they are Accidents, yet have an Aſtral and Elementary Vertue or Spirit. 3. They are not ſubject to varity, but adminiſter Eternal Food, not pleaſant to view only, but of higheſt uſe.

3. What they are like. 1. They are like the almoſt Infinite variety of Trees, Plants, Flowers, productions in the Out-birth; for the outward World is the Image of the holy World. 2. They are like and agreeable to all the deſires of the moſt pure Spirits and Angels, a glimpſe whereof is in our moſt enlarged curioſities; for they are made ſuitable to them to whom God gives them; to them they are tangible and compleatly adequate to the Holy Men and Angels, as the Mothers Nutriment is to the ſucking Child. 3. They are like the Holy Trinity, as at large might be ſhewed.

4. Whereunto do they ſerve. 1. To be the Material Word of God; this is that every word that proceedeth out of the mouth of God by which Man lives, alluded to by our Lord, when he ſaith, *And not by bread alone*; for by This the unſearchable Abyſs of God's Goodneſs is to the bleſſed partakers of it in a ſort comprehenſible. 2. To be the Eternal Food of the Men made perfect, and of the Angels, who hereby eat the Paradiſical Vertue in the mouth wanting no Beſtial Stomach nor Guts. 3. To ſhew the Creatures tho' moſt glorious, to be but Creatures, not Almighty, but to have dependance on the Womb of Infinite, Incomprehenſible Bounty; hinted by theſe words, *Of all the Trees*, &c. *thou maiſt freely eat*. And in the *Canticles*; *Eat, O Friends, yea drink abundantly*, &c. for the Fountain is an Ocean. The Trees of the Lord are full of fruit. *Pſal.* 104. 16.

5. Whence are they, and wherein ſtand they. 1. From and in the Properties of the ſeven Fountain-Spirits, according to the holy Impreſſion or ſecond Principle. 2. From and in the Ten Forms of Fire, (*viz.*) Love-fire; both the former and This are figured by the ſeven times Ten Palm Trees. 3. From and *Exod.* 15. 27.

in

in the Divine, Living, Almighty speaking Word or sweet Power-world, or Divine third Principle.

6. Thus if Man contemplate what these Trees are exempted from, what they serve to, and whence they derive, or where they stand: He may find them to be the same with *Adam's* Body, which was pure, and to have existed in Eternity, as are the new Bodies of those who are risen and ascended with Christ.

Q. 57. *What was the Tree of Life, and also the Tree of Knowledge of Good and Evil, each in its Power, Essence and Property?*

A. 1. We read of Cherubims (with a Sword turning every way) placed to keep the Way of the Tree of Life: who then can describe it, that hath not first passed the Sword of the Cherub? And if all Mortality be as Fuel to that flaming Sword, who in the Body (by Human Wisdom) can (without danger of being burnt) approach the Way to that Tree?

Gen. 2, 9.
Rev. 22. 2.

2. The Tree of Life is said to stand in the midst of the Garden, and also the Tree of Good and Evil. The Tree of Life is also said to be in the midst of the Street of the New Jerusalem, and on either side of the pure River there, bearing twelve Fruits, one every Month.

3. How can it be more clearly shewn? For the Tree of Life stands in the midst between two Kingdoms, two Worlds, or two Principles, *viz.* Between the Fathers, or first, fierce, wrathful, mighty Principle, and the outward or third Principle.

4. The first as its Root, the other as its Shadow and Figure, dimly representing both the Root and Tree; though more obscurely the latter, since the Curse.

5. And the Holy Power of God which penetrated the outermost, and swallowed it up (as Light doth Darkness) This Holy World is the Tree of Life it self, which in its Original should have been unknown to *Adam*, even as the Tree of Good and Evil, should have been unknown to him.

6. He should have kept a Child-like resigned Mind which is attained, after the corrupt Man (consisting of the fierceness of the first, and vanity of the third Principle) is cut off, by the sharpness of that Sword, or become Fuel to the flame of it. Then the New Man entreth irresistibly by that Guard, and Eateth freely and for ever of the Tree of Life: till then, his Food is of the Tree of Good and Evil; and what that Tree is follows.

7. The Tree of Good and Evil was the only Tree of that sort that grew in *Eden*. This Tree was Good, as partaking of the Vertue of the second Principle, though it self grew in the third, and it was Evil as partaking of the dark Impression of the first Principle, whereby is Poison, as the Gall is the Exciter of Life in living Creatures. and so that Death and Corruption is in this Worlds Fruits.

8. Therefore was it forbidden *Adam*, as being a Production of the Stars and Elements over which he was to Rule; for though *Adam* was in the third Principle, he was above it; as Eternity is in yet above time. God willed *Adam* to have remained in the Happy State; therefore commanded his not touching that which would be Contagious and Mortal, as it proved to be by opening in him the Evil of the divided Properties.

9. It was in the midst of the Garden, (that is) in the midst between the first and third Principles, partaking of both, as doth also the Tree of Life; but this of Good and Evil hath not the vertue, but shadow of the second Principle.

Q. 58.

The 177 Theosophick Questions Answered.

Q. 58. *Wherefore did God Create this Tree, seeing he knew well that Man would offend, or lay hold on them, and hurt himself thereby?*

A. 1. The considering God's foreknowledge (unto whom nothing can be casual but all Events, which Time divides into past, present and future, are one instant act) should make it seem, that God's infinite Goodness would have inclined his Omnipotence, to forbear the Creating the Tree of Good and Evil, or have restrained it that exquisite Garden, that it might at least have been no tempting bait to *Adam* or *Eve's* Curiosities: Had not the Creator willed such dire Effects, as that it should be the Eternal Perdition of so great a part of *Adam's* Offspring; such Reasonings Human frailty calls Wisdom.

2. But Predestination and Reprobation may not be here discussed, because it falls under the seventieth Question; (whoever shall live to answer it) wherefore it would be here Digressive.

3. The Answer of this must be restrained to the Cause of God's creating that Tree of Good and Evil, whereby the Transgression was occasioned.
In Answer whereunto it must be understood, that when the Almighty willed to become Creaturely, or to behold Himself in Images of Himself, He moved the *fiat* in every of the three Principles, (*viz.*) according to the first and second in the Triumph of all the seven Properties, in the Eternal Nature or Temperature, the Holy Heavenly Thrones, Powers, Dominions, Princes and Hosts of Angels.

4. Also according to the Out-birth or third Principle out of the great Mystery with the seven Properties but much less sublime, was produced the Astral World in so beautiful order, yet with such adverse qualities, as they were for their excellency adored, by some Ancients as Deities, and deemed for their Contrarieties. Immortal Gods at Civil Wars.

5. Who yet being but an Image of the third Principle, must by the Wrestling-wheel of Nature, be resolved into their Æther, not being allied to any Soul which can invest it, or it self in a Root of the Eternal Band, as *Adam's* Body was.

6. Next out of the Astral for Matter by the insinuation of the Astral Spirit were the four Elements produced, and with them and the Astral Spirit the Transitory Creatures, and as an other Out-birth the Mineral and Vegetative Commonwealths.

7. Lastly, According to the three Principles, with the seven Properties in due Temper and Harmony; with a Soul out of the Potence of the first, a Spirit out of the Holiness and Glory of the second, and out of the out-flowing vertue of the third Principle, was Man made a complete Image of the total God; in his first and second he was an Angel, in his third lower, yet Lord of that Principle; also his glorious Body had this excellency above the outward Sun, that it was United to an Eternal Soul, and so exempt from suffering any Recess, but capable of Eternal Splendor.

8. From what hath been said, it is Evident, That the same cause why the Almighty Imaged Himself in the first and second Principles, moved Himself in the third also; part of which was the Trees of Good and Evil, as our outward Eyes witness to us. And the like Motive which induced *Lucifer* to Image in his Will the potence and strength of the first Principle which was his Root, and whereof (by the Grace and Glory of the second) He was Lord in His glorious Body; the like Motive induced *Adam* to Imprint in his Will, the Lust after the fructifying Vertue of the third Principle; whereof by right of Creation he is part, and by Donation hath right of Soveraignty over it.

9. And if there yet rest so eminent a Vigor in the Reliques of Man, as appears

in Women with Child, and common Sympathies and Antipathies, what was out of *Adam*'s reach, especially in the third Principle, over which he was Lord, being himself subject to none but God? Could not his Magical Desire raise that unhappy Plant which he should not have done nor known? Then came the severe Inhibition, That of the *Tree of Good and Evil thou mayest not Eat; for in the day thou Eatest thereof, thou shalt surely Die.*

10 God created Man compleat, which he could not have been (especially as His Divine Image) without the freedom of his own Faculties, which the very Brutes have; but left in that one Tree he should harm himself unwarily, or by ill exercise of his freedom, the dangerous Tree is named, it's Situation described; he is warned, he is threaten'd on pain of immediate Death. What can be more?

11. If his Will had been chain'd, it had been to take it away, or as to speak a Contradiction, What had that been but to Uncreate Him? What had that been but to inflict the utmost severity on Him who was never yet a Sinner?

12. What could confine *Adam*'s Magical Will to call up such a Tree; for *Moses* dividing the Sea, *Joshuah*'s stopping the Sun, *Eliah*'s calling down Fire, his, and *Elisha*'s dividing *Jordan*, were but Fragments of *Adam*'s perfect Piece.

Q. 59. *Why did God forbid Man these Trees, What was the Cause thereof?*

A. In the 57th Answer appears what this Tree is, and why said to be in the midst of the Garden. In the 53d, is shewn what this Worlds Fruits were when at best. And in the last preceding Answer, what introduced it into the midst of *Adam*'s Garden, and where that is; to which severally, to avoid Repetitions, this referr'd.

1. Which well pondered, little may suffice for Answer of this: For though *Adam* was God's total Image, by having the third Principle on him; yet he was not in it, nor of it, but Lord of it, and it, as it were hung, to him. As the Lord Jesus Christ was in the outward World, but not of it, but of and in Heaven: So was *Adam* in the Garden of *Eden*, but not of it, but of, and in Paradise.

2. Again, *Adam*'s Body was no otherwise one with the Astral Spirit than as allied, or as Brother to it (proceeding from the same Holy Element) yet was to out-live it even for ever; because his Body was conjunct with an Eternal Soul, and Divine Spirit; whereas the Astral Spirit hath its Age, and recess into its Æther.

3. But the Tree of Good and Evil was Corruptible, having it's Root in the Elementary World, influenced only the Astral, in which the separated Properties were so awakened, as it consisted of Heterogeneous Good and Evil Parts: Even those of the Dark World radically impressed.

4. So that it was Death and Poison to the Paradisical Heavenly Man; for it generated Putrefaction, and a filthy Draught and Bestiality; wherefore the Gracious Creator did so severely or expresly and strictly forwarn and forbid Man that Tree.

Q. 60. *Wherefore should Man rule over all the living Creatures or Beasts of the Earth? How, and to what End could that have been?*

A. Negatively it is answered, That *Adam* while he stood, had no need; neither.

1. Of their Milk or Carcasses for Food, or Skins or Fleeces for Cloaths; because Corruption contributeth nothing to Incorruption and an Incorruptible Body: as Heaven wants not Earth.

2. Nor their Strength for Labour or Culture; for the Productions needed by him were

The 177 Theosophick Questions Answered.

were Pure and Heavenly. The Effect of the Curse it was that it was said, *in the sweat of thy face thou shalt eat thy bread.*

3. Nor their Courage or Velocity for offence or speed; for no Opposition needed no Counter-force, and no Extremity needed no Speed.

4. Nor their assimilating or Antipathetick Powers for Medicine; because no Sickness needs no Physick; no penetration of Bodies, nor impairing of Parts; no need of assimilating or restorative Applications.

(1) 5. They wanted not him. 1. To be Justice of the general Peace; for tho' they were of adverse qualities, yet innoxious, till ushered in by the Curse (as the effect of Sin) irritated and arm'd them against Man, and against each other. Their innocence was their defence, their Contrarieties were no more offensive to each other than contrary Colours are, or Flowers of different Kinds.

2. 6. They wanted not him to raise them a subsistence; for their Creator had provided so for them, as they should be no burthen to him, nor his Divine Offspring; he cares for the Ravens.

A. 7. Positively to shew how, and to what end his Rule should have been? (2:) It's answered, *Adam* and his Heavenly Offspring should have used all the Creatures as Letters standing in several Volumes, Sections, Sentences and Words in the Book of the Creation; declaring what the Creator is, what He willeth, and what He doth.

8. And though the Creatures are Dumb, as are Characters of Letters; yet the Divine Powers of the Spiritual Worlds are spoken in and by the Creatures more expresly than are our Minds signified by Writings, or our Passions by articular Sounds: And hath Art fram'd Accents, Aspirations, Liquids, &c. Much more hath the Infinite Powers spoken themselves, and the Holy Names of God in the several Pieces of the Creatures, shewing the Principles, Properties and Figures of the Eternal Worlds.

9. And as *Adam's* holy Offspring had blessedly Multiplied, and Paradise gloriously open'd it self; so the Creatures had (in their low Sphere) born a part in that Triumphant Theatre; nor had they been subject to Vanity, Pain, Impotence and Misery, by Want, Weakness or Drudgery; for that the Curse subjected them to.

10. But during their respective times, had sweetly delighted themselves and Man in Ecchoing, and in their measure assisting, the High Praises of the Infinite Gracious Lord, and when their Parts were acted, have gone off the Stage with Swan-like farewels, into their first Principles and Æthers.

11. *Adam* gave them Names according to their Roots and Designs, wherein they shall be in their Idea's before the new Blessed Men successively produced, and as it were perpetuated by the wresting of the Properties; for neither in this sence shall Man's Disobedience frustrate the purpose of God, or give Period to the Glory of his Creation Work; for the Spiritual Worlds will obtain their Desires of imaging themselves for ever.

As saith our Apostle, Because the Creature it self shall be delivered from the Bondage of Corruption into the Glorious liberty of the Children of God.

12. Nor are the Creatures uselefs, but serve our God's Designs. And 'tis observable even Sathan useth (if he may) the most accute Wits, while God by Men of low Parts doth confound the Wise; for so, though Sathan used the Serpents apt Wisdom in his cheating Imposture, God honoured the Ass, the silliest of Creatures to divulge such Truth as was necessary for a Prophet's Instruction and Reprehension.

Whence we may observe, if under their Vanity they are of such excellent uses, what would they have been, had they retained their Primitive Excellencies?

Q. 61.

Q. 61. *Why did God say, it is not good for Man to be alone, whereas yet in the Beginning he lookt upon all his Works and said, They are very Good; yet of Man only he saith, 'Tis not good that this Man should be alone; Why was it not good?*

A. In the 43 Answer, it is shewn why God created but one Man at first, and not Man and Woman together, and in the 45th Answer, what Form and Fashion he was when he was neither Husband nor Wife, but both. In the 46th appears *Adam*, had not at first Man-like Members, Guts, &c. In the 47th, That had such been, he could not have stood in Eternity; whereof it cannot be denied he was by Creation capable.

1. All which duly weighed, evidence why it was said at first all was very good; for then was Man a compleat Image of God in all the three Principles, illustrated by the second, (viz.) his Soul in the Eternal Band, his Spirit in the Divine Holy Triumphant World, his Body out of the Holy Element, having both Tinctures of Fire and Light enriched and fortified by all the seven Properties. Having further the Authority over the Creation like a God, the Intellect of an Angel, and Innocency of a Dove.

2. And whereas afterward it is said, It is not good for Man to be alone; it was not from any defect in the Creator's Work, for that (as above appears) was perfect to a high degree; but the Creature had ceased his Progress, as no other Creature had; for of none of them was it said as of Man, though not a few of them were ordain'd, and still do propagate themselves otherwise than by distinct Male and Female, as well in the Sensitive as in the Vegetative and Mineral Republick. See the 54 Answer, v. 1. and 43 Answer, v. 3, 4.

3. And the being not good, may be noted from the Consequence of dividing the Tinctures, that it succeeded as to an Army broken, or a Besieged City, one part Parling with the Enemy, without Privity of the other; concerning which, the above quoted Answers speak much.

4. Yet so propitious was Infinite Goodness and Wisdom at this Stand and Ebb of his Creature, as to provide so suitable an Expedient; not only that might prevent a worse state, but which might also bring forth an Incomprehensible glorious Master-piece and Miracle of astonishing Love and Condescention, the Lord Jesus Christ; of, and for whom are all things.

5. Thus is it manifest, how at first it was very Good; after that, how it was said it was not Good: which may lead them that list, to penetrate that when the End shall find the Beginning, how the undivided Tinctures making the Virgin state shall be again and for ever very good; as saith the Lord himself speaking of the Children of the Resurrection, that they neither Marry, &c. but are (in that respect) as the Angels of God.

6. Which state is amply signified, that it should have been, by the Lord's recommending it to all, to whom Power for it should be given; also, in that it was a Way traced out by his own Example, pursued by our Apostle and others, and Prophesied in the Revelations.

Q. 62. *Why caused God, or did suffer a deep Sleep to fall upon* Adam *when he built a Wife out of his Rib? What doth it mean?*

A. 1. Sleep is a Perquisite or Appendix to Time, a Foreigner to Eternity, the result of a Conflict or Strife, whereinto the vanquished retireth, as doth the Matrix or watry Element, when it is over-powred by the Fiery or Astral.

2. And though *Adam* had not actually tasted the Fruit afterward forbidden, yet had

had his Imagination penetrated into, and his defire drawn forth the Tree on which followed the Severe or earneft Inhibition. Then he (as one overcome) flept or fwouned, which the Divine Life in the Refurrection knoweth not.

3 He flept to the Angelical World, and awakened to the outward; for Sleep is a refpite, or an arreft of the exercife of the Divine and Rational Faculties: alfo, as Death is to the Elementary outward Life.

4. Not that it was impofed by Power without him from foreign Will and Neceflity, but was a neceflary Supplement with reference to *Adam* himfelf; which is the thing meant and taught us by this deep Sleep which God is faid to have caufed to fall on him.

Q. 63. *How was the Wife or Woman made out of* Adam? *What doth the Rib* [taken] *out of his Side fignifie, of which God made the Wife, as* Mofes *writeth?*

A. 1. *Mofes* faith, God took one of *Adam*'s Ribs out of his Side and thereof made a Woman. Will any underftand the Text fo grofly as that his Bones were then as ours are, dry, dead, rocky, obnoxious to the penetration of Fire, diffolution of Time, &c. Such a Thought is rather applicable to Beftiality than the Eternity.

2. We are therefore to know the Rib whereof the Woman was made, fignified part of *Adam*'s Strength; for fuch were the Bones he then had, and not fuch dead petrified, weighty Subftances as ours: no more than his Flefh, which was created for Eternity was like our Beft:al Flefh, at the Root of which is a Worm.

3. And becaufe *Adam*'s Bone or Strength was a Compofition of all his Effences, Principles and Properties; therefore it is r ghtly faid, a Rib, or Bone and Subft:nce: nor is it any new Phrafe to put one part for the whole, the Scripture abounding in all parts of it with that manner of fpeaking.

4. Alfo that it is faid to be taken out of *Adam*'s Side, may fignifie the procedure to be from the Noble and Central Part, and into the Side literally did enter *Longinus* Spear, when the Lord of Glory was Crucified.

5. *Eve* was that Child which *Adam* fhou!d have glorioufly produced, which had he done Divinely, Powerfully, Actively, Magically (according to the excellency of his Creation-right) it might have been call'd his doing it awake; then alfo had that Child been as compleat as himfelf: but being brought forth by an affifting Power, and (as to him) paffively and unknowingly may we be call'd his Sleep; therefore lefs vigorous and perfect than his own Structure. Thus the fecond Temple which was raifed in an Eclipfe of Times, could not reach the excellent Fabrick of the firft Temple.

6. Yet, forafmuch as *Eve* was brought forth (though in fome weaknefs yet) with no offence to the Modefty and Virginity of the Divine *Sophia* of God's Wifdom; therefore was fhe Holy, though by the reafon of her feeblenefs, very near to a precipice of Danger.

Q. 64. *Did* Eve *alfo receive a Soul and Spirit from* Adam'*s Soul and Spirit, or a n w ftrange one, peculiarly or feverally given of God?*

A. 1. Had nothing been taken from *Adam* (whereof to make *Eve*) but a Rib, and that had been fuch a Bone only as ours is come to be, *Eve*'s Production had not been from all *Adam*'s Effences; but fuch fhe was, only Man hath moft efpecially the Fires Tincture, and Woman moft efpecially the Lights Tincture. The Man more of the firft, or Souls Principle, the Woman more of the fecond or Spirits Principle.

2. Thus

2. Thus *Eve* cannot be said to have a Soul and Spirit new and peculiarly from God; but to partake with *Adam* of the same Soul and Spirit, as may be proved as follows.

Argument 1. 3. To deny *Eve* part of *Adam*'s Soul and Spirit, because for her Structure the Text only mentions a Rib, would with like force argue that she was not of his flesh.

Arg. 2. 4. If *Eve* were not of one Soul and Spirit with *Adam*, their Posterity must either (every of them) have new created Souls, and so be unconcerned with their first Parents Transgression, or uninclined to their immediate Parents Good or Evil habits: The former of which, opposeth Religion; the latter, Sence and Experience: Or else the Children must have each two Souls and two Spirits, one from each of their Parents, which were a Solecism, and morally a Contradiction by making two Eternities.

Arg. 3. 5. If the Woman had another Soul and Spirit, then that with *Adam* it must be out of other Principles, but other Principles whence Soul and Spirit can be, there are none; for it were as absurd to make new Eternal Principles, as to make new Gods.

Arg. 4. 6. If the Soul and Spirit of *Eve* had not been one with, and part of that of *Adam*'s, then the Lord Jesus, who took a Soul from the Virgin *Mary*, had not taken Man's (or the Male) Soul, and so Men were not redeemed, which is contradictory to Law and Gospel, Faith and Reason.

Q. 65. *How was the dividing of* Adam *into the Wife or Woman effected?*

A. 1. Had the parting been natural, genuine and according to the blessed Paradifical state, it had been as voluntary and delightful as is the Sun's diffusing its Radiance, or the Olive tree and Vine putting forth their Fruit.

2. But the Text calls it [casting him into a deep sleep] so as the Phrase may be compared to the manner of Chirurgeons, about to make some deep Incisions which the subject of their Skill would not without great Impatience, if awake, permit.

3. And whereas *Moses* saith, [took out one of his Ribs] signifieth a violence and force, not only as before without the Privity; also not only without the consent and concurrence of *Adam*, but implyeth some unwillingness in him, and may be compared to the cutting the outer and inner Bark of those Trees a little above ground, whence issueth the Rosin: and those also yielding Frankincense, or drawing the Blood of a fruitless Vine for some singular use.

4. And the Phrase of [closing up the flesh again] signifieth, there to have been a rending, wounding, or laceration of *Adam*, all against the Nature of a Blessed Eternity; which may be likened to Gardeners rending the Roots of Flowers, or cleaving with a hard Wedge or Pin the Roots of drowzy Fruit-trees.

5. So that from the whole, 'tis apparent, that, whereas *Adam* was created perfectly with both Tinctures of Fire and Light, Masculine and Feminine in Virgin Modesty, Purity and Chastity; which appears in the 45th Answer, that he was to have propagated a Progeny and Virgin holy Race out of himself, is proved in the 54th Answer.

6. That he did not so is apparent; That therefore the Woman was separated from him by a Holy Violence, is evident by the above Discourse; and that the *Fiat* took not only part of one part of him, is proved by the last precedent Answer, but part of every part; and it is visible, that though the Woman is the weaker part (which should strongly incline Man compassionately to bear with her, affectionately to assist her, earnestly to Pray with and for her, she being and bearing the weaker part of his Essences) yet hath she every of the four first Forms of the

The 177 *Theosophick Questions Answered.*

the Eternal Nature also, every of the Principles and every of the Faculties, Powers, Passions, &c. were all as truly imparted to her from *Adam*, as was the Spirit of *Moses* to the Seventy Elders, or the Spirit of *Eliah* to *Elisha*, but the manner how it was done was much otherwise; being unknowingly, as to him, violently, and with notable penetration.

Q. 66. *Why did* Adam *presently take his* Eve *to him, and said she was his flesh? How could he know her?*

A 1. If a rent or cut divide the flesh of a living Creature, both parts earnestly will to attract each the other, and sement; with like Reason did *Adam* take his Eve; for while he was whole, and married to the Divine Virgin of Modesty, the Wisdom of God, he remained as the Sun in a Cloud, not doing what he was enabled unto.

1. But changing Love for Lust, his heavenly, dear, mode't Love, Delight, Joy, and fixed Satisfaction, hath now a great aloy of Astral Precipitancy, Fancy, Immodesty, and deceivable seeming Satisfaction; for the Tinctures, when thus divided into two distinct persons (tho' as yet not throughly infected, but having only the above aloy) expected to find each in the other the Virgin of Purity and Modesty, and from that mistake the Magical Ardency, introducing and belonging to the deformed Bestial Image arose and insinuated it self.

3. So when he but saw her, he faith, *She is*, &c. and straightway without interposing reflection on his former State (for any thing appears) he took her, where was then his Purity and Virgin Modesty, accompanying the Heavenly Man. This declension was so great, that the second *Adam* was conceived without the Masculine concurrence, bringing again the Purity and Modesty of the Heavenly Virgin, the first Image which *Adam* had caused to disappear.

4. The Man acknowledged her to be his flesh and bone, and took her, and they were Husband and Wife; and Posterity are told their duty, that the Man leaving Father and Mother, must cleave to his Wife, and they be one flesh.

5. And the Birth of *Cain* following in the next verse after their expulsion the Garden, yet the Conception must precede, with due gradation of interposing Time.

6. But that the knowing *Eve* and her Conception are spoken of after the expulsion, may have this Mystery; as being so unsuitable to the Paradisical State, as not fit to be recorded till after their being driven out of the very Garden.

7. And why might not by the Conception the Woman be the easier swayed to a libidinous tasting the forbidden fruit?

8. In sad commemoration whereof the Tyranny of Womens Lusting so much inconvenienceth them, as not seldom to frustrate the Conception, other times to destroy the formed fruit, other times to impress forreign marks on them, and sometimes the Magical Lust is so rampant and voracious, as like a Storm it blows down the Abortive Fruit, Tree, and all.

9. And for *Adam*'s knowing what and whence she was, the cause is plain, he knew his God, and by That knowledge knew himself, in the same Light discerned her; for his Intellect was very radiant, it must be more bright than *Noah*'s, who (tho' in an ill sleep) knew what every of his Sons had done to him, whilst he so slept, which sleep of *Noah*'s is a pregnant figure of This sleep of *Adam*'s.

Q. 47. *What was the Serpent on the Tree of Knowledge of Good and Evil which deceived or seduced* Eve?

A. 1.

The 177 Theosophick Questions Answered.

A. 1. The less is requisite to answer this, because the blessed propounder in His own Answer to This 8th Question shews what the Devil is; and in His Answer to the 11th Question saith what the Dragon is, that strove with *Michael*. Shortly then, it little concerns us to know whether the Serpent that tempted *Eve*, were the Old One forming himself into That Animal's figure imitating his particularities, or whether actuating the very Creature to insinuate his design. But it greatly concerns us to know what the Tempter or Temptation was; tho' *Eve* should not have known it.

2. The Tempter is a Will resulting from the Central Fire of the Dark impressed Forms of the first Principle, without enkindling the Love-fire of the second, thereby becoming separate and broken from the Infinite Inseparable Unity into Self-lust.

3. It therefore imageth it self into a hunger after knowing the multiplicity; (*viz.*) after entring into, possessing of, or rather being possessed by the divided Properties of the Out-birth or third Principle, without enkindling the Love-fire of the second, thereby becoming separate and broken from the Infinite, Inseparable Unity into Self-lust.

4. It therefore imageth it self into a hunger after knowing the multiplicity; (*viz.*) after entring into, possessing of, or rather being possessed by the divided Properties of the Out-birth or third Principle. Will it be said the Tempter should have been character'd, and here is only the Temptation?

5. It's answered, we may know the Evil Tree by the corrupt fruit. Again, the Tempter is dangerous to us for the sake of the Temptation: What could the Fisher do without his Net or Bait? Again, tho' *Eve* were but little, and *Adam* less propense to the sugar'd potion, yet we have abundant thirst, like one in an inflaming Fever desires drink.

6. 'Twas therefore necessary our Second *Adam* should be able to say the Tempter cometh, but findeth nothing in me. To prevent Ruine, we must imprison our domestick Foes to avoid their betraying us to the common Enemy.

7. Every man is tempted when he is drawn aside of his own lust, and enticed; which faith not only that our own lusts are our Temptations, but that it is what every man is obnoxious to.

8. It is of sad consideration, that many who abandon the Wit, Craft and Subtilty of the Fox in great measure, may yet betray themselves to the curious Art, Contemplative Ingenuity, and Innate Wisdom of the Serpent, falling also far below the Divine, especially in This.

9. That the Wisdom from above is not only good-natur'd, as peaceable, gentle easie to be entreated, full of mercy and good fruits; but is also high-born, (*viz.*) pure, humble, self-emptying, denying, annihilating, mortifying, judging condemning, leaving, loathing, witnessing for God against it self and all others. Adding to Faith Patience, to Experience Hope, with which Faith, Patience and Hope enduring all things, waiting in extremity with quiet resolution.

10. True it is, that much penetrating speculation, and knowledge, natural and acquired for advance of reputation, with improvement of Property and Self-pleasing, is the Serpents Dust and Meat, but the former are bits he cannot rellish, they are his bane, poison and death.

Q. 68. *Why did the Serpent perswade Eve, and not Adam, to lust after the fruit? What was the fruit on which they both did eat death?*

A. 1. Whether an envenomed Shaft pierce the heart through the breast, or through the side, it is equally mortal; Such was the Serpents Temptation, and
Eve

The 177 Theosophick Questions Answered.

Eve might more easily be seduced, becaufe the breach was begun in her very Structure and Constitution by the feparation of the Female Tincture. Again, the Woman was as a fcattered party, who are more fuddenly made a prey of than the Body of any Army.

2. The Temptation might take hold of her moft readily, being her felf a kind of Temptation, having drawn *Adam* from his pure, chaft, precious, dear Virgin-ftate; therefore the Tempter awaited her, and prevailed by a kind of affimilation.

3. Naturalifts obferve Affimilation effects much in motion, as in the haftening of Bodies to their feveral Centres, not only in rarity and denfity, and the verfion of the Needle, but in velocity and penetration; that the Arrow headed with Wood, and the Woodden Wedge fhall pierce and cleave Wood by more ready infinuation than Iron.

4. And This fquares moft with the Apoftles humbling charge on that Sex, that the Woman was firft in the Tranfgreffion, *&c.* not barely with refpect to the Serpent or Temptation it felf, but her declenfion, inclination and propinquity to curiofity, which ftill is found amongft them, preparing her to fwallow the Bait.

5. But I fpare them, for the above hints pondered may fuffice; rather adding that men fhould be the more compaffionate and affiftant, knowing they are Man's weaker part, and of his own Effences.

6. To fay farther what was the fruit on which they did both eat Death, little is enough, but refer to the 7th, 8th and 9th verfes of the 57th Anfwer concerning the Tree of Good and Evil; which fhews it to be of the third Principle, no better nor worfe than That we eat of, yet mortal Poifon to their Paradifical Life.

7. And (a little to digrefs) let it be confidered, that the Lord's bleffing the Meat when he did eat with his Difciples, teacheth us to know and remember the peril, left the Evil Properties in the Creation fhould fo fteal themfelves into our Meat or Drink; as to affociate with, heighten and ftrengthen the Evil Properties in us.

8. Therefore we find fome character'd who make provifion for the flefh, to fulfil the lufts thereof; and of the Rich Man, that fared delicioufly every day; and of others feeding themfelves without fear.

A fin prevailing by Affimilation with our voracious, licencious, wanton Appetites, willingly indulging our felves to forget that the Provifions for our Lord and his Difciples were a few Loaves, and a few little Fifhes, and thofe he multiplied or augmented by Miracle, yet the Loaves were but of Barley in a Country abounding with Wheat, Milk, Honey, *&c.*

Q. 69. *What was the fin, and how is it become a fin, that the fame is an Enmity of God?*

A. 1. What the Tree of Good and Evil was, and why forbidden, the 7th, 8th and 9th verfes of the 57th Anfwer explaineth. How excellent *Adam's* firft State was, is fomewhat diftinctly in the whole 52 Anfwer. How he fell, and how low, is touched in the 51 Anfwer; a review of all which will be eminently affiftant to the fearcher, and a large contribution to the Anfwer of this. Yet farther 'tis anfwered,

2. That as *Lucifer* and his Angels by imaging in their Bodies the Forms of the firft Principle, left the glorious holy 2d Principle, whereby their Tincture became not only impure, feparate and unclean; but falfhood and filthinefs in the abftract.

3. So *Adam* being Ruler (by Creation right) in the third Principle imaged in the Spirit of his Will, Mind and Soul, a hunger of the same third Principle, grasping the shadow (as painted Food) instead of the substantial Quintessence and Bread of Eternal Life, departed out of the Unity wherein he possessed all and every good perfectly at once for ever, into a few little parcels of fading good blended and interlaced with Volumes of multiform exquisite, real, steddy, permanent Evils.

4. What the Will is, the Man is: Thus the Will of *Lots* Wife's captivating her by the Accommodations of their late opulent Seat; she is by the Astringent Property fixed a Pillar of Salt. Also *Nebuchadnezzar* placing his chief Glory in such stuff as must be rubbish, becomes a Beast or Fowl; for the Magical Will hath (as even in Witches appears) the over-match to the Forms of Elementary and Astral Concretes; because the *Magia* is the Power of the Will, or Hand of the Mind, having its Root in the Potence of the first Principle or Eternal Band.

5. Thus our first Parents, by impressing in their Originally Noble Breasts the Good and Evil Properties, could not retain the Divine Image: As the Eye looketh not at once upward and downward; therefore the pure Love, Delight, Joy, and Heavenly Man disappeared, and the Dead Form resigned. The Apostle saith, *Death reigned.* As Iron, when the Lustre of the Fire is gone, or a Lamp extinguished, so no more could he be Divine, and Sensual, Earthy and Heavenly.

6. This departure was his sin, and the impression of Lust introduced the departure. And this eager impression and departure from the second Principle deformed his Soul and Body by awakening the Properties of the Good Beasts, which at best are but partly good, and that but transitory; because their Æthers must resume them.

7. The same departure, at the same time also awakened in him the Properties of the evil, cruel, voracious, crafty, hateful, wrathful, envious, poisonous Creatures, which, tho' they are resolvable into their Æthers also, yet being ingrafted on his Everlasting Root, they were eternally his, and he theirs.

8. Thus is it an Enmity against God, and had so remained irrreparably (as the the anguish of Frost, and fierceness of Fire are at Enmity against the sweet harmonious Temperature) had not Infinite Grace inspoken again the word of Reconciliation, which is the promised Seed and Regenerator.

Q. 70. *Why did not God hinder it from being effected, being he did forbid it them?*

A. 1. The Answer, if full, should open the true sense and plain meaning of God's Predestination, and the Election and Reprobation, which hath so much perplexed Mens Minds, tortured their Inventions, filled so great part of their Volumes, imployed so much of their Time in Oratories and Pulpits, exerted so much Ardency in their Grave Disputes, whereon hath been founded such confidence in their Censures, raised so many curious Distinctions in the Schools, so constant Agitation, different Results influencing their Lives and Demeanour; that it hath been as *Sicilis* to *Rom*· and *Carthage*, or the Philosophers Stone in Divinity.

2. And tho' some of each Opinion are eminent for holiness and integrity of Life, innate and acquir'd gravity and Wisdom, happy Education, deep Speculation, yet each party in diametrical opposition of the others Maxims sit down abundantly satisfied with their own.

3. Making Predestination and Reprobation like the Mysteries couch't in the *Revelations* so folded up, as may stir up mans industry, exercise his utmost abilities, humble him to the dust in his highest flights, teach him not to contemn the minute parts of Divine sparklings, exercise his faith, patience and love, and stir him up to prayer.

4. It

4. It may not be expected here should be an abridgment of the controverted Arguments suited to the depth and heighth of the reason, expositions and deductions they have made, or a ravelling into the knotty intricacies and labyrinths, their tacit impeachments of supream Justice, their deriving the Origin of crimes from the Fountain of purity.

5. Instead of all which is recommended to the studious and unprejudiced inquirer *Jacob Behmen*'s Book concerning Election and Predestination, where (if the bottom will satisfie) he may find the depth as convincingly evident, as the profundity of the Subject will permit, and the Inquirer penetrate.

6. But not daring to leave it thus; let me be as plain as a Child, and as regardless of content, and in the Lords behalf, and do hope by his guidance, must say,

Our God is perfectly good, one intire Will, not Yea and Nay, but from Eternity and in Eternity never did nor ever can will Evil, for such a will were a breach in the intire Unity; he made man very good, had he will'd him to have been sinfully evil, impotently evil, or penally evil: Either to act evil, be unable to good, or suffer evil, would he have exempted him from these? But contrariwise hath monish'd him of his danger, menaced his running thereinto, and when he fell, shew'd infinite pity by gracious power to restore him.

7. To admit a contrary thought of God is ingratitude, to plead for it borders on Blasphemy, and makes us as the Devils Advocates; for *Adam*'s shifting his sin on the Woman, and her loading it on the Serpent, was evil; but for any to cast it on God, is a boldness which the Serpent did not presume on; for we find not him to say God had reprobated him, and therefore he must needs be what he was.

8. Our destruction is of our selves, our Salvation of God. It was wrought above our conception, and we contributed not to it: But our aversion, as it could not frustrate, so it did enhance the inestimable value of it: Yet our Salvation is not ours without us but wrought in us, with us, tho' not by us.

9. The Christian must simply, plainly and readily obey as little Children do; a Father calls his Children, they ask not, whether tho he calls them all, he wills that some only should come? But all, one out-running the other, according to the degrees of strength hasten to him: He bids them go this or that way, they go, calls them out of the dirt, they come: This Food they eat and that they forbear; for he tells them this is good and that will make them sick. They play with a Bird, but fly from a Toad; for he saith this is harmless the other hurtful. They admit not the least thought that he saith one thing, and hath a secret contrary will.

10. And certainly all Mankind are more truely Gods Off spring than a natural Child is of his immediate Parent, and are accordingly all call'd upon.

11. Gods Voice is in Mens Hearts, Ears, before their Eyes, they are surrounded and inclosed in it, and penetra ed by it. Sometimes it stops mens career, here it whispers, anon it thunders, there it leads, by and by it draws or drives, to one it glanceth convictions, to another it gives succours, one it warneth in his sleep, another in his solitudes.

12. Thus it strives with man, wrestleth to Gain him, standeth in the door of the Soul, calling all the day long from Morning to Evening of our Life and where it is not hearkened unto it withdraws, and is grieved at resolute impenitence, and that ceasing to strive is call'd Gods hardning, leaving the Soul a Briar or Thorn; for where men mistake wilfulness for wisdom, and become not as a little Child, that wisdom is their snare and seducer.

13. Thus we see so astonishing grace and condescention is in the Mighty God,

that

The 177 *Theosophick Questions Answered.*

that he is greatly desirous, exceedingly concern'd and sollicitous to restore his disappeared Image in Man. It is not therefore a cross direct force and violence to the Scripture which saith of Christ, he tasted death for every man, to restrain it from many, yea by far from the greater number? Do those that so restrain it speak the thing that is right concerning God? Ought we to believe God or such contradictions?

14. Let us consider that to have made *Lucifer* and *Adam* unalterably what at first they were, had been to have made them more than Creatures, *viz.* rather Gods; or else less than Inferiour Creatures, (*viz.*) with Imprison'd wills. But there is no room left to doubt that the true Interest and Highest Good whereof any Creature is capable, is to be what the Gracious Creator design'd him.

15. Let us be so plain as to make the Precepts of our Gracious Lord to be the best comment and discovery of his own Glorious Sublime Nature. I am to believe evil must not be done that good may come, and that this Principle is derived from the Holy God: May I yet believe that from the same Fountain issued reprobation of an indefinite number of Angels and Men compelling them to be really guilty black Criminals, abandoned wholly to hardened sinful resolutions, adverse blasphemous will, and to be fuel for everlasting Burnings; that the good of shewing his power and wrath might thence be extracted.

16. The will of the Father is the reason of the Child. And God commands me to forgive, that I may be like him, do good for evil: And that I, who am less than a drop to his Infinite Abyss and Ocean of Mercy, should yet shew so much Mercy, as to help the Beast of my Enemy fallen under his Burthen. How can I then think that this God of Infinite Bowels did from Eternity reprobate any of his Intelligent or Rational Children and Creatures to be Back-broken, or design snares and pits into which they must necessarily fall and be precipitated?

Rom. 9. 22.   17. It is written what if God willing to shew his wrath, *&c.* having endured with much long-suffering the Vessels of Wrath fitted for destruction. It saith not that God fitted them for destruction: But it saith of God, that he had endured them with long-suffering, but in *ver.* 23. It is written of the Vessels of Mercy that he, (*viz.*) God had afore prepared them unto Glory; which distinction is very weighty and significant.

*Matth.*25.34.   18. Again the Judge himself tells us the manner of the great irrevocable sentence, (*viz.*) *Come ye blessed of my Father, inherit the Kingdom,* &c. But in *ver.* 41. *He saith, Depart from me, ye cursed, into Everlasting Fire,* &c. But saith not, ye cursed
ver. 41. of my Father, as before ye blessed of my Father; signifying evidently, that men make themselves accursed which deserves heedfully to be pondered. See the answer of the fifteenth Question throughout particularly the ninth verse.

     Quest. 71. *How were the Eyes of* Adam *and* Eve *opened that they saw they were naked, which before they knew not?*

1. It is manifest *Adam* and *Eve* were an Image of God in all the three Principles, but they should have lived a resigned life in the second, contemplating the Greatness and Glory of God in the first Principle, but not have entred into it, as *Lucifer* had done, also should have seen how the third did Image God, and over that *Adam* was to rule, but not subject himself to it by becoming an Image of it, or receiving nourishment from it; for his so doing (as in the foregoing answers hath often been inculcated) the transitory Food having in it the divided properties, is Belial, Mortal and Putrefactive, and *Adam* and all his Off-spring became thereby as the Beasts.

     2. Therefore entring into that unsuitable state their Eyes were opened to behold
the

The 177 Theosophick Questions Answered.

their Nakedness; for they were appointed to a Paradifical Glorious state, else they had been furnished with Hides, Fleeces, Furrs, Feathers or Scales.

3. But falling into the principle for which they were not provided, they were as naked and unfit as we are to fly into the Air, whereto Wings are requisite, or to live in the deep, whereto Fins and other peculiarities must adapt Creatures.

4. But their Eyes were so open'd to the Out-birth, as shut them to the Divine Birth. My Hand is but a small part of me and given me for good uses, as was the third Principle given them, but with my Hand I can hide the whole Heaven from my Eyes, and so did they; for by shutting the Divine Eye, they opened the outward dark one, as on departure of the Sun we see the Houses, Trees, &c. obscurely.

5. Had I lived in the time before *Adam*'s death, and had spoken with him, I might have found him groping by the strength of his memory after the things which I should have sued to him for the knowledge of; all which he by the infallible Light saw distinctly, and had exquisite knowledge of before he Fell: Like one who hath a Candle in his Room, and seeth every thing plainly, but that once extinguished must by memory direct his Feet and Hands to grope out any thing he would find.

Q. 72. *What was Adam's and Eve's Shame, that they hid themselves behind or by the Trees of Paradise? Whence came their fear and terrour?*

A. 1. When they had imagined into the third Principle, that is so far penetrated into it as to Lust after it; then did the Eye affect the Heart, for the strong Magical Will and Mind conforms the whole Man; especially the Body which is as the shadow of the inner Man, who is the Substance.

2. This Lusting, when it proceeded to actual Eating, awakened the Properties of the first and third Principles (that is the Hellish and Bestial) in the innermost Man, which was before irradiated with Divine Love, and true Sublime Wisdom, filled with the Spirit of Holiness, Tranquillity and Angelical Excellencies: this most inward Image of God (according to the second Principle) was invaded by the inletting of the four Forms of the first Principle, which compose the Kingdom of Wrath.

3. Their outward Man given them out of the one Element (whence proceeded also the Astral World) receiv'd by the awakened Lust the Wi'l of all the Evil Beasts in the divided Properties; as of Goats, Cocks, Boars, Bulls, Foxes, Dogs, Wolves, Bears, Tygers, Lions, Crockodils, Vultures Serpents, Vipers. Toads, &c.

4. Thus, Man who was the Quintessence and exquisite Abridgement of the Creation as to the third Principle, in having their total Energy in pure Heavenly Harmony without Admission into him of any of their divided Evils: now by Lusting hath taken into him every of their hateful Properties, and become a Beast of all Beasts.

5. For their imperfect Evil Properties by Transplantation into his excellent Nature are sublimed into real Wrath and Obstinacy, and Premeditated Rebellion against the Kingdom of Divine Love and Grace? defiling him with bestial Lusts; which in them is filthy, but in him sinfully so.

6. And *Adam* and *Eves* Body which was heavenly before, hereby became dark, opake, sluggish, bony, deadish and fragil, obnoxious to wounds, sickness, the *Turba*, Mortality and Dissolution into Ashes.

7. No wonder then their shame, horror and fear should drive and pursue them to hide behind the Trees, from that glorious Face, whence they had

with-

withdrawn themselves, and before whom they were no longer able to look up.

8. For their Monstrous Image was notorious, even such as made them contemned by the very brute Creatures; who withdrew the awe, fear and service from them, which they were to have paid, they were scorn'd by the Devils, a shame to themselves; how much more then were they sunk in the All-observing Eye of the Infinite God.

Q. 73. *How did Adam and Eve really Die in the Fall to the Kingdom of Heaven and Paradise, and yet live naturally to this World?*

A. 1. To answer this, it must be told what the Life of God was in *Adam* and *Eve*, which Life consisted in an entire Union with the Universal Will; which Union is so absolute, compleat and perfect, that the Holy Angel's and Blessed Men may be said to have no Will at all, and their Unchangeable Happiness is their resigned Life, wherein they lose themselves, and find all for ever.

2. As a Family is wholly at the guidance of the Lord of it, so are they; but on setting up an adverse Will, the makers of the breach dye to the Will and Conduct of the Father of that Family; and those making themselves their own Lords, cut themselves off from the Family.

3. Or as a Twig while it continues in the Fruit-tree hath one Will with the Tree; but when once it is rent off, and grafted into another Stock, it gets another Will and another Life to bear other, be it bitter, sour or otherwise Evil Fruit.

4. Thus *Adam* and *Eve* impregnated themselves with the third Principle, receiving a bestial Life from it, and putrefying Nourishment; their Divine Will, Appetite and Knowledge did thenceforth immediately Die and was Extinguish'd. Thus a well Educated Child apostatizing from his first Principles, degenerating into contrary Practices, dyeth to them, and loseth his first Love.

Q. 74. *What was the Voice of God in the Word when the Day grew cool? How did God recall Adam? How is this to be understood?*

A. 1. By the cool of the Day, is understood the time when *Adam's* Eternal Day was grown cool (that is) his Temperature was fain to Extremities of heat and cold: also alluding to the End of a Natural Day, which though hot closeth coldly.

2. By the Voice of God, is understood God's Anger in their Essences; for they had awakened the *Turba* or Wrath in themselves; Heaven they were at Enmity with, 'twixt it and them was a firm inclosure of a whole Principle, they might see Devils deriding them, and Fear the Fate of *Lucifer*, the Holy Angels had quit all intercourse with them, nor could they help them.

3. While this sad Knell was rung them, their Fear of God's Voice was not only at that of his Wrath in them, but that of his Love and Pity, to which they were estranged, such as the Earth trembled at when the Blood of the Lord descended on it from the Cross.

4. The Voice of the Lord moved and walked in the Gates of the Deep, in Fire and Light in the first and second Principles, and recalled them. But concerning the recalling them, the following Questions will require to Discourse of.

Q. 75. *What is the Seed of the Wife or Woman, and bruising and Treading upon of the Serpent? What did God speak or breath again into them? Was the same nothing else but an outward Promise, or an Incorporation of the effectual working Grace?*

A. 1.

The 177 Theosophick Questions Answered.

A. 1. The Womans Seed is not the Fire Soul, which standeth in the first Eternal Principle. (1.)
It is not the Astral nor Elementary Principle or Power arising thence. (2.)
It is not the Eternal Son of God the second Person or Divine second Principle, though the Lord in humbling Himself, to take our Nature, often calls Himself the Son of Man. (3.)
It is neither of these; for the first is too hot, the second too cold, the third infinitely too high.

2. But that which is properly the Seed of the Woman here intended, is the Heavenly Humanity, or true Virgin Image of God, the pure *Sophia* consisting of Divine Wisdom and Modesty, which was Married to *Adam* till his Transgression made a Divorce.

3. This is that Grace which was here again inspoken into *Adam* and *Eve*, and this is the Pearl which is to be searched after with all diligence, which was not only barely promised but brought in the Word, and ingrafted into the Light of their Life.

4. This is the Lamb slain from the Foundation of the (fallen) World, not only intentionally but actually; for being in every of *Adam*'s Offspring witnessing for God, was resisted and slain in its strivings with the old World and downward.

5. But where ever the bent of the Will inclines to obey and subject it self to the Divine Councils, in such was restored the joy of their Salvation, ever pointing at the Lord, who being the true Son of the Virgin, in the fulness of time bringing this Virgin by taking *Maries* Essences, consisting of all the principles and properties and making of two one, by that power which is able to subdue all things unto himself.

6. But so heavenly and pure is this, that one that hath it cannot shew it to one that hath it not, much less give it to such; but he that hath it can stammer and speak by parcels, and darkly by Parables, for such what he saith will seem, tho' it be not far from every one of us.

7. He can give the other some directions where to dig for it, also what it is like, and what it is not like. But Men are exceedingly perverted from it by the many Images their Astral Spirit imposeth on their Understandings: So that the Invitations of pure simple, and self-emptying Truth can hardly get audience, more hardly obtain to be considered and penetrated, but with highest difficulty get obedience from us, and due Soveraignty over us.

8. Men use their outward Senses so much, and are so full of Objects occurring to them, that they are strangers to the very existence of the Inward Sences, forgetting what the Apostle saith, *That which we have seen with our Eyes, heard with our Ears, and our Hands have handled of the Word of Truth*, &c.

9. The Men guided chiefly by the outward Sences are Sensual and Brutish, and yet too much of that sticks to us all: Such Maxims will not believe a Rock to be a shadow, and Faith a substance; they consider not that Visibles are transient, and that which is not seen is Eternal, whereof Faith is the evidence.

10. Thus is the Lord from Heaven call'd the Son of God, Son of Man, and Seed of the Woman, and is so at once perfectly and unchangeably.

11. And fallen Man when once reunited to God by the death of the monstrous Image, and restored to this new, first, pure, Virgin Image, are by this Seed of the Woman made the Sons of God.

See more to this purpose in the 81st and 90th Answers.

Q. 76. *What is the Curse of the Earth, what is thereby brought to pass?*

A. 1. This Earthy Globe is very much unlike to what it was; as our Bodies are also to that *Adam's* was; for as *Adam's* Body was the Epitome of the whole Out-birth; So this Globe was an Image of the Astral World, and all the Properties, and the Divine Principle did penetrate it as the Sun doth the Fruits, so that the Earth was as much paradisical as it was capable to be, but it had these bounds.

(1.) 2. That it could not be purer than the Root whence it proceeded, (viz.) the Astral and Elementary, and of those Heavens it may be said, they are not pure in his sight.

(2.) 3. That it could not be more permanent than its Root, and none doubts but of these it may be said, they shall pass away, and be folded up as a Scroul.

(3.) 4. That it was a compaction of the Mass of the Salitter, Sulphur and *Mercurius* of the deep, all of which were much darkened, corrupted and confused by the Fall of the Angels.

5. Yet was this earthy Globe in its first make before the Curse very Beautiful and Good.

6. And as in Mans Body so much of it is dead, hard Bones, foul Guts, stomach and gross Flesh, so that its first contexture seems worn out, yet it was and shall be glorious, though sown in dishonour.

7. Thus also this Globe consisting now of much raging deep, the unhabitable frozen North and South Extreams, other parts of parched Wildernesses and Desarts, also rocky useless places: and barren Heaths, sandy and Montainous Territories: Yet is a remainder of Fertility and Excellency here, seeming to be left so, to shew something of what once it was; as *Vespasian* is said to have left two or three Towers undemolisht tho' desolate, to shew what *Jerusalem* had been.

8. The Earth before the Curse must have known no sterility, the Air no storms nor intemperature, the Seasons no unhealthiness, the Brute Creatures no hostility nor hurtfulness.

9. For tho' the properties were in all, yet had the Gracious Creators blessing so ordered and bounded them, that they could not be manifest to divide and discord among themselves; for the good properties had the Dominion, and the other were serviceable in their places to the great ends of the Creation, viz. That the Divine and Spiritual World might be expresly Imaged in such exact order as the great variety of the Creatures and Creation were fitted for.

10. But *Eve* and *Adam* biting the Apple divided the properties so that the evil became prevalent, and the good (disturbed thereby) could not influence as before, and Gods withdrawing the Vertue and Influence of the Spiritual World from them the transitory Creatures which were of their own Nature passive, became penetrated throughly by the evil: Thus those of hot, and others of cold quality were made such, in an intense degree, and consequently destructive Poyson, and Venom also in Vegetables, thus came the destroyers in the Earth, Air and Seas.

11. *Adam* and his Race should (if they had stood) have been as the Angel which *John* saw with one Foot on the Land and the other on the Sea; so should *Adam* and his Race have had one Foot on this Principle, and the other on Eternity, but transgression set us adrift and sunk us, and for our sakes the whole Creation.

Q. 77.

The 177 Theosophick Questions Answered.

Q. 77. *How was Adam and Eve cast out of Paradice into this World? What was the Cherub with the naked Sword before Paradise?*

A. 1. *Job* from Opulency and Renown, washing his steps with Butter, and the Rock poured him out Oyl, falling to Nakedness, Sores and Contempt, had this vast disproportion to *Adam's* Fall, that his Inward Man not only retain'd stability but shone the brighter.

2. *Nebuchadnezzar's* degenerating and transforming into a Brute, was also exceedingly disproportionable ; because he had little to lose, wanting the Indowment, especially the Internals wherewith *Adam* was glorified.

3. And Men that taste of the good Word, and of the powers of the World to come, yet after that fall into final Apostacy and Darkness, which from the best a fallen Man as Man can attain, to the word a damned Sinner falls into, hath yet a great disproportion to *Adam's* Exclusion had not Infinite Grace interposed; for, as no Sinner mounts higher than feigned Happiness, but *Adam's* was real and sublime, so no Damned Wretch sinks more or comparatively but few with him, but *Adam* sunk a World, which must add to him a world of Woes.

Thus far I have digressed to give some glimpse of the greatness of the Fall.

4. Now to shew how they were ejected Paradise into this World, the review of the 71 answer will be very helpful. We must farther know that it was not a precipitation from a more lofty to a more low or other local station, but a departure out of one principle into another asleep or dying a Nescience or Oblivion of Divine Tranquillity and peaceable Fruition of Eternity, and an awakening to the Turmoils, Impotence, Discords, Pain, Care, Sorrow, Enmity and Anguish of Mortality and Confines of time in the third principle or Out-birth, and by an Inviolable connexion fixed to the Everlasting wrath of the first principal or dark Abyss.

5. To know now what the Cherub and Sword before Paradise is, it must be fore-known that Cherubims signifie Images, *(viz.)* Gods Image particularly that of his Justice, that is Gods Righteousness and severe Justice this hath a Sword cutting off or away whatever cannot stand in the proba, all such are as Fuel to that Flaming Sword.

6. Will any say these are Novel Allegories, not demonstrable but of uncertain found, let such consider, 1. What we fell from, our Reason faith from a pure state, capable of Eternity. 2. What we fell into, our Sences answer to an impure Bestial Mortal one. 3. How may we re-enter, the reason common to all rational Creatures, tells it may not be by the old filthy Garment we thus got, for a weight that presseth us down must be put off, if we would rise again, what thus we foolishly put on, we must wisely put away.

7. The Sword of Divine Justice cuts off the Monstrosity, because the Mortal Earthy cannot enter the Heavenly. Having put on Immortality it may, but that Robe is Christs Heavenly Flesh and Blood, his Holy Heavenly Body, or Gods Body, in this we pass the Cherub.

8. But this Cherub and Sword is in us. Thus the Lord saith, No man hath ascended into Heaven, but he that came down from Heaven, the Son of Man, (he saith not the Son of God) which is in Heaven ; for the Divine principle was not only in him, but he in it, and he was it.

9. Let us know Heaven is in us *(viz.)* the Divine principle is in us, yet we may be far from being in it, until following the Captain of our Salvation we yield (in his strength) to have our Earthy man Crucified ; otherwise keeping

our

The 177 *Theosophick Questions Answered.*

our Right Eye, Right Hand or Foot, we with both Eyes, Hands and Feet shall be Excluded; shutting our selves out for ever.

This 78th Question begins the Fifth Grand Distribution.

Q. 78. *Why was or did the first Man Born of a Woman become a Murtherer?*

A. Before *Eve's* Conception of *Cain* the following things did precede, viz.
1. *Adam's* non-exerting his power to produce a glorious Race of Intellectuals to succeed for ever the room of *Lucifer's* secluded Angels, which defect of *Adam's* came from his somewhat declining to the third principle, and Eclipsed his Magical Vertue and Lustre.
2 Next follow'd the dividing of the Tinctures, and thence forming *Eve*.
3. The departure of *Adam* and *Eve* from the pure Virgin Modesty, and going into the wanton Lust of the Out-birth, or Beastial principle, making a false Tincture.
4 A Self-will to Rule, for *Eve* would have been a Goddess; hereby making an evil Root.
5. Thus tho' they had in them the word of promise in its own principle, yet leaving the resignation they walk'd in their own will, strongly drawn by the four Stars of the first principle, also by the Out-birth or third principle; thereby making an evil Tree.
6. This was the Tree, now what fruit could be expected from an Evil Tree but evil. Is the Tincture spoil'd, the Root must be Infected, the Tincture through the Root Influenceth the Tree, and the Tree affects the Fruit. Thus in them the Fires Tincture being strong, suck'd to it the Bestial Out birth, their Will remained no longer in the resignation, but was a Self-lord, and joyning in the four forms of the first principle, becomes a raging Murtherer.
7. To which *Eve* would stir him up, who her self had at first an aspiring lawless Will, also misjudging her Son *Cain* to have been the promised Seed which should subdue the Serpent, she might cocker him to lordliness and power, whence he might be provoked to Jealousie and Envy, lest his younger Brother *Abel* should usurp the Soveraignty, the rather seeing *Abel's* Sacrifice accepted and his own rejected.
8. And the Serpent who had an open Door into *Cain's* Essences when his False Tincture operated in him, was no less active to poison him, than he had been to infect and deceive *Eve*.
9. All which is a dismal prospect to all living in Beastly Lusts, a startling check to all Immodesty, a sad consideration to all Conjugal Irregularities, and a serious Looking-glass to all, for all that are or shall be Born of Women.

Q. 79. *What was* Cain *and* Abel's *Offering? Why did they Offer Sacrifice? What did they do thereby?*

A. This Question hath three parts requiring respective answers, which seems most proper to be distributed thus, the first and third together, and after to speak to the second part.
Q. 1. *What was* Cain's *and* Abel's *Offering? And what did they do thereby?*
A. *Moses* saith *Cain* brought of the Fruit of the Ground, *Abel* of the Firstlings of his Flock and the Fat of them.
2. We are to understand that Mans Fall had brought him to be Earth; for his Body which was out of the Heavenly Eternal *limus* or substance became vile, elementary

The 177 Theosophick Questions Answered.

mentary and beſtial. Now in that Body, and in the Matter Sacrificed, was a double parity and likeneſs, viz. both in one Principle, and both under the Curſe.

3. Again, we are to underſtand that the Soul tho' ſince tranſgreſſion is as ſubtile and immaterial as a will: Between which ſince the Fall and the Angelical powers (by the Miniſtration of whom the Law was given) is as to the Souls originala parity, but as to the erroneous bent of the Soul a diſſimilitude.

4. Now to introduce the Soul into the Univerſal that it may be reclothed with its diſappeare'd Body it had of the Heavenly *Limus* (the Image which the Son of the Virgin reſtoreth, wherein the Bleſſed after the Reſurrection ſhall be cloathed) the Soul muſt have Matter as a Medium, it ſelf being Spirit, whereby to reunite to its true reſt, which Medium muſt be the Divine Subſtance.

5. Thus the Fire from Heaven (repreſenting the Heavenly Subſtance) laying hold on the Unctuous Property in the Sacrifice and Fuel) repreſenting the remainder of the Right Humanity in us) converts it into its own Magical flaming Property of Seraphick Love, figuring the Reſurrection, and the deſtroying the groſs Earthy part, ſeparating its Form into Aſhes and Vapour, figureth the cutting off of the monſtrous Beſtial Image by the Sword of the Cherub, becauſe That cannot enter Paradice.

6. The Smell in the Sacrifices is the Sulphur of the Body which requireth the ſweet Incenſe of the Divine Property to perfume it ; the Taſt is the Saline Spirit of the Out birth.

7. The Offering and Tranſmutation thereby, ſignifies the dying to Self-will, and uniting to, and living in the Univerſal Holy Will, whence Man was ſtrayed. Quite croſs hereunto *Cain* dying to the Reſignation, and living to Self-labour Will, and Agitation in his Tillage found no acceptance.

8. Whereas *Abel* giving himſelf up, or loſing his own Will, was taken up into and found all in the Univerſal Will ; which is an Eternal Truth, not ſpeculative, but real and practical through all Ages, here and in the World to come, the ever enduring Divine World.

9. Now for the ſecond part of the Queſtion, Wherefore did they offer ? *A.* If (2.) Q. A. the Anſwer of the other part of the Queſtion be well pondered, this is alſo anſwered ; for Man being ſtrayed, cannot be brought home but by dying to Self-will, which the Offerings did clearly repreſent, as hath been ſhewn.

10. Yet may we not think theſe and others of the Antients did This without Divine Precept, tho' not recorded when or how given, till after the coming out of *Egypt* ; for God rejects our Will, and weans us from it, as the Sacrifices evidently demonſtrate ; ſo the ſtraying Self-will may be deemed Captain of all the Armies fighting againſt God.

Q. 80 *Why was Cain's Murther for the Offering ſake ? What was the ground of it ? What Type are theſe two Brothers ?*

A. 1. In the immediately preceding Anſwer is ſhewn what moved *Cain* to murther *Abel*; which the Apoſtle ſaith was, becauſe his works were evil, and his Brothers were good.

1. There being predominant in the Soul of *Cain* the four Forms or Stars of the firſt Principle, he did not by dying to their prevalence enkindle the Love-flame of the ſecond Principle; becauſe it is done only in the Reſignation whereto he would not bow his Will: So that all the diſcording Properties might in him have met in a Harmony by enkindling in them a Light Joyful Luſtre.

2. Therefore was it that the Spirit of his Mind remained in the wrathful Dark
Fire-

Fire Principle, to satisfie, allay and quench his immoderate Lusts ready to proceed to a Hellish Anguish; he would in That Spirit suck in the third Principle by his labour and tillage, yet would hypocritically offer That to the Lord.

3. He might climb up in his claim of Primogeniture, to a Will of Prerogative over his Brother, and when he not only fail'd of Precedency, but of Equality with him; for that *Abel* found merciful acceptance, whilst his Offering was rejected; his Countenance fell, his Pride finding a repulse, turned him to Wrath, That to Envy, and That to Murther.

4. Thus the Parents Disobedience is visited by the wickedness of their firstborn.

Now what Type these two Brothers are, is evident: They were both Sacrificers, only *Cain* had no more but the Form of Religion and Devotion, joyned with a hatred to him who had the Form as himself, but had the Power like his God, which makes men as distinguishable from others, as the accepted Offering was from the rejected one.

5. *Cain* is the figure of all who causlesly hate another; for That being in the heart, is heart-murther, if it enflame the Tongue but to detraction, it hath one considerable aggravation, if it move the Brain to devise mischief, the Foot or Hand towards doing it; it is still greater, if it perpetrate the purpos'd Evil, 'tis heavier yet.

6. If it extend to many of the True Worshippers, or (if it could) to all, it is become the Blackness of Darkness; drawing on themselves all the righteous blood-shed from *Abel* to the day of doing or willing the Evil.

7. What need much be said, the Hunter or Persecutor is known; for tho' the Goatish Creature may undiscerned associate among the Sheep till the Judgment of the great day, yet the Wolf is notoriously distinguisht from the Lord's Flock of Lambs.

8. They are the figure of the Christian and Antichristian Churches to the end of time. Also here to the considering mind it is evident, that cruel Persecutions rise not but from the strong, stern, lofty, bitter Forms of the first Principle, who are so cruel each to other in an Intestine Wrath, that it is exceedingly more facil for the Sons of the Humble Light Principle, sweetly to yield up themselves a Sacrifice, than for the Evil Ones to perpetrate it, and still or quiet their own clamorous Consciences in and after the fact, but such bitter persecuting Spirit existeth not in, nor resulteth from the third Principle or due Natural Magistracy.

Q. 81. *In what Grace was the first World saved without the Law? What was their Justification?*

A. 1. Tho' the 75th Answer contributes much to the solution of this Question, yet the more plain, full and direct Answer of this is, That the Lord Jesus Christ, the Eternal Almighty Son of the Father, was, and is, and is to come, the only alone Redeemer, Justifier and Saviour (by him, for him, are all things, to whom all Knees shall bow, and all Tongues confess him) by uniting the Heavenly Humanity to the Seed of the Woman.

2. In the Volume of the Book it is written of Him: He is in His own holy Principle in the Light of the Life or Heart of every Man that cometh into the World; He cannot be comprehended by space; for all Heavens are comprehended by Him; He is a Branch in the Infinite second Principle, whence is the Divine Virgin of Wisdom.

3. He was inspoken by the Father into *Adam* and *Eve* at That needful Time as a Refiners Fire, or as the Holy Fire which descended and transmuted the material Sacrifices,

Sacrifices, or as a Tincture ennobleth Metals; He is to the Soul as it is to the Body, to the Understanding as the Light of the outward World to the Eye; to the Deadness of the Soul the Animation, Food to its Hunger, an Appeaser to its Tumults, reducing her of meer Grace from the Multiplicity to the Unity; such was He to the Old World; and in the fulness of Time the Divine Wisdom and Purity assumed the Woman's Seed.

4. For at the instant of the Father's inspeaking, Christ did re-implant Himself in the Light of the Life of *Adam's* and *Eve's* Souls to dispossess the Strong Man, and through all Generations doth stand in the Door of the Heart of every Child of theirs (none excepted) reproving Sin, warning of the Judgment to come, and Preaching Salvation: This is the Light shining in a Dark place; the name of This is Infinite Love, and it is also the Word of Reconciliation: To Him give all the Prophets witness, and also all the Holy Ones which have been since the World began.

5. Here are no Novelties, nor in any of the blessed *Jacob Behmens* Writings may such be found. But whereas men have dark confused notions of God, like those of *Athens* dedicating their Altar to the unknown God; of Him therefore whom men ignorantly worship do *Jacob Behmens* Writings give a clear, certain, demonstrable and distinct knowledge, and of all things and Worlds; also of all Creatures, from the most holy Angelical Princes of Eternity, to the most despicable excrescence of Time.

Q. 82. *Was* Cain *condemned for his sins? Or whether did* Cain *become damned in respect of his sins? What was his doubt or despair of Grace?*

A. 1. The heinousness of his sin appears; 1. That *Abel* provoke't him not, who in truth of heart offered, but *Cain* only in shew; the one really did what the other only pretended to do.

Aggravation, that on fall of his Countenance, and rising of his Wrath, the Lord reprehended and warned him before his perpetrating the fact. 3. Aggravation, his false and stubborn Answer after he had done it, before Sentence, I know not; Am I my Brother's keeper? 4 Aggravation, his desperate Answer after Sentence; My punishment is greater than I can bear; or, my sin is greater than can be forgiven. 5 Aggravation, that he went out from the presence of the Lord to marrying and building. So that were there no more in the Text, it had left him in a most desperate, forlorn state. His sin therefore under these Aggravations must of its own Nature, and by its own Writ condemn him. [1.] 1. 2. 3. 4. 5.

2. But *Cain* is under a twofold consideration; one as to his own Person, and so he was a Sacrificer, a Priest and Worshipper of the True God: Nor may it be doubted but that the Offering in it self was well warranted; for God's approbation of *Abel* shews it had Divine Institution; yet was *Cain* a Worshipper with an Evil Heart; that is an unresigned Spirit, but a Self-will, and therefore not accepted.

3. *Cain* is to be considered as a Figure of the Formal Hypocritical Worshippers and of them, 1. Such who pretend to worship the True God. 2. That in the Outward Form of what they do, suit their Worship much according to the Letter. 3. That yet are strangers to the Spirit, Life and Power of Divine Worshipping. 4. That have some Outward Dignity, Priority or Authority over the humble, resigned Worshippers. As *Ishmael* and *Esau* had the Primogeniture of *Isaac* and *Jacob*. 5. That they have a strong disposition and preparedness to Anger and Envy against the Faithful Worshippers, and do make all such Approaches to their hurt as they can: As did *Balaam* and *Corah* with whom *Cain* is ranked. 6. Such as when they can hurt or kill, have so great impenitence as hardens them against Self-accusing, and impudence to deny their Evil Facts. [2.] 1. 2. 3. 4. 5.

P 4. Now

The 177 *Theosophick Questions Answered.*

4. Now to close the Answer, It is true, all such Churches or Persons as are figured by *Cain*, are, whilst they continue unregenerate, seeking to please the Self-will in a lost, desperate state under the first four Forms, and shut up in the first Principle.

5. But forasmuch as God did set a Mark on *Cain*, thereby defending him against the destroyers; all this may be without his particular personal condemnation.

Q. 83. *Why did God make a Mark on* Cain, *and said, he, or whosoever that slayeth* Cain, *his blood shall be avenged sevenfold?*

A. 1. *Cain* said, *From thy face shall I be hid;* also *every one that findeth me shall kill me.* It could not be the Outward Man there meant, for that could not be hid from God, but the Inward might fall into Darkness, and so be as it were hid. Nor was it the Outward Man that he feared they that found him should kill him; for there was no Man besides him but *Adam*; but it must be the Inward Man that might be kill'd; for to That there were Enemies enough.

2. The Mark God set upon *Cain* must not therefore be understood to be on his skin or flesh, but on his Inward Man, to withstand the Spiritual Enemies; That Mark therefore must be an Opposite Power to that of the Evil Spirits, which must be confessed to be the Covenant of Grace, Jesus Christ, which was inspoken, imprinted and set upon him.

3. The Threatning; *He that slayeth* Cain, *vengeance shall be taken on him sevenfold;* must be an Inward Vengeance, for Outward it could not be on Inward Enemies; but to be understood thus, that if any Spirit slay *Cain's* Inward Life, vengeance shall be taken on him sevenfold, that is, Eternally in all his seven Forms of Life.

4. Thus Grace was extended to *Cain*; nor may we think *Cain* was the Only Cause of that Murther; for his Propagation in the divided Properties was his first mover; and as *Cain* had Grace extended to him, he being the figure of the False Church: So is Grace extended by Christ to such of That Church as shall come out of it into the Resignation.

5. And *Abel's* sincere giving up of himself, as well as the Offering, enkindled the Love-fire in his Lifes Forms (who by propagation was otherwise out of the divided Properties) but therein he was the Figure of Christ's Humble Church.

Q. 84. *Wherefore said* Lamech, Cain's *Successor, to his Wives* Zilla *and* Ada, Lamech *shall be avenged seventy and seven fold; what doth this mean and signifie?*

A. This Mystery prophesied by *Lamech* calls for these Considerations.

1. What he was from *Cain*; viz. 1. The seventh. 2. Why to his Wives spake he this; viz. because by the Woman came the first Evil and Vengeance: And to his two Wives, pointing at the divided Properties.

2. The next is the thing spoken, *I have slain* [or would have slain] *a man to my wounding,* or in my wound, --- *and a young man to* [or in] *my hurt.*

3. No one is named to have been slain actually, but That and the other Reading [would have slain] signifies an Internal Slaughter. And if *Cain* be avenged seven-fold, truly *Lamech* seventy and seven-fold, shews the Vengeance was not against the person of *Lamech*, as it had not been against That of *Cain.*

4. Whence we are to know, that the Holy Ghost signifies by the Man, or young Man slain, or that he would have slain the Heavenly Man, against whom *Cain* was the figure of Enmity.

5. And *Lamech* the seventh from him saw the holy Power World (acted by the Mental Tongue or Language of Nature) would withdraw, and vengeance
should

The 177 *Philosophick Questions Answered.*

should be taken by the dividing of the High Tongue into seventy Languages, which was done at *Babel.*

6. And under This Hurt and Evil the World still groans. But where the Divine Power Rules, men speak one Language, tho' imperfectly; but they who are under subjection of the multiplicity, speak Confusion, and run into the Abyss of Disorder and Enmity: Concerning which I here say the less, because it will be met with if God will open in any one understanding to answer the 89th Question.

Q. 85. *What was the greatest Sin of the Old World? or first Terrestial Human World?*

A. 1. Their greatest sin was their leaving the Divine Substance of the second Principle, and going into the Out-birth or third Principle; which is only a shadow, figure, image, or representer of the Substance, whereby they mistook that for their chief food which is not so.

2. It is written, *All that is in the World, is the Lust of the Eye, the Lust of the Flesh, and the Pride of Life*; and they are charged with the Lust of the Eye, and the Lust of the Flesh: And after it follows; *God saw that their wickedness was great on the Earth, and that every imagination of the thoughts of their hearts* [or desires and purposes] *were only evil continually.*

3. The Heart is the Parent, the Thoughts the First-born. And as Water is best known by tasting at the Fountain; so is the Heart by the Thoughts, Imaginations [or makings] for so signifies the word Imaginations, shewing Man's Soul to have a kind of Creating Power.

4. And if Man chuseth (as they did) the things of This World for their Chief Good, that his Choice is his God, and his Love makes him to be the Propriety of the thing chosen.

5. Such men are therefore call'd the Children of This World; for that, Man rather lives where he loves, than where he is. And what Man chuseth for his Chief Good, loves and lives in his desire unto, puts confidence in; here during all the Union of the Soul with the Body, That is the Substance his Will feeds on, and That is his, and all he hath for ever.

6. If it be God, it is heightened and perfected; if it be the World, it is more wretchedly depraved; which being a Substance fixt in his Will, the same he shall for ever insatiably desire, but never reach, and therefore be his Torment and Anguish in Eternity.

7. Who hath bewitched men therefore; that they chuse not and practise what their Reason cannot but dictate to them (as depraved as it is) to be best? And That is That Divine Love and Eternal Life, which Christ in God is more elegible than the Lust of the Eye, the Lust of the Flesh, and the Pride of Life.

8. What cure is there when men depart from God's Goodness? God is but one, and hath but one Son eternally generated of his Substance, and That Son can die but once; our resistance of his Calls, makes God by Ezekiel say, *I am broken with their whorish heart, which had departed from me, and with their Eyes which go a whoring after their Idols:* Like to what he said to the first World; *It repented the Lord that he made Man, and it grieved him at the heart,* &c. Ezek. 6. 9.

Q. 86. *What is the Henochian Life? What is become of Henoch? or where hath Henoch remained; so also of Moses and Elias?*

A. 1. Not without many hæsitations come I to this (almost singular) Question: Many Recoils from my attempts to adventure speaking of so secret a Mystery: My heart meditateth terror to see it self groveling. But it must be said the Henochian Life

The 177 Theosophick Questions Answered.

Life is a Life of Faith; for the Holy Ghost saith, *Henoch was translated that he should not see death, and was not found,* &c. And tho' the Administration of the Henochian Life be so rarely found as it is, and hath been, and that the Writing on it might seem to anticipate and forerun the discovery of it, yet for the sake of the Sons of Wisdom, to whom only it shall appertain, it is answered, and let such be directed.

1.   1. To consider Christ's Life in the Wilderness, who after his abandoning the Food of the divided Properties in the third Principle forty days (being in the temperature) was then ministred unto by Angels.
2.   Let it be considered that this was no Life separate from the Elementary Body, but as well it, as the Essences of the Soul remained unchanged.
3.   That *Henoch's* Time and Ministration shall be within the Circle of Time, signified by this, that he lived just so many years as are days in one year.
4.   It shall be in and under the six Forms of Nature, not entring (as such) into the Sabbath as himself was, the sixth Generation only excluding *Adam*, who should so have generated.
5.   The whole Essences of the first Principle, and the whole Elementary Body of the third Principle, (remaining really such) shall be throughly irradiated and penetrated by the second Holy Love-Principle, yet so secretly (tho' absolutely) as shall not be reached by the outward Eye.

3. But in This Administration shall not be *Henoch's* Translation, much less the change or mutation spoken of by the Apostle *Paul*; but they, tho' being in, shall be yet unknown to the World.

4. To the second part of the Question, What is become of *Henoch*, so also of *Moses* and *Elias*? I readily confess to have an impulse and clearness to speak only of *Henoch* and *Elias*, and concerning them,

Do answer; they are no farther from us than the third Principle or Out-birth can be removed: I speak not of Mathematical Distance, but Metaphysically of Principles; and tho' the Out-birth or Astral World, in its divided depravity, imageth Hell and Death, blended with the Divine Powers, yet in its due place it imageth the first and second Principles in sweet Harmony, yet still is but an Image.

5. *Henoch* was not transmuted or risen again, but translated, and hath the third Principle in or on him; it is not as with the Saints, raised at the period of the Sufferings of our Redeemer; for it was with them then raised, as it will be with us in the Resurrection. It is not with him, as with Christ risen and ascended, but rather as with Christ when transfigured, but not wholly so neither; but he is in the Astral Man (without the *Turba*) a Substantial Image of the Spiritual World in the Heavenly Harmony.

6. It is said of *Henoch, Gen.* 5.24. he was not; which is expounded by the Holy Ghost, *Heb.* 11.5. he was not found; so and no otherwise is it understood of him and *Elias*.

7. They are not in highest Exaltation, as those who having laid down their Astral Man, and are raised, receiving it again in the New Body, or Christ's Heavenly Flesh and Blood, in the One Holy Element the Divine Substance, whereof the Astral World is the Spring and Image, which Off-spring and Image *Henoch* and *Elias* retain, tho' (haply) in the highest Glory the same Image is yet capable of.

8. Therefore was *Elias* Ministration expected to return, as it did once in *John* the Baptist; and again his and *Enoch's* are yet to do. For thus, what the Lord Jesus saith of himself, is in this state also a fixed Truth, *John* 12.24. *Except a Corn of Wheat fall into the ground and die, it remaineth alone; but if it die, it bringeth forth much fruit.*

The 177 Theosophick Questions Answered.

Q. 87. *What doth Noah's Flood for Sin typifie and point out?*

A. It points out the Judgment of the Great Day: (1.)
1. That shall be (as the other was) inevitable.
2. That Day, after many Warnings through all Ages, shall yet come suddenly, even as the Deluge after 100 years premonition came as a surprize.
3. That Day shall hasten and be shorten'd, even as the other was promised to be forborn 120 years, came in the one hundredth year after.
4. There shall be as safe a Deliverance to all the Children of the Faith of *Noah* by the Antitype of the Ark, as was the Ark to *Noah* and those with him.
5. The True Ark of the Covenant having the first, second and third Principle, composing and establishing one Eternal Power or Heavenly World, is typified by the first, second and third Stories of *Noah's* Ark.
This World will be much less excusable than that was, among a multitude of Instances producible in this; that the Judgment to come is News to few, nor hath been, as appears by this, that tho' in the first publishing the Gospel to the Gentiles many laughed at the News of the Resurrection, yet find we none so doing at the Judgment to come. Nevertheless how few enquire for the Ark; whereas in the first World, the Deluge could not be foreknown but by believing the one only *Noah.*

1. It figures Fallen Man as followeth; 1. It points out, That by Man's departure from the Order wherein he was set, his Out-birth over-mastered him, as did those Waters overwhelm all. (2.)
2. As Waters, whereof some are sweet, others bitter, fresh, salt, stinking or poisonous, make all one Flood; so all the Properties, when separate, though various in themselves, make up one uncleanness.
3. It figures the Universality of Man's Apostacy, leaving no Man, nor any part of Man exempt from the general Confusion, like that of the Flood.

Q. 88. *What doth Noah's Drunkenness signifie, by reason whereof he cursed his Son Ham?*

A. 1. *Noah* represented *Adam* several ways, particularly as he was the beginner of the Second World or Monarchy, as *Adam* was of the First. Again, Record is made of the Names of but three Sons of *Adam*; (viz.) *Cain, Abel* and *Seth,* whereof one (viz.) *Cain* only bare the Image of the Apostacy. *Noah* had also three Sons, whereof *Ham* only bare the same Cursed Image.
2. *Adam* Lusted after This Worlds Property, thereby falling from his Divine Understanding, Creating, Gratifying, or Living in the Sensual Image, which is signified by *Noah's* Drunkenness, which clouded his Holy Image, and uncovered his Shame and Brutish Image, which is so evident as needs no enlargement.
3. *Ham* was cursed, for he was the Figure of Introduced Bestiality, whereunto the Curse was annexed; This was That False Lust taking pleasure in Shameful Nakedness; therefore of *Ham* came the filthy, and more than beastly Sodomites, and the vile brutish *Cananites* whom *Joshuah* destroyed.
4. But *Ham's* admission into the Ark shews, that the very Mocking-spirited men are not of purpose reprobated, but Salvation is tendred them.
The farther Answer is referr'd to the 34th Chapter of the *Mysterium Magnum,* &c.

Q. 89. *What is the Tower of Babel; and wherefore were the Speeches there altered?*

A. 1. The Tower of *Babel,* is Fallen Man's Confidence, his Home and his Defence: Yet is a mistake having no Foundation but one continued Cheat; for whilst

The 177 *Theosophick Questions Answered.*

Adam stood in the Temperature, he needed no Tower; for himself in God was a strong Tower, standing as the Image and in the Might of all the three Principles and Harmony of all the seven Properties.

2. But when Man had run into the multiplicity of the divided Properties, the Holy United Powers could no longer be imaged by him, as a Branch cut off a Tree retains a little of the worser part, but nothing of the vigour of the Tree. He became a degenerate Plant, and was like a City infested with Intestine Fatal Broils, so that it can hold no commerce abroad, or like a man distracted, who cannot advise nor be advised, being a stranger to himself as well as to common Prudence.

3. For Man having passed from the Unity into Self, became a God to himself, and so there were as many Gods as Nations, as Families, yea as Men: Then could they no more speak the One Language, than abide steddy in One Power, whereof they had deprived themselves.

4. Therefore was the One Language confounded into many, as One United Power was distracted into many feeble ones. But to shew what the One Language was, and the possibility, or impossibility, or restoring it, and way how, cannot come under the present Question, but falls of its own accord under the 145, 146, and first part of the 147 Questions, whoever God shall enable to arrive at their solution.

Q. 90. *What was the Covenant of or with* Abraham *concerning the Blessing, and also the Circumcision? What doth that signifie?*

A. 1. It was not a Litteral or Verbal stipulation as the Covenants amongst Men are, and as we are too apt to conceit and deem it. Yet is it the subject of many, and in some respects of all the holy words and writings imparted to us.

2. It is the again inkindled holy power of the Eternal Divine World, which was ingrafted and inspoken into the darkened Souls of *Adam* and *Eve*; creating peace and order there, as the Light had done in the Chaos in order to the Creation of the Out birth or World, figured by the Tincture which transmuteth and innobleth base Metals to Gold: And as the holy Fire inflamed the Sacrifices, the Inspoken Grace set on Fire Mans cold Affections; for he was given to that end * as a Covenant to the people.

42. 6.

3. This was the Holy Seed sowed into the Light of the Life of *Adam* and *Eve*, which was their Salvation: Yet pointing to and being the Lord Jesus Christ, who was, and is, and is to come, yesterday, to day, and for ever, but at the time of the limit of the Covenant took Flesh.

4. This according to the Flesh was to descend and be in one line only from *Adam* to *Seth*, thence to *Sem*, *Abraham*, and Tribe of *Judah*, and took the Womans Seed in the Virgin *Mary*.

5. But according to the Spirit and Divine Life (wherewith, and by which it was in the fulness of time begotten) it was not only in that Line, but in every of *Adam*'s Children as an Ingrafted Word, as truely in *Cain* and in his Race, as in *Seth* and in his Race.

6. This was grieved at the Heart, by the old World, vexed by the *Israelites* in the Wilderness, and (as Gods formed Word) is his witness in Men, judging and importuning from Age to Age. This, like the small Grain of Mustard-seed, grows up to such a Tree as whose top reacheth Heaven.

7. This was the Covenant and Blessing given *Abraham*, and with respect to the Union it hath with the Son of God, was both the Food of *Adam's* Soul, and of *Abraham's* Faith, and the Author of his Faith and Confidence.

8. And

The 177 Theosophick Questions Answered.

8. And now being come to the Circumcision, having set a Law to my self to avoid repetitions (all I can) do refer to the 8th and 9th Sections of that short Tract call'd, [*Considerations on the Scope of* J. Behmen] compared with the 41st Chap. of the *Mysterium Magnum*, is said to be Epitomized or Abridged in the Book of Extracts, in every of which it is so largely opened, that to touch it here would be Tautology and superfluous recitals.

Q. 91. *What Figure is the destruction of* Sodom *and* Gomorrah? *How was it effected?*

A. 1. The destruction of *Sodom*, &c. is the Figure of the destruction of *Babel*, sometimes call'd the Antichrist, sometimes the Whore, sometimes the Man of Sin; a Man for his daring Courage, a Whore for Unfaithfulness and Impudence. And these do figure *Sodom*, &c.
2. 1. In their State and Grandeur. 2. In their Sin. 3. In their Downfal. (1.) 1. 2. 3.

Their State consisted, 1. In their Opulence being richly perfectly Scituated, thus do *Babylon*, Antichrist, and the Whore covet and possess the Fat of the Earth.
2. Their State and Grandeur; *Sodom*, &c. were Cities, Royal Cities, having Kings and Pomp.
3. In their security by their numbers as Cities in a well watered Land. Like the second, thus doth Antichrist ally it self by Policy to Chief Magistracy. Like the third, thus doth Antichrist establish her self by outward force.
3. In their Sin; *Sodom*'s Sins were, 1. Pride. 2. Fulness of Bread. 3. Idleness. (2.) 1. 2. 3.

Thus *Babylon* and the Whore is said to be in Scarlet, with a Golden Cup in her Hand, not got by Industry, but already in her Hand. And is distinguishable and an Enmity with the Servants of Christ; for, 1. Christs Servants are like their Lord, humbled to the Earth. 2. If not poor outwardly as for the most part they are, yet are always as having nothing. 3. Not Idle; for they are working out their own Salvation with fear and trembling.
4. In their Downfal, sudden and unexpected, *Sodom*'s was not in the silence (3.) 1. and horrors of the Night Season, but when the risen Sun had renewed their hopes of Safety. Thus is it said of *Babylon*, who said I sit as a Queen, &c. in one hour Rev. 18. 17. is her, &c. 2. That *Sodom*'s Ruine was immediately from above. Thus the A- 2. postle saith of Antichrist; Whom the Lord shall destroy by the Spirit of his Mouth 2 Thes. 2. 8. and Brightness of his coming. Therefore shall *Babylon* fall irresistibly.
3. The Fall of *Sodom* was total, final and irrecoverable or irreparable, in every 3. of which it figures Antichrist; for to express it it's said that a Mighty Angel took up a great Stone like a Mil'stone, and cast it into the Sea, saying, thus with violence Rev. 18. 21. shall the great City *Babylon* be thrown down, and shall be found no more at all. Rev. 18. 4.
4. In the fall of Antichrist those that will come out of her shall be received; fi- 4. gured by the escape of *Lot* and his two Daughters, as saith the Holy Ghost, Come out of her my people, that ye partake not of her sins, nor receive of her Plagues. Thus Antichrist and *Babel* might well and fitly be call'd Spiritually *Sodom* and *Egypt*.
5. To the second part of the Question, (*viz.*) How it was effected? It's answer'd, 1. Not by the Hellish Fire, for the Fuel and Matter of that Fire must be Eternal. 1, 2.
2. Not by the Fire which shall sweep and reduce the Out-birth to it first princi- *By what it* ples before the last Judgment; for that would have dissolv'd the Elements. *was not effected.*

6. But

The 177 *Theosophick Questions Answered.*

By what it was effected. 6. But it was effected by the flagrat of the Elementary Fire, which was fully sufficient to execute Divine Vengeance on the Elementary part of *Sodom*, &c.

Q. 92. Wherefore did Lot's *Wife become a Pillar of Salt, how is it to be understood?*

A. 1. For a dreadful warning to all succeeding times, of the effect of Covetousness. We are not to be trusted with the World till we are dead to it, as *Paul* saith he was, then, as tho' two dead Bodies come not of their own accord one to the other, they may be brought together, but they embrace not each other, and being parted again, grieve not.

2. Man is what he wills; for the Magical power of the Will, especially if it be strengthened by the Astral Spirit, is (by far) an over-match to the Elementary, as is the Eternal Soul to the Astral, now, and especially after dying of the Body. Therefore when *Adam* and *Eve's* will were gone into the Out-birth of the third principle the Lord tells him, Dust thou art.

Luke 17. 37. 3. *Lot's* Wife looking back was a captivating her self again, so directly against Gods goodness and Mercy, that it is said, Remember *Lot's* Wife: And is a figure of all Apostates; like those *Israelites* after the *Babylonish* Captivity, who returned to *Egypt* to their own destruction.

4. Thus those who in their simplicity are come a little way out of the Antichristian Yoak and Cheats, yet suffering themselves to be drawn back by the advantages of this World are near *Lot's* Wife's condition: So the *Israelites* long'd for the Flesh-pots: And *Demas* and *Judas* drew back to perdition.

Q. 93. Wherefore did the Daughters of Lot *lye with their Father, and first made him Drunk, that they might be with Child by their Father; whence arose two Potent Nations; what doth this Figure signifie?*

A. Such as can see no more in *Noah's* Drunkenness than what the Letter recorded, nor in this of *Lot* but the Incest, &c. would make the Holy Scripture to be only a bare Narrative like other common Histories.

1. But the figure of *Lot* shews how *Adam* (and in him we all) went out of the Paradifical order into the Beftiality of the Out-birth: whereby we were overwhelmed and as one drunk, and hath made his and our propagation so far estranged from the Divine purity in which *Adam* before the dividing of the Tinctures should have propagated his holy Race, as may be best figur'd by inordinate, incestious, Bestial Lust.

2. And whereas this came in his sleep, shews the sleep of *Adam*, and our death, neither of which should have been, had the Divine order been observed.

3. Again, as of this came two potent Nations, *Moab* and *Ammon*, we see how near of Kin the faln, impure, incestuous, bastard brood of faln Mankind are to the holy Seed the Lord Incarnate; for *Lot* was *Abram's* Brother *Ha-ran's* Son, so they were of Consanguinity as betwixt *Abraham* the Man of the Covenant, and *Lot* the Figure of the Lords sacred ones and redeemed, of whom came these Incestuous productions.

4. For *Ammon* and *Moab* were not so forreign to *Israel* but that God commended to them the care of his people to be their covert from the spoiler in requital of *Abraham's* rescuing *Lot* from the four Kings.

5. This openeth a Door of hope to all the faln Mankind tho' in *Adam* sinfully conceived as *David* confesseth, yet the Covenant placeth it self in and near unto us, (*viz.*) in our Souls and the Lord himself humbled himself to become our Brother. 6. And

The 177 Theosophick Questions Answered.

6. And laſtly, Whereas the two Daughters of *Lot* did this to preſerve a holy Seed of their Father, which was but an impure Baſtard Seed, thereby they figured *Eve*, who thought her firſt-born had been the holy promiſed Seed, ſaying, I have got a Man the Lord, which was *Cain* the accurſed Seed.

Q. 94 *What doth the figure of* Moſes *ſignifie that he muſt be drawn out of the River or Lake of Water, and be preſerved to ſuch a great Office?* The Sixth Grand Diſtribution.

A. 1. What can figure the wretchedneſs, miſery and helpleſs ſtate of all faln *Adams* woful Offspring more to the Life than *Moſes* lying in an Ark of Bulruſhes amongſt the Flags in the River *Nilus* : Where neither his Father or Mother after they had hidden him three Months could better provide for him.

2. To an Infant caſt out in the Green Field was even *Jeruſalem* compared, but this figure was ſomething more, for the Field will ſupport the Body, but not the Water without an Ark. The Earth alſo hath beſides Men, ſeveral Creatures that may ſhew kindneſs to an out-caſt Infant, but the Water hath none, alſo that River wanteth not devouring Creatures.

He was ſentenc'd to die as ſoon as he was born, his very Exiſtence was a Capital Crime.

3. The figure thus conſidered hath theſe expreſs ſignifications, viz. 1. *Moſes* his ſo forlorn Eſtate, is the true circumſtance of every Child of *Adam*. 2. *Amram* and *Jochebed*, are *Adam* and *Eve*. 3. *Pharaoh*, Gods ſevere Juſtice. 4. *Pharaoh's* Daughter, the Divine Virgin *Sophia*. 5. Her Maid Servant the Inſpoken Grace in us, and outwardly the Prophets, Apoſtles and Preachers of Righteouſneſs. 6. The Ark of Bulruſhes, all the conveniencies our firſt Parents could leave us. 7. The Siſter of *Moſes*, our dearly affectionate Guardian Angel. 8 The River, the diſſolution and mortality of our Aſtral and Elementary Man. 9. The devouring Crocodiles the Evil Angels. 10. His being drawn out, ſaved, nurſed and honoured, the Regeneration.

1.
2.
3. 4.
5.
6.
7. 8.
9.
10.

4. The figure tells us that all Perſons and Nations, *Jeruſalem* as others, are by the heavy Fall as wretchedly helpleſs in as abſolute peril, and of themſelves as ignorant of the ſame as was that out-caſt Infant: With this grand addition, that as they grow in the wiſdom of the World they wade deeper into the miry Flags, are more hazarded and ſinfully hardned, till in a moment they go down into the Grave as a prey to the Deſtroyer.

5. Virgin *Sophia* ſtirs up the Inſpoken Grace, by the Miniſtry (ordinarily) of the outward publiſhers of the Glad-tydings, whereby Man is carefully nurſed, and ſafely preſerved notwithſtanding the Decree gone forth againſt him by the ſevere Juſtice from periſhing by the River or evil Monſters; the mortality of our Aſtral and Elementary Man from the Devils.

6. And the ſweet loving bleſſed Angels figur'd by the Siſter of *Moſes*, are concerned Spectators of our calamitous ſtate, and willingly ready by their Miniſtry to help, ſave and retrieve us. But all ſuch dark obſtinate Men and Women who will not quit their Ark of Bulruſhes, but load themſelves with the ſlime, and be defiled with the pitch wherewith it is covered, do grow unactive and unweldy as to Divine Works and ſtick faſter and ſink deeper into the filth, becoming an unavoidable prey to the Deſtroyers. Out of which perſwade us, O Lord, to ſuffer our ſelves to be drawn.

Q. 95. *Why did the Lord appear to* Moſes *in a fiery flaming Buſh when he choſe him?*

Q

A. 1.

A. 1. It hath been often shew'd that Man's Fall was his going into the third Principle or Out-birth, therefore did God doom him to the toiling about Earth; which was by the Curse made Barren; for the first Principle meekned and glorified by the Properties of the second, doth where it entreth into the third Principle (triumphantly) make it a Paradise.

2. But the afflicted Sons of *Abraham* groan'd under the toil of the third Principle, which they inherited from *Adam*, and travel'd to be deliver'd from the Bondage of it, crying to God because of the Rigor of their Servitude; as the Poor where-ever they are oppressed may do, assuring themselves their cause is weighed.

3. In this needful time God appears to *Moses*, in the Fire of the first, the Flame and Lustre of the second, in the Bush representing the third: both to shew them what they had lost, and that as the Fire could burn in the Bush without consuming it; so could the first and second Principles have well consisted with the third, had the due order been kept.

4. For when the Harmony was preserv'd, the first with its four Properties was as a Root to the whole, the second as a Life to the Root and the whole, the third a Fruit or Vertue of and in the whole.

5. Whereas in the Severation and Disorder, the first was a fire to the whole, the second only as an incomprehensible unknown Life and Witness: and the third a Life of Vexation, Sorrow and Pain, and loaden with the Curse.

6. Therefore was it the Lord appear'd in the Idea of the two first Principles, and so appearing sanctified the third, which was meant by the Command that *Moses* should put off his Shoes; because the place was Holy Ground.

7. By the first Principle is signified the Lord's Jealousie and Zeal, and by the second his merciful Love and Pity. Therefore is this Figure (as are many others) repeated over a thousand times (from Age to Age) on and towards the Souls of all God's ransom'd and Redeem'd ones.

Q. 96. *From or out of what Power did* Moses *do his Works of wonder before Pharaoh?*

A. 1. The Apostle saith, I can do all things through Christ that strengtheneth me. But to shew what Power enabled *Moses* to do his Wonders; It must be known whither go the Groans and Complaints of the oppressed? It is answered, into the Principle of God's severe Justice, such time as wicked Oppressors destroy and devour Wicked Men like themselves.

2. But when cruel Beasts grind and hunt the Lord's Flock, who are not of their Game: (though they also have the Beasts Hide on them) but return Good for Evil, Praying for their Persecutors. This passeth into the Principle of fierceness with respect to the Enemy; but the Holy World, the Fountain of Grace and Compassion, is strongly prest upon, with respect to the wronged Children.

3. And unless the Oppressor enter into the Grace Principle by humble, earnest Repentance; all his Works, Words, Thoughts, and every their Aggravations go into a Substance, and are treasur'd up for God's Judgment, and then these that sow the Wind shall reap the Whirlwind.

4. And from the Holy World is it said, I have seen, I have seen the affliction, &c. I have heard, &c. and am come down. So that *Moses* ability lay in the Abyss of God's Power and Holiness; that is, in both first and second Principles.

5. For whereas the Avarice, Haughtiness, Envy and Cruelty of the Driver goes into the Treasure of God's Wrath, so the Patience of the Lord's Family goes into the Treasure of God's infinite Love-Principle, and Holiness; as we therefore reap Wheat or Cockles whence we sowed them, so is it here; thus *Moses* had Power, out of his first Principle of awakened Zeal to Muster the fierce Qualities in the third Principle,

The 177 Theosophick Questions Answered.

Principle, and bring them like a Victorious Army upon *Egypt*; and out of the Treasure of Divine Grace to visit, secure and exempt *Goshen*.

6. Yet God is but only One; thus the sweet Odour of fragrant Herbs, and the fumes of foetid Weeds, differently ascend from one fire wherein they are burnt.

7. Is it occasionally ask'd, whence is the Power the Magicians did their Wonders by? It's answered, it proceeded out of the divided Properties and Powers of the spoken formed Word or Out-birth, which the Ancients were skill'd in; yet was theirs impotent, when in competition with the might *Moses* exerted, for his was the speaking, forming Holy Powers, whereof theirs was a Figure and Representation.

8. But our Modern Pretenders to Wisdom in Nature, are Men of Words, having neither Divine Substance, as was in *Moses* and the Prophets, nor true Knowledge of the figure or formed outward Powers, as had the Antients: but pretending Divinity to Umbrage their shallowness, do call God's Power in the Out-birth Diabolical, and pretending Philosophy fill their Schools and Books with an empty Sound of vain words, fictitious and fabulous; neither knowing what they say, nor whereof they affirm; first Coin feigned words, then contend about their Etymologies; thus fighting with a shadow themselves give being to, instead of seeking the Spirits of the Letters of the Holy Tongue, whence we departed by our Confusion at *Babel*.

Q. 97. *What figure is the Departure or bringing forth of the Children of* Israel *out of Egypt?*

A. 1. Man exchanged Paradise for the third Principle; the Substance for the figure or obscure Representation: and thereby his (till then) immortal Body became by the Contagion of the Fruit of the same like the Beast, an Accident, no longer a Substance.

Whereunto was added a Curse, that by toil and sweat he should gather his sustenance out of the barren Earth, which himself was near come to be.

2. A taft and earnest figure whereof was *Israel*, whose Males were either to be Drown'd as soon as Born, or Vassals as long as they Lived, which yet was but a figure of the best Life Man hath in this World, compar'd with that we departed from, and whereof *Solomon* writes his black and pale Characters, that it is altogether Vanity, and Vanity of Vanities, Vexation of Spirit, and sore Travel.

3. And whereas God tells *Abraham* his Seed should be in Bondage 400 Years, it is a figure that all Poor Mankind undergoeth the Servitude of the four Forms of the first Principle, and the four divided Elements.

4. And now the figure of their departure out of *Egypt* stands thus; As Man by falling into the third Principle stood with his Astral Man in the four Elements, and his Soul in the four Forms of the first Principle, which either murthered them at first falling to them, or kept in rigorous Vassalage till laying off the Body.

5. Out of which, a series of Miracles only could deliver: So Man can no more ransom or deliver himself, than these poor oppressed ones could by their own Power call down the Ten Plagues, guide their way, and divide the Sea and *Jordan*.

6. And the spoiling the Egyptians by borrowing and bringing away their Jewels, shews that God's Children shall carry out of the place of their Captivity under the first and third Principles, a Soul and Spirit wholly resigned to God, signified by the Jewels of Gold, and the Quintessence or Divine Tincture of the Humanity signified by Jewels of Silver, the Seventh or Lunar Property.

7. And that *Moses* the Son of *Amram* of the Tribe of *Levi*, one of their Brethren should be their Deliverer; hath this Signification, That God raiseth up in Man a Prophet

The 177 *Theosophick Questions Answered.*

Prophet of his Brethren out of the four Forms of the first Principle, blowing up his Light and Love Form, which is a fifth, as a Brother to the four, who becomes a Leader, a Deliverer as was *Moses.*

8 And whereas the Red Sea was no other of its own Nature but a hindrance to them, yet by Miracle became Defensive and Instrumental to their safety, by overwhelming their Enemy *Pharoah,* &c. hath this meaning, that Man's fragil fleeting, earthy Life shall be driven out of the way, as was the Red Sea into two Parts, signifying the parting of Man's Astral Spirit from his Elementary Body, giving open passage towards *Canaan.*

9. And whereas the Sea was on each side a Wall to them, and such a defence as overwhelmed their Enemies, it shews that their inward and outward Enemies can follow us no farther than to the dividing of our Astral and Elementary Man, but are there stop'd and over-whelm'd.

10. Spiritually also was the Sea and Cloud a figure of the Baptism, and we (that is) our first Principle is Buried with him in Baptism, in and by the Spirit of Holiness and Love.

Q. 98. *Why must* Moses *remain Forty Days upon Mount* Sinai, *when God gave him the Law?*

A. 1. To signifie a certain Proportion of time, wherein *Adam* was in the tryal or *Proba,* and the which Mount *Sinai* was a figure of Bondage, in which *Adam* enthrall'd himself and us all: which was often repeated; As, (1.) By *Moses* remaining once and the second time forty days in the same Mount. (3.) It rained forty days, then came the Deluge. (4.) *Esau* lived 40 years, then Married two Evil Women. (5.) *Israel's* forty Journeys in the Wilderness. (6.) Their being forty years there. (7.) *Goliah's* challenging the Host of *Israel* forty days, and then kill'd. (8.) *Eliah's* fasting forty days. (9.) Christ fasted forty days and was then tempted. (10.) Was forty hours in the Grave. And, (11.) Was forty days on Earth after His Resurrection.

2. This forty days stay of *Moses* once and again on Mount *Sinai* the Mount of Bondage, as the Apostle construeth, shews us that the whole time of Man's Life is a time of Straits and Thraldom.

3. And whereas *Moses* was twice on that Mount, and each time forty days, and did neither Eat nor Drink, it shews that Mankind was doubly distrest; that is, in his Soul by the four Anguishes of the first Principle, and thereby is kept as *Cain* said, lest whosoever that meets him should kill him, (viz.) in fear of Eternal Separation from God, it's true Life.

4. And by the second time of *Moses* remaining forty days on the Mount, is pointed us how also Man's Body is imposed on, influenced by, composed of, and subjected unto the four Elements; that is, to its rigorous heat and extream cold, oppressing and swaying it to Pain, Sorrow, Sickness, and Mortality.

5. So that hereby both Soul and Body are excluded the true Food, and detained in a place of Abstinence and Deprivation from the Paradifical Eating and Drinking, whereof *Moses* fasting was a Representation.

Q. 99. *What is the Law in one Total Sum?*

A. 1. The Lord Jesus teaching which is the First and great Commandment, saith, *Thou shalt love the Lord thy God with all thy heart, with all thy might, and with all thy strength;* and that the Second was like to it, *Thou shalt love thy Neighbour as thy self;* and that *on these two hang all the Law and the Prophets:* Again reneweth it, giving the

New

The 177 *Theosophick Questions Answered.*

New Commandment, that *you love one another;* and that *so shall all men know you are my Disciples.*

2. And our Apostle saith, *Love is the fulfilling of the Law.* But seeing the Law Rom. 13.10. was given because of Transgression; therefore to the restoring that Love which is the fulfilling of the Law, it is necessary we know what kind of Love our Transgression deprived us of; and how, and what an ill Bargain we made, that deprived us of that Love.

3. But to avoid Repetition of things, I refer to the 45th, 46th and 47th Answers; for should I give my self liberty to wade in this sweet River, it would be a Volume, and swell more deep and high, till it issueth into the Ocean of Eternity, where dwells that Love which casts out Fear, for Fear hath Torment. My Soul, for ever bless the God of Love, who hath Pitied and Redeemed thee.

Q. 100. *What were the Offerings of Moses? How was Sin blotted out and appeased through these Offerings?*

A. 1. The 79th Answer contributes largely to the Answer of this, to which this (1.) is referr'd. It is further answered, That the legal Sacrifices were of three grand sorts, viz. (1.) The Burnt-offerings. (2.) The Peace-offerings. (3.) The Sin- 1. 2. 3. offerings answering to the three Principles. The first, or Burnt offering consisted of four Kinds, viz. (1.) The Herd. (2.) The Flock. (3.) The Fowls. (4.) The 1. 2. 3. 4. Meat-offerings; figuring the four Forms of the first Principle. [2.] The Peace- [2.] offering, which was only of two Kinds, viz. (1.) The Herd. (2.) The Flock; 1. 2. signifying the two Tinctures Male and Female, United by Jesus Christ interposing the Peace of the second Principle. [3.] The Sin-offering, which was only of one [3.] Kind, viz. A Bullock signifying the third Principle, which is but one only, and that a figure of the inward Spiritual Worlds, and should only have accompanied Man as his shadow doth.

2. By these three Distributions, was the whole Man, consisting of Soul, Spirit and Body, offered up; and what had he more? It was therefore accepted, wherever heartily done, and sincerely intended; but the bare Performances had no Acceptation, as we see by *Cain's* offering, but a coming under the Lord's reprehension, as the vain Repetitions, and thinking to be heard for much speaking.

3. Such Offerings the Prophet compares to the cutting off a Dog's Head, and to Swine's Blood. Sincerity without meer outside Service and Hypocrisie is intimated by the inwards that were strictly charged to be offered, but the skin was the offerer's part; only in the Sin-offering it was to be burnt as the World, thereby signified, shall be.

4. As for Acceptance it is plain in the Epistle to the *Hebrews*, That it was impossible the Blood of Bulls, &c. should do away sin. But the Acceptation, Value, and Vertue was in the Sacrificer's Faith and Hope, Expectation and Affection to the one Sacrifice, signified by the Incense and sweet Odors offered on the golden Altar, v z. The true High Priest, offering up Himself outwardly once for all, and inwardly often to every one.

Q. 101. *What is the Ground of the Prophetical Prophesyings? By what Knowledge and Spirit did the Prophets in the Old Testament Prophecy?*

A. 1. In the Old Testament the word Prophesie is not always restrained to future Events, nor is it in the New; for as the Prophets Exhort to present Duty, Dehort from prevailing Sin, and on Obedience or Rebellion prophesie Good, or denounce Evil: So in the New Testament Prophecy, is understood in the same sence

(viz.)

The 177 Theosophick Questions Answered.

(viz.) to Exhortation and Monition, as we read: one Praying or Prophesying, &c. Also, He that prophesieth, let him prophesie according to the proportion of Faith.

2. But this Question intending chiefly things to come, we must know, There are two sorts of False, and two sorts of true Prophets; viz. First, to describe the false;

(1.) *The first sort of False Prophets.* (1). They are such as do Lying Wonders, and predict Events of Publick and Private Importance, going no farther than into the imaged formed world, the occult qualities of Nature and outward Causes and Consequents contracted to wonderful Good and Evil Uses, into which Satan can easily insinuate himself.

(2.) *The second sort of False Prophets.* 3. (2.) Such as have a Spirit of Prophesie, but not a Spirit of Holiness; such was *Balaam*, and such the Lord mentions, who shall say, *Lord, Lord, we have prophesied in thy Name,* &c. And these have their Water out of the Fountain, but receive and keep it in foul Vessels. God is so bountiful a House-keeper, that his Wine is given running over; so that some falls into such Mens old Bottles.

(3.) *The first sort of True Prophets.* 4. (3.) The Children of Wisdom, the regenerated holy ones, who live in God, and have their Names written in the Book of Life, having Divine senses opened. These Prophesies according to their proportion of Faith; for Love and Faith begot them: They prophesie of their own Death, which comes to pass for they die daily, they are Priests and Prophets, what they want in 'kill and Power they have in love to his Service. These as Priests and Prophets shall have boldness in the day of the Lord, which they wait for, being Children of the day: and are true Prophets, yet without that Gift of Prophecy this Question levels at; and yet of these it is said, the Spirits of the Prophets are subject to the Prophets.

(4.) *The second sort of True Prophets.* 5. (4.) Those of the Lord's Holy ones who are gifted by the Spirit of Prophecy, some more eminently, familiarly, frequently, and as it were continually, before whom the Doors of the spiritual World lye Night and Day wide open.

6. They as Watchmen see the contest of the Properties, and what weight of sin over-ballanceth the contra-ponderating Wrestlers: for the Magical Power of their Souls uniteth with the Universal as the Tincture of Gold doth with the Sun's Tincture, they as evidently see the Displeasure of the Almighty, as by Man's face may his delight or dislike of any extream occurrence be discerned.

7. This is so intimate, that the Lord saith he doth nothing, but what he tells 'or shews to his Servants the Prophets. For as there is but one God, and his Spirit is but one, and that Man is a compleat Image of the whole Almighty God, and having the Work of that one Spirit begetting in him the true Divine second Principle, he can as clearly (when gifted to this distinct office) hear and see the Power whence himself and all things are, as a Glass can reflect a Face; for all lyes in himself, though (like *Hagar*) we see not the Fountain, till God's Angel shew it, though it be (as that) in and before us.

For such a Man is as a well-tun'd Musical Instrument, the Sounds are all distinct, ready when ever the Spirit of God shall play on it. And the simile sutes well. for Man's original Numbers and Measures answer exactly to the Number of the Notes in Musick, which are 3 and 7, and not one more or less; and this Harmony is signified in the Harp, Organ, &c. used in the legal Administration.

9. And as Men are affected with the elevating of the Airs to Delight, and with the solemnity into seriousness, with the harshness into regret, and with the solid composure into excess of Melancholy, so ought all to be with the Lord's Voice in his Prophets.

10. To such it is shewn many times what time, place, manner and other circumstances may fitly hide the Lord's redeemed ones, if the Decree be not gone forth, for they see where, when, and how the Destroyer comes; by which such may escape, who are not to witness by their Blood, and be Crown'd with Martyrdom.

11. Some

The 177 Theosophick Questions Answered.

11. Some have been Leaders, as *Moses*; Deliverers and Judges, as *Samuel*, &c. And as a figure of the Heavenly Worlds concurrence and assistance to the Magical Vertue of the faithful Soul was the Oracle near the Mercy Seat, the Urim and Thummim, Ephod, &c.

Some have been Prophets for more private and particular Occasions; as *Agabus*, &c.

12. We are farther to know, he that liveth the Life of Jesus Christ, lives at the Fountain of Wisdom, having all the Principles and Properties in due subordination to the Divine Life; whereby he knows God, the Creation, Heavenly, Hellish, the Out-world and Himself.

13. Yet all this in part; he comprehends not that wherewith himself is comprehended, he seeth a part of every thing, but not the whole of any part. As a Mathematician hath a true distinct knowledge of both Globes which he can describe and measure, while yet he knoweth not fully that spot of Earth whereon his Feet tread.

14. And though the Natural Philosopher penetrateth much farther, and the Divine Philosopher deepest of all; yet how little a part know we of him even of things existent; how much less of Futurities?

15. And if *Daniel* heard the Angel praying, *How long wilt thou not have Compassion on Jerusalem, against whom thou hast had Indignation these threescore and ten years?* and if the Lord Jesus said, *of that day and hour knoweth no man, no not the Son;* which I submissively understand to be meant thus, (*viz.*)

16. Not the Son as he is the opened Treasure of Grace and Love of the second Principle; but the Father, that is, as he is the secret Treasure of the Justice and Vengeance of the first Principle. How very little and poor, is the utmost, faln Man's Race can attain?

17. But hence we discern that the Knowledge and Spirit whence the Prophets in the Old Testament did Prophesie Good, was by the Spirit in them opening those things out of the second Principle; and the Spirit and Knowledge whence the Prophets either brought Evil Denunciations, which should succeed, was out of the first wrath Principle, or by which they call'd down immediate Evil, as *Eliah* the Fire, was the same.

18. But that it might not as a Coal burn the hand of the Bearer, it was wrapt up in the Prophets holy Divine second Principle.

19. For as it is hard for a Captain who hath Personal Enemies in the adverse Camp to carry on his Force vigorously, and at the same time pursuing his Success, wholly lay aside the Sentiments of all personal private Wrongs: so is it hard for a Prophet to bring the *Turba* on others, without his own entring into it, either before, in, or after the stroak. How needful is it therefore that sinful men should be inhibited to revenge themselves?

Q. 102. *What is Christ of whom the Prophets Prophesied in the Old Testament?* The Seventh grand Distribution?

A. According to the constant design of avoiding Repetitions, the Answer of this Question is referr'd to the review and perusal of the 75th, 81st, and 90th Answers which laid together, are a compleat Answer to the present Question, according to what I have attain'd.

Q. 103. *What was* John Baptist, *Christ's forerunner?*

A. 1. The Lord saith of him, That among them that are Born of Women, there

there hath not risen a greater Prophet than *John* the Baptist; that is, in the Father's first Administration; nevertheless, *he that is least in the Kingdom of God, is greater than he*; that is, in the more clear day and Manifestation of Christ.

Mal. 4. 5, 6.
Isai. 40. 3.

2. The Lord saith also of him, *This is Elias which was for to come*: as saith the Prophet, *I will send you Elijah the Prophet*, &c. And *Isaiah* saith, *The Voice of him that crieth in the Wilderness, Prepare ye the way of the Lord*, &c. The same saith *John* of himself.

Let it be said, What is the Voice that crieth, and what the Wilderness wherein he crieth? And the Question lyeth open.

1.
2.
3.

3. 1. The Voice is not properly the Voice of Jesus Christ; for this was Preparatory to his coming. 2 Nor was it the Voice properly of the Holy Ghost; for his Administration succeeded that of Christ's. 3. Nor a bare Human Voice; for so much Power and Conviction was in it, that all men acknowledged him a Prophet; and his Baptism not of Men but from Heaven.

4. The Wilderness was not of Earth, Rocks and wild Beasts; for such are not prepared for Christ: But Man stray'd out of the Garden, is the Wilderness here meant, that was cried in and unto, to repent; because of the near approach of the Kingdom of Heaven.

5. The Voice crying in the Wilderness is the Father's drawing; as saith the Lord Jesus Christ, *No man cometh to me except the Father draw him*.

6. *Elias* in the Spirit of Zeal is *John* the Baptist's Antitype, figuring (as did *John* the Baptist more eminently and immediately) the Father's fiery Zeal, in the Holy first Principle; for *Elias* and *John*'s Administration was in the Father's Property.

7. The great Confluence of all *Judea*, &c. to his Baptism shews the Universality of the Father's Applications, Convictions and Drawings.

8. The reprehension of the Scribes and Pharises, calling them *Generation of Vipers*, &c. Shews the Father's drawings to Repentance to be not only general, but particularly in and to his resolved and designed Enemies. Also shews the rejection of Man's Wisdom and outward Formality, even in the true Religious Institutions.

9. Thus the Groans of Penitent Souls, and Impenitent Mens Gripes, the Mournings of the one, and the Stings and Horrors of the other, proceed from the Father's condemning Convictions; whereof *John* the Baptist's Ministry and himself is the representation.

Q. 104. *What kind of Virgin was* Mary *(in whom God became Man) before she Conceived?*

A. 10. The Virgin *Mary* was of low Estate and Degree, Daughter of *Joachim* and *Anna*, not (as such) wholly pure, as some feign, but came from faln *Eve*. Much less was she the Virgin *Sophia*; for the first *Adam* had repudiated himself and all his from that Heavenly Virginity, and gone into Adultery, into Lust.

Dan. 2. 30.
Acts 3. 12.

11. So that of *Mary* it may be said as *Daniel* of himself. *This is not revealed to me for any Wisdom that is in me more than in any living.* Or as *Peter* saith of himself and *John*, *Why look ye on us, as if by our Power and Holiness we had done this*, &c.

12. But though *Mary* before she conceived, was in Soul and Body such as other Daughters of *Eve*, who by the Regeneration were in the Holy Element. Yet to say what she came to be in, and after her conceiving, will fall under the Answers of the two following Questions.

The 177 Theosophick Questions Answered.

Q. 105. *Why must Mary be first Espoused or Betrothed to Old Joseph before she Conceived of the Holy Ghost?*

A. 1. An Espousal (of the sort here signified) is a solemn mutual Contract, between two of different Sexes, exclusive of all others; such was This of the Virgin to *Joseph*, a thing usual with the Jews: To which allude both the Prophet, *The Love of thine Espousals*; and again *Paul, I have Espoused you to me.*
The above definition hath these parts; (viz.) 1. It must be mutual, between two. 2. Of different Sexes. 3. Exclusive of all others. 4. Solemn.   1. 2. 3. 4.
  2. By this Espousal is signified; that the Virgin of Wisdom, the promised Seed, was Espoused to Man's Soul. This Virgin *Sophia* is the Tincture in the Holy Element in Paradise; viz. the Holy Ternary or Heavenly Earth.
  3. As the Spirit, or (as some have call'd it) the Soul of the Outward World, is to This Out-world and Elements a giving Mind, Sense and Virtue to the Creatures: Such is the pure Sophia in the Eternal Glorious World. The Soul and it, were as one, but by the Apostasie became two.
  4. Again, This Holy, Pure Virgin is Espoused to Man's Soul or Fiery Property, her self being of the Tincture of the Light World, and so were they of two Sexes.
  5. Also This Espousal is exclusive of all others; for the Soul must cleave to her, and not joyn it self to the first or third Principles.
  6. And the Solemnity is no less than that which either enters the Soul into the Life Eternal and Love Kingdom, which else is precipitated into the fierce Wrath.
  7. Now that *Mary's* Espousal should precede her Conception by the Holy Ghost, was,
  To shew what Infinite Grace did immediately on the heavy Fall: For Man even   1. ready to be devoured by the third Principle, and to devour himself by his first, is by this Espousal (the Covenant of Grace) stayed from the Abyssal Fall, which stop or betrothing must needs be now or never.
  That it was only an Espousal, and that before the actual Conception, was, to   2. shew that Man could not be entrusted (at least not yet) with so inestimable a value.
  To signifie an intermission or intervention of Time or Ages, to pass and occur   3. before performance of what had been promised; being, as the Apostle phraseth it, the end; viz. us upon whom the Ends of the World are come; as had said the Angel to *Daniel*.
  To shew what a vast distance Man had removed himself, that his Restoration   4. must be wrought by tract of time, as men creep out of Chronical Diseases, so that the time of Espousal was, as saith the Apostle, *My little Children, of whom I travel in birth again,till Christ be formed in you*;as till an *Embrio* mature to a compleatness, or a Seed to be a Tree.
  To attest the Genealogy of the Lord's Earthy Humanity to be of *David*. For,   5. besides the express, frequent, plain and full Testimonies by the Prophets and Apostles concerning Christ's Lineage, both Genealogies in *Matthew*, from *Abraham* for satisfying the Jews; and in *Luke*, to *Adam* for comfort of the Gentiles, do pitch on *Joseph*, wherein *Mary* is included; because none married out of their own Tribe, and consequently none Espoused out of it.
  The certainty of *Mary's* Genealogy is demonstrated only by her Espousal with *Joseph*, to keep humble that Sex, who being the divided Tincture,were first in the Transgression.

Q. 106. *How was God; viz. the Word made Flesh? What hath he assumed from Man?*

R   A. 1.

The 177 *Theosophick Questions Answered.*

A. 1. In the 75, 81, and 90 Answers, and in the 15 particulars of the 21th Chapter of the little Treatise call'd *Considerations,* &c. *on the Scope of* Jacob Behmen, much relating to the present Enquiry is opened. Yet it seems fit to say farther; (*viz.*) 1. That because Man's going into the third Principle, had subjected him to the Mortal Bestial Flesh, in the Wrath and Curse; if the Word had not assumed and been made Flesh, the Plaister had not been as broad as the Wound. The Elementary part; (*viz.*) that of the four Elements, must for ever have remained Captive in Death, and passed away with the melting and dissolution of them, into their Æther, without Recollection or Resurrection.

2. At the same instant therefore, of the Virgin *Mary's* Conception, the Word in or of the second Principle, was by the Vehicle or Medium of the Holy Element Conceived in the Light of her Life, taking her's, (*viz.*) our Eternal Human Soul and Spirit, or Light generated out of the Souls Essences, and both Soul and Spirit became as one in an Eternal Band with the Word, like as the Masculine and Feminine Tinctures unite in ordinary Conceptions.

3. In the same moment also, by the genuine Right of Nature, as the Divine *Lubet* of the two Principles breath out the third Principle, attracting the Powers thereof for their manifestation, and by the same immutable Law, as by which common Fire attracts Air, did This Holy Divine Conception call to it the Astral Powers and Spirit, and those (for their Associates) brought, as their house and clothing, the four Elements, being of the like necessity, as the Body of a living Creature follows the Head.

Thus the Word became Flesh, yet as incomprehensible not only to the Flesh, but also to the fallen Humane Nature as the Eternal Soul is to the Astral, or as the Astral Spirit is to the dead Earth.

4. But as truely as the Eternal Humane Soul and Spirit, the Tincture, the Astral Soul, the Animal Spirits and Sences, and the Elementary Body or Bulk compose and form one Man, so truely did the Word of the Almighty Son of God the Virgin of Gods Wisdom: the disappeared Image of the Heavenly Humanity assume and unite with Mans Humane Soul, Spirit, and Tincture, enter also into the Astral Vigor and Powers, also enter and assume the Elementary Flesh, and consecrat, circumcise and hallow them; and thus become one perfect compleat person God and Man.

5. The decay of the Lungs is hard to be restored, because applications thither are obstructed, their Porter so curiously guards the entrance, as that Air only may have admission; wherefore the Wall is sometimes broken by Inscition to send injections to the part impaired, tho' with great hazard.

But our Almighty Restorer hath entred the whole Man: every crevice and secret of Soul and Body is all Superficies, an open Field at Noon-day to the Omniscience of gracious Love.

6. When my dull Spirits a little penetrate this incomprehensible condescention, my powers yield up themselves prostrate, tremble and flame, my Soul finds himself as one living among the dead; it hath something to say and do which it wants apt Organs to express and prosecute. And if my obscure Soul find himself unequally yoaked, what a stoop did Infinite Goodness make to bear our griefs and take on him the chastisement of our peace, be as a Lamb dumb before the Shearers. Yea under the Mercile's Murtherers and Tormentors pour out his Soul? He hid not his sweet Face from shame and spitting, that by his stripes we his cruel Enemies might be healed.

Q. 107. *Wherefore would God become Man? could he not forgive Man his Sins without becoming Man?*

A. The

The 177 Theosophick Questions Answered.

A. The Minds of Men have been very apt to err about the Doctrine of forgiving sin, thinking it to be like verbal Remissions among Men, or at a Bar of Judgment.

1. One party pretend possession of the Keys of the Kingdom of Heaven by succession to *Peter*, who himself had no promise of them but as he was one of the Apostles, which when it was performed was to him and the rest alike: Yet still that Party plead prescription, and saying a form of words like a Charm, great sinners are told they are pardoned, yet probably by such who are often greater sinners than themselves.

2. Another party less gross in words, yet no less remiss in Practice and Conversation expect pardon of an Age of sins, by a Death-bed pretended sorrow, and words of hope and confidence in the Merit of the Lord Jesus without, any conformity all their Life to his Death and Resurrection.

3. Had the putting sinful Man into a Blessed state been so easie; Would the only begotten Son of God have taken our disorder'd Souls and vile bestial Bodies, born the Curse, fulfilled all Righteousness, encountred and been slain by Death, a shameful death, passed through a Sea of streights, grief and pain, exerted a Series of miraculous power? No, No.

4. Man was estranged from God, had lost his noble Image, was partly a Devil, and partly a Beast, it was then absolutely necessary he (who alone was mighty to save) should do all he did: Or Man was past any help, and all hope of Restoration and Pardon.

5. Therefore did God become Man, the Word was made Flesh to appease the wrath of the forms of the first principle, by inkindling Divine Light in them, therewith also was Mans Spirit (which was like a Phantasm, or like a foolish Night Fire) inflamed with Sacred Love, and Mans Astral and Elementary parts were Tinctur'd into a due Subjection to his more noble part as they to the Divine.

6. Thus the great Captain entred through Death to break the Gates of it, restoring the Virgin Image in our Humanity; of himself he saith, *John* 17. 19. And for their sakes sanctifie I my self, that they also may be sanctified.

The pardon of sin produceth a mortifying of self, a rising in a new Life, a sacrificing every Lust, a Love sickness to the Lord, a War with the Enemies, a Heart broken and melted, a new tender one receiv'd, this is true Gospel forgiveness.

Q. 108. *How was the uniting of the Deity and Humanity in this becoming Man?*

A. 1. God Created *Adam* an Image of the whole three principles, both first and third, fully illustrated by the holy second principle, yet was his very third principle of the holy Paradisical Element wherein was the pure, modest, chaste Virgin of Divine Wisdom vouchsafed to Man as his Bride.

But neither is the Virgin, holy Element nor Paradise God, but the Virgin is the Tincture of the Light, and the holy Element the Flesh and Blood of Christ, whence was *Adam* and the Angels.

2. These things foreknown, way is made to answer the Divine secret sought after in this Question, and requireth the Eyes of all the three principles as they stand in the Spiritual World: which are open in some measure in all the humble Holy Ones, but to others (tho great Proficients in Knowledge) if of Old *Adam* only; I am dumb, and these things are idle Speculations; they are lockt, bolted, sealed.

3. But to the Children of the Kingdom it is answer'd. The Deity united it self to the Humanity in the holy part of the Humanity in every of the three principles, (that is) in the holy Element, where his third principle in his Creation stood else could he not have rul'd over the siderial, had he not been in their Root; for they

they but Imaged the powers of the holy Element, and Eternal Nature, or great Myftery

4. We are not to be fo ignorant as to fuppofe the Deity took into union our Beftial part; for we fee in tranfmutation of Metals the drofs or ruft is not affected with the Tincture. The regenerate new Man feels while we are prefent in the Body we are abfent from the Lord.

5. The Infinite Deity or Heart of God the fecond principle of Love createth nothing, being himfelf the end of nature, (*viz.*) as out of himfelf; for he is the perfect *Summit* of all, yet doth comprehend all, penetrate all, only the perverfe will blindfolds it felf.

6. But tho' the holy Love principle or Deity createth nothing: As neither doth the outward Sun generate any fubftance out of its own pure Body but furthereth pre-exiftent Matter. Yet, becaufe Man had eftranged himfelf both from the holy Element and Virgin of purity, who was his Image, being the Tincture of the Light, as himfelf was the exprefs Image of the Father; therefore did the for ever Bleffed Deity (to the Eternal Admiration of humane Nature, and of the Angelical World) Unite himfelf in the holy Element (which is his Heavenly Flefh and Blood) and in the Virgin of Wifdom (the Spoufe of the Soul) unto miferable, fallen, blind, diftreffed Humane Nature.

7. Hereby meekening the rage and diforder of the darkned Soul, illuminating the unfetled Spirit and Underftanding, and Tincturing the very Siderial Soul, or Aftral Spirit, or Man: Extending alfo his Abyfs of Infinite Grace to the very Elementary Body. As *Aaron*'s precious Oyl ran down to the Hem of his Vefture.

Q. 109. *How did Chrift become Born of Mary to this World, without prejudice to her Virginity? How could fhe after the Birth remain ftill a Virgin?*

A. 1. This pure Virgin Conception may fhew all who are not wilfully blind, what *Adam*'s exchange of pure Virgin Love and Modefty for Luft (in the divided properties) was,

I refer to the 54. 61, 62, 63, and 65. Anfwers, ftudioufly fhunning recitals of things written in any of them, how pertinent foever hereunto.

1. 2. The Virginity of *Mary* remained intire after the Conception and Birth of the Lord; 1. For, it may be confidered that this moft admirable condefcention, was a work begun and perfected by Infinite Divine Love on the one part, and holy awe and profound humility on the other; more above wanton Luft, than do the Coeleftial Rays excel the foul Kitchen Fire, in purity.

3. Obfcurely figur'd by fome eminently holy Men, who were the Children of Old Age, fuch as *Ifaac* and others after long barrennefs. So was *Jofeph* given to *Rachel*, and others after Wreftling with God by Prayer, as *Samuel* to *Hanna*. And *John* the Baptift given to *Elizabeth* who feemed to be proverbially call'd Barren. Now in the holy Parents of fuch the wantonnefs of Flefhly Luft was withered, which in the Virgin *Mary* had not been excited.

2. 4. Let it be confidered, that the accefs of Increafe of Homogeneous Vertue and Power doth not nor can weaken, impair or leffen the vigour of the property it
(1.) hath; as, (1.) In a Houfe where burns a common Fire, the hot Sun and Seafon makes the heat more ardent, tho' that Fire lefs penetrating and fcaldirg. Or, (2.) Into a Room where burns a blinking Candle, or other fmall Light, a Beam of the Sun entring makes the place more luftrous, tho' that faint Light,
(3.) lefs luminous. And, 3. Pure Water poured into Water fomewhat foul, makes it not lefs, but more pure.

5. Thus the holy Element feeding the Life of *Maries* regenerated Soul, and in

the

The 177 *Theosophick Questions Answered.*

the same pure Element the Virgin of Gods Wisdom being the Tincture of the Light and Spouse of Jesus Christ. In the same pure Element with that pure Virginity of Gods Wisdom the Infinite holy second principle the Son of God took for an Eternal propriety the Essences of *Maries* Humanity, and did (of all) form one Divine and Humane Holy One, Holy Thing, Holy Child, &c.

And all this could no more detract or impeach her Virginity than the *Elixir* put into common Wine or Water, can debase and debilitate it, and decline it towards the disesteem and inefficacy of common cold Water.

Q. 110. *Why did Christ walk or converse Thirty years upon the Earth before he took or entred upon his Office? Why did he increase in Age and Favour with God and Man, seeing he is God himself; and needed no growing or increasing?*

A. 1. Infinite Wisdom saw Thirty years neither more nor less than necessary; wherein compleat obedience might actually be rendered by the second *Adam* to all the parts of the Righteous Law breken by the first, and all this before the Lord took his Office.

2. For in these Thirty years the ten forms of Fire in the active Life signified by the ten Generations beginning in *Sem* and ending in *Abraham* had their perfect work, three times; because as Man had miserably estranged his Life forms by actual Transgression in every of the three principles: So accordingly did the Son of God (who was now also the Son of Man) graciously travel with his (which were our Lifes forms) in and through all the three principles by the several steps of the ten forms of Fire in the active Life. *The Angels served Christ ten times.*

3. Bringing thereby the first, second, and third principles which were stray'd from the will of the liberty (as the first of the ten was figured by *Sem*) and introduced the Humanity through the desiring, anguish, and all the rest into the tenth (that is) into the Holy Flesh and Paradifical or Angelical World figur'd by *Abraham*.

4. Thus *Joseph* the Type of this Glorious Thirty years, (wherein were fulfilled all Righteousness) endured Bondage, and a Series of Sorrow, and when he was Thirty years old stood before *Pharaoh*, and was put into Office next unto him. *Gen.* 41. 46.

5. *David* also another Type of this, after passing many tiring hardships and almost invincible difficulties and hazards, was at the same Age of Thirty years Crowned King. 2 *Sam.* 5. 4.

This is represented again by *David*'s Thirty Worthies, and three more Honourable than the rest figure the years after the Lord took his Office.

6. *Noah*'s Ark and *Solomon*'s Temple, were each Thirty Cubits high pointing us these Thirty years. *Gen* 6. 15. 1 *Kings* 6. 2.

Now for answer to the second part of the Question, why Christ did increase in Age and Favour with God and Man, &c.

7. This signifies and points out to us his process and passing from one part of the Law of Righteousness which he fulfilled, into another to fulfil that; as the Ark was gradually Built, and the Temple erected Cubit after Cubit.

8. *Joseph* and *David* had first a youthful privacy, and then severe figures given them to bear; sometimes to be as it were given up and lost, and again, passing that, almost swallowed up of another. Thus also is the Christian taught to add unto Faith, Patience, Experience, &c.

9. The Lords process from state to state is the Epitomy of the Birth of the Eternal Powers; the liberty of the will floweth into a desiring, thence into sharp attracting, thence into anguish, thence into the Eternal Nature, &c. through all the forms of Fire to the 10th, or Crown and punctum of *Sol*.

10.

The 177 *Philosophick* Questions *Answered.*

10. As out of the Anguishes of the first principle, is generated the love and joy of the second which the Christian feels, and the searching mind sees in every (very) outward power.

Now for that the subsequent Questions will lead to inquire into the admirable process of the Lords humbling and emptying himself. What is written may suffice to this answer.

Q. 111. *Why did Christ suffer himself to be Baptized by* John *with Water, whereas he himself was both the Baptism and Baptizer which should Baptize with the Holy Ghost?*

A. This Question made, *John* the Baptist, adding, I have need to be Baptized of thee, to which the Lord answered, Suffer it to be so now, for thus it becometh us to fulfil all Righteousness; for the Lord of the Law by taking Mans fallen Nature on him, having so far made himself subject to it as that he must fulfil it, and that thereby he might introduce into the Humanity a suitable will of walking agreeably to it, found Baptism part of that Righteousness.

2. And yet in *Moses* according to the Letter, yea until *John* is no mention of it in express words, only the Apostle makes this Baptism to be meant by their passing through the Red Sea, and under the Cloud.

1 Cor. 10. 2.

3. Christ Jesus by taking on him fallen Mans Nature, took on him that which stood and consisted in and of all the three principles, and every of the three principles in the faln *Adam* were depraved standing in need of Baptism.

4. The first principle or Soul stood in need of the Baptism of Repentance from dead works; for Mans Soul had stray'd, imaging in it the dead Out-birth which is dead to it.

Mark 1. 4.
Acts 13. 14.

The second needed the Baptism of the Holy Ghost working Faith in or towards God, which was it *John* meant, when he said I have need to be Baptized of thee.

The third or Astral and Elementary Man of the Out-birth, needed the outward Baptism, which outward is as a Medium to the other.

Heb. 6. 2.

5. And we find all three in one Breath, orderly by the Author to the *Hebrews*, viz. not laying again, *&c.* (1.) Repentance from dead Works. (2.) Faith towards God. (3.) The Doctrine of Baptisms; thus stand the principles in the regenerate Man.

6. And as the Sea was the Instrument to cover the Enemy for his destruction, and the Cloud cover'd the *Israelites* for their defence; so the outward Baptism shews us the burying of the old Man, and the washing and arising of the new Man.

7. In the first sence we are defended from the oppressing disorders of the old Man shut up in the first principle, and in the other we are restored by the rising of the second principle in the new Man, which is the first Resurrection; teaching the Song of *Moses* and of the Lamb.

8. And tho' the siderial Man comprehend not what is done to it, yet seeing it shared in the disobedience, it is buried by the Baptism of Water: Seeing also it shall share in the Resurrection and Eternal Salvation, it must be washed in Baptism.

9. Thus see we why Christ suffered himself to be Baptized with Water, as in the Question is demanded, also why all his Servants under the Evangelical Administration are to do it, not only as a Litteral, but also as a Foundation Duty.

Q. 112.

The 177 *Theosophick Questions Answered.*

Q. 112. *Wherefore must Christ after his Baptism be tempted Forty days in the Wilderness? What doth it mean that a God-man should be tempted? And why must the Devil tempt him before he began his Works of Wonder?*

A. 1. *Adam* was tempted and fell in it, and his fall open'd a Door in the Humane Nature, through which the Tempter entreth; for his first principle is drawn by the Forms (whereof it is compounded) into an adverse will against the meekness and resignation, so that the Tempter entring the breach widens it: And the third principle, which Man Imageth in his Soul, is the Kingdom whereof the Prince of Darkness is a God.

2. The Devil useth the passive powers of the out-world, in themselves good, to his direful Machinations and other powers, which by their being separate (and in that respect) in themselves evil, are as Tools ready made, wherewith to exercise (as far as his Chain reacheth) fatal designs, to bring Tragedies on Places and Persons.

3. And all Men whose Intellects (the remains of their second principle) are confin'd in the limits either, of their disorder'd first or third principles, how politick, speculatively penetrating, seemingly wise, or rigorously superstitious soever, are all yet Vassals, Drudges and Ear-bor'd Slaves to the wicked one at his will.

4. But where ingenious Nature simply follows its own dictates, as undebauch'd Childhood or Youth, that Intellect is little serviceable to the Hellish powers, even as the outward Sun and Moon are little useful to them. Tho' at the same time the Spring that feeds that ingenuity derives from the first, not from the new Man and second *Adam* or Regeneration, nor is its Life from the Divine Light.

5. It is also too manifest that the Children of the day, in whom Christ is form'd, being immur'd in Bestial Flesh, propagated by Apostate sinful Man and Woman, and having the Tincture of their Souls impaired, lye open to the Tempter, and have great necessity of Divine aid, continually to humble themselves, pray, fast, watch, fight, strive, wrestle and use all diligence, lest they enter into Temptation.

6. Now the Lord Jesus taking the Humane Nature on him, did undergo the evil, and bear the load of Temptation, being one eminent part of his process for us; but the Tempter, not seeing the purity of his Conception; being quite another principle, too deep by far for him, might conceive hope of like success as he had against *Eve*, who was a kind of Virgin, and the Lord being made of a Virgin: But the Lord saith, the Tempter cometh, but hath nothing in me.

7. Now that the process of Temptation should succeed the Baptism of the Lord, teacheth us, that the New Man's Advances in the Way of Obedience, is a time of holy fear, care and humbling the Soul, it being the more not the less liable to various, multiplyed, terrible Temptations, and in that the Lord was tempted he is able to succour them that are Tempted.   *Heb.* 2. 18.

8. Why the Temptation lasted forty days is referr'd to the 78 Answer. Also why a God-Man should be Tempted is shewn above.

His Temptation must needs be of the Devil, or otherwise as from without, his Divinity and Purity exempting him from such variety, as we poor miserable Creatures are surcharged with from within our Souls and outward Man, and Objects of our Sences are as so many Snares, Serpents and Devils in us, about us, and waiting way-laying us.

9. And lastly, that all this must precede his working of Wonders and Miracles, teaches us the method of the Eternal World, also is manifest in all Created Existencies, viz. That from the anguishes of the first four forms should result the glory

ry, of the second Principle, or other three Properties. But I close here; because (if God will) that I live to meet with more of the dear, precious, golden, inestimable Contemplation of the Process of Christ, it may fall under the 117 Question.

Q. 113. *How was Christ in Heaven and also on Earth both at once?*

A. 1. Men may not think Heaven and this World to be so sever'd, as that Heaven cannot be said to be here, till the present World pass away; for though this World cannot be in Heaven by reason of its Impurity, yet Heaven is in this World, for it comprehends it, and is the whole second Principle; where-ever the Infinite God is in his Love, there is Heaven.

2. This understood, it must be acknowledged Heaven is in every Heart that loves God, but every Child of God is not yet in Heaven; for they are so present in the Body, as that they are absent from the Lord: that is, their love, &c. hath an allay of Dross.

3. But the Lord Jesus Christ, and also the first *Adam* before his Fall, were as Men, or in their Humanity in Heaven, for their love was perfect, and it must be noted, that the Lord saith not *the Son of God*, but *the Son of Man which is in Heaven*. I farther refer this Answer to the 77th and 108th Answers.

Q. 114. *Why did Christ upon Earth teach before the People concerning the Kingdom of Heaven in Similitudes or Parables?*

*Mat.*13. 34.
(1.)
*Psal.*78. 2.

(2.)
*Mat.*13. 11.
(3.)
Mark 4. 24.
(4.)
Mat. 7. 6.
Mat. 13. 13.
Acts 28. 27.
Isai. 6. 10.

(5.)

A. 1. We read, *All these things spake he to the multitude in Parables, and without a Parable spake he not unto them.* (1.) Adding, *that it might be fulfilled,* &c. *I will open my mouth in Parables*, seeing therefore the Text gives that for a Reason, must we not receive it as such?

The second is, The Reason the Lord Himself gives His Disciples, *To you it is given to know the Mysteries of the Kingdom; but to them it is not given.*

The Text also gives (viz.) *with many other Parables,* &c. *as they were able to hear it.*

The fourth is drawn from the Lord's warning and inhibition; *Cast not Pearls before Swine, nor Holy things to Dogs,* of whom it is said by the Lord, *I speak to them,* &c. *because they seeing see not, and hearing they hear not, nor do they understand.* Of them also it is said, *Make the hearts of this People fat, make their Eyes heavy,* &c.

2. Summarily then, the Children by means of their weakness were not able to hear it otherwise than in Parables, though to them apart they were open'd; and the Multitude, by reason of their Wickedness, were not worthy to hear it otherwise; because the proud Rejecters of God were inwardly devilish, and outwardly bruitish, and are call'd Dogs and Swine, to whom the Childrens Bread might not be given; for God resisteth the Proud.

3. Because Man was fallen into the third Principle, over which he should have been Ruler, so that the regenerate themselves were outwardly bruitish;and in their inward and best part were as young Children; to them the Gracious Lord vouchsafed to bow down, and as it were lisp, and to feed them with Milk.

4. For as much now as Man was gone out of the Unity into the Multiplicity, God of infinite Bowels follows him into it, and there teacheth him by the Earth, Corn, Fruits, Stones, Thorns, Sheep, Fowls, Ants, &c. Making them speak to him, pursue, convince and judge him, by the Good and Obedience of the very Oxe and Ass, gratefulness of the Earth for Rain, and Bounty of Heaven in the Seasons, and when nothing will do, he makes the Stone cry out of the Wall, and Beam out of the Timber to answer, leaving such, not only without excuse, but accused by

the

The 177 Theosophick Questions Answered. 135

the whole Creation. Neverthelefs, by thefe Parabolical Applications, call'd the foolifhnefs of Preaching, was Power found to fave them that Believe.

Q. 115. *Why hath not Chrift himfelf defcribed his Gofpel with Letters in Writing, but only taught and left it afterwards to his Apoftles to write down?*

A. It may be fuppofed and argued, who fo fufficient as the Omnipotence of the Son of God? Who could fo exactly difcover the Myfteries therein, as the Author thereof? Who could fo challenge and command Belief, as he who is Truth it felf? with the like reafonings.

1. But we muft know, that the Three glorious Perfons, have Three diftinct Operations, *viz.* The Almighty Father, or Infinite firft Principle doth Eternally beget and generate as his Love, Delight or Heart, the Eternal Son whom he giveth. The Almighty Son or Infinite fecond Principle is Eternally begotten every where in the Abyfs, giving Himfelf, who is the Light of Divine Life, having Life in Himfelf, is Himfelf the Gofpel written in the Heart; *Ye are manifeftly declared to be the Epiftle of Chrift.* 2 Cor. 3. 3. The Almighty Spirit, Holy Ghoft, or Infinite third Principle, doth Eternally proceed from the Father and Son, and Eternally publifh, propagate, figure, declare, image and manifeft the firft Principle and the fecond; alfo the firft in the fecond infinitely, through the whole Abyfs.

2. Thus was the carrying on, publifhing abroad, or profpering this wonderful Work of the Arm of the Lord to reftore loft Man, being like making dry Bones live, the proper operation of the third, not of the fecond Perfon. Therefore faith the Lord to the Difciples, *What I tell you in the ear, preach you on the houfe tops.* Again, *He that believeth, the works that I do fhall he do, and greater works, &c.* And faith, *the Mat. 10. 27. Spirit when he cometh fhall convince the World, &c.* John 14. 12.

3. Thus *Abraham* figured the Father's property or operation, giving his Son a Sacrifice, *Ifaac* the Son's property giving himfelf; but *Jacob* that of the Holy Ghoft multiplying firft into 12 Branches, then became as the Stars, and the Evil Seed only profeffing are like as the fand for multitude, fand for their earthinefs.

4. Thus as the Lord faith, *the Father hath born witnefs of me;* And again, fpeaking John 5. 37. of the Holy Ghoft faith, *for he fhall take of mine, and give it unto you;* not fixing Jerufalem only, *but the whole World with his Doctrine*.

Q. 116. *Why muft it be the very High Priefts and Scribes or Scripture learned (who taught the People) that muft fpeak againft or contradict Chrift; and would readily mock him, and condemn him continually to Death? Why muft not the worldly Magiftracy do it or the common People? What doth that fignifie?*

A. 1. The worldly Magiftracy expect Civil Duty and Obedience; their grandeur is their Idol, and having the outward Obeyfance and worldly Advantage, it fufficeth.

2. The common People expect moral Juftice and common Honefty, and finding that, are quiet; efpecially if no bait of Profit by Treachery offer to accrue to them.

3. Now Chrift's Difciples in imitation of their Lord (whofe Kingdom was not of this World) do fubmit to Magiftracy in all civil Concerns, grudge them not Civil Honour, and all the Profits they can reafonably challenge, and all this for Confcience fake.

4. Alfo to the common people, they give readily what commutative Juftice guides to, and have a propenfene's to more, *(viz.)* to be Good as well as Juft, to give and forgive, wherewith the common people are not only fatisfied, but
S (though

The 177 Theosophick Questions Answered:

(though in their tempers brutish and dogged) are often obliged to Peace and Gratitude. And as for Profit by abusing Christ's Followers, there is usually little; for the Cross and Poverty is their portion here, as it was their Lord's, and his first and eminent Followers.

5. Therefore though *Herod* on the Wise-mens Enquiry was by mistake afraid of Christ, lest the new-born King should supplant him of his Regality, the latter *Herod* and his Men of War set the Lord at nought; and what the common people did in their Acclamations against Christ, was by the incitement of the Priests, &c.

6. Now why the High Priest's and Scribes or Scripture-learned were Christ's cruel Persecutors, was grounded on, and proceeded from the following Maxims offer'd to Consideration.

(1.) The nearer one approacheth a much desired Object, the more hot and sharp is the Desire.
(2.) He of two Rivals for one excellent thing that misseth it utterly; his Desperation is Anguish at his own falling short, and Envy at the success of the other.
(3.) The contrariety of Darkness to Light, moves the Workers Hate of being detected.
(4) The Expulsion and final loss of the possession of an Ineftimable Good, is the highest provocation to Rage.

7. These things duly weighed, shew why the High Priests and Scripture-learned were the Lord's implacable Enemies, sharpest, hottest and most furious Persecutors, even to Death.

8. From *Cain*, the first False cruel Worshipper till then, Christ as Christ, Truth and Integrity met no such Adversaries (among Mankind) as the Apostates, pretending to the true Worship, and from that day till now, none so real haters of the humble Children of the day, as the Blind Zealots, making themselves believe they are doing God Service, by destroying those who bear the most express Characters of His Divine Image. They Kiss and Betray, and are muster'd by the Craft and Malice of the fallen Angels, and make up the Antichrist: concerning whom, I may not here enlarge, nor character him; because whoever God shall use to answer the 162 Question, will meet it as the only Enquiry there made.

Q. 117. *Why must there be such a way and Process observed towards Christ, with Mockings, Reproaching, Derision, or Scorn and Scourging before his Passion? Why did God suffer that to be so done?*

A. In regard none of the Questions past nor behind lead to the opening the whole Process of Christ as doth this, I may be permitted to digress by way of Retrospect from the present part of the Process, this Question searcheth after: yet not so far back as the Conception and Incarnation whereof *Jacob Behmen*'s Book of the Incarnation discourseth; as doth the 21st Chapter of the Considerations of, &c. But what is here intended, is only the Mysteries of His Infancy, Circumcision, and Flight into *Egypt*. 2 Of His Youth. 3. Of His Thirty Years Privacy, and then come to the present Disquisition.

Mystery I. 1 The Mystery of his Infancy, Circumcision and Flight, wherein we must see his Sufferings.

1. (1.) 1. *Privatively.* 1. His divesting, Self-emptying, deep humbling and becoming only as an Object of Compassion, Pity and Charity, as are Infants; figur'd by *Isaac*, who went as his Father willed by Submission, not by Choice.

(2) 2. His proceeding into a state of Ignorance or Nescience to be guided and guarded by others, who were to monish His Danger and prevent it from *Herod*. Particularly he was, 1. as wholly unknowing in the first Principle, viz. The Jealousie

The 177 Theosophick Questions Answered.

lousie, Subtlety, and Cruelty of *Herod*, and to ward that stroke, is fully resigned to the Father, by the ministration of Angels. 2. He was as wholly ignorant in the third Principle, *viz.* Whither to fly, and how to be furnished for the Charge incident to a Necessary Flight, and constrained Exile; unto which the Presents of the Eastern *Magi* seem to furnish *Joseph* and the Virgin.

3. *Positively.* His becoming Wretched, 1. By taking on him our naked, help- 2. (1.) less, shiftless state; for Man's Fall renders his Offspring the Epitome of Misery and Nakedness, more than the rest of the Creatures, who all bring their Clothing with them. 2. Wretched by Suffering, as was the Circumcision, requiring Patience, and the Danger in the Flight, requiring Resignation.

4. Thus this Child-like state, as it consists of Simplicity, Humility, Innocency and unspotted Purity, is the absolute Universal Refuge and Retreat of all that enter the Kingdom of God; as the Lord saith, *Except ye be converted and become as little Children, ye shall not enter,* &c. For the top of the Gate entring into Glory, is so low, that only the humble stoop so low, kneel, creep and enter, and none else.

5. We see a Child, a stranger to the griping Covetousness, Pride, Envy and Rage of the first Principle: So is the truely new-born Christian. It is also careless of heaping up; the Infant wills no more than the wants of Nature, abandoning superfluity. A Child takes no hurtful Impressions into the Mind, to enrage the Passions through the Doors of the Senses; but when the Countenance of things smile or frown, their Affections of liking or dislike, are disengaged and dead to them as soon as removed.

6. Thus are we taught to be, to praise and dispraise, to flattery and contempt; for the one must be as a Song to a Child, at once ended and forgotten, the other as the snarling of Dogs in an outer Court, which concern us not; for neither the Wrath of the first fierce hellish Forms, nor the lying Cheats of the third Principle are less dangerous where prevalent, than Fire or Water getting mastery.

7. Thus is the Infancy of this blessed Babe, such a Mystery as teacheth Divine living Doctrine, and is the impregnable Fort or Bulwark which Hell hath ever in vain besieged; for while we keep faithful to this holy integrity, our peace is perfect.

8. The second Mystery is that of his younger Years, or Youth; wherein we be- *Mystery 2.* hold and learn his Patience and Subjection or Obedience. The true root of Patience, is Humility; the root of right Subjection, is Reverence; and of Obedience, is *Love*.

9. Here may be noted, that never was Subjection, Patience, Humility and Obedience to Parents, and all placed over us, enforced by any so cogent and irrefragable Argument, as it is by this Subjection of the Lord Jesus Christ to them; *Luke* 2. 51. Even to *Joseph*, no otherwise His Parent than by Espousal to *Mary*: and that not for a short time, but a Tract of many Years, even after His being among the Doctors about the Business of the Almighty Father.

10. In admiration of this Condescention behold here! Oh my Soul, the only Son of the only God, the Soveraign of all Worlds; that He might pluck thee as a Firebrand out of the Fire of thine own kindling; content to burn Himself, that He might Redeem thee from dark Chains of Everlasting Vassalage, became Himself a Servant subject to His Inferior Subjects, because Man revolted from his Obedience to God; God obediently subjected Himself to Man. The Wisdom of God learnt Obedience by the things which he suffer'd.

11. Doth my Soul beg to know His sweet Name? Where dwells He, and who or what is He like? I am told He was like a Servant, no Thing, Creature, or World may be liken'd to Him; but that His dwelling is with the humble, many times in old Cottages and strong Prisons. And that one of His great Names is but a Monosyllable, *viz.* LOVE. S 2 12. A

12. A Name that calls for Love, and commands Obedience for the delight found in Love. That Heart therefore that reading and meditating this and weeps not, the heart that groans not, bleeds not, melts not, breaks not, flames not, is not the Heart of a true Man, but of a Beaft or a Devil Metamorphos'd into Human shape.

Myftery 3.   13. The third Myftery is of His Thirty Years privacy, the Types of which are in the 110th Anfwer; and in the firft part of that Anfwer is the Ground why Thirty Years was the due proportion of time for compleating actual Righteoufnefs.

- 14. El.e it may feem marvellous, that He who was the Light of this and all World's, could with-hold any of His infinite diffufive Vertue: Alfo, that feeing He was only the faving Light and Fountain of Salvation without whom the World perifheth, fhould conceal His Glory; His Omnipotence not being obnoxious to the Contagion of Sinners with whom He might converfe, which our impotence expofeth us to.

15. May we not on this occafion be warn'd to put a ftrong bridle and reftraint on our Tongues (the Herald of our impetuous Lufts) in our Applications to others? knowing how often it wounds us and others, and inverts the End for which it was vouchfafed us.

17. May I not hence alfo convince my felf, that very much of my Work is within rather than abroad, and that God's Holy Work with us is entirely within Men? for the beftial part of us is the Monftrous Image, got by departure from God, fo alienated, that all Communications and Approaches to it muft be Image-like, if intelligible to us faln Men.

17. And whereas the Divine Work is agitated in Man's fuperior part, it caufeth a departure from the brutifh Man; therefore was this of our Lord's moft inwardly a Sacred filence, privacy or fecrefie for fo great a part of his Pilgrimage in Flefh on Earth, wherein he was literally feparate from Sinners.

18. How crofs to this is the precipitance of our rufhing to fpeak our fuppofed Knowledge, and of unmortified Mens hypocritical Stage-Plays in Pulpits, and other publick Oratories?

19. How oppofite to this is our needlefs affociating (for Curiofity) with Company to whom we cannot do, and from whom we may not hope for Good?

20. How diametrically thwart to this, is that River of Thoughts, like fwarms of Locufts, which are uncontroulably allow'd to confume our precious Fruit, and thefe Thoughts are moftly generated in the ftinking Lakes of difcompofing converfe with beftial people.

Direct Anfw.
Myftery 4.
(1.)   21. Chrift's fweating Blood in his Agony was, when his Sufferings came to the breaking of the fourth Form, which is the Fire; for then did the other Forms feverally grow prevalent, furrounding him with Death: that ftate being fuch as Men mean when they fay the Heart is broken; for in the Heart is the Fire-life. All which did our dear Lord bear; becaufe *Adam* had enkindled in himfelf a Fire, which (had not Gracious Love even then interpofed and been infpoken) had foon devour'd him.

Myftery 5.
(2.)   22. The Lord was betray'd by *Judas*, his pretended Friend and Servant; for fuch feemed the Serpent to *Eve*. and by a Kifs, a fatal falfe Friendfhip of *Eve* to *Adam*; thus we ftill fall by miftaking Enmity for Friendfhip, perifhing for want of Knowledge.

(3.)   23. Our Saviour was apprehended and bound; for *Adam* (our Undoer) going out of the Liberty, was bound by the prevailing Anguifhes of the firft Principle, and Mortality of the third Principle.

(4.)   24. Jefus the Eternal Light was thus dealt with by Night; becaufe *Adam* went

out

The 177 Theosophick Questions Answered.

out of the Eternal Day into Eternal Darkness; therefore was the Lord carried to the Murtherers by Night.

25. Our King the Lord of Glory, was mocked, reproached, derided and scorn'd (5.) by vile Men; because *Adam* had introduced such odious shame, as made him the scorn of the Devils.

26. The Prince of our Peace was scourged, though the Innocent Lamb of God; (6.) for *Adam* awakening all the Properties, made not only the Essences to be inwardly Raging, but his outward Body (as that of the Beast) to be subjected to the Whip; which the gracious Lord refus'd not to endure for us.

27. The Son of God, Heir of all Things, and King of Immortality was Crown'd (7.) as if he had been a false King with Thorns; because *Adam* would in his Pride be like God, and wear this World's Crown.

28. And as all these were but Fore-runners or Entrance of *Adam* on the borders (8.) of Everlasting Destruction, whereinto he was plunging his whole Man and Posterity; so all these things were done to the second *Adam*, and meekly endur'd by Him before His Passion.

29. And all this was to make a plain and terrible Demonstration to all Mankind, (9.) that Sin unrepented of, becomes a Substance; crying for all inward and outward Vengeance for ever. See 25 Chap. of the Three Principles.

Q. 118. *Why must the very Teachers of the Law bring Christ to the Judgment, and yet must be put to Death by the Heathenish Magistracy? What doth that signifie?*

A. 1. That so it was, appears: Now to answer why it was so; Let it be noted, that Persecutions proceed not out of the second Principle, for in that all are United in Love and Meekness, nor out of the third, wherein Civil Magistracy standeth; for that of its own Nature (if not unwarily heated) persecuteth none: as is found in Christian Republicks, who have no oppressive Interest to advance or support, Persecution introduceth not its sting.

2. Nor in such only, but in the Mahometan Monarchies, is not Religion as such persecuted, but Conquests made for the greatning their poor outward Momentary Power. And this is found not only among the Turks, but Persians, under whom the Christians enjoy the rich and large Country of *Georgia*, and those Christians not leven'd and perverted with Idolatry.

3. But Persecution stands rooted in the first Principle, in which it is apparent how Brethren in Profession betray Brethren in Truth and in Deed; because they all consist of the self-same four Forms and part asunder only in the Fourth; for the Children of the day only generate out of their Fire-civine Eternal Light, and the other proceed no farther than the Fire; generating no other Light than a false one (viz.) as may consist with the false Maxims of the third Principle, a Serpentine Wisdom.

4. Thence is it that from the natural strife of those divided Properties and Rage of the Fire proceeds the cruel Persecutions; therefore the High Priests and Teachers of the Law with the unbelieving Jews were the Lord's bitter Enemies. As was *Cain* the false Sacrificer to *Abel*; for that *Abel* by enkindling the true Light, sacrificed his own Affections, Will and Heart, which *Cain* reserved, and so his offering was lame and disregarded.

5. Nor may it seem strange that the Teachers of the Law should be at Enmity against the Fulfiller of it: for they were only Ministers of the Letter and the Letter killeth. Thus Antichrist who succeeds the Jewish Priests in killing Christ in his Members, would bind the Children whom God hath made free, but cannot.

6. Thus *Ishmael* the Son of the Bondwoman persecutes *Isaac*, and would have been

The 177 *Theosophick Questions Answered.*

been the Heir. These if they can acquire Power in the third Principle destroy the Sons of the free Woman: if they cannot, they call the Civil or Military Assistants whom they mis-inform as *Haman* did, then stir up such a Fox as H rod, whose jealousie of losing, what the Lord would not foul His fingers with, prompts him to Cruelty.

But more particular might I have been here, would it not anticipate what will fall under the 154 Question concerning the titular Christian, and the 162 Question concerning Antichrist, by whomsoever God shall open their Answers, which is therefore here forborn.

Q. 119. *Why must Christ suffer and die? Was God to do it for such a revenge sake, that he might attone and reconcile or appease himself? Could he not otherwise forgive Sin?*

A. I have no reason to vary my often mention'd design of declining Repetitions; therefore must refer the Solution of this to the 107 Answer.

Q. 120. *What is the figure of the two Murtherers which hanged on a Cross on each side of Christ? And why must Christ die on a wooden Cross and not otherwise?*

A. Adam's terrible Fall was accompanied with dividing the Tinctures, as is manifest in the 43d Answer, which brake and parted him into a Woman, as is shew'd in the 65th Answer. And (as more links of that heavy chain) follow'd the extremities of Heat and Cold, as appears in the 50th Answer, agreeable to the separate Properties in the Tree of Good and Evil, discover'd in the 57th Answer. All which is made more obvious in the Birth of *Cain* and *Abel:* to every of which Answers, for laying open the thing sought in the first part of this Question, I refer my self.

1. Yet farther for Answer we must know, that *Adam* when fallen hung between the enraged Properties of the first Principle and the third Principle, as it were leaning on both, using the Out-birth to meeken the extorting Provocations of the four Anguishes. And having lost the Divine Vision, had his doleful abode betwixt Hell and this World: which is the thing figur'd by the two Thieves; the one whereof was forgiven.

2. Thus is it that Publicans and Sinners, signified by those of the third Principle, enter the Kingdom of Heaven before the Scribes and Pharisees, who (as in the 118th Question is clear'd) do stand in the Zeal and Wrath of the first Principle to persecute and worry them in whose Hearts the Day-Star or second Principle is risen.

3. Now that the Lord did die on a wooden Cross and not otherwise, was, That as the Civil Magistrate is God's Ordinance for Execution of vindictive Justice; as being of the third Principle, which third is the Instrument or Figure of the first and second, as is evidenced in the first part of the 118th Answer. So the wood of the Cross was of a Plant of the same Principle, by Eating the Good and Evil Fruit whereof *Adam* fell thereinto.

4. Therefore was it proper to be the bitter and Blessed, or Evil and Good Instrument, framed for the Lord's suffering Death, whereon in him hung all the three Principles, who, though he was Lord of Glory, yet like a patient Lamb for the Slaughter, bare this unexpressible Anguish, as if himself had been a Transgressor, to the pouring out of his Soul to the Death.

Q. 121. *How did Christ slay Death on the Cross? How came that to pass?*

A. 1. That

The 177 Theosophick Questions Answered.

A. 1. That Christ the Son of the Blessed God should Die, offends the Turks and Pagans. That He lived so humbly, and died so contemptibly offended the Jews; but the Proud lives of us Professors of the Name of Christ (we in the mean time believing Him so meek and lowly a Master) must needs offend not only Jews and Turks, but Christianity it self, and above all the Holy God.

2. What consideration can tread down Mans loftiness, if the looking on our crucified Jesus will not? Who can chuse but (infinitely rather than *Toomas*, concerning *Lazarus*) say, *Let us go, that we may die with him?* No less than thus to do, can secure us against the second Death; for he that is dead is free from Sin. Wherefore saith the Apostle, speaking of this Death, *I die daily.*

3. Christ did slay Death on the Cross with his Dying, by laying off the filthy Garments *Adam* had wove himself into, that is, carrying the Monstrosity wherewith the Souls Essences were charged, clog'd and immured as a Sacrifice into Death, and through or out of Death again into the Liberty of Immortality; as the burnt Sacrifices precipitating their dark Matter arose into a Radiant lustrous flame.

4. *Adam* made himself and us justly Debtors to Death, but the Lord not only discharged, but brought Death into his Debt, as at large might be shewn. He disarm'd it and takes away his Dominion, so that he reigneth over it: thus hath this Rose of *Sharon* perfum'd our Graves.

5. It is in the   Answer said we may as easily return the Sun backward over us, as change Nature's regular Motions of proceeding from a Seed to a Root, then a Fruit, and then a Seed, which Seed must first die before it multiply.

6. Wherefore it was that faln Man's monstrous Image was necessarily lead into Death, and the monstrosity left there before the new Image was raised; for the new ariseth by the falling off of the old, as saith the Lord, *a grain of Wheat bring-* Joh. 12. 24. *eth not forth much Fruit except it die, but abideth alone.* Thus came Death to be slain by the Death of the Lord of life.

Q. 122. *Why must Christ be nail'd to the Cross? And why must his side be open'd with a Spear out of which Blood and Water ran? How do these signifie in the Figure.*

A 1. Christ being nail'd to the Cross (a Plant or Product of the third Principle) shews us how we are fixed to the loading burthensom part of that Principle, whence we cannot dis-engage or free our selves, though being over-loaden therewith we should greatly desire it, but must patiently wait the whole time of our life till God shall do it.

2. And as Christ refused not His Cross, no not the carrying it, though the Burthen exceeded the strength of His afflicted wounded Body; for that one was compelled to help him to bear it; thus neither should faln Man refuse his own, nor help to bear another's Burthen.

3. And as Christ refused neither to be nail'd to it, nor did remove His blessed Body from it, but thereon meekly poured out His very Soul, and breathed out His Spirit, and was taken off by others; so will the regenerate Man spend and be spent for his God.

4. And as out of *Adam*'s Side (being rent open) went out a Female Property, which Wound (otherwise incurable) was repaired by the piercing Jesus holy Innocent Side; because as the separating the Female from the Male Property introduced so great an Evil, the Consequence whereof was Defilement, Misery, Lamentation and Wo.

5. So the piercing the Lord's Side was the opening the Divine Fountain, whence issued Blood and Water, that is the Virgin Tincture of Soul and Spirit, the holy Fire and Light, the first and second Principles in Inseparable Harmony, which

introduced

introduced that Good, *viz.* the bringing forth Righteousness, Salvation and sacred Love, wherein consists the pure Heavenly Virgin Image (that out of which *Adam* departed and died, or disappeared to him) the Bride of Christ, and Joy and Delight of the Eternal World and General Assembly and Church of the First-born.

Q. 123. *Why must Christ be reproached on the Cross?*

A. 1. One accounted it the Complement of Misery, when a Captive in much Torment beg'd his severe Governess (whose Slave he was, in old *Rome*) for Ease or some Mitigation, who was so wholly regardless as to be all the while Painting her Face: a Scene calculated very fitly to the present Mother of Harlots in *Rome* Antichristian.

2. But what is the anguish and torture all Creatures are capable of, if compared with this super abundant grief sorrow and load, the weight of a World of Sin pressed our Lord with. To all which, that (no part might be exempted) was added, that His blessed Eyes where Love and Mercy sate Triumphant, and His Prayer-hearing Ears must see the scornful gestures of Prophane Heads, wagging at Him in Scorn, not bowing to Worship Him, and hear the Taunts of vile and blasphemous Spectators: the very Passers by, and a Thief under Execution joyning to aggravate it. So was the 53 of *Isaiah*, fulfill'd in the 27 *Matthew*.

3. And what shall we say, was not the Cup bitter enough till cruel Mockings were wrung into it? but thus it was, that as *Adam* by the loss of his Innocence, purity and brightness, fell into guilt, filthiness and scorn; reproached by the Devils, by the first and third Principles, by the Sin of *Cain*, his own and the rest of his sinful Posterity, by every Essence, whence he fell, and every separate unclean Property into which he fell.

All this did He who hid not His Face from Shame and Spitting, receive as if it had been His own Due, and His own Procurement.

4. And into this Shame, Mocking and Reproach must every Child of the Regeneration submissively enter, and accompt it their peculiar Privilege to suffer their own Shame by the Lord's designation, we suffer righteously yet the Lord calls it a suffering for Him.

5. His reproach was *Moses* Riches and the Apostles Joy, His Chains are all pure Gold, but all the Lord's Children must remember that their Cross is fully as long as themselves; being the Principle into which they fell, and that they are nail'd to it. But though the Lord's Crown were Thorns, there is at the End of our light and momentary Afflictions and Cross, a Crown of Righteousness, and Eternal weight of Glory, coming by the meer, free Gift of gracious Love.

Q. 124. *Whether was also the Divine Power in the Blood, which Christ shed or poured into the Earth?*

Q. 125. *Why did the Earth tremble when Christ hung on the Cross?*

A. The latter of these Questions depends on the opening of the former, so that one Answer will suffice to both.

1. The whole scope of the Gospel teacheth us, that Christ was truly God and truly man; for that the Deity graciously United it Self to the Humanity in the Incarnation of the Lord Jesus.

2. We are also to know, that though God may be distinguished as into three, yet not at all divided; Seeing therefore that God assumed the Humanity and became Man; we may not after that Unity, divide Him from that Humanity which He United himself with, though we distinguish the Deity from the Humanity; lest we

The 177 *Theosophick Questions Answered.*

we seem to divide Him from Himself. What therefore *God hath joyned together, let no man put asunder.*

3. By the Incarnation of the Lord Jesus Christ He Himself, who is God Blessed for ever, became a God-Man, in an inseparable indiff luble Union. A d (a little to digress) the Human Nature of us poor Men is so strongly allied, espoused or betroathed and adopted by the same Incarnation, that it is most stupendious, admirable and ravishing. How can a poor Earthen Vessel bear the serious contemplating of it?

4. For were Man sensible how near God is to us (who as of our selves are wretchedness and vanity in the abstract) it must be with the re e erate Children as it was with the Women departing quickly from the Sepulchre with Fear and great Joy, and with others as with the Souldiers, they would be as dead Men.

5. But the third principle is an Eclipse to the prospect of the Soul awakened by the Sun of Righteousness, and an allay to their holy affecting Meditations, and is also a mitigation and flattering gilded Dream to the willingly deluded Captives.

6. And now to step back to our Work, we must say, that the Humane Soul of the Lord Jesus being of Divine Conception was inseparable from his Deity; therefore the Blood he shed for us Sinners had Divine power in it; for that Souls Masculine Seed was out of the Fountain Spirits, pure before God, as of the Eternal Divine substance of the Holy Ghost.

7. And as Fire kindleth combustible Matter; So was the Feminine Seed he receiv'd from the Virgin *Mary* (which was also our Soul according to which he is our Flesh and Blood, and our Brother) united and incorporated with the Divine substance, making one Heavenly Humanity in an indiff lub e Band.

8. Thus as a Child receiveth a Soul from the Souls of Father and Mother, so this Heavenly Humane Soul of the Lord Jesus, dwelling in his holy precious Blood, was one and but one, received from the Holy Ghost and the Virgin *Mary*. Therefore was it that when the Lord did shed his Blood for Mankind he is truly said to pour out his Soul; that Blood being the Chariot of his Soul. Also out of his side pierced by the Spear, came Water, the Signifier and Chariot of his meek, pure, Spirit of dear love and purity, as the Blood of the Soul united unto the Infinite Spirit of Love.

9. When therefore this Water and this Blood fell to the Earth, the Divine power being in and with it, caused the Earth to tremble, the Rocks to rend from their dark Coagulation, the Graves as Prisons to open. For the captivating power which the Salitter from the Fall of the Angels sustained, and was invaded withal, causing rocky coagulation, and the Curse and Death by the Fall of Man, casting the Earth into a deadly stupor and sterility; was as it were dismay'd, broken, enfeebled by the holy powers coming on it.

10. This could not be concealed; but as *Jordan* fled from *Eliah*'s Mantle, the Graves ceased to be Prisons, opening their Doors, the joynts and cement of the Rocks were loos'd, and they clave asunder, and the drowsie Earth awakened and trembled.

11. For as the wrath had shut up the Divine power in the Creation, in Death, in an inactivity or obscurity: So the Divine Love hath by his Conquest over Death on the Cross, with irresistible Might and Puissance, opened the Doors, broke the Chains, and proclaimed the acceptable year, leading Captivity Captive.

Q. 126. *What did the Darkness signifie, which at that time came over all Nature?*

T   A. 1.

The 177 *Theosophick Questions Answered.*

A. 1. The Root of five of the other seven Planets is the Sun, but *Saturn* hath a distinct Centre. Now the Sun is out of the Magical Spiritual Fire and Light World, and that Worlds Fountain is the incomprehensible power of the Fathers property, and the inaccessible Light of the Sons property. And the Spiritual World is figured, imaged, represented, actuated and expressed by the Sun and *Saturn*: Especially by the Sun as it were by a Nature God.

2. And therefore as if you stop the Efflux of a Fountain the stream ceaseth; or if the Sap be obstructed, the Fruit soon feels the defect, or if you withdraw the Face from before a Looking glass, the Glass retains not, but loseth it. Thus was it that the Out-birth of the third principle was over-cast, ceasing its Lustre at the instant of the Lords Passion.

(1.) 3. The things signified by it were, (1.) That as *Adam* departed out of the Eternal day into the temporary Darkness; so did temporary Darkness here shou'der out or exclude the day.

(2.) And as *Adam* Exchang'd a blessed repose, exact order, perfect peace, and sweet rest for a state of Enmity, Horror, Torment and Death: So now did the Lord enter into that Death, Enmity, *&c.* to pass us through into Life and Rest.

(3.) Again as *Adam* went out of the holy first and second principles in to the Bestial, separate, prophane Out-birth: so did the same Out-birth pass now into Death and Impotence, discovering it self thereby to be only a shadow, their Order and Beauty borrow'd and dependant wholly on the Internal World, and that no Creature, World or Angel hath a Self-sufficiency, so least of all hath this, which is but a Picture of Eternal things.

(4.) It also signified the wrath of the first principle invading the second or out-breathed holy Life, prevailing to the shutting up the Eye of the third principle. Yet that after three hours, *(viz.)* from the sixth to the ninth, *(viz.)* after a three-fold domination in and over the faln Humanity; the Soul, the Spirit, and the Astral or Elementary Man, making the Divine Man cry out and p'ead, that it also might not be forsaken;straightway upon a second cry and a resignation made,*(viz)* the second principles out-breath'd Image entreth Death and strook it dead; then the Internal Light figur'd by the outward riseth again.

Q. 127. *Why did Christ in his Death commend his Soul into his Fathers Hand? What is the Hand of God?*

A. 1. As previous to this Answer it must be enquir'd, 1. What may be understood by Souls in general? then what by this most holy one. 2. What various acceptation we read concerning the Hands of God? And come to the direct Answer.

1 *Thes.* 5. 23. 1. Souls in general are, (1.) Sometimes intending the Eternal Soul, distinct from Spirit and Body;
Levit. 7. 21. (2.) Sometimes it means the Body, distinct from both Soul and Spirit.
Jam. 5. 20. (3.) Sometimes it's understood of the Soul and Spirit, distinct from the Body.
Josh. 10. 28. (4.) Sometimes it extends to the taking in of the whole Man, as of the most ho-
Exod. 1. 5. ly Soul, Spirit and Body of the Lord Jesus Christ, who yielding up himself wholly unto his Father, was as a whole Burnt-offering. or Lamb without spot, sacrificed as the one alone, once for all, and for ever, intire Sacrifice and Altar also, and Incense, fully making Atonement and Entring once, and thenceforth Eternally into the Holy of Holies.

2. Thus as the true High Priest, he entred the most holy place bringing in a new Priesthood of another Tribe (*viz.*) not of *Levi* but of *Judah*; also another order, not

The 177 Theosophick Questions Answered.

not of *Aaron* but of *Melchizedeck*; by change of the Priesthood, changing also the Law, of direct necessity, putting a period to figures; as the daily Sacrifice the anniversary entring of the High-Priest into the holy place, but rending the Vail, &c.

3. Of all which the Epistle to the *Hebrews* (as that they were most immediately concerned to know) doth copiously inculcate and convince

2. What may be understood by the Hands of the Father here spoken of.   *Deut.* 32. 27.
1. Sometimes it means his Mighty Power, invincible strength, &c.   1 *Kings* 18.
2. Some times are sign fied by it his Infinite Omniscience and Omnipresence.   46
3. Sometimes are intended his most wise and gracious ordering and providence.   *Psal.* 95. 5.
     Acts 4. 28.
4. Sometimes it speaketh his most loving, merciful, careful preservation, and shielding of his Children.   *Psal.* 31. 15.
     Deut. 33. 3.

4. In serious view of all which the Fathers Hands whereinto the Lord Jesus Bequeathed his Soul, Spirit and Body, may not only be taken in all these Acceptations but an infinitely more vast comprehension than all Creatures, Saints or Angels can fathom or enumerate.

5. Now to the answer it self, be it known that the dear and only Eternal Son of the dear Eternal love of the Father, having given his Disciples and all his purchas'd holy ones, his peace for their incomparable privilege as the legacy of the Prince of Peace by Testament: To the end it might never be frustrated, ratified it by the Death of the Testator, gives himself up wholly at once, entring into death who himself was the Fountain of Life, and breathing his last cry and groans into the Bosom or Hands of his Ever-living, Infinitely loving, Omnipresent Father, and thus through death re introduced life into the Humane Nature.

6. And is it ask'd why? It is answer'd, Who but the whole Father could receive the whole Son? Who less than the Infinite first principle could receive the Infinite second principle? For tho' the Humane Soul as it was deriv'd from *Mary* was finite, yet as he was conceived by the seminal substance of the Holy Ghost it was Infinite, being wholly so united to the Infinity.

7. Behold, and sink down, and drown thy self, Oh my Soul, in the sweet Ocean of this free Master-piece of Matchless love, see the heighth, depth, length and breadth! Know what passeth Knowledge, Conception, Comprehension! Make thy Heart the Footstool of it, thy Soul a Sacrifice to it, thy Spirit the amazed Witness of it, thy Mind and Thoughts the Waiters on it; thy Tongue and Pen the Trumpet of it.

Let Heaven and Earth adore it, let Time and Eternity record it, let Hell and the Children of Pride tremble at it, but let the humble Man and broken Bones Inherit, Inhabit and Rejoice in it for ever.

Q. 128. *Why did some convert and turn again when they saw what was done at the dying of Christ: And the High-Priests not? Why must they be blind and hardened as to this Work?*

A. 1. By the High-Priests are meant him that was such, and those Rulers of most Eminence assisting and concurring with him. This Question is double, (viz.) Why some did convert? And why such as the High-Priests, &c. did not?

That some did as the Centurion, &c. *Matth.* 27. 54. seeing that which was done feared greatly, saying, Truely this was the Son of God, *Luke* 23. 47. 48. And *Luke* records, That the Centurion and all the people seeing, &c. Glorified God, and all the people smote their Breasts and departed.

2. For their dark Centre was terrified, then stirred by remorse and compassion

T 2   with

with and unto so patient and innocent a Lamb and that stirring, moving on by conviction to great grief, sorrow and mourning, begat love. and the love enkindled the holy Light of the second Divine principle, of which number it's said *Longinus* was, who with his Spear pierced the Lords blessed side.

3. But in the High Priests, &c. The dark Zeal had like Fire, drunk up the meek Water of Tenderness and Compassion, so that the Light could not enkindle, but they remain'd a dark Fire. For it is manifest they by their impetuous Lusting, proud grasping for Grandeur and Rule, and their griping after heaping up abundance of the outward principle; had by Covetousness like greedy Dogs or Swine, formed their very Souls according to the four Auguishes of the first dark Hellish Impression.

4. As Antichrist also (whose Forerunners and Antitype these were) hath done and still doth. Therefore to distinguish a resolv'd hardened Persecutor from the Creaturely Devils is thus to be done; that the persecuting Man hath on him the Bestial part of the Out-birth for mitigation, which is a Door, through which it is possible Grace may enter, unless the impardonable sin hath judicially wholly shut him up.

5. But the mitigating third principle excepted, (*viz.*) the worst part of it, the Antichristian Spirited Man having shut out the second principle; the Evil Angels and he are in one and the self-same principle.

6. It is also certain that the Antichrist, sometimes call'd the Whore, sometimes *Babylon*, sometimes the Mystery of Iniquity and Man of Sin, is as such, incureable and irrecoverable; for it is an Enmity against Love and Meekness.

The Art of Physick gives that Disease for Incureable which is grounded on the Constitution, the Disease of Antichrist is such, and therefore Incureable, for he is compos'd of the Enmity of the four forms of the first principle, and is Enmity in the Abstract, against the Divine Kingdom of Humility, Meekness, Love, Peace, and Divine Light and Joy.

Q. 129. *What was Christs going to Hell where he overcame Death and the Devil?*

A. 1. Great is Mans Misery on Earth, by reason of wilful blindness. When we hear of Christs going to Hell or overcoming Death and the Devil there, we blindly grope with our Conceits imagining in our Reason a local motion to a place far off. But that it may be plainly told what Christs going to Hell was; it must first
1. be orderly said, 1. What Hell is, and where? Which is referr'd to the 17th.
2. Answer the 19, 20, 21, 22, 23 verses. 2. What the Conquering Captain Christ is, that Vanquished all the Devils every where? It is answered, It was Christ as he had made himself a Creature; for his Body as a Creature is the whole holy pure Element, which comprizeth this whole World. The holy Body hath Heavenly Flesh and Blood, and Water of Eternal Life, which feedeth the Faithful Soul at the Lords Table.

2. And tho' it comprizeth this World, Heaven, Paradise, and the Angelical World, yet is a Creature, but such a Creature as can be every where in the Deity; for unto this Creature of Heavenly substantiality hath the Almighty Son of God espoused himself, as a Body to remain in Eternity (as in the time the Sun doth unto the Moon) as in his own Body. In every part of which Body the Trinity is always manifest.

Objection 3. But this crosseth the received Divinity, which assigns ubiquity to be the peculiar distinction of the Creator, from the Creature. Also an imposing

upon

The 177 Theosophick Questions Answered.

upon the Senses, that one Creature is at *London* and at *Quinsay* at the same moment of time, a thing denied to be in the Sphere of an Angel; whose Wings are only illustrations of his almost instantaneous local motion; implying he cannot be in two places at once.

Answer 4. The least divisible Body requires place and space; and magnitude is the uniting of two or more divisibles. 1. My Foot is not where my Head is, but I am where either of them is. 2. If my Head only is in the Air, my Body only in the Water, my Feet only in the Earth under Water, yet I am in every of these at once. 3. My Hand is at the Helm, my Eye on the Star, my Heart with my God; then am I at once in two Worlds. 4. Again, my Elementary and Sensual Man is in pain, my Siderial Man in care, the unmortified properties of my Eternal first Principle or old Man (or Root of the Soul) in much stubbornness, anxiety and frowardness, my regenerate new Man or humble meekened Spirit is rejoicing under the Cross in hope of Eternal Blessedness. Yet am I but one little poor Creature, tho' I am at once in one Visible and three Invisible Worlds.

1.
2.
3.
4.

5. Now tho' what the new Man sees or feels, hath or hopes for, meets with resistance in the unmortified part of the first principle or earthy Vessel, yet is it not so in Divine Bodies of Angels or perfected Spirits: Who all by prevalence of their consonance and uninterrupted holy will have their Heterogeneous parts swallow'd up by their lustrous Harmony.

6. All these things penetrated and pondered; shall our straitned Souls confine the Immense Heavenly Humanity of the Lord Jesus Christ? For his becoming Man or Incarnation wherein he assumed our darkened Souls, uniting them with the Divine Virgin of Wisdom, as one Creature in himself; did not straiten, lessen, debilitate or commit a Rape upon that Virginity, which is the Tincture of the holy World, according to which he was Begotten by the Holy Ghost; but it exalted to the highest the assumed Soul.

7. Nor was his uniting our frail Astral and Elementary, and Sensual Man unto the holy pure Element, any Impeachment to the holy Element, which (in the instant of the Virgin *Maries* Conception) was like a Tincture, blessedly put into our Body in him; but it was as the first Resurrection to our impair'd, divided, sleepy, impure, mortal Man.

8. For thus the Soul in the Virgin was taken into the Trinity, and the Body in the holy Element (which is every where present and evermore pure before God) was made Lord in the Heavenly World.

9. Yet is this whole Heavenly Man a Creature, tho' the First-born of every Creature, and is the Food of our Souls, neither is this a confounding the Deity with the Humanity of Christ, no more than the Apple is the Tree: Or the living Vertue of the Sun in the whole deep is the Sun it self.

10. This Virgin of Wisdom is the Image of God, the Delight of God, the Spouse of Jesus Christ and of so high descent as to be possessed by God in the beginning of his way, *&c*. Read *Prov*. 8 from the 1. to the 31. verse, but yet is not God or the Infinite Almighty Deity.

Thus see we how Christ was on Earth and in Heaven as Son of Man, or in his Heavenly Humanity at once, and is so still, and it is his Office to expel, bind, vanquish and chain all Devils every where, and reign in the Throne of expulsed *Lucifer*, to kill Death, and take away the Sting, for Hell cannot withstand him.

11. This is demonstrated by the Operative *Astrum*, particularly by the seven Regal Stars. See we not how *Saturn*, tho' most remote, is equally potent in coagulating, petrifying, giving weight, *&c*. as in Lead, Stones, *&c*. as if he were at the nearest distance. Also how *Mercury* in *Jupiter* causeth Sensitives and Plants to sprout up tall, *&c*. And how *Mars* Influenceth Men, and confines Plants, checks

Oaks

The 177 *Theosophick Questions Answered.*

Oaks to be crooked knotty, dwarfy Shrubs: And how calmly and serenely *Verus* influenceth every where, how the Moon asts Bodies, the Circulations and Fluxes of Blood, and the Tides which some call the Pulse of that Element. How also the Sun chearfully bears witness to himself. All these do variously work through all the Creatures within their principle (or as 'tis term'd, the Sphere of their activity) all at once in all places of all kinds.

12. And shall we straiten the sacred power of the Body of the Lord Jesus Christ in the holy principle, to narrower bounds than we can do the outward Sun which is his outside Image, which at once dwells in all the Stars and whole deep in every Creature on, and many under the Earth and in every piece of Grass.

13. It is demonstrative in the four Elements; the same Air fills all Crannies, and (with degrees of purity) so doth it the deep, as also the other three Elements in the Out-birth.

Only within or above the Firmament is another principle, understood to be a holy Birth, of which it were digressive to speak here.

14. And shall we think the one holy pure Element, the vertuous Eternal Mother of the more Impure, Prophane and Mortal four Elements, to have less vigor to operate in the holy principle as the Eternal living Body of Christ, than they in the drowsy Trave's of Mortality, for Productions and Dissolutions.

15. The like might be demonstrated by the outward principles of *Sal, Sulphur* and *Mercury* : And how they operate in degrees of Purity according to their several Subjects. And in a word it may be demonstrated in whole Nature at every Travel it hath: But it's better to be contemplated than exposed into many words.

Thus the Lords descending to Hell to overcome Death and all Devils, is evident not to have been a going a great way off, &c. but what and how it was and is effected.

Q. 130. *How did Christ* 1 Pet. 3. 19, 20. *preach to the Spirits ; which in the time of Noah believed not ?*

A. 1. Truth hath found worse Entertainment than the Lords seamless Coat; for some pretenders to it have rejected, what other pretenders have wrested. Thus as Man's wick dness makes him unworthy so makes it him unable, to hear the truth. But tho' we are justly offended at the fictitious Purgatory which Covetousness promps to tell of, yet we must submit to God in his Word ; all which magnifieth his Mercy and Goodness.

2. The Spirits mentioned by *Peter* were of those overthrown in the Deluge, which tho' *Scaliger.* * one interprets (expressly against the Text) to be the preaching before the Flood : The Error and Vanity thereof will appear, by the following Particulars.

3. 1 This Preaching was to Spirits, not to Men in the Flesh ; and certainly they 1. that perished in that Sort were Men living and dying in the Flesh. 2. The Text 2. takes notice there were of all that World but few, to wit, (eight Souls) saved which hath a serious consideration, like that of God to *Jonah* concerning Populous Nineveh. 3 It is said Christ was put to death in the Flesh, but quickened by 3. the Spirit : By which also he went and preached: It is not said that Spirit 4. by which Christ was quickened, went and preached but he that was put to death and quickened, went and preached. 4. The first World Imaged the first Principle and Real, *Jacob*'s First born Figured the first World. And yet *Reuben,* (tho' other infirmity are high'd of) was the only innocent of all *Joseph*'s Brethren of the Severity used against it only, which might open a Door to them, viz. the first World figured to second principle graciously inclineth to inlighten

the

the firſt. *Reuben* is alſo readieſt to reflect on their ſin againſt *Joſeph* in their diſ-
treſs in *Egypt*; for he was the firſt Worlds figure. a: *Joſeph* was the Figure of Je- 5.
ſus Chriſt.   5. It was to Spirits in Priſon not to Me that large, Chriſt when quickened from the dead did Preach; which the ſame Apoſtle explaining according
to this meaning ¦ faith, 1 *Pet*. 4. 6. For this cauſe was the Goſpel preached to
them that are dead, not living   6.
   6. The Apoſtle ſaith he preached to Spirits which were but ſometimes diſobedi-
ent, alſo telling us when, (*viz*.) in the days of *Noah*, while the Ark was preparing; implying they were not diſobedient at this time of preaching.   To this *Zech*. 9. 11.
ſence are refer'd the words of the Propheſie of *Zechary*.
                                                                                                Mat. 27. 63;
Q. 131. *What doth Chriſts reſt in the Grave ſignifie; that he muſt lye Forty Hours* 64.
in the Grave?

In the 98th. Anſwer concerning *Moſes* being Forty days on the Mount is what
may be the compleat Anſwer hereunto, to which this is referr'd.

Q. 132. *Why muſt Chriſts Grave be guarded with Watchers? What doth that ſignifie that the High-Prieſts ſhould reſiſt or oppoſe Gods Power and Might, and would keep
Chriſt in the Grave?*

A. 1. If it be clearly known what the High-Prieſts were, and what Figure they
bear, it may alſo be known why they would reſiſt God and ſtrive to keep Chriſt
in the Grave. And what they were and figur'd is manifeſt in the 128 Anſwer.
They were, as to their fiery Zeal, Captives in the Properties of the firſt Principle,
without enkindling the Light of the ſecond, which makes Men free: Their heat
(as to their Law) was rooted in Enmity, which is the true cauſe of all Perſecutions.
   2. For if they had been moderated by the Maxims of the third, as obſcure as
they are: Tho' the Divine Light had been withheld, and not enkindled, yet cruel
Perſecution could not, would not thence naturally have proceeded.   See 118 Anſwer.
   3. It is written, Caſt not Pearls before Swine leſt they trample them under
their Feet, which Swine are the Beſtial Men in the third Principle. Again, Caſt
not holy things to Dogs, leſt they turn again and rent you. Theſe are they of the
Wrath Principle or firſt Principle, whoſe Root is in the dark fiery property and
anguiſh of that firſt Principle. So that a Hog is better than a Dog.
   4. Whenever we are ſhutting out the Rebukes of God in his Providences againſt
our wilful Contrivances, or the Convictions from his Word Preached or written,
or the juſt Reproofs of good or bad Men for our faults, or the checks of our own
Hearts, and Gods Witneſs in our Conſciences; and would, by our partiality and
indulgence to our ſelves, flatter our ſelves, hide our evils like *Adam*, ſeek ex-
cuſes, ſtifle, ſilence, extenuate, or any way palliate the Matter charg'd on us, then
are we as thoſe Watchers keeping Chriſt (as much as in us lyes) from the Reſurrection out of the Grave.

Q. 133. *Why did the Evangeliſt ſay that the Angel remcved the great Stone from the
Door or Mouth of the Sepulchre? Could not Chriſt have riſen elſe out of the Grave?*

A. 1. This is the eighth Angelical Miniſtration to Chriſt recorded by the Evan-
geliſts, there being ten in all; *viz*. 1. To *Mary* before the Conception. 2. To   1. 2.
Joſeph concerning her. 3. To the Shepherds at the Nativity. 4. To *Joſeph* to fly   3. 4.
from *Herod* into *Egypt*. 5. To return on the death of *Herod*. 6. To the Lord after 5. 6.
                                                                                            his

The 177 *Theosophick Questions Answered.*

7. his Fasting and being Tempted. 7. Again to the Lord in his Agony in the Garden.
8. 8. This removing the Stone. 9. Two Angels in the Sepulchre after his Resur-
9. rection. 10. Two Angels at the Ascention.
10.

2. By reason of Mans folly and slowness of Heart to believe the great and important Doctrine of Christ's being risen, did it please the Lord to condescend this way to help Mans Infidelity, and confirm their weak Faith. And therefore came the Angel of the Lord and rouled back the Stone, and sate upon it, and there was a great Earthquake, and the Keepers did shake, and became as dead Men; for the countenance of the Angel was as Lightning.

3. There was no need on the Lords part to roul away the Stone; for his Heavenly holy Body (which entred to the Apostles the Doors being shut) could not be detained by the Stone of the Sepulchre.

For the Heavenly Humanity is not included nor exclusible by any thing, but passeth unapprehended through all things; being Lord of all, living in himself in his own holy Principle the Eternal Liberty.

4. But the poor Earthy Children of fallen *Adam* being Captives in the third Principle have need enough of all Gods gracious Condescendings to work Faith, and confirm our Confidence, a devout soud our hope; for which gracious coming was the glorious Messenger of Irresistible Majesty sent on this Errand. But so obstinate and great is Mans hardness of Heart, that all this and what so lower were needful to settle a Foundation for his Apostles and Martyrs to build their and our Faith upon: But for ever blessed be the Almighty God, that all his gracious Promises and Purposes are abundantly ratified and opened; for he is for ever the yea and *Amen.*

5. Thus, as *Adam* in the Face of good and bad (viz.) of the Holy and Hellish Worlds, fell into impotence into the Out-birth of the third Principle. So the second *Adam* by the Ministry of the glorious Ambassador of the mighty power World whose Countenance was as Lightning, and in presence of the astonished Souldiers figuring the Hellish Principle, raised the right Humane Nature. And thus also must we, if we will arise with our Head, be as Passives suffering the Lord to exercise all his Rights in and on us, with a resigned sense of our inability, wretchedness and vanity.

Q. 134 *What is the power of Christs Resurrection through Death? How did he make a Triumphant shew of Death on his Body? What was it then that he did with it?*

A. In the 45th Answer is shew'd what *Adam* was before his Fall. In the 69th Answer is what *Adam*'s Fall plung'd him and us into; and in the 111st what the death of Christ (and effect of it) is: Every of which three Answers being duly consider'd, will conduce much to the opening of this.

We come to search what the power of Christs Resurrection is, whereby he Triumphed over all opposite Powers and Principalities, and made a shew thereof in his Body.

1. The Fall and Curse brought wrath into *Adam*'s several Principles, (viz.) the four properties of the first into Enmity and Rage. Also so captivated, obscured and buried the Tran parency of his second Principle, that the Virgin of Divine Wisdom (totally disappearing) retir'd into her own Heaven, thenceforth he became wholly impotent and utterly dead to the Divine *Magi*, only the Siderial *Magia* did sit as Councellor in his Earthy Reason, whereinto the Serpentine subtilty can familiarly infinuate.

2. But so much of the Tincture remained in him as is inseparable from the several Existencies, and for the sake whereof, the very Out-birth of the Creatures

shall

The 177 Theosophick Questions Answered.

shall in their Idea's have a Resurrection, by Vertue of the Tincture in them.

3. His third Principle was also as wretched as its Capacity extended to; for the Astral Man was under a series of Evil, Cross Conjunctions and Aspects: The Elementary was brutish, degenerate and like the worst of Beasts. Where was now the dear, first, precious Image of Modesty, when he was now half Devil, and half Beast?

4. Of this fierce State and Death it is said, *O Death, I will be thy Death*; which is done by introducing of Life, and the Life thus enkindled is as the Tincture transmuting Metals, by feeding their hunger by such part of the vertue of the second Principle, which the hunger longeth after, and is capable of.

5. And the Divine Love-fire begotten and arising in the Soul, is the Soul's Resurrection, of which it is said, *Blessed and holy is he that hath part of the first Resurrection, for of such the second Death shall have no Power.*

6. The great Doctrine of the Resurrection hath had many Enemies (besides the Athenians) who laught at it; for the Sadduces amongst the Jews believed it not, and too many at this day oppose it, because they misunderstand that and other Divine Truths; so that may still be the Lamentation, *My People perish for want of knowledge.* They that said in the Apostles days *the Resurrection is past already*, were not (perhaps) aware that they overthrew the Faith of some, it being the same as if they had said *there was no Resurrection*.

Obj. 8. Some may say, Man having a visible, palpable, elementary Body, and an invisible, astral Spirit or Soul Author of the five Senses, at least that acts the Organs: neither of those parts can share in the Resurrection; for the Stars shall fall and the Elements dissolve. Let them tell me too, our Flesh is Grass, Dust we are, of the Earth earthy, and like the Beast that perisheth. If therefore the Syderial Root and four Elements return into their Æther, can the Products thence, subsist, his Body being dependant on a transient Principle whereof 'tis compounded. With what Body therefore shall he arise?

A. 1. 8. Christ had a visible, palpable Body as ours from the astral World and four Elements, though by reason of his being begotten of the Holy Ghost was infinitely Superior and more Noble; yet in his Resurrection was his Elementary also raised to Immortality and Glory.

9. The Apostle saith, *If the Dead rise not.* (1.) *Then Christ is not raised.* (2.) *Your Faith is vain.* (3.) *Ye are yet in your Sins.* (4.) *Our Preaching is vain.* (5.) *We are found false Witnesses.* (6.) *Those that sleep in Christ are perished.* (7.) *Our hope is vain.* 8. *We of all men are most miserable.* But therefore *that Christ is risen, and become the first fruits of them that slept.* 2 Cor. 15. 12. *Tour to the End.* *(1.) (2.) (3.) (4.) (5.) (6.) (7.) (8.)*

A. 2. If our Body (as far degenerate as it is become) had no higher Extraction than barely the astral World and four Elements, it might have no other Resurrection or Perpetuity, but be as the Beast: But how then was it to have endured to Eternity, had not Sin broken it? It had therefore its Root in the Eternal spiritual World, whereof the outward World and the Spirit thereof, (*viz.*) The Spirit of the great World are a figure and Representation.

A. 3. 11. It is relatively Eternal, being United to the Eternal Soul joyned to the Holy Body it obeyeth and beareth, suffereth and doth the Holy Will of God, as the Souls Instrument and Companion. And the wicked Souls direful confederate in all their black Machinations, beastly selfish Maxims and sordid Prostitutions; and therefore in both must have a Resurrection to receive according to their Works.

12. But the Bodies of wicked People are as a ready prepared Engine, whose every part is curiously composed by Exquisite symmetry, liberally oy'd to whirl as an *Automata* down a steep Mountain: whilst the Bodies of holy Souls are as a Bullock unaccustomed to the Yoak, or a lazy Ass to struggle through a narrow

U   deep

The 177 *Theosophick Questions Answered:*

deep way, with a leaden load, up a weary heighth. So that look how much of extraordinary Assistance, or rather violent Inducement, the Evil man's Body is to his Soul, so much perplexing Impediment hath the regenerate Child from his Body.

13. Infidelity suggests so many Improbabilities, as may make one Impossibility of the Resurrection, to which is opposed Omnipotence; Shall that Infinite Power, whose Hand gives Being to every thing and World, from the Angelical Thrones to the vile Insect, and Minute-parts of every pile of Grals, be insufficient to rally Man's dissever'd Limbs, number the Hairs, and not the Members, record all Mens Actions Words, Thoughts, and forget the whole Bulk and Fabrick?

14. As to the last part of the Objection, with what Body shall they rise? To this the Apostle replies, *Thou Fool, that which thou sowest is not quicken'd except it die,* and the Body which shall be (*viz.*) not the self same Grain, but the self-same Kind riseth, be it Wheat or any other. and the self-same Tincture in the Crop as was in the Seed, only our Corruption, Dishonour and Weakness is changed into Incorruption, Glory and Power.

15. The Sons of Wisdom can see the Transmutation of Metals. The Naturalist, the death, dissolution and reforming and vivifying of Craw-fish. The curious Observer, the Transmigration of the Silk-Worm. Every one that kindles a fire, the triumph of the flame, on change of the Accidents of the Fuel. The Physitian the consent of Bodies and Parts by sympathy, and of Actives and Passives. Who sees not the Loadstone single out one filing of Steel from a heap of Sand. The Plowman and Gardener see out of the dark Earth arise Corn, Fruits, Flowers of other colour, odour, taste, *&c.* than the Earth; yet acknowledge they the Earth hath all the Vertues, Properties and Powers of them obscurely in it.

16. Why then should it seem impossible, that He that raised up Jesus Christ from the Dead should be able to quicken our Mortal Bodies, though literally mortified when Death shall be swallow'd up of Victory; as saith the Prophet, *Thy dead Men shall live, together with my dead Body shall they arise; Awake and sing you that dwell in the dust, for thy dew shall be as the dew of Herbs,* &c.

Isai. 26. 19.

Q. 135. *What manner of Door hath Christ through Death opened in our Humanity, in the Anger and Righteousness of God. whereby we may enter into God? How is that done?*

A. 1. As it is not the Wind abroad, but that in the Earth that causeth Earthquakes, so neither could Man's mortal inward Wound be cured by outward Applications; for, because Man was become inwardly a Hell to himself, and outwardly lock'd up in the Curse of the Out-birth: wherein he had secluded and shut up himself from the Divine Light, as in the 69th Answer is discoursed

2. It was therefore past all Remedy, unless Heaven would mercifully introduce it self into the Soul in the light of his Life. Then did the gracious Principle of Love by bringing the Eternal Virgin back into the lockt up Humanity become a Saviour: Like as the *Fiat* or speaking Word did in the Beginning by the Light compose Order amongst the Confusions of the Properties of the Chaos. So the Lord of the Light-Holy-World came into the averted Will of the Humanity, and there imparted it self as a Tincture, being Himself the Omnipotence of the Kingdom of Divine Love into the Anger and severe Righteousness of God in Man.

3. Thus came it into Man's enraged first Principle, like sweet Oyl or Incense into a dark hungry fire: which raiseth it into a Radiant sweet flame and lustre. As when the Humane Intellect returned into *Nebuchadnezzar,* his bestial Image was exalted. So when the Divine, dear Love embraceth, and is enkindled in Man's angry fierceness, it potently attracts by assimilation some Divine Breathings,

The 177 Theosophick Questions Answered.

ings, and makes impressions of it self: As in *Esau* at his meeting *Jacob*.

4. The Door by which the Soul goeth into God is opened, as *Jacob* by yielding up himself, passed through a Death, appeasing *Esau*; for by this the Soul's bolted and barred-up Door, is unshut and set wide open. So that in the resignation, it lives one Life with Christ in God, and hath its passage through one Death with Christ to God, and is in the Resurrection thus begun, in one Spirit by the Eternal Spirit, the heavenly Flesh and Blood or Humanity of Christ is its Food, it is God's Body or Christ's Body, the pure Element and Virgin of Wisdom and Modesty is his Companion.

5. For thus his violent griping Astringency is sated by the Lord's infinite giving, yielding Power and Vertue, this causeth him instead of violent Attraction to be like a water'd Garden, breathing out his sweet Odours. His Anger and Rage is foil'd and kill'd by calm, serene, Meekness, Humility, Patience and Sweetness; His Envy by Love, which grows to a kind of Emulation to give, if it were possible, more than any Saint or Angel; yea, as much if he could, to God and for God, as he receives from him.

6. This Soul loseth himself; for he is not his own, but in an excellent sence is besides himself: as the Brethren of the dear Jesus said of him. and would have laid hands on him. This Door thus opened gives such access, that the Soul once and ever, and once for all, gives all, without the least reserve, and so hath nothing, and yet then and for ever receives all, and hath all for losing his own poor, narrow, miserable, beggerly all, he finds himself rich with Eternal fulness, which still he surrenders with deepest Humility.

7. But how can words export what the Soul cannot contain, or broken Letters express, what a broken Heart breaketh and melteth in the Contemplation of? How can the shallow brutish outward Man fathom, what the New and Spiritual Man is swallowed up with? These things are the matter at the time of Sacrifice; but what! it is always the Hour of Prayer, it is always the time of Sacrifice in this Temple. *Amen*.

Q. 136. *What doth the Pilgrimage or Journey of the two Disciples from Jerusalem to Emaus signifie, where they complained in Anxiety for their Master, and yet Christ walked among them, and enquired of them, and taught them: and yet they knew him not?*

A. 1. This Journey is fitly compared to that of *Hagar*; who by leaving her Mistriss *Sarah* was in great Anxiety, and then comforted and instructed by the Angel, and shew'd the Well *Lahairoy* and that both with respect to *Hagar*, whose hope concerning her only Son, was like to the over-whelming sorrow of these two Disciples: their only hope (being on the Lord's restoring the Kingdom) was reduced to a great degree of despair, distrust and offence at their fail'd hopes. Also with respect to the Angel appearing to *Hagar* at the needful time of her despair, and which is the first recorded to have appeared. So is this at as needful a time, and on a most important Exigent of Despair, and the first day of the Lord's Resurrection.

2. And now founding the Discourse by alluding to this Parallel, it will be obvious what signification this Historical Occurrence hath, (*viz.*) That as *Hagar* figured the state of Bondage, as did Mount *Sinai*, which our Apostle teacheth us, were an Allegory. Only by the way it may be noted, had not so good Authority expain'd it thus, but that the self-same Exposition had been made of it by a Modern Pen, though guided (in some measure) by the same Spirit, our letter Wise men would probably have call'd it Enthusiasm. So doth this Journey of the two Disciples from *Jerusalem* to *Emaus* signifie the offence of a Christian, quit-

ting Divine faithful waiting on God in any obscure Dispensation, when the Providences are too deep and high for their faint, feeble dull disquisition and reach, then they depart from *Abraham*'s abounding stedfastness of precious Faith to *Hagar*'s dry Bottle of Reason; but like *Cleopas* in Anguish say, we trusted this Man should have redeemed *Israel* (viz.) this or that should, or should not, have been, &c. implying their trust is expiring.

3. The Bridegroom was taken from them, now was the day of fasting and heaviness: the Shepherd was smitten, now were they scattered: This was the hour of the power of Darkness, such as God's Children usually meet with especially the beginners, who having tasted a time of love, think presently to have all they hope for; Dreaming of the Journeys end at first setting out, when contrariwise their Mr. is taken from their head, inward or outward. Temptations, perhaps both, like a Torrent sweep them downward.

4. Then are they apt and usually do let go the exercise of the Divine *Magia*, where Faith and Love support each other, and betake them to the Astral *Magia*, their own Reason, where in disconsolate anxiety, they shew their Hope is giving up the Ghost.

5. The Lord's joyning himself unto them, signifies such a time of recollection as is a day neither dark nor light: they are seen and that in mercy, but their infidelity with-holds them from seeing. It is neither Day nor Night, their Understanding out runs their Eye, their Hearts burn, but till farther discovery their fire gives little light, but in the Evening it shall be light; it was so with them, (viz.) when our Reason, the Issue and Child of the third Principle doth set, as when their Evening was come, then the true Eternal Light in Jesus discovers it self, breaking the heavenly Bread: and the same hour they return to *Jerusalem*.

6. But let all such offended poor Disciples know, the Lord may be with them while they are surrounded with Laments: let them stay for he will not tarry long, but if they wholly depart, they may lye down sadly 60 Furlongs from *Jerusalem*; as is too grievously to be seen in the Potent Eastern Nations: who are lain down under the Doctrine of Siderial Reason, their Regulation of the third Principle. As far also as the Western World is with-held by Antichristian Maxims, they feed upon Ashes, the Trash and fictitious Formulas's of the same third Principle joyn'd with the cruel Properties of the first.

7. And lastly, It must be noted, that by the Lord's appearing to them in their anxious state is signified, the natural Production of Divine Power and Glory out of the anxious wheel, the struggling of the four mighty Forms of the first Principle, as out of its natural Root or Centre. More might be said, but none will deny that which is said to be according to the Analogy of Faith.

Q. 137. *Why did Christ after his Resurrection first appear to a Woman, and not to his Disciples?*

(1.)   *A.* 1. More generally. (1.) To shew his Prime and Particular regard to a Soul excelling in Love to God, did he first shew himself to *Mary Magdalen*, to whom much had been forgiven, therefore she loved much.

(2.)   And (2.) it was to proceed in God's usual Method, who standeth not in need of the Wisdom, Ability and Excellency of Men to work his Designs, but doth it

(3.)   for and in Babes, and by them to and for others. (3) Again, to give preference to the Holy Zeal and Fervour, which excited by earnest Love is successful, passionately to enkindle Divine Light in such proportion of speed, as the heat is in degree; for great Divine Fervour having Anguish for its Root, hath always according to its own Nature, eminent Light and Glory for its Fruit.

2. More

The 177 Theosophick Questions Answered.

2. More particularly, (4.) To shew his immediate care of the feeblest; as tender Mothers do to their weakest Children : So here to a Woman. (5.) To demonstrate his gracious Condescention to the separate Image of the Humanity, divided from *Adam*, and first in the Transgression, like to the saying, *Tell my Disciples and Peter, who had so lately denied him, that it was as the setting of a dislocated Joint.* (4.) (5.)

6. To try the Faith of his most eminent Followers; who should first only hear (6.) of this glorious Resurrection once and again by the words of others, than after the sence of hearing, follow'd their seeing him; then touching, then tasting by their Intellect his heavenly Teaching, then participating of the Spirit by his breathing on them Thus became they Witnesses, not only of Christ's swallowing up Death by Victory, by gradual assurance past all shadow of doubt : but also be Witnesses against themselves of their own Diffidence, till their Faith was enforced to act its office by Mediation of all the Senses.

Q. 138. *Why did Christ after his Resurrection eat of the broiled Fish with his Disciples, and entred in unto them through a shut Door, and taught them?*

A. 1. The Text saith, *They gave him a piece of broiled Fish and a Hony comb, and he did eat.* The first part of this Question may seem curious as well as obscure ; but it must be noted, that all things God discovereth are not alike plain, but must be sought out by diligent search, comparing and inferring, as amongst many the offering strange Fire was not forbidden: but God consuming the Sacrifice by his own Fire, did by Consequence forbid the other, the Error herein cost *Nadab* and *Abihu* their lives. The carrying the Ark on a Cart was not forbidden, but *David*'s not considering and inferring a Prohibition of that by the Direction for carrying it on the Priests Shoulders, cost *Uzzah* his Life.

2. And now here the Lord after his Resurrection eats broiled Fish and Honycomb, as before he twice fee's the Multitude with Fish by Miracle, we may not think the Eating of Fish insignificant, and that again having wrought the Miracle of the great Draught of Fishes : after the Resurrection their Dinner was Fish. All which hath a double signification.

(1) 3. More general, That as *Adam*'s Fall had laid the Creation under Universal Disorder, such as was most aptly represented by the confused troubled Sea, and all his Posterity by Fishes, one devouring the other, as saith the Lord on this Allusion to his Disciples, *I will make you fishers of men* in this sense concerning the New Heaven &c. Viz. At the reducing to Paradisical Order, it is written, *there was no more Sea.* Rev. 20. 1.

(2.) 4 More parti'ularly, whereas Fish was never us'd in Sacrifice, and Honey directly forbidden to be in any Offering to the Lord by Fire, this, with rending the Veil of the Temple, as to shew the Jews the time of their Sacrifice was finished: But Men, signified by Fish, were in a more excellent way to be the Lord's, and the Kingdom of Heaven like a Drag Net to catch them. But their not considering this their gracious Visitation, and persisting in their obstinate Sacrificing, and wilful Ignorance of the signs of the times, cost not the lives of a *Nadab* and *Abihu*, or *Uzza*, but those of Priests and People, City and Nation, Desolation of *Jerusalem* and *Sion* Temple and Altar, and suppression of their supposed Offspring for so many Centuries to this very day.

5 Now as his Eating was Paradifical in the Mouth only, So his entring (the Doors being shut) was his being now only in the Divine Principle not to be shut out ; for the World is as nothing before him. The Condensations, fiercest Attractions, strongest Constringencies are all open High-ways to his Omnipotence; (5.) for his Conquest was over Hell, and he goeth into all the wrath of the first Principle,

The 177 *Theosophick Questions Answered.*

Principle, as well as the third, all Power in Heaven and Earth being his for ever.

Q. 139. *Why did not Christ after his Resurrection shew himself to every one, but to some only?*

1. A. 1. 1. By every one must be intended. 1. Every of those in *Jerusalem*, or
2. 2. Every of the Lords Disciples. 1. But so to have done in the larger sence had been cross to his own Inhibition, *Cast not holy things to D gs, nor Pearls before Swine.*
(1.) (2.) It had oppos'd the Method of his Proceedings with Men, from the time of his Conception to his Ascension. (1.) His Conception was a Secret imparted only to the Virgin after in a Dream to *Joseph*, then Prophetically to *Eli/ b th*, *Simeon*
(2.) and *Anna*, and Prophesies had Obscurities. (2.) His Birth was discovered to the poor solitary Shepherds after that perhaps above two Years to the Wise Men; but presently veil'd by his Flight and Absence. Thence no more is said of him till he attained to about 12 Years, and then, though the Doctors were astonished at his Understanding, yet they knew him not. Neither understood his Parents his Answer on that occasion, but he went with them and was subject unt o them, from that time till he began to be about 30 Years : So that for 18 Years nothing ap-
(3.) pears but as if he had been a common Child of *Adam*. (3.) Then the Observation of what passed at his Baptism, was instantly shrouded by his Forty Days with-
(4.) drawing from all Men, into the Wilderness. (4.) And after his calling of the Twelve and Preaching the Gospel, he often retreated from the Multitudes, divers times from some of the Twelve, and sometimes from them all, especially
(5.) for Prayer, and all this while, unknown to his very Brethren. (5.) And when his exalted Glory was so conspicuous upon raising of *Lazarus*, that the High Priest *&c.* began to say *the World goeth after him*; that it seemed to threaten the hindering the Baptism, he was graciously straightned to be Baptized with, and that they feared the People; then offered he himself up at once, checking the mistaken Hopes and Confidence of Jews and Gentiles. This was the Method of the humbled state of the Only, Eternal, Almighty Son of God.

3. 3. 3. The Reason of his thus much concealment was, the abuse by vile Man-
(1.) kind of the sparklings of his Glory; As, (1.) *Herod* begins by shedding the Blood
(2.) of Innocents. (2.) The Sharers in, and Beholders of his Miracles, were obstructive to his other work of gaining Souls; therefore he so frequently chargeth
(3.) Privacy on them. (3.) The Multitudes that he fed by Miracle, offered so much interruption, as to obtrude on the Eternal Soveraign of all Worlds such Advancement, as to be King of a Dunghil, and render him obnoxious to the silly Jealousie
(4.) of Earthy Kings, those Gods of Clay and their beastly Tyranny. (4.) The Splendor naturally arising from the Eminence of his necessary Evangelical Work, sharp-
(5.) en'd the Spirits of the Priests, *&c.* with Rage. (5.) We see with horror what the Obj. Effect of *Judas* knowing him was. *Objection.* But these are not significant to his Ansew. state after the Resurrection. *Answ.* Though the Objection be Digressive, yet then
(6.) consider, (6.) What use Antichrist makes of her Knowledge of this profound Humiliation, Life, Passion, Resurrection, (*viz.*) to be wholly solicitous in the outside, 1. Of Things. 2. Times. 3. Places, *viz.*

(1.) 4. 1. That the Things may be Figur'd, Grav'd or Painted, and those Products of Humane Fancy adored. The finer Antichrist Talks, Preaches the Things as a History: Believing which imaged History do flatter themselves to secure Eternal Blessedness, though they live and die unmortified, and in another Principle;
(2.) and propose to themselves (to wit) the third Principle and Self, yet Pride themselves with Words. (1.) Time, they devise for Idleness, Licentiousness and Prophane

phane Riotou[n]efs, call'd Saints Days. (3.) Places, (they hallow) of Affembling; (3.)
Confecrating ftone Wal's and Structures, and one part of thofe muft be more Sacred
than the reft, and name the Places by Saints Names, &c.
 5. Whether any of the Difciples during that Forty days had not beheld him is II.
not faid, therefore it may feem they all faw him; and why not, being feen of 1 Cor. 15.
above Five hundred Brethren at once.
 6. But there is one thing ftill to be faid, which may be read and heard of, but
not known by Human Wit or Art, or comprehended by Aftral Reafon, (viz.)
That Chrift had, nor hath more, nor fewer Witneffes of hi[s] Refurrection, than
thofe who were rifen with him, rifen in him, and he rifen in them; thefe Children of the Day witnefs his Refurrection, by his Voice to and in them, they know
his fhape and moft lovely form; for his true Image is in them; they Dine with
him, his heavenly Humanity is the Flefh and Blood their hungry Souls really, truly
and fubftantially do Eat and Drink, their fiery Property is allayed by the meeknefs
of his Living-water, they, as the Hem of *Aaron*'s Vefture partake of fome of the
Holy Oil poured on his Head.
 7. Of thefe things Man's fharpeft Penetration, without Regeneration and Mortification difcerneth, as the blind, finful, hardened Multitude would have done,
had they viewed the Lord after his Refurrection: perhaps to gaze or adore the
place they faw him at, but perfecute his Image never a jot the lefs. Or be aftonifh'd, as *Saul*'s Company were, feeing only the Light.
 8. This Refurrection is the fubverting, gaining upon and over the Diforders of
the four Forms or Properties of the firft Principle, which without the vertue of
the fecond, would image the third Principle in them, or Image themfelves therein, getting on meer Fig-leaves. But in fuch where this Refurrection is beginning,
though in fome it is like the uncovering of Fire; for the Paffions catch and burn
the more, being curb'd and put under a Law, yet light is the natural confequent of
that Combuftion.
 9. In another Form, Clafs or Degree of Chriftians who have made Progrefs,
this new life is more apparent, who yet fometimes by their Droufinefs their
habitual Evils return and foil them; for fuch are left a while as thofe *Canaanites*, as
Thorns and Gnaes to exercife their Faith Diligence and Circumfpection, &c.
 10. But in thofe excellent Souls, the fealed ones, where the Refurrection is moft
confpicuous, there (as in Torches or Candles) is little trouble intrinfically in
emitting their flames of light from any inward Defects, but their burthen and
difturbance is from blafts without, either of the Sins of others, which like many
bordering Vapours confpire into a Fog, to hinder the executing their Holy Purpofes (and bent of their Souls, to enlighten the Spirits of thofe they converfe with)
perhaps by Calumnies. Or elfe their crofs is from ftormy Perfecution to terminate their Courfe, or torment them in it; in all which they are with the fweet
Spirit of the firft-born from the Dead, to encounter Oppofers, and with unconquerable Patience to offer up themfelves, and abide by it, content to pafs through
many Deaths, be Partakers of their Lord's Entertainment, hold their Teftimony
and finifh their Courfe; for the day is breaking in fuch which may have Clouds, but
never fhall Night invade it; for it is the entrance on the holy, pure, Paradifical Life.

Q. 140. *Why did Chrift after his Refurrection converfe Forty days on Earth before he
went or was taken up to Heaven? What doth that fignifie?*

A. 1. This Queftion Demands, 1. Why Chrift converfed 40 days, &c. Alfo, 1.
 What it fignified? 2.
 To the firft, the Caufes obvious to common underftanding were, 1. To con- (1.)
firm

(2.) firm the Faith of the Diſciples, And, (2) To found the Faith of ſucceſſive Gene-
(3.) rations concerning the Reſurrection. (3.) To Leave the obſtinate Jews and others
inexcuſable.
(1.) 2. To the ſecond what it ſignified, (1.) That as *Adam*, in his time of tryal,
went out of the Eternal ray into the two Principles of the dark Abyſs and Out-
birth, ſo Chriſt now brought back the ſame two Principles harmoniouſly into the
(2.) Eternal Day. (2.) To ſhew openly in his Body (that was dead and is alive for
(3.) ever) the Victory over Death and Hell. (3.) To ſhew the Holy Paradiſial Life
which *Adam* ſhould have continued in, (viz.) The perfect Image of the Almighty Trinity in every of the three Principles; That is, how his firſt, illuſtrated by
the ſecond, was to be imaged and figured by the third, over which he was to
(1.) rule; (1.) By conſerving his Pure, Holy, Virgin ſtate as the ſecond *Adam* did.
(2.) Alſo, (2.) To Eat and Drink as the Lord then did thoſe 40 days in a Paradiſical
Heavenly manner, in the Mouth only, not with filthy Guts, &c. but as did the
(3.) Angels with *Abraham*. (3) To have comprehended and been able to paſs through
all the compreſſed or condenſed Bodies, irreſiſtibly, unapprehended not excluded
but as light through Cryſtal, penetrating all Aſtral and Elementary Exiſtences, as
the Eye of Eternity doth time.

Q. 141. *What is Chriſts going or Aſcenſion to Heaven: that he did viſibly aſcend?
Whither is he arrived, and where is he now at preſent?*

A. 1. This Deep is our World, here was the Throne of *Lucifer*, and in this
World or Space is our Heaven, yet not in this World, but in the Heaven that
comprehendeth this World; but this World cannot comprehend it, as Time cannot comprehend Eternity.

2. The ſharp Power and Omnipotence of the Father is the true Centre, as of all
Worlds, ſo of Heaven: and the gracious Omnipotence or true ſecond Principle,
is the true Centre of Holineſs and Purity in the whole Abyſs of the Father, and
eſpecially (if it may be ſo ſpoken)the Heaven of Heavens: who as he is the Mediator, the Chriſt, the Firſt-born of every Creature, is on the Throne, and is himſelf the Throne, ſitting on the right Hand of God; that is, at the place of the
quenching of Wrath with Love, he ſitteth in the Throne, and is himſelf the
Reconciliation.

Q. *Is it askt, what is the Kingdom, City, Palace or Seat whither he aſcended, and
where he is?*
A. 3. He is himſelf the Seat, Palace, City and Kingdom.
Q. *Is it askt how can this be intelligible to Mortals, living in Houſes of Clay?*
A. What is, and where are the Bounds in the outward World of the Light?
The ſhining Sun is its own Palace and Throne, it alſo is in the whole Deep in the
ſeveral Elements and Concrets, as far as any thing is capable of it; yet is it but a
Figure or Repreſentation of the true Eternal Son.
Q. It is ſaid, concerning his viſible circumſcriptive Body, which roſe again, and
was ſeen by his Diſciples on Earth during his Forty days converſe whom the Diſciples ſaw aſcend, and of whom the two Men in ſhining Garments ſpake, that he
ſhould in like manner deſcend, *Where is that Body?*
A. 4. It is anſwered, it is in its own Eternal Throne: But it is to be conſidered,
if we in our aſtral Man, can view in our Intellect the whole Globe of Earth and
Seas, and the whole Deep of the third Principle. And, were our more noble
part freed from the Images our Syderial Spirit frameth, what a view could it take
of the Principles and Fountain Spirits whence it all ſprung, eſpecially that which it
lives in, and delights in; as how much of the Eternal World may a glorified Spirit

The 177 Theosophick Questions Answered.

rit know; for the Child knows and seeth his Parents, and the Lords very outward Body was Begotten of the Holy Ghost as Masculine Seed.

5. It therefore such a poor finite Creature as Man (the lower sort of Intellectuals) who is the thing formed or building, can mount so high, and apprehend so much. Whither cannot he ascend, what cannot he do and comprehend, who being Conceived of the Holy Ghost, is the Builder of the House? Who, tho' he humbled himself to the form of a Servant, and ascended as such to shew he was our Brother, yet is Lord of all, and in his Heavenly Humanity is not exclusible of place, as Eternity is not excluded out of time.

Q. 142. *What signifie the two Men in Shining Garments, who said; Te Men of Galilee why look ye up after him: This Jesus who is taken from you to Heaven will come again, as you have seen him ascend or go into Heaven?*

A. 1. *Moses* saith, Out of the Mouth of Two Witnesses shall every Truth be established. And the Lord saith if he will not hear thee, take with thee one or two more. Thus in the Temple were two Cherubims stretching out their two Wings, and the Lord sent out his Disciples two and two.   *Deut.* 17. 6.   *Mat.* 18. 9.

2. The signification of all which is that when the first *Adam* by not acting his Powers caused the dividing the Two Tinctures into distinct Male and Female, which should have remained but one, Error and Falshood soon crept in; for the Two Tinctures were neither of them true, but Deceit introduced it self into both, because the true Virginity disappeared.

3. And the Two Tinctures were united only in the second *Adam* to bear one Voice or Testimony; for he Married the Humane Soul to Virgin *Sophia*. Thus the two Men in shining Garments bear but one Testimony: Hence was it that in Sacrificing of Fowl, the Male and his Female made but one Offering.

4. Also thus, as the Lord, who was then taken up into Heaven shall in like manner return again; so the holy pure Virgin *Sophia*, the Wisdom of God, and Tincture of the Light, who left the Humane Fire Soul of *Adam*, and withdrew from him into her own Heaven: But by the Incarnation of the second *Adam*, the same Eternal Virginity came down and returned again to the Humane Soul of us poor, unworthy, miserable Men.

Q. 143. *Why must the Disciples of Christ yet wait ten days for his Ascention for the sending of the Holy Ghost? Why was not that done instantly?* Here begins the Eighth Grand Distribution.

A. 1. It was, 1. To compleat the Antitype, being the time pointed at by the Feast of Weeks, which Feast of Weeks is commanded several times, (*viz.*) from the Morrow after the Sabbath of the Passover reckon seven Sabbaths is 49, and 1 is 50, (or the Feast of *Pentecost*) from the Lords Resurrection. At the end of Forty days the Lord ascended, and the Disciples were to wait at *Jerusalem* till the coming of the Holy Ghost, which was ten days after.

The ten days to make up the Feast of Weeks, was that they might be a secondary illustration whereto the seventh day or weekly Sabbath is suited.

2. Nine of these ten days points at the whole course of the Race of a Christian in this World, and the tenth is the Crown, Summit or Perfection. As the nine first forms of Fire are Crowned with the Heavenly Birth of the Paradifical Earth and Water of Life in the holy World, which is obtained by adding thereunto the tenth form.

3. This is figur'd by the nine Generations beginning with *Sem*, and *Abraham* is
X the

the tenth, in whose Seed cometh the Blessing upon all. In like manner find we Angels Ministring to Chrifts Incarnation nine times, and the two at his Afcention was the tenth. See the first Verse of the 133 Answer. So there were ten Lepers cleansed but one only returning with thanks, it is said where are the nine. Thus was the tenth day of their waiting the day of the gracious and glorious coming down of the Holy Ghoft.

Q. 144. *What is this that the Difciples muft wait and continue together till the Holy Ghoft came?*

A. 1. Will any say it was for their outward safety; 'tis true, obedience is the safe path: But this was of its own Nature most hazardous, againft *Jacob*'s method who divided his Family and Subftance to preferve fome, but this keeping them together was, as to Mans Judgment, an expofing them to danger; for firft an Affembly is lefs fecret than one, alfo more obnoxious to the Jealoufie of evil Eyes: From the confequence whereof they had no outward defence of their own, or Followers, or the People which fomewhat fwayed with the Priefts, &c. in their time of rage againft the Lord, whereas they were not entered fo far into their Miniftry as might promife popular refpect. Therefore their being together might be deemed by the Bloody Perfecutors of the Lord a fit feafon, at once to extirpate the Lords Sacred Embaffy and Embaffadors.

(1.) 2. Their waiting and continuing together was therefore an Eminent Touchftone of pure Love, and incomparable Faith. (1.) In refpect of their Work which was to witnefs, what the Lord was Crucified for acknowledging, (viz.) that himfelf was the Son of God.

(2.) 3. (2.) In refpect of the place, *Jerufalem*, the ftage where the Shepherd was fmitten, where the Murtherers were Rulers, whofe Streets lately Confecrated with the holy Lord's walks, Miracles and Heavenly Doctrines: The Temple where he had often fpoken like God, not like Man: Where was a Garden which he had often frequented: The Judgment Hall, where he had been reviled, crown'd with Thorns, mocked, fcourged and condemned: Alfo *Calvary* where they mercilefly crucified Mercy it felf, remained all Monuments of the greateft Love and Patience, and extream Malice and ferine Cruelty: In this City which fhould have worn Sackcloth, with thefe fad Objects and under thefe Rulers were they to dwell and be confined.

(3.) 4. (3.) With refpect to the time, being that of the Bridegrooms being taken from them, of their having Tribulation ten days, the time when their Enemies were Flefht, by having their Hands Embrewed in the Blood of the Lord Jefus: As cruel wild Beafts tafting the Blood of their prey, and the time before defcending of power from on high to revive them.

5 But they muft wait on this fervice, in this place, at this time, fignifying to us that the time of the Chriftians Life is the exercife of Faith, Obedience and Trial of the fincerity of Love; a time of beholding fad Objects as was this of theirs, of hearing finful founds, the being haraffed by Oppreffive Rulers, converfe with or amongft malicious, enfnaring, dangerous Enemies, inward Terrors and Tempefts, and outward Storms and Outrages from the powers of the dark World.

6. So that the diftreffed Soul can find no fuccour or guidance from the Imaged Powers of the outward Aftral World, but muft fink down from them, and conftantly wait the Breathings of the true fpeaking Light World, left if the outward *Magia* be our level defign and home, the dark *Magus* do by it infinuate into us, and we thereby form the will of the Spirit of this World into our Eternal Souls, which neither can feed them, cloth them, nor guide them, but if thus they proceed

The 177 Theosophick Questions Answered.

ceed till the four Elements fall off, they shall find themselves miserably cheated. This waiting of the Apostles directs us therefore, to wait for the Whispers of the Word behind us, so call'd; we having gone out from it, and turn'd our Backs on it.

Q. 145. *What is the Feast of Pentecost? How was the shedding or pouring forth of the Holy Ghost effected? And how did the Bands of the Tongues of the Lords Disciples become unloosed?*

A. 1. Our Fall in *Adam* brought us from the Paradisical Feasting to the toilsom Life, to a state affording no other Food for the four properties of our first Principle (which was the Centre of the Soul) but the third Principle: Which is rightly a feeding on Ashes and a Shadow. If Men can live by looking on their own Picture, so might *Adam's* Soul by the third Principle. It was worse with him than it is with an Elementary Body who can subsist a little while by feeding on it self.

2. Now the Feast of *Pentecost* was bringing back through the Lords Incarnation the vertue of the holy World, (viz.) the Paradisical Bread and Water of Life, for the Soul to feast on: The true Flesh and Blood of Christs Heavenly Humanity, this pure Water of Meekness is in the Soul a Well of Living Water, springing up to Eternal Life.

3. The pouring forth of the Holy Ghost was thus effected; The Darkness into which the Soul had cast it self caused a violent anguish, that anguish of its own Nature generates a fierce hungry Fire. And higher than this the Humane Soul of its own ability since its Captivity goeth not. Now such Souls as can get no satiety in the Spirit of their will from God, but go to the third Principle, do as *Saul* who waited not for *Samuel*, but considering his streights Offered a Burnt-offering himself, and so lost the Kingdom. *1 Sam. 13. 6.*

But so did not the Lords Disciples, for they waited till the Lord came. Where is he that learneth the lesson this Mystery unfoldeth? He shall hear and understand the things which none of the divided Languages can possibly express, and sometimes may see and penetrate what it is not lawful to utter.

4. Pluck out the Earthy guessing and pretended seeing, stop the Ear against the delusive Charmer, then shall not the outward Reason (like the Sun) dazle, nor Thunder, or the roaring of the Sea amuse; the raging Waves shall be countermanded, and thy Ark will be in inward Tranquillity.

5. The pouring out of the Holy Ghost did enkindle the Souls Anguish and Fire into a Light and Divine serenity of meek Love. Now as the blinking Lamp flaming from a small spark, enlighteneth a little Room, and the greater Fire of a Torch yields a more eminent Lustre: So the greater the Anguish the greater the Fire, and the greater also is the Light, when the Lord enkindles it to a Love flame, that according to its exalted vivacity it be proportionably as it were Tinctured, reaching hard after the Resurrection from the dead.

6. Now were the Bands of their Tongues unloosed by their opening the power World in this World; for by how much we are by wrath and death Captivated, by so much are we impotent: But where the Spirit of God unites with Mans Spirit it frees him from all restrictive Ligaments, that with the Word there may be power. But the following Question treating of this Subject, more is not here said to this third Branch.

X 2   Q. 146.

The 177 Theosophick Questions Answered.

Q. 146. *How is the difference or distinction of Languages among them to be understood; that they have all at one irst int spoken all Languages at once in one sence; so that people of all Nations understood them?*

A. 1. Man's Fall cast him from the unity into the multiplicity: Before which Fall he stood in the one holy power; his Word being in God, was by his Almightiness Mighty, ruling in, through and over the multiplicity, his Words were as many Arrows in a Quiver, penetrating all things: As the Arrow out of a Bow of Steel doth the Air. But Mans Fall into the multiplicity, disarm'd him, render'd him impotent, only some have a little power to see into one property, some into another, but were all Mens Abilities united, it were but some pieces of the multiplicity far short of the Unity.

2. Man is an Image of the whole Trinity, and the Astral and Elementary Worlds Image, Heavenly Things and Places, while Man therefore kept his station he was in the Divine Centre, but his departure thence dejected him into the circumference, Wheel of Nature or Out-birth, thenceforth was the Centre or Holy Fountain hid.

3. The Lord Jesus Christ as he is the only Begotten Son of God, is the Eternal speaking Word, which may be understood to be Eternally generated out of the Eternal Father, or first Principle, as our four Forms or Anguishes generate naturally the Liberty or Light which is call'd the fifth. This is the first Word the creating speaking holy Word from Eternity, 1 *John* 1, 2, 3.

4. The next is the created Word the holy World, wherein the Almighty Word doth through the Virgin of Divine Wisdom Image himself. It may be compared to a holy Eternal Book, whereof the Angels are Golden Letters, founded in Divine Harmony: In which Book the Almighty with delight reads his own glorious ineffable, tremendous Name.

5. But *Lucifer* making an harsh jarring Tone, and changing his Golden Letters into black of poysonous composition, raced himself and his whole Hierarchy out of that fair Record. Then did the creating Word speak or incert, and interline Man into that part of the Book out of which *Lucifer* and his Angels had been raced, which with the additional skill of Interliners had the Out-principle as an adjunct to him, this was the second race of Intellectuals.

6. And tho' the skill of the speaking Word were perfect, yet as usually it is in Interlinings, the obliterated Letters had left some flaws or scratches (tho' not in the holy Book, yet) in the adjunct, shadower or cover. (*viz.*) the Out-birth, which being new bound and the lacerated pieces cemented; in the cover rested such stains and rents, that thereof came the perillous, poysonous, stinging Animals and Vegetables, and Beasts of prey bearing the impressions of the clauses of the dark World.

7. Whereinto when Man fell their contagion so affected him, that he could not sound a due consonance to the Harmonious Dialect of the Holy Book, which as to him became so close and sealed that he could not read, open, nor so much as look thereon. But as Men Illiterate cannot Spell nor Read, so the Language of Nature of the Heavenly Holy World (our true Mother Tongue) was lost; he had no Ears to hear the Angelical Ravishing Voices, nor Tongue to utter it, till the Fiery Cloven Tongues descended.

8. Now come we to the Holy Language it self, which if any could speak, would not some say this Man is full of new Wine. But we may mournfully tell of our Losses, easier than regain them, we must say that Language was one and but one. For its Nature it is pure, for its extent it is comprehensive of all, and therefore no wonder all understood it, for its power it hath Authoritatively Omnipotence in it, actually

actually or executively it hath the Keys of Life, and Inflruments of Death, this Word flew *Ananias* and *Sapphira*, and freed *Tabitha* from the Bonds of Death.

9. Now as in Mens ordinary Affairs the Reafon and Underftanding prevail to move the Mind, fo that after Debate a Will is formed, this Will is the Refult of all confideration, and is the Man. the Soul, the Spirit, the Body, the Paffions, Affections, all make one Intire Will, and the Magical driving power of all this becomes the Word, this Word is the Executive Inftrument, and not barely the Herauld of the Soul or whole Man. It is the Energy and exprefled Vigor of all the Powers ; wherefore it is faid. By thy words thou fhalt be juftified, and by thy words thou fhalt be condemned.; for the word is the work and the worker.

10. Thus and no otherwife is the Divine Language which the Holy Ghoft opened in the Apoftles, (*viz.*) the Refult and Law or Abridgment of all the Powers of the hidden Holy World, it was the Opener of all Doors, the Epitomy of all Openings, the underftanding of which is offered by this fimile.

11. The Intricacies of the perverted perplexed, confufed Tongues in the multiplicity is compared to the Night feafon, wren a Man can only fee the Houfe or Room that contains him, and that not without the aid of Fire or Candle Light where is much fhadow, many uncertainties, fome colours not diftinguifhable. And the explicating, opening and voice of the holy one Language is compared to the Noon-day which fhews every thing at once without Door and within.

12. Thus the Divine Word or Language comprehends all, opens all Doors ; therefore was it that all Nations underftood them ; for the unity contains the multiplicity , as every Genus doth every of its own Species, or as the Element of Fire doth every Spark of Fire. This hath the Life of all openings, as the Vowels are the Spirit of the whole Alphabet. All the founds Mufical or otherwife are contained in three and in feven, both Concords and Difcords: All Voices or Tones expreffing the Paffions and Affections in the two Extreams of Joy and Sorrow, and the Mean of Equiponderating Solemnity of Humane Creatures, or others are comprifed in the fixth Fountain Spirit, or property of the Eternal Nature, and muft have its efficacy in every formation.

Q. 147. *What doth this fhedding forth of the Holy Ghoft out of Chrifts Refurrection and Ajcention to Heaven profit or benefit us ? How may that be alfo effected in us ?*

A. 1. When the *Ephefians* (who had been Baptized by *John*) were ask'd, Have ye received the Holy Ghoft fince you believed ? Anfwer'd, We have not fo much as heard whether there be a Holy Ghoft, they may not be thought wholly ignorant of the Eternal Exiftence of the Holy Ghoft ; for all the Holy Men from the Creation were guided by him : But that thefe knew not of this glorious and plentiful Effufion of the Holy Ghoft on the whole Affembly. *Acts* 29. 2.

2. And now how the pouring forth of the Holy Ghoft profits us, is not only that records deliver this to us, as once done in the main ; but that the fame is vouchfafed more or lefs Eminently, as thofe facred Vifits are more or lefs welcom'd by joyful Obedience, or grieved by ftubborn Refiftance. For as the precious Ointment going down to the Hem of *Aaron's* Vefture is not faid to be fpilt on the Rocks or fterile Earth, fo neither doth the Holy Spirit always ftrive with Gainfayers.

3. Again, the coming of the Holy Ghoft out of Chrifts Death and Refurrection profits us alfo, that whereas it finds us in as many pieces as there are Properties in Nature, and drawn by as many contradictory wills as there are fubordinate Species in thofe Properties, figur'd by the confufed Languages at *Babel*, this Holy Spirit unites us as Fire unites all forts of Fuel into a like Flame.

4. Thus it found fome of them in one form and extream, fome in another, fome

some Busied with Curiosities, others Brutishly Ignorant and Remiss, some seeking by fraud or otherwise to establish their particular propriety, some making Ambitious Designs their Idol, &c. 'The sacred Spirit putting out their several false Fires, and Gloworm fictitious Light, brought them, and willeth to bring us into one Kingdom, by one Spirit to mind the same things, leads us by one will to be imploy'd in one work, for our scatter'd Interests, extravagant Desires, and private selfish Contrivances must as Rubbish be removed, before the Lords House be Erected, or as Weeds be eradicated before the good Seeds flourish.

5. 'Tis true our Humane Powers, and the Spirit of the great World in us, and the Tincture convey'd us thereby may be used by the Almighty Architect as unhew'd Timber, rough stone, and other Materials whereof to frame a Building, like as the Principles and Properties were extracted out of the first Chaos: So may our confusions be consecrated and made conducible to the work of the new Creation which is effected in us by dying of our first wilful desires. For by giving up the might of our first principle into the Intellectual Light of the second Principle there is generated in us the pure Love of the third Principle, of which Love the Holy Ghost is the Author, by this the Law is fulfilled, and in and by it the Holy Ghost graciously seals the Regenerate to Eternal Salvation: Who having been fed by the Flesh and Blood of the Lord Jesus have in part got his Heavenly Body on them, which is attaining a measure of the Resurrection from the dead.

6. This brings in Universality in the Room of Propriety, one instead of many, signified by the Tongues, which tho' Cloven were all but one united, and one only in every Language, here see we the Kingdom on Earth as it is in Heaven, and the new Man thus progressed is the true, and in some sort perfect Image of the Trinity, for it is the first disappeared Image which *Adam* fell from. And in this most excellent way doth the glorious Trinity work in Eternity in all Divine Creatures wherein the Three Persons Image themselves.

Q. 148. *What is the Litteral Word and the Living Word Christ; in his shedding forth one with the other: How became they distinguished; seeing all did not hear the Holy Ghost teach from the Mouth of the Apostles: for one sort of them said, They are full of sweet Wine; these heard indeed Mans Word, but not Christ teaching in his Resurrection.*

A. 1. The Literal Word did signifie in the Jewish Administration the Law of Circumcision, &c. call'd a killing Letter, tho' even that were glorious as is intimated by *Moses* Face. The Evangelizing by Preaching or Writing must then be much more glorious, the Holy Writings of the Prophets, Apostles and Saints are therefore exceeding precious, and require great care and diligence to learn the Mysteries there intended and taught, they are so good and important, their Efficacy, Majesty and End so Divine, that the living Word and it, are used as terms convertible, but yet Metonymically: As by the Cup is meant the Wine, or by the Bag the Treasure.

2. But the Living Word is the Eternal Creating Word, and tho' no Language contains yet every Word of Men is of it and by it, and when the Lord Jesus saith of the Holy Spirit he shall take of mine and give it unto you, he means the so speaking as the Spirit should give utterance. Such was this when the God of Spirits fell on them; other speaking sprung from *Babel*, is as far below the Life and Power of that as the Consonants are below the Vowels, which produce but mute Hissings, &c.

Rom. 2. 17, 29.
2 Cor. 3. 6.

1 John 1, 2, 3.

3. And

The 177 Theosophick Questions Answered.

3. And we may expect, when God shall give to his, one Heart, one Soul, one Love, one Life of Faith, Holiness, Meekness, Patience and Self-denial, accounting nothing their own, but as Members of the one Body to live as that white, sweet, first Age of those Guests at the Feast of *Pentecost*: When God shall do this, we may expect he will restore the Spirits of the Letters, and give us Water at the pure Fountain; until then, as one people know not the Language of others, so all people are strangers to this, and as falshood causeth Men not to know others Minds by their Words, so do Mens false Hearts make them unknown to themselves.

4. Now why some of them who heard the Heavenly Tidings said these Men are full of sweet or new Wine, was because themselves were Captivated in another Principle than that wherein the words were Born: perhaps some in the deceits of the third Principle, others in the wrath of the first; so that they could no more comprehend the words of the Children of the day, than the Creatures of the corrupt terrene Salitter can converse with the Aerial Creatures, or the aqua-strish with those of the Fire, or then we poor Offspring of faln *Adam* can skill the Dialect of Angels.

5. Mans Heart is naturally prepossest against Divine Understanding, and the simplicity of truth not only from his disorder'd Original, but especially by Maturity of Growth to fixedness in the humane Apostacy; for Youth stands in a true Ground which makes Angels delight in them, until the Serpents, Foxes and Goats, their Tutors, Companions and Tempters have gravely taught them to be Fools in Fashion, also false, and by degrees to be obscene and impudent of Conversation.

O how great is Mans Misery on Earth, how innumerable his Snares, how multiply'd his Perils and Sorrows in this great and terrible Wilderness?

How Infinite is the forbearance of a contemned Father! How compassionate the Redeemer to his daily Murtherers! How long-suffering is the grieved Holy Spirit!

O, the Heighth and Depth, and Length, and Breadth of that Love so abused by us!

The subsequent Question excuseth saying more to this:

Q. 149. *How doth Christ himself teach presentially in the Office of Preaching, and yet sitteth at the Right Hand of God? Or among whom doth Christ teach, what is a Shepherd or Pastor in the Spirit of Christ, and a Teacher of the Letter without the Spirit of Christ, each in his Office?*

A. 1. How Christ is in Heaven and every where on Earth at once according to his Heavenly Humanity the 119 Answer from ver. 3. to the End, sheweth: Also it is elsewhere shew'd the sitting of Christ at the Right Hand of the Power of God, is at the place where Love quencheth Wrath; therefore are the Sheep at the great Day placed on the Right Hand of the Judge.

2. But now to the next part of the Question, among whom doth Christ teach, it must be answer'd, the Light which bringeth Salvation hath appeared to all Men; for as every Countrey on Earth is visited by the splendor of the Sun, and every Plant and Pile of Grass Influenced by him, and so hath been from the Creation; so also from *Adam* to the last Man, hath Christ the only true Light shined, and will shine.

3. And as there are many places in some Countries, and some Angles in every Countrey, whereon the Suns Beams beat not directly, yet is there no Vegetable which his Vigor Influenceth not: Such is the Preaching Vertue of Christ to all present, past and future. 4. Again

4. Again, as every Mineral is not Gold, nor every Fruit folar, that the Suns vertue should be totally prevalent in them, but they all are helped the more to grow thereby in their own Property, so that it is not the Suns fault that many are spoil'd. Thus tho' Christ stands in the Door of every Mans Heart, calls them, waits the whole time of the Life of many, and very long on all, as a Judge, as a Councellor, and as a Monitor, yet many grow hard, and (as evil Creatures) the stronger in their own property, by the desireable access of the Suns Rays: Thus Impenitent Men do from Gods goodness treasure up wrath, blese themselves, say we shall have peace, cry the Temple of the Lord, &c. and grow the more evil because God is most good, and are the more daring, the more they are intreated and strove with.

5. Now to the latter part of the Question, what is a Shepherd or Pastor in the Spirit of Christ. It is answer'd, Christ is the alone Shepherd of Souls; for alluding as before to the outward Sun. As the Sun directeth the Creatures to get good and prevent evil by his daily steddy course, such is Christs providential guiding us by his working for, and sacred Epistles written to us, and by assisting us by some loving Brother he substitutes, this is his outward Pastoral Office.

6. Again, as the Sun not only directs the Creatures to the place of their Food, but by his vertue makes it to be Food, so that they are fed by his secret vertue in the things fed on, and the things themselves are but the Medium. Thus is the Soul fed by Christ by whom the Medium is caused, and the Soul by him also hath a preparedness and capacity thereunto, and the good Shepherd thus gives his Life and Vertue for and to the Sheep, and they feed on him But Men calling themselves Shepherds are only at best as Ink and Paper wherewith the Lord Jesus writes his good pleasure, teaching others to read it. So is the Church call'd the Epistle of Jesus Christ.

7. And to the last part of the Question. What is a Teacher of the Letter without the Spirit of Christ in his Office; It is answer'd, he is dead, (for it is the Spirit only that quickeneth) both in respect of himself, is sensual, not having the sacred Spirit, and in respect to his Work, the Letter killeth. Therefore tho' a regenerated Child may receive some strength from the Teacher of the Letter, yet the Divine Principle by him who is himself only in the Anguish of the first Principle, (viz.) the Covetousness, Pride, Envy and Anger, or in the Image or Shadow thereof the third Principle properly call'd the Valley or Shadow of Death the unregenerate Souls are by such misled into the Ditch.

8. What is that power then, whence the Blind Guides issue and derive Authority? From the holy Spirit of Christ it is not; for that is pure, peaceable, gentle, easie to be intreated, full of mercy and good fruits. If they were founded in the Regeneration they would proceed in the Divine Impulse, but being sprung in the Astral *Magia* which is but the Figure or Shadow of the Eternal World, the driving is from without, and being so from beneath cannot ascend higher. Preachers in that Spirit are only the Apes and Counterfeits of the Divine Living Spirit, and the Super-intendents or Ordainers of them are Men neither Authorized by the Law nor Gospel. Thus after the choice Youth of Christian people are prepossest with *Aristotle's* Heathenish, and dry Breasts of Philosophy, like the Children prostituted to *Molock*: They are spirited by Men who by a fatal Name are call'd School-Doctors.

Doctores Scholastici (i. e.) illusorii vel ludicri.

9. These come abroad with unmortified Lusts, imperious Wills, imposing Principles in contempt of the humility, simplicity, and plainness of the Doctrine of Christ, and of the Self denial, Charity and Love in the practice of Christianity, but will be Teachers of the Multitude, yet being ignorant of God, of Nature, and of themselves; being very great strangers to Christ, in whom only are all the Treasures of true Wisdom.
Q. 150.

The 177 Theosophick Questions Answered.

Q. 150. *What is the Office of the Keys? How may they become rightly used, or who is worthy or fit for this Office, or whether is he himself the Office? Or whether hath he freely given it to man, so that he may without Christ's Spirit forgive Sins, or how is it done?*

A. 1. People of the Roman Communion say, Their Bishop hath the Keys of Heaven left him by *Peter*; but why they derive from *Peter* they should shew, for *Peter* was the Apostle to the Circumcision. they were Gentiles: and *Paul* was the Apostle of the Gentiles. Thus far they are as the Jews, that as the Jews Persecuted the Head, these do the Members.

2. But were it so they derived rightly from *Peter*, which cannot be, and *Peter* only from the Words of the Lord Jesus; which were a direct Error (as of such who know not the Scriptures) to think : yet let it be observ'd, the Lord said to Peter, *I will give thee the Keys of the Kingdom*, &c. It is not there said, *I do give*,&c. *Mat.*16. 19. Nor seems he then fit being ignorant of, and offended at the Notice of Christ's designed Sufferings, his Answer on that occasion caus'd the Lord to say, after this Promise, *Get thee behind me Sathan*, &c. But when that Promise was performed, it was to the other Apostles equally with *Peter*; for when the Lord Jesus shew'd himself to them, he breath'd on them, saying, *receive ye the Holy Ghost; whose Sins* *Joh.* 20. 21, *ye remit*, &c. 22.

3. But we read of the Lawyers who took away the Key of Knowledge, as these *Mat.* 18. 18. do ; for the Pardon of Sin is not like the Remission of Mens Penalties by a Magi- *Luke* 11. 58. strate at a Bar, but is a great Work ; therefore said the Jews, * *Who can forgive* * *Mark* 2. 7. *Sins but God alone?* And *Moses* interceeding for *Israel* saith, *Let the Power of my* *Numb.*14.17. *Lord be great, and Pardon*, &c. It was Power that created the World, but great Power goes to the forgiving of Sin.

4. But Power of Remission and Retention of Sin was given by the Lord Jesus *Obj.* to the Apostles, together with a Commission to go and Preach the Gospel : wherein more was meant than what was conferred on the rest of the World ; for it was not only a Power of bare Verbal Declaration which others might do, but a Delegation of Commissionary Authority.

All Sin is against God ; those against Men are against God, as Men stand related *A.* to God, and as they Transgress the Righteous Law of God. Therefore no Sin can be Pardoned but by him against whom Sin is committed. And 'tis the Infinite can extend Infinite Mercy, which only can secure a sinful Creature against Infinite Wrath.

5. Men may as Ambassadors declare their Lord's terms of Reconciliation in general to all, and they may ratifie Peace with particular Persons, if they are directed by the unerring Spirit of God to discern them from all others : but *Samuel* himself was mistaken by the goodly Presence of *David*'s elder Brother: Such an Error in this Case may both invalidate the Absolution and Shipwrack the Man into a Lethargy, Presumptuous Dream, Slumber, or translate him to Fools Paradise.

6. And it may be doubted this discriminating Eye is dimm or shut when the Concomitants disappear ; for now the glorious Effusion of the Holy Ghost enabling to take up Serpents, drink any deadly thing, heal the Sick, eject Devi's, Prophesie, *Mark* 16. 17. speak with new Tongues. are all controverted as a misunderstood History, rather 18. than to be things practicable by the Pretenders to that great work of Pardon.

7. Let it not therefore be thought a designed Sacriledge of part of Ecclesiastical Authority, to warn all to see they have salt in themselves, and not be led by the Eyes of others, and those also Eyes confessedly defective. But that the Apostles did this, was because they had an open Door into Hearts, that could see who was in the Gall of Bitterness, and who had Faith to be Healed : so infallible was their
deep

deep penetration, whereas the now Pretenders have their own Hearts shut against them, and many ('tis to be feared) themselves fetter'd in the Bonds of Iniquity.

8. I compare the Apostles continuation in the Lord's Work of remitting after his departure, to *Joshuah* succeeding *Moses*, who passed the Tribes through *Jordan* as *Moses* had done through the Sea, but the succeeding Judges (though Prophets) did not so, and the Allusion so fits, as the one is the plain figure of the other.

Jam. 5. 20. 9. *He that converteth a Sinner from the Error of his ways, shall save a Soul from death, and cover a multitude of Sins.* As many therefore as God useth for Instruments of Converting Sinners so many Absolvers, Remitters, Pardoners and Coverers of Sins are there ; yet not one of them is so, but God alone enkindles his Candle, and puts a Treasure in such Earthen Vessels, sometimes by Preaching the Gospel, which who so reject, do reject the Council of God against themselves. Some others are
Acts 2. 38. used by holy Conversation to the same end; so is the unbelieving Husband by the believing Wife, &c. Some by faithful Monitions. Some by patient and constant Suffering. But many by Writing (according to the measure of Grace vouchsafed) which is a loud way of Preaching, ringing to the largest distance of the habitable Earth, and living to the longest space of time it self : opening Heaven to several Nations and Ages, influencing dark Souls, and subjecting them to the Scepter of Jesus Christ.

10. All these and the like blessed ways, doth God the Holy Ghost consecrate and sanctifie to touch and change Hearts ; these are the Keys, the Evangelical Keys of the Kingdom of Heaven, to unlock Imprison'd Souls. But if any pretend to have Keys to open Heaven to the Unregenerate Man, the old unchang'd Nature, and to bring the Serpentine Man in, as once the Serpent entred *Eden*; those are Thieves, and their Keys, Picklocks, Heaven is exempt and above them that would break through, and enter not in by the Door.

Q. 151. *What is Christ's Testament, together with the last Supper with Bread and Wine: How is Christ really enjoy'd? what manner of Flesh and Blood is it? and what is the Mouth to eat it with.*

A. 1. The Question is double, 1. What is Christ's Testament together with the last Supper with Bread and Wine, what manner of Flesh and Blood is it ? 2. How is Christ really enjoy'd: and what is the Mouth to Eat it ? To the first, it's answer'd
(1.) Negatively. (1.) It's not his Almighty pure Deity, the infinite inaccessible Light
(2.) or true second Principle ; this no Creature can touch or reach. (2.) It is not the Body, Soul and Spirit he received from *Mary* descending from *Eve* ; for so he is
Acts 1.11,12. our Brother, and remains a Creature, not so swallow'd up as to be confounded in his Deity ; but must so return as the two Men in white testified ; nor is it eaten or swallow'd (Cannibal like) into our foul Carcasses. As the Jews rightly said, *How can this man give us his* (meaning this) *flesh to Eat.* But affirmatively,

2. The Last-Supper Bread and Wine, Flesh and Blood, is the pure chast Virgin of Wisdom, or Heavenly Man, or Holy Humanity which *Adam* fell from. The Tongue of an Angel might tell what this is, but there must be a preparedness in the Intellect to receive the thing spoken, or he would be as Dumb to the Hearers; yet for the sake of the serious Desirers it is answered,

3. It is the created Tincture of the Light World, That, out of which Angels were spoken or breathed forth, the Food of Angels ; as every Creature feedeth of its Mother, the Child of the Breast, and the Elementary Creatures of the Elements: Man's outward Body on the Tincture of the Elements, Soul of the World, or Astral Powers, but if his inward Man hath no higher Nourishment as the Unregenerate hath not, the Soul starveth ; for its Will hath an inferiour false Tincture,

declining

The 177 Theosophick Questions Answered.

declining to Sensuality, and with the Fool faith, *Soul take thy rest, eat drink and be merry*. And though by reason of the noble Extraction of the Soul, Man hath Eternity, as also the Devil remains an Angel. Yet is the Tincture of both, false and degenerate, man going into the Wrath in the Looking-Glass, and the Evil Spirits into the fierceness of the first Principle, and both out of the Light.

4. While the regenerate New Man feedeth on the true Divine Tincture, which is the Bread that cometh down from Heaven, or the Flesh of Christ and Water of Life, or Divine Meekness, (*viz.*) The Blood of Christ, which quencheth the wrath or thirst of the Fire-Soul. It is the Quintessence of the Paradifical Angelical World every where for ever pure before God, evidently figur'd by the Quintessence and Tincture in the outward World, which that Man only who is taught of God knoweth, or can know?

5. The second part, *How is Christ really enjoy'd, and what is the Mouth to eat it with?* 2. *A*. The Mouth is the great, earnest hunger and thirst of the Love-sick Fire-Soul, and the enlightned Human Spirit, both sharpened into so vigorous desire of Food proper for them; that they are dead (while thus awakened) to all the drivings of the outward *Magia*.

And Christ is really enjoy'd while the outward Bread and Wine or Elements are received by such a Soul. The way, and manner how, The Divine Power-world, or Paradifical-Tincture or Virgin of Wisdom and Purity, which are meant by the Flesh and Blood of Christ, gives it self by and through the Tincture of the Bread and Wine, not through the Elementary Bread and Wine which are Mortal, and so under the Wrath, but through the Tincture thereof which is Immortal, and for the sake whereof, the Creatures shall in their Idea share in the Liberty of the Children of God. Therefore this Tincture or Kind of Quintessence doth the Holy Power use as the Medium to conveigh it self into the Mouth of the Human Soul and Spirit.

And as the right Tincture transmuteth inferior Metals into the noble solar one, so doth this Body and Blood, through the above Medium, transmute the half-dead Image into revived Vertue, the Eternal inward Man into a holy lustrous Love-fire, and Love-flame, that the Man may thereby be exalted into an Image of the three Worlds, in due weight, harmony and regiment of the Holy World, or Divine second Principle, the Almighty Infinite Son of God.

2 Q. A.

Q. 152. *What is the place in Man, wherein Christ's Flesh and Blood continueth; He himself saith*, Whosoever eateth my Flesh and drinketh my Blood, he continueth in me, and I in him; * *Also*, If you do not eat the Flesh of the Son of Man and drink his Blood, then you have no life in you? *Joh. 6. 56.* *Verf. 53.*

A. 1. What the eating Christ's Flesh and drinking his Blood is, and how it is really enjoy'd; also what we are if we eat it not, and what it brings us to be if we do eat it, is the Substance of the immediately foregoing Answer.

The place in Man wherein Christ's Flesh and Blood continues, is the whole Man, for all is the Lords, (*viz.*) the whole enlightned Man, though in all parts of him God is not alike manifest.

2. As he who sits on the Throne of a Kingdom is in Possession of the Regality of the whole Territory, yet especially resident in the Palace Royal; thus, though the Flesh and Blood of Christ sit as Soveraign in the Spirit of the Mind of the new born Child of God, which is as his Throne in Man, and that wherein he is peculiarly present; yet is he thereby Owner and right Proprietor of the whole Man, and where this is received all is new. And whereas it is written, *Behold I make all things new*, yet is it extended only to all things now capacitated to receive this Renovation. 3. It

The 177 *Theosophick Questions Answered.*

3. It is true, the Body hath the Honour to be the Antitype of the outer Court of the Temple of the Holy Ghost, or the thing signified by a place without the Camp, where the Sin-offering was to be Sacrificed, the Body hath a rich and blessed hope, not only to be raised again, but that *he shall change our vile Bodies, and make them like his glorious Body.* Now though God was without the Camp as a Wall of Fire, and in the Camp as Captain of his Host, yet was he in his holy Place as at Home.

4. The New Man (strengthened by the Virgin of Wisdom) is in its Wrestlings both with the Anguishes of the Fire-Soul or first Principle in us, and with our Mortal, Sensual, Astral and Elementary Man or third Principle, like to the good Properties of Nature labouring (as it were in the very Fire) to rescue themselves from the Curse and Wrath of the Dead Earth, and indefatigably struggling to produce living Paradisical Fruits, Precious Stones, Odours, *&c.* in Power, but cannot; because the Curse hath introduced Corruption and Instability. Thus goes it with the Divine stirrings, where (as it were ineffectually) they approach our bestial Man; so vastly unsuitable hath our Fall render'd us to the pure Paradisical State.

5. But as the good Properties are much more prevalent in the benign Influence of the Syderial World; where they find a flexible Will strenuously active, and a kind of pure transparency and uninterrupted Serenity in the Form of Eternity. So is the sacred Energy of Virgin *Sophia* approaching our Superior part, *viz* our Spirits, after Holy enkindlings in them: whereas all those Applications to our vile Carcasses work so obscurely and faintly, as sufficeth not to Tincture them to be out of the reach of Worms and Putrefaction.

6. Thus is seen in what place or part in Man Christ's Flesh and Blood continueth: which though before our Fall, and when we shall attain the Resurrection of the Dead, we stand as a well tun'd Instrument, but now under the Fall as an Engine pull'd all in pieces.

7. And whereas it is said continue *IN* us, as usually we say the Soul *IN* the Body: it is much more true and proper to say the Body is in the Soul, for it comprehends the Body. So, and much more are we also in the Flesh and Blood or Body of Christ, or in God's Body; therefore it is written, Put on the Lord Jesus Christ, by whom our whole Man, Soul, Spirit and Body are comprehended.

The farther Answer is referred to the Book of the Two Testaments.

Q. 153. *How is Man, and how doth he become a Branch on the Vine Stock of Christ? How doth Christ dwell in him, and yet sit at the right hand of God in Heaven? Also, how can he sit at the right hand of God in Man, and yet the outward Man not be he?*

A. 1. Man was a noble Vine, and became degenerate by his Fall into the Outbirth. which shut him up from the Divine Birth into Enmity, and under the Evil Influences of the Astral World over which he should have ruled: The third Principle was that he took root in; no wonder then that he bare Fruit to himself, but concerning the Fall, the 71, 72, and 73 Answers are clear.

2. And that Man might be grafted into the Vine Christ, the Almighty second Principle took the Heavenly Humanity the Virgin Image (whose love *Adam* exchanged for the Lust of a Woman) and reimplanted it into the half-dead Humanity in *Mary's* Essences, and so ingrafting fallen Man into the true Vine. See 75 Answer from *v.* 3. to the 7th.

To the second part of this Question how Christ dwells in Man, and yet sits at the right Hand of God in Heaven, is shewn in the 77, 108, 113, 129, and 141 Answers copiously.

3. To the third part, *How can he sit at the right hand of God in Man, and the outward*

The 177 Theosophick Questions Answered.

ward Man not be he? Is anfwered that the outward Man is the Image of Wrath and Love, & yet he who fitteth at God's right Hand in Man (viz where Wrath is quenched by Love) is not the outward Man; for he is the Image or expreſs Character of God according to his Love. 'Tis true, Man he is, but is the Heavenly Man: who by Uniting to the outward Man, became our Brother, by killing the Will of the Erring Brother, preferved the Brotherhood, by cutting him off, implanted him.

4. In like manner we fee the Fountain of all Natural Philofophy is the very knowledge of a certain real skill to ſtay an expiring Spirit at home, where it is eminently neceſſary, to tranfplant it into another of the ſame kind, which wants the out-going Spirit to reinforce that other Species.

And what is all Sacred Theofophy, but the very underſtanding of a certain Divine Art, to receive and aſſimilate the evermore over-flowing Effluence of God's Bounty. This is the regenerating and the receiving the Divine Univerſal Will, which grows, over-tops, and Commands to the irradicating the private perverted one: This is that Holy One fitting at the right Hand of God in Man; which though it refemble the outward Man as a Subſtance doth its own fhadow: yet is no more the outward, than a good potent Tincture is a decay'd or impotent thing to be tinctured, becauſe its Application is continually about fuch: or than a Phyſician is a Malady, becauſe his Buſineſs is about Diſtempers.

Q. 154. *What manner of Chriſtian is the titulary Chriſtian in Name only, without or out of Chriſt: who only comforteth himſelf; and imputeth Chriſts Merits to himſelf, and yet is unregenerate of the Spirit of Chriſt, and liveth beſtially? Whether alfo doth he in ſuch working or dcing belong to Chriſt? Or what doth he receive in Chriſt's Supper?*

A. 1. He is one who knoweth nothing as he ought to know, nor doth what he ought in any thing; for all that know God worſhip him in Spirit, which this Man is a Stranger to, and is alfo no leſs a Stranger to himſelf: and God of fuch a one will fay, *I know him not*. Oh may we never know a ſtate of entring Hell by Heaven's Gate.

2. Many Volumes are extant concerning Regeneration; fome difcovering the Old Eſtate fome the New, fome the Proceſs from the one to the other: whofe parts (after Information) are, of terror for awakening, Exhortation, Direction, Tryal, Caution and Encouragement, and doubtleſs all whoſe fincere Love to God draws them to this Imployment are profecuting the End of Gods Creating and Redeeming Work, and are as truly, though weakly, at what pleaſeth God, as the Holy Angels are; but all Pretenders to teach Religion, who are neither inſtrumental to call in the Sinner, nor to feed the Flock, are titular Chriſtians, but truly Antichriſtians, yet would be accounted Paſtors and Leaders.

3. Mens Induſtry for fading Toys, gives Evidence againſt the lazy titular Chriſtian, what a feries of Pains, Study and Patience have Men emulouſly ſtrove with, to acquire Trades and Arts? What Extremities others encounter chearfully to difcover new Countries, paſſing torrid heat, and ſtone-cleaving cold? What daring attempts Ambition hath fet Men upon, by cruel force like Wolves and Vultures, to wade through Rivers of Innocent Blood, to add more clods to their field of ufurped Soveraignty, for a larger Stage to act a little while with more Elbow-room, the tyranny of their impetuous luſts over their Brethren?

4. And how little Price do Men fet on Treaſures, talking only of them: whereas only ta'king of Work all Day, gets no Wages at Night. The profeſſing Faith, but practically denying the working Life of it, is the Damnation of titular Chriſtendom at this day, the Form of Godlineſs denying the Power, is to be turned from in others, but eſpecially in our ſelves. The ſtate of *Chorafin* and *Bethſaida*,

was

was more intolerable than that of *Sodom*; for they had the found of the Gofpel, which it feems was all they defir'd. And who doubts but the foolifh Virgins were as certainly fhut out as the moft lewd Harlots. The meer outfide of Religion is as profitable as painted Fire and Food to warm and nourifh.

5. The Titular Chriftian is the more inexcufable, becaufe if he will he may know himfelf to be only a counterfeit (tho' the fincere Child may by reafon of his Allay and Imperfect Work, have caufe enough to doubt himfelf) the reafon whereof is, becaufe the unregenerate Profeffor doth out of the four Anguifhes of the firft Principle only generate the third Principle, which is but a cold fhadow or reflected Light moft fenfibly difcernable. And not to conceal the very truth, an Hypocritical Titular Chriftian hath but a noife of words, a feigned reprefentation of the very third Principle it felf: Lefs of Faith than the Devils, whofe Faith caufeth trembling: And lefs of the figur'd Powers of the Out-birth or World than the Heathen Magicians; for thofe could imitate *Mofes* in many things from the powers of the formed Worlds Properties.

6. But the Regenerate Child is enabled, out of his firft Principle, to generate the true underftanding, and real ravifhing Fervour of the Divine Love of the fecond Principle; and fo crucifies the Old Nature confifting of the firft Principle imaged in the third, and lives in the New Nature; (viz.) the firft Principle illuftrated by the meek facred fecond; having the third only hanging, fticking or adhering to it, and clogging it a while, whereunto it is more and more dead; as the Fruit is to a withered Leaf, which hangs on the Branch with the Fruit, but when the Fruit attains maturity, and is gathered, the difregarded Leaf falleth.

7. And to tell what the Titular Chriftian receiveth in Chrift's Supper: He receiveth what fufficeth his hunger; for his Soul defireth only a Form of Godlinefs; it hath therefore a Form of words, a fhadow of the powerful Worlds word. His Body would conform to the fafhion of others; it hath the fafhioned, mortal, Elementary Bread and Wine, a dead figure of the Heavenly Food. Thus in both Inward and Outward he hath a fhadow, form and figure fill'd with Wrath, Curfe and Damnation.

8. Thefe participate with Chrift in his Anguifh, but die not to their Lufts; they would rife with Chrift, not to a New Life, but that Sin might reign with him in them; and thus tread they on His Blood, but the Blood of the Paffover was not to be on the Threfhold to be trampled on, but on the Lintel and two Side Pofts. Thus did *Judas* eat the Sop, as thefe the Supper.

Q. 155. *Whether alfo may Chrift's Flefh and Blood become enjoyed by Believers, without, or out of the Teftamentary Ordinance and Obfervation, or how it may be done?*

6. 63.

A. 1. That the Flefh and Blood of Chrift is the Living, Holy, Powerful Word, is manifeft; that This was given His Difciples before the Inftitution of the laft Supper, is alfo manifeft by the fame Text, and their believing on Him. That This was the fame Spiritual Meat and Drink which the Rock Chrift gave the Ifraelites in the Wildernefs, is plain: And what other Spiritual Food had all from the Creation, to make and nourifh the Holy Souls; for This was in-fpoken into Man immediately after the Fall, elfe had he been fwallowed up of the Anguifhes of His own Root.

2. And that This may be enjoyed by Believers out of the Teftamentary Ordinance, is clear; how elfe come they to be Believers? How elfe alfo in all Nations are fuch as fear God and work Righteoufnefs accepted? Now how This is received by the Soul, the Inward Eye only feeth, for the Outward Man and Aftral Soul comprehend Chrift's Spiritual Flefh and Blood, no more than the grofs Stone doth the Tincture of fine Gold that is in it.

3. This

3. This Flesh and Blood of Christ is His Heavenly Humanity, a Divine Love-fire, or a Holy Tincture re-enkindling *Adam's* vanished Virgin Image, as precious Oil put into common dark Fire, gives it a shining glance. So This Spiritual Paradisical Humanity, Christ's own *Mummia*, freely presseth into the Soul, as the vertue of the Sun into the Plant. This is the Spiritual Flesh out of which the Visible Image groweth. As Fire falling into Tinder turns it into Fire and Light. Thus is Christ the Light of the World, and doth substantially inhabit in the Soul. See more of this in the little Book of the two Testaments.

Q. 156. *Why hath Christ Ordained and Instituted This Testament, and said, so oft as we do it, we should do it in remembrance? to what profit and benefit is it done with Bread and Wine, and not without? Or whether may it also become enjoyed or participated without Bread and Wine?* 1 Cor. 11. 25.

A. That it may be enjoyed and participated of without Bread and Wine, appears in the last preceding Answer. It remains here to answer why Christ ordained This Testament, saying, &c. which was; (*viz.*)

1. That the Antitype Christ might be received in a way suitable to the capacity of the Receiver. (1.)

2. In a method suitable to all his gracious ways of condescending to men in all Ages, by Sacrifices, &c. (and by the Pascal Lamb in particular) by things palpable, but the Lamb was eaten as in haste, and with bitter Herbs: The Supper, as in a Table gesture of such as have attained rest, not by violent killing, as That, but by a free Issue of the highest and sweet Tincture as is That producing Bread and Wine, and remaining in them. (2.)

2. So high is it, that it hath been thought by some of the Learned (tho' erroneously) that the Spirit of Wine is the true Fire of Nature. (3.) That it might be a *Medium* for conveyance; for so great was the Precipice down which Man fell, that he must be followed, or for ever lost; but tho' he fell into the Mortal Elementary State, and the Elements of Bread and Wine blessed for his use; yet these are not the *Medium.* The Tincture is a Virgin, a Servant to Virgin *Sophia,* who tho' it be not purely Divine, yet is such a Servant indeed, as in whom is no guile. (3.)

3. The Tincture (whence issueth the Corn and Vine) is the middle Earth betwixt the Heavenly or Paradisical Earth as the most superior, and the Mortal as the most inferior; This is therefore the proper *Medium.* Here the Souls fiery hunger in the Promise meets the Divine Love and Grace, the Living Word or Power World, bringing in and with the Flesh and Blood of Christ's Heavenly Humanity; which is the *Emmanuel,* the Hope, the Joy, and Eternal Spouse of the Fire Soul, and the Lord, Husband and Crown of the enlightened, renewed, meek Spirit; fore here the two Tinctures are united for ever, and is neither Male nor Female, but our Christ is all in all.

Q. 157. *Whether is the True Testamentary Enjoyment or Participation bound meerly to the Apostolical Practice and Observation; or whether also men may have Power or Authority to alter and change This Ordinance, as is done now-a-days?*

A. 1. Amongst men, the Law making Power only hath Authority to change and alter Laws. And a Testator dying, no one may alter the Will and Testament ratified by the deceased: On much higher and surer Reason is it therefore, that no man, or all men may alter or change This Ordinance, or reject any of God's Institutions, no more than two or three School-boys can root up the Basis of Philosophy, or two or three Thieves or other Criminals change the publick Statures of a State or Kingdom. 2. This

2. This will be acknowledged in words; but when men come to measure Heavenly Mysteries by the Form of Words, and Those Words by the Standard of Reason, and that Reason corrupted by their Lusts; disputes are raised without end, and Obstinacy is the Disputant; for the unregenerate man hath a perverse Will; so that such of them as can attain the most exact Form of Godliness, are only thereby the more confirmed in their Ungodliness.

3. Could such do every Outward Ordinance, with direct exactness of every gesture, speak the words, and only those spoken and done by the Lord himself, without the Regenerating Spirit of Christ they would transgress the Rule still, be in the Livery of Christ Traitors to Him, fight against Him under His own Banners; the Lord's Supper will be to such as the Sop to *Judas*, who did after kiss and betray. Such men receive the Heavenly Dews, but bear fruit to self, and That fruit the Grapes of *Sodom*; they err in every work of their hands; their very plowing is sin; their Metonymies and other Tropes are airy distinctions of the words of the Institution; like the endless Genealogies of the unbelieving Jews.

4. Thus we see men guided by the Properties of the first Principle (clothing their Hypocrisie by the Images and Maxims of the third) do turn That blessed Ordinance which was to be as a Bond of Peace, into Enmity. And what wonder they should endeavour to impose their dark notions on others by hostile force (as wild Beasts are to be dealt with) not having the Light of the second to guide their Understandings, as Children of the day. But the new Nature of Gods Child is fed by that whereof it is Begotten, and because the love of every such is sincere, their hunger is earnest, and is in proportion satisfied as it is in power and vigor excited.

Q. 158. *Whether also is the Testament powerful in the alter'd or chang'd Ordinance or not?*

A. 1. The misapprehending of this Question may either on the one hand encourage to make unwarrantable alterations arbitrarily, or persist in them after being found to be such: Or on the other hand unnecessarily to decline all Communion, or despair of Vertue from the Ordinance, because something said or done at the Administration, seem not expresly commanded in the form recorded in the Institution. Wherefore,

1. 2. To make way to the Answer, (1.) Something must be said to the Institu-
(1.) tion of the Sacrament it self. (2.) Something to the partakers, (1.) In the Sacrament are, (1.) The Form and Materials. (2.) The Force and Vertue. (3.) The Medium. (1.) The Form and Materials are meant in the words, take
(2.) eat this, and take drink this, [this] intends the Elements or Accidents of Bread and Wine. (2.) The force and Vertue meant by the words this is my Body, is my Blood, viz. are that Heavenly Flesh and Blood of Christ the Food of the Eternal Soul. It is Christs Spiritual Humanity whereby he doth substantially inhabit the Souls of all who open to him their hungry and thirsty Mouth, sups with them, and is himself the true Bread and Water of Eternal, Paradisical, Divine Life.

(3.) 3. (3.) The Place or Medium, and this is not Christ himself, tho' in his Heavenly Humanity he is not shut out of any Heaven; for he is in or rather is, all Heavenly Places. Also the Medium, neither can be the Elements of Bread and Wine; for they are Mortal, Accidents not Substances. But the Tincture whence groweth the Bread and Wine is the Medium; for that is Pure and Immortal, and for the sake whereof the Idea of the Creatures shall be raised into the Glorious liberty of the Children of God.

4. Some-

The 177 Theosophick Questions Answered.

4. Something (preparatory to the Answer) is, concerning the partakers of the Sacrament be the subdivisions how many soever, there will be found at last but two sorts: The Wise and the Unwise, both call'd Virgins. The one really and in Heart, the other feigned and only in shew. The one those of the day generated in the Glory and Love of the second principle, the other of darkness in the works of the first principle.

5. The Child of wrath can eat only and drink the Elementary part, which hath in it the good and evil properties, the Imaged Powers of Wrath and Love extending only to his Mortal Elementary Life: wherewith neither his Eternal Soul, nor Eternal Spirit of the Mind are really fed, but starve; and therefore so eats he and drinks he Damnation to himself, not discerning the Lords Body; viz. not receiving nourishment from the Heavenly Food the Lords real Body, but only the Elementary. And his Astral or Siderial Spirit cannot receive so much as the pure Medium, and keep it so; because the evil properties domineering in the Soul makes the Tincture false, which in its self is true, as also it is in the Devils.

6. Thus we see the Air, of its self sweet and wholesome in a City greatly infected with the Plague, is by the Emanation of many Sick and Expiring Bodies by that contagion, corrupt. So the discord of the dark Soul invades the serenity of the Tincture, and maims it of its Inclination and Ability to good, and Invigorates it with the Rage of its own perverse Affections.

7. Now to the humble, obedient Child the Supper is a Feast giving nourishment suitable to his Hunger; his Fire Soul and Principle of strength is meeken'd; his drooping Spirit cheered, his Astral Spirit composed into order; some of the Properties restrained, other properties stirred on, and others sweetly encouraged, and the disappeared Image of the Virgin by the Body and Blood of the second Adam restored.

8. Come we now to the Doubt, Whether the alter'd Ordinance retain power to do good. It is answer'd, That if the alter'd Administration fall short of shewing the End of its Institution, or hath so great additions (as so) to cloud the thing signified as it cannot be rightly discerned, or the change be such as doth race out the Ordinance its self, the Essentials are departed, and it is no more an Ordinance of Christ than a dead Corps is a Man, the power disappears when the thing it self is not.

9. It is true if the Soul remain so doth some measure of power, as a Man may live yet have lost a leg or Arm, but dismembering is often Mortal to the Natural Body, and not seldom so in lameing the Service of God, carry such to the Ruler will he accept it. But wo to such who innovate, to them are the Curses of Gods Book added: Also where Sacriledge is found it rends that Name out of Gods Book of Life, and where the intire alteration is, there Hell hath enlarg'd it self.

10. Yet in every Age and Place where the Divine Love is or hath been begotten, the hunger is ever a receiver of such quantity of Manna as is according to every one's eating. We see the outward Sun through Clouds, Showers and ill Vapours, in and under the Earth and Seas, doth great good work, and shall we streighten the unlimitable Divine Grace and Power? Is the holy Child at any time driven into the Wilderness, and goeth not God thither with him? He that instructs us in Dreams, in the Creation, in evil Creatures, and by many things evil as in themselves, that brings good out of evil, confirms us by our falls, that brought Almonds out of *Aaron*'s dry Rod, shall not he also out of weakness create strength? He doth out of the cruel Anguishes of the Lion-like first Principle, bring the most sweet Honey of the holy second Principle: Which is still a Riddle, but the day of God dawneth, and will proceed to a perfect day, in all such in whom he, of whom *Samson* was a shadow, shall slay the enmity of the four dark forms, by introducing Divine Light and the holy Power World.

Q. 15.

Q. 159. *What do the Learned when they reproach one the other about Christs Testaments, and the precious Covenant of Grace: And disgrace one another, and give up one another to the Devil about it? Whether do they also manage the Office of Christ; whether is that right or wrong, whether also is this done as a Minister of Christ? Or whom do they serve thereby?*

A. 1. Their reproaching each other usually proceeds either from outward prosperity, or desire of Superiority; whence come Wars, which come they not from your Lusts which War in your Members? When *Joseph* had open'd to his Brethren a prospect of approaching prosperity, he seasonably warn'd them not to fall out by the way. As soon as *Constantine* had given the Christians a general Jubilee from the frequent Persecutions of more than two hundred years up riseth *Arrius* and other Hereticks Titular Christians, persecuting the real Christians: As saith the Apostle, He that was after the Flesh (*Ishmael*) persecuted him that was after the Spirit, for which there are many Reasons, briefly thus;

2. The counter Christian being shut up in the first four forms of Nature; to stifle his intestine tumults sallies out into the third Principle, which is the great figure of his proper radical disorders, the World therefore being his only home, he will be Master there, especially over them who both are and own themselves to be strangers.

3. But God keeps peace among his Children by his Rod, which is so Moral an Argument of conserving peace, that the penitent Thief urg'd it on the other, *viz.* Dost thou not fear God seeing thou art under the same condemnation? On the swelling of *Severn* by a great Flood Islands were made, on some of them Lambs and Foxes saved themselves, where the very Foxes tho' hungry were observed to keep a Civil Community with the Lambs, being all under one Conservation.

4. Mans departure from the Unity into the Multiplicity brings his Lifes forms into Enmity: But Heavenly Peace the Sister of Sacred Love is Born at the reducing him from the Multiplicity into the Unity again.

5. If therefore the love of the World and the things of the World, *viz.* as it is figur'd and impressed by the evil dark Powers, be the cause of strife introducing the contrariety and multiplicity: Then the Love of the Heavenly Father whence we departed being regenerated in us by his only Son in the method of Self-abasing, which is the Cross of the Christian as far as he is unmortified, This love thus begotten makes peace, and this appeased mind (which also was in the Lord Jesus Christ) divides the World into two parts only, *viz.* the humble afflicted Children of Sacred Love, those of the day, and the proud unmortified Workers of evil in the Kingdom of Darkness: Whereby it is that the renewed Image hath only Enmity for its Enemy.

Q. 160. *Which is the very mark of a right Christian upon Earth, whereby Men may distinguish him from a Titulary Christian?* Here begins the Ninth Grand Distribution.

A. In the 154 Answer is much to the opening of this.

1. The Christian in Heart and Life is very precious, and as secret as precious: Thus precious Metals are the most secret being resembled by base:, so precious Stones have their counterfeits, and Nature is much of it imitated by Art, even as the out-issued or out-flown Nature of this World is but a Figure of the two Eternal Worlds; all therefore to be seen here are not the things themselves,

bu

but Shadows, Figures, and Representations, and those, but as in a Glass darkly.

2. What wonder then that the Christian is unknown to others, and to himself also in great measure when *Paul* saith of himself, left while I Preach to others I my self be a Cast-away. The new Man is not very apparent to him in whom he is, when yet is at a good growth, and sometimes wholly obscur'd; for the Astral Man hath a very Dim sight, and sees such things only by similitudes which impose mistakes: And the Eternal Soul is like jarring untun'd Strings of an Instrument: So that the holy new Principle is buried, drown'd and out-founded.

3. How may the Heavenly Man be distinguisht from all pretended Christians, seeing there is given him a white Stone and a new Name which none can read, but he that hath it? And how obscure the Characters ingraved in that white Stone are, may appear in this, that when the Lord said to the Twelve one of you shall betray me, they all severally askt, Master, Is it I? So that he only who had not the white Stone was able to know who it was, and by consequence who were not Traytors, but Faithful. And yet notwithstanding all that hath been said the right Christian may be known partly by comparing him with the contrary Characters of the Titulary Christian, and partly by something visible in him, who is the Christian in Heart.

4. The Character of the Titulary Christian is, he makes the profit, pleasure and pride of things on Earth his great and constant aim, and it cannot be otherwise, (pretend he what he will) for this is his home, his all, his treasure, where else can be his Heart?

5. His first Principle is uneasie to him unless he hath somewhat to go into; for his first four Properties being by his loss of the Divine World (in the Fall) at perpetual enmity, and in respect of his dark Principle separately considered he is a Tormentor or Hell to himself; therefore laying hold on the third Principle (which is all he can reach) his hungry Fire and Rage is mitigated; as Men in pain and grief are a little eased by delightful Objects diverting the regret of their Melancholy, as Children by Toys do cease crying.

6. Thus the prosperity of the Fool shall slay him; it made him say, Soul take thine ease, eat, drink, and be merry. Did I not studiously shun many words much might profitably be said, shewing how according to this the Lord Jesus doth Character the Scribes and Pharisees, which were Hypocrites, and what the whole reprehensions of the Prophets and Apostles in all the holy Records say of this out-cast state; who all with one continued cry, did in all Ages perswade. recal. and warn Man, from the Image and Shadow to the true Eternal holy substance, and condemn his obstinate refusal: The Holy Ghost convincing him of his stupid Lust to his Chains and Prison, willing him to leave off his grave Cloths.

7. But the Faithful Christian is distinct from the Titular Christian in this, that his main aim, bent of his will, stream of his affections, bottom of his real designs, desires and longings are not after, and stay not in the figure, but penetrate into the substance, lives to, groans, and thirsts after, the Inward Man.

8. Nothing he finds can compose true peace but reuniting the Light World to him, which is done only by the death of the Enmity, not the death of the Enemies; for then the Soul were Mortal if the Powers or Properties could be kill'd; but the Regenerate Man dies to the Self-will and Lusts, to which the Titular Christian is a great resolute stranger. And that it is said he dies to the Sensual Man is so true that it cannot be otherwise; for the sensual Life is to the Life of the new Man, the resigned Inward Man, as sickness is to health, which by the true Physician is drove away.

9. And tho' Men have the Heavenly and Hellish Properties in them, that which
soever

The 177 Theosophick Questions Answered.

soever they awaken that Fire burneth, and becomes the Life of the Man suppressing the contrary property, yet is not the prevailing Property of these two easily distinguishable in the Out-birth, but very obscure: Even as the Light of the Sun, by the interposition of gross palpable Fogs and Exhalations, is less visible than the Lustre of a Bright Moon in a serene Air.

Q. 161. *What is properly a Christian within and without? How is he a Temple of the Holy Ghost in which the Kingdom of God is inwardly revealed or manifested? How doth he walk and converse in Heaven and upon Earth both at once?*

A. 1. The last preceding Answer distinguisheth a Christian from another Man, so that to the first, second and third parts of this it may suffice to say, that the Christian properly such, hath inwardly his first principle (consisting of the four Anguishes, the Root or Fire and indissoluble Band of the Soul) illustrated and regulated by the Love Fire (which is the Divine Holy Life) out of the second principle. In respect whereof he walks and converseth in Heaven as in an Angelical state in great purity and simplicity, as such are they dear Children and were not the third Principle annexed to them, were in the Holy Eternal Paradise already.

2. But were they not invested by the Out-birth or Astral World, they could not be the compleat Image of the Trinity, which in that respect the Angels themselves are not. Therefore according to the Astral Man the regenerate Soul is properly the Temple of the Holy Ghost, but the Holy Angels themselves wanting that Principle are not said to be so.

3. Thence it is our Apostle dehorting from polluting it by Harlots; But that we keep our Bodies pure and chaste, tells us, they are the Temples of the Holy Ghost, which if we defile, we destroy Gods Temple, and that who doth so, him will God destroy; for as the whole third Principle is the propriety of the Holy Ghost, so peculiarly is Mans Outward Man or Astral Man his Temple.

4. In the outward Man of some of Gods Holy Children, therefore the inward Power World so manifesteth it self, that it giveth vigour of the Eternal Holy World into the Tincture of their Astral Man (as in the Prophets and Apostles) to enter into their Diseased Brother, and bring his weak Faith both into a potent and good order, with such Energy as fortifies the Paralitick, separates the impurity of the Leper, calms the rage of the Calenture, revives the drooping, stays the departing, and sometimes recalls the departed outward Life; Gods Spirit awakening the Magical Virtue of his Children, all things are possible.

Q. 162. *What is the Antichrist upon Earth under Christianity?*

A. 1. Although the Holy Ghost describes Antichrist, his Rise, his Character, and the method of his destruction adding that there are many Antichrists: Yet so mysterious is he that it is proverbial that Antichrist is the Philosophers Stone in Divinity. His shelter is the Darkness, his defence the Word and Power of Hell and wicked pretended Christians. Of this Vizard of Darkness the Divine Light divests him, and the Divine strength consumes him, the brightness of the Lords coming discovers him, and the Spirit of his Mouth destroys him. How then can any be deliver'd from the Tyranny of Antichrist who are strangers to Christ, or any know Christ who are willingly in servitude to Antichrist?

2. The time of Antichrists discovery and destruction is certainly come; but as the Sun gradually prepares his way from the dark Morning, by making step by step in his Chambers of the East, so are the Heavenly approaches made. While the

The 177 Philosophick Questions Answered.

the Pope points at *Mahomet*, the reformed Christians at the Pope, and at that or the other Party : how unlike are we all to the Lord's Disciples, when the Lord said, *One of you shall betray me*, they said not, *Is it he*, but *Is it I, is it I*?

3. Antichrist is not by that Name known in the whole New Testament, or Epistles of the Apostles or Holy Pen-men, but in the first and second Epistles of *John*, and in them five times, and no more. The Mystery whereof may be his prevalence in all the Five Senses; thus understood, the Astral Man is his which should be the Temple of the Holy Ghost, therein Antichrist sits as God, and there shews himself that he is God *(viz.)* in them.

4. But *Paul* knows him, 1. By his Names. 2. By his Character. 3. By his time of being revealed. And, 4. By his time of being consumed. (1.) His Names, *viz.* 1. *a* Man of Sin. 2 *b* Son of Perdition. 3. *c* Mystery of Iniquity. 4. *d* Strong Delusions. (2.) By his Character. 1. Unbridled Pride and Self-Exaltation, *(viz.)* above all that is called God, or that is Worshipped. 2. He whose coming is after the working of Satan *(viz.)* with all Power, Signs and lying Wonders. 3. With all deceivableness of Unrighteousness. 4. That it should make Men believe a Lye, that they might be Damned. (3) By his time of being revealed, *(viz.)* upon the withdrawing, of the Glory; which while it was so present as to let and hinder, yet even then did the Evil one begin to work. (4.) By his time of being consumed, and means how *(viz.)* by the Spirit of the Mouth of the Lord, and his being destroyed by the brightness of his coming.

2 Thess. 2. (1.)
a v. 2.
b v. 3.
c v. 7.
d v. 11.
(2.)
(3.)
v. 7.
(4.)
v. 8.

5. Those who understand the four Forms composing the first or hellish Principle, can well and distinctly see the signification of the four Names given him by the Holy Ghost mentioned by the first of the above four Heads. And those who can view the Operations of those four Properties exclusive of Divine Light, can also well know the four Characters of the second of the above Heads. And those who understand the third Head, see the Birth of the *Turba* in the Soul, which *Adam* introduced by shutting out the Light of his true Humanity. But those Children of the day who follow the meek Saviour in Faith, Purity, Patience and Simplicity, know no more of Antichrist than the Eleven did of *Judas* Treason, but are received into another Life and Principle; for the Essences of their Souls have generated the Love-fire, and they dwell in that hidden brightness and serenity by which Antichrist is unveiled; yet these know no more of him than the Day doth of the Night.

6. The appearing of Antichrist upon the withdrawing of the Divine Unction, the holy Light World, may be understood not as Night to day, but as followeth. A Man's noble Intellect departs, yet may remain his Proportions of Body, and a Capacity of imitating externally what others seem to do understandingly: and what also himself was formerly able to do rationally. yet now his words are rather those of Parots, and his doings the gestures of Apes, than those of Prudent Men. Thus Antichrist speaks the words of Christ, but without the Power, Bows, Kneels, Prostrates yet without the Presence of Christ.

Simile.

7. Again, a Tree dead at Root, may seem by the Branches and Leaves too (for a little time) like a growing Tree: so the reflection in an opposing Cloud of the Rainbow, represents another, yet is but a meer shew of the true Rainbow, and so have we *Parelii* or Mock-Suns; Such is the Antichrist, but with this difference, (among other important ones) that Antichrist dwelling in the unmortified Affections, hath Enmity against what it seems to be, which none of the above Similes have any thing of.

8. By many of the like Contemplations and Similitudes may be apprehended, how Antichrist was revealed upon the departing of the Peace-proclaiming Light of Christ; which every Soul sadly Experiments in its Declensions, turnings aside,

lookings

lookings back, slumberings and unfaithfulness; but where it proceeds to final Apostacy and Enmity of Spirit, it is Antichrist in Epitomy, as the outward Hypocrisie is Antichrist in the Mirror or Looking-glass. See the 139 Answer, *v.* 3, 4.

9. Thus may be seen that Antichrist is the result or Law decreed and ratified by the titular Christians Reason. And Reason is the general Knowledge of things, attain'd and taught by the collected Observations of the Senses; for their particular Acts and Experiments are the Materials of Reason, as Letters are of Books.

10. Antichrist in the high Exercise of his Reason may have a Name to live, but because that his Reason is the Child of his Senses, it must needs be true that he is Dead (*viz.*) to the Divine Life; for he is only sensually rational, which a Dog (now hurt by a Stone thrown on him, flying from the offer of throwing anon another) partaketh of.

11. Wherefore Antichrist not having the Spirit of Christ, confirms himself in his own; as it is written, sensual, not having the Spirit, for the Spirit of Life and Holiness is vouchsafed us only in the fifth Form, whereunto the regenerate only reach, and whereof every unmortified Soul can attain no more but the Counterfeit, as it is written, A grain of Wheat remaineth alone, and is not quickened except it die.

12. And as Antichrist is Dead to the Holy Life by being alive to himself : So those who enter the Holy Life are Dead to the sensual, and consequently to the Earthy rational, and in that respect may in an excellent sence be said to be besides themselves, and according to the Maxims of Astral Reason are Fools and Madmen, to give all their present Professions and the Advantages of their Acquirements, Emoluments and whole Man, in exchange for unseen Futurities and Hope of them; for such see plainly that Reason and the Senses, are such things only, as the more accomplish'd a Nominal Christian is in that inferior Principle, the more strong a Beast, the more dangerous an Antichrist is he.

13. 'Tis true, Man falling in *Adam* into this third Principle God's immense pity met him in Sacrifices, a worldly Sanctuary, Perfumes of Incense, *&c.* That his Senses should be Witnesses of Divine Condescension, but when the Lord became Flesh, he led to Sublime things, (*viz.*) Spiritual Worship, not confin'd to places, *&c.* Holy Faith and the new Creature, wrought by the Almighty Spirit of God.

14. Therefore, Man's having begun in the Spirit, declining as if he would be made perfect in the Flesh is the Essential Character of Antichrist; for as *Lucifer* fell thus into his central Fire: so falls Antichrist into his circumferential Fire, or Astral Out-birth, (*viz.*) from the Holy Eternal Light, to the figure of it in the sensual part, which readily uniting with the four dark Anguishes of the first Principle, becomes a fixt Enmity to the Holy Powers. See the 118 Answer, *v.* 5.

Antichrist as it is a fixed Enmity is incurable, being like a Disease grounded on the Constitution; See the 128 Answer, *v.* 6.

Q. 163. *What is* Babel *or* Babylon, *the Beast and the Whore in the Apocalypse or Revelations* ?

A. 1. *Babel* the Beast and the Whore is the World's Trinity; for all that is so in, as to be of the World is the Lust of the Eye, the Lust of the Flesh, and the Pride of Life; the best of the Evil World (as far as the Holy Powers are withdrawn, lock'd up, or excluded) is in those three Lusts Comprized and Anatomized.

The Root of the three.

2. The Beast hath its Foundation in the Elementary Man, *Babel* in the Astral, but the Whore in both, and all of them in the Dust, and are themselves no other Dust but such as the Wind from above shall scatter and drive away. Thus the inquiring Mind may, by considering, find what these three are, and how varied in their

The 177 Theosophick Questions Answered.

their Root and Original. It is next to be shewn how they are diftinguish'd in their Progrefs and Operation.

3. The Beaft becomes more and more Senfual, fome more coveting reft and felf-pleafing, like fuch Beafts who greedily covet fulnefs, in contempt of the Creator's Defign, and wilful Ignorance of the ftate the (ftarving) Soul loft by the Fall, and the means conducing to its recovery being far from p.eafing and pampering the Flefh but thefe Swinifh Lufts would fain be fated with the Husks of things. Another fort are fierce, dogged, unfociable; others haughty; others luftful, filthy, &c. But the Apocalyptical Beaft includeth all thefe, adding fuccefs by great accefs of Power among wretched Mankind, who either by Fraud or Force obtain outward Magiftracy or Soveraignty, thefe the World goeth or wondereth after. *Their Progrefs.*

4. The Progrefs or Operation of *Babel* is the exercife of Man's Reafon in things truly known only in the Regeneration; thus *Babel* is the Centre where all the ftraight or arch lines of Confufion drawn by the Beaft or Whore meet. Here all Ages, and all Nations and Languages do agree in difagreement, and are fo far from knowing the true God, that they know nothing truly, much lefs themfelves or others, feeming and but feeming to be ever learning, but ftill at Enmity againft Truth.

5. The Progrefs or Operation of the Whore is that Spirit in Man which diffembleth the inward Naughtinefs, with the outward guife of Holinefs, Purity and Devotion. this Whore never was a Wife but in the time and place of Efpoufal was rejected, abandoned and feparated, or repudiated, called a Divorcement but improperly. never being really Married, for her Filthinefs fo clave to her, that her unfteadfaftnefs and unfaithfulnefs appears in her adulterous Eyes, her impudent Forehead, her feigned Dialect, her difdainful Deportment. Now as the Whore is fenfual, fhe rooteth in, and as one with the Beaft; for which caufe the Antichriftian Spirit ever ftrengtheneth it felf by Uniting with the Temporal Magiftracy and Authority. And as the Whore is the Ape or Counterfeit of the Holy Work wrought in Mens Wills. it being only pictured in her Intellect, without affecting the Soul or Mind, much lefs fubjecting the Will; fo is the Whore a Builder of *Babel*, concerning which Whore, reference is made to the laft foregoing Anfwer concerning Antichrift.

6. It feems fit alfo to fay fomething of the Attainments, Refults or Summits of thefe three. The Whore can attain to fit as a Queen, to ride on the Beaft. to induce the Kings of the Earth to drink the Wine of her Fornication, in all this fhe deceiveth others; but fhe is not a Queen; alfo the hope concerning her felf, that fhe fhall fee no forrow, fhall fail; for fhe fhall be hated. they fhall eat her Flefh and burn her with Fire, fo fhe deceives her felf as effectually as others. *Their higheft Attainments.*

7. The Beaft having its Rod in the Elementary World, and its fatiety therein being filled therewith is (when broken by the *Turba*) refolved thereinto; fo that fuch as ftill the Out cries of their Eternal Souls therewith, have their whole Life but a deceitful Dream, and when the Elements drop off, awake into Horror and Nakednefs.

8. The Summit and Refult of *Babel* is to be alway doing what cannot be done: as that figure the Tower, was never finifhed, they are the foolifh Builder, which is ftill beginning, but never compleats any one thing; inftead of compleating order, they end in Anguifh.

9. The Fulnefs and Attainment of the Beaft is of the three, the moft truly effected; for as in the Mire and Duft he dwells, of that he fills himfelf he hath no higher Luft; Profit, Eafe, Pleafure and outward Honour he Defigns, and if he hath it, and can bound his Defires to the Proportion obtainable by him, he is beft of the three; for his Life is a pleafant Dream, his Mifery is out of his prefent view, his Eternal part being choak'd, cries not out, but he rejoyceth in the good fuccefs

his Craft, Violence or Cruelty hath: the present is his Heaven, Futurities are in his Esteem airy Speculations, but the Evil Day (if perhaps at the Door) seems to be very far off; his Misery is, that sure-footed Death must come and undeceive him, and convince him that his Thoughts having perishing Objects, do themselves perish. Thus the Beast, like the light of a Gloworm, being only the issues of the Senses. *Babel* being like the Light of a Candle as the Product of depraved Reason, these two Lights are United by the Whore, who undertaketh by them to shew Heaven to others, which is as easie and demonstrable as it is with a Candle in a close Night to shew the clouded Stars: whereas Heaven can only be seen by its own Light, as even the outward Heaven is.

Q. 164. *What is the Ruin of the Beast, and how is it effected that the seven headed Beast should become cast into the Abyss?*

A. 1. When a Vegetative as a Tree or Plant attaineth its fulness, it issueth into Flowers, Fruits, &c. whereunto if its vigor inable it not, it declines and steps backward towards its first Mover, so do Sensitives and rational Creatures. But because the Astral Worlds that they may figure Eternity have a Prerogative Royal, it is only required of them in Conformity to the Universal Order, to condescend to a resemblance of the rest by Revolutions.

2. The Number of the Beast is 666. far below the 1000 the Crown Number. And all his seven Properties are included in the six working Forms, never attaining the true Seventh, which is the only rest: So that the Beast wants Vigor to bear Fruit, but having brought all his seven no higher or farther than the limit of six, there grovelleth, therein is bounded, and those bounds are as those *Lucifer* and his Legions find themselves immutably confin'd by, as by Adamantine Chains of condensed Darkness, the Beast is not so near rest as 6 is to 7, but as 666 is to 1000. And as the Evil Angels having secluded themselves from the meek Majestick Order, will yet be as Eminent in their Evil as they can; so Man being become bestial, willeth to be as extreamly and vigorously a Beast, as he may. He is conversant about the Dictates of the sensual Man seldom proceeding but so far as the depraved rational, which yet were he, they both would not only fall utterly short, but indispose him to the true Light: as a Man brought out of a dark Dungeon is surprized, and sees not in the dazling Sun.

3. Now how the Seven headed Beast is cast into the Abyss is thus done, he is destroy'd by Intestine or as 'tis call'd, Civil Discord. A Beast hath many things like to a Man, so the Apocalyptical Beast hath the Notion of Grace, making room in the Regenerate by Combat and Warfare, to destroy the impure depraved Lusts, and cleanse the House, that the King of Glory may enter. The Beast flatters himself. finding a disposition in him to be rid of some Sins, though it be as Men are of troublesome Tenants; without design of receiving a Heavenly Guest as the Regenerate do, for Grace is none the Beast desires not, for he knows no such, but doth it only to ease himself of such who are unprofitable Associates. Nor is there in the bestial Man a Warfare betwixt Grace and Sin, the pure Spirit and sinful Flesh, the Holy Virgin Image, and the unmortified or revivings of Lust; Though in the Astral Man (as it is more nearly the Instrument of the Eternal Soul) there is something better than is in the bestial Man as in a more simple ingeny, where the Tincture is less incurvated, or the Mind byassed, than in the sensual bestial Man. So that unto that Man, the Heavenly Applications have readier intercourse, more familiarly to impart it self, and diffuse its beams; therefore was it, and still is it, that the Soul is often spoken to in Dreams; the Visions of the Night finding her best at leisure, and emptied in some sort of the bestial Man's Clamors and throngs

of Impositions. But the War in the unregenerate Man is between the adverse parts and properties wherewith his Soul is endowed, or whereof rather it is composed, and as resulting from them the strife is between that natural Intellect, which distinguisheth him from the Transitory Brutes on the one hand, and his impetuous Lusts on the other.

4. This Intellect may be call'd his Natural Conscience whereof the Apostle speaks, that in those things which they understand, as [viz. little differenced from] natural Brute Beasts, in those they corrupt themselves. Now in this contest where the depraved Intellect sentenceth that or this to be evil or good, the will resulting from the Rebel Affections (which will is regent, and by Prerogative deems himself unaccountable) calls the evil good, indulgeth it, delights in it and assimilates, becomes one with it. This natural Intellect the Beast deceived by the Whore, calls the new Creature and Regenerator, and flatters himself to be fighting the Fight of the Faith of Gods Elect or precious Ones : Whereas their dark Heads and inimicitious Hearts are only engaged in Intestine Broils, from the disorder of their native contrary Parts or Faculties. And this Light is that whereof the Lord speaks, *If the Light that is in thee be Darkness, how great is that Darkness?* viz. If the Eye be evil and not single the four forms all this while proceed not to enkindle the true fifth but are compassed by the sparks [of Fire] of their own private Spirits] enkindling, not Flames of Light blown up by the Spirit of Divine Love. And other times the Affections enclined by their good Astral Man or Constellation, or perhaps by some surprize of Sympathy have a warmth towards compassionate and righteous Actions; but yet at the same time the Mind is abstractedly darkness; for death and disorder reigneth there. These may give some Light to the inquiring Observer by what ways the Beast deceives, precipitates and destroys himself, plunging himself into the Abyss of Confusion, for all his seven Heads, Forms or Properties being so many implacable Enemies to each other, rend and ruine him.

Q. 165. *How doth Christ take the Kingdom when this Beast becometh slain?*
The Tenth Distribution.

A. 1. Here we are come to enquire how that is done which we are taught to pray for, [*Thy Kingdom come*] out of that Kingdom, we, like the Prodigal, wandered, and became as he, into a most wretched state ; desirous to eat of the Swines meat, but no one gave even that, shewing us he had no right or title to it, but either must beg it, or steal it, having not to pay for it, and yet must have it or perish for hunger In this very state, and nothing better is every man till Christ introduceth his Kingdom into the Soul: And Man's going out of himself, is in this Parable call'd a coming to himself.

2. But Reason can neither speak what This Kingdom is, nor understand the written or spoken Language concerning it, be it spoken with all possible plainness, or written with ample demonstration; for Reason hath but one Eye, and that looks downward like the Eye of a Beast, and the Lust of Property and incessant Thirst to gratifie the Flesh (by self-pleasing, its own exaltation, self-avenging &c. like manifold Cloths of Pitch, shuts it up from the Kingdom of Christ; so that all it can by this reach to, is but as a swiming in the brain, the receptacle and working-shop of the Sensitive Astral, and Depraved Rational Spirits: But the Eternal Word is spoken in the Heart, which in opposition to that of the Brain, is only mentioned; and it's not without signification, that the word Brain is scarce found in the whole Bible, but always the Heart as that which the Lord regardeth to mention.

A a 3. The

3. The Knowledge how Chrift takes the Kingdom will be much advanced, by clearing how *Adam* loft it. For as the Spiritual World breathed it felf through the Outward, which is its Image; fo the Divine World filled the Effences of *Adam*'s Soul, alfo fwallowed up his Aftral Man then capable of Eternity, fo that his firft four Forms were fweetly united in the Image of Holinefs and true Righteoufnefs; and thus themfelves were as it were hidden. The Aftral Man alfo was only ferviceable to its Illuftration, and thereby compleatly happy; fharing (according to its capacity) the Glory together with his noble Soul, replenifht with his Divine Spirit.

4. And his departure from the Eternal Subftantiality of the Divine Life, was to live according to Aftral Reafon, as to his Inward Man, and no higher: And according to the Senfual Beftiality in his Outward; both which are but the Figure or Shadow of the true fubftantial Spiritual World; thereupon he died to the Divine Life. And the Magical Power of his Effences being Thofe Properties whereof his Soul is compofed, wanting Heavenly Food, became a dark, hungry, fierce, inimicitious Will, fpoiling his Tincture, as is feen in raging, furious, defperate men; from thenceforth wanting a Mouth capable to eat Paradifical Food; therefore God curfed the Earth, that it alfo fhould no more be able to produce, nor be intrufted with Living Holy Fruits of the Heavenly Power-World; for the Heavenly Humanity once withdrawn, Man was no longer a Subject, Member, Citizen or Child of God's Kingdom, but a Beaft, and in the Beftial, Aftral and Elementary Kingdom at Enmity with the Holy, Pure, Sweet, Eternal Order.

5. Therefore Chrift taketh the Kingdom by bringing again the holy difappeared Power-World, or Heavenly Humanity, into the captivated, dark, debilitated Humanity, call'd an Ingrafted Word, alfo a Seed growing to a Tree: A Leven levening the whole: A Refiner, and is as a fparkle enkindling the whole; and as in germination of a Seed, the grofs matter (given it from the Elements) dieth, or as of the burnt Sacrifice the Elementary part is by the fire of the Altar, feparated into a Vapour and Salt: Juft fo Chrift entred the corrupted Man, and leading it through Death, became the true Separator. He brought the holy Virgin Image, the alone Heavenly Virginity, which is fignified by the Salt thrown by *Elifha* to heal the Fountain, into the Stream: For This Divine Power healeth the Tincture, and the Tincture being cured, (like the healed Spring) by its new got Magical Might and Puiffance, is a Co-worker with God in regenerating the whole Man: As the Subterranean Fire doth draw one way with the Solar Fire in propagating and advancing the Generation of Metals, ejection of Fountains and fanative hot Baths.

6. This Kingdom is not taken but purchafed by the Blood of the King of it, and what this Blood was, fee the 124 Anfwer 2, 6, 8, and 9 verfes, but this Kingdom is fuch that it is the fcope of all the Writings of the holy Ones from *Adam* the firft Man, to the unknown day and hour of the end of this dying World. Men who would fain be Atheifts have faid the great ingredient of their mortal, fatal, contagious Madnefs, hath been the obferving how little affected the Converfations of fuch fhew them to be, who profefs the knowledge, love and fear of an Infinite, Powerful, Omnifcient and Omniprefent Glorious and Gracious Father, Son and Holy Ghoft, thinking they could not fo converfe did they indeed believe what themfelves fay.

7. But the reafon thereof hath been the deceiving Spirit, for there hath all along been fuch Sacrificers as *Cain*, fuch as have the Faith of *Simon Magus*, the Prophefyings of *Balaam*, the Humility of *Ahab*, the Repentance of *Judas*, the Abftinence of the Foolifh Virgins, the priviledge of the Tares, to be the Gueft without a Wedding

The 177 Theosophick Questions Answered.

ding Garment, the Branch yet wither'd and cut off, the Wife but Divorced, the Building without Foundation, those who after cleansing take seven worse Spirits, whose goodness is like the Morning Dew; Stars, but either fallen or wandering ones, Teachers, but yet at last Cast-aways. All these professing themselves of Christs, are really of the Devils Kingdom.

8. For that which these attain, is at highest but Faith as it is an act of the understanding: which gives a false faint Light without Life and Heat; while the Faithful Subjects are actuated and moved by a Faith that purifieth the Heart, and subjecteth the Will, proceeding from strength to strength; for as purifying Faith worketh from Love, so it increaseth Love, Simplicity and Innocency, and there is founded the Kingdom of Patience. It is true Mahometans, the dark Ethnicks and Barbarians call those things Vices and those Vertues which we call so, and by that Rule, They accuse or excuse themselves or others. But the Doctrine of our Lord Jesus Christ the Son of God, not only condemns our evil, but tenders us Life Eternal, it kills us to save us, that is, it sends us out of our selves by resignation of our separate, perverse will; that we may be regenerated unto the holy universal comprehensive will. Whereby is obtain'd and convey'd not only self-abasing but purging and saving Mercy of Free Grace, as only of meer Alms from God; This Grace proceeding from pure pity and undeserved goodness, is of all things in the World the most disagreeable to Mans unmortified proud Heart, most cross to his own will, therefore the most sublimely, divinely true.

9. Faln Mans dejecting himself may be call'd Humiliation, Anguish, and a Spirit of Bondage, but the top of this is but uncloathing the Man, who is thereby neither wash'd nor cleansed, but the Conscience still polluted, the proud Devils must yet see their own deformity with Anguish; thus this Spirit in Man shuts him up in the first four Forms or Properties: But it is the Spirit of God by the Faith of the Gospel which is generated in the fifth, growing to a Flame of Love by the Holy Blood of the true second *Adam* only washeth the Soul, and sprinkleth the Conscience from dead Works. How miserable then must those Men be who are willingly ignorant of the power and infinite value of Christs Heavenly Blood? and yet themselves undervaluing it, are pretended Perfectists, yet declare so great an aversion to this as if they would know nothing of that which the Apostle *Paul* desir'd only to know. Contemning the inquiry into that Mystery which the Angels desire to look into. But to help the sincere Mind towards the Understanding of the Heavenly condescention in the Lords Incarnation, the reperusal of the 106 Answer is seriously recommended. And what kind of Subjects Christ taketh into his Kingdom are Character'd in the 117 Answer from ver. 3. to the 8th. And what the inestimable Blood of this Lamb of God is, see the 77th Answer, ver. 7, 8, and 9.

The Kingdom is taken by the Glorious King of it without hands: As the Angel faith of the Stone to *Daniel*; even as the outward Sun conveys not his Light and enlivening Heat by the violence of stormy Winds, but is calmly and sweetly his own Vehicle, under whose glorious, dear Sway and Scepter may the Lord bring our whole Man and every part of it for ever, that this which is the Kingdom of Gods patience may be that of his Power; concerning things pertaining to this Kingdom the Lord discoursed with his Disciples in the forty days after his Resurrection. But yet this Kingdom suffereth violence, tho' it doth none, and the violent take it by force, for it requires that all diligence be used, that Men work out their Salvation with fear and trembling, that they ask, seek, knock, search, dig, watch, fight, strive, wrestle, suffer, wait, (comparatively) hate Father, Mother, Wife, Child, and our own Life: Pray without ceasing, looking to Jesus, &c. for as the King entred by the Cross so must the Subjects.

Q. 166.

The 177 *Theosophick Questions Answered.*

Q. 166. *What is the true new Regeneration in the Spirit of Christ ? Is it done in this time, or after this time ?*

A. 1. Here is a question consisting of two parts. 1. What the true new Regeneration is? 2. What time is it wrought in? Both of them are secrets; the first done by the Almighty Power of the Holy Ghost, the latter perfected and consummated by the same Power, concurring with the Gracious Providence of Infinite Wisdom. The first so great an inward Divine Work, as none but such in whom it is wrought can speak more of it but as Parrots, so that the Experimental Work only enables rightly to see, taste, feel and know it: And the Spirit working it, can only rightly open the Mouth and guide the Hand to tell, and describe it. And this being spoken in the plainest, simplest way, can yet be received and profitable to such only, who by the same Spirit are not only enlighten'd, but made alive by the new Regeneration.

2. Therefore in answer to the first part of the Question, we are to know that God made of one Blood all Nations of the Earth, and all Men in one Principle, *viz.* the third, consisting of the first four Properties for its Root: But the second was Mans Paradifical Garland, his Heaven, his Crown and Divine Image: This, our Root and common Father the first *Adam*, suppressed, extinguished and caused to die, and disappear. Thenceforth Man became like the Cursed Earth, whereof some plats bear Thorns and Briars, others fetid Weeds, others poysonous Plants, others less noxious Products, according to the prevalency of every of which the plat is named. So some Men are hurried by the impetuous storms and fury of the four Anguishes of the first Principle, and so are Devilish; others are swallow'd up of the voluptuous Lusts of the Elementary Spirit, and thence rightly called sensual; others steered and regulated by the Maxims of the Siderial World, and these can be no more or better than Earthy.

3. Now out of all these the Divine Power ingenerating Faith, not only acting in the understanding, but swaying the Scepter of the Will; also self-denial, both as from abhorrence of the defiling self, and also from self-interest, property, and self-pleasing, which is as the Flower of Grass; then cometh a hunger after the unseen *Manna*, which is the Root producing the meek resignation of self-pleasing desires, patient submission to the Cross, which as it were insensibly enkindleth in the Soul, the sweet, dear, silent retirement, rest and peace, the passing into the fifth form, and this walkt in gradually regenerateth and tinctureth the dark perverted Soul, with the noble new universal Power and Might: And these are as different according to the procedure of Men, as years distinguish the growth and stature of Children; But done so silently by the Holy Spirit in Mans Spirit, as the Blossom issueth and after it the Fruit.

4. The true new Regeneration in the Spirit of Christ is always new; and that continually and successively renewed, if indeed it be true, not as the natural Birth of Children into this World, who are so Born but once, but rather as the growing of the Embrio in the Womb to a formed, animated, perfect Child: Nor as an Arrow flying through by the force of its first push, but as a Ship sailing through successive Perils, and always returning to its latitude from various aberrations, and passing through raging Surges, as over so many Deaths. Or as young people recover out of, escaping from and through many Sicknesses and Relapses. For the Lord himself teacheth, saying to his Disciples, who none doubts were before that converted, *Except ye be converted, and become as this little Child, ye cannot enter into the Kingdom of God:* Which then they were not; for their quest was who should be the greatest; thus tho' Metal upon Metal be false Herauldry, Conversion upon Conversion is true Christianity. 5. Nor

The 177 Theosophick Questions Answered.

5. Nor is this less plain and evidently real in it self to the Children of the day, (tho' *Nicodemus* the Night Visiter misunderstood it) than that the outward Suns Diurnal appearances on the Earths Revolutions, make so many new days; and every advance of the new Born Soul towards Perfection is such another thing than was the former, as this Harvest is than the last was; for the Soul can no more continue to grow by the first stirrings of the Heavenly World in it, than the Body be nourished and supported by the Food it received the last Month, or the Plants by the Rain they imbibed the last year, or the *Manna* gathered one day be Food the following day when grown Verminous, Thus God saith, Behold I make all things new.

6. Such therefore who pinfold their apprehensions of the new Regeneration by the Gage and Glass of the Natural Birth of Children, may as equally infer the Mortification or Dying to the corrupt Man to be one only act: Contrary to the Apostle, *I die daily*. Whereas we both die daily, and are daily regenerated, as Night and Day, Winter and Summer are successively perpetuated. Among the *Roman* Ecclesiasticks their Novices are under an absolute Arbitrary Subjection to the Tyranny of their unaccountable Superiors, but the higher the Soul advanceth to the superior parts of true Regeneration, the more simply and resignedly obedient is he, till he actively, passively and compleatly become as a little Child.

7. And now to the second part of the Question, Is it done in this time, or after this time? It is answer'd in the immediately preceding Discourse on the first part of this Question, That the Regeneration is not wrought by one act as neither is Mortification done at once, but gradually by little and little effected, as a Summer hath its Spring, a Day its Dawning, a Vintage its sprouting out.

Obj. 1. 8. Is it objected Omnipotence may perfect the Regeneration at once by one single act?

A. Without the Censure of confining Infinity it's queried on what Ground is this presumption Built? God shews us his way by all his gracious Discoveries; for instance, that of the Creation of the Out-world leads us as by the Hand, to the view of the progress of the new Creation, in which not to touch particulars which were repeating what is elsewhere done and digressive, it may not be denyed but the Light call'd for at the beginning might have been multiplied into the inkindling of the whole deep, that all had been as a Sun, and so the alone figure of the Heavenly World, but how then had this Out-birth figur'd both Worlds or both Principles, wherein the seven properties should impress themselves in their distinct powers? Therefore was that Light collected, and the place of the Sun ennobled with the preheminence of the Empire of the Out-world; as the Representer of the Holy Infinite second Principle the Son of God. And the Darkness which before covered the Deep, was conserved by condensation of the Terrestrial Globe whereon we creep, and the Crassitude of the other Stars, to figure the Infinite Eternal first Principle, whereinto according to the dark impression thereof Man fell, and out of which he is gradually recover'd, as by way of similitude, the Suns lustre attenuateth the gross Air by his continual variation by steddy, orderly and regular approaches toward either Tropick.

Obj. 2. 9. But God new regenerateth the Spirit of Christ in Man at dissolution of the outward Life at one instant, and by the same dissolution is it effected and compleated.

A. What Omnipotence may do is not for vile dust to comprehend, for it is written, I know thou canst do all things, and the Thief on the Cross was a Monument of unsearchable Grace, yet by the words of that Thief there seems not only a preparedness, but a good degree of Conviction of guilt, penitence, sence and anguish under it; inlightening to know the Lord Jesus, Faith to direct and fortifie

his

his petition, and a seeing the unseen Kingdom; yet so late a Repentance tho' thus manifested is the one only singular president on Record.

Q. 10. *But it may be enquired what the dissolution of the outward Life of its own Nature contributeth hereunto?*

A. It must be acknowledged that it banisheth for ever the outward Objects of our misimployed Affections, and yet it followeth not that it takes away the desire, gust or lust after them, for the breaking of the outward Life, or Elementary and Siderial Man, or the Obligations and Ligaments of our Souls and Spirits, is but as taking away the Skreen, and opening to us the two inward Worlds, which is as the unraking of Fire, and enraging the Souls native forms of the unregenerate, which the Astral and Elementary Man had been before the separation a mitigation of the Anguishes of, so far is Mans dissolution from contributing to a Foundation or Beginning of the Divine Birth. As it may be conceived by noting, that tho' a proper Soil and apt Season may shoot a Mustard-seed sown unto a tall, large stature: Yet the richest Soil, concurring Elements, liberal Season, benign Astral Influences with the Solar Rays uniting, transmute not Tares into Wheat, Thistles into Fig-trees, nor Thorns into Vines.

11. But where the Soul like Flax only smoketh with the Holy Fire, and the Souls Fire is irradiated with (true, tho' weak) Divine Light, rightly directing the Eye of the Mind: Causing the Will and Affections to press forward, mourning, sowing in tears, smiting on the Breast in Anguish, heaviness and good earnestness; the dissolution of such a sincere beginning Pilgrim may be but as plucking up a Thorn Hedge to make the way more accessable, disburthening an over-laden Ship the better to secure the whole, the alighting from a froward, unbroken or tired Horse, which will neither carry the Rider, nor can be carried by him. So unsuitable a Companion doth the Soul (begun to be regenerate) find his Body with the distrustful cares, distracting fears, worldly sorrow, and hateful pollutions thereof. And so adverse are the Maxims of the Sensual Man to those of the New, that they are on terms of Hostility; so that if we live after the Flesh we shall die, but if by the Spirit we mortifie the deeds of the Body we shall live. The Body's Vileness is pointed at by that Statute in *Moses*, that the Holy Anointing Oil was not to be poured on Man's Flesh, tho' not only both the Altars, the Table, Laver, all the Vessels and Candlesticks, but also the very Tabernacle was to be anointed therewith.

12. How much are we less provident than the Brutes, who know and use their season, the Stork, the Ant, &c. and under flattering Hopes of doing all at last, neglect all for ever; but when Harvest is come, begin to sow, regardless of what is written, *To day if you will hear his voice, harden not your hearts.* But besotted, lost Man will promise himself that it is enough at death that the Priest can absolve me. Others, to say, I believe Christ hath done all for me; or because they acknowledge that all are sinners, indulge themselves to be always sinners, neglecting the great End of their Creation, and of Divine Patience, till the Creator is calling them for Accompt of His betrusted Talents, as if they would then work out their Salvation when themselves are passive and unable to action, and the night come when no man can work.

Obj. 3. 13. But we are told, and that by some who detest the Roman Purgatory, that something may be done to compleat the perfection of separate Souls after their separation from the Mortal Body; who produce several Texts out of the Old Testament, and out of the New; also out of the Apocryphal antiquity to point at it, or rather expresly to confirm it; as out of the Old, *Deut.* 26. 14. *Isa.* 61. 1. *Zech.* 9. 11, 12. out of the New, *Matth.* 12. 32. 2 *Tim.* 1. 18. 1 *Pet.* 3. 19. 1 *Pet.* 4. 6. out of the Antient Writings call'd Apocrypha, 2 *Esdras* 7. 37. *Ecclesiasticus*

Justicus 7. 33. 2 *Maccab.* 44. 45. Let us therefore post-pone the first step to the New Birth, till our bodily Letts be removed, when without the obstructions of the Rebel Passions ending with cutting of the Temporal Thread we be adapted thereunto.

A. The Objection supposeth not that one who at separation of the Soul from the Outward Body, after rejecting the Gospel, being in fixt Enmity against God, and the Kingdom of Resignation, is remediable; nor suggesteth that he who soweth himself a Tare, Thorn or Thistle, shall rise a Wheat Corn, Vine or Fig-tree; how therefore may it seem incumbent on me to oppose my self to the dint of the Texts produced?

14. But rather as the Lord Christ in answer to the Question of the Disciples; Wilt thou at this time restore the Kingdom? It is not for you to know the times and seasons which the Father keepeth in his own Power, but prophesieth and chargeth on them on that occasion their immediate concern and business. How much less is it for men to know what the operations of Father, Son and Holy Ghost will be in perfecting separate Souls when out of the Circle of Time and Seasons? For so strong a Fort hath Satan built in mens resolute Self-wills, so impierceable are their Rocky Hearts, that like Leviathan, they laugh at the shaking of the Spear; and as the Servants of Atheistical *Benhadad*, diligently catch every word seeming to favour their flattery of Impunity, that they may treasure up wrath by impenitence more and more against the day of wrath.

15. To these am I sent with happy Tydings, that howsoever the Abyss of Mercy hath winked at the faults of the days of Ignorance, yet now commandeth he all men every where to repent; also with heavy Tydings, that if in this their day they neglect so great Salvation, how shall they escape? Which Question none in Heaven, Earth or Hell answereth. Again, if they that sinned against *Moses* Law died without Mercy, and it might seem the bottom of Misery to die a merciless Death, of how much sorer punishment shall they be thought worthy who have trampled under foot the Son of God, and (blasphemously) counted the Blood of the Covenant an unholy thing, and done despite to the Spirit of Grace? of how much sorer punishment is that Question, but which either is unanswerable, or which Eternity can only unfold?

16. A murthered Body is the sorrow and pity of the Country; a Self-murtherer their shame and indignation, but the unknown number of wounded Souls, and self-murthered Souls, are not regarded; tho' it shall be more tolerable for *Sodom* and *Gomorrah* than for such Gospel-Apostates and Haters of Christ. The malicious Enemy of Mankind (who wounds himself that he may murther Souls, so greatly he hates Man) draws into the Anguishes of his Central Forms whole Harvests of Reprobates (in whom he hath no true Right or Propriety) by his offering Baits and Cheats for Food and Realities, while (woe to the World) the most glorious, gracious and adorable only Son of the only High God, whose we are by Absolute Propriety, and whose Love to Mankind was so immense and unsearchable, as that He made Himself vile, and a Sacrifice, to whom He offereth Real, Highest and Eternal Blessedness; yet hath only the gleanings of the Harvest or Vintage, while the World lieth in wickedness, and their Posterities approve of their saying, calling the proud happy, and perpetuating the Black Art of Self-murther; like Fish hasten greedily to catch the same Bait wherewith others had been hookt: or Birds speed to be taken in an evil Net; so throng Men to be ruined, reject the only Hope, precipitate into irreparable desperation. Others seeming less obstinate, are as fatal Foes to themselves, telling and flattering of to morrow, while such futurities of safety expose them as Fools to perish to day, while Wisdom saith, To day if you will hear his voice harden not your hearts, and that This is the accepted time, This

is

is the day of Salvation. The time of the coming of *John* the Baptist was in the year of *Jubilee*, yet then faith he, The Axe is laid to the Root of the Tree.

17. Our gracious God infinitely out-doth, and out-bids all, to make us his, and restore his Image in us; for in Man's Creation he did much more than for any or all the visible Creatures of the Out-birth or third Principle: in his Redemption for restoring the Divine Image, he did infinitely more for him than any or all the invisible Creatures of the first Principle, the Apostate Angels, for whom is given no Sacrifice nor Mediator: Also in Man's Consummation, Perfection, Sealing and Glorification and Preparation thereunto, is much more done for him than for the Holy glorious Angels (the Sons and Inhabitants (as morning Stars) of the bright Heaven, the Holy second Principle; for the Spirits of just Men made perfect, the general Assembly of the Church of the first born are Fellow-Citizens with the Angelical Worlds, and so share of the infinite Goodness of God as they, and also have this more that they have had in the Lord their Head, the Bowels of infinite Pardoning Mercy drawn out for them, which is peculiarly extended them and treasur'd up only in the Emmanuel for them.

18. This most dear, boundless Goodness calls for the highest and deepest Contemplation; 'tis so profound, so large, so adorable. So admirable that neither can the Earthen Vessel bear it, the Syderial Man find any thing whereunto his Bounty may be likened, the Immortal Soul be properly said to know it, for it is what passeth Knowledge, but the Soul is known by it as it is more or less enlighten'd therewith, and Man's intellectual Spirit is so far from through'ly penetrating it, that it only shines and flows by Influence and Reflection of it, for it self is as a drop of the Abyss enlighten'd by a beam of the Eternal Sun, it burns and flames in the self-evidencing splendor of that incomparable inexhaustible Treasure and excellent Majesty. This poor vile hand lyes prostrate at the Footstool of this Grace the Elementary, and Astral Man, the Eternal Soul and Spirit is herein swallow'd up once and for ever.

Rom. 12. 1.

Rom. 2.

19. How reasonable, necessary and natural was what our Apostle faith, *I beseech you Brethren by the Mercies of God, that ye present your Bodies a living Sacrifice, holy, acceptable unto God.* This is the Riches of his goodness, forbearance and long-suffering to lead man to Repentance. There is a Promise that Men shall fear the Lord and his Goodness. Man's contempt of Bowels of Infinite Mercy shews him less rational than the Bruits, than the Insects, who all shew the desire of Self-defence; while he refuseth to be shielded from the greatest of horror, by the free goodness of his God purchased by his own Blood, with sorrows aggravated to unexpressible mysteriousness: yet is Man offered all at the cheap Price of Acceptance, and importunately besought to open his Hand, Mouth and Heart to receive Pardon (from day to day, perhaps for many years) still in vain; whil'ft he riseth early, compasseth Sea and Land with his Life in his hand, sweats, freezeth, bleeds, frets, wounds his Conscience, and sells himself. What therefore can the account of such Rejecters of the Invitation to the Marriage Supper be? seeing to Ungratitude is added Stubbornness, to that Despitefulness, and consequently desperate Madness; being one, who having more done for him than for the Holy Angels, and yet thus doth more against the glorious Grace of God in Christ by exalted Wickedness, than the very Devils.

20. Behold this, and Blush, ye Heavens, ye Sun and Stars, gather blackness, let the Earth be moved; let the Stones of the Streets and Walls be Witnesses, let the Brutes and Animals stand amaz'd; melt, ye Rocks of Adamant, relent and sigh, ye Mountains of Ice, let Marble and Pummice-stones weep, come hither, discover your inward Forms, ye savage Bears, cruel Tygers, Vultures and unnatural Vipers. The Heavens, Sun and Stars were never Witness of the like Tragick Stupidity, for

had

The 177 Theosophick Questions Answered.

for had they seen the Angels that fell become Devils, yet had they not known them refuse Mercy freely, continually and importunately tendered; the most brutish Animals reject not, but greedily snatch what they want; the Adamantine and Marble Rocks are all easily dissolvable by their proper Separators and Dissolvents; the Mountains of Ice are as unwilling Captives; Bears, Tygers and Vultures are not only kind and friendly to themselves, but compassionate to their Young; the Viper, though he destroys his Genitrix, yet seems to do it of necessity to preserve its own Existence; where therefore can be found so obdurate a thing as the Impenitent Heart of Man? so great a Monster? so ferine a Brute? such a Prodigy of Ingratitude? so implacable a Creature as the hardened obstinate Sinner? No such Ingratitude and Cruelty can the Astral World demonstrate in the contrary Wills of the Martial, Mercurial, and other cross Constellations, nor in the Elementary Offspring of them, nor all whose Differences result to Harmony in the Earth or Deserts, Air or Seas; no, not in Hell, the dark Abyss or Devils, no Sinners against so great Mercies and means for Recovery, no Sinners against a Redeemer, against the bleeding Love and Bowels of a Saviour there, but Man; the Devils are those for whom nothing of Mercy is prepared. Oh therefore that Men were wise, that they knew this, and would hear that their Souls might live, and not sink into everlasting Indignation, Wrath, Tribulation and Anguish, who can dwell with devouring Fire under the Wrath of the Lamb?

Q. 167. What is the Dying of a true Christian? What of him Dyeth?

A. 1. The Dying here inquired is call'd a Sleep, which alludes to *Adam*, who (not exerting his Power) became as one fainting, and fell into a deep Sleep, in which time his Female Property was divided from him, and he slumbered to the Unity of the Paradisical Life, and then was opened in him the divided state, partly (and but partly Paradisical; for it was a begun Declension into the Dividings of the Astral Multiplicity: And by *Eves* and his Eating the Fruit of the third Principle soon wrought in them dismal Effects; for he lived no longer according to the Universal Will, but set up a private Self-will as Law-maker, ceasing to Rule over the Astral Powers he fell under them, and so sadly as to be relieved, and collect, support, and food from them given up to their contrary Properties, and became a Beast as to his outward Body, the deadness of part whereof degraded him so far as to render him by his Bones, Skin and other insensible Parts to the baseness of Vegetatives, and all this not transient as are some Astral Impressions; but as a strong Prison out of which is no escape but by demolishing the Walls and Fabrick. This is the desolate Wilderness which was signified by the going of the the Lord Jesus out of *Canaan* into the Wilderness to be there Forty days tempted of the Devil after Fasting.

2. Thus may a glimpse be seen what *Adam*'s Sleep, and after that his Fall introduced. It chang'd his first Principle by darkning the Divine Eye of his second from great Power and active Vigor, such as is that of the mighty Angels, into Discord, Rage, Envy, Fury, *&c.* and it chang'd his third Principle from so great Purity, Transparency and Aptitude to have done Eternally the Offices of his great Soul and Divine Spirit into a gross obscene, filthy, palpable, feeble, sickly, bestial, perishing Carcass, or Sack of Worms.

3. Now when the Sun of Righteousness descends into this dark Dungeon, he more or less, according to the growth of the Regenerate Child, by his pure meek Spirit appeaseth the Disorders of the Soul and halloweth it, directing, correcting and confirming a resolved will to obey as simply as a little Child, and to persevere as a strong Man in Christ, by which the Internal Man is in great part made God's

Child and Image, reaching toward the Love flame, pressing strongly thitherward, and groans to be with the Lord, but still is the Body as little affected as the Bark of a Tree with the Virtue of the Fruit, or as a Candlestick with the lustre of the Taper, or as the Earth with the Astral Vertue rousing the Principles of Sulphur and Mercury in the saline Spirit in and through it.

4. What can be done with this Body? If it were possible to affect it so as the *East-India* Nut-tree doth, that the Mercurial Vertue arising with Sulphur into a Nutmeg on a Clove for the Stud, the Bark should be a Cinnamon, it were somewhat; but our Carcass is as senseless of the inward Man's Divine Work, as the Bone is of the Respondence and Intercourse the Spirits have through the Arteries and venal Channels, or as the Beasts Hide is of the Astral Impulses moving the Animal. Therefore it must like a Husk shell off, and the Natural Body as a Grain of Wheat be sowed into the Elements, whence it is derived, as the Corn into the Earth and die before it can increase and rise a spiritual Body.

·5. Thus dieth the Elementary part of the true Christian. How dieth the Wise-Man? as the Fool, returning into the Mouth whence it was spoken. The Astral Body also rather disappears than dies, but being dissolved from the ancient Obligations to the bestial Body, it may remain at the Will of the Noble Soul to be its Chariot, wherewith (as a Medium) it sometimes doth vouchsafe a loving Visit to his dear Christian Friend, yet in the Body: but most easily when such a one sleepeth as to the Elementary Man, and seeth, heareth and toucheth with his Astral Man; for then may the precious separate Soul (if it desires it) as familiarly have access and converse with his dear Friend or Brother, as two Men of one Language may, and this hath been and may be to the great Satisfaction and Edification of the surviving Christian, though not frequently, because of Mens unworthiness, or for fear of Impostures, and especially because the Lord only is abundantly and infinitely all-sufficient by his own Omnipotence and Omnipresence.

6. As *Adam* slept to the Holy Paradifical Virgin state, and awaked to the bestial World's Adulterous state: so the true Christian's Death is a sleeping to that sleep of his, *viz.* The filthy, sickly, cumbring, prophane, Elementary Life, and an awaking to the pure, holy, triumphant, dear, sweet child-like, angelical, Endless Life; it transfers him out of the howling Wilderness of Temptation into Eternal *Canaan:* out of a Dungeon into the glorious Liberty of the Sons of God : out of the *Turba* of perplexing Multiplicity and restless wrestling of contrary Properties, into the equal Temperature and Calm harmonious complete Unity, the private Self being extinct he entreth the Universal sacred Freedom of the Lord's Redeemed ones.

Q. 168. *What is the Dying of the wicked, in that it is called an Eternal Dying?*

A. 1. It hath been often inculcated in these Writings, that all Men are in all the three Principles of one Blood, but their difference is notorious; for though they are almost the same in their first and third Principles, and much what alike (though not without great distance of degrees) in their second Principle, yet here is the immense difference, that in some their second Principle, like the House of *Saul* impairs and gradually (as it were insensibly) extinguisheth to a dismal blackness to be felt at length, and in others the Regeneration calmly (yet with irresistible sweet force) more and more opens that Principle, which as the House of *David* improves and flourisheth.

2. From these dear Children, if their Progress hath been Crown'd with Perseverance their third Principle, is like Trash and dusty Rubbish scatter'd about a firm built Structure fully finished, which Death like an impetuous Storm with rapid Motion

The 177 Theosophick Questions Answered. 193

Motion disperseth: or as a mounting Torrent of Water violently bears away, leaving the Fabrick unconcern'd; But the third Principle is to the other his Fortress, Confidence, Retreat, Refuge, Rest, Joy, Hope, Treasure and his all; therefore Death at once surprizing him, and snatching that away, he and it perish together, his only home falleth for want of Foundation, the Cistern he hath hewn is broken, having no Water in it, nor can hold it if any were entrusted thereinto, which shews the fault to be in the very bottom, else it might hold some Water, but the truth is, it hath no bottom at all. The World to the one, is either as it is to some a Pageantry, a Comedy, a Feather in his Cap, or as to others, or to him at other times; his Burthen, Snare, place of Tentation, Care, Sorrow, occasion of Sin, Shame and Punishment, his place of Exile, and at best, more or less, his *Dalilah*, and many a Groan it costs him whose Home and Treasure is elsewhere.

3. But to the sinking Man it is his Harlot, his Leaden Weight or Milstone, his Idol, his only Heaven, and though he sees it disappearing and vanishing, it being his sole Attractive, he hugs it, courts it, lives for it, dies for it, and dies Eternally for it. That which is the Quintessence of Tragedies is his only Comedy, nor can it be otherwise; for neither hath he any thing else, sees, loves, knows nor longs for any thing beyond it, but ever looks on all Futurities through the Glass made of Materials here. He would have endless Stores obtain'd to satiate his insatiable Covetousness, a boundless Dominion to gratifie his proud Lusts, vast Power to execute his Revenge and Malice, that all Creatures might be Instruments, and if he could, the Creator too might contribute to his Will of raging Fury.

4. From which Root it is that the most abject People, because they cannot rend in pieces all they impotently hate, will not fail to imprecate and causelesly Curse, which extends mostly to Image in their own Souls, only the Model of Hell, though sometimes it toucheth the Tincture by the *Magia* exalted (yet in the dark Impression of it) and so reacheth both in the inward World, and in the shadow of it the outward Principle, unto such Persons and Things as are subject, and stand as a Harmony with the Impression themselves are of, that is, within the reach of their Chain: Hence dark Witchcraft springeth.

5. Now when those fall short of the subject, they level at, every such falleth out with himself; for his Eternity is a continual greedy desire of what can never be had, accompanied with like constant despair of obtaining it, producing consequently a perpetual Rotation of Rage and Fury, all which like the parts of a Wheel shut him up at the Nave or Centre thereof immoveably, unalterably. A glimpse whereof is, when Men in this World are arraigned by the Out-cries of guilty Consciences let loose upon them.

6. Thus is it with the dying of the Wicked, who fall into the Central implacable Forms of the first Principle, and the God of Life (dwelling in the infinite Light and Glory of the all-comprehending second Principle) being for ever withdrawn to the distance of a whole Principle from them, because the Darkness comprehendeth him not; that Life of theirs must needs be an Eternal Dying, and they be kill'd in their own House, as for a figure *Ishbosheth* the Son of *Saul* was. And 2 *Sam.* 4. 7. as the sleep of the Holy Children is the Death of their Disease, so the Dying of the other is the Life of their Disease, and the total Privation, extinguishing or extermination of the slender Remainders of their Health. This Life is a Sickness to both, only the one feels it to be so, the other is insensible of it, and the passing hence is to the one a forgetting of the sickness and sorrow here, and to the other an awakening to the sick frame, whereof here he had no Sence or right Apprehension.

Q. 169. *Whither goeth the Soul when it parteth from the Body, be it Blessed or not?*
A. So

The 177 *Theosophick Questions Answered.*

A. So evident is this in the Answers of the 11. 23, 24. and 26 of *J. Behmen's* Book of the Forty Questions, and in other parts of his Divine Self-Evidencing Writings. Also in the Answer of the 166 Question particularly in the 9th Verse, and elsewhere in these Answers, that it is here wholly forborn.

Q. 170. *What are the Doings and Life of Souls till the last Judgment Day?*

A. 1. The Answer of the 22th of *Jacob Behmen's* Forty Questions of the *Soul* is totally a Solution of this Question; something also concerning it is in the Answer of the 166 of the present Questions, which if accurately inspected, might lead the Enquirer to the Summit of his Desires. But this Question restraining to the time present, as to the Doings of separate Souls in that state, without the outward Body simply considered, without either Retrospect to their passed state, or Prospect to their Futurities (although the Hebrew admit no Present Tense) yet thus abstractedly divested of past and to come as far as is possible, something may be told only by way of Representation in some low Similitudes, pertinent hereunto, for hardly otherwise can the dull Reason penetrate such a Secret, or the enlightened Mind either.

1. 2. 1. The Reapers cut down Wheat not fully ripe, and Tares green, the keeping of both some time may prepare them. one for good use, the other to be scatter'd by the Fan; but the solar Spirit in the unripe Wheat, and Martial Spirit in the Tares sleep not, but proceed to conquer the adverse Properties, and mature
2. the Mass or Territory whereof they are Regents. 2. There are two Trees Fell'd, the one for Timber for curious Uses, the other a knotty unsound one for Fuel: the lying of them both a while, makes as well the one as the other, more fit for
3. their several contrary uses. 3. If this Life be a Seed-time and Heaven the Harvest,
4. there interpasseth some time which is a patient waiting time. 4. If this Life be the Transgressing time, the Night of Violence and committing Facts, and the Lake of Fire be the Execution, there useth to pass some Occurrences requiring Deliberation between the Fact and Judgment, as between the Fact and Execution or Re-
5. compence for the Fact. 5. If this Life be a time of Sacrifice, and the glorious Kingdom the returns of God to those Petitions, which is the time of the restitution of all things: the Sacrificers must allow some time of waiting at, or under the Altar for the returns of those Sacrifices.

3. But from all these it follows not, but the state of the Perfect may be exceedingly Good and greatly Blessed, though when they shall put on their new Garments it shall be best of all; for that is the time of the restitution of all things, nor doth it follow but in that very state there will be degrees of Happiness, according to the degrees of their passing into the fifth Form (where is the opening of the Divine Power-world) as there are of Stars in Glory: Neither also doth it follow, that the state of the accursed is capable of mitigation; for their estate is not so bad, but that it is capable of being more wretched, yet not of being more tolerable, and yet 'tis so Dark as admits not the least glance of Light, as even in this Life they grow actually more and more Vile: So in that state, though it be the worst, they ever knew, yet still posteth it on without stop, recoil or respite, ever hurrying them on towards the Tempest of Eternal fierceness.

4. Here is the Antipodes to the black Fiction of Atheists and Sadduces, who would make themselves believe that the whole inward Man is Mortal and annihilable, such who not only judge themselves unworthy of Eternal Life, but uncapable of Eternal Existence, while they grant it to this Mass of Crumbling Earth and Mortal Water; and are so extreamly degenerated from the Divine Image Man was ennobled with, that, as their outward Life extends not to that length, activity

The 177 Theosophick Questions Answered.

activity and occult Excellencies of many Brutes, as Beasts, little Animals and some Birds, so the infatuated Atheists would that their Souls and Spirits might also run the same Fate, and be as transient as the vilest of Insects. Here is also Diametrical opposition to others, who say, the whole inward Man is fellow Prisoner with the bestial Flesh till the general Resurrection; but the Answers of the two immediately preceding Questions shew what of the Blessed sleepeth, and what of the Wicked is Arrested by the King of Terrors. And for farther Answer hereunto, see the Answer to the 22th of the 40 Questions of *J. Behmen*, of the Soul.

5. The Doings of Souls till the last Judgment may stand here in the very words of the Book of Extracts, (*viz.*) " They.all (meaning the Holy Souls) abound with " great inward Joy, and wait to put on their bright, fair, new Body out of the " old, their Joy and Hope is different as Labourers Expectations are; who at the " End of the Week receive every one according to their degrees of Labour and Dili-" gence. Those who have put on Christ's Body here, are as one, who having " overcome his Enemies in Fight, represents the Victory before his King, who re-" ceives him with great Joy and Honour. The Expectation of the wicked Soul, is " as an imprison'd, condemn'd Malefactor, still listening when any thing stirs, and " the Executioner comes; all their passed Wickedness stands before them in such " different Aggravations as they had here.

Q. 171. *What is the last Judgment, how is it Effected?*

A. 1. That there shall be such a great general final Day of Judgment grates on the Ears of Atheists, but against them the very Devils will rise in Judgment: but others there are who would be accounted more religious than many, who shut up themselves from the acknowledgment of that Judgment Day, and though they are not practically Atheists who put the Evil Day from them, yet do these raze it out of their Intellect, restraining the Judgment Day of God to his declaring for, or against us and our actions here only, during this our Pilgrimage; all, in their Judgment, is the Judgment before Death or Resurrection. To whom may be said, that as they who said the Resurrection is past already, did thereby overthrow the Faith of some, so they that say the Great Day of Judgment is past already, undermine the Faith of many, overthrow the Faith of some, and direct their force against Truth it self, whereon is founded all true Faith which is well founded.

2. It is true that Christ in the Light of our Life is from from Age to Age, and for ever, till Ages cease, a Judge in the sain Humanity, speaking by his living Word in the Consciences, and written Testimony in the Intellect and Memory, being the words of his Prophets and Holy ones, and evidence of our rightly informed Brethren and Fellow-Members in our Ears; his being a swift Witness, by severe Visitations before our Eyes, also by Eminent gracious Providences; and in the Creation, the Earth, Elements and Creatures, to our other Senses, wherein may be read frowns and smiles variously dispensed, which are perpetuated in their Seasons as long as Sin is perpetrated unto all reclaimable Transgressors; this God doth by his Stars who have a Voice which every Nation hears, for with them the Psal- *Psal. 19. 3.* mist saith, he reacheth by them, and by them both judgeth and fighteth.

3. Again, the Lord teacheth us to judge our selves, which is every ones part, but not to judge others, for Man's Judgment must be restrained to things, not extended to Persons from which we are warn'd and caution'd: yet are Men very propense, apt and sharp to the latter, but very averse, partial and slack to the former. More judge Men, which is to be noted both after the dark and light Worlds Impressions; after the dark thus, the four Anguishes composing the first Principle judge each other; thence is it that from the Astringency the Covetous judgeth and

is judged by the Prodigal; again, the Covetous as he is a Self-lover, and so is timorous, judgeth and is reproached by the rash fiery furious one; again, the Covetous as he is drawn (shameless*ly*) to base fawning ways for profit fake, judgeth and is judged by the haughty Proud one: Again, the insatiable Thirst of heaping up, taking from the covetous mind his rest, renders him the trouble of his own Life House and Cohabiters, yet prompts him to judge the contrary inclination for sloth and dronishness, while that other judgeth him so wretchedly slavish, that he distrusteth (almost) his own hands to hoard up his Idols: And so of the rest of the Properties resembling the Builders of *Babel.*

4. But God hath given all Judgment to his Son; some glimmerings of His Infinite Glory are found in them whose four Forms generate the fifth; for in the meek Resignation arising to the Divine Love-fire and Pure Breathings directed by Heavenly Light, Judgment proceedeth toward Victory. And it is represented by the fifth Letter in the Hebrew Alphabet, which is only as an aspiration or breathing from within outwardly; conforming exactly in that respect to the Language of Nature. Standing united to That of the New Nature; for the fifth Form producing the second Birth, and being produced by it, leads the Creature to the giving up its all in a flame of Love in Jesus Christ to the Father, which flame he feels blown up by the Holy Ghost.

5. Thus we have seen what God's judging in This mixt World is, also what Man's judging here is, according to the Dark World's accusing dividing Properties, and also what Man's judging is according to the little part of the Light World we share of here; by which it is evident that all this is to That day of days, as a blinking Candle is to the Sun it self. Such was the report *Paul* gave of That day, as made *Felix* tremble, tho' an Infidel; for, as it hath been elsewhere noted, tho' some have laught at the Doctrine of the Resurrection, none have been so fool-hardy and mad as to slight the report of the General Judgment. *Enoch* the seventh from *Adam*, figuring the end of the six working days or Properties, and by his Translation and Son *Methusalah*, the entring on Eternity, prophesied of This day; all the Prophets, Apostles and Holy ones confirm it; Christ the Judge himself preacht it, with the order, manner, and particularities of it: The Devils knew it, and therefore argued, *Art thou come to torment us before our time?*

6. He that would say what That great Judgment is, can never do it but by parsels, and then also cannot stretch beyond the sphere of his own activity; and what if it be said, an Angel can do but so, were he to speak it; for all Eternal Creatures live either in the holy or prophane Worlds, or in both. They that live in the Light-World, as far as they see the Centre of the Dark-World in themselves, may speak, and no farther; *viz.* not what That Darkness is in others, or what the perplexed Hellish Charms, Cheats and Intricacies are; for the Holy ones live far above them, and the Battle managed by *Michael* and his Angels against the Dragon and his, is not with the Dragons Weapons, but with the quite contrary. As bright Torches fight with black Vapours, or the starry Region with opposing Exhalations.

7. We must come then to consider them who live in both Dark and Light, making a third Principle by their mixed production, and in them may be found the figure of an Umpire or Interpreter. As he who reads two Languages can tell him who knows neither, what is written in both, if he hath the Tongue also That third person is of. Thus was it the first *Adam* could give names to all Creatures; for he had the Properties of them all in himself, either according to the Forms of his first Principle, or according to the Astral Powers of his third; wherein he was infallible, having the splendor of the second for his Guide; but his departure from his Pure State degraded him of the Judicatory, as a man is deprived in the
night

The 177 *Theosophick Questions Answered.*

night of the view of what the Sun priviledged him with, or as one immured in a dark Cavern sees not what a lofty Mountain gave him prospect of, or as *Nebuchadnezzar* ceased as to Royalty when he had only a Beasts heart.

8. And in this State all *Adams* posterity find themselves (as of themselves) ignorant of the Creator, and therefore also strangers to themselves, and rightly knowing nothing. Therefore the Son of the Virgin, that he might be the Light of the World, brought again the Virgin Image into the Humanity, openeth the pure Eye, and gives such a proportion of discriminating Wisdom as our hunger adapts and capacitates us for in the Regeneration; hence it's written, the Spiritual Man judgeth all things, but he himself is judged of no man. But to which of the Angels hath God said at any time, Be thou a Judge? Those glorious and mighty Agents are Princes in one only Principle; *viz.* the Holy Divine One, not in the first, nor third, tho' some of them are enthroned according to the Holy Impression of Potence in the first; and others have the Dominion according to the Infinite Variety of the third Principle, but all breath only the Air of the second, yet are neither the one Hierarchy, or the other Judges of Men or Devils: While yet the Lord saith of his Twelve, they should sit on twelve Thrones judging the twelve Tribes; and our Apostle faith, Know you not that we shall judge Angels; (*viz.*) Evil Angels?

9. Now to say how this Judgment is effected: It's answered, 1. The Principles (1.) and Properties are all wide open unto the second *Adam*; for out of them He created every World, as without Him was not any thing made that was made, and this as He is the Son of God, before whom all Worlds and Individuals drawing Air, and living of, in or from either Principle or Property shall stand at That day, and ever did as open as a City on a Hill, 2. The Principle and Properties are all re- (2.) ally in Him as He is the Son of Man, and His throughly penetrating them is a consequence of His perfect knowing Himself, His own Heavenly Humanity. 3. The (3.) Principles and Properties will be at That day known to each other, as well as each to its self. Now is the Dark World much hidden from the Light World, and the Light wholly incomprehensible to the Dark. Now also the Hellish and Heavenly Principles are under a disguise, so that men catch at the Bait of the Dark World, and eschew and flie the cross leading to the Holy World: The Treasures of *Egypt* weigh down the Reproach of Christ. But then shall the Principles and the Good and Evil of the Properties be so open to the Holy Children, that they may penetrate and contemplate the Wrath Kingdom, without being impressed, incited or imposed upon by it, and they shall view, contemn, scorn and judge the fixt Enmity of those burning in the Wrath of the Dark Central Fire. Then also the Love flame of the Holy Virgin Souls united to their raised glorified Bodies, shall be so evident to the Vassals of the inimicitious World, as may fully convince them to their eternal anguish and shame what kind of Birth-right, Glory, Felicity and Blessedness (which must endure to perpetuity) they profanely, desperately and madly sold and exchanged for a Mess of Pottage, and Death in the Pot, for faded, painted, imaginary Toys, Trifles and Cheats.

10. But what need more to convince of the Truth that there must be such a day, or to shew the order how it is effected, seeing the Holy Scriptures abound with Accounts of This Judgment which is spoken of, where it is call'd a fearful looking for of Judgment. Again, the Judgment was set, *&c.* – may have boldness in the day of Judgment, *Heb.* 10. 27. *Dan.* 7. 10; *&c.* 1 *Joh.* 4. 17. *Mat.* 11. 22. 2 *Pet.* 2. 9. *Rom* 14. 10. 2 *Pet.* 2. 3. Also see the Answer of *J. B.* to the 30th of the 40 Questions concerning the Soul, and the 27th Chapter of the three Principles.

Q. 172.

The 177 *Philosophick Questions Answered.*

Q. 172. *How is the Resurrection of the dead effected? What riseth again?*

A. 1. It may justly be complained that reading is oppress with excess of enlarged Writings being therein as unsuccessfully transgressive as the hopes of the Hypocrite to be heard for his much speaking. It therefore seems more suitable to the shortness of Mans Life, straitness of his leisure, discomposure of his Spirits, feebleness of his penetrating faculty and weakness of his retention, to avoid all vain repetitions, and commend the reperusal of things once read as the most ready, rather than to new shape (many ways) that which is but one thing and once done already. In order therefore to the clearing of this Answer let it be considered, what *Adam* was before his Fall, which is discoursed in the 45 Answer. Next what dire Effects that Fall of his had, treated of in the 69 Answer. Again what Mans Death and Resurrection is, as in the 6th verse of the 121 Answer. And what Mans faln State, Death, Christs Resurrection and raising of Man, and what of him riseth, are, which is the substance of the whole 16 verses of the 134 Answer. So that the Answer is made, before this Question comes in its Order here to be considered.

2. Yet because I dare not dismiss this important Doctrine being so much opposed even at this very day, not only by many Hellish Atheists transforming themselves into Brutish Animals, but not understood by some pretending to be risen with Christ, and guided by his Light within them. Let it be observed, by such who wilfully oppose, or not regarded, at their Peril: And for satisfaction of such who are willing to know the truth, *viz*. That Christ had a true Natural Humane Body of Flesh and Blood from *Mary*. Heb. 2. 24. *Forasmuch then as the Children are partakers of Flesh and Blood, he also himself likewise took part of the same, that through Death he might destroy him that had the power of Death, which is the Devil.*

Q. 1. A. 1. Q. 3. But is it askt how is this Body and Humane Soul the same of ours? It's answer'd, 1. By way of Concession, that it was so far other than ours as it had the Holy Ghost instead of Mans Masculine Seed. 2. Yet took he (as the above Text with many others plainly tell us) part of our Flesh and Blood, and so was our Brother, that is such as the Children had part of, were of, or are partakers of, and this is also ours of what Nation soever we are, for it is written, *Acts* 17. 16. *God hath made of one Blood all Nations of Men to dwell on the Face of the Earth.*

Q. 2. A. Q. 4. *Is it ask'd what of this was raised again?* It's Answer'd all of it; for the Women, and after that the Disciple whom Jesus loved, and *Peter* saw, there was nothing left in the Sepulchre after the Resurrection but the Linnen Cloaths wherein he had been wrapped.

Q. 3. A. Q. 5. *May it be fully so with other Bodies?* Answer, Matth. 27. 52, 53. *And the Graves were opened, and many Bodies of Saints which slept arose and came out of their Graves after his Resurrection, and went into the Holy City, and appeared unto many.* And it must be remembered that it shall be so with ours at the last day, it was the Faith of *Martha* who faith unto him, *John* 11. 24. *I know that my Brother shall rise again in the Resurrection at the last day.*

Q. 4. A. Q. 6. *May it not be otherwise with us; our Bodies must putrifie, and the Incorruptible only rise?* Answer, our Apostle saith, 1 Cor. 15. 53. *Our Mortal shall put on Immortality, and our Corruptible shall put on Incorruption,* and all this as a consequence of *Christs Death and Burial according to the Scriptures, also of his rising again; and after his rising again was seen of Cephas, then of the Twelve, after that of above five hundred Brethren at once,* 1 Cor. 15. 3, 4, 5, 6.

Q. 5. A. Q. 7. *Shall it be a Resurrection of all?* Answer, The Lord saith, *Marvel not at this,*

The 177 *Theosophick Questions Answered.*

this, *for the hour is coming in the which all that are in the Graves shall hear his voice, and shall come forth, they that have done good to the Resurrection of Life, and they that have done evil unto the Resurrection of Damnation.* Let it therefore no longer be charged justly on us as formerly on the Jewish Rabbies, *That we err, not knowing the Scriptures nor the power of God.* 1 Thes. 4. 14, 15. *If we believe that Jesus died and rose again, even so them also which sleep,* &c.

Q. 8. *How is it effected?* Answer, As *Lazarus* was raised. That voice which Rev. 20. 5. gave Being to all call'd him up, and that voice shall call all up, every one in his own Order. May it never be said of us as of the Jews, *Because they knew not him, nor yet the voices of the Prophets which are read every Sabbath-day, they have fulfilled them in condemning him.* So may it not be said now, *Because they consult not frequently, nor heedfully regard, nor will understand the holy Words and Writings of the Lord, his Apostles,* &c. *which they may daily read, they yet sit down with a confused Notion of this great Doctrine, and bury their drowsie Intellect, some with dark Heathenish Maxims begetting Atheism in Judgment and Practice, a degree worse than Devils.*

9. Other some there are having a glimpse of a true Light wherewith they think themselves rich, and to have need of nothing, and there shut it and themselves up, without persuing it by searching like the *Bereans,* and without improving it by trimming their Lamps: But not imploying themselves in the Lords methods, do obscure or bury their Talent, and so by degrees let their foolish Heart be darkened, not only in this but in many other of the plain and precious Truths of the Kingdom of God; which great evil and defection is (as ever heretofore in all other forms) accompanied with sharp Censures of others, and peremptory unwarranted Injunctions of their own Reason. Whereas the more we approach the Divine Life, the more comprehensive is that Soul, the more ready to bear and forbear, to do and suffer, to become all or any thing to all, that it may beget of that meek Spirit in others, to be swift to hear, to have an open naked Breast whereon it begs the Lord Jesus to write his whole Pleasure, is so vile in his own absurd Judgment that is easily induced to think highly of others.

Q. 173. *How doth this World pass away or vanish? And what doth remain thereof afterward?*

A. 1. To some this Question may seem only curious, and to others so occult as if incogniscible, to a third sort, such, as if possible to be resolv'd, were needless; because it fruitlesly anticipates (say they) the thing which in its season shall demonstrate it self. But on serious mature inspection it is found possible, important, and greatly necessary to be known and believed.

2. It is said that when *Cortes* with a Brigade of Spanish Horse and Infantry Invaded the *West Indies,* and had charged them of the Republick of *Tlaxcallan,* upon the Fall of any *Spaniard* either Man or Horse, care was taken so to bury them that the *Americans* might not know it, which made them despair of withstanding such, whom they thence concluded to be Immortal. Thus not to discover the end of this present World (which the dark World and the Prince of it would conceal) were to insinuate as if it were indissoluble and consequently uncreated, and so Brutishly to introduce Atheism; and Atheism is that fatal Evil, which may be justly accounted the worst of Errors of the worst of Men.

3. But this World had a beginning, and shall have an end, as it is written, Psal. 102. 25, 26, *Of old thou hast laid the foundation of the Earth; and the Heavens are the works of thy hand. They shall perish,* &c. *They all shall wax old as doth a Garment.* &c. Heb. 1. 10, 11, 12. And tho' no History scarcely records any who mock'd at the coming of the Lord, yet is it Prophesied, 2 Pet. 3. 3, 4. *That in the*

C c *last*

The 177 *Theosophick Questions Answered.*

last days Scoffers shall come (even at that which will then be at the Door) *saying, Where is the promise of his coming?* &c. For such Mens Lusts Bias them to abuse Gods long-suffering, ver. 9. Who is *not willing that any should perish, but that all should come to Repentance,* Ezek. 18. 31, 32. 2 Pet. 3. 10. And it is told us how this World shall pass away, viz. 1. Unexpectedly as a Thief. 2. Suddenly, in the Night. 3. Violently, with a great noise. 4. Universally, the Heavens, Earth and Elements. 5. Irreparably, *The Elements shall melt with fervent heat, the Earth be burnt up, and that the Heavens being on Fire shall be dissolved,* ver. 12. And this tremendous Truth is not only really and litterally, but demonstrably so.

4. To the second part of the Question, viz. what remaineth thereof afterward, see the Answer of the 30th Question of the 40 Questions of the Soul, and the 27 Chap. of the three Principles, ver. 6. and ver. 20.

But to speak yet farther on this latter part, what remains of it [the World] afterward, viz. after dissolution of the present frame or fashion? I must seem, and but seem to digress; which tho' to some it be obscure, will be plain to the Mind initiated into and irradiated with the Theosophick Wisdom. The Out-birth is the Figure of the two Eternal Worlds or Principles, having all the Properties according to the two different contrary Impressions: And this Out-birth in the Womb of the Eternal Mystery, was by the earnest Magick longing and will originated, which will is as the Voice or Mouth of the great Mystery, and the properties are as the Instruments or Fingers of the creating word; the first, viz. the Voice is the Father, Soveraign or Lord of the Separator or Father of Nature; and the latter, viz. the Properties, are his Limbs or Members, working by the Astral Powers for Generation of all the Creatures of the Out-birth.

5. This Father of the external Nature or Outward World (invigorated by the might of the Properties) hath ability unweariedly to work universally in and through the whole Out-birth, and being the Image of the first-born of every Creature (who standeth incomprehensibly in the Eternal Rooting Powers) this his Image and Servant is innobled with such energy as both to form and animate the productions of the whole Out-birth, yet who will be so foolish as to take him either to be the First-born Son of God, or the Father which is in Heaven whom the Son teacheth us to direct our Prayer to as the Object of all Adoration, or the Holy Infinite third Person or Subsistence, tho' his Office is in the third Principle, but is a Creature potently furnished and fortified to stamp, engrave, delineate and shadow Living Images of the two Inward Worlds: And hath the Seals and Magical impresses, but not the Eternal, Holy, Incomprehensible *Magia*; for that the Divine Virgin of Wisdom is a Possessor of, generating the real Worlds themselves for ever, whereof this is only the figure,

6. And this Father of Nature call'd by some the Soul of the outward Universe hath a Tincture under his dispensation, such as of which the Out-birth is capable to be enriched with: And this also of both Impressions, viz. of the light and dark Worlds Figures, but it hath not the holy, meek, divine Tincture; for that the Divine *Sophia* the Virgin of Wisdom is glorified with. But the Tincture and *Magia* which the Father of Nature is distributer of, is yet so noble as to be holy in the holy Vessels, but not so fixed and compleat as to hallow unholy Vessels, but so flexible as is vitiated into a false *Magia* and counterfeit Tincture, and so applicable to the Impostures of Evil Angels, and their Humane Vassals that they (to their Eternal Damnation) may and do prophanely abuse and prostitute this Tincture and *Magia*.

7. Thus what the Virgin of Gods Wisdom is in the Heavenly Birth to the Angelical World, and other Paradisical Inhabitants, such is this Father of Nature in

the

The 177 Theosophick Questions Answered.

the Out-birth, and not only the two Eternal Worlds have their Figures and manifest Portraitures in this, but the very holy creating Word and Virgin of Wisdom (of which no visible figure can be) hath above all this grand Separator or Father of the External Nature for it's plain audible Herauld, immediate substitute and express Representer: Yet so secret as only to be found by the Inlighten'd Mind, and tho' seen in all things, yet discerned, understood and perceived by very few, and for the sake of those very few are these things thus opened.

8. From all which it may easily be deduced what of this World shall remain, *viz.* Nature. in its Virtual, Form and Dress, the real Entities with their Tincture, their substantial, tho' not palpable Bodies; that is to say, the true substance of every Individual Figure, the Idea of every thing which the Father of Nature hath produced to shadow and reveal the hidden Holy and Power Worlds; therefore of necessary consequence the Father or Separator must needs remain, to Marshal his Hosts in their Eternal successive Scenes; for the most High and Holy God will not lose the end of his Work: But his goodness must be for ever extensive, diffusive communicative for his Glory. *Amen.* Nor is it possible he should lose the least part of the Order by him fixed of declaring himself, but that by the things he hath made may be shewn his Eternal Power and Godhead, because for that purpose they were produced.

9 I compare the World to a Seed, which tho' it die, having lost its Husk, Chaff, and very Sulphurean and Saline Body, is yet regenerated by its Mercurial renovation into another, yet as it were the self same; hence saith the Lord, *There is nothing hid or covered which shall not be made manifest.* The Idea of the Drunkards Horie like *Balaam's* Ass shall convince the madness of the Rider, and Eccho his own repeated causless Sufferings and Groans under the Tyranny of his more Savage Owner. The Flocks shall bleat again, and shew how their Lives have been lavished to satiate the voluptuous Gluttony of their Wolvish Owners. The Vine and Fatness of the Field shall shew how their Blood and Strength was exhausted for the Lusts of the proud while the Bellies of the Indigent were shrunk up. For as by the Chymist the Flegm of the Plant is separated away, and the fæces precipitated, yet the Spirit, Essence and Idea retained, so is it here. Also as the washing of a Man who hath many Wounds in his Body covered all over with Blood, shews how many, how great, and where those Orifices are, so is it here. Likewise as the drawing back of the extended Shadows and Curtains of the Night, lays open and exposeth like *Ezekiel's* Vision the Idols, and undermining Works of Ezek.8.8,&c. Darkness, so will it be then. Or as the wiping of the slime and filth sticking to a Looking-glass makes all appear therein clearly, so will that transcendent work be, yet neither is the Seed perished, the Plant utterly lost, the wounded Man quite expired, nor the Looking-glass broken in pieces.

10. Therefore as the Lord would preserve a Pot of *Manna* wherewith the Tribes of *Israel* had been sustained in the Wilderness, and as the Lord Jesus would have the Fragments of the Bread and Fish Basketed wherewith he had fed by Miracle so many in a desert place, how much less will he lose the noble Tincture it self, nor for the sake thereof the Earthen Pot in which (like the *Manna*) it is intrusted, but Ransom by his Mighty Power the Tincture (like a Captiv'd Turtle) from the power of the Dog, for his own glory sake, and therewithal every Idea it hath been imploy'd to animate and hath spirited?

Q. 174. *What shall be after this Worlds time when God shall be All in All; when the Dominions shall cease?*

A. 1. (1.) The Answer of this may be censur'd as curious, as the preceding Question (1.)

The 177 Theosophick Questions Answered.

(2.) Question seemed at first to be. 2. To be also so hidden, as to be inscrutable from the perplexedness and ambiguity of it, being so far (as may seem) beyond
(3.) our measure. (3.) To be sterile and unfruitful: And in incountring such imputations it runs parallel with the discouragements of inquiring into the last pre-
(4.) cedent Question, but to this one is added, *viz.* that, (4.) It is a Tautology, repeating the former Question.

2. But to clear all successively, the Matter here inquire I must be confess'd to be our great End, Mark and Object we should level at; therefore not unnecessary

1 Cor. 15. 24, and curious, and accordingly it is the subject of that of our Apostle, therefore not
o ver. 28. unprofitable for us to get the knowledge of, being our particular concern. Nor is it unsearchable seeing the Holy Ghost in that Text teacheth us that Mystery; can therefore the Explanation of it be unacceptable? Lastly, It is no Tautology, for it must be heedfully noted and distinctly understood, that the former last preceding Question intends the first Administration, step or transaction immediately following the general Resurrection, comprizing that formidable, final, irrevocable, general Judgment, but this Question intendeth the second step or administration as consequent of that Judgment, or (as may be expressed) the Executive result of that Universal Judgment, being the compleat summit of the perfect Worlds, wherein the end hath not only found the beginning, but is entred thereinto, resteth in, and possesseth it.

3. We come now to speak of that most holy, pure, desireable state. It is most undeniable that God shall not then only be All in All, but ever was and is so either in his love or second Principle, or in his Wrath or first Principle, therefore it is no News, but that it is said he shall then be so, also how and why is clear in the following part of this Answer, particularly in verse 23, 24, 25. being its proper place whither it's referr'd.

4. This state signified by the Sabbath, Jubilee, &c. in *Israel* is, when all the six Properties or Forms of Nature give up themselves into the seventh, that is, into the Throne or End of Action and Work. Thus as by the gracious Creator the captiv'd Properties were ransom'd out of the dark confused Chaos, and by him disposed into orderly Contexture, to Image the hidden Powers of the Holy World, and seven Fountain Spirits, which made the Morning Stars sing their Psalm of Adoration, Thankfulness, and Shout for Joy : So out of the Confusion the Creation had hurried themselves into by the direful Fall, this state is the compleat Restoration; there being afore begotten in every thing capable thereof, something conformable to the new Birth, which is the superior part of the Lords Children according to the capacity of the things themselves.

5. And as in the Out-birth are such Fruits, Products, Precious Stones, Seasons, Localities, Properties, Auspicious sweet Astral Influences in the animate and inanimate Creatures, all which are the footsteps of the disappeared Paradisical World, and the Figures and Pointers toward the state here intended : So are there in the Out birth on our Terrene Ball, (and why not on other Stars?) Certain Inhabitable Climates, as toward both Poles, Inhabitable places in the Habitable Latitudes, as terrible Wildernesses, raging Deeps, also there are cross fatal Conjunctions, malevolent Astral Influences, with their various Productions a- mongst us, as may figure and point out the state of the dark Abyss, where the Ear bor'd are for ever Slaves.

What re- 6. But because some may think this Discourse to be too remote from the Mat-
mains after ter here sought, it must therefore farther be said, the Demonstration of what re-
the last diso- mains after the general Dissolution, may be found in every Man, whether wicked
lution. or holy; for instance, the Prophane Soul who turns all God's Goodness to him into Gall and Wormwood, when ever the influences of gracious Bounty cease,

and

The 177 Theosophick Questions Answered.

and God's tender Pity and great Long-suffering with him terminates, the Serpent is grown in such a one thereby, but the more strong and lusty; for that in him which by the allay of this World's intermixing Divertisements, and the Holy World's Neighbourhood, was only bitterish; wil then, when this World as to what it now is, is vanished, and that wholly and for.ever withdrawn, become bitterness in the Abstract.

7. As, prick or bruise an angry Man's finger only, and you see his Choler; but rend his several Limbs, and judge what his severe Fury will be. Take from a griping Man but a few Shillings, and see his Anguish and Repining; but take all his Idol gods at once, and he is as a Bear bereaved of her Whelps. Disregard but the presence of an imperious spirited Man, and he will wish to make a Sacrifice of all that do so, and all they are and have, like *Mordecai*; but render him as vile as really he is, and what would he not do could he revenge himself to the full: Thus may we see what remains to the Dark Impression, when this World's time is ended. *1 Simile of what reping Man but mains.*

8. But now according to the Divine World (which is the thing in this Question intended) it is very evident thus, Let the Man who is raised in the Spirit of Christ, retire himself but a little while by submissive resignation, quitting his being at Home, and from the Images there swaying in the outward Man : also from the Desires and Remembrance of them, let him then approach the holy Intercourses, enter into the Contemplation of the infinite Love kingdom, and he shall see and feel what he cannot speak or write; he shall, like a little Child, act purely, and will uninterruptedly, the Passions of the Principle in which he lives, if they may be call'd Passions; he shall also, like a little Child, move simply according to the Dictates of his Father's Universal perfect Will, for himself and his own Will averted are as if neither had ever been: and thus according to the Question, what remains after this World's time, such a one throughly penetrateth, the Spirit of this Man experiments how God being all in his poor little all, causeth all other Dominions to cease in and over him, and he breaths the holy Air. *2 Simile of what retire mains.*

9. The contrary Properties in him are in a measure so attoned and in harmony, as they are in the infinite Abyss of Almightiness; for they are all really and truly in him. he consisting of them, yet all is but one Power, because the Divine Love in the Wisdom hath swallow'd them all up, and that Love is soveraign for ever over them. And though this be most conspicuous in the mortified and daily dying Child of God, who hath made good Progress in the Regeneration, yet is it in some degree and measure in the Child of a Day old, or a Span long; for these have pure (though much interrupted) Breathings, their Love may be very Ardent, as the Love of Espousals, though often and variously perverted : these are begun to enter into the new World, by the new Way, in the new Nature, and have thence by Interval's a fair Prospect into what cometh after this World, all such are in a measure my Witnesses, for what is above spoken in Answer to the Question.

10. Now more particularly come we to the latter part of the Question, (viz.) *When God shall be all in all, when the Dominions shall cease.* What therefore may most undeniably be said on this, shall be drawn from the Words of the Holy Ghost by our Apostle. wherein are taught us, 1 Cor. 15. 23. to v. 28.

1. That Christ having raised himself as the first Fruits, raiseth also them that are his at his coming.   2. That he shall put down all Rule, Authority, and Power.   3. That then is, or cometh the End.   4. That then the Kingdom shall be deliver'd up to the Father, and God shall be all in all.   To every of which a few words in their order. 1. 2. 3. 4.

1. That our risen Christ shall raise all his, and after, all others at his second coming; For, (1.)

II. We

The 177 Theosophick Questions Answered.

11. We ought assuredly to acknowledge that the great Work shall once be Universall, accomplish'd by *Jehovah's* Almightiness, in Raising, Judging and Determining the state of all *Adam's* offspring, and the actual delivering up the Kingdom to the Father, and God shall be all in all, and that all this is openly, literally, really and universally a Foundation Truth, to be confessed before all men: and next shall be spoken according to the same Method (as Demonstrations thereof) the work particularly done and doing (*viz.*) in the Divine meek Spirits and regenerated Souls of all God's new born Children, from the first Holy Man to the last that shall be.

12. Now that Christ having raised himself as the first Fruits, shall also raise them that are his at his coming, is such an immoveable Foundation Truth, as neither Atheists or Apostate Christians (those fallen stars) nor any fallen Angels, nor all of them United can ever resist, but it is an Eternal Truth to the Glory of God, the Joy of all his in their Pilgrimage, and matter of Divine Contemplation and Adoration for ever. Read and Meditate among many others, 1 *Thess.* 4. 14, 15, &c. 1 *Cor.* 15. 23. *Rev* 20 4, 5, 6. 1 *Cor* 15. 3, 4. and Review the 134 and 172 Answers.

The general Resurrection demonstrated by the first.

13. This great general second Resurrection is also done and demonstrated by the first Resurrection; when God awakens the Sinner by unlocking the inspoken Grace, and makes the Word a Refiner's Fire, and as a Tincture transmuteth the Mass, and leaveneth the Lump, then the Soul dies to the old and lives to the renewed Image, by the Visits of the Virgin, becomes a Virgin, by looking on Christ comes to look like him; the Bottle is made new into which the new Wine may now be intrusted, and the King of Glory comes into his Temple, his new made Vineyard and Garden, and imparts himself, his Heart, his Whispers and Counsels when the Ear is opened. For the sake of the Virgin Image thus Begotten shall the whole Man be crystalliz'd and tinctured with solar Power at the Resurrection; mean time no Tongue or Pen can more than smatter, at the recital of the love-inspired Words formed at every of the Masters sweet Visits, when he comes to feed this Infant-birth and Sup with it.

14. The Reason why we cannot tell it when we come out from the Holy Place, is, because our Astral Man knows not of what Dignity the Guest is that comes to the inward Man, for he enters farther, and our Astral Man or outward Reason is as a Porter, whose office being at the Door, hears not the Holy Treaty held within, in the Closet, and were it he could, he understands not the Language, but if a loud word be spoken, which he hears, then only when the sensual Man sleepeth, then doth he either tremble, as if he feared to be dismist his office, for our Reason is like *Gillio*, no Judge of these Matters: or else he frames Images of what he as it were over-hears. And if a Letter to the Virgin be intrusted with the Astral Man (the Porter) he only reads the Superscription, but sees not what the inside is, he thinks it all as the outside with ordinary Ink, but within 'tis all golden Letters mixt with Blood, and legible in the dark Night, for the Characters all shine and flame; and none can read them but those who share in the first Resurrection, for the old Eves are dim: these are convinced, and somewhat more or less see how the second Resurrection will be, having a sensible lively feeling of the first, and passed the Danger and Power of the second Death. See the 8th and 10th Verses of the 173 Answer.

(2.)
1 *Cor.* 15. 24.

15. That our Lord shall put down all *Rule, Authority and Power*, this is meant to be after the Resurrection, when he (as the Sun in his strength) obscures not only Glowerms, but the Candle and Torch light: Men shall then no longer abuse lawful Power, nor acquire lawless Authority, nor violently or subtilly usurp undue Rule, the Hunter and his Dogs shall no longer chase Lambs as if they were

Foxes,

Foxes, but the tyrannous Monarchs and the wronged Captives stand on the same level each in his own Principle: and the Principles are as different, as a dark Sulphurous Fire is from a sweet Radiant Lustre; then also shall the Evil Angels, whether they shall be Seducers of Men, or other spiritual Wickednesses in High Places, or Rulers of the Darkness as God of this World, be all thrust out; for he is come whose right it is, both by Original and Purchas'd Propriety.

16. This great general Manifestation of *Jehovah*, Christ's Natural Soveraignty, is also done and demonstrated in the whole Creation; by his sitting among the Gods, turning the Heart of the Mighty as Water, stopping all Mouths, bowing all Knees, being above the Proud, rescuing the Prey from the Teeth of the fiercest, feeding the Hungry and Helpless, the young Lions and young Ravens, showering on the parched Wilderness, stilling the raging Deep, opening his Bottles in their Season, treasuring his Snow and Wind, and marshalling his Host of Stars. But above all it is demonstrable in his Family, who not only have ceased Hostility against him, but taken up Arms for and under him, out of weakness are strengthened to do, suffer, live, die for him, and in him; their Health is to be Love-sick their Life to die daily; he is their Fear, Love, Hope, Repose, Strength, Wisdom, Song, their Springs and Treasures are in him for Time and Eternity, their four Forms are attoned by his Light, their Discord by his Unity is composed, his Presence kills their lofty Thoughts, it also makes them alive to him, his Fire refineth them, they are always prostrate at his Feet, mortified and mortifying continually and makes them a Living Sacrifice day by day, till Death become their intimate associate, and safe retreat from the Storm. Yet these things are so secretly done in the new Heart, that the Heart it self can better conceive it than the Brain; but how can the Idea thereof be comprehended by us who are comprehended by it? When we would form it we cannot, for we (*viz.*) our new Man is formed by it. How can we express it, seeing we are the Letters by which it expresseth it self? It is far above the Languages got at *Babel*; but when the Spirits of the Letters shall be restored, the renewed Spirit shall find a Tongue to be a Herauld for the King of Kings, put to silence all contrary discording sounds, and Dethrone all other Rule, Authority and Power in us, *Amen*.

3. 17. That then is (or cometh) the End; the Judgment being ended, the End hath found the Beginning. When the Six Working Days of the Week are ended, Masters use to Reckon with their Hirelings, and give them their Wages, then followeth the Day of Rest. When the six working Properties have wrought their designed end in any Creature, they give up themselves into the seventh wherein to rest; the doing whereof, bringeth the End into the Beginning, when the Wheat is in the Barn, and the Tares cast away, the Harvest is ended.

18. A few words are offer'd to be consider'd concerning the End. 1. *Whether the Elements shall be dissolved at the instant of the Resurrection, or not remain till the compleat End of the Judgment Day?* *Answ.* It may seem otherwise; for they must as Conservatories be opened; that is, the Earth, *viz.* Hell or the Grave must deliver up the Dead which shall be therein; or how else shall the Mighty men at to the Rocks to cover them, also the Sea deliver the Dead conserved therein, the Air the words it treasur'd in it. 2. *Whether the Elements may not remain, and yet the Sun, Moon and Stars be resolved into their Æther?* *Answ.* As there was Light the three first days of the Creation, out-spoken by the Word which was as a dispersed Light, before the collecting the same into the Sun, Moon and Stars: so may the collected Light pass back into the dispersed Light, to form that one Great Day, which is not to admit of Revolutions of Night and Day, but only the Day and Night of the two Incomprehensible Principles; which may be both in one place at one time without justling one the other, and be the full End of Specifick and revolved Time, may

(3.)

Q. 1.
A.

Q. 2.
A.

may be at the Commencement or Morning of that Day, and the full entring on Eternity not be till the End or Evening of that Day, when the Judge shall give to each World the Inhabitants thereof, as their Magick Wills have severally tinctured and formed them thereunto: whether of the Day, Love and Purity, or of Blackness, Wrath and Abominations: And this is the absolute Period of the Genus and Thing which we call Time.

End of Time demonstrated 1. 19. The End of Time may be demonstrated in the regenerated Children, thus; When the Holy Fire of God on the Altar in the Soul, hath separated the Earthy part from the new Man, so that by resignation of the Will, the Love-flame is raised up, the Spirit of that Man entreth into God, and in a measure into such rest as ends the multiplicity, and possesseth the Eternal Unity; for his earthy, salt, corrupt Sulphur, and Mortal Mercury is changeable into the Saline Property, Paradifical Flesh or Sulphur and Spiritual Mercury, by the Holy Tincture whereof in this Separation the renewed Image becomes capable. And if the inward new Man be enabled to press forward, it may in this very most secret Path attain the Resurrection from the Dead in the outward Man, and be translated into the Life of *Enoch.* Thus also we see that Antimony calcin'd by the solar Rays through Burning Glasses, may both be augmented to almost half in weight, and also changed from a strong, rank, great Poison to a vigorous Balsam and potent Fortifier of decaying Nature, shewing us how the Mutations of time cease, and how to enter into a fixt serene Eternity.

End of Time demonstrated 2. 20. The End of Time may be also demonstrated in the Sons of Perdition thus; That after all Warnings, Judgments and Convictions they have met with, they finally fix in Enmity, and are Imaged into a private perverse Will, the Circumferential Applications are restrained by the Central Fire, which also stops up the Fountain of pure, meek Water, and clouds the Divine solar Influences of Light, and therefore receive no increase, as was said of Antimony, but are subjected to a perpetuated Vanity; nor can such be renewed but are obdurated, they are not like Antimony transmuted from Poison to a sublimated Cordial, but recede more fiercely into the endless Anguishes, as Evaporation by Heat makes cold Poison the more deadly, here also the Times of successive Good and Evil, strife of Flesh and Spirit, Resolves and Doubts are ceased, and these Men are become Sensual in the most outward part, stubborn and obstinate in the Astral, which should be the rational part, and furious, haughty, false and filthy in the Will of the Eternal Man. So in the most outward sensitive part are meer Animals, in the rational part stubborn, besotted Fools, and in the Immortal Souls, Devils; and all fixt so, that if the Divine Sun should graciously shine on him, he would but as a filthy heap of Horse-dung, or a stinking watry Ditch, generate the greater and more dangerous venomous, loathsome reptils continually.

(4.) 21. That then the Kingdom shall be delivered up to the Father, and God shall be all in all. The Lord's Prayer Establisheth all the parts of it with this word, *For thine is the Kingdom, the Power, and the Glory for ever:* of him and from him are all things, and therefore also all things are for him; they are the Manifestation of his Power, and of his Love. Infinite Power were Defective without Infinite Wisdom, also Infinite Wisdom were impotent without Infinite Power; again, Infinite Power, and Infinite Wisdom were infinitely Dreadful without Infinite Goodness; but all three United, is infinitely sufficient to support the weakest of the Lord's little ones and blow to atoms the highest, vastest Puissance of the Princes of the dark World (the God of this World) and hold them shut up for ever.

John 17. 6. 22. The Lord Jesus saith in his Prayer concerning his, to his Father, *Thine they were, and thou gavest them me:* but that Grand Administration must be such, as if it were said by the Lord, *Mine they are, and I give them back to thee;* where lies a Mystery fiery not obvious to any but the enlightened Mind, which shall be spoken in a simple familiar way. Consider common Fire it is not Light, no more than a Rose is a Tree, or the Root of a Lilly is the Flower: Tho' by the way we may digress, to observe that an Eminent Pen, endeavours by many (in their kind ingenious) Arguments to prove Light to be Fire in a less degree; but granting the vigour of the Fire to be in the Light, or by the affluence of the Air to be the enkindler of the Light, yet will it not follow that the Light is Fire, unless the whole Deep is therefore the Sun, because the Sun's vigour enlivens it: For, grant That Author's Arguments to arrive at what he levels them, the distinct Properties will result into a Chaos, whose various Vertues mutually produce, consubstantiate, figure and cohabit each the other, yet the one no more the other than Heat is Cold or Light is Darkness. It would also confound the Son with the Father, and those two to be only terms convertible, a thing so far from truth as not to be esteemed only short of it, but rather diametrically opposite to it: But passing by this, consider we (as was said) common Fire, that hath an attractive, hungry *What Christ's* fierceness in it like that in a heated Stone, and that fierceness must be perpetuated, *delivering up* if the Light be not generated by it, but is the Fire of Hell; but when the Light *the Kingdom* begotten by it (as from a Fountain) is resigned unto it, and shineth in it, then *&c.* and there is the meek Vertue united with the strong might of the Fire, thereby turning all into a Majestick splendor, so bringing the Copy as a fit due conformity to the Original; because the alone perfection of the multiplicity is its arriving at the Unity.

23. Now come we to the last [and God shall be all in all] here may be taken a (5.) prospect of the Holy of Holies. An Angel's Royal Hand were well employed in drawing these Lines and Measures, but then still it must be with a Reed, and the Computation must suit with the Cubit of a Man, the Language also must be stammering, wretched, and as it were foolish; else it descends not to the fallen Human Understanding. And as none knows the things of a man but the Human Understanding Spirit; so none those of God but the Holy Spirit of God. What is vile dust to penetrate this? Woe to us that we are of unclean Lips, and vain in our imagination.

24. Truth tells us that our Omnipotent God hath three Delights; *(viz.)* 1. In *Prov.* 8. 30. his Son, in whom is his delight. 2. In the Excellent made so by his Son. *Isa.* 42. 1. 3. In Exercising Mercy. The two last; *(viz.)* the Excellent and Exercising of *Psal.* 16. 3. Mercy dwell in the Son as in their Ocean, Centre or Fountain, and issue through *Micah* 7. 18. him as Sap through a Tree, and That Tree grows in our Impotent Humanity. Now (after the delivering up the Kingdom to the Father) God's becoming all in all, is the uniting all these three Delights to the Almighty Power-World, where the Joy is incomprehensible, and the Increase of it Endless and Infinite; for then Almightiness of Strength and Wisdom hath replenisht it self with Almightiness of Love and Goodness, the Unity hath reassumed the Multiplicity; What words may express This most Holy Dominion?

25. Can it be pourtrayed by the Joy of a tender-hearted Parent, all whose dear Children having been miserably captiv'd by a barbarous malicious Enemy, are by the prudent Conduct, and prosperous Atchievement of their eldest Brother compleatly rescued? May it be apprehended by the Joy of the Harvest, when the loaden Sheaves crowning the Fields, do seasonably enrich the Barns and Granaries: Or of the Vintage, when the bowed Branches dropping into the Press overflow it: Or by the lost Son, the lost Groat, the lost Sheep, the Joy of the Bridegroom over the Bride; all which are faint resemblances and dim shadows of the Delight of the Eternal Father. Also what is the Content of an Earthly Monarch, whose Victorious Arms subject his Enemies, and his seasonable Succours secure his Friends:

What is the Triumph of the Sun in the Firmament, when his Spicy Beams revive the Face of Nature grown pale by his long absence, and call up a smiling Spring? These are weak figures, and dark similes of the Delight of the Sun of Righteousness. And what is the sweet Satisfaction the tender Mother hath by seeing all her dear Babes for whom she travell'd, to whom she had drawn out her Breasts, over whom she had long unweariedly watcht and cared, of whom she had been a compassionate Comfort and Assistant in their Froward Fits, various Anguishes, Sicknesses and Hazards, as so many Deaths, at last all thriven to perfect stature of Body, excellent Endowments of Mind, exact, chearful Dutifulness to their Father, and by Him all advanced to wear Crowns? By this may be, tho' obscurely, represented, the Delight of God's Holy Spirit. Lastly; What was the Joy of the lately oppressed Tribes, when delivered at the Red Sea, and occasion'd the Song of *Moses*? What was also their Joy when God turned back the Captivity of *Sion* from the *Chaldean*, when they were as men in a dream; and what the Joy of them, who having washed their Garments in the Blood of the Lamb, and had been brought out of Fiery Tryals, do come to receive their White Robes and Palms? by which may be seen the Joy of the Redeemed of the Lord in that Holy of Holy days. Thus are the sublimest Affairs offered in a most familiar homely manner, with a low voice, and flat style, for so the Wisdom of God descends, and delights to cloath it self; while Man's Wisdom would flourish in enticing words puft up with empty sounds.

Obj. 26. But some by way of opposition may say, that God ever was, is, and shall all be in all; as it is written, Of him, for him and through him are all things; and in him we live, move, and have our Being.

Anf. A confused knowledge of things doth but little difference men from Brute Creatures. Let us therefore summarily remember what disperfedly in the Answers foregoing, and the blessed *Jacob Behmens* Writings, is large and clear; *viz.* That the gracious Creator spake the Paradifical or Angelical World out of himself, according to every Property of the Eternal Nature, and according to the holy second Principle, which till there was a rent, by the receding of *Lucifer* into the by-path of his private Self-will, the whole remained an exact Image and true Copy of the Original, where the Name of God was perfectly spoken, and God was all in all.

27. And out of, and as an Image of the Paradifical Principle, and with the Properties of the Power-World, did God speak forth the Aftral-World an Image of both Inward-Worlds, which as a Child of the other two had (as the Children of Men have) a Centre of its own; and tho' it were a Copy of the Inward-Worlds, yet was another a third Principle issuing into the multiplicity, and as far as it so remaineth, God is all in all in it also.

28. In and over this Principle *Lucifer*'s Throne had Jurisdiction substituted by the Son of God himself, till on *Lucifer*'s Heresie he became uncapable to derive Power from the Holy World, but introduced Anarchy in the Principle over which he was to Rule according to Divine Order; thence all faces of his Legions, and This very Deep, gathered Blackness, and the Deep tumbled into a Chaos: Here then God, as He is Purity, Holiness and Goodness, was not all in all, but they were now captiv'd in him as he is the Ocean of all Might and Power, the Abyss of the first Principle, according to which He is called a Jealous God, and Consuming Fire; and thus is He in That Profane Dark World. But God is all in all in the Holy World and Creatures, as far as they are Holy in his gracious majeftick Light and Goodness, the thing in this Question intended.

29. And now that the whole Deep (being God's inoffensive Creature) was impos'd on, suffering the sad Effects of the Rebellion of the Apoftate Angels; it
pleas'd

The 177 Theosophick Questions Answered.

pleas'd the God of Grace (whose Angel pitied *Balaam's* Ass, and who made merciful mention of the very Cattle in *Nineveh*) to ransom this great space, that as it had been the Tragical Stage of the Impure Spirits, it might, by introduction of Light, be the Theatre of Mercy and Goodness. Then was the New (which Men call'd the Old) World founded, or a New Principle revealed ; such a one, that as the Evil ones having profanely left their Habitation ; (*viz.*) the Holy second Principle ; To were they in a great measure excluded. This New one ; the Light of the Outward Sun being no advantage, but rather opposing them ; and the Moon, tho' but a Looking-glass reflecting the Sun's Light, not serving, but rather thwarting them ; for no Light fits them better than that of the Lightening, from the astonishment that comes with it.

30. And whereas the Out-World was like a Boat built of the pieces of a wracked Ship, and that it was formed of the Properties which *Lucifer* had divided ; therefore were the fierceness of *Mars*, the strong Bands of *Saturn*, the sly quality of *Mercury*, figured distinctly, and not harmoniously, in the cruel and other Creatures of this World, at enmity with the noble *Jupiter*, amiable *Venus*, and royal *Sol*. Seeing now also here was an empty Throne, whereof *Lucifer* was as uncapable as of That Estate which he had not kept, then did God create a Prince who might Image the Trinity, His Soul having the Properties of the first Principle, His Divine Spirit the Holy second, His Royal Transparent Body (capable of Eternity) figuring the third ; in This Noble Person, while he so stood, was Power and Suitableness to fit in the Throne of the third Principle ; for in him was God (whom he compleatly Imaged) all in all.

31. But when This Prince divorc't the Pure Virgin of Divine Love, and degenerated into Bestial Lust, God his Creator was no longer all in all in him, but he was a Mock-God to himself, a Captive to his own Lust and Tyrannous Self-will : So that his dear Virgin could no longer trust her self with him, but he died as to her, and she withdrew her pure Modesty into her own Heaven, leaving his Soul among the Murtherers (whereof *Cain* was afraid) like to the state of the Out-cast Legions, and his Body like the dark confused Deep before the Almighty call'd for Light ; where was now the Holy Image wherein God is all in all ?

Q. 32. But is not God all in all in His Converted Children here, of whom it is said, *He that is born of God sinneth not ?* And *as many as be perfect*, (*viz.*) meaning 1 *John* 3. 9. them, *be thus minded.* Again, *He hath perfected for ever them that are sanctified* ; and *Phil.* 3. 15. is not God all in all in such? *Heb.* 10. 14.

A. Well were it for us if it were so, but our too high thoughts keeps us dwarfy, and greatly aggravates our wretchedness, proceeding very much from our ignorance of that State we fell from, of which Treats the 45th Answer, 8 and 9 verses, and the 52 Answer throughout ; and how miserable Man's Fall made him, is traced in the 72 Answer in all the 8 verses of it. The dividing of the Tinctures into distinct Male and Female, is an Evil, men are willingly ignorant of ; where began the dismal breach, whence *David* as a Prophet lamenteth his *Psal.* 51. 5. Extraction ; (*viz.*) *I was shapen in iniquity, and in sin did my Mother conceive me* ; that also is signified by our Apostle ; (*viz.*) *There is neither Male nor Female, but Gal.* 3. 18. *Christ is all in all*.

33. The present State of God's Holy Ones, subjects them in a great degree to the prevailing hot fury and wrath of the first Principle ; and the fleeting, wavering, ambiguous unsteadiness of the third, against both of which is the Apostle's caution ; (*viz.*) *I will therefore that men pray every where, lifting up holy hands, without wrath and doubting*, that is, without the predominancy of either first or third, but in the Resignation, Love, Meekness and Faith of the pure second Principle. Thus, as this World is a part of us, the God of this World hath a party in us, which

Dd 2   entails

entails on *Adam*'s Posterity vast loads of sorrow, misery, vexation and woe; for so far are we wandered from the Holy Powers, and Magically formed, and degenerated into so corrupt a Bestial Body, that the awakened Soul finds her self not only unequally, but sinfully and shamefully yoked to a strange deformed filthy Companion, instead of the pure Paradisical Virgin Image capable of Eternity, bearing only the figure, but that we lost was to have been the Ruler over, and Epitome of the Out-world, and was invested with Dominion of the Works of God, and all this to that degree of wretchedness, That to be present in this vile Body, is to be absent from the Lord. And that through much tribulation we must enter into the Kingdom of God.

2 *Cor.* 5. 6.
Act. 14. 22.

34. Hence is it that the Wise man tells us, Wisdom and Sorrow joyntly grow up; for he that encreaseth Wisdom, encreaseth Sorrow. So that *Heman*, who was wise to a Proverb, that it was said of *Solomon*, He was wiser than *Himan*. This *Heman*, the Pen-man of the 88 Psalm, shews his frame to be composed of mournful parts, and that Psalm as the Glass, Door or Issue of him, is as the Epitome of unexpressible grief, as a night mantled over from any the least glimpse of day. It is ignorance, stupidity or madness that transports men in the Vale of Tears into wanton fleshly merriments; for this is the time of budding, and extendeth but to green fruit, wherein the bitter, four, undigested Properties prevent by their crudity the Solar Influence. And lest we deceive our selves, we ought to know this is the watry Seed-time, the place of the Childrens being in the birth, of working with fear and trembling, fighting, wrestling, watching, of receiving many a wound and discouragement, of suffering reproach, many reluctances upon the rallying and re-enforcing of our domestick Enemies, who (impudently almost continually) return upon us our old Habits. The Evil One is also ready to imbitter our way, double our crosses, aggravate our scandals, pervert our purposes, and make much sorrowful, if not shameful work for Repentance. So that the Pilgrim who is in real earnestness, had need to pray without ceasing, bear his Lord's Cross, tho' in anxiety of his own Soul, live the life of humble Patience in passing through this so Thorny a path in our comfortless Desert, beset with snares, pollutions and deaths; also to bear with the infirmities of others, to shun Evil Influences from them; and that the Love of our dear God may sink the price of our own Repute, our desire of Ease, and of our whole self, that God, and only God may be at last our all in all in us and over us, which the God of Grace and Infinite Compassions assist us in unto the end.

Q. 175. *What will the Holy or Saints, and Damned each of them do and leave undone?*

A. 1. The blessed *Jacob Behmen's* Answer of the 32 Question of the 40 Questions of the Soul, sheweth the condition and glory of Souls in the Life to come, and the Answer of the 34th of those Questions, telleth the miserable, horrible Estate of the Damned. The Answer of the 167 of these Questions, treats of what concerns the Holy Ones, and the 168th is of the Wicked, as is also the 9th verse of the 166. On this Subject review the 170 Answer.

2. Yet without reciting the Reviews, something must be added: That the Holy Ones being gathered into the Unity, do the work of the one in their various measures; and having one Will with the Eternal One, have a proportion of the Wisdom and Power of the one, and in That Wisdom and Power can enter into the Variety; and as the Variety is part of the Infinity, they have a creaturely prospect and open door into the Infinity.

3. And for as much as they are the Image of all the Principles, and an exquisite composition of all the Properties, therefore when the Resignation of their Will

in

The 177 *Theosophick Questions Answered.* 211

in Jesus Christ translates them into the Kingdom of God, what can then withhold it self from them, but that all the Properties should operate triumphantly in them? Only this is their limit, that as their Life is the Holy Kingdom, they can skill nothing but the Works of the Principle wherein the Holy Kingdom standeth, but yet are comprehensive of all the Principles in the manner of Creature-comprehension, according as when the Three in One was the profound Harmony before the speaking forth of the Multiplicity; but they cannot see into, much less Image in themselves the separate, impure, divided Properties; as neither can the Outward Sun see Darkness, tho' the Eye thereof go into every Country, because where ever it looks, the Darkness disappears, so that in the Light the Image of Darkness cannot be impressed, tho' the Light can impress its Image on the Darkness, and shine in it.

4. And seeing the General Assembly of the Lord Jesus Christ the first born, hath the Power, Wisdom and Love of the first-born in an Eternal Community, as the Natural Body hath the Animal, Vital, and Nutritive Spirits in an intire Community, what then can be too mysterious for them to contemplate? for in themselves is the Echo or Pulse beating of every thing, World and Existence; they can therefore at once (as it were) dissect every thing, and what can be too strong for them to sway who are in Jesus Christ compleatly furnisht with ability for working the works of God, which is the highest Good the most excellent Creature is capable to do or to will.

5. Now to tell what the Damned do and leave undone, is unfolded by knowing, 1. The Principle in which they are comprehended. 2. Themselves. 3. By knowing and considering God. (1.) The Principle they are shut up in is the first, the strong might of the dark Abyss, consisting of the fierceness of the four Anguishes, they are everlastingly under those Adamantine Chains, and must needs leave undone those things which are out of the reach of that Chain. And it may be understood thus; there are Lands and Seas near both Poles where the extremity of condensed cold arrests the Seas, and they are an Icy Rock, and the Lands and Mountains are bound by Stone-cleaving Frosts, and under a Region of Snow, so that Sea and Land are in a fixt Barren inactivity, and while continued darkness dwells on it, the Principle of the dark Abyss (as sever'd from the other Principles) is in part figur'd by it.

6. (2.) By considering the Damned themselves, they are as utterly unable to enkindle the least glance of Divine Light in them as the Icy Seas and Mountains of dark Frost are to create to themselves another Sun, and Fructifie to the production of the Rich Vertues and Ornaments of *Eden* the Garden of God. (2.)

7. (3.) By considering the Holy God from whom (as he is the Infinite Goodness, the One Gracious Will and Abyss of Love) they have rent themselves, and become dead to his Divine Life, and at the same instant are become alive to his Wrath: As one awaking to rage and fury dies to patience and meekness, hereby they become a sweet savour to the hunger of that anger; as it is written upon the wicked it shall Rain Snares, Fire, Brimstone, and an horrible Tempest, for the Righteous God loveth Righteousness. The rise, progress and perpetuity of the fierceness of Gods Wrath, tho' an Eternal Principle, is yet Gods strange Work, and is their only Work, wholly their Life tho' a dying one, their Centre and home tho' a horrid one. (3.)

8. All they think is confusion and distracting Anguish; all they do is the outward Expressions of their inward fierce Impressions, they are resisting the Infinite Power of Omnipotence, and in their fixt Enmity against the Gracious, Holy Love of God are united and become one with the Devils in the Principle of Gods devouring Fire and consuming Fierceness: As Molten Glass hath one will with

the

the Fire to scorch and burn as it. And tho' Damned Humane Creatures and Devils are one with themselves, and one with, in or under the Principle of the wrath of God, it is not with them as with Molten Metal, which by the action of the Fire are made conforming Passives, and all the contrariety hereunto evaporated, separated or transferred into it; for Man was Imaged in a Divine, Pure, Paradisical Principle with all the three Principles powerfully fixt: For the Creator willed not to lose the end of his Creation; having given him a Soul rooted in the Eternal Band of the forms of the first Principle, a Spirit out of the Eternal Substance of the Light, a Tincture out of the Spiritual World, and a Body out of the Eternal Nature, whereof the Astral Heavens are a figure. So that his second Principle is not volatile or evaporable, tho' capable of being darkened, nor his third Principle so to be separated as to be annihilable, tho' Mortal for a time; therefore the fiery Property of the Soul is such as subsisteth in the devouring fierceness of the Wrath Kingdom, and the second and third Principles subsist in and with, and are tormented by the Anguishes of the Soul, as are the Souls themselves by the contrarieties of their own four forms.

9. Thus also are Devils and the Damned a Torment each to other, tho' in one Principle, and one with the Principle; as the Holy Angels and Saints are a Crown of Joy, and Transcendent Delight and Triumph one, to and with the other, being all in one Principle, and one with the Principle in Nature, *viz*. the new Nature, and all the seven Properties making in them all one Property. The same contrariwise do the Devil and Damned torment themselves, and one the other, laying one his Blood on the other, and all at constant Enmity against the Principle which comprehends them, Blaspheming the Infinite Omripotence.

10. *Obj.* But will some say here seemeth a contradiction that the Faln Angels and Damned Men are one in Nature and Property with the Principle of Gods Wrath wherein they are comprehended, and yet at Enmity with and in the same.

A. It is truely so, and easily made obvious; for the Principle is that of stern Astringency and violent Attraction, also Exaltation whence Covetousness and boundless Pride in the separate Properties originate; now how ill do griping covetous Men, and other covetous Men each scraping from the other agree, and proud Men with contrary proud Men? But the resignation of the Spirit, and emptying and divesting of the Soul, thereby becoming as a little Child, frees from those direful Extremities. The Principle is that of Darkness, and the dark Spirits only are suited to, and fixt in it; but those in whom the Divine Light is generated and inkindled cannot be detained thereby, for that were a real contradiction. The Principle is also an Eternal Desperation and Anguish, above which they in whom the Faith of Gods Elect is begotten are exalted; but the rest are therein plunged. The Principle is Rage, fierce Wrath, and implacable Enmity, from which the Humble, Meek, Dear, pure Love, translates and ennobles the Soul, giving another Centre, another Life, so that he is dead to all these and to the prevailing Dominion of this whole Principle, and lives a new Divine Life, which this Principle cannot see, apprehend or conceive the Idea of, much less comprehend and fasten upon. But the Vassals or Parts of the dark World sink as Lead into that Abyss, and as poysonous, venemous, filthy, and other cruel Beasts, cannot but do or endeavour hurt, for it is their Life, and their Forms of Nature have no other will, so are these dark, fierce, damned Souls, one in Will, one in Nature, one in Act with the Inimicitious Principle, and therefore must ever be at Enmity therein and therewith.

11. And this thus enkindled is the Kingdom of Gods fierce Wrath, Fury, Vengeance, Consuming Fire, the Blackness of Darkness; this is that Fuel which the Breath

The 177 *Theosophick Questions Answered.*

Breath of the Lord like a River of Brimstone doth kindle. The Principle of Wrath as it is in God is not only not Evil, but very Good in it self in its Original, as is the heat in the outward Sun, or the Gall in living Creatures, the former giving Essence to the Light, the other strikes up Life in the Animal, but as the one in Burning-glasses consumes, so the other separated from the other Properties is a bitter, raging, tearing, fierce Enemy to the Tranquillity of Life, as hath in these Answers been remember'd.

Q. 176. *Where shall Hell, and also the Eternal Habitation of the Holy or Saints be?*

A. 1. When depraved Reason hears this Question, it straightway imploys the Imagining Faculty to dig a Dungeon for the place of Hell, either in the Bowels of the Earth, or under the Poles where the Suns absence causeth a desolation; and to find the Habitation of the Saints it soars up to an imaginary *Zenith*, and if it be not so gross as the fiction of the *Elizian* Fields, yet placeth them by local defiance from the Circle of time, and remote from the roarings and fumes of the smoaky Pit.

2. It is true to say up to Heaven and down to Hell, but let the same imagination remove this Ball of Earth and Water, and the starry Heaven is without *Zenith* and *Nadir*; no Star is above or below. And the local Apprehensions are as near the Truth as those *Americans*, who by an Inaccessible Ridge of Mountains are shut up, do (as 'tis said) promise themselves to be Translated by Death only to the other side of that Ridge. It is not unlikely that *Mahomet* might have heard of the mention St. *Paul* makes of the third Heaven, and thence form in his gross Imagination an Ignorant Idea of his Travels through the Silver into the Golden Region, and giddily feign those Varieties to be fenced out one from the other, as Beasts be fenced out one from the other in their Inclosures.

3. The [where] in this Question must therefore have quite another [there] and solution than what local distance gives; for Hell will be Everlastingly comprized in that Principle of fierceness, wrath, and blackness of darkness; where the seven Properties are in a fixt Anguish, Enmity and Radical or Original Discord, wherein all and only Extreams are ever Existent, and so possess the Powers in the dark World, whereof the fierce Properties in this are a Figure or Shadow; for in the third Principle or Out-birth hath the first or dark World as really, as the second, the holy pure World, powerfully impressed its Image. In that place, therefore are the Evil Angels and Damned Reprobates, and when their filthy Bestial Bodies shall have a Resurrection to Condemnation, as they were the Figure, and Tinctured by their averted wrathful Inward Man, they shall possess the Dregs, Fierceness, Anguish and Odious Properties of the same third Principle, as the Filthiness, Bitterness, Stink, Venom, Contrariety, Poyson and Extremities of the Out-birth, which shall be resumed after the dissolution by its Æther, not annihilated, but remain Monuments of the Power of the Infinite Creator, and Figures of the Spiritual dark World or first Principle; as the *Caput Mortuum* of the Chymists: Nor is it any Impediment but Exciter of Life, that the bitter poysonous Gall is in the Bodies of Animals; nor prejudice to the day when the Sun is in the *Zenith* of the *Æquator*, that darkness is also in that instant on their Antipodes and both Poles, yea on Caverns of Rocks and Ships holds if shut up, and on the inside of every Mans Glove, and under the Eye-lid as soon and as oft as it is shut; thus as to Locality Hell is in Heaven.

4. And concerning the Eternal Habitation of the Holy or Saints, it must be said it is wheresoever the seven Properties are in Harmony and triumph; for
there

there the first four in Eternity generate the other three, whereby calmness is transported into triumph, and peace ascendeth into excess of highest delight, joy and ravishment. Hereby diminutives of Affection (if sincere) are exalted and blown up into Angelical Flames of burning Love: Thus dwell they in and are united to the Divine Powers of the Infinite glorious holy World, of which World all the best, innocentest, most lovely, excellent Creatures and Things here are a faint dead shadow. And when the holy Souls shall have again, and put on their bright pure Bodies, being raised and conformed to the glorious Body of Jesus Christ, then shall the Paradisical Substance (which is the Essence or Quintessence of the best Properties here) be the Eternal living Food of those new Bodies. Nor shall the Vertues of Concretes here be annihilated, but resumed, sublimed and spiritualized, the holy World being their proper Æther, where they shall remain in their Essence and Idea for the glory of the gracious Creator.

5. Thus we see the distance of Heaven from Hell is as far as from Wrath to Love, from Anguish to Triumph, from Night and Darkness to the day, not locally but a whole another Principle; for it is not like, or to be compared with the distance of those Stars which are lift up in our Zenith from those in our Nadir, for they unite in their operation in one Individual Flower or Plant, and by their Light continue to kiss each other; but the distance here meant is an incomprehensible one. Thus is it in the Creation as in Man, the mixture of Spirits compelleth to Compassion, and Compassion (by assimilation of an Artificial Identity) generateth Love, but this distance consisteth in a Total and Eternal Separation of Spirits, so alien and diametrically opposite one to the other, as Life and Death are.

6. It may be with this our Globe when the Elements dissolve, as with an Herb whose Ligaments being loosed, and the Properties thereof by the Artist segregated into Spirit, Oyl and Salt; for then the Creatures which now groan after Deliverance from their Subjection to Vanity, and the good Properties here captiv'd, may, the Creatures in their Ideas, and the Properties in their Energies, by the Tincture of them all unite with the Spiritual World, and shew forth the Infinite Wisdom of the Gracious Creator and Mighty Redeemer, being part of the Spoils and Trophies of his powerful Redemption. And here may in the place of this self-same Ball, yet in another Principle, be separated away, all the filthy, impure, abominable Creatures and Properties, as the Fæces, Dregs and Ashes of an Alimbick, which confused Mass of Reprobated Properties must dismally adhere and be ingulphed with the fierce Horrour and Anguish of the dark World, the Image whereof they bear, and that not fully as sickly Complexions by their ill Constitutions fall by the Plague when there comes a Pestilential contagious Air, but they unite with that outer Darkness as they are a Plague-sore to themselves.

And now to avoid Repetition, see concerning the Locality of Hell in the 19, 20, 21, 22, 23, and last Verses of the 17th of these Questions. Also concerning the Locality of Heaven. See the 2d, 3d, 4th, 7th, and last Verses of the 18th of these Questions.

Q. 177. *What shall be the Eternal Joy of the Holy or Saints, and the Eternal Pain or Torment of the Wicked? Or also may there be any alteration effected?*

A. 1. The three Parts of this Question require only a few words, or rather Quotations severally; as first, what shall be the Eternal Joy of the Holy or Saints, the knowledge whereof may be collected by the serious Mind from Meditation of the Discoveries of it Recorded in the Sacred Scriptures, as amongst many these following, Psal. 16. 11. *In thy presence is fulness of Joy, at thy Right Hand are pleasures*

for

The 177 Theofophick Queſtions Anſwered.

for ever more. Pſal. 36. 8, 9. *Thou ſhalt make them drink of the River of thy pleaſure, for with thee is the Fountain of Life, in thy Light we ſhall ſee Light,* Iſai. 64. 4. *For ſince the beginning of the World, Men have not heard nor perceived by the Ear, neither hath the Eye ſeen, O God, beſides thee, what he hath prepared for him that waiteth for him,* which words are recited in 1 *Cor.* 2. 9. adding v. 10. *but God hath revealed them,* &c. Rom. 8. 18. *The ſufferings of the preſent time are not worthy to be compared with the Glory that ſhall be revealed in us.* 2 Cor. 4. 17. *Our light Affliction which is but for a moment, worketh for us a far more exceeding and Eternal weight of Glory.* 1 John 3. 2. *It doth not yet appear what we ſhall be, but we know that when he appeareth, we ſhall be like him.* Jude 24. *preſent you faultleſs before the preſence of his Glory with exceeding Joy.* And the 21 and 22 Chapters of the *Revelations*.

2. Much alſo may be found by pondering the Anſwer of the bleſſed *J. Behmen*, to the laſt of the 40 Queſtions, and 32 Queſtion of the Soul. Something alſo conducible and pertinent hereunto may be found by Review of the 18th and 19th Anſwers of the preſent Queſtions, the laſt Verſe of the 40th Anſwer, the 45th Anſwer throughout, the laſt Verſe of the 49th Anſwer, the 5th Verſe of the 57th Anſwer.

3. The Eternity of the Joy of the Holy ones ſhall be the alone Unity without Fraction; ever new, ever young, one only conſtant ſpring and uninterrupted Autumn, their City as pure and undefiled, as is the inward Holy ſpiritual World, their Kingdom incomprehenſibly vaſt, being one with the illimitable ſecond Principle. The precious Stone call'd *Lapis Galliſtoneus*, is ſaid to be unable for its warming, cheering vertue unleſs ſet into Gold, nor hath the Cryſtal any intrinſick Light, till the influencing Solar or other luſtre hath acceſs to it, which then is multiplied by it: and to paſs by infinite inſtances producible, the perfection of the ſeven Properties is attained by the United Conjunction of the ſix Actives in the ſeventh, which is as their Paſſive Work houſe.

4. Things and Perſons here, though partly good, are partly otherwiſe; and that either by an Evil commixture or want of ſome good thing or Property; or by inequality of the Proportions of their Compoſition; or the feebleneſs of the parts United; or want of Time to perfect the Creature or thing; or by a corruptible quality: or by the inſufficiency of its Origin; or by its undefenſibleneſs; or if very good may yet be only ſo in and to it ſelf but incommunicable; or the participation interruptible, and not always ſo alike; or (which is often) a good Influence may exhauſt over much, as that Aromatick Herb Baſil, by ſtanding long in the Sun, may degenerate into Wild Thyme, or ſome other Neceſſity the Creatures of the Out-birth are incident unto, their whole Principle being but a Figure of the excellent World whence it was effluenced. But all theſe and all other Exceptions the ſtate of the Saints tranſcends, and is for ever exempted perfectly and at once.

5. To the ſecond part of the Queſtion, what ſhall be the Eternal Pain and Torment of the Wicked. Let the Records of Sacred Scriptures be pondered as amongſt others theſe following, *Iſaiah* 3. 11. *Matth.* 5. 22, 29. 2 *Pet.* 2. 17. *Iſaiah* 30. 33. *Jude* 6. & 13 *Luk.* 10. 14. *Rev.* 20. 10, 14. *Rev.* 14. 11. *Iſaiah* 33. 14.

Much alſo may be underſtood by conſidering the Anſwer of the bleſſed *J. Behmen*, to the 34th of the 40 Queſtions concerning the Soul.

Something alſo apt and pertinent may be found by review of the 17 of theſe Anſwers fr. m Verſe 8th to 19th. The 21ſt Anſwer throughout, and the two firſt Verſes of the 22th Anſwer.

6. The Eternal Pain or Torment of the Wicked may be thus in part apprehended. That as the Saints are inveſted with Eternal Joy by the Uniting of the Tinctures, and Harmonizing of the Properties in them by the gracious *Immanuel*, and ſo the ſad Rent in the firſt *Adam* abundantly is made up, united and reſtored by the ſecond *Adam*, by introducing and reviving in our Humanity the diſappeared

Virgin Image, which had been as a Lamb slain by dividing of the Tinctures; so that Man is again the compleat Image of the Holy Trinity, with an intimate real indwelling of the Eternal Son in them.

7. Thus the Eternal Torment of the Wicked, consisteth in the irreconcileable, implacable Enmity of the Properties in them, at first divided and disordered by *Adam*. It is observed, old Friends once at variance are the more hardly appeased, by how much the Bonds of mutual Amity and Endearments have been violated; how much more is it here, where the old Union is separated into Diametrical Opposition in its self to its own Structure and Existence, and the Antipathy of the same Necessity of Nature, as are the Properties themselves of Perpetuity.

8. That Duel is most vigorous, doubtful, durable and fatal, where the Combatants are of equal Force and Activity; thus at the meeting of two steady contrary Currents is a continual Whirlpool, and the Strife of contrary Elements is as impetuous as Life and Death, the congress of opposite Properties bursteth out Thunder Claps, and Air pent stirs up Earthquakes, and Gunpowder dissipates by violent Expulsion, the Opposition wherewith it stands charg'd.

9. What outragious fierceness then, like a Torrent, must the Enmity of the damned Soul Burn in, what Thunders must their Horror vent it self by, whose Parts are not barely divided but Discordance it self, not Enemies, but Enmity? For as those Souls had whilst with the Body no Food but that of the third Principle, which was no more proportionable to their Hunger than painted Food to sustain the outward Life of Man or Beast, or painted Fire to heat us; So then the Soul's extream Hunger incessantly, yet necessarily (as it were) devours it self; as Men Famishing to Death, are said to gnaw their own Flesh, and the damned Souls Flesh or Food is its own Faculties, which are filled with the four Anguishes of the first or dark fierce Principle; and in this respect, is the Associate of all Devils: and as the outward Body is encreased, and as it were composed of the Vapour of the outward Elementary Food of the third Principle producing it: So these Wicked Souls are as it were composed and consist of the Anguishes of the dark World.

10. The Spirit of such Souls and their Tincture, which is as the Eye or Treasure of the Soul, looketh, imageth and impresseth in it self the uncontrouled dark Powers, (*viz.*) all impious, blasphemous Lusts, and impure, proud, wrathful Desires; this is in the inward Centre of the Soul; also in his Spirit and Tincture stands (as a Memory or Record as to the out-birth) the vile depressed Will of all cruel Bears and Tygers, the insatiable desire of the Swine, Wolf and Horseleech; the Malice of Dogs and Toads; the Wrath of Vipers and Dragons; for they had imaged in themselves by the Magical degenerate Lusts of the separate, private Self-will, the Properties of all fierce, cruel, horrid, griping, poisonous, filthy, loathsom, hateful Creatures.

11. In the Spirit of the Soul remains a Will to Voluptuousness, Superiority, Revenge, *&c.* which may break out into Malediction, Blasphemy and Monstrous, Malicious Abominations, but can proceed no farther than the Will and insatiable consuming Desire; for the desire to Good or Evil, and in Good and Evil is real, and the Genuine Natural Issue of the Soul: Actions may be dissembled, Words gilded, but Desires are entire solemn things, thus their restless Desires and furious impetuous Wills are their real all: and though the Magical Might and Power of the Will in the Spirit of a Zealous Soul is very puissant in all such who have all the Principles in some Harmony; yet in those abandoned vile Wretches, where all is depressed into Discord under blackness of darkness, the Will is under Chains and Impotence, only of Power most abundantly to torture it self.

12. All

The 177 Theosophick Questions Answered.

12. All the Horrors here are weak resemblances of the inexpressible Hell of the Damned, and above all, the Rebels against the Gospel, that reject and defile that Garment which the God of Grace hath spun out of his own Bowels, and dyed and washed in his own Blood. For if all the Dreadful things here, as the wasting Sword, poisonous venomous Beasts, insulting domineering Tyrants, cruel voracious Wild Beasts, devouring Fire, astonishing Thunder and Earthquakes, sudden Inundations, wretched Famines, desolating Contagions, general Plagues, and other noisom Messengers of Mortality, if all these and such other, are but Counterfeits, Similes, Figures or Shadows of the true, real, substantial, everlasting, dark Abyss, what are the Originals and very Essences themselves which Form that fierce Principle, where the Worm dieth not, nor is the Fire quenched? where Death flyes from them, and Omnipotence establisheth a Life to subsist under the infinite Wrath of Omnipotence, call'd *the wrath to come*, and shall after a Million of this World's Ages be still call'd *the wrath to come*.

13. To the third and last part, May there be any Alteration effected? To resolve which we should first consult the Sacred Scriptures. That the Joy of the Saints shall be Eternal; who but the Lord himself must we hear in this thing? *Matth.* 19. 29. *John* 10. 28. Chap. 3. v. 16. Chap. 4. v. 14. the like amongst many others is found, *Isaiah* 61. 7. *Rom.* 6. 12. And that the Torment of the Wicked must be Everlasting also, is told us by the Judge who is Truth it self, *Matth.* 25. 41. and again, v. 46. also it's found, 2 *Thess.* 1. 9. *Isaiah* 61. 7. *Jude* 6. & v. 7. *Rev.* 22. 11.

14. This, though it need no Confirmation, yet it may be profitable (by way of illustration) to consider the Answer the last of the Forty Questions made by the blessed *Jacob Behmen*, also somewhat pertinent thereunto in the 175th of these Answers, from Verse 5. to the end. Again, in the 16th of these Answers, from the 7th Verse to the 12th Exclusive.

15. Now that Truth may appear what it really is, how apt soever Man is to flatter himself; Let it be considered that there is but one only Infinite Original of all Power, Eternally generating his Delight, the Son of God, in whom is the Infinite Original of all well pleasing and Wisdom, the Process of both which, is the Infinite Original of the All-holy Love and Goodness, in these three is one Infinity, yesterday, to day, and for ever; by, in and for whom are all the seven Spirits or Properties, generating Harmoniously and Triumphantly at once and ever, and in the United accord of their Powers subsisteth the Holy World. Also in the separate Properties of six of the seven Spirits standeth immutably the Abyss of the Dark World, which though in their Union is truly and really existent, yet till the Separation, is for ever unmanifested, as in the preceding Answers is often most conspicuous, as in many places of the Writings of the blessed *Jacob Behmen*, and particularly in the 15th of the Answers, v. 3. & 4.

16. And here are the two Eternal Worlds or Principles of Love and Anger, Darkness and Light, known only in the Separation of the Properties in the Creatures; so that either both or neither is Eternal, they having the Self-same Eternal Root and Consistence: and the effluenced Creation is Imaged either by all the seven Spirits in Harmony, or by all of them in Discord, where one or more potently tyrannizeth over the rest, and thus stand the Heavenly and Hellish Powers with the Holy Glorious, and contrary Impious black Inhabitants. And when the Out-world (*viz.* the Astral) was formed, the two Eternal Worlds impressed their Images therein, over which Man, as the second Race of Intellectuals was natural Lord substituted to hold the Dominion, wherein while he stood, was no more subject to Mutation (having his habitation in the Holy World) than Eternity is to time, which it comprehendeth, but is not measur'd by, for Eternity and the Eternal Inhabitants are never old; but as their Worlds are ever new, so themselves ever

E e 2　　　　　　　　　　　　　　　　young;

young; there being no to Morrow, but all is to Day, with and in them. And this is firmly true in both Worlds.

17. But his Fall subjected him to the various Alterations of Time, his Out-birth, becoming subject thereunto, which (how Evil soever) is not the greatest Evil; for as on the one hand, it (as it were) cut him off from the firm Land of Holiness to be like a floating Isle of Vanity and Vexation; so on the other hand, the tossed Turf is not so swallow'd up as immediately to sink, nor is so far driven, but there remains a possibility by the sweet gales of the Holy Spirit to be reunited to the firm Land, whence it had broken it self: whereas the Apostate Angels, like a piece of a Rock sank into the Deep, without hope of reverting and cementing for ever, having deprived themselves of all but one Principle, and are destitute of a Medium, having no salt in themselves; whereas in Man (on this side fixt Enmity) there is United to their first fierce dark Anguish, an intrusted Talent of infpoken Grace, like a Tincture of the meek, humble Principle of Love, both inward Worlds being Imaged in the outward transient floating Life.

18. Thus, was it that, Infinite Goodness moved Infinite Pity and Compassion, that the Son of God himself took our Humanity, and made it a Sacrifice to attone in us the enraged Forms of our first Principle, being the Father's Property, according to which, he is call'd *a consuming Fire,* and reunite us in the Kingdom and second Principle of Love, Peace, Meekness, Purity, and true Wisdom, for without the Out-birth (which is the place of Mutation) no change can be, because in the Astral Powers are the Alterations effected, for there are the Figures of both the hidden Worlds; therefore the least thought of transmuting the state of the Holy to Prophaneness, or the Wicked to relaxation of their Torment, were to admit or suggest a Contradiction no less absurd than to assign Eternity to the Vanity of the present, transient, momentany Life, or to impeach Eternal Omnipotent stability with a possibility of Annihilation. See the part of Answer of the blessed *Jacob Behmen* to the 15th of these Questions in the four first Verses; also the rest of that Answer to the End.

Meditations

Meditations and brief Contemplations on some of the Preceding Questions Propounded by Jacob Behmen.

On the 14th Question and Answer, *What is* Lucifer's *Office in Hell with his Legions?*

1. MY Soul, first ponder thou God's Immensity; as it is written, *Whither shall I go from thy Presence?* This Globe of Earth and Sea is great, but to the Deep from Stars to Stars is a Point to a vast Circumference, and that vast Deep is a Point to another proportionably greater than this is to our Ball; and all that and twenty or twenty Thousands of such Deeps compared with him is nothing, for if spoken out by him, it leaves him nothing the less, for he is still Infinite as before. Again, Meditate thou his Omnipresence, for no Point or least Centre of the least imaginable Circle exempts him, but in every such part is the same Infinite undivided *Jehovah* entirely present; his Omniscience is hence undeniable, for he that made the Eye shall he not see? Behold again his Omnipotency, whereby he from Eternity and in Eternity generates his only Son, and by him all Eternal Glories, and in the Abyss of his Infinite Power is the Dark Abyss; If I make my Bed in Hell thou art there.

2. Concerning Man, reflect thou (my Soul) with Grief and Astonishment. What a God is he who the black Mouths of vile crawling Worms and proud Dust do desperately abuse by Prophane Swearing, as if that Holy and fearful, awful Name were a common thing, wherewith they make Blasphemously bold with Hellish Execrations. Again, what a Hell doth the Lord's Redemption free all from whose discording Forms of Life in the first Principle are attoned by kindling the saving renewing Light of Life in them of the Holy second Principle, being a fifth Form and Quintessence, turning by the Supream Tincture, Everlasting Dying, into Eternal Life, and Regenerating a Holy bright Child, out of a Corrupt dark impure Mother. Again, what can the Summit of selfish Skill, sharpest Speculation and Penetration into Divine Sacred Mysteries avail, if thou arrive not into the Holy self-same Principle by Mortification and the first Resurrection? what short of that can make thee better than the Devils? what can the exactest Form of Godliness advantage thee more than it doth him who can transform himself into an Angel of Light?

3. Then (O my Soul) proceed on to Meekness, Integrity, Faith and Love in Holy Fear till thou come to the Feet of thy Jesus: Or move not at all; but remain a Swine, a Dog, a Beast, inwardly a Devil, for if thou goest part of the way only, thy Fall is of a Stone from a high place is the most heavy, but to persevere will make thee more blessedly Happy, than Hell is miserably Accursed.

On the 15th Question and Answer. *Hath Hell a Temporary Beginning, or Eternal,* &c.?

1. Here opens a wide Prospect into the Abyss of Eternity, for as the Dark World originates from the Abyss of Infinite power of the *Jehovah*; so neither can it terminate.

minate but that second Death be ever a Dying Life, while the God of Life liveth. This is that King of the Kings of Terror, this shakes the heart of a Rock of Adamant, this as a World of Lead lyeth on the dark Troops; while yet the most exquisit Tortures, if transient and finite, bring Cordials with them to the faintest of Christ's Followers, sugaring the bitterest Pills to the humble, patient, tormented, persecuted Children of whom the World is not worthy; this also serves Gall in every Dish to him who could engross the Out-principles Delights for *Methuselah*'s Age. But Eternity is as Incomprehensible as the Eternal God, as far beyond Men and Angels as Infinity is beyond our short, narrow, shallow and superficial Measures. This God, this Christ, this Holy Principle is our God, our Christ, our Holy Life, for ever and ever, and were there any thing after for ever, it were ours too.

2. Look then (O my Soul) fixedly on this Freehold, and disdainfully, on all visible and invisible melting Idols and airy bubbles, breathe, press, pant, sweat, freeze, suffer, fight, run, watch, persevere, till thy dry husk crumble and fall off, and thou shalt reap once and for ever, more than Eye or Heart can see or conceive.

On the 16th Question and Answer, *Why is God's wrath Eternal,* &c?

Let God be true (and every Man a Lyar) who saith he is Light, in him is no Darkness at all. But yet if the Creature shall put out its own Eyes it is Darkness, having extinguished the holy Light in it self. Again, he that dwelleth in love, dwelleth in God for God is love, but when Evil Angels and Men fix themselves in Enmity, they causelesly quarrel with God, live no more in that love, but enter into wrath in their own Evil Principle. This being so (O my Soul) search thy self, what black veils are there excluding the bright, holy, eternal Light of God. See also if there be an unmortified, impenitent, repining, impatient Spirit swaying and prevailing in thee, that thou be estranged from the meek love of God, leading thee Captive in the inward Kingdom of dark Fierceness, and then that the Devil perswade thee not, that God willeth thy Destruction, and thou to excuse thy wilful Rebellion, Blaspheme the God of Eternal Light and pure Love.

On the 17th Question and Answer. *What is God's work in Hell, is Hell a local place?*

1. The Holy Eternal *Jehovah* is in himself undivided, yet as he operates in all the seven Forms of the seven Fountain Spirits, moving to make himself Creaturely, so all divided Properties derive from him, and are radically in him, and the multiplicity is as a very little thing comprehended in the infinite Unity. Thus the Fire which is the Life of all Creatures is often their Death, but when it generates, the Light is the Joy of such where it so proceeds: if it generate the Holy intellectual Light, the Fire is made Holy, and the whole Existence is Angelical and Paradisical: but if it dwindle into an Image or meer Representation of the true Light, it degenerates into a Shadow, and if the Light that is in any be Darkness, how great is that Darkness?

2. Come up hither (my Soul) and see what Light thy Fire yieldeth, grows it toward the Harmony, resigning it self into the Unity? then thou hast thy Fruit unto Holiness, and thy End everlasting Life. Or is it captiv'd in the Wrath of the divided Properties, laboureth it in Building *Babel*, striveth it to be its own Lord and Law-giver, is self its first Mover and Ultimate End? then shalt thou of the Flesh reap Corruption; the Disunion makes Disorder, the Disorder causeth Aversion, that again begets Anguish, that issues into utter Enmity, that finally into Rage.

3. Oh then (my Soul) return into thine impregnable Fortress, step back into thy Child-like Innocence, Meekness and Simplicity. Hast thou in *Adam* lost thy

dear

Meditations and Contemplations.

dear Virgin Purity ? yet blush away thine adulterous Apostasie, and with torn Hair, flowing Eyes, and a broken Spirit, acknowledge thy unworthiness, implore to be as one of the hired Servants, and thou wilt find thy Father hath bowels ; a kiss of his will break thy Heart, melt thee as Wax, impress in thee his New Life, wherein the various Properties draw all one way. Divine Love will crucifie Self-love and Self-will, and kill the Enmity as the fresh blushing morning doth the Fogs of the night. With-hold nothing from him whose are all things and all Worlds, whose thou art, and who spared not his One Only dearest dear Son for thee, to attone thy divided, inimicitious Properties, ransom thee from the Principle of Wrath, exempt thee from the Eternal Dark Abyss, free thee from the Hell of Hells, thy exceeding sinfulness, and to bring thee who wast a Devil inwardly, and a Beast outwardly, to be a Child among the Spirits of just men made perfect by his Mighty Salvation!

On the 18th Question and Answer. *Where is Heaven? Is it a local place?* &c.

1. What a taking Travel were it to pass with and thro' Temporal Pleasures to Eternal Joy? If so, what throngs would resort by treading down the side banks to widen that narrow way? But thou hast learnt (O my Soul!) that the pleasing of the flesh is the Paradice of Fools ; consider thou therefore that it is abundantly sufficient advantage by passing through as many deaths as are days in thy Pilgrimage here, and through as many horrid Hells to, at last to step safely into our Fathers House. How acceptable were the contemplation of Heaven, if it were enough to entitle us to it, without wetting a foot, to sit on an easie Chair, and take a prospect in the Holy Scriptures and other Books of what some Travellers thither have left on Record, which will do the work when the viewing the World on a Card will entitle us to the Kingdoms of it ?

2. But because there are Legions of Lusts binding hand and foot, there is much to be done, and much help to be sought, striving, mortifying, working, crucifying, fasting, resigning, patience, lying low, being often in the furnace. And becaule there is a devouring Lion opposing maliciously, there is need of great Faith, constant, strong Prayer and Watching. Because also the Wisdom and Glory of this perishing World opposeth, there is need to become Fools, to be accounted the Off-scouring of it, to pass through the Good and Evil without being impressed and swayed by either, but in meekness blessing them that curse us, praying for despiteful Persecutors, and lying dead to present desirable things, that thou maist be raised by the first Resurrection. And now (my Soul) thou seest that Heaven is no empty speculation, but entring is opening Heaven: And the Lord Jesus, who is the Heaven of Heavens in thee with a mighty Power utterly unconceivable to the top of Man's Wisdom, and the acutest deepest search of all the unregenerate World, and to the Children of the Resurrection known but (as in a Glass) darkly.

On the 19th Question and Answer, *What are the Dominions of Angels Evil and Good?*

1. David meditating the Heavens, is transported into admiration: *What is Man?* &c. But what place may be found low enough for Man to prostrate himself in, who seriously considers his loathsom deformity by sin ? he is so far baser than the Outward Heavens, which yet must pass away, that he is viler than the Beast that perisheth ; for his subjection to vanity he owes to us, is also viler than the Earth, which bearing our Curse, yet gratefully pays what it can for the Blessings showering on it, and willingly serves the higher Influences of Nature to generate noble Concretes ;

cretes; and were it delivered from our Curse, would gladly travel for Paradisical Productions; but our heavy Curse is so eating, that it hath entred the Timber and Walls, therefore must this House needs, as that having the incurable Leprosie, be pull'd down. We are also viler than the poisonous abominable Reptiles, for they are but figures of the Forms of the Black World; but sinful Man is really united to them. Man also considered as Reprobate, is worse than the Devils, both as he is lower by Creation, and higher by aggravated transgression, having trampled on the Only and most excellent Remedy freely offered for his recovery, the Sacrifice of the most Holy of Holies, the Only Eternal Son of God.

2. And is there no Creature so vile as Man? Hold this (O my Soul!) for thy Contemplation remain confounded and astonished: Let not thy Tongue smother what thy Intellect sees, nor thy Pride refuse thy just Reproach; flatter not, paint not, indulge not, but depart out of thy self as now clothed with thy shame and filth; cry to him whose Eternal Mercy is infinite for pity to cast his skirt over thee now in thy Blood. And when thou contemplatest the sublime Wisdom, excellent Power, and irresistible Activity of the Angelical Hosts, and remembrest that the subtilty of a Fox, the strength of an Ass, the nimbleness of a Fly, the skill of a Bee surpass thee, yet know, (if regenerate into the Image of Jesus Christ) thou maist by humble Obedience and willing Child-like Resignation to the Conduct of the Councils from above, obtain That Wisdom which the Old Serpent is short of; thou maist hate sin, in a measure, as the Holy Angels do; (viz.) really, because it is sin, and universally; thou maist love Holiness, Purity and Modesty sincerely, in a measure, the perfection of which Love is the Glory of the Heavenly Hosts. Let not therefore the shame of thy nakedness so sink thee, but that thy humble thoughts may offer up Volumes of Blessings for any possibility of recovery. To Thee therefore who art all in all, and infinitely above all, be offered up my wretched all: To Thee who art all pity be presented my mournful earnest prayer, graciously lay hold on my feeble Faith; let thy Wind blow Life on my dry Bones. To Thee, O Fountain of Goodness, be given all my weeping praises, and my whole Soul for ever.

On the 20th Question and Answer. *Out of what is the Visible World created?* &c.

1. This Visible World is originated out of the Eternal; thence sprung the Stars, and four Elements of the one Element; the Fire actuates separates and digests the other three Elements; and the Father of Nature forms all according to the Will modell'd by the Wisdom, and giveth the Tincture. Thus the Fire-life in Man's Mortal Body, helps three Concoctions; the first in the stomach as the Chilus nourishing by assimilation answering to the Air; the second in the Mesentery and Liver, as Blood answering to Water; the third Concoction is the passing by the Veins into the gross Members, and by the Arteries to the more fine, and to add to the Bones, answering to Earth and Stones; in each of which is a separation of the unprofitable part. This Contemplation well raised *David* to say, *I am fearfully and wonderfully made.* And as in our Mortal Man there is something surviving; viz. the Tincture; so in the Out-birth, the Soul of it and Tincture being out of the Eternal Nature and the first Principle, is indissoluble, but the Bestial Man sees not that, but greedily catcheth at the Husk and Hogs-meat, the excrementitious part.

2. But thou (Oh my Spirit) shew by thy humble meekness thy high extraction. shew by thy Resignation to the universal Will of thy Creator, that thou art his Child, keep thy Lamp clean, that being enkindled by the Fire from above, thou maist enlighten the dark Forms of my Immortal Soul to know and live to God, and

Meditations and Contemplations.

and will purely his will; that my Souls heat may be a Love fire, and that Love-fire may be a conſtant Fountain for thy Love-flame. That as every individual Creature in their degree do unawares to themſelves ſhew the Almighty Power and Infinite Wiſdom of God, thou being intruſted more than they all with five Talents, maiſt prove them to ten; and ſhew (underſtandingly) not only his Infinite Power and Wiſdo n but Infinite Goodneſs, Grace, Clemency, Condeſcenſion, Pity, Love, Bounty and Sweetneſs. And thou, Oh my Aſtral and groſs Body! beware leſt the poor Brutes, by ſerving thee while they live, and dying to keep thee alive, out-ſtrip thee not ſo far as to witneſs againſt thee, that thou haſt prevented the end of thine own Creation, and theirs by inſatiably luſting to indulge and ſerve thy ſelf thereby, robbing thy Soveraign of the fruits of his Vineyard.

On the 21th Queſtion and Anſwer. *Whence proceeded Evil as poiſonous Creatures here? &c.*

1. Out of the Dark Confuſion by the Apoſtaſie of *Lucifer* and his Legions, the *Fiat* moving by the Separator to bring forth, every Power ſtrenuouſly willed to make it ſelf creaturely; ſo was it the ſeven Planets ſeverally bear the ſeven ſeparate Powers, and according to them are impreſſed the Evil and Good Properties on Plants, Minerals and Senſitives; not that any one is wholly one, but one is prevalent, and the reſt ſubſervient. Thus evil, venomous, loathſom, voracious, fierce Creatures and things have exiſtence, yet ſhineth the Sun, deſcendeth the ſweet drops on them, and ſpringeth up the fatneſs of the Earth for them.

2. Behold here the overflowing Bounty of the gracious God who feeds the young Lions and young Ravens, the Dragons and Serpents of the Wilderneſs. Behold here alſo his Long-ſuffering, who not only ſpares but heaps up outward bleſſings on far worſe; (viz) obſtinate, hardened, ſeared Rebels, for whom he hath not ſpared his own Son, and on whom he hath waited, counſelling, entreating, convincing, reſiſting and dropping Line upon Line, perhaps twenty, forty, and on ſome fifty years; for ever bleſſed be that abuſed Creator, that bleeding Redeemer, that grieved Holy Ghoſt.

3. Come hither all my Inward Powers, proſtrate your ſelves, be enkindled by this Holy Fire; learn to do good for evil, bleſſing for curſing. Be aſtoniſhed (O my Soul!) that ever thou didſt return black ingratitude, and trample on heavenly Blood and Bowels of Mercy, that thou haſt not only been as the worſt of Beaſts, but much more vile, and haſt had ſomething in thee to ſtout it out againſt the Charms of Divine Love. God glorifies his Almightineſs, Wiſdom and Goodneſs in Evil Creatures. his Juſtice by the Devils; ſo that if we be wicked, what loſeth he? and if we be righteous, is it not for our ſelves?

On the 22th Queſtion and Anſwer. *Why muſt there be Strife in Nature?*

1. By Nature is meant the Outward Nature, where ſtrife ariſeth out of contrariety, and contrariety founded in the dividing of the Properties, which dividing ſhould have been hidden from *Adam*, had he continued in the Harmony; but his Fall opened the Enmity in his Soul, in his Spirit, in his Aſtral Man and in his Body, which then was become beſtial. And the Peace, Man compoſeth is the conſequence of ignorance or ſtupidity, which our Saviour when he comes breaks and draws a Sword againſt.

2. The reaſon is, becauſe the Peace of our making is a ſtifling or violent ſtopping of the Natural Iſſues of the Striving Properties, no more like the true Reſt than *Adam*'s Sleep was like the Paradiſical Life; but the Lord's Reſt and Peace is when

F f the

Meditations and Contemplations.

the fix working Properties refult in the feventh, and the four Forms generate the fifth; yet neither the fixth nor the fourth ceafe to be, or to work, but in their working attain the true end of their work.

3. Is it thus, O my Soul? beware of indulging. drowning and burying thy felf in ftupid eafe, but as the Infinite Father worketh hitherto, generating the Son, and the Son worketh in the Father, and the Holy Ghoft goeth out continually with Power and Vertue; fo alfo in thy very little, wretched, poor faculties, co-operate with higheft longing and defire in this happy ftrife; bring the ftrong Forms of thy firft Principle, into the meek Light of thy fecond, and let all iffue into Divine Love and Delight, which will be a third, till thou flame, and thou be as fuel, dying and rifing again always more bright and flaming. Fear not to die daily, but ftudy, prefs, pray and practife it, that thou maift every day be renewed and transformed into the Image of him, a glance of whofe gracious countenance hath a ravifhing Power, and covers thee with fhame and confufion, and yet with excefs of humble trembling Joy it fhakes, yet confirms, it kills, yet revives. And if a glance be fo noble and powerful, what were a fteddy look? and then what lofeft thou ftraying into outward divertifements, thofe deluding flatterers? Lookeft thou on any thing without a defign to fee thy great Lord in it? it renders thee lofs of time, bows thee down like the Beaft, is thy fnare, and thou doft unnaturally lay hands on thy felf, be thine own deceiver, making thy fences thy tempters, left there fhould be want of Devils; but to ftrive againft this is a Holy War. Art thou (my Soul) unwilling? pray the Divine Will may make thee an impreft Souldier. Fainteft thou? Love hath Eagles wings. Feareft thou? Faith hath a whole Armoury, Thinkeft thou this Combate is above Thee to atchieve? what were all the Spirits of the Juft made perfect, but the Children of finners, and themfelves finners pluckt out of the Fire, Captives redeemed by our Lord Jefus? Look on that Eye (my Soul) who ever looks on thee, and all days will be holy days, all places holy places, and thou ever in the beft company thou art capable of, fuch as will teach thee to lead thy natural ftrife into fupernatural triumph.

On the 23th Queftion and Anfwer. *On the Dividing the One Element into four.*

1. Like as the Monuments of former Ages, the Tower of *Babel*, the Egyptian Pyramids, the undertakings of *Archimedes*, &c. do commemorate the Atchievements and Skill of the Framers; fo do the works of God fpeak the great *Jehovah*: Whence the Pfalmift; *The Heavens declare the glory of God, and the Elements fhew his handy-work.* The four Elements are according to the four Forms.

2. Behold how out of one are all things infinitely proceeded, for out of the Unity is breathed the multiplicity, fo that when we bring our multiplicity forward, as we ought, we return into the Unity. O my Soul! let the multiplicity of the very Out-birth of the third Principle be but taught to know its diftance, and thou maift live in the Unity, rule over the Multiplicity, and bring out of the four Elements their Glory and Vertue for the praife of the Almighty Soveraign, that in an outward way (yet having Eyes within) they, like the four Beafts before the Throne, without ceafing fay, *Holy, holy, holy,* &c. And again, when thou dieft to the Tyranny of the four Forms of thy Root, thou afcendeft by their Harmony into the feveral branches bearing good fruit.

3. What tho' thy Sting be fharp, may it but ftir thee up the more vigoroufly to the work of God in thee? What tho' thy Fire be hot, may it be the incentive to a radiant Love-flame? What if thy Anguifh be greatly ponderous and oppreffive, if it ballance, fteddy and fix thee to a glorious perfeverance? Courage then, thou art on a fhort Voyage to a vaft Country. Are not all the Elements doing their
feveral

Meditations and Contemplations.

several Offices? Is not every Pile of Grafs obeying its Ordinance, and levelling at the End of its Inflitution? Is not the whole Family of the very innocent Creatures preparing themselves to live and die for thy pleasure, profit and necessity: And wilt thou not do and suffer for him whose thou art, and who hath vouchsafed to make himself (of meer Grace to be) thing, and which conformity in thee is for thine own absolutely necessary, overflowing Eternal, superabundant Advantage; thou hast but these three things, make thy choice, either to go back into *Egypt*, stand still and fall in the Wilderness, or go on after thy Captain into the Land flowing with Milk and Honey.

On the 24th Question and Answer. *Wherefore, and to what Benefit are Stars Created ?-*

The Stars are the Revelation or Immense, palpable, finite, diffolvible Body of the Infinite, Eternal, Holy, Substantial World, and that, 1. In their Splendor, especially in the glorious shining Sun. But how dirty and vile is Man? O my Soul, how art thou darkened, every little Storm clothes thee in Rags, and casts filth on those Rags; every recess of true Light leaves thee languishing as one Foot were in the Grave, whilst their Beauties are (in their Principle) lifted far above such mutations; fix then thine Eye on thy Sun, and like the Flower of the Sun turn ever to him, and only to him wherein alone lyes thy chief good. 2. In their variety wherein they are admirable, particularly in the seven Royal ones. So are there in *Saturn, Mars, Mercury* and *Jupiter* when cross aspected, an intolerable ligation, anguish, rage and proud elevation, in the *Sun, Moon* and *Venus* a scorching Fire, Inconstancy and Impurity, in all which the Eternal dark Principle openeth it self, but in their benevolent Aspect is an Harmonious, Noble, Transcendent Excellency figuring the Paradifical Holy Principle. But how much in thee, O my Soul, is there, not only to figure, but of the real substance of the dark World? So much as thou hast of Covetousness, Envy, Anger and Pride, so much art thou not a representation but a part and limb of the dark Abyss, an essential portion in thy proportion of the black, raging, blaspheming, burning Hell of the Damned, radically, virtually and potentially. What is the Long-suffering of God who bears affronts and despights from vile wretched Man, while the whole Hosts of Stars punctually observe his Ordinance, and are at his beck. 3. In their (as to Man) Infinity they figure the Angelical Hosts. And as every Angel is as one whole Kingdom, so is every Star as one whole World; how little a proud Worm then is the dirty piece of Clay call'd Man? How dare any the greatest of them admit a thought of being his own Lord and Law-giver to enter his foolish Head and deceitful Heart? And how much less darest thou (my Soul) who art of the least, lowest, and most unworthy of Men, why delayest thou to give thy whole will, thy love, thy life, thy self to him, from whose word thou sprungest, by whose word thou subsisteth, on whose word anchoreth thine only hope for Time and for Eternity: Deceive not thy self by giving up the guidance of small and indifferent things, whilst thou swayest the weighty imports of thy Life, and resentest a disappointment there as a dismembring, but faithfully, stedfastly, willingly, submissively bow with equal resignation to every of his Providential Determinations, those of the nearest and most sensible concern as of the least; so shalt thou dwell in a peaceable Habitation. 4. In their steddy duration, their Morning commenced with what is call'd time, and their Evening compleats it, and then (resolving) Eternity resumes all, but I am of yesterday, or last hour, and do post away with the next, yet so feeble as cannot watch with our Lord one Hour. A weight of Glory is at the Goal, yet I would have it before I run; more than

than Heart can conceive is prepared for perseverance, but I would have all before I well begin. O my dear holy God, and must I stay enquiring after thee? Must my short time seem long to me? Must my hope be deferr'd till I faint? Must my sick Soul be Imprison'd too, and none to visit her? Have I but one in my Heart on Earth and in Heaven, and must I be so throng'd with Strangers as not to touch the Hem of his seamless Garment? While I pine away for thee I do yet tremble and blush to approach thee; how can so foul unclean a Creature come into so pure a Palace, or Stand before thy Holiness? Shame covers me, yet Passionate Love makes me bold and impatient. I will not, I dare not plead modest in excuse of disobedience. if I withhold my self I die, for I cannot live in thy absence. What kind of Life is this that keeps me from my Life, when shall thy Banished be recall'd? Oh let not time with-hold Eternity, let not many days lengthen my Night. Is my presence in this Body absence from my Lord? for how can the dry Breasts within the reach of this vile Body satiate my thirsty Soul? What kin is the perishing lump of this Body to me? it is dead, why should my living Spirit be tyed to the dead? Yet will my Lord continue me under the load of mine own making, bury me under so sad a Vail, leave me in Anguish nail me to the Earth, deny me the view of my one only most sweet, dear, precious and desirable Object? It is the Lord, he doth all things well, who having himself but one only Begotten gave that his only Beloved for me; and shall not this silence me, cause me
5. to acquiesce and swallow me up for ever? 5. In their order, not justling, starting, losing, over running nor fainting. but regularly, steddily, jointly ever proceed on their Creators great designs: Their Motions, Aspects, Courses, Positions and Variations so exactly precise (to the praise of the God of Order) that all or much of that they are about, is easily fore known, But among Men what Kingdom tho' in Peace, or Army when their Life depends on't may be found without strange disorders, what Town, what Family without it, what Man but for a very few steps treads order? for we having by transgression lost it, are both ignorant of it and obstinate against it; so that to introduce the right order is requir'd in forming of the Intellect, alluring of the Affections, and subjecting of the Will, and there is also requisite clenching of a Nail, and driving in of a Goad, or else order ether starts or dies. But who is that Man dwelling in a House of Clay, who upon an unerring Intellect is used to the Divine Order so as to conform an unwavering will thereunto. How many faintings, recoils, runnings back, and Apostacies hast thou (my Soul) sadly Experimented what hour hast thou continued only the Lords without mixing Linnen with the Woollen? And must the Holy Spirit be grieved with so vile a wretch must thy Bones be set and dislocated by a continued Succession? Oh thou Fountain of Goodness when shall thy will be done, here as it is in Heaven, when in the outward Man as in the outward Heavens, when in the inward as in the holy Heavens? Let thy sweet Order bury my con-
6. fusions that in thee may be my Resurrection. 6. In their energy, strength, and active vigour, so are they the immediate Parent of the four Elements, being the same in the outward Principle as the strength of their Root and Originals is in the Inward Worlds; the four anguishing Constellations also afford matter, and in the Moons property exhibit it into palpable substance, this the solar power exalteth according to the kind the Separator disposeth every thing unto, in Minerals, Vegetatives and Sensitives generating, animating, maturing, invigorating, ennobling, irradiating, and again exhaling their volatile parts, and dissolving the Fabrick. All strong couragious Creatures owe their compaction and fortitude instrumentally to them. But what am I who cannot by all Humane Art or Policy, or, by any Fortress or Arms be defended against a Fly, who if Commission'd to Hostility can enter such Organ as may suffocate my Breath? How inevitable my,

Misery

Meditations and Contemplations.

Misery that I at once nourish my Life and the Seeds of my Mortality brought forth of the Womb with and in me, and after have with pain, hazard, care and sorrow struggled a few years, my Constellations having wrought their course, it must be said to me, return to thy dust as all other the Sons of vain Mankind. 7. In their Vertue which is so conspicuous that from them every Creature of this whole Principle derive their Excellency; The Elements their simplicity, the outward Heavens their purity and serene Beauty, they enrich the Fields with Fruits, clothe them with Flowers, replenish the Sea with Inhabitants and precious Things, the Air with foul, penetrate the Bowels of the Earth, so as to produce and generate precious Metals, Stones and Sanatives, give Excellency to Sensitives from the Ant to the Elephant, their activity, comeliness, usefulness, cunning and seminal Power. But above all to man a vigorous beautiful Body, a prudent capacity and prosperous success, furnishing him with such Abilities as may be applicable to preserve himself and others, by implanting, improving and repairing things profitable, and extirpating and preventing the noxious, also ennobling him with such Endowments whereby he may rule over and give conduct to the Inferiour Creatures, and use the Creation, the Earth, Water, Air, Fire and Wind as his Servants to do his Work without Wages or Limitation of Time, &c. The Ruler of the day and Mistress of the Night are his Directors.

On the 25th Question and Answer. *Of the Temporal Natures, Light and Darkness whence they sprung and exist.*

Seing they sprung from, exist by, and are manifestations of the two incomprehensible Principles, the holy Light World and the dark Wrathful World, how large a Field of Meditation is here to us Men who are little Worlds?
The Experience of one Man hath been, that his Closet approaches in the Evening hath been more confused, perplext and impure, and his most early Morning access more simple, chearful and vigorous; the former seeming not only toucht with the days contagion, but at the entrance of the figure of the dark Abyss; whereas his Morning hath been a Sally of the Soul out of a Dungeon, more transported with a new Glory figuring the Resurrection. Which seems to be one reason the Christians about an hundred years after the Incarnation used to meet at certain days before Sun rising to Sing Hymns to Jesus Christ, &c. Hence those in whom Christ is risen are the Children of the day, for New Jerusalem knows no Night. If therefore thou (my Soul) art risen with Christ, the things over which thou art risen are to thee: dead, dry, withered trash, and thou art entred by the first Resurrection into the new fruitful growing state. But where are the steps of thy growth is it in the figure or similitude of the New Birth? Hast thou a Lamp without Oyl? A fair Building not rightly founded? Livest thou on the Letter without the Life? Art thou receiving Seed, but choaking it with the outward Principle? Art thou one of the Grains that shall be fann'd away? Or hast thou entred the true second Principle? Do thy Original forms generate the true Light whereof the outward Light is but a shadow, and therewith the Divine Love whereof the highest outward delight is but a weak Similitude? Is there in thee a deep humble foundation, and a springing out of Life through Death as a structure on that profound Basis. If so the day is dawned, and the Day-Star risen, else not; a dim weak sight, yet infallibly informs when 'tis day, and when not, and why should it be so mysterious to our Intellect? But so dismal is Mans Fall that the Children of Darkness may more unerringly doom themselves such than those of the day can be assured of their progress therein: While that often good beginnings are flatter'd as if the Prize were won, and yet themselves degenerate into wild Grapes and

wild

Meditations and Contemplations.

wild Olives, and the awakened Souls are often under various Misrepresentations, fears and impressions proceeding sometimes from real, and sometimes from supposed causes; as it happens to a distressed Traveller in an unknown Countrey, or as to a laden Ship labouring under successive Surges. Seeing therefore the day and night we carry about in our Botoms (figur'd by the natural day and night) is truely Heaven and Hell, what highest diligence is necessary to introduce and stir up the one, and what dreadful earnest cautions are requisite (like Sea marks where the Ships have been split) to shun the other.

On the 26th Question and Answer. *Of the separation of the Water above the Firmament from the Water, which is underneath the Firmament, and of the Created Heaven in the midst of the Water.*

1. The Created Heaven out of the midst of the Water (being the outward Heaven partaking of both Waters) is like the Tree bearing the Forbidden Fruit which stood in the midst of the Garden between the inward and outward Principles, and partaking by Figure of the inward but really was of the outward. The Water above the Firmament is a part of holy Paradise, and that under the Firmament our palpable Mortal Water, yet a similitude of the other ; for as this is our condensed Air, and our Air as the Breath of Fire, so is that holy living Water the meekness of the Heavenly, which Air is exalted from the Incomprehensible Forms of the holy Fire. And as our Water hath a cleansing property to the outward Man, so hath that a purifying power to the inward. As ours gives reception to the Light, which no sooner looks on it but through it : So is that the Vehicle or Transparent Habitation of the Eternal Light not to be understood so grosly as the Blood is of the Life of Creatures, but in a sense agreeable to the Spiritual Power and Property thereof.

2. And as *Lucifer* not obtaining his inordinate desire excited his Central Fire to the drying up of his meek Water wherein his Light shone, his Light thenceforth disappeared. So when Mans dark implacable Lust thirsting for Domination, Revenge, or to compass some other evil (according to the fierce Anguish of the Fire-Soul) is quenched, overcome and kill'd, by the sinking down, humble subjection and true resignation of the Will to the Divine Councel and Conduct, a new Life is generated of Childlike Obedience by the arising of this Water of the upper Springs which cleanse and become in that Soul a Well of Living Water springing up to Eternal Life. For this Water is the Eternal Light and Eternal Love substantiated in such degree as this holy living Water can be capable so to be signified *Exod.* 30. 18. by that in the Brass Laver between the Tabernacle of the Congregation, and the Altar wherein the Priests were to wash that they died not.

3. Why (Oh my Soul) are thy daily and hourly thoughts so low and impure? It is not the defect of a Fountain of that above the Firmament, but because thou usest it not. Why sometimes feelest thou the Fire of prevailing Wrath proceeding from Impatience, that from Pride, that from Ignorance of God and thy self, but because thou drawest not by an earnest thirst this living Water, nor sinkest into it ? Why is it by the returns of thy old Habits thou so often defilest thy self, and so seldom washest in these Waters ? Did not the Priests wash as often as Sacrifice was it not daily Morning and Evening, wants not the Earth the former and latter Rain ? So let (Oh my Lord) my cleansing be frequent and constant as was that of the Priests. Let it be real as the Fire of the Altar and the Water in the Laver was real. Let my cleansing be universal and extend to all the active Properties as they washed both Hands and Feet, and their Fire consumed the whole Burnt-Offering. Let me (Oh thou God of my Spirit) neither

ther begin, much less end with the outside washing, which is my self washing of my self: But let my Soul, my Inside, my Heart, Will, Designs, Desires, and my secret Thoughts be washt by thee, for without that, I have no part in thee. Let this washing last longer than the possibility of my polluting my self can endure: And let me be washt from my self, which is the foulest sink on this side Hell. Then, and not till then shall I know, what the Water above the Firmament is and can do for such a black Creature who of himself must cry unclean, unclean.

On the 27th Question and Answer. *Of the Male and Female Kinds, Whence is their Desire to each other? And of the necessity of it.*

1. We are taught to pray, *Thy will be done on Earth as it is in Heaven.* But seeing that Man hath (now by dividing the Tinctures, who till then Imaged the Divine Kingdom) got such a will as is on Earth among the Brute Beasts, losing the Heavenly Image, what remains but that the will be taught subjection, and long for, groan after, earnestly desire, and accordingly pray to be restored here to be as they are in Heaven, where by the reunion of the Tinctures they Image their God. Yet tho' the Rent of the Tinctures be irreparable in the bulk of Mankind here, and that God of pity to his Creatures hath extracted Good out of Evil, bearing by Divine Patience that in Man whereof Nature it self as deprav'd as it is shameth at: It nevertheless remains our Souls Work and Duty to learn what his dear disappear'd Virgin Image is, studiously and sollicitously to seek that, his first Love, the Free Woman, the *Jerusalem* from above which withdrew when *Adam* slept, bitterly to bemoan that loss, and account the finding that precious Pearl worthy of all pains, care, and highest diligence, and having found it, then to sell all to buy it.

2. But now (my Soul) seeing thou art so Beastly in thy Earthy, Elementary and Astral part infecting thy noble Eternal part, behold with abhorrence thy filthiness by a true impartial Glass. Where is the Modesty of a Virgin state which doth the will of God in Heaven? That purity which descended from Heaven, and when Men became degenerate returned thither. Why hast thou suffered the Virgin to wait at thy Door and Window, calling as to her Bridegroom? Exciting sometimes a Transport of Love, other times shame, again Joy to Trembling, or Grief to Astonishment. Finding thy self in so strange a Lodging as was *Nebuchadnezzar* when a Beasts Heart was given him. If thou compare thy self with thy self in some days past, perhaps thou maist flatter thy Judgment into Partiality, and if thou compare thy self with others seeming more filthy, thou maist be apt to pride thy self, but if thou reflect on thy pollutions, and the pure holy Virgin, how great will be thy monstrosity, how wretched vile and naked? Come therefore daily to this perfect Standard, just Balance, true Glass, and bewail thy defection. bear the shame of thy deformity, be humbled to the Dust, as great Malefactors and miserable Captives whom nothing but Death can set free and redeem are dejected.

3. And will nothing till Death intirely free me (O my God) and that my Soul hath no share of the natural Death, which could it taste would only reprieve, not deliver? Let therefore that Death of Death, the Mysterious Death of the Cross which opens the Door to the first Resurrection be powerfully vouchsafed, so shall I be saved from this Mother of Harlots and Abominations of the Earth, and my Heart and Mouth be fill'd with thy pure praises for ever.

Meditations and Contemplations.

On the 28th Question and Answer. *Of the Principles of the Spirit of this World.*

1. The Psalmist meditating the frame of his Body, saith it is fearful and wonderful. The Fabrick of the whole Creation must needs be so likewise, for 'tis a Mirrour shewing evidently and distinctly all Worlds Powers and Properties not as a dead record, but in a living Image by an Articulate voice, with as many demonstrations and Tongues as here are forms: All convincing that Man of great stupidity who sees not God, hears not his voice, reads not Lectures of his Infinite Wisdom, Power and Goodness in this his Theatre. The day is the Child of the second Principle, the Night derives its Fountain from the first, time is not fatherless, the Principles of the Spirit of this World being various such must needs the Creatures be

2. It went with Man as with one drunk regardless of the top of the Stairs missing the first falls down all the rest; or as one sleeping on the Brow of a Precipice or brink of a River, whence if he tumbles it is to the bottom; thus he who should have had Dominion over the Astral Powers losing the Reins is not only hurried by them but subjected to the Extremities of the Elements, and domineer'd over by the sickly Humours, Wants and Excesses of the Bestial Flesh, and corrupting uncleanness of this Bag of Worms.

3. If thou (my Soul) delightest in this, 'tis as a Fool in throwing Darts; art thou proud of thy Bodies features as well may an unsound Man of his Ulcers, or a Vassal of his Shackles; thus to be present in the Body is to be absent from the Lord, whose gracious presence removed makes Hell. Return then (Oh my Soul, my Spirit, and my Inward Powers) into your rest, live in the incombustible Body, put on the Humility, Modesty, and Sacred Flaming Love being the Heavenly Flesh of Jesus Christ; then will this Worlds Spirit own Subjection, no longer be a Clog or Lord, but a Staff and Servant. To this, O thou Almighty Arm strengthen me, O thou Glorious Sun, inlighten me O thou Sacred Breath, enliven me; for without thee what can I do, who am faln to be weakness, darkness, and dead under this outward Worlds Tyranny?

On the 29th Question and Answer. *Of the Sperm or Seed of the Generation of all things.*

1. The Psalmist complains, *I was shapen in iniquity, and in sin did my Mother conceive me*; but the Sperm or Seed of all things is without iniquity standing in the fifth form of Fire, being in its Existence a Mirror wherein the Abyssal Will beholdeth it self, and in its operation a transition unto or imager of the Multiplicity.

2. But how much doth Man who was created Good, by seeking out many Inventions run against the order of Nature: for out of the dark Earth sprout excellent Vegetatives, with various cheering Odours, delightful Colours and Tasts, and nourishing Vertues, out of the Mortal Waters are generated vast numbers and kinds of Fish; also Amber, Pearl, Coral, &c. all more excellent than the Water their Mother, which is corrupt as is the Earth. Yet Man, tho' proceeding from an Immaculate Sperm or Virgin Seed originally is become vile and filthy, moving retrograde, and is more and more degenerate, earthy, sensual and devilish.

3. Wert thou (O my Soul) the Image of thy God, how wouldst thou study, strive and practise the turning a less degree of good into a greater, not better into worse but (like thy great Guide and Pole-Star) improve not impair, turn to
him

Meditations and Contemplations.

him in whom only ceaseth thy variation, thou mayest in his Power find the Evil fall, and the Good have a Resurrection.

On the 30th Question and Answer. *Of the Distinction or Difference of the Sperm or Seed of Mettals, Stones, Vegetatives, &c.*

1. Behold we here, God's Infinity, how little a part whereof is this vast deep from Stars to Stars, the whole being but a Point to the infinite Abyss, and in this Deep how sure and demonstrable is God's Omnipresence and Universal Grace? How to be adored and with most profound Humility to be admired, and that with sincere transport of exalted inflamed Love; which is to begin Eternity, and be lifted here in the Roll of Celestial Worshippers.

2. Behold we also, how Omnipotent Goodness first spake the Sperm in the great Mystery and ever speaketh little Beginnings (scarce visible) into great Attainments, like as those large big-bellied Clouds which overcast the Sun, is a Cloath wove of most small Threads spun of the breath of the low Lands. Man, even thus, who ruleth the gentle and tameth the wild Beasts governing the Terrestrial Globe, is the first Six Days (as observ'd by the curious) as Milk, the second Nine Days as choaked Blood, in a few more Days by the commixture of the Spirits and the Blood, coagulates into a thin Skin like that within an Egg shell, in which, three little Swellings like Bladders floating arise, in them are formed the Liver, Heart, and Brain of that Proud Beast, who when formed is fed at the Navel, till wanting nourishment and room, breaketh the Panicles letting in Air and following it, having it self been the substance of venom: with wretched Pain enters the World like a poor Worm in a most forlorn, frail, tender, deplorable manner; and being the Epitomy of the whole, shews us what is that Power that ripens such pitiful Beginnings, and keeps it so long from returning to its Dust, whereto by very little means it is obnoxious? This we are before we have sinned, but what doth Sin make us after, if our Teeth be on edge by our Father's eating four Grapes, what doth our eating of them make us to be?

3. And now (my Soul) who is like thy God, who (thus base as we are) became like us to make us like him, as once we were, and passing over the more noble Creatures the Angels, became the Brother to us Worms, and because to be born and live like us was not wholly enough, was pleas'd *(Oh admirable!)* to die like us, thereby opening in us the Door of Eternal Life, what an Abyss of pure Love is this?

On the 31th Question and Answer. *How is the Conjunction of Feminine and Masculine Kind effected, whence the Seed and Growth existeth?*

1. The Meditation on this Question and Answer will continue the sad complaint of the last preceding; for how far are we fallen from the Virgin Image, into a state whereof depraved Humane Nature is ashamed, and at which the remainders of Modesty (which are not wholly defaced) are offended. The shiftless manner of our entrance on this Stage, shews us more wretched than Birds or Beasts. The Murther done by the First born of Woman, the strict Law for Circumcising of Men, and for Purifying of Women after Child-bearing, the Womens Confinement to one place at the Temple, with many things of like import, all shew what the breach of Modesty following the dividing of the Tinctures was.

2. But on the growth proceeding from the Conjunction, the Soul may a little stay it self from utter sinking, that though it is written, *who can bring a clean thing out of an unclean? not one*; yet all things are possible to Omnipotence; the God of Might

Might and Goodness hath, by bringing a clean thing into an unclean, cleansed the unclean, and so brought Good out of Evil.

3. Teach us (O Lord) that Divine Skill to fetch Honey out of the Devourers Belly. Let the sore Anguish of Soul, the New Man travels with, as consequent to the rent made by the dividing of the Tinctures be a little eased; let that bitter Cup have some of the sweet pure Water of the Fountain (open'd by the Son of the Virgin) be put thereinto. Let his Skirt be thrown over our Shame; Let after a Night of Mourning and Heaviness come some glimpse of Daunings; Let the Beast as well as the false Prophet be cast out, to make room for the dear Precious Virgin Image, the true Bride, Joy and Glory of the Fire-Soul, and is that signified by the Apostle, when he said, *the Woman is the glory of the Man*, but the Earthy Woman ought to have Power on [or over] her Head, because of the [pure Modest Virginity] of the Angels.

On the 32 Question and Answer. *Of the Tincture in the Spermatick Kind or Species, whence Growing and Lustre ariseth.*

1. Of the Tincture may be said as of the Wind, thou hearest the sound thereof, but seest not whence it cometh, nor whither it goeth, by it Clouds, Seas, Ships, Trees, *&c.* are driven, overthrown, rent and hurried, and Earthquakes caused, yet it self invisible to the outward Eye; So by the Tincture, not only Vegetables, Minerals, Animals, Men, the Elements and Stars, but Heaven, Earth, Hell, Angels, Saints, Devils and damned Creatures are acted, affected and distinguished, yet who may be said to see it, for it is above the Horoscope of the Senses; It must in Man be look'd for in the Eternal part, by the Eye of the Intellect.

2. The ball of the Eye seeth all things visible, but seeth not it self, so may it be apprehended of the Tincture in us, which seeth the Tincture in the Stars, and in the Terrestrial Stars the Pretious Stones, Metals, Vital Spirit of Animals and Vegetatives, yet cannot penetrate their own Tincture, unless the inward Eye be divinely opened to that Vision which how few are, and of those few, how imperfect? Natural Philosophy is exercised in the Inclination, Vertue, Variety, Power, Connexion, Sympathy and Antipathy of Nature, but it is Theosophy that is Comprehensive of the Spirit, Root, Mystery and Property of every Essence, and how, and why they transform into variety, whither they tend, what they figure, and how they transmute into more excellent, by subliming the Tincture when set at liberty, how the exalted Tincture is fortified to the Salvation of one, and how vitiated to the Damnation of another, for so rich is the Treasure, so large the Talent, that it must be accompted for with Usury.

3. And is this (O my Soul) entrusted to thee, regard it as thy life, beware thou do not as doth the fallen Angels; if the Light that is in thee be Darkness, how great is that Darkness? If thou use thy Members to unrighteousness, it is sinful and an unpenitent habit ruinous, as a Man may Bleed to death by one vein; but if the precious Tincture be once marr'd and prophaned, it is as a Dart thrust through the Liver, the Fountain of Blood; the Hair and Nails will after being cut grow, a Tooth may supply a former Tooths place, but the Tincture spoil'd, is as the Heart and Brain pluck'd out. Salt savours all things, but if it hath lost its savour, wherewith shall it be salted? Of the Tincture comes the Growth and Lustre, and so is as our Mother, if any one reproach and prophane it, he becomes mortally guilty, *He that curseth his Father or Mother shall surely be put to Death.*

Meditations and Contemplations.

On the 33 Queſtion and Anſwer. *Of the Original of the Creatures of the mortal Life.*

1. When I look towards the Circumference and ſee the winged Troops, ſhould not I find Cœleſtial Inclinations in all of them, where yet I find many filthy, many cruel, many ravenous; I look towards the Centre, and are there in the Deep any but dark undigeſted uncleanneſſes? yet there I obſerve almoſt all clean, many fair, more greatly nouriſhing, ſome adorn'd with rare Pearls and in the dark cold Earth the Triumphs of Nature in precious Stones and Minerals: And looking round me, my Fellow-Commoners are ſo various as to figure all Principles, all Worlds, all Properties to Infinity. No Star ſo noble but it's Energy is Imaged in ſome; no Conjunction ſo malevolent but is figur'd on others.

2. The dark World hath its Subjects and Idea's, *Saturn* in that Impreſſion owns the Wolf, Horſeleech, &c. *Mercury* the Fox and dangerous Reptils, *Mars* the Tyger and Dog, *Sol* the Lyon, *Venus* the Oſtrich and Vultures, *Jupiter* deformed Apes, Baboons and Monkeys, *Luna* unweldy Bruits. And among my Brethren of *Adam's* Apoſtate race, *Saturn* ſways the Meagre, Griping, Carking, Raking Inſatiable; *Mercury* the ſly, circumventing Crew; *Mars* the inſociable, outragious Rabble; *Sol* the daring ſeeker of Self and Domination; *Venus* the ſhameleſs obſcene cruel Adulterers; *Jupiter* the filthy Hermaphrodite and *Semihomines*; *Luna* thoſe who are a burthen to others and over-load to themſelves. Yet according to the Light World is a Book written with ſhining, living Letters accurately Engraven according to all Properties, in which our Old Man may meditate his derogating from the Copy, *viz.* The ſimplicity of the Dove and Lamb; and in which the New Man may (as in a Glaſs) behold his own Face, may obſerve how the Heavens hear the Earth groaning for Drought, and deſcend in ſweet diſtilling Bottles, the Earth hears the ſhriveling Seed and drying Roots, and the Corn and Fruits hear hungry Men and ſtarving Beaſts, and when all are filled by the overflowing of Infinite Goodneſs, how do the Bloſſoms breathe, and the laden Boughs ſhew their Satisfaction, the Herds return with flowing Udders and in the Flocks the Ews pay their Lambs what bounty lent them, how do the Subterranean Minerals extend their ſtretch'd out Arms towards the four Cardinal Points, and the hidden Treaſure excite Man's Diligence.

3. But what part beareſt thou (my Soul) in this Harmony? Art thou Hoarſe? Is thy ſound only like that when the Earth is knockt on? Doth all flow to thee and for thee, and art thou only as a Grave to bury them in, run they all to thee as *Jordan* into the Dead Sea? Muſt all theſe Voices of Divine Love be heard, ſeen, felt, taſted, ſmelled, renewed, increaſed and continued, and thou as Barren as *Arabia's* Sands, thy Heart as impenetrable and ſenſleſs as the Mountains of Ice, and Rocks of Adamant. Wo were me, if every Pile of Graſs muſt be a Witneſs againſt me. Hath thy Redeemer not only given thee all theſe, but open'd for thee, to thee, in thee Heaven it ſelf, and his own Heart, which is the Heaven of Heavens, and art thou on Earth and Cold? Why burneth not thy Heart? why flame not thy Affections? why dyeſt thou not as a Burnt offering, and riſeſt not in this ſweet Fire of humble, earneſt, endleſs Seraphick Love?

On the 34th Queſtion and Anſwer. *On the Separator of every Species of every Property.*

1. This Meditation exalts my grovelling Thoughts towards him, without whom was not any thing made that was made, yet this *Archeus* is no more than the great Inſtrument of Omnipotence; who when call'd the Father of Nature, it's only meant

the

Meditations and Contemplations.

the Father in Nature, bearing the Image of the Father, who alone is God, bleſſed for ever. Nor are the Aſtral Powers (though various, infinite and different alſo ſeeming oppoſite) to be call'd many, becauſe not one is broken from the United Harmony, but mutually embrace each other, no perverſeneſs among them; that is left to the Prince and Legions of the Abyſs of the dark World.

2. All the Properties and Aſtral Powers are an Egreſs of the Fountain Spirits as they are of the one Will, and by figuring and propagating their Energies, are as a Body Politick, whoſe many parts compoſe into a Republick. Thus is the whole one only Separator, Father and Mother in Nature, for whole Nature is an Hermaphrodite, in it the Tinctures being inviolably United, potently proceed in Magical Maſculine and Feminine Virgin Purity, doing all as *Adam* ſhould have done, and with ſo equal a hand, that the Excellency of one is ballanced by another kind of Excellency in another: The Pith and Brain needs the Bark and Skull, is Gold moſt valuable, Iron is moſt uſeful; the Powerful hand that lays the Contexture of the Whale and Elephant is altogether as admirable in the little Inſects.

3. Now as by a numerous well-accoutred Hoſt is ſhewn the Puiſſance of their Prince,by the greatneſs of a River the large Tract of Land whence it deſcends:So by this ſteady,unwearied,ſkilful,proſperous,mighty Architect is demonſtrated the Eternity,Wiſdom,Infinity & Omnipotency of the Glorious Creator,who is repreſented by this his excellent Agent. And as with Veneration Men receive the Decrees of the Wiſdom of a State with ſubmiſſion, the Commands of a Soveraign Authority, and with Circumſpection obſerve the Precepts of Phyſick, wherein life is concern'd with how much greater reaſon are we obliged, or rather by genuine ſweetneſs charm'd to the Laws of Nature, to be Loyal to the Government, ſtudious of the Inſtitutions, and faithful in holding the Secrets thereof, if entruſted to us; for as the Eternal Nature is in God,ſo the Temporal Nature is of God, in which alſo God and Heaven, is as Eternity is in time ; Grant therefore, O our God and Father which art in Heaven, that I may hallow thy Name in Nature, leſt if I do not thy Will ſhewn on Earth in things ſeen,I be not entruſted with the Knowledge of things in Heaven, which are not ſeen.

On the 35th Queſtion and Anſwer. *On the ſix days work of the Creation, and the Sabbath.*

1. The ſix days Work demonſtrate the ſix working Properties, and they being diſtinct, do yet every of them generate another, and all ſix meet to generate the ſeventh,yet when they concenter in the ſeventh,do not there ceaſe to Work, which were as impoſſib'e as for them to ceaſe to be ; but if they Work in the ſeventh,their Operations are heavenly,ſweetly, harmoniouſly, triumphantly ; as ſaith our Lord, *My Father worketh hitherto, and I work.*

2. Hath not Man brought himſe f in a moſt wretched degree of the Curſe by the Fall, of Toil and labour and Confuſion of Language, it is on the Work and Word, what hath and is man more ? A great aggravation of this Miſery is, either when we ſit down under Bondage in Soul and Body, feeding among Swine, having a Beaſt's Heart, as *Nebuchadnezar*, and groan not after working in God and for God, which would gradually deliver from the Curſe. Alſo when we miſtake our preſent working-time, and flatter our ſelves with undue and imaginary reſt, whereas we are here in the Seed time, in a Journey in the ſix days of Work.

3. But thou (my Soul) ſpare no pains, ſpur thy lazy Aſſo iate, my Body,ſubject it to the Croſs, to free you both from the Croſs, endure patiently, die daily, and having done all ſtand, empty thy ſelf, loſe thy ſelf, pour out thy ſelf ; Let not thy

Meditations and Contemplations. 235

thy Will be bought, but pay it to the Owner, give and refign it gladly and irrevocably. As to thy Name, be content it fhould wither as if blafted with the Eaft Wind, be willing to be namelefs, the Memory of it to be as written on the Sand, and (while here) to be a Fool, a Child, an off fcouring, any thing or not; yet muft not thy work ftop, let it proceed chearfully, till thy Body like the Matter of a Taper be confumed; if then thou art found fo doing, no fooner fhall this Candle expire, but the Sun will rife who fhall never fet, and the Sabbath enter at the end of the Week.

On the 36th Queftion and Anfwer. *Of the difference of the Mortal Creatures their Chaos, kind, and how diftinguifh'd.*

1. Had we the Intellect of an Angel, the diftinct Properties would be as an Index by their Idea to the voluminous Book of the great Myftery, and the Idea of the Creatures as it were pourtray the Potent Will and Properties of the Abyfs. Or had we *Adam*'s bright Eye, we might read their Names in the Language of Nature, and in them the Names, Power and Vigor of our own three Principles; but falling fo far below both, as that many of the Bruits themfelves may inftruct us in feveral things. How weak are our Enquiries, how perplext our Aphorifms and Procefs. The ancient *Magi* direct us to know the feven Properties by the feven regal Stars and Governors, which are the Spirits of the feven Metals, and imprefs the Vertues of the feven precious Stones, while many of Modern Pretenders to Wifdom (having loft the Spirit, Life and Effence of Nature) fill their Heads only with the Names, Mood, Figure, and Grafp at Shadows of things.

2. Behold how various are the Species, how curious the Symmetry, how agil the Compofure even of many Infects, how wonderful the Tranfmigration and Product of the Silk-worm, the Confection of the Bee with her Feminine Monarchy, how crafty the Nets of the Spiders, how providently laborious the Ant, wherewith our Lord upbraids our flothfulnefs, and we gratifie our Pride with the Silk, and our Palate with the Honey, inftead of fearching out and adoring of the moft High in thefe his little Creatures: yet are thefe little ones great, compar'd with thofe (to the bare Eye invifible and only vifible in good Glaffes) which fits fpinning in Sage leaves and yet how many Atoms may that Creature be divided into. Confider we their Sympathy and Society not only of Flocks and Herds, but of Birds of Prey, as Rooks, Stares, Storks, alfo their Antipathy as the Threfher and Swordfifh againft the Whale.

3. But now how highly neceffary is it that from this open Door all fhould impartially fearch themfelves to fee whether their Spirits are imaged according to the Evil Creatures, and if they find the Powers of the dark World predominant, that they learn to die to them, elfe they die in them, fhall rife in them, and live everlaftingly in them; and of what infinite concern endlefs Mifery is, all reafonable Creatures may judge. Whereas, if by the Spirit of Life we mortifie the Deeds (that is, the lufts) of the Body of Sin, we fhall by the fame Spirit be raifed now in the firft Refurrection, which excludes the fecond Death, and begets the Divine Life fpringing up through Death, by felf-emptying, where no Creature nor all of them hath any room but the Lord, and thofe only to Contemplate his Grace and Infinity in.

On the 37th Queftion and Anfwer. *To what end, and wherefore were the mortal Creatures made.*

1. When the gracious Creator placed Man here, it was in a Farm well ftockt, but

but that which meets my Meditation on the present Subject in the last Paragraph of the Answer, which is the Eternity of them in their Idea, how fading and transitory soever they are. The glorious Work of the Creation is not a bare Pageantry, it must cease as to its present Forms, but not vanish into a non-entity; for it shall bud forth for the sake of it's Tincture, by the strife of the Properties, to the Glory of the God of Glory, and as Instances or Trophies of the Victory, the weak Members of the Almighty Lord Jesus Christ have obtain'd by their Lord's strength, fortifying them to tread his steps, and follow him in the Regeneration.

2. By the reverting of these Figures, shall the blessed see how meekly the patient Lambs and other good Creatures pour'd out their lives, how quick and punctually the Fowls contributed, as did the Quails and Raver, how readily the Inhabitants of the Water yield themselves as those to the Apostles Nets, how liberally the Olive and other Fruit Trees pour'd forth their fatness, and the Elements their several Stores. And to the cursed Rejecters of God, shall all Creatures be plain material Demonstrations of their Abuses by Man's Excess and Cruelty; the toil of the laborious Oxe, the sweat of the macerated Horse, the life of a multitude of other Creatures profusely lavished away to pamper base sordid Lusts, run as with one cry, not as the Lambs against a devouring Wolf, or the Turtle against the Vulture, but that as those Devils in Humane shape should ransack the *Indies* and four Elements to humour their insatiable Lusts.

3. What Arguments (my Soul) may be drawn hence for Sobriety, Moderation, Humility, Thankfulness, Improvement of the Strength given us, liberal breaking to the Poor, and Mercy to the Dumb Creatures, of doing all not only as before the Omniscient Eye, who will be a swift Witness, before the good Angels, Devils, our own Consciences, but the whole Creation also, who as they (the Creatures) partake of the Properties and Tincture, are branches of the whole Astral and Elementary Creation, shall in their Æthers be more than a meer History, (*viz.*) an express, material Representation and Witness for or against thee in the other Country, though the Fool and Atheist will not know it.

On the 38th Question and Answer. *Of that whence Man's Body was taken.*

1 *Cor.* 3. 16, 17.
Ames 2.

1. If they to whom the Word of God came, are called God's, what was Man's holy Paradifical Body, in which that Word was? If the Tabernacle and Temple (being transient and of perishing Materials, and were dead Figures) had a Sanctity, How holy was *Adam*'s Divine Body which was taken out of the great Mystery or Heavenly Earth, and (had not the Fall been as a Worm at the Root) might have so flourish'd Eternally? If these dying Bodies are call'd the Temples of the Holy Ghost, that therefore he *that defiles the Temple of God, him will God destroy;* Also if Barbarity perpetrated on the meer Skelleton was pursued with Divine Vengeance, (*viz.*) the burning of the Bones of the King of *Edom* into Lime, What account shall the *Nimrods* give, who (as common Enemies to Mankind) empty Cities, waste Countries, make the World an *Aceldama*, her Inhabitants a Sacrifice to their insatiable all-devouring Ambition. What account the pretended Physitians, Chirurgeons, &*c.* those legal Slaughter-men, who arbitrate their unhappy Patient's Substance to their own mercenary Avarice, for protracting and heightening the Distempers, and finally killing the Sick; less generous than avowed Enemies, less just than common Robbers? What accompt shall be required for Self murther, and that which is worse, (*viz.*) enslaving it to unmortified Lusts, either pampering it to gratifie Pride, Filthiness, &*c.* or macerating and wearing it out by Envy, Malice, Revenge, Covetousness, Impatience and other Works of the Flesh, the end whereof as is the process therein, is Bitterness, and Death.

2. Why

Meditations and Contemplations.

2. Why should we be so greatly ungrateful for the betrusted Talent, as basely to derogate from the Noble Extraction of it? To which we are Debtors not to live after its Lusts, for they are (on pain of Death) to be resolutely and impartially mortified, to make it serve by chearful doing, and meek suffering the pleasure and designs of our great Soveraign, to keep it for his sake with Care and Conscience, nurse and nourish it for its gracious Father, wean it at his order, and at last resign our trust into the hands of our Faithful Creator, in whose Book all its Members are written, and who hath promised to raise it a Spiritual Body.

On the 39th Question and Answer. *Of the Imbreathing whence Man became a Living Soul.*

1. When the Paradifical Body was prepared, as in the last Meditation is said, it is written, *God breathed thereinto the Breath of Life, and Man became a Living Soul.* What the Soul is can be no News to the serious Perusers of these Writings; and what the Father is may be in part known by knowing the Child, and the Apostle saith we are his Off-spring, and if the Father be (in our very small measure) known and the Child, why not the Working and Inspiration? But the Father is unknowable by his Creatures, otherwise than as he is pleas'd to unvail himself in his only Son whom he Eternally hath, doth and shall generate, for the Infinite Father generateth in himself the Infinite Son in Eternity; and Man should even so have generated in the Soul a meek, loving Spirit as the Father generateth the Son in whose Infinite Lustre and Majesty is all his delight. Thus should Mans four forms of his Fire Soul have enkindled the Love Flame as the common Fire doth, the common Flame and Light, the defect whereof makes us ignorant of God and our selves, for what is seen without Light; this is it makes the vast distance of Heaven from Hell.

2. If the Body be so great a Trust (as in the preceding is noted) what is the Soul? As the Root is better than Bark, so is the Soul than the Body, and as both Root and Bark are unknown but by the Fruit, so are the first and third Principles without the second. The Soul as it is Immortal is Invaluable; and not to preserve and improve a vast Trust, and Treasure is a high contempt of the Trust. Not to enkindle the Flame of Love in the Soul, and going out of self by resignation of the Will by Union of the Divine Will, not to do this, is to deal with that Trust as the Devils did, who getting a covetous proud Will in their Spirit extinguisht, the Majesty thereof, and shut themselves up in Enmity and Rage of the dark forms of their Life.

3. O may my Soul be none of mine, for my Wisdom is Madness; may my Will be the Will of an humble Child; may the forms of my Life all be given out of my keeping, for my Father *Adam* having lost the Divine Eye, what folly were it to trust mine own Eye; but let me die to my Seeing, to my Reason, to my Senses, to mine own Conduct, and know what the second *Adam* openeth in the Regeneration, and no more, nor otherwise.

On the 40th Question and Answer. *Of Mans Immortal Life, his Soul, Mans Spirit, and his outward Life what all of them are.*

1. The last Question gave matter of Meditation on that part of Man sprung out of the first Principle. The 41st will offer the like on the second, or Spirit of Man; this opens a Door to the third, *viz.* his Mortal Life. And of that first its beginning consisting of Sin, Contemptibleness and Misery; to the first *David* saith, *I was shapen in iniquity, and in sin did my Mother conceive me.* Next the poor contemptibleness

temptibleness of his beginning, which the curious Observers tell us is, for the first six days as Milk, the next six as a thin Skin next the Shell of an Egg laid untimely; certain days after it is as Blood, and there riseth three little Bladders like Bowels floating in Water, wherein are form'd the three most noble parts, the Brain, Heart and Liver: Then gaining substance of choak'd Blood is nourisht by the Navel, yet so frail as may perish by the Mothers smelling the stink of the snuff of a Candle. Thus originateth the proud Beast, and when with great hazard and pain he cometh abroad, how wretched is he? Like a poor Worm coming out of the Earth, then growing up he is a commoner for Water, Air, and the product of the Earth with the Brute Creatures, a Companion of Devilish Men, and among Devils who is call'd the God of this World, loaden with Sin, Temptations, Sorrow, Care, Pain, and after a short Dream of the bitter sweets here, becomes a prey for Worms, Fishes, or perhaps a more Tragical Exit.

2. How Fantastick is Hope founded in the Dust? How multiplied are our well grounded fears? How fixt our Sorrows, which are as long as time? How Contagious our Disease, that not one escapes it, making also the whole Creation groan with us? How fatal our Languishing, which no weaker Physick than the King of Terrors can terminate? Some he cures in the Womb, others meets at the Door, others overtakes on the way, but at longest lodgeth all in the Evening. When as we began contemptibly of weakness do end in rottenness, as we sprung wretchedly, consume, disregarded and forgotten, our place knows us no more, and perhaps the Grand-child kicks the Skull of his careful Grandfather, the Fruit of whose cares, vexations, pains and troublesom sleep he prodigally lavisheth.

3. Come dwell here or hereabouts (my Soul) 'tis not vain to behold and consider what Vanities Incircle thee. What fierce or desperate Men madly venture on which they can try but once, and what Men overwhelm'd with the painted present pleasures do with a Transport of Consternation undergo, that do thou neither Court nor Fly. Man here is like *Jerusalem* when Besieged by *Titus*; the Devil and his Engines, the Snares of the World like the *Roman* Legions begirt him, waiting at all his Avenues: And his Domestick disorders, like the three Sects within, are at Mortal Enmity. God hath sent thee (my Soul) a voice warning hence, and directing whither, hear and obey, and the outward death shall land thee at *Jerusalem* which is from above, learn thy general and thine own particular Business, find thy Constitution Sin, do thy Days Work studiously, calmly and cheerfully, dwell at home (that is) within, and the vigorous, eager Maxims of the Worldly-wise, and their Storms as well as the flattering shews abroad, and other Mens Opinion of thee, will be to thee as Tragedies and Comedies in the Antipodes.

On the 41st Question and Answer. *The Idea or Express Reflex Image of God in Man wherein God worketh and dwelleth.*

1. This Image was figur'd by the Tabernacle, Temple, *Jerusalem*, and Mount *Sion* their Holiness, Exquisiteness, and Impregnableness, a glance of it shone in *Moses* Face. This when *Adam* fell into the outward Worlds Principle withdrew; and had not the same been reimplanted, he had remained part Devil and part Beast; and but that it continueth striving in Man he should still be so, and where final resistance is, that Man is a Devil and a Beast Everlastingly; for Men without Humane Intellect are Brutes, and without the Divine Image Devilish; for this Seal differenceth the Sheep from the Goats. Mans rejecting this is Gods rejecting of Man, for tho' the want of it makes the Devils miserable, yet Mans despising the

Meditations and Contemplations.

the tenders of it is an Aggravation to the opposition the Devils make against it. This is the Light that cannot be hid, why should it? What were Men without Eyes, or this deep without the Sun? What business hath Mortal Man here but to get it? Blessed is he that hath part of this first Resurrection, and that so shineth as to lead any other into the knowing and love of it, and living in it.

2. Contrariwise wretched are those who sit down with the Image, Shadow or Similitude of it, this is every where in reputation; Antichrist adorns it self therewith, the Politick Statesman pretends to it to ratifie his Magistracy over the Persons of his Subjects, as Antichrist ever Mens Consciences; while the real, pure Image of God in Man is every where decry'd and persecuted: Thus did the Jews kill the Prophets, and Men of the same Spirit garnish their Sepulchres. Men deal in matters of this vast import, as if that glorious Spiritual Image were like the Wooden Gods of the Blind Heathen, or as if it were as some Flowers Beautiful to the Eye, but without Smell or Taste. Thus while the holy Souls of Christs Followers went for the perishing Loaves, the Souldiers had his Garment, and the Relick-Mongers pretend to some of the Wood of the supposed Cross. Therefore is the outer Court given to be trodden down of the Gentiles.

باب
۱م

EXTRACTS
Of several of the
WORKS
OF
Jacob Behmen,
Beginning with his first Book
CALLED
AURORA,
OR,
𝔐𝔬𝔯𝔫𝔦𝔫𝔤 𝔎𝔢𝔡𝔫𝔢𝔰𝔰.

CHAP. I. Page 33. v. 1. *Of searching out the Divine Being in Nature of both the Qualities of Good and Bad.*

1. Though Flesh and Blood cannot conceive the Being of God, the Spirit (when enlightened from God) may. By considering the Powers in Nature, the Outward Heavens and Earth, Holy Angels, Men, Devils, Heaven and Hell. By considering all which are found the two Qualities Good and Bad, one in the other in all the Outward World.
2. A Quality is the Mobility, boiling, springing or driving of a thing. *Page 34.*
3. The seven Qualities are call'd sometimes seven Sources, Species, Kinds, Man- *What a Qua-* ners, *lity is.*

Aurora.

ners, Circumstances, Conditions, Powers, Operations of Faculties; also the Fountain Spirits which give Model, or Frame the Power, Vertue, Constitution, Substance, Essence, Being, Figure, Shape, Colour, Taste and Distinction to all things which ever were, are, shall or can be, in, from, or to Eternity, in all Creatures, Heaven, Hell, or this World. Also the Forms or Properties of Nature, which is the Salitter or Power of God, and call'd the seven Spirits of God in the *Revelations* four times.

Heat. 35. 4. *Heat* consumeth, expelleth or hardeneth. Light in it, is its heart and joy, making all things living and moving, fierceness maketh the Light moveable, the Light subsisteth in God without Heat, but not so in Nature.

Cold. 37. 5. *Cold* is the allay of the fierceness of Heat, making all things pleasant, but hath a fierceness which is the House of Death; from Heat proceedeth Air, which temper'd with Cold doth in the bitter quality become dewy, from Cold comes Water, which temper'd with Heat would else as Earth, &c. be congeal'd, Heat consumeth the Water, Cold crowdeth the Air, in the Meekness of the Air reigneth the Holy Ghost, but Air in its fierce Elevation destroyeth, in the fierceness of the Water is a deadly Spring in which all living things rot.

Bitter. 39. 6. The *Bitter* quality is the Mother of Life; for it a tracteth the Water, and dissipateth it, and becomes separable; from this quality have Leaves and Grass their green Colour, where it dwelleth meekly it is the Heart and Joy, a glimpse of Heavenly Joy, the Holy Ghost moveth in it, but in its fierce Elevation it is the very House of Death, for it kindleth the Element of Fire.

Sweet. 40. 7. The *Sweet* quality is a Joy of the Life, the Mansion of the Holy Ghost, 'tis Love and Mercy, Fragrant, good Taste, giveth Fair, Yellow, White, and Ruddy Colour, but in the fierce source 'tis Death and Corruption, if kindled in the Water Bitterness, it breeds the botchy Plague or Pestilence, if in the Heat, Bitterness, it ingendereth a spreading Plague, infecting the Air.

41. 8. The *Sour* quality cooleth, is a still joy to the Spirit: But in its evil source, it beginneth sadness.

9. The *Astringent* or Saltish quality is a good Temper to bitter, sweet, and sour: But in its fierceness in the Fire begets the Stone or Gravel, if in the Water, Scabs, Pox, Leprosie.

CHAP. II. *The Visible Heavens and Earth, and all Creatures, have a good and evil Source or Will, except the Holy Angels and Devils.*

44. 1. THE *Sun* is the Heart, King and Joy of the Stars and all Creatures. The whole Creation is the Body of God, being enlightened by the Holy Ghost, which they only are who relye not on themselves, but set their desires on him: Man comes to know God by the Creation; for as Mans Spirit informs and replenisheth his Body, so doth the Holy Ghost dwell in the good qualities of every thing.

46. 2. We are to conceive that in the Body of the Stars is the Triumphing Holy Trinity, which is the Light, Holy, Eternal Fountain of Joy, but is Infinite. Nor must we conceive God not in the Body of the Stars, and this World, but is all

Man resembleth the Creation.
and in all, So Man his similitude, whose inward hollowness signifieth the whole deep: The whole Man, Heaven and Earth: The Flesh Earth, the Blood Water, the Breath Air, the Windpipe and Arteries, the deep from Stars to us, wherein Fire, Water and Air qualifie, the Veins the Astral Influence, the Guts the consuming

fuming power of the Stars, the Heart the Element of Fire: The Liver Water, the Hands Gods Omnipotence, the Feet near and far off, the whole Body to the Neck all within the Sphere of the Stars, the Head Heaven, with its Imperial Organs, and all the Sences in a soft, meek power, as the Brain is; Heaven gives to the Stars, they to all Creatures Life and Spirit.

3. When we nominate the whole Creation, Heaven, Angels, Men, Visibles, and all above Heaven, is nominated the total God, which hath made himself creaturely, tho' God in Trinity is unchangeable. 51.

Obj. Will you say, is not good and evil in nature, and is evil come from God?

4. *A.* There is a Gall in Mans Body without which he cannot live, it making the Aftral Spirits moveable and joyous, but when it over-floweth and runneth to the Heart it kindleth the Element of Fire, and the Fire kindleth the Aftral Spirits which reign in the Blood in the Veins, in the Element of Water, and then the whole Body trembleth by the Wrath and Poyson of the Gall. The bitter quality is in God, but not as in Man, but is an Everlasting Power and Triumphing Joy, which springing up maketh Heaven, out of Heaven the Stars, out of the Stars the Elements, out of the Elements the Earth, and Creatures moveable. Whence also were Created Angels before the Creation of the Heavens.   *Good out of Evil, as Life out of the Gall.*

CHAP. III. *Of the Property of the* FATHER, &c.

1. **W**Hen Chrift prayeth (*Matth.* 6.) to his Father which is in Heaven, he doth not mean that Heaven can contain him, but diftinguifheth him thereby from the Father of Nature, which the Stars and Elements is, and becaufe in Heaven the Fathers Luftre is very bright and pure. God is the immediate Father of the Soul, which therefore hungereth after him. The Father of Nature, is the Father of our Bodies, and thence comes their nourifhment. All Powers and Properties in Heaven and Earth proceed from God the Father, who if he may be likened to any thing, it may be to the Globe of Nature, as by the Wheels in *Ezekiel* 1. for all the Powers are in the Father, one in another, as one Power, in unfearchable Clarity and Glory, his Immenfity and Infinity no Creature nor Angel can fearch into.   *God the Father.*

2. Of God the Son; he is not another, and yet his Property is other than that of the Father; for he is the Heart and Caufe of fpringing joy in all the Powers of the Father, a fimilitude whereof is the Sun which enlighteneth the whole deep, Heaven, Stars and Earth moving in the midft is the King and Heart of all the Stars, fo fhineth the Son in the whole Father, being a felf-fubfifting Perfon. The Father from Eternity to Eternity ceafeth not to generate the Son, and the Son ceafeth not to enlighten the Perfon of the Father, but the Son is not fo mixt in the Father that his Perfon cannot be known nor feen; if fo it were but one Perfon, but is another Perfon, not another God.   58. *God the Son.*

3. Of God the Holy Ghoft; He proceedeth from both, is the holy Fountain of Joy, a meek, pleafant Breath, or ftill Voice, which muft be fhewn by a fimilitude. As the innumerable Stars and Sun created out of the Stars, refemble the Father and the Son, fo the three Elements, Fire, Air and Water proceed from one Body, *viz.* The Fire fwells from the Sun and Stars, the Air expands and flies aloft from the Heat, and the Water from the Air, and in this motion is the Life of all Creatures that can be named, and fignifieth the Holy Ghoft; who caufeth the living motion in all the Powers of the Father. The Son and Holy Spirit are nothing lefs or greater than the Father.   64. *God the Holy Ghoft.*

The

Aurora.

The Trinity.

P. 68.
The Trinity represented.

4. This Ternary is manifest in Man's Body and all Creatures, also in Wood and Vegetables, and in Stone and Minerals. In Man's Heart, Veins and Brain, is a Spirit and all the Powers which move in the Heart, Veins, and Brain signifie the Father, thence springeth up a Light of Understanding, in the Power of which Knowledge, the whole Body moveth, signifying the Son which shineth back into the Heart, Veins and Brain, as the Son into the Father, and from both Powers, proceedeth forth Reason, Skill and Wisdom to govern the whole Man, and distinguish all that is *extra corpus*, which is thy Spirit, wherein thou excellest the Beast, and wherein the Holy Spirit rules if thou be not a Child of Darkness, *v. 97*. The Father is signified by the Power of thy whole Mind, the Son by the Light in thy Mind, the Holy Ghost by the Spirit of thy Mind. The Soul containeth the first Principle, the Spirit of the Soul the second, the Astral or outward Spirit the third. So in a Beast, only Man is made by God himself, out of the best Pith or Kernel of Nature, to be his Angel and Similitude. The Beast is made out of the wild Nature of this World, through the Motion of the Stars and Elements. In all Creatures are, 1. The Power out of which the Body comes. 2. The Sap or Heart, 3. The flowing springing Spirit.

CHAP. IV. *Of the Creation of Angels: And first, Of the Divine Quality.*

1. ALL the Powers are so in God, as no Man can reach; but by the Creation it may be clearly known. Though all Powers are in the Father as the Astringent (or harsh) soft (or gentle) heat, cold, bitter, sour, sweet, light, sound or noise one in another as one Power, yet not in the manner as in Nature; for *Lucifer's* Elevation made the Powers impure, separate and unclean; but in God all are mild, soft, triumphing, if he may be likened to any thing, it must be to the Soul of Man, enflamed by the Holy Ghost, as a glimpse, but in God all is Spirit. The Light and Glory of the Son goeth into all the Powers of the Father and the Holy Ghost is a glimpse, but in God all is Spirit.

2. The Light and Glory of the Son goeth into all the Powers of the Father, and the Holy Ghost moveth Eternally in all, which in the Deep of the Father, is like a Divine Salitter or *Salnitrum* to be likened to the Earth, which before its Corruption was such, not hard, cold, dark, &c. but like the clear, pure Heaven, in it all the Powers were fair and heavenly, till *Lucifer* spoil'd it. But the Fathers heavenly Salitter doth generate all manner of Divine Trees and Plants, bearing Fruits of Life, with heavenly colours, smells, tastes, different, every quality bearing his own Fruit: as Nature doth endeavour to produce in this dark Dungeon or Den of this World, hard, dark, dead, Trees and Fruits, and precious Stones, Gold, Silver, which are all but dark shadows of the Divine Being mixed with hellish qualities and smells, but the Trees meant here are Heavenly and Spiritual, and yet truly and properly such.

In which Holy Kingdom are two things mainly to be consider'd.

1.

3. The Salitter which are moving springing Powers. 2. *Mercurius* or the sound, which is the voice and sound of all Creatures, and that in the Earth (which causeth the growing of Gold, and all other Metals) shadows out. All the exquisite Musick of this World compar'd with the Harmony of that Sound, is as the howling of Dogs. 4. For

4. For though Nature hath always from her beginning used highest diligence to produce heavenly Forms in Power, in all Creatures and Productions, also in all Delicacies and Arts; for it would fain be delivered from this Vanity, that it might procreate Holy Forms in Power, but Death hath entered, and doth and must hinder it; for Man's infectious Lust to Eat of both the Qualities of Evil and Good spoil'd the Salitter, and stopt his Ears against the Sacred sound, whereas the Divine Salitter and *Mercurius* is the Food of Angels.

5. *Of the Creation of Angels.* Philosophers, who supposed Angels were created only out of the Light have erred, for they were made out of all the Powers of God. The total Holy Trinity made by its moving a Body like a little God out of the Salitter and *Mercurius*, that is, out of the Exit and Excrescence, and being made are a distinct Substance. As while a Mother hath a Seed in her self, it is hers; but when it is become a Child, it is its proper own, though cannot live but by the Mother's Food; but the quality External without the Child's Body is not the Child's Propriety, the Mother nor the Mothers Food, but what the Mother out of love gives, thus are the Angels. And the Mother may well thrust from her the rebellious Child, and with-hold her Food from it. Thus was it with *Lucifer*, God withdrew his Divine Food when he elevated himself, then must a Spirit faint, and can no more subsist as before, than a Man without Air, nor can the Angels without their Mother. *Angels made out of all the Powers of the Father.*

CHAP. V. *Of the Corporeal Substance, Being, and Property of an Angel.*

1. TO answer what their Figure, Body or Shape is: They and Man bear the like Image; how else must we be like them in the Resurrection? And *Moses* and *Elias* were in their own Form on Mount *Tabor*, and *Elias* was taken up alive. And Jesus shall come again as they saw him go. As in God we observe, 1. The Salitter, or Divine Powers out of which the Body or Corporeity is. 2. The *Mercurius*, Tone or Sound; so is it in an Angel, who have as Men the five Doors of that we call Senses. *Angels are in Human Form.*

CHAP. VI. *How an Angel and a Man is the Similitude of God.*

1. AS is the Being and Divine Body of God, so is the Being and Body of an Angel and a Man, with this only difference, that the Angel and Man is but a Creature, not the whole Being, whom if he resist, the Father may justly cast him out.

2. The whole Father speaketh out of all the Powers of the Godhead, the Word (that is) the Son of God, this Word is the Father's Glance and Majesty, proceeding out of his Salitter and *Mercurius*, which being spoken turneth back, and ever is in all the Powers of the Father as a glorious Eternal splendor. Now that Word hath so swift a sharpness, that instantly it goeth through the whole deep of the Father, and the sharpness is the Holy Ghost.

3. Now in an Angel and a Man the Head is the Council-seat, signifying the Father, whither all the Powers rise, for higher they cannot; and the five Senses as Counsellors agree, and what they decree, is concreted into a Judge, as a word in its Centre, the Heart as a self-subsisting Person signifying the Son of God. And *How Angels and Men are Images of the Trinity.*

that

that goeth from the Heart to the Mouth and Tongue, with its Mercurial sharpness to distinction, and that signifieth the Holy Ghost.

4. The Mouth sheweth an Angel and a Man not to be Almighty, for through that, both must draw in the Powers of the Father, or cannot live, an Angel as well as a Man, only theirs is the Spirit whence the Air of this World exilteth, which he must do, or cannot be a moveable Creature, he Eats (as men do) the Heavenly Fruit, and hath a Body in the same Form as Man with all the Members (except those of Generation Guts and Fundament) but all spiritual and heavenly; Man had need of those only by his Fall.

Paradifical Fruits.

5. Out of the Divine Salitter and *Mercurius* are produced Trees, Plants, Fruits, Flowers and all sorts, not a shadow of such but really substantial: yet as the Angels are, such is the Vegetation, but not in the two Qualities of Evil and Good, but only in one, the Good. Those Fruits the Angels pluck with their hands and eat, but need no Teeth, for they are Divine Powers, and whatsoever they have Externally or without them is not their corporeal Propriety, but God's Gift to them.

CHAP. VII.

1. GOD at the first made three Kingdoms of Angels, their Kings were *Michael*, *Lucifer* and *Uriel*. The whole Deep betwixt the Stars is one, the other two are without and above it according to the Trinity: in the midst of all which is the Son of God, yet no part of either further or nearer to him, yet are the three Kingdoms circular about him. In all which the Father is Power and Kingdom, The Son Light and Splendor. The Holy Ghost Moving or *Exit*. Seeing in the whole Creation in a Gold-stone, the Salitter and *Mercurius* signifieth the Father, the Gold the Son, the Virtue the Holy Ghost.

CHAP. VIII.

Of Angels.

1. THE Angelical Kingdoms are formed according to the Divine Being, only their Bodies are Creatures, and their Kingdom, Court or Locality is not theirs, for a natural right as their Bodies are, but belongeth to God the Father, out of whose Powers it was made. 2. And as the Father generateth the Son, and as the Holy Ghost goeth forth from both: So do the Angels in their Power generate the Light and Knowledge in them, and by them the Spirit goeth forth from their Heart, Light and all their Powers. 3. The Corporeal Body of one Angel is as it were one Kingdom, or as the Holy Trinity. All Power is in God the Father, he is in his Deep, the Fountain of Light and Darkness, Air, Water, Heat, Cold, Hard, Soft, Thick, Thin, Astringent, Bitter, Sweet, Sour, Sound or Tone, all which are in Angels and Man: but Man hath corrupted it, to us the Light of the Sun is intolerable, so is our unqualified Heat, Cold, &c. 4. And when the Creature willeth to elevate it self in the Light above the Humility of Love, he kindleth a Fire which extinguisheth the Light, and falls into Darkness (which as the snuff of a Candle is hid in the Centre of the Light) as is apparent in *Lucifer*. 5. Now how we may conceive that God is an angry Zealous God, and a gracious merciful God, the seven Species or Circumstances must be known to wit,

7 Species. 1. 2. 3. 4. 5. 6. The 1, Astringent. 2. Sweet, 3. Bitter, 4. Heat, 5. Love, 6. Tone or Sound.

7. 7. The Body generated out of the other six Spirits. 6. The

Aurora. 247

6. The sweet Quality flyeth from the bitter, which is the cause of the growth of Fruit in Vegetables, and the Astringent and bitter eagerly pursue it, cloaths it, and is the cause of a stalk, and when it overtakes it, strives to hinder its farther flight, and so comes the knot in the stalks, through which is a small Orifice, the sweet Quality gets through that, and then comes more stalk, leaves and blossoms, which by the external heat and light gets colours; but the sweet Water is not a Mother strong enough to produce Fruit, but the blossoms being fallen off, the outward Heat with the united aid of all the Qualities bringeth the Fruit. *P.* 133. 134. 140. 141. *Vegetations.*

7. The Light riseth up only in the sweet Quality, no thing can be kindled but that in which the sweet Quality is predominant, for the Spirit riseth up only in the Water. A Stone or Earth cannot be kindled, because the Astringent and bitter Qualities are predominant in them, only. The Earth when the earthy quality is boyl'd out, is brought (as in Gun-powder) to give a flash of Terror, wherein the Devil in the anger of God representeth himself. 8. But that the Water will not burn, is because it is not the sweet Water, but Elementary only: Else Water were not Mortal. Flesh shineth not, but fat doth, the sweet quality prevailing; therefore lean Creatures are not merry. 143. 144. 8. 145.

Q. *Where are the seven Spirits?* 172.
9. A. All Heaven and this World, and all the Creatures in Heaven and Earth are comprehended in them.

Q. *Seeing God is every where, and is himself all, How comes heat, cold, wrath, and fierceness among the Creatures?*
10. A. The first four Forms are at Enmity with each other without the Light, and yet are the cause of the Life. 11. Know, that all within the Stars was a holy Salitter and the place of *Lucifer*, whose proud Elevation kindled the seven qualifying and Fountain-Spirits, all was burning. The Astringent compacted so vigorously that Stones were generated, and so Cold, that the sweet Water became Ice, and part thick stinking and raging Poison.

12. Whereupon *Lucifer* was thrust out, and instantly insued the Creation of this World, and the hard, spoiled, corrupt matter, which had wrought out it self in the kindling the seven Qualities, was driven together, whence Earth and Stones came to be, and after that, the Creatures were made of the kindled Salitter of the seven Spirits of God, their kindling made the fierceness of one Property against another, and the Creatures from the same impulse do bite and annoy each other. *The direful Effects of Lucifer's Fall.*

13. Upon which, the Universal God hath Decreed the last Judgment, to separate the Good unto the meek Delight, which was before the kindling by *Lucifer*: and give that which is fierce and wrathful, to be an Habitation for the Devil for ever. The Good Men being Eternally with their King Jesus Christ. 175.

CHAP. X.

1. THE sixth Fountain Spirit is the Sound, Tone or Noise. 1. Whence is the singing Melody of the Angels, and all Colours and Beauty are from the Tone or *Mercurius*. 2. Hardness is the Father, but the whole Salitter is the Mother; for if the hardness were both Father and Mother, a Stone would sound and ring. 3. But where the Light is generated out of the Heat, there riseth the sound (viz.) The Astringent Quality rubbeth it self with the bitter, making Heat rise up in the sweet Water, the flash of Light distinguisheth there, and impregnateth the bitter and Astringent, so that the moving Spirits would speak. Then the flash coming from 176. 2. 3. *The 7 Spirits of God. 6 still generateth the 7th.*

from the bitter, breaketh open the hard, and the Tone goeth forth as it was decreed in the Centre, in the middle of the Circle, the Council of the seven Spirits. 4. Therefore all the Veins and Powers go into the Tongue that the Noise may go forth gently.

P. 187.   5. Of the seven Spirits, six always generate the seventh, without every one
 6.   there would not be any one. 6. But the Author saith, his naming of but two or three to the Nativity of a Spirit is (though he saw them all seven well) yet, because of his weakness, he could not bear the speculating them all at once in their
 7.   Perfection, but in part. 7. Otherwise if a thought through the Centre of Nature, could penetrate all the Forms, it were free from the Bond of Nature.

Majestick   8. From the flash comes the Light of the Majesty; therefore if any one could
Light.   in his flesh comprehend the flash, kindling it self in the central Fountain of the Heart, which the Author saith he very well saw how it is, that Person could clarifie or transfigure his Body therewith, and be like the Angels: and no more bestial.

192.   9. The Soul hath the first Principle, the Spirit of the Soul hath the second, the Astral Spirit hath the third in the Elements.
          10. When a Fire riseth up in one of the Fountain Spirits, it is not concealed from the Soul, which may awaken the other Spirits, and it hath a Prison, and (if the Fire become too big) can shut up the kindled Spirit in the Astringent quality till it be allay'd and extinguished: Else the Sap that is in the whole seven will become dry, and then thou art a Hellish Firebrand. But if thou take the evil Spirit, and imprison it, and turn a submissive Heart and Will to God, contemn-
The 7 Spirits ing Honour, Pleasure, Riches, Wantonness, by bearing the Cross and being the
in Harmony. Worlds Fools, then will not the Fire at the last Judgment Day stick to thy sappy Spirits, but after this anxious trouble God will in the Resurrection Crown thee, and thou wilt be a Triumphing Angel.
          11. Q. *Is there in God also any contrary Will, amongst the Spirits of God?*
          12. A. No, tho' the great earnest severity of God may by the former Writings of the Spirit be seen, yet in God is no disunion, in him all the Spirits Love and Triumph as one Spirit; but in the innermost secret geniture (not apprehended by any Creature but in the flash) it must be so, for Life and Omniscience is thus begotten; for tho' *Lucifer* kindled the Spirits of this World, and made it all faint and half dead, yet this World belongeth to the Body of God the Father as well as
13.   Heaven. 13. And the whole Trinity is generated in the Heart of all Angels and Men, except the Devil and Damned Men, and in such a manner is God Almighty,
14.   All-seeing, &c. and proveth the Hearts and Reins. 14. Thus also all the Devils and Damned must in the Salitter which they have corrupted be his Eternal Priso-
15.   ners in Torment and Reproach. 15. 1. The hardness gives extream cold. 2. The sweetness gaspeth and fainteth. 3. The bitterness teareth like a hot Plague as
The Discord of Gall. 4. The Fire is as a wrathful Sulphur. 5 Love is turn'd into Enmity.
the 7 Spirits. 6. Sound is as a crackling Fire or Thunder out of a hollow place. 7. Their Region a hole of Mourning. Their Food is the fierceness of all the Qualities.

CHAP. XI.

1. THE seventh Spirit is the Body wherein Heaven and Earth, Beauty and Joy rise up, being generated out of the other six; in colour Azure or Heaven Blew; were it not for this, there would be neither Man nor Angel, and God would be an unsearchable Power.

2. All

2. All the seven Spirits without the rising up of the flash, were a dark Valley, but when the flash riseth up between the Astringent and the Bitter, in the Heats shining in the sweet Water, it makes all living, and the Power which riseth up in the flash is the Love, and all the seven Spirits thus enlightened, become a palpable Body to speak after an Angelical manner, and this is the Body of Nature, wherein all heavenly Creatures, Idea's, Figures or Vegetations are imaged or fashioned. *P. 202. The 7 Spirits in the Light are Omnipotent.*

3. The Light is the Life of all the seven Spirits, it is their Son and Heart, they are its Father, him they Eternally generate, in him triumph. This Light or Majesty is the second Person in the Trinity, and is another Person from the seven Spirits, and the seven Spirits rise up continually in the Light, and are the Father. *206.*

4. And this splendor of the Light in the seventh Nature-spirit, (viz.) the going forth of the Powers to form and image all in the seventh Spirit, this out-going or Exit of the glance, is the true Holy Ghost, proceeding from the Father and the Son.

5. This the Jews, Turks and Heathens might find in their own Life, and by these three they must rise again.

6. But that the Christians boast not, and scorn them; Know, that if the Turks be of an Astringent Quality, and the Heathens of a Bitter, yet if they stand in the anxious Birth, seeking Rest and Grace (though not in the right place) God is every where. And the Christian is generated in the Heat, where the Light springeth up in the sweet-water, yet take heed by drying up the Water thou extinguish not the Light and be burnt.

7. The six Spirits rise up alway in a compleat Birth in the seventh, and the corporeal drying of them is called Divine Salitter.

8. The Angels are not all of equal Power, though every one hath the might of all the Fountain Spirits, but in every one there is somewhat of one Quality more predominant than another, wherein he is glorified. *232. The various Excellencies*

9. Such as the Salitter was in every place at the time of their Creation, in such *of Angels.* is the Angel strongest, and according to which is he named.

10. As Flowers in Meadows receive colours from each ones Quality: So the Holy Angels, some are strongest in the Astringent quality, and are of a brownish, dusky grey, white light, like Twilight, and nearest the Quality of Cold, and when the Light of the Son of God shineth on them, they are of a brownish purple flash of Lightening, very bright in their Quality. *Astringent.*

11. Some are of the Quality of Water-light like the Holy Heaven, and when the Light shineth on them, they look like a Chrystalline Sea. *Water.*

12. Some are strongest in the Bitter Quality, and are like a green precious Stone or Emerald, sparkling like a flash of Lightening, and when the Light shineth on them, they appear as a greenish red, as a Carbuncle, or as if the Life had its Original there. *Bitter.*

13. Some are of the Quality of Heat, and they are brightest of all, yellowish and reddish, and when the Light shineth on them, they are like the flash or Lightening of the Son of God. *Heat.*

14. Some are strongest in the Quality of Love, and are a glance of the Heavenly Joyfulness very bright, and when the Light shines on them, they look like light blew azure lustre. *Love.*

15. Some are strongest in the Quality of the Tone or Sound, and are bright also, and when the Light shineth on them, they look as if something would lift up it self aloft there, in the rising of the flash of Lightening. *Tone.*

16. Some

Total Nature. 16. Some are of the quality of the total Nature, as a general mixture, and when the Light shineth on them, they look like the Holy Heaven formed out of all the Spirits of God.

p. 234. Arch or Throne Angel, what he is. 264. 17. But the King is the Heart of all the qualities, and hath his Court, Province or Circumference in the Centre, as the Sun amongst the other Planets, so great is a Cherubim or King of Angels.

18. The Author saith this Revelation was given him of God, not that he had gone into Heaven and beheld it, nor had any told it him; for if any, yea tho' an Angel he could not have understood or believed it, but have doubted whether it had been an Angel sent of God or no, but because it is generated in the Centre or Circle of Life, as a bright self-evidencing Light like the Heavenly Birth or rising up of the Holy Ghost, with a fiery impulse of the Spirit, he could not withstand it, at which let him that mocketh fear, left he soweth mocking and Eternally reap it.

19. Worldly Wisdom is Born Blind, therefore must all be Born again, which new Birth begets the flash of Life in the sweet Spring or Fountain Water of the Heart, and then it seeth.

Cause of Baptism. 266. 20. And therefore hath Christ ordained the Baptism in the Water, because the birth of the Light riseth up in the Water, which hath from the beginning of the World been a Mystery till now.

21. This World is a Type of Heaven.
22. The Stars denote the Angels being unaltered.

How the outward World figureth the Eternal World. 23. The Elements in the deep between the Stars and Earth, by their often alterations of being bright, and sometimes louring, blew, whitish, duskish, wet and dry signifie the wonderful proportion, variety and change of the posture of Heaven, yet all according to the rising up of the Spirits of God, and the Glory of the Son of God shining Eternally therein.

24. The Earth sheweth the Heavenly Nature, or the seventh Spirit of Nature, in which the Ideas rise up.

25. The Birds, Fishes, Beasts, Worms, Trees, Plants and Flowers set forth the forms in Heaven, tho' they are in clarity and brightness, who rise there and go away again, not being compacted as the Angels are? but a figure, and if imaged in one Spirit, the same by wrestling with another Spirit is divided and altered, therefore also the Creatures in this World are created Transitory.

CHAP. XIII. *Of the Doleful Terrible Fall of* Lucifer *and his Kingdom.*

269.
275.
1. WHen *Lucifer* saw his own Excellencies, then his Heart or Life Spirit exalted it self, aspiring to triumph over the Divine Birth, the Son or Heart of God.

2. For the seven Fountain Spirits who are the Father of the Light were pleased to become creaturely in him, and gave him the superior Primacy, in whose bright Light was perfect understanding.

Lucifer's dismal fall gradually shown. 3. But he, seeing himself so Triumphant, moved the Spirit generated by the seven so hard and strongly, that it became very fiery, climbing up in the Fountain of the Heart.

4. But had it moved gently and lovingly, as the seven did before they became creaturely, there had been generated a lovely, mild Son, like to the Son of God, and then the Infinite Light, the Son of God, would have been delighted in, and played

played with the small Light in *Lucifer*, as with a young Son or dear little Brother.

5. But let not the Devil make any believe, Gods will was that he and some Men should be loft, and so pervert Gods Truth defending the Devil by Lies.

6. For know, the whole Deity hath in its innermoft Birth or Pith, a very tart, terrible, sharpnefs, in which, 1. The Aftringent quality is a very hard, dark, cold, attracting like the extream Froft, congealed Water, when fuppofe the Sun totally taken away, which auftere attraction, caufeth fixation of the Body, and the hardnefs drieth it up fo, that it fubfifteth creaturely. *P. 281. Tyranny of the four firft forms.*

7. The bitter quality is tearing, cutting and penetrating, driving the Aftringent to Mobility. From the fierce rubbing and raging of both which,

8. A wrathful kindling proceedeth.

9. And in this eager ftrife exifteth a hard Tone or Noife penetrating all like a Tyrant, according to which God calls himfelf an Angry, Jealous God, and in this confifteth Hell, Enmity and Eternal Perdition : And fuch a Creature is the Devil come to be.

10. And in thefe is God an All-comprehenfible, All-fixing, Sharp God.

11. But in the ftrife and heat of thefe qualities arifeth the Light, and in the Light and the Sweet Water the Flafh of Life, wherein all the foregoing qualities are made pleafant, as a four Apple by the Sun is made fweet and good, yet the Tafte of the other qualities remain in it. *285. Evil producing good. 290.*

The Head Spring and Fountain of Sin.

12. *Lucifer's* qualifying Spirits, having an Imaging Power in that Royal Body, vehemently affected the high Light, fo triumphantly that they lifted up themfelves to Pomp and Statelinefs, leaving the Angelical Obedience, whereby the great bright flafh became, fo bright as was intolerable to the Fountain Spirits, againft the right of Nature. So that the bitter quality which Exifteth in the fweet Water, and is the caufe of joy trembled and rub'd it felf fo hard in the Aftringent, that the Fountain or Quality of Heat was eagerly kindled : Which bitter and hot Quality caus'd the Aftringent to dry up the fweet Water, wherein the Heavenly Heat and Light have their Being. And thenceforth could not the Heat rife to a Flame or Light (for the Light exifteth in the Oylinefs of the Water, thus dryed up) but glowed, as red hot Iron, or rather a very hard Stone, in the greateft Heat. *299. Lucifer's dreadful, voluntary and irrecoverable Apoftacy, and of his Legions demonftrated.*

13. Not that the Spirit of the Water was devoured, but its quality was turn'd into a dusky, hot and four Quality: Which introduced extremity of Cold alfo, whereby the whole Body grew fierce and wrathful. And the bitter Quality raged and became a Poyfon, hence fprung the firft Poyfon; which bitter poyfonous Death comes alfo into poor Humane Flefh.

14. And now was *Lucifer* an Aftringent ; hot, bitter, dark, cold, four, ftinking, poyfonous Fountain. And the Tone rofe up through the bitter Qualities, penetrating the Heat and Aftringent hard Quality, as a clap of Thunder.

15. God created Angels out of himfelf, that they might be harder and dryer compacted than the Ideas or Forms, which, through the qualifying of the Spirits of God in Nature rife up, and through the moving of the Spirits pafs away again, that their Light in their hardnefs, fhould fhine brighter, and the Tone of their Body fhould found clearer and fhriller than it did before (either fhine or found) in the Salitter, which was thin and dim. And therefore they lifted up themfelves (tho' they knew themfelves to be but a piece of the total God) fuppofing, they were a fairer little Son than the Son of God himfelf, and that they could qualifie, operate and elevate themfelves above the whole God, and Rule and Govern all without Corrival or Supream Comptroller. 16. Here *305.*

Aurora.

16. Here lyes the Root of Covetousness, Envy, Pride and Wrath. All *Lucifer's* Angels fell with him; for he was created out of the Kernel of the Salitter, out of which they were created, he their Lord, they were all of one will with him, which they would not suffer to be taken away.

17. Q. *Did not the Universal God know this before the Creation of the Angels?*

18. A. No, for if so, it had been a Predestinate Will in God to have it so, and had been no Enmity against God, but God had created him a Devil. God made him a King of Light, and for Disobedience spewed him out of his Royal Throne.

19. God knew this according to his Wrath, in which he is not called God but a consuming Fire, but knew not this according to his Love, according to which he is called God, into which no fierceness entreth, and so God is alone called God or Goodness.

20. And what Gods Love knoweth sensibly or feelingly in it self, that it also, and that only it willeth.

P. 385. 21. The Devils Prison is in, upon and above the Earth up to the Moon, till the last day; And,

The Devills present and future Prison. 22. Then their House will be in the place where the Earth now standeth, and this will be called the Burning Hell: but not in such a Form as it now standeth, but separated in the kindled wrath Fire into a dark, hot, cold, rugged, hard, bitter, stinking Relicks, dregs or dross.

CHAP. XVIII. *Of the Creation of Heaven and Earth.*

396. Composition of the Terrene Globe.

1. WHen the Astringent quality was predominant, the hard, dry Stones came to be.

2. But where the Astringent and Bitter were equally predominant, there sharp Gravel and Sand.

3. Where the Tone and Astringent in the Water, there Copper, Iron, and Rocky Oar.

4. Where the Water, there the wild Earth : But the Bitter Spirit is the chief cause of the Black Earth.

5. Yet the Heat in the Astringent chiefly helped to make the hardness, and there it generated the noblest and preciousest Salitter in the Earth, as Gold, Silver, and precious Stones.

6. But when the hot Spirit in the sweet Water was predominant in the Love, the Astringent made the Oar of precious Stones, *&c.*

CHAP. XIX. *Concerning Heaven, what it is, where it is, and how it is.*

429. The dear and Transcendent Heavens.

1. THat there is a pure glorious Heaven in all the three Births aloft above the deep of this World, in which is Gods Being and the Holy Angels, he is not Born of God that denieth: Which comprizeth the Kingdoms of *Michael* and *Uriel,* and continueth as it was from Eternity, with which the innermost and holy Birth in this World uniteth, being all one Body of God ; one Heart, one Will, one God all in all, for the true Heaven is every where.

2. When thy Spirit apprehendeth the innermost Geniture of God, and presseth in through the Astral and Fleshly Geniture, it is clearly in Heaven.

3. But

3. But the Out-birth of this World was *Lucifer*'s Kingdom to the Stars, and so far is the Wrath of God ; between which outmost Birth of this and the outmost Birth of that, is a great gulph, and are one to the other as Death is to Life, or a Stone to a Man: So that as to the Out-birth we cannot see the Angels, nor they dwell with us ; but in the innermost they dwell with us.

4. The second Birth or Geniture, *viz.* the Astral, standeth in the seven Fountain Spirits of this World in which the Holy Ghost also ruleth and helpeth to generate the third Holy Birth.   *P.* 432.

5. The which third Holy Birth, is the clear Holy Heaven, which uniteth with the Heart of God, and holdeth the Devil Captive in the Out-birth in the Anger Fire.

6. Out of this Heart, Jesus Christ, in the Womb of the Virgin, went into all the three Births, that he might with his innermost take the Devil Captive in the Out-birth, overcome the Wrath of God as a Victorious Prince, and in the Power of his Birth in the Flesh, press through all Men, whereby he is become Lord and King of our Heaven and Earth, over Sin, Devil, Death and Hell ; in whom, we also press through the sinful corrupted Out-dead-birth of the Flesh, through Death and the wrath of God into our Heaven, in which Heaven now sitteth our King Jesus Christ, as an Almighty Son on the Right Hand of God, being present in all the three Births in this World in all corners and places, bearing up all, ruling in the Throne of the once potent (and now expelled) *Lucifer*.   *Whence our Lord Jesus came, and where also he now sitteth.*

7. When *Stephen* saw Heaven opened, and the Lord Jesus at the Right Hand of God, his Spirit did not swing it self up into the upper Heaven aloft, but penetrated into the innermost Birth.

Concerning the Constitution, and Form of the Earth.

8. Every thing must have a Root. The Earth is come from the corrupted Salitter of the outmost Birth ; for in Earth and Stones is Death, and in it is also a Life ; else Gold, Silver and Vegetables could not grow therein.   438.

9. Three Births are in it, the outmost is Death, the second is Life pressing through it, being in the Wrath Fire, and that of Love ; and the third is the Holy Life.   *Three Births of and in the Earth.*

10. In the outmost is Gods Wrath, else why engendereth it poysonous, venemous Worms and creeping Things?

11. The Earth hath more than one kind of Life ; for Herbs and Wood are not Earth, nor is Fruit Wood, nor is the vertue of the Fruit God ; for the outmost Birth containeth him not, but he containeth the Out-birth.

Q. *Why is the Earth so Mountany*, &c ?   441.

12. *A.* Where the sweet Water was chief, much earthy palpable Water came to be.

13. The corrupted Salitter was more abounding in one place than another. Also,

14. Where the Astringent Quality was chief in the bitterness in *Mercurius*, much Earth and Stones were compacted.

15. Where the Heat in the Light, much Silver and Gold, and some clear Stones.

16. Where the Love in the Light, the most precious Stones and finest Gold.

17. Where are great Lakes and Seas, over that *Zenith* (there being not much Salitter) there came to be a Valley, for which resting place the thin Water sought ; resembling the Spirit of meekness, not elevating it self as in the Bitter Fires quality the Devils did.

On

P. 446.   On the words, the Evening and Morning were the first day, is said.

18. Evening and Morning reacheth only up from the Earth to the Moon, taking its Original from the Light of the Sun, which maketh the outward day and the outward Night: Not that there was then a twofold Creation of Evening and Morning.
Query, Whether by it be not meant, by once turning about of the Earth, whereby the Evening and Morning came to be, that is, by one Revolution?
19. *A.* Man having a Threefold Birth, tho' with his inward he uniteth with the Light of God, cannot bring it perfectly back to his Astral, and less to his outward Birth, which tho' *Moses* did in part, when his Face shone, but could not see God perfectly and live; even as an Apple on a Tree cannot bring its Smell and Taste back into the Tree nor Earth.

CHAP. XX. *On the Creation in the Second Day,* Let there be a Firmament in the midst of the Waters, *&c.*

456.   1. THis Firmament divideth the impalpable, inward, pure Water from the outward, palpable, corrupted Water: Wherein is Death, which lyeth Captive below the Moon; and is the House of the Devils, Death and Hell where the fierce Wrath of God becometh kindled daily by the Devils through the great Sins of Men, which mix with the Astral Birth in the Deep.
2. But even those pure Waters, have some of the Wrath in them; and is that meant, where 'tis said, *The Heavens are not pure in his sight.*
3. The innermost holds the outward Water strongly Captive, and the outward Earth also, else with the Revolution of the Globe, the Water would be divided or dissolved, and the Earth crumble away. Which Firmament is between the clear Deity and corrupt Nature.
4. Yet the Deep above the Earth may be said to be a place where Gods Holiness dwelleth, for the whole Holy Trinity dwelleth in the Centre under the Firmament of Heaven, tho' that cannot comprehend him, but dwelleth not there fully, bodily, and creaturely, as the Angels and Souls of Men do.
467.
471.   5. The Third Birth is the Almighty Holy Heart of God, wherein Chrifts Natural Body sitteth; for his Natural Body is not as *John Calvin* thought, such as reacheth no farther than a little circumscribed place wherein it is.
6. For if every Man in his Astral Spirit comprehendeth the whole Body of this World, should not the Fountain Spirits in the Natural Body of Christ being out of the Fountain Spirits of Nature, and his Heart out of the inward Birth, *viz.* the Heart of God which comprehendeth all Angels and the Heaven of Heavens, *viz.* the whole Father should not it comprehend the whole World, and uphold it as the only Head, Heart and King of it, in his Hands are his Sheep whom none can pluck out.

CHAP. XXI.

485.   1. MAN is made out of the Seed, *viz.* Matrix of the Earth, wherein the Eye is Twofold, one in God, the other in this World out of the three Principles,

Principles, not out of the Wrath, but out of the Birth of the Earth, in the Aftral Birth in the part of Love, but Wrath hung to him, which he fhould have put forth from himfelf, as the Fruit putteth forth from it felf the bitterrefs of the Tree, but that he did not, but reached back from the Love into the Wrath, and lufted after his Dead or Mortal Mother to fuck her Breafts, and fo brought his outermoft Birth into Mortality, and his Aftral Birth or Life into the part of the Wrath. *Man whereof made, and what his Fall was.*

2. Man's Soul or Spirit is generated out of the Aftral, and is the third Birth in him: As an Apple on a Tree is the third Birth, which though it be United with the Word of God in its innermoft Birth, yet the Wrath being in the Mother of its Body, it remains palpable muft dye and rot: but at the laft Judgment Day, the Power of the Principle out of which the Apple groweth, fhall fpring anew in Paradice, and be a Fruit for Men in the other Life.

3. And Man's Body hath the fame Hope, for though the beftial Body muft putrifie, yet its vertue liveth in the four Elements in the Word: and there grows out of it beautiful Roles: and if thy Soul ftandeth in the Love, thou canft while thy Body liveth here, live and reign with God in Heaven, according to the Spirit of the Soul, which the Devil feeth not. *What in Man the Devil hath accefs to.*

4. But for that thy Aftral Birth ftandeth one part in the Wrath, the Devil feeth into that part (*.i&*) of the Wrath into thy Heart: where, if thou give him any room he teareth that part of the Aftral Birth which ftandeth in the Love, out from the Word, and then thy Heart is a dark Valley, and if thou labour not quickly to kindle the Light again, he kindleth the Wrath-fire, and then thou art a Devil, and into what thou haft fowed thy Seed, that is thy Soul, and in that part fhall thy Body arife.

The ftriving of the feven Spirits in the Earth, the Depth in the Centre. 498.

5. In the ftrife of the Aftringency, bitternefs and fweet water the Aftringency is Predominant, which is dry. The fweet quality is extenfive and yielding; yet the bitternefs and fweet quality ftruggle till the Aftringency dry and harden them, and thence, (from their unwilling Captivity) Anguifh rifeth up: juft as in a Dying Man, in this anxiety Heat rifeth, whereby a Sweat exhaleth as in one yielding to the Captivity of Death. That Sweat the Aftringent and bitter qualities lay hold on as their Son, which they had begotten on the fweet quality, which they had killed. *Strife of the 7 Spirits caufeth Vegetation.*

6. However the Aftringent being ftrong, and the Bitter fwift, from their Joy in their Son do ftuff it, that it fwells and grows full and great. And when the Aftringent ftriveth to captivate the Bitter, and the Body begins to be too ftreight or narrow, and that the ftrife there be too great, the Bitter muft yield, but cannot be kill'd, but leaps afide, and breaks out of the Body into Strings or Threads: taking the Son's fap with it. And this is Vegetation and growing of a Root in the Earth.

Q. *How can God be in this Vegetation?* 500.

7. *A.* That is the Vegetation of Nature, and if the wrath Fire were not in the three Qualities, *(viz.)* Aftringent, Sweet and Bitter; God might plainly be feen, but the Wrath makes the Aftringent a cold Fire, and its Attraction to be too hard: and maketh the Sweet too thick and dark: and the Bitter too raging and fweling, elfe they might kindle that Fire from whence the Light would exift, and from the Light, the Love, and from the fame Fire-flafh the Tone, and then would be a Heavenly Body, wherein the Light of God would and doth fhine, and then would be a Heavenly Fruit, as it fpringeth up in Heaven and the Light would generate it felf in the fweet-water, and there would be a bright fhining Heavenly Body where God is.   K k   8 But

8. But being the first three Qualities are benummed in Death, they remain a dark Eternal Prison, God's Wrath, Death and Hell a source of Torment. Not that the three Qualities are reprobated even to the innermost, but only the outward palpable Body, and therein the outward Hellish.

Commixture of Good with Evil,

9. Thus is seen how the Kingdom of God and of Hell hang one to another as one Body, and yet the one comprehendeth not the other, but the Heat, Light, Love and Sound are a kind of second Birth, making the outward moveable, and in the inward standeth the sound of God's Word, which seeing it riseth up through the Astringent, bitter Death, and generateth a Body in the half-dead Water, that Body is therefore Evil and Good, which may thus be demonstrated.

Demonstrated

10. One taking a Surfeit by any mortiferous Herb, Water, or unwholsom Flesh, let the same kind of Water, Herb or Flesh be distilled or burnt, whereby the outward Poison which standeth in Death is gone, the Astral Vigour remaineth (that Dead Body being gone) wherewith if good Treacle be mixed, which holdeth Captive the Wrath in the Astral Birth, and give it the Sick in warm Drink, then operateth the innermost Birth which hath diseased the Person, and Cureth. Whereby is seen, that the Power of the Eternal Life wrestleth in the Dead Earth in Anguish, but cannot bud till the Death be severed, which hangeth to it, for the Wrath is the Life of Death and of the Devil, wherein standeth their corporeal Bodies or Being, for the Dead Birth or Geniture is their Eternal House.

CHAP. XXII.

P. 533.

After other things in this Chapter, are the seven times Refining of Silver, and especially Gold, till it become Triumphing.

CHAP. XXIII.

342.

1. THE earnest and severe Birth or Geniture, out of which the Wrath of God, Hell and Death are come to be, hath been from Eternity in God: but not accensible nor elevable, not kindled or domineering, without which, severe Birth would be neither God, Life nor Heaven, Angel, nor Creature.

555. *The Gate of the Holy Trinity.*

2. The whole Birth of the Heaven of all Heavens, this World, the place of the Earth and of all Creatures, and wharever can be thought of, all that together is God the Father. And in every the least circle imaginable is the whole Birth of God perfectly perpetually and irresistably: but if in a Creature or Place the Light be extinguish'd, there is the Austere Birth, which lyeth hid in the Light in the innermost Kernel.

The Ubiquity of the Trinity.

3. The second Person is the Light, which is continually generated out of all the Powers, and enlighteneth again all the Powers of the Father; an instance whereof, is in the kindled Fires in this World, the innate Son is the meek Joy and Delight of the Father. Now the Father and the Son are equally great, the one could not be without the other. If the Jews, Turks and Heathen will convert, the Light will rise up in them gloriously.

4. The third Person is the moving Spirit of Life. Thus there is One God and Three

Three diſtinct Perſons, neither of them can comprehend, with hold or fathom the Original of the other.

5. If any will be Saints, and not Devils, let them generate in the meek, holy Law of God, elſe they ſhall Eternally generate in the auſtere ſevere Geniture of God's Wrath. But the Deity is a very ſimple, pure, meek, loving quiet, unanimous Being, through which the ſharpneſs of the innermoſt Birth can never elevate it ſelf, but remains hidden.

What the Deity is.

CHAP. XXIV. *Of the incorporating or Compaction of the Stars.*

1. GOD moved the whole Body of Nature contained in the Extent of this World, (on the 4th Day) which (though it was benummed) yet the Life was hid in it, and generated the ſtars out of Nature, ſo the Light roſe up making its Seat in the Houſe of Death, which Death could comprehend as little as Wrath doth Meekneſs.

2. As a Tree hath Life, Vegetation and Sap producing Fruit, which the dry Bark hath little of, through which the living Power thruſteth forth Twiggs, while the withered Rind harboureth Worms, which at laſt deſtroy the Tree. It is the Love which breaketh through the Houſe of Death, and is one Life with God.

3. The Stars are come out of the Power of the ſeven Spirits of God, for the Wrath of God was kindled by the Devil: and the Out-birth as droſs and ſcum was driven together, whence came Earth and Stones; for the Body of God as to this World could not remain in Death, but the corrupted Nature with its palpability, hath remained in Death, and is the Houſe of Devils; therefore God created new Angels, (*viz.*) *Adam*, and would bar up *Lucifer* in the outer Darkneſs.

P. 568.
Stars whence.

Q. *Why had not this been done inſtantly, and then he had not done ſo much Miſchief?*

4. A. God purpoſed to make an excellent Angelical Army out of the Earth, and all Vegetations after a Heavenly manner, and then Extract the Heart or Kernel at laſt, and ſeparate it from Death, and the Death of the Earth and Wrath therein ſhould be *Lucifer's*, who in the mean time ſhould, and now doth, lye Captive in the Deep above the Earth.

570.
Lucifer's Place at preſent.

5. But that there are ſo many Stars of differing Operations, ſhews God's Infiniteneſs, and their continuance ſhews there ſhall be a conſtant Uniform Birth.

Q. *When the Devil and his Angels fell, why had not God inſtantly bolted him up in the place where he fell?*

6. A. What Sin hath the Salitter committed that it ſhould ſtand totally in Eternal ſhame? None; therefore God willed to uſe it as a Dwelling for the new Race of Angels, *Adam* and his Children, and leave only the kindled fierceneſs to the Devil, which had it been all left to the Devil, out of it could not a new Body have been built.

7. The Stars are a ſharp Birth and innermoſt Geniture, which had their firſt kindling from Heaven, and God uſeth them as an Inſtrument to the wreſtling fighting Birth, and to anxiety, for on the third Day the anxiety in the Birth of this World, rub'd it ſelf, whence the Fire flaſh exiſted, and the Light of the Stars kindled it ſelf in the Water of Life, till the third Day Nature was a dark Valley, and then Life brake through Death, and the new Birth began; for ſo long Jeſus Chriſt reſted in Death. The old Body which ſtandeth in the auſtereneſs is a Houſe to the Devil, but the new to the Kingdom of Chriſt.

Stars and for what.

K k 2   CHAP.

CHAP. XXV.

P. 590. 1. Every Star hath a peculiar Property, as may be perceived by the various curious Ornament of the blossoming Earth, which variety should have kindled the old Body into so many Powers to break forth through the Wrath, that the new Life might have all the Powers, that ever the old had before the times of the Wrath, which new Body blossomed at the Creation, but Nature being by Man more corrupted, God Cursed the Ground, for Man took hold of the Fruit of the old Body; wherefore the Fruit of the new was hidden, and the bestial Body had *Eves* Wrath Apples to Eat.

594. 2. Concerning the Sun. As far as the middle Point or Centre hath kindled it
What the Sun self just so big is the Sun, for that is the Sun. The Light of the Meekness of the
is. Sun uniteth with the pure Deity, and were the great Heat taken away from the Sun it would be one Light with God, but the Heat cannot comprehend the Light; therefore the place of the Sun remaineth in the Body of God's Wrath.

598. 3. The Sun hath its royal place to it self, whence it moveth not, but the Earth
The Sun moves rolls about every 24 Hours: and compasseth the place of the Sun once every
not, the Earth Year, as do the other Planets; but *Saturn*, *Jupiter* and *Mars* by reason of their
rouls as do the great height, cannot do it so soon.
Planets. 1 The Life of a Creature is in the Heat of the Heart, so is the Sun to the whole
606. Deep. 2. The Gall is not exiled from the Heart, but yet is the Mobility or stirring of the Heart, by a Vein that goeth from the one to the other; so is *Mars.* 3. The Brain is the Power of the Heart, so is *Jupiter*. The Astral Birth stands with one Root in the Holy Heaven, and with the Corporeity is in the Wrath.

CHAP. XXVI.

609. 1. Saturn is Cold and Astringent, and takes not his Power from the Sun, but
Saturn what. as the Sun is the Heart of he Life, so is *Saturn* the beginner of Corporeity, and of all Formings, and as *Jupiter* is of the Brain, so is this of the Skull: his place is in the midst between *Jupiter* and the general Sphere of the fixed Stars.

612. 2. *Venus* is a gracious kindler of Love in Nature: for when the two Spirits of
Venus what. the Life and Mobility were risen up out of the place of the Sun, *viz.* *Mars* and *Jupiter*, then the Meekness as a Seed of the Water, pressed downward with the Power of Light, whence existed the Love of Life, or Planet *Venus*: mitigating the fierceness of *Mars*, and humbling *Jupiter*; else the Brains would break through the Brain Pan: and transmute it self in high-mindedness, in the manner of Proud Lucifer.

617. 3. Of *Mercurius*. The seven Spirits of God are perfectly in every place, but if in any one place they wrestle not triumphingly, in that place is no Mobility, but
The Ubiquity a deep Darkness: such a House is the House of Flesh in Man, such was the whole
of the 7 Spi- space of this World, when the Deity, in the 7 Spirits had withdrawn it self from
rits of God, the Devils: and had so continued, if the seven Planets and Stars had not risen
from them from God's Spirits. but the Heart of the Deity hideth it self in the Corporeity
came the 7 and Out-birth of this World; which therefore is in great Anguish, till the Heart
Planets. of God will move it self again in the seven Spirits of God in this Word, and
kindle

kindle them, and then the Sun and Stars will pass away again, to their first place, and the Light of God shall fill all the Body of this World, and when the anxiety tasteth the sweetness of the Light of God, all is richly full of Joy, and the whole Body triumpheth, which now cannot be: because the fierce captive Devil keeps House in the Out-birth of this World, till the last Judgment Day, and then the Heart of God with his Fan will cleanse his Flour, and breaking through, Proclaim bright Day.

4. The Earth is the Fruit of the seventh Spirit of God, but Man's Body is far more Noble, being an Extracted Mass out of the Salitter, out of the seventh Nature-Spirit. *P. 627. Man's Body.*

5. When the Seed is generated, the Astringent Spirit draweth together a Mass out of the sweet Water: that is out of the Unctuosity of the Blood of the Heart; which Oyl or Sap hath in it the Root of the whole Man; as Tinder cast into Straw. *630.*

6. But if the Light had kindled it self in the Birth of the Soul, all the Fountain Spirits (according to the right of the Deity) had triumphantly United with the Deity, and had been a living Angel: but because the Wrath had already infected the Salitter; that Danger was to be feared which befell Lucifer; therefore, the Extract whereof Man's Body was made, was not become Earth, though it was of the Salitter of the Earth, but was held by the Word, till the Love-Spirit, out of the Heart of God glanced on the Salitter of the Mass: then did the Salitter become impregnated in the Centre of the Soul, and the Light abode in the Centre of the Mass, and the Word flood in the Mass in the Sound. *637. Man's Body whereof made.*

This Book was Written by *J. B.* in the Year 1612. Being his first Book. It was taken from the Author, and not finished, but that Defect supplied in his other Writings.

Auroræ Finis.

THE

THE
Three Principles
OF THE
Divine Essence.

CHAP. I. *Of the First Principle of the Divine Essence.*

1. Though God generateth the Essence of all Essences out of Himself; for through Him and in Him are all things, yet Evil is not God. And though the first Principle be the earnest Fountain of Tartness, and Cause of all Mobility; yet if that be irradiated with Divine Light, it is no more Wrath or Tartness, but great Joy.

2. Though also God hath no Beginning, it is here set down as if he had, to distinguish the first from the second Principle. Although it cannot be said that Bitterness, Sorrow, or Hell Fire are in God; for God made no Devil nor Death, yet those things are in Nature, and Nature originateth from God, according to the first Principle of the Father, whoso is call'd Angry, not in himself but in the Spirit of the Creature, which hath enkindled it self, and the Wrath of God burneth therein.

3. God is the incomprehensible Infinite Spirit. A Spirit doth ever nothing but ascend, flow, move and generate it self, in a Threefold Form, *viz.* Bitterness, Harshness, and Heat, neither of which is the first or last; for a Spirit is like a Will which rising up, beholdeth, perfecteth and generateth it self.

4. Three things are in the Original, whence all things came to be, Sulphur, Mercurius and Sal. In Sulphur is Soul or Spirit and Matter. In Mercury is harshness, Bitterness, Fire and Water, of which four Sal is the Child. From harshness, bitterness and fire in the first Principle, come wo, torment, trembling, and burning; yet from those three, is also generated Water. But in the first Principle God is not called God, but a devouring Fire.

CHAP. II. *Of the first and second Principles, what God and the Divine Nature is.*

1. THE Divine Essence cannot be expressed by the Tongue, the *Spiraculum vitæ*, the Spirit of the Enlighten'd Soul seeth it; for every Creature seeth no farther, than to its own Mother, whence it originated. The Soul was breathed

out

out of God's first Principle into the third Principle (*viz.*) into the Syderial and Elementary Birth, it is not therefore marvellous that it should see the whole depth of the Father in the first Principle; it so seeing only it self in its rising. The Devils also see and know it, they wish also they neither saw nor felt it, but themselves shut themselves up from the second Principle.

2. The Sydereal Spirit which cloatheth the Soul, and the Elementary which ruleth the Fountain of the Blood, see only into that whence themselves are. But the Spirit of the Soul enlightned by the Holy Spirit of God, seeth into the Holy Divine Birth, the Heavenly Essence, the second Principle. This Door can be opened only by Prayer, seeking and knocking.

3. In the Syllable phur in Sulphur are signified, the four Forms of harshness or astringency, bitterness or attraction, anguish and fire; but in the Sul of Sulphur, is the Soul or Spirit meant, which when it attaineth the Light, the fifth Form of Love springeth up, the Bridegroom embraceth his sacred Bride.

4. Hence by the Water Spirit in *Mercurius* ariseth the sixth Form or sound, so are all in one Heavenly Harmony united in the Divine Nature, yet every Form retains its own Property, so that here existeth a cross Birth, for the fire goeth upward, the Water downward, the Essences of the harshness sideways, as it were East, West, North and South.

CHAP. III. *Of the endless and innumerable Productions of the Eternal Nature.*

1. Such as by reproach forbid a search what God is, prosecute the Devil's deceit; that it might not be known what the Anger of God is, nor what the Devil is, and what properly it is which God Abhors. Ability is in Man to speak what God our Father is, and what the Eternal worketh.

2. Every of the six Forms generateth more; for in every of the Fountain Spirits is but one Centre, and each generateth more, as out of one branch issue many sprigs and buds, and out of one root many threads.

3. Out of the harsh Spring proceed five Springs, (*viz.*) Bitterness, Fire, Love, Sound and Water, and in their Co-operating through Anguish, the Light and Life arise, and the Anguish becomes in the sixfold Form, a great Joy: in a meer pleasing Tast, delighting Sight, reviving Smell, ravishing Sound, the softest Touch all unutterably Excellent. So as if one were instantly snatcht out of the bitter Pangs of Death and Torments of Hell into the Triumphant Light of Divine Joy.

4. For, the Forms of harshness, bitterness and fire being perfect in Love, become totally Glorious, and a Highest Joy, and yet their various Properties remain, all perfectly irradiated.

CHAP. IV. *Of the Eternal Essence generating Infinity of Existencies.*

1. The Eternal generating hath neither Beginning, Number, End, Bottom, nor is it Corrupted: The Mind of the Syderael and Elementary Spirit seeth only a glimpse of it, which Mind is the Chariot of the Soul, without which Mind the Soul were feeble and cruce in the first Principle; but if the Soul be regenerated in the Light of God, that Light is its lustre in the second Principle, wherein it liveth Eternally.

2. Man's Body was made out of the one Element, the Quinteſſence, whence alſo the four Elements, Stars and Heaven of the third Principle were created. But the Soul was breath'd by the Holy Ghoſt out of the Father's Light, which Light being the Name of God is the Light of Life, and enkindled out of the four Anguiſhes; therefore is the Soul God's own Subſtance.

3. If therefore the Soul elevate it ſelf back, into the Anguiſhes of the four Original Forms into Pride &c. it becomes a Devil. But if it elevate it ſelf forward, in the fifth Form of Light, Meekneſs, and lovely Humility, it is fed by the Word, the Heart of God, and its own ſtrong fierce Original becomes Paradiſical, a ſweet Fountain of Eternal Songs of Praiſe, it is an Angel, a Child of God, and hath Ability to ſpeak of the indiſſolvable band, but not of the infinite generating; for the immeaſurable ſpace of the Deity hath neither Beginning nor End.

Of the ſublime Gate of the *Holy Trinity.*

(v. 56.)
4. The Father is the Original Eſſence of al Eſſences, in whom, if the Son the ſecond Principle were not Eternally generated, the Father, according to the firſt Principle, would be a zealous, wrathful, dark Principle; for the Son is as the Light out of the Fire, the Heart, Brightneſs and Love of the Father, who is in his Son merciful, reconciled and well pleaſed. The Son is another manner of Perſon than the Father, hath another centre of meer Joy and Love. The Holy Ghoſt proceedeth from both in the enkindling of the Light, as out of the Water Fountain of Humility, is alſo an Almighty Spirit making out of the vertue of the Light an infinite number of Centres, of a ſweet ſmell and ſweet taſt.

The Deſcription of *Lucifer,* &c. I Abridge not here, having done it more fully in the 13th Chapter of *Aurora,* page 250.

CHAP. V. *Of the third Principle the Creation of the Material World, and farther clearing of the firſt and ſecond Principles.*

1. A Principle is a Birth. Therefore he that is Born of God, may know the third Principle by his own new Birth. The terror of God's Wrath, the horror and anguiſh of his Eſtate, Sin and Darkneſs was his firſt Principle. His pure Divine Joy in being born again, is his entring into the new Life or ſecond Principle.

2. In the firſt Principle is the indiſſoluble band, which is a Genitrix in it ſelf inanimate, wherein, by the moving Spirit of God, out of that incomprehenſible Matrix, the comprehenſible viſible Water proceeded, in ſuch various manner as the Spirit willed: for out of the fifth Form of it, was enkindled the fiery Heaven and Conſtellation or Quinteſſence, where the Light originateth, whence the Sun was Born, which opened and enlivened the third Principle of the Material World; as the Heart of God in Paradiſe doth in that pure immaterial Heaven, opening the Eternal Power and Wiſdom of God.

3. The outward third Principle is the Similitude or Repreſentation of the inward Paradiſical World, in which Angels and Man were Created, and ſhould not have known the Original of the four Elements, wherein by the Fall of *Lucifer* was Evil and Good, but now the Knowledge of it is highly neceſſary that we may fly from the beſtial Man, and learn to know the true Man.

CHAP. VI. *Of the Separation in Creating the Third Principle.*

1. BY the Separation of the Creatures the Sun, Stars, Elements, yea in our selves and in all things, and their particular Properties, the Eternal Mother is seen.

2. The generated World becomes a Genitrix, not sundered from the Eternal, but by the Sun hath attain'd another Light, and Life, but is not the Eternal Light, Life or Wisdom it self.

3. Out of the Paradifical Heaven, Water, Spirit or Matrix is the Material Heaven created. For, when *Lucifer* would Domineer, the dark Matrix attracted so, as the Earth, Stones, Metals, Salt, &c. proceeded: which shut him up, but the vertue remaining in the Matrix producing Light, made also Gold, Silver, Copper, &c. The Spirit of God without departing from his own Eternal Paradifical Seat, by the *Fiat* moved on the Material hath deadned Water, and created the Heaven, which once separated from the dark Mist whereof was the Earth, the Elements of Air, Fire and Water, though one in another, appeared.

CHAP. VII. *Of the Eternal Birth of Heaven, and generating the four Elements, &c.*

1. NO Spirit nor Man can (of his own Power) possibly see into any other Principle but in which he is, or is regenerated into. Man whose Soul is out of the first Principle his Body outwardly of the Stars and Elements, and inwardly of the one Element (if illustrated by the second Principle) hath great might of Miracles, raising the Dead, &c. such may well see into the three Principles; the Spirit of which it is Born searcheth the deep things of the Deity.

2. Other Men Swim between the Vertue of the Stars and Elements as the Created Heavens do, between the Divine and Hellish Kingdoms, as doth Man also, and to which of them he falls and yields himself, in that is he regenerated.

3. The Light of God is a cause of all the three Principles. But for that, there would be no longing and attraction in the dark Eternity, and the Father is the first desiring and longing after the Son, thence the Eternal Nature is ever longing. So the brightness or Heart of the Father in the dark *Matrix* generateth the third Principle, for so is God manifest, who else would be Eternally hidden.

4. Therefore, O Noble Man, though thou art stept with *Adam* out of Paradice into the third Principle, set thy great desire and longing of thy Heart, on the Heart of God, and his Kingdom will be taken by force, seek God in thy Soul, there stands all the three Principles: The Divine Birth it self, the Pearl, the Paradifical Garden do all stand open in a holy Soul.

5. The true place of God is every where, the Centre of the Earth, he comprehendeth Hell it self. All things are of him and from him. And yet the out or procreated Birth is not from his Essence or Substance, but from the Darkness,

The Three Principles of the Divine Essence.

And, 1. The Fountain of the Darkness is the first Principle. 2. The Vertue and Power of the Light is the second Principle. 3. The Out-birth generated out of the Darkness by the power of the Light is the third Principle. In a similitude.

6. 1. Your Soul-giving Reason representeth God the Father. 2. The Light shining in the Soul, represents the Son. 3. The vertue proceeding from that Light, whereby the whole Body is directed, represents the Holy Ghost.

7. 1. The Darkness in you, which longeth after the Light, is the first Principle.

2. The power of the Light, by which you see in your Mind, without Bodily Eyes, is the second Principle.

3. The vertue proceeding from the Mind, impregnating it self, whence the Material Body groweth, is the third Principle : Between each of which is an inclosure, knot or stop.

8. God sever'd the Fiery Starry Heaven or Quintessence, from the watery Matrix; else there would have been no end of generating of Stones : That done, the watery became clear, and still the fiery longeth after the watery as the Husband of it, and the watery as the Wife is impregnated thereby, by which the Elements and all Minerals, Vegetables, *&c.* as Children, are proceeded.

9. Every Form in the Matrix hath its visible Creatures, but invisible to us, unless they will manifest themselves; for tho' the Elements are Members one of the other, and receptacles one of the other, yet each comprehendeth but it self: Nor do the Spirits of the Air, Water, and Fire comprehend more, than of their own Birth or peculiar World. As the Body seeth not the Syderial and Elementary Spirit, nor that the Soul tho' one be in another.

CHAP. VIII. *Of the Creation, Vegetation and Constellation, and Original Substance of this World.*

I Forbear Abridgment of this Chap. contenting my self with research of the Extracts of the 4th, 5th, 6th and 7th Chapters of this Book, and of the 18th and 19th Chapters of *Aurora*.

CHAP. IX. *Of Paradise.*

1. A Dam was in the Garden of *Eden*, and in Paradise, but *Eden* was not Paradise. The Tree of Good and Evil in *Eden*, grew as those whereof we eat, which are Evil and good. But Paradise is another Principle. The Spirit of the World cannot, much less can any Creature comprehend it.

2. It consists in exact Perfection, no Evil Creature or Thing can reach it, Angels Knowledge and Tongues are requir'd to express it. None can come therein but by the new Birth, and true resignation. The Holy Ghost hath, and is the Key.

3. Paradise is not corporeal and palpable, but consisteth in the Vertue and Power of God, its corporeity, is like the Angels bright and transparent Substances, its Birth immeasurable, immutable, a constant Spring in perfect Love.

4. Fruits grow there in such Figure as here, but not in such property, its Root is the Heavenly Matrix. The Eternal Father is instead of the activity of the Stars. The Light of God instead of the Sun. The Holy Ghost is the Air. No years nor time

The Three Principles of the Divine Essence.

time is there. There is a figur'd substance of all this Worlds Creatures, and the figur'd substance of all words that came from the Divine Root stand there also.

The Holy Gate.

5. Nothing is nearer us than Heaven, Paradise, and Hell: There is a Birth between them, yet both Gates stand in us. The Devil stands in one calling and beckening, and in his hand is Power, Honour and Pleasure, the Root of which is Death and Hell Fire. God calleth in the other Gate, and in his hand are Crosses, Persecutions, Poverty, Misery, Ignominy and Sorrow, and the Root of these is Fire also, and in the Fire a Light, and in the Light a Vertue, and in the Vertue Paradise, and in Paradise the Angels, and among the Angels Joy: Take which of the two thou wilt.

6. The third Principle of us belongs not to Paradise, and sees it not, till it rot in the Earth, and rise a new Vertue: But the regenerated Soul sees it, being a Child of Paradise.

7. After the time of this World the Out-birth returns to its Æther, but the Figures of all Creatures remain, as also of all words and works in either Kingdoms, in which they were sown, and then Angels and Blessed Men will remain in the Birth of the Divine Light, and the Devils and wicked Men in Eternal Darkness, for being Created out of the harsh Matrix out of which the Light of God existed from Eternity, they cannot go back into Transitoriness. Therefore seek the Pearl of Divine Meekness and Patience, and finding it you will be throughly taught, and in it find Paradise and the Kingdom of Heaven.

CHAP. X. *Of the Creation of Man, of his Soul, and of Gods Breathing in.*

Though I have met with more of this Subject in the 21 ft Chap. of the *Aurora*, and in the 5th Chap. of the Book of Election. Also in the 3d, 4th, 5th, to the 8th Chap. of the Book of the Incarnation, and in the 16th Chap. of the *Mysterium Magnum*, yet taking it also briefly here, do observe and collect as follows.

1. *Adam* was Created with the Vertue of all the three Principles in him, the Heavenly Centre was fixt, and was to have remained so, and the Earthy not to have been awakened; for though as the similitude of God, he had the dark Fountain or first Principle, and the Out-birth, viz. the Properties of all the Creatures in him, yet was he to live and act in neither of those two, but in the second Principle, that of Light and Paradise only: And in that Divine Light, rule over the Stars, Elements, and all Creatures.

2. For *Adam's* very Body being of that holy Element or Quintessence whence the Stars and Elements originated, besides the Royal Soul he had, he was to have been incorruptible, tho' the Stars and Elements had returned into their Æther.

3. He was without distinct Female, to generate out of his will (without rending or dividing his Body, or Anguish, or Misery) an Angelical Hoft.

4. His Bones, were Strengths or Powers, no need of Guts and Entrails, Teeth or Bestial Members, no dark, opake Body, nor hardness, no sleep, sickness, or any kind of evil, which arose by the prevalency and inequality of the afterward divided Elements.

5. This

266   *The Three Principles of Divine Essence.*

5. This God did for *Adam*, and intended most mercifully towards him, and gave his own Heart to redeem him. He fell not by reason of Gods Decree, as the Devil suggesteth: Nor was the Tree of Good and Evil planted to try him but the Tree sprung up in the will of *Adam* and *Eve*, and standeth yet in us, not in God. Nor cometh the punishment from his Hand, but from *spiritu majoris mundi*, the Macrocosm the third Principle.

Ver. 34.

Q.

A.

6. To attain this knowledge, see, in the mind of Man lyeth, and thence proceedeth Joy and Sorrow, Hope, and Doubting, Love and Hatred, Meekness and Wrath. The Question is, May not the Mind stand in one only Will and Essence? A. If it did so, then it would have but one quality, an immoveable stilness, no will to any thing, a meer nothing, no knowledge, wisdom or joy.

7. Therefore in God (whose Image Man is) is an Eternal Mind, which generateth the Eternal Will, and the Eternal Will generateth the Eternal Heart of God, the Eternal Heart of God generateth the Eternal Light, the Eternal Light generateth the Eternal Vertue, the Vertue generateth the Spirit. And again the Spirit generateth the Mind, this is the Eternal, Almighty, Unchangeable God.

8. So in Man, the Mind standeth in Anguish, and the Anguish maketh a longing, and that longing is the Will, the Fathers Property. The Will conceiveth the Vertue and Light, and is the Sons Property. And in the Light, out of the Vertue, proceeds the Spirit, and is the Property of the Holy Ghost, which again generateth the Mind and Will, so is made the indissoluble Band.

9. Thus *Adam's* Mind and longing Will should have abode in the Vertue of the Light, which had ill strated his first Principle, and by his Spirit should have ruled over the third Principle, did by going into the third Principle, and eating thereof, subject himself thereunto, and had not his noble Soul hindered, had become a meer Beast.

10. But the Gracious God inspoke his Word again into him, and to redeem so fair a Creature, sent his own Heart, that the unchangeable purpose of God might stand, to bring again the same Image in the Resurrection into Paradise, which was at first created in it and for it.

11. But *Lucifer* generated a fiery Will in the first Principle, who should have generated a Loving, Meek, Angelical Will, and extinguisht the Light, which was the end of Nature. No help was for him, for to give him more Divine Light, were but as Water to increase his Fire. And God willeth to have no fiery Spirit in Paradise, his Brimstone Spirit is inkindled, and remaineth unquenchable, desiring to get above the Meekness of the Heart of God, which shuts him up Eternally.

CHAP. XI. *Of all Circumstances of the Temptation.*

1. WHen God did set the *Fiat* in the Will to Create Angels, he separated all the Properties as hard, four, bitter, harsh, fierce, soft, *&c.* (as we see are in the various properties of the Stars) and created the Princely Throne Angels as so many Fountains. Then in each Fountain came forth a Centre, in many Thousand Thousands, and every Host got a Will, such as was the Fountain or Prince whence they proceeded, giving their will to him as the Stars do to the Sun. Tho' all thoroughly irradiated with Divine Splendor, yet had every Host some one of the Properties of the first Principle, most Eminent in them.

2. Of the Princes one is fallen and his Host; for, standing in the fourth form his Fire Elevated him above the End of Nature.

3. The

The Three Principles of the Divine Essence. 267

3. The *Fiat* in the Creation, separated the Matrix also of the Out-birth, created after the other according to the forms of the inward World, and out of the Properties of the first Principle, came Creatures of all sorts good and bad as Lambs, Doves, *&c.* as also Wolves, Toads; also in the separation of Vegetables are good, and hurtful Plants. And that the evil is also profitable, is seen, for that in every Creature is a poysonous Gall, being the cause of Life.

4. *Adam* was created of all the three Principles, but in perfect clarity an Image of his Creator, and Epitomy of all Creatures.

5. In the Garden of *Eden* were all Paradisical Trees, pleasant to look on, and good for Food, wherein, tho' they sprung out of the Earth, yet in them, was imprinted the Divine Vertue of the second Principle, and yet were truely in the third Principle. Death stuck only in that Tree of Good and Evil; that, was able to bring Man into another Image.

6. God willed not *Adam* should eat of it; for he not only barely warned him of the danger, but forbad him with a severe Menace.

7. Nor was he Created with a distinct Female as other Creatures that on his Fall he might the better be helped.

8. Nor will'd, he should need any other clothing than Glory, else would have given him a Hide as other Creatures. But as a Heavenly Man he should have eaten Heavenly Fruit. Now follows the Gate of the Temptation.

Adam had all the three Principles or Worlds in him, and in all he looked on without him.

9. The Heart of God would have him to abide in Paradise being his similitude. The Kingdom of Wrath would have this great Lord because he proceeded out of the Eternal Mind of the Darkness that through him might be shew'd great power. The Kingdom of this World would have him be his Housholder for that he lived in it, and was part of it, saying, Eat and Drink not only Divine Food; thou art not yet a meer Spirit, eat not that which is incomprehensible. Eat my sweet, drink my strong which is comprehensible.

10. Here *Adam* thought, seeing I am on the Earth, and that it is mine I will use it as I list.

11. Then came the Inhibition, on pain of Death, not to eat the Earthy Food, wherein was mixt the evil, for the Tree was neither better nor worse than that we have. But God saw his eager imagination so set on the Earthy Fruit, that he could not generate a perfect Paradisical Man, but an Infected one out of himself, that would fall to be corruptible, did let a sleep fall on him.

CHAP. XII. *Further of the Circumstances of the Temptation.*

1. **M**Oses at the Bush was commanded to pull off his Shoes shewing his Earthy Birth.

God gave the Law at *Sinai* and establisht it in clarity, but by Thunders, *&c.* in the Spirit of the great World (for in Gods Heart is only Love and Kindness) because after the Fall Men lived therein, *viz.* in the Spirit of the great World.

2. The Law demanding obedience, and the false voluptuousness of *Israel* were in strife Forty days till they fell to their sinful Calf. And Christs tryal Forty days, *&c.* * shew the time of *Adam*'s Temptation.

Of Adam's Sleep.

1. *Adam*'s sleep was his being Captivated by the striving Stars and Elements, whose

* *See Chap.* 18. *of Mysterium Magnum.*

The Three Principles of the Divine Essence.

whose wrestling so far overcame him, that his Tincture became enfeebled, and he as dead, who should (as we in the Resurrection) have Eternally with open Eyes beheld the Infinite Glories. This God so greatly loathed, that *Adam* could not long continue in Paradise.

The Highest Gate of the Life of the Tincture.

What the Tincture is.

2. The Tincture is that which separateth the pure from the impure, and graduateth to the highest all sorts of Life in all Creatures: Yet in some strong in others weak. Its Birth is from the Vertue of the Deity, and imprints it self in all things, yet so secretly, that none of the ungodly can know it: It is Eternal, but the Spirit given it by the *Fiat* is according to the kind of every Creature. At first it was implanted in Jewels, Gems, Metals.

3. It was generated in the fifth form, that of Love out of the Heart of God. And tho' its Spirit in the third Principle abide not for ever, yet, for the sake thereof, the very figures of this World shall remain for ever. But in the second Principle, the Tincture standing in the Spirit and Substance in Angels and Men is Eternally fixt.

The Tinctures Essences.

Tinctures Essences.

4. It is the flash of Life and Lustre whose Root is Fire causing the faculty of seeing in all Creatures. It Chrystallizeth impure Water, separateth the Light from Darkness, imageth it self in what it hath made pure, making it also sweet, shining like Oyl and Fire. Mixt with the Matrix of Water by the mixture becomes fixt and thick, and by the Property of the Fire is colour'd Red, and is the Blood in which the Noble Life existeth.

Of the Death and Dying.

5. In so great and hourly danger stands the Noble Life in the Tincture, and hath so many potent Enemies, that either on the Efflux of the Blood the Tincture flyeth away, or on the over-prevalency of any one of the four Elements, or ill Conjunction of the Constellations darting their Poisons the Band of Life breaketh and the flash goeth out in Meekness.

How the Heavenly Tincture was in Adam *before the Fall, and shall be in us after this Life.*

6. *Adam's* three Principles whereof he was, were three Births, the one not comprehended by the other, *viz.* The Worm or Brimstone Spirit, generated out of the Eternal Will of the Father. The Virgin or Wisdom of God. And the Spirit of this World. The two latter were given to him, to his right and left.

Heavenly Tincture.

7. The second was to illustrate the first, in the power whereof he was to rule over the third. It is possible for a Soul, by reaching back into the might of the Fire or first four forms, and becoming false to the Virgin (the Wisdom of God) to shut the Door of the Virgin, and lose the good of the third Principle; which cannot be obtained again, but by a new Birth wrought by the Holy Ghost. Such a Regeneration restores true Honour and Joy, but without it, at the Death of the Body the Soul remains a Serpent, or Worm that never dies, and the figures only of the other two principles remain, to compleat its horrour that he may see what an Angelical Form he hath irrecoverably lost. Thus *Adam* lost the Virgin by his Lust, and got the Woman in his Lust.

8. By

The Three Principles of the Divine Essence.

8. By the above appears what *Adam* was, *viz.* having the Tincture of the perfect Male and Female Properties.

9. The Temptation was the Spirit of the VVorld being the third Principle, like a young Man of good Complexion, Vertuous and Beautiful, having forty days and nights sweet Converse and Embraces of a perfectly Fair, curiously Featur'd, modest Virgin of Gods Wisdom, in meer Joy, with command that their Will be most stedfast, so as not in the least thought to desire one another, but as chastly as if they were each unknown or unseen to the other, and so to remain in the *Proba* forty days and nights.

10. The Spirit which God had breathed into *Adam* was the chast Virgin, which *Adam's* worldly Spirit should have loved with a pure Mind, but he desired her with Terrene Lust, which was his Fall.

11. But by being Born again, of Water (which is in the Centre) and of the Holy Spirit, the Soul is cleansed from impure Affections, and inflam'd with Divine and Sacred Love.

CHAP. XIII. *Of Creating the Woman.*

1. *Adam's* Tincture being wearied in the strife of the three Principles, his Lust Spirit prevailing, he sunk into sleep, his Heavenly Body became Flesh and Blood, his strength Bones, the Virgin withdrew into her Heavenly Ether, where she waiteth to see if any will by the new Birth receive her for their Bride.

2. *Adam's* Angelical Kingdom was gone, he now must generate a worldly Kingdom, by a Female, as other Beasts: Which that God abominated appears by his making Man at first without a Female, and said all was very good, also that the first Child was a Murtherer, and that God cursed the Earth, *&c.*

3. But God, that he might help vanquisht *Adam*, of one of his Ribs built a Woman. That is. * The *Fiat* stood in the Centre, and sever'd the *Matrix* from the *Limbus*, took part of *Adam's* substance, *viz.* of his Spirit, Flesh and Bones, which then were not so hard till *Eve* did bite the Apple: So they were two, yet undivided in Nature, and both must generate one Man, which before one should have done.   * *Ver.* 12.

4. *A pleasant Gate.* As little as the Spirit of the Soul could be helped except the Virgin by entring into the Abyss of the Spirit of the Soul (which is near the Hell of Gods fierce anger) had regenerated by Jesus Christ, so little could the rent in *Adam's* hollow side (whence the Rib was taken) be made perfect, except the second *Adam* had suffered the Wound in the same place to pour out his precious Blood, and so repair the first *Adam's* breach made in the same place.

5. *Further of the Woman.* *Eve* was not made of the Rib only, but of all *Adam's* Essences, yet of no more Members than the Rib, which causeth her feebleness, and is by Gods command in subjection to the Man, and to be friendly to him. Also the Man must help her, and love her as his own Essences. And they being but one Flesh, Bone and Heart, must have but one will: And their Children are neither of the one, nor of the other, but of both: As if only of one, which causeth the severe command that they honour and be in subjection to Father and Mother on pain of Temporary and Eternal Punishment.

6. *The Noble propagation of the Soul.* The Tincture is generated from all the three Principles, yet hath neither, for its own, but is a bright Habitation in which the Spirit dwelleth. It reneweth the Spirit that it becometh clear and visible. Its Name is Wonderful, known only to them that have it. It giveth Vertue to, *What the Tincture is and doth.*

and

and is the Life and Heart of all things. It is the fragrancy of Herbs and Flowers, and causeth them as also Silver and Gold to grow; though of all the Children of Nature it be a Virgin, and generateth nothing out of it self. It is the Friend and Play-fellow of God. The way to it is very near. Whosoever findeth it dare not reveal it, nor can he, for no Language can express it, yet it is not God. It may be over-powered and uſed in Metals, if it be pure, it can make pure Gold, of Iron and Copper, and make a little grow to be a great deal. Its way is as ſubtle as the thoughts of a Man, for thence riſe the thoughts.

7. *The propagation in the Fleſh.* So great is the ſubtilty and might of the Tincture as to penetrate the Marrow in the Bones of another, which Witches know and practiſe; for their Maſter *Lucifer* thought to exalt his falſe Tincture above Gods.

8. The Male and Female Tinctures, tho' different, yet both long after the Virgin the Tincture of the Male goeth out of the *Limbus*, that of the Female out of the *Matrix*. And in the delicate Complexions where the Tincture is moſt noble and clear, the ardent vigour of each thinketh to find the Virgin in the other, tho' it be in neither. And from the mixed deſire proweth the Body, and in the wreſtling the Conqueror giveth the marks of diſtinction. The Spirit of the great World thinketh it hath the Virgin which it hath not.

9. *The ſecret Gate of Women.* The Seed is ſown in the Luſt of the Tinctures, and the harſh, ſour *Fiat* ſuppoſing it to be the Virgin, attracteth the Seed to it with great joy, deſiring the *Limbus* of God in Paradiſe, but the Spirit of the great World inſinuateth and filieth the Tincture with the Elements, whence comes a loathing againſt the fulneſs; for the Virgin Tincture reliſheth not ſuch groſſneſs, but retires into its Ether. Then the pirit of the Sun, Stars and Elements doth by the *Fiat* attract and foſter the Child.

Saturn. 10. In the firſt Month the harſh *Fiat* in which ruleth the Spirit of the Stars perceiving the Blood of the Mother wherein is the Tincture to be ſweeter than its own Eſſence, it longeth to image it ſelf therein, and Create *Adam*.

Jupiter. In the ſecond Month the Matter is ſever'd into Members according to the predominance of ſuch Stars as are then moſt potent.

Mars. In the third Month, the joy the *Fiat* got in the Tincture of the Blood withdraweth, and the harſh Eſſences in Terror would fain like a flaſh depart, but are withheld and made hard making the Skin incloſing the Child, then the Tincture flaſheth upward, in the Terror taking the power of all the Eſſences with it, all which the *Fiat* holdeth faſt, thereby Creating the Head, &c. And by the hard Terror is made the ſkull, and in the Conteſt and Terror of the departing Eſſences, come the various Veins.

11. The ſtifling in the *Matrix* is the firſt dying, by which the Eſſences ſo ſever from Heaven, that the Virgin cannot be generated, which *Adam* ſhould have done without Woman, or rending his Body

12. *Further of the Incarnation.* The *Fiat* ſo holdeth in the Terror, that the filling in of Elements hardeneth to be Bones. So the Elementary Man riſeth and the Heavenly falleth. And the Stiches and Aches Women feel come from the Sympathy the Tincture of their Bodies have with the Tincture in the *Matrix:* In this Anguiſh a ſhrg enkindleth a Fire, and in the Fire a Light of Joy which is the beginning of Life.

Sol. 13. In the fourth Month, the Light of Life makes the harſhneſs calm and meek, here ſpringeth a longing and vertue coming from the Light, and this delight in the Love is the Noble Tincture which is the Childs own. And the Spirit generated out of the Anguiſh in the flaſh of the Fire, is the true real Soul.

CHAP.

CHAP. XIV. *Of the Birth and Propagation of Man. The very Secret Gate.*

1. MANS Paradifical Life sprung up in the Holy Ghost in the Divine Light in the place of the four Elements. Whence when he departed into the Principle of the Spirit of this World, that withdrew, and this made him like other Beasts, desiring only to fill it self and propagate. By that Spirit is he figur'd in the Mothers Womb, Life, Birth, Nourishment, good or evil success is given; and at last corruption.

2. And were not Mans Essences out of Gods Eternity, he, like the Spirit of other Creatures, had gone into its Ether, and in this Life had worn the rough Hide, but he is left with full Power to yield himself to which of the first or second Principle he will. Hence is it that Regeneration is of absolute necessity to the blessed Restoration.

3. *Of the strong Gate of the indissoluble Band.* The three Essences, *viz.* Harshness or Sourness, Bitterness and Fire make like the Trinity the indissoluble Band. The first is the *Fiat* and sting of the second, and both the cause of the third, and from all three in anxiety ariseth the twinkling flash, out of which the Angels are Created, who by their longing after the Heart of God were enlightened by the Divine Wisdom. But *Lucifer's* Pride cast him back into the anxious Fire without Light.

4. *The Gate of the Sydereal or Starry Spirit.* By the great longing of the darkness after the light was this World Created, which desire must continue, else no good Creature could be.

6. But the Starry Spirit would be King of the Essences of the Soul which ought not to be. It longeth to find the Virgin in Man where once it was, but the Virgin consisting in the vertue of the second Principle is out of reach.

6. Every thing groaneth after the Divine Vertue to be freed from the Vanity of the Devil, which panting should it cease, the World would be a meer Hell.

7. But that the Creatures may attain it, they must wait till their dissolution, when in their Figure, and in their Ether, they get a place in Paradise.

8. The more the Spirit of the World wrestleth, and that the Soul (by approaching the Heart of God) resisteth, the more eager still is the Spirit of the World. There the King, the Vertue of the Sun is so triumphant, that it *sublimeth* all the Essences of the Stars to their highest *Summit.* And here the Essences of the Soul can see in the Light of the Virgin its own Original.

9. *The depth in the Centre.* That Fire we see with our Eyes is not the Element of Fire, but the fiery Wrath, come to be such by the inkindling when the Devils fell out of the one holy Element, in which one Element is Meekness and Rest, not Heat and Cold which have a contrary will.

10. Because therefore the fierceness would rule over meekness, God caused the Sun to come forth, thereby opening four Centres. 1. It made the harshness thin and pleasant as Water. 2. By the Water the fierceness in the flash was extinguisht. 3. The Motion and Egress whereof became Air. 4. And what the four fierceness had attracted to it was thrust out as the Earth swimmeth in the Water, these seek in anxiety to retreat again into the one Element, which cannot be till the number to the praise of God be full, according to the Eternal Mind.

1. *The most precious Gate in the Root of the Lilly.* 1. The longing, (or attracting) willing and desiring are the three beginningless and indissoluble Band. Hence originateth

ginateth the Eternal Mind, in that the Will goeth out of the attracting Activity into Meeknefs. Hence alfo originateth the Eternal Anguifh Gods original fiercenefs. Hence likewife originateth the Eternal mixture where the flafh difcovereth it felf in many thoufand thoufands. The going forth out of the darknefs without intermiffion opening ftill a new Centre or Principle *in infinitum*.

2. *The Gate of God the Father.* The attracting of the Will impregnateth it felf with meeknefs, being deliver'd from darknefs, wherein ftandeth the pleafant joy, for in the appearing of the fharpnefs breaking the darknefs, ftandeth the Omnipotence, and is as when a Man is inftantly come out of a fcorching Fire to fit in a temperate refrefhment, herein is the perfection of the higheft Joy and Meeknefs.

3. The Will of God is, that whatfoever inclineth it felf to him, he will create in meeknefs. To which the Worm in the Spark inclineth whether to the fharp fiercenefs in the Fire, or the fharp flafh to the Regeneration in the fecond Principle of meeknefs, in that it ftandeth in Eternity,

4. The deep of the darknefs and of the Light are alike great, and are both without beginning and end, the firm Bar of a whole Principle is between them. And the will to Love, Refignation, Meeknefs and fharp Regeneration, is the bound or limit of thefe two Principles.

The Exit of the Will by the fharp Fiat caufeth the Effences.   5. *The Gate of the Son of God.* The will from Eternity impregnateth it felf, and hath an Eternal Defiring, and bringeth forth Eternally, the Eternal Son and Child of Meeknefs, Vertue (or Power) expreffing and fpeaking forth the depth of the Deity, and the Eternal Wifdom of God.

6. *The Gate of Gods Wonders in the Rofe of the Lilly.* The Holy Trinity, dwelling in it felf, generating out of it felf, comprehended by nothing, having no place of reft or limit, but is the unfearchable Eternity and Infinity; hath an Eternal Will, going forth of the Mouth and Heart of God by the Holy Ghoft. In which going forth, by the fharpnefs of the *Fiat* all Effences are, and yet this is not God, but a chaft Virgin of the Wifdom of God. This Virgin openeth Gods Wonders in the Eternal Effences. Thefe reveal'd Wonders become a fubftance. And this fubftance is the one Element, wherein all Effences are. And the fair, chaft Virgin of Gods Wifdom difcovereth her felf infinitely, without number or end in Powers, Colours and Arts, at which the Deity rejoiceth. And that Joy is call'd Paradife, becaufe of the fharp generating of the infinity of the pleafant Fruit of the Lilly. What it is no Earthy Tongue or Pen is fufficient, all we can fay of it is lefs than Drofs to Gold, and our Speech is as a drop, or glimpfe, or fparkle.

CHAP. XV. *Of the Knowledge of the Eternity (in the Corruptibility) of the Effence of all Effences.*

1. IN the Original Effence of all Effences, we find but one, whence is from Eternity generated the other, both are in Divine Omnipotence, have different Inclinations, mix not, nor can be diffolved.

2. In the Eternal Original is alfo the Virgin of Wifdom, whofe longing after a Similitude Created the Angels, opening a Fountain to every Effence, whence came the Names of Principalities, Thrones, *&c.* And out of each many thoufand thoufands.

3. But *Lucifer* and his Servants like a Tree and its Branches, moved by the ftern Matrix, bearing only the guilt of his own Fall, kindled the Element (whence came the four Elements, and out of it came Earth and Stones) and became execrated out of Paradife.   4. But

The Three Principles of the Divine Essence.

4. But the Virgin redisсovered, in the Out-birth the Similitude, which the *Fiat* made substantial a meer *Quinta Essentia*. And God Created the Sun, the Similitude of his own Heart, which put all the Out-birth into Meekness, that all this after dissolution might in Paradise be a shadow of his substance, and not only made the outward Creation, but also out of the *Quinta Essentia* figur'd Spirits.

5. And in the room of the fallen Angels made Man of all the three Principles, but to live in the second, and rule over the other two, to whom the Virgin of Gods Wisdom Espoused her self, opening in him a Centre to many thousand thousands, in perfect chaste Meekness, without rending his Body, but the Spirit of the great World so overcame *Adam*, that he became Earthy, the Virgin departed.

6. But still the Virgin calleth, and is ready to return to all that seek her with humble earnestness. 'Tis a Lie to say one is not elected; the possibility of humble seeking is in every one. Pride enclineth one more strongly than another, but forceth none. There is need of the Treader upon the Serpent in the Womb; because all the three Principles do there imprint themselves.

7. And tho' the Devil dare not Image himself till Mans understanding inclines to evil, yet let no one presume on the Devils Impotency; for tho the Child be in Innocence, the Seed is not, which is of fearful consideration to Parents, especially evil ones.

8. *Diligently and deeply to be considered.* Pure Love which reacheth Paradise is wholly modest: As in two young people whose *Limbus* and *Matrix* have attained the Blossom of the Noble Tincture, how hearty, faithful, pure Love bear they to each other. But after they take each other, the burning Love infecteth, and the Ashes of Lust turns them oftentimes to spiteful Enmity. Whence may be seen, God willed not the Bestial Copulation, but the pure, fiery, Paradifical Love.

9. When all the parts of the Child are formed, 'tis still so Bestial an Image, that if it perish before the enkindling of the Light, *viz.* the Spirit of the Soul, nothing of the Figure appears before God at the Restitution, but its shape and shadow.

10. *The Life of the Soul* standeth in the three Principles. The first discovereth it self in the Fire flash, standing over the Heart in the Gall: The second is generated of the first, and is the pleasant joy, Oh happy they who experience the governing power of it! The third Principle presseth after the Tincture of the Soul, but attaineth only the Light of the Sun and Stars, whose qualifying with the Soul, brings many Diseases into the Essences, as the Plague, &c. and at last Death.

The Extracts of the rest of this Excellent Chapter I forbear, contenting my self with what hath been done in the *Aurora*, &c. on that subject.

CHAP. XVI. *Of the Mind, Understanding, Senses, Thoughts, Threefold Spirit, Tincture, Inclination of a Child in the Womb, of the Divine, Hellish and Earthy Image,* &c.

1. THE Mind standeth in three Kingdoms. The first is Eternal, the second is Eternally generated, the third transitory. If the first generateth not the second, it goeth into the Abyss: The Gate of the second goeth into Paradise.

2. So can our Mind, being a sparkle breathed in from the Eternal Mind, speculate things remote from the Senses, and penetrate Wood, Stone, Bone and Marrow, without rending the dark Bodies. The third Kingdom, that of the Sun, Stars and Elements, wrestle with the first Kingdom, yield themselves to it as to their Father.

3. The second standeth between these two Regions, from the Rays whereof,

spring

spring the Gates of the Senses, filling all with joy. The Tincture whereof, causeth all Vegetation. And in Animals, especially in Man, the Blood of the Heart, in which the Soul Swimmeth is incomparably sweet; therefore God forbiddeth eating Blood; for the Bestial Life ought not to be in Man, left the Spirit be infected by it.

4. The Constellations make not a Child an Image of God, but at highest a lusty, subtle pleasant Beast. In some the Image of a dangerous evil Beast, in others of a tame, merry Beast, according as the Constellations stood at the Incarnation and Birth of the Child.

5. The first Principle saith, Go forth in stern might. The second in Love and Wisdom. The third in sustaining and adorning the Body, to which the Soul obeys of these three, his Servant he is.

6. If thou desirest the second Birth, know thou art here in Prison, call to him that hath the Key of the Gate of the Deep, and thou wilt break through as the day breaketh, and find the chast Virgin waiting for thee, who is ever warning thee of evil: Whom if thou follow, despising the good and evil of the World, she will joyfully conduct thy wandered Soul into its true Native Countrey.

CHAP. XVII. *Of the Lamentable Fall of* Adam *and* Eve *in Paradise.*

Ver. 47.

1. ADam stood forty days before his sleep in an Angelical Image, yet had a Body out of the one Element, out of the which one Element issued also the four Elements, and of the Quintessence of the four are the Stars, and are as the Husband, and the four Elements the Wife. The Heart of both is the one Element, and of the Essence and Vertue of that one Element is Paradise.

2. *Adam* had the Eternal Essences of the first Principle behind him. The Divine Light of the second Principle before him, both were as Fire and Light. The outward World of Stars and four Elements under him, and were impotent as to him, his Breath was that of the Holy Ghost Paradifical.

3. As long as he set his Heart on the Heart of God, the other two Kingdoms as to their divided properties were hidden. But in his reflecting on the great hidden Wonders of the great World he lusted, the potence whereof remains in the Lust of a Woman, by which is impressed a mark on the Child in her Womb.

4. His so Lusting enfeebled him that he slept and became impotent as to generating Magically with the chast Virgin of Gods Wisdom. Then God built a Woman out of him, whom when he awaked he took as the Beasts do, he drew Breath of the four Elements, and kindled his Astral Spirit therewith.

5. But the fierceness did not yet stick in them tho' the longing did, which *Eve* (by her little regarding the Commandment) soon shewed. And thus entred Sin, Shame, and the Evil from the divided Properties, from the Elements to which disobedience had subjected them.

6. For the Devil is this Worlds Executioner, the Stars are the Councel, and God is the King of the Land: Such therefore as depart from God, fall under the Councel who send some to the Rope, Water, Killing, Stealing, *&c.* in all which the Devil is very active. And at best the Councel helps to vain turmoil, discontent and vexation.

The farther Extracts of this profound Chapter is here forborn, being copiously treated in the 20, 21, 22, 23, 24, and 25th Chapter of the *Mysterium Magnum.*

The Three Principles of the Divine Essence.

CHAP. XVIII. *Of the Promised Seed,* Adam's *Exile, and Gods Curse.*

1. WHen fallen Man stood in great shame and horror, fast bound by the Devil, God the Father appear'd to him with his angry Mind of the Abyss into which he was now fallen. And his most Gracious and Merciful Heart oppos'd it self to the Wrath, placing it self highly in the Gate of Mans Life, re-inlightning the Soul, which yet stood trembling to hear Gods Sentence, *Because thou hast eaten of the Tree,* &c.

2. Thenceforth the Holy Element withdrew, from the Root of the Fruit, and left it to the inkindled fierceness of the four Elements producing Thorns, *&c.* and the Fruit issuing in the Out-birth, made for the Beasts, became Mans Food, who was become Earthy, and now God would not cast his Heavenly Food (which belonged to Angels) to the Bestial Man.

3. Now rose the Enmity of the Beasts to Man; he was a Wolf to them; and they as Lions to him.

4. Before the Curse, the tame Creatures were very near akin to the one Element with whom Man should have delight, and others (the wild ones) to the four divided Elements.

5. Now also the turmoiling Life of digging, *&c.* was necessary; for death, frailty, *&c.* in the four Elements succeeded the continual living Vertue of the Holy Element which was departed.

6. God laid the burthen of managing the Creatures on Man, when he was become like them, but had God willed to have Bestial Men he had Created them such, and given them no Commandment, as neither have the Beasts any Law.

7. God could well have Created Creatures to have the charge and labour of managing the Beasts as already there are Creatures in all the four Elements without a Soul, yet somewhat adapted to such a conduct, while Man might in Paradise have retained his Angelical Form.

8. *Eve's* Sentence, *Thou shalt bear Children in pain,* &c. establisht her perfectly to be a Woman of this World. It should have been without a Woman and impregnation; therefore was the Lord Jesus without the Seed of Man, the Son of the Virgin.

9. *Of the Incarnation of Jesus Christ* out of the Heart, Word and Promise of God the Father, through the chast Virgin of Gods Wisdom, is proceeded the Treader upon the Serpent, who imaged it self in *Adam*'s mind, and Espousing therewith, openeth Heaven for the Soul, giving the Virgin for a Companion to instruct him in the way of God. But because Mans Soul was too hard inkindled from the first Principle, did not so instantly imprint it self therein, but stood opposite to the Hellish Darts; and in the Minds of these Men that yielded to Gods Wisdom, did break the Serpents Head.

10. But after long Tryal whether Men could by this way wholly yield themselves to God, there came to be Murtherers, unchast and domineering Spirited Men, and but few clave to God, then came the Deluge.

11. The dread of Gods Judgments not prevailing, God chose the Children of *Sem* to erect the Office of Preaching, but Mans self-will (ruled by the Stars) prompted their blindness so, that they would secure themselves by a Tower, which God stopt, by making their Language as confused as their Thoughts: That by their scattering, the holy Seed might be preserved, but that not reclaiming them,

The Three Principles of the Divine Essence.

them, God out of the fierceness of the first Principle burnt *Sodom* and the five Kingdoms, yet Sin sprouted as a Green Branch.

12. Then God promis'd the chosen Generation to multiply them, if they would obey him, and prospered them in a strange Land, to see if they would depend on him, rais'd them up a Prophet, wrought Wonders, fed them from Heaven, gave them a Law in the Zeal and Fire of the Spirit of the great World into which they were fallen, gave them Circumcision and Sacrifice; for that Man was Earthy, their Prayers (with a Token of Acceptance) were heard, through the Consumption of the Earthiness of their Sacrifices and Incense, forbad them Meats, especially Swines Flesh; which in the Fire giveth a stink, as also it doth in the Souls first Principle, and fuming darkeneth the Gates of the breaking of the Light.

13. But nothing could ransom the Soul, nor attain the Resurrection of the Body, and bring the new Body out of the Holy Element, till regenerated in the Son of the Virgin. Therefore in the 3970. year the Angel *Gabriel* saluted *Mary* with that precious Message, to her Astonishment and the Angels Admiration.

14. Think not, that the Word descended from the highest Heaven above the Stars, and became Man. No; but the Word which God spake in Paradise which imaged it self in the Door of the Light of Life, waiting perceptibly in the minds of the holy Men, that same Word is become Man, the same is entred again into the Divine Wisdom. And the same Wisdom of God in the Word of God gave it self into *Mary*'s Virgin *Matrix*, uniting it self as an Eternal propriety into the Essences, and into the Tincture of the Element which is pure before God. And it was a going forth with the whole fulness of the Deity, whence also the Holy Ghost goeth forth, making it greater than *Adam* or ever any Angel was, being the blessing and might of all things in the Father Eternally.

15. Not then, nor ever separate from the Father, every where present, and is become a new Creature in Man, and called God, which new Creature is not generated of the Flesh and Blood of the Virgin, but of the total fulness and union of the Holy Trinity, and filleth all the Gates of the Holiness, whose Depth, Number and Name is Infinite.

16. Yet the Corporeity of the Element of this Creature is inferior to the Deity, for the Element is generated out of the Word Eternally. And that the Lord should go into the Servant is against Nature, and the greatest Wonder done from Eternity, and rightly called LOVE.

17. This Divine Creature in the Holy Ghost was in a moment made a perfect self-subsisting Creature in the same moment the four Elements, Sun and Stars in the Tincture of the Blood, and with the Blood, and all the Humane Essences of the Virgin. *Mary* in her *Matrix*, received the Creature wholly as one, and not two Creatures. The Holy Element was the *Limbus* or Masculine Seed.

18. Every form hath its own source, yet the Divine hath not so mixed as to be the less; but what it was that it is, and that which it was not, that it is, without severing from the Divine substance, and the Word abode in the Father, and the Natural Humanity in this World, in the Bosom of the Virgin *Mary*.

19. *Of the three Regions of the Incarnation*. First, There is the Word which hath its forming from Eternity in the Father, and in the Incarnation so continued.

20. The second forming is done naturally (when the Virgin said to the Angel, *Let it be done to me as thou hast said*,) in the inward Element like the first *Adam* before the Fall, who should have generated such an Angelical Creature, which was done perfectly at once in a moment.

21. The third forming was done also at once out of the pure Element, and this new Creature in perfection of the Element was the Masculine Seed of the Earthy Man, which was conceived in the Earthy *Matrix* of the Virgin.

22. But

The Three Principles of Divine Essence.

22. But the Word of the Deity so separated them, that the Masculine *Limbus* of the new Creature was not defiled by the Earthy *Matrix* of the Virgin.

23. Yet this Angelical Image as to the *Limbus* of it, came by commixture of the Earthy Essences of the Virgin, which claveto it, to be Flesh and Blood, and at the end of three Months attained his Natural Soul: As all other of *Adam's* Children, and hath resumed the Princely Throne again, out of which it departed by Sin in *Adam*.

24. Thus Christ was the Natural Eternal Son of the Father, the Soul in the Word was a Self-subsisting Natural Person in the Trinity. Christ (the true breaker) through continued in the second Principle, and the new Body in the third Principle, and at Nine Months was Born of the Virgin. Here the Light shone in the Darkness of the outward Body.

25. Thus came he to, or into his own, and they knew him not, nor received him, but to as many as receiv'd him, gave he power by him to be begotten to the Kingdom of Heaven; for his is the Kingdom and Glory for ever, *Amen*.

26. *Of the distinction between the Virgin Mary and Jesus Christ*. Tho' God in former times permitted Miracles of seeing the Saints departed; for vindication of them and their Doctrine, of another Life after this, for converting the Heathen: Yet Invocation of them hath no ground in the Nature of the first Principle: Is vain in it self; for they having attained the still rest, load not themselves with the Miseries and Sins of the Living. It is also a disrespect to the Omniscient Mercy of God, which without their Intercession, and without ceasing, with stretched out Arms, inviteth by his Gracious Call, all Men to come to him freely.

27. The Virgin *Mary* is fabled to be taken up to Heaven Body and Soul, but such take this World to be Heaven, for the Earthy Body belongs to the Earth. She is in Glory in the new Body of the Holy Element, and her Lustre is above the clarity of the Heavens, as one of the Princely Angelical Thrones, for out of her Essences, went forth the Body which was the Saviour of all the World, and that attracteth all the Members to it, and who now standeth in the Holy Trinity, and she, as a Virgin of Chastity, is highly blessed by her Son Jesus Christ. But Invocation belongs not to her; for the ability to help cometh only out of the Father through the Son.

CHAP. XIX. *Of Souls entring to God and to Perdition, and of the Bodies Breaking.*

1. THE Soul hath the Eternal Essences of the first Principle. Regeneration opens the second Principle; The third Principle is the Region of the Stars and four Elements. When Man's first Principle hath been wholly taken up about the third, *v. g.* This World, and that the Brimstone-Spirit which kindleth the Tincture of the Heart is choaked, and the four Elements break off from the one Element, then doth the Soul keep the starry Region, still as its dearest Jewel; in the Power whereof they appear, and think to find rest in settling things relating to their Wills and worldly Businesses. But when the Stars have compleared their *Seculum* or Course, and that the Treader upon the Serpent hath not hold of the Soul, by guiding it through the Sufferings, Death and Resurrection of Christ, it remains naked without the third Principle, which it hath left for ever.

2. *Of the going forth of the Soul.* When the Body breaketh, the right Soul which was breathed into *Adam* is in its Principle, and is so subtil as cannot be comprehended

hended by Matter, as Flesh, Bones, Stones, &c. only by an earnest Promise (not recalled in the time of the Body) it may be comprehended.

3. Those that by true Re-entrance ingraft themselves into the Heart of God, do instantly at breaking of the Body, lay off all that is Earthy, and comprehend the Mercy of the Father, and love of Jesus Christ, and enter into the Element before God, where Paradise shall flourish, waiting without irksomness for the Restoration.

4. But if Souls have been defiled with gross Sins, and not rightly passed into earnest Regeneration, yet do hang as by a thread of Faith, and will not let go, but when the Bridegroom calls, answer, I cannot trim my Lamp yet. These Souls may after a long time be ransom'd out of the Putrefaction by the Passion of Christ, but the Glorification of such shall not be in Eternity, like that of the true born Saints; but Antichrist's juggling Masses for Money avail not for these.

5. But the earnest strong Prayers of such as are entred into the New Birth, especially of Parents, Children, Brethren, Sisters or Kindred of the Blood, who have one Tincture with him, who have all one Tincture, enter the Combat more freely than Strangers, and help to wrestle off the Devils Chains, especially before departing of the Soul from the Body.

6. *The true Door of the Entrance into Heaven and Hell.* The Soul departed from the Body need not go far; for in the place where the four Elements break, the Root standeth, which is the Holy Element, the Soul entreth through the Door in the Centre into the Kingdom of Joy, and is in the Arms of Christ in Paradise. So the Damned needs no flying far away, it remaineth in that which was outermost, without the four Elements in the Anguish of Darkness, in the strong might of the grimness.

CHAP. XX. *Of Adam's going out of Paradise, also of the true Christian and Antichristian Church.*

1. ADam having a Garment lent him by the great World, is let go out of the Garden, and a Cherubim with a flaming Sword is set to guard the Way to the Tree of Life: which is the Kingdom of the fierceness in God's Anger, which must cut away the Earthy Body from the Holy Element, that the new Man may press into the second Principle, the Way to the Tree of Life in Paradise. Our gross Flesh is the Hedge before the Paradise. Would you enter? press through the Sword of Death, Christ the great Champion will help you; who though by his entering hath shew'd and made the Way more easie, yet the Sword stili before it.

2. Christ took the Book of the first Principle out of the hand of the Ancient of Days, and opened the seven Seals or Spirits of the Operation of God. The seven Candlesticks are his Humanity, the seven Stars the Deity. See the four first Chapters of this Book.

3. When *Eve* bare *Cain*, she said, *I have a Man from the Lord*: meaning what the Apostles thought of Christ, that he should erect a Worldly Kingdom, and break the Serpent's Head, by the Spirit of this World and its might. And here lay the Foundation of the two sorts of Churches, one as *Cain's* standing in the might of the Spirit of this World, the other of *Abel* pressing on the Mercy of God in Faith and Resignation. But from the Evil Tree of *Adam* and *Eve's* lust, sprung the evil murtherous branch *Cain*.

4. That *Cain* the First-born should be so wicked and a Murtherer, is, for that *Eve* was the Child which *Adam* should (if he had not been overcome) in great Modesty have generated, but his Matrix being impregnated by the Spirit of the

great

The Three Principles of the Divine Essence.

great World; therefore first was framed out of it a fleshly Woman, and her first Fruit became Evil, as well as the *Limbus* of *Adam*. After *Abel*'s Death 70 Years passed before *Seth*.

CHAP. XXI. *Of* Cain'*s Kingdom and Antichristian Church, and of* Abel'*s Kingdom and true Christian Church.*

1. THE two Eternal Principles of Fierceness and Meekness, do strive from Eternity to Eternity; for without the fierceness, the Meekness would be a still nothing, without Mobility; and without the Meekness the Fierceness would be a dark gnawing as in Hell. *Adam*'s first Principle was throughly illustrated with the second, and his Body out of the one Element, out of which Element came the four Elements.

2. *Adam* was drawn of both, and so is Man still, but Man hath the ballance of both Scales. The Mind is the Centre of the ballance, the Senses or Thoughts are the Weights, which the Mind passeth out of ore Scale into the other. The one is the Kingdom of the Fierceness, the other of the Regeneration. Thus hath Man the Kingdom of Heaven, in the Word of the Divine Vertue given into his Power: the Kingdom of Hell (in the Root of it) in a Bridle, and the Kingdom of this World, according to the Humanity from *Adam*: Consider we well, which we suffer the Mind to be charged with, and over-ballanced by, for of that we are the very Image.

3. Man is a Field, the Mind the Sower, the three Kingdoms the Seed. Look, which thou sowest, for that thou reapest, and at the dissolving of the Body that thou art. If thou give thy Field (thy self) up to this World, thou standest only in two Principles that of this World, and that of the fierce Wrath.

4. But he that is generated out of Darkness into the Light, knoweth both the fierce Eternity and the Out-birth, but cannot search out the Light; for he is therewith environ'd, and therewith ruleth like a Prince in Heaven, over Hell and Earth, and all are profitable to him; for by the first, his high exulting Paradifical Joy springeth up, and in the third are God's variety of Wonders (as in Glasses) represented.

5. Thus may be seen, how *Cain*'s Evil worldly Kingdom, and hypocritical Antichristian Church is founded. Also how *Abel*'s meek Light, righteous Kingdom, and his regenerated and resigned spiritual Church is perfected.

The victorious Gate of the poor Soul.

In the three last Pages of this Chapter, is a sweet and consolatory Incitement and Exhortation, that the Soul advance by Perseverance, with disregard of the Old Man, compar'd to a Wild unruly Beast, that it may attain the victorious Garland of Pearl to Crown the New Man with.

CHAP. XXII. *Of the new Regeneration in Christ out of the Old Adamical Man.*

1. THE Scripture saith, Christ was conceived and born without Sin of a pure Virgin. But since *Adam*'s Fall, no pure Virgin is generated of Man's Seed; therefore the pure Eternal Virgin of God's Wisdom, putting it self into *Mary*, became not thereby Earthy, but *Mary* by putting on the chast Virgin, as a pure Gar-

ment of the Holy Element, or as a new regenerated Man, the Soul of *Mary* comprehended the same, and in that same she conceived, and did bear into the World the Saviour of all the World.

2. And as *Mary* bare the Heavenly, in the old Earthy Man (which was her own) yet comprehended not the new: So the Word entred into the Eternal Virgin, in the Heavenly Matrix, in the Body of *Mary*, and became a Heavenly Man, out of the new regenerated Man in the Soul of *Mary*, and hath brought the Soul of *Mary* again into the Holy Father, so that the Souls of Men, were new born again in the Soul of Christ.

3. The Soul of Christ was no strange Soul brought from Heaven, but as all Souls are generated, so was Christ's, though in his Holy Body which was become *Maries* own. And Christ with his entrance into Death, sever'd his Holy Man from the fierceness of the Anger, and from the Kingdom of this World.

4. As the pure Element which is truly every where, in which God dwelleth, hath attracted to it this World as a Body, and yet this Out-birth comprehendeth it no more than the Body doth the Soul: So truly hath Christ in the Body of the Virgin *Mary*, attracted to him our Human Essences, and so is our Brother: which Essences comprehend not his Deity, nor can the new Man comprehend it otherwise, than the Body doth the Soul.

5. In our Human Essences Christ died, and his Deity of his Holy Man in the pure Element bereaved Death of its Power, and opened a Gate for us all, to be separate from the Devil, the World, and the bestial Body of the four Elements, whereof only the shadow is to remain. Who then, shall not have the Image of our *Immanuel*, shall have the Image of that which his Heart hath been set upon here.

Illustrations by Similitudes.

6. To Demonstrate Highest things by a Similitude;
(1.) The Almighty Father, is as the Fire of the whole Holy Constellations.
(2.) The Son, as the Sun, which is the Heart and Joy of the Deep.
(3.) The Holy Ghost, as the Air.
(4.) The Virgin of God's Wisdom, as the Spirit of the great World.
(5.) The Holy Ternary, as the Earth.
(6.) The Heavenly Aquaster, as the Water, call'd also the Holy pure Element.

7. In the holy Ternary and pure Element, spring the Paradifical Fruits, and the Virgin of Wisdom is the great Spirit in the whole Heavenly World, and the Holy Element is her Body. But the Deity is Incomprehensible, yet as a Soul to a Body in the Holy Ternary. The Virgin of God's Wisdom Christ brought with him, to be a Bride to our Souls, and the Holy Ternary which is his Body, is the Food of our Souls. *Amen. John 6. 56.*

The Cause of the Baptism with Water.

8. Baptism was not instituted in respect of the Earthly Man, which belonged to Earth, nor of the Heavenly Man, which was pure already, but for the poor Souls sake; for though we may have a new Body, we cannot have a new Soul, that being out of the Eternity. Therefore as the Holy Ghost over-shadowed and impregnated *Mary*, so the Water out of the Heavenly Matrix coming out of the Holy Ternary in the Baptism over-shadoweth and filleth the Soul, and so reneweth the Earthy Water (of the Out-birth) washing it clean, that it is in resignation a pure Angel, and may eat of the Heavenly Fruit, which is the cause of Baptism. Thenceforth if it incline it self forward into God, this World is only bound or tyed to it till it enter into Death.

CHAP.

CHAP. XXIII. *Of the Testaments of Christ, Baptism and the Supper.*

1. Christ said, he would be with us always, and would give us his Body and Blood for Meat and Drink.

2. The Deity is not divided, and if the Father be every where, so is the Son, his Heart, nor is the Son divided, and a spark of the Deity in his Body, and the rest every where. When Christ sat with his Disciples, he gave them his Flesh and Blood, (viz.) His holy Heavenly Body in the second Principle, and his holy Heavenly Blood, in the pure Element, wherein is the holy Tincture and Holy Life.

3. The holy pure Element is every where, and substantial, generated of God, therein is the *Ternarius Sanctus*, and that is the heavenly Body of Christ, with our here assumed Soul in it, with the fulness of the Deity therein.

4. Thus the regenerated Soul putteth on the Body of Christ, (viz.) his Eternal Humanity which is out of the holy Element, and which giveth the new Body, Meat and Drink. The Father every where from Eternity to Eternity doth generate the Son, and from both, doth the Holy Ghost every where proceed.

5. The inward Element which comprifeth this World, became Christ's Eternal Body: the Deity espoused it self thereunto, and acteth the Heavenly new Humanity, which is an Omnipresent Creature, such as captivated all Devils. Thus all Men who earnestly and stedfastly draw near to Christ, are in their new Man in Heaven, who acteth their new Humanity, Christ hath taken this Pledge of us, (viz.) our Souls in *Mary*.

6. Christ began his Baptism by *John* his fore-runner, who was born before Christ, signifying, that Water is the cause and beginning of the Life, and in it, by the Tincture, cometh Sulphur, wherein is vital Motion. And in the Sulphur and Water, the Tincture after causeth Blood.

7. In the same order is the Regeneration, that the Soul be Baptized in the Water of Eternal Life, and then the grain of Mustard-seed of the Pearl be sown, that it become a new Fruit in God.

8. Children ought to be Baptized, or the Covenant is contemned; for though Children know not that which is done to them, yet it is not in our fore-knowing, but in God's, that the Covenant stands, and if thou, as the tree, be in the Covenant, so may thy Child as the branch; thy Faith is its Faith. Art thou a true Christian? Thy Child, at the kindling of its Life, passeth into the Covenant, yet omit not to Baptize; for when 'tis born 'tis sever'd from the tree, and thou must with thy Faith and Prayer present it. *Why Children must be Baptized with the outward and inward Water.*

9. And because the outward Body is in this World, therefore the outward Water is requisite, and with the inward Water of Eternal Life, the Holy Ghost in the Covenant baptizeth the inward Man.

10. Yet if after the Soul depart, the Virgin passeth into the Centre of the Light of Life, but if it again return is receiv'd. And therefore was the other Testament of the Lord's Body and Blood left, in which the outward Man hath the outward Elements of Bread and Wine. The inward new Man feeds on Christ's heavenly Flesh and Blood, and the Soul feeds on the pure Deity.

11. The unworthy Receiver feeds outwardly on the four Elements, and inwardly on the Wrath of God, having departed, as did the fallen Angels out of the Love.

CHAP. XXIV. *Of true Repentance.*

1. TO enter into true Repentance, the Mind with all the Thoughts, Purposes and Reason must be collected wholly into one will, resolution and earnest desire, to forsake all Abominations, and fix the Soul in a stedfast Confidence in God's Mercy.
2. That which terrifieth and with-holdeth arising from the greatness of Sin, is of Sathan, but every (though but the least) thought inclining the Will towards God, and that it would fain enter into Repentance, is not from self, but the Love of God draweth, his Spirit inviteth, the noble Virgin calleth.
3. Neglect not to give the Lord a meeting, who will certainly give a hearty welcom. Come, Knock, Pray, he knows the Language of a hearty Sigh. Depart not, press from Sin; so doth the Kingdom of God press into thee, wait from day to day; the greater the earnestness, the greater will be the Jewel.
4. But this Seed is not instantly a Tree. The Devil would root it up, many Storms rush on it, every thing in this World is against it, sometimes Sins cover it, Conscience upbraids the Traveller, even God's Children themselves rush on him, he sometimes doth what he reproves in others, even against his own Light, and Purposes.
5. When it is thus, the Tree of Pearl is hidden; for not being sowen in the outward Man, which is not worthy of it, but is Sathan's Seat, that doth what the Soul opposeth. It is sometimes done by the Spirit of the Stars in Man. So that a Christian is not known to himself, how much less to others, and is often wounded in the strife; for the Field in which the new Man grows, is barren, harsh, cold, sour and bitter, but the new Man arm'd by the sharp Sword of Christ's Death, is Conqueror, growing as the Herb or Flower out of the Earth, by the pleasant Sunshine.

CHAP. XXV. *Of the Dying, Death, Resurrection, Ascension of Christ, and his sitting on the right Hand of God his Father. Also our Misery, and the Divine Power of his Love.*

1. THE outward Man and its Actions, Thoughts, and Intents, are Instruments of the Spirit of the great World, which after Corrupt.
2. None therefore should scorn another, having our several Compositions, Habits and Mutations according to our Constellations and Influences, which are not wholly rooted out till Dissolution: though Regeneration oppose the falshood of the outward corruptible Man.
3. But the outward Man's not doing what it would, is not from its Wisdom, but the Heavens Contra-conjunctions.
4. But if it be restrain'd from Sin, that is not by the Astral Aspects, but by the Regeneration, whose strife cannot yet swallow up the earthy, but the fire is sometimes blown up again.
5. So great is our Misery! Let none be secure; for sometimes the whole Man running to Evil, loseth the Pearl.
6. The Soul is bound with two Chains, the one is the root of its original Poison and Anger, remediable only by him who is Love it self; the other, that of the
Flesh

Flesh and Blood and Region of the Stars; therefore God assumed a Human Soul from ours, and a new heavenly Body like to our glorious Body before the Fall, and not only to cloath the Soul with it, but really Unite it in the Essences, and so became a Creature in all the three Principles. And by separating the third, passed thence by Death as a flower out of the Earth, captivating Death by treading on the Head of it in the new Body.

7. So by kindling the Love in the Soul captivateth the Devil in the Eternal Prison of Anger, for in the Light is the Holy Trinity, which the Devil neither can nor dare behold, so saith *Paul*, *O Death where is thy Sting ? O Hell where is thy Victory ?*

8. The causes why Christ must not only die, but in so many sorts suffer, are as (*v.* 17.) follow. Man's Fall made all the Essences of the first four Forms predominant; so that had not the Eternal Word given it self into the Centre of the fifth Form, opening another Centre of Love, the Soul in this Body, had been captive in an Eternal Prison.

9. And when in Jesus Christ the fourth Form came to be broken, all the Forms (*v.* 22.) stirred and environ'd him, and in him, us, with Death, which made the bloody Sweat, and the outward Man cry, *Father, if it be possible, let this Cup pass from me.*

10. And as *Adam* by going out of the fifth Form, *viz.* the Angelical into the fourth became the scorn of the Devils; so the Pharisees who lived in the Spirit of this World must have their pleasure on Christ, for a terrible Example. That what we fill our Souls with, becomes a substance in the figure, and must come under the Judgment of God.

11. And as *Adam* would in his Pride be like God and wear this Worlds Crown, Christ must in this World be crown'd with Thorns, as a false King of, or in it.

12. And as after *Adam*'s entring into the Spirit of this World, he had a Rib broken from his Side, for a Wife; so did Blood by scourging flow from Christ's Body, and his blessed Side pierced and opened.

13. And as *Adam* departed out of the Eternal Day into the Eternal Night : so was Christ bound in the dark Night, and carried before the angry Murtherers.

14. And as *Adam* chang'd his Angelical for this gross Body; so was Christ loaden with the heavy wooden Cross.

15. And as upon *Adam*'s Disobedience the fierce wrathful Essences pierced him; so must Christ be pierced in his Hands & Feet by sharp Nails, fixing him to his Cross.

16. And as when *Adam*'s Soul entred the fourth Form, the Cross-birth was stirred: so hath the Man on his Brain the one half of the Cross, and the Woman the other.

17. And as *Adam* then hung between the Kingdom of Hell and this World: so did Christ between the two Malefactors, the one whereof was forgiven, entring with Christ into Paradise.

18. *The great Secret.* The Love of God or the second Principle became Man taking the Human Soul, which was out of the first, (*viz.*) the Anger, and Body out of the third, (*viz.*) the Out-birth; so there hung on the Cross all the three Principles then commending his Spirit to his Father, *he bowed the head and departed.*

19. His Father is all the Kingdom, Power and Glory. So the Love is his Heart and Light. His Anger is his strength and darkness, the Father took the Soul into the Trinity, and in the Soul the lost Paradise sprung up.

20. And by the rising of another Sun in Death, (*viz.*) in the Father's Anger, the outward Sun (which was generated out of the pure Element, the Body of Christ,) lost its Light.

21. And at the Holy Lifes going into Death the Rocks rent. And those who had put their trust in the *Messiah*, as Patriarchs, Prophets, *&c.* when Christ's Mortal had put on Immortality, got their new Bodies out of Christ's Holy Body and Vertue.

22. *Of Chrifts reft in the Grave.* That the Soul of Chrift leaving his Body in the Grave, defcended into Hell; a great way off, and there chained the Devils, is nothing fo: For all the three Principles hung on the crofs; why not alfo refted in the Grave with the Body forty Hours? for the Heavenly Body was not Dead, but the Earthy only. His Soul came with the Light into the Anger, caufing Paradife to revive, which made the Devils tremble, and captivated them, for the Light is their terror and fhame.

23. *Of Chrift's Refurrection.* There was no need of rolling away the Stone, fave to ftrengthen the weak Faith of his Difciples, for he comprehended all things.

24. He appeared a Creature in our Human Dimenfions, yet the fulnefs of the Deity was in him, and his Body is the whole Princely Throne of the whole Principle, without end or limit.

25. As our inward Body is unlimited in the Refurrection in the Body of Chrift, yet vifible and palpable in Heavenly Flefh and Blood, and fo can in the Heavenly Figure be great or little without hurt or want; there being no need of compreffing the Parts of that Body.

26. Vain is the Contention about the Sacrament, for Chrift's Heavenly Flefh and Blood is really received by the Faithful, and it is as great as Heaven.

27. The Forty days before his Afcenfion, of the *Proba* or Tryal, was fuch a life as *Adam* fhould have liv'd, having all the Principles except the four Elementary ones: He fhew'd himfelf without outward Glory, did eat, yet all Heavenly and Paradifical in the Mouth, not into the Body, and entred the Doors being fhut.

28. So fhould *Adam* have liv'd in and above the World, above the Stars and Elements in Meeknefs and Divine Love, without Death and Frailty.

29. To this ftate we make fome approaches, when in Obedience to Chrift's Laws we do Good for Evil, and overcome the World by being Dead to it.

30. *Of Chrift's Afcenfion.* Chrift afcended in fight of many to fhew he is our Brother. Will you afk, whither afcended he? Into his Throne, the right Hand of God, (that is) where Love quencheth Anger and generateth Paradife in the whole Father.

31. But the place of this World, according to the Heavenly Principle, is the Throne and Body of Chrift, alfo all the third Principle is his.

32. And the Devil who dwelleth in the place of this World in the firft Principle, is our Chrift's Captive; for the Father is the band of Eternity, but his Love (in the Body of Chrift) holdeth the Anger, together with all Devils Eternal Prifoners: as Darknefs ftands fhut up before the Eternal Day.

CHAP. XXVI. *Pentecoft.* *The fending of the Holy Ghoft.*

1. ON the feventh Day after *Mofes* afcended the Mount, was he call'd, and the Lord fpake with him. And Chrift when he was afcended into his Throne, was on the ninth Day glorify'd, and the Holy Ghoft went forth from the Centre of the Trinity, into the whole Holy Element, alfo opened the Doors of the great Wonders.

2. So that the Apoftles fpake with the Languages of all Nations, for the Holy Ghoft went out of all Effences, and filled the Effences of all Men who had but an earneft defire to it.

3. And the hard palpable Body of Chrift was received into the Holy Ternary, only the fource of this World was deftroy'd in Death. And though he be fwallow'd up as to our fight and apprehenfion, yet fhall he come again at the laft Judgment Day, and manifeft himfelf in that fame very Body to good and bad.   CHAP.

CHAP. XXVII. *Of the Last Judgment.*

1. AT the time before the Fire of Nature causeth every thing to dissolve, melt and pass into its Æther, cometh the Judge of the Living and Dead, and with him the Angelical World. Then all not comprehended in the Body of Christ shall howl, tremble, yell, roar, blaspheme, gnaw their Tongues, and would hide themselves in Holes and Caves from the Terror of the Lord. They Curse the Heavens, Constellations and Stars that inclined and drew them to Evil, they Curse the Earth that bare them, and buried them not sooner: They Curse their Parents that brought them up, and had not strangled them. They Curse their Priests that flattered and misled them; They Curse their Superiors, whose Cruelty and Evil Example influenced them; They Curse their ungodly Associates that accompanied them. The Tears of those they had oppressed, like fiery Serpents sting them. Their abused Authority, Wealth and Might, stand in the Tincture; in the Substance of Eternity.

2. The Devils also stand trembling, they see how every Fire burneth in its own life, in themselves they feel the Hellish Fire, in the fierce Wrath.

3. The Angelical World in the Light, Lustre and Brightness is as the Sun in Triumphant Hallelujahs.

4. The Angelical Quire of Holy Men, stand there before the Eyes of them that Murther'd, Oppress and Reproacht them for the Truths sake, whose Guilt like Mountains of Lead, holds them down, and Speechless.

5. And then the King calls and enthrones all his Members. And pronounceth that formidable and irrevocable Sentence on the Wicked, that they depart from him, &c.

6. At the Moment of Departing pass away the Heavens, Sun, Moon, Stars, Earth and Elements, and time shall be no more.

7. Nor can the Holy Principle touch the other any more to Eternity; nor conceive a Thought of the other. The Parents of their wicked Offspring, or Children of their wicked Parents or Relations, but Eternal Joy fills, surrounds, and Crowns them.

See more in the Answer of the 30th of the 40 Questions.

AN APPENDIX,
OR THE
Threefold Life in Man.

I. *The Life of the Spirit of this World.*
II. *Of the Life of the Originality of all Essences.*
III. *Of the Regeneration and Paradisical Life.*

1. BY the *Ternarius Sanctus* in the *Aurora*, and the three Principles, is not meant Holy Earth, but the Holy Body out of the Vertue of the Trinity, and properly of the Gate of God the Father, whence all things proceed, as of one only substance.

2. For in the Creation proceeds from one only Fountain, good and evil, life and death, joy and sorrow, love and hate appearing in all things, especially in Man.

3. So find we the Threefold Life in Man in the Gate of God the Father. See we also, how joy is turn'd into sorrow, and again joy return'd, and by the prevalence of either a substance is made according to which the Mind commanding the Thoughts, and collecting them sets the Hands, Mouth, Feet, *&c.* to obey what the Mind willeth, and though all the forms of Nature are in Man, yet that which is predominant causeth all other to lye as if dead, and become as a nothing.

4. There are (especially) three forms in the Mind, all superior to the outward, for the Mind is anxiously desirous, and can see, feel, smell, taste and hear what the outward Senses know not.

5. And if the Divine form be Paramount it is in God, and the other two are as half dead.

6. But the Mind can raise the Spirit of this World, of Covetousness, Pride, *&c.* which instantly openeth the first form out of the Eternal Indissoluble Band, in falshood, envy, malice, *&c.* To whom therefore you yield your selves Servants, his you are, whether of Sin or Righteousness.

7. This Life is the sowing and growing time, and in the time of this Elementary Life the mind may open, which of the three Principles it will, but at the dissolution of the Body the Mind standeth in one only Principle, having lost the Key of the other two; for when the stalk is cut it is no longer a Plant, but a Fruit, and can stand no longer, nor open no other Principle, but be Eternally in that which he here kindled. 8. But

An Appendix.

8. But if God hath regenerated us, to enter through the Death of Christ, into his Life, then hath our *Immanuel*, who abased himself to enter into our Humanity, exalted us, to enter into the Holy Flesh and Image *Adam* lost, which is out of the pure Element. And then the Trinity worketh really in us, and we stand in the Life, Body and Property of Christ, and our new Man standeth in that, out of which Heaven and Paradise is generated, and the Earthy Man doth but hang to it.

9. Put on therefore a true earnest purpose, desire and resolution, which is Repentance, and the Regenerator is ready, deep in the Mind in the Light of Life, to help the earnest Wrestler, and so soweth himself, as a Grain of Mustard-seed, or as a Root to a new Creature, and if the Souls earnestness be great, the earnestness in the Regenerator is also great.

10. But this is known by them only, that feel and experiment, how the Regenerator changeth the proud fierceness, into humble Love; for the new Man is not of this World, but hidden in the old.

For the true knowledge of God is in no Man till he be Regenerate.

11. Christ gave not the Flesh and Blood of his Creatures to his Disciples, but the Body of the pure Element (wherein God dwelleth, and is present every where, in all Creatures, but comprized in another Principle) to eat and drink under Earthy Bread and Wine. And as the outward Man is Baptized of the Elementary Water, so is the new Man with the pure Element, which appeareth only in the second Principle.

12. No Reader understandeth this Author rightly, unless he be Born of God, it is not folded up in an Historical Art: But as Earthy Eyes cannot see God, so neither can a Mind not enlightened by Divine Light, reach them; for like must be comprehended by like. And tho' Heavenly Treasure be carried in an Earthy Vessel, yet there must be a Heavenly Receptacle, hid in the Earthy, or the Heavenly cannot be comprised.

13. Eternal Life is in a Twofold Source. First, That of the Originality, *viz.* the fierceness according to which God calls himself a consuming Fire; and this Principle we must have, or else we should not be alive. Yet if we stay in this, without generating the Love and Humility, our abode is in Pride, Covetousness, Envy and Anguish as the Devils.

14. Let us look to it, that seeing the Life in the Originality is both Inimicitious against it self, and against the Regeneration, and that the Life in the Love, is Heavenly; therefore we be content to be pierced, wounded, and to bear the Cross in Meekness, and expect, till at the day of Separation, the Field of the first Principle in which groweth the Heavenly Fruit of the second Principle, shall be taken away, for then shall the Life, springing up through Death, be a Fruit to God in the new Man, and thereunto dedicate our selves, in our Meek, Victorious Saviour.

THE
THIRD BOOK
OF
Jacob Behmen,
CALLED THE
Threefold Life in Man.

CHAP. I. *Of the Root, Beginning and Forms of Life.*

1. Seeing there is in us an incorruptible Life wherein is a Principle capable of the highest good, yet by its Original is also in danger of Eternal Perdition and Misery, and that here we are strangers posting away, how necessary is it to search whence all these originate? And this may be by going up the Stream to the Fountain.

2. The outward Elementary Life is a Living Heat or Active Fire, enlivening the Body and sustained by the Body, the Body by the Food, the Food by the Earth, the Earth by the Water, and the other Elements, the Elements by the Fire of the Constellations, their Fire inkindled by the Sun causing a Boiling in all. So should that first outward cause cease the sude or seething, and Generation of all, also of Metals, Fruits, &c. would cease as the Food failing the Body, and its Life extinguisheth.

3. Now this perishing Life hungering after a higher Life shews there is such, and that is the Eternal Life of the Soul. As is said in *Moses*, God breathed into Man the Breath of Life, and Man became a Living Soul. The Soul is also an ever induring Fire, and must have Food, which it presseth after, from its original, which is the Eternal Band, the Forms of the Eternal Nature, the Property of the Father, but that Band of those Forms is of it self as a dry Breast, whence it is that the Soul would have the Food in its own power, but that also is as impossible as for the Eternal Nature to have the Light in its own power, which cannot be; for the Love shining in it (or into it) remaineth Lord therein, because the Eternal Nature doth not comprehend it, but rejoiceth in the Light which is another Principle, which when it is received into the Soul it is a new Birth ingenerated in the Soul, and this is done as truely as the Soul like a Branch is come from the Tree of the immediate Parent.

4. And

4. And because *Adam* fell into the Aſtral Kingdom, and our Elementary Body is infected therewith, as sometimes the Body is with the Peſtilence, it was out of the power of the Soul to enter into the Divine Principle; therefore of meer Infinite Grace did the Love the Son of God take our Humane Soul, and brought it into the holy Life, that we might every one by or for our particular ſelves preſs with our Soul in the Life of Chriſt into the new Regeneration in the Spirit of Chriſt. No Meritorious Works on the one hand, or lifeleſs feigned words of believing on the other avail at all, but only a ſtedfaſt earneſt reſolution in the new Created Will, bearing the Croſs, killing the old Will, and ariſing in the Life of Chriſt bringeth the Glory, Food and Paradiſe of the Soul; elſe the Soul remains in the four Anguiſhes or Forms of the Eternal Band for ever, wherein ſtands the Eternal Wrath and Hell Fire for ever. And thus ſee we the Original in the firſt Principle, and the Divine Light making the ſecond Principle; why then ſhould not the Man to whom this Knowledge is gracioully given ſpeak of this as his Native Countrey not as of things afar off, but that wherein he ſtandeth, and himſelf really is, and not to be learnt of another Man (as is barely an Hiſtory) unleſs himſelf enter into the new Birth in the Life of Chriſt, that the Divine Light may ſhine in him.

5. The Root whence is inkindled the Vital Fire conſiſts of two Forms only, the four which is a ſtrong ſhutting up, and the bitter ſting is an opener, and thoſe are what the Eternal Will in the deſiring attracteth, and is the wills ſomething and darkneſs. Then the ſting of the bitterneſs would get looſe, which the ſourneſs captivateth with ſtrife, tho' like a woe is yet no pain, for they are immaterial forms of Nature in the Eternal Will, and this contrary commixture is as a confuſion of Eternal Mobility, and cauſe of the Multiplicity of Eſſences, and are efficiently the Eternal Eſſences and Eternal Band.

6. The vaſt infinite ſpace deſireth narrowneſs or comprehenſion wherein to maniſeſt it ſelf; as a Map doth in a few Inches a huge Territory, a ſhort Speech or Scene Abridge a large Hiſtory, a Minute Model Epitomize the Terreſtrial and Celeſtial Orbs. And as all pourtraying Figures have ſhadows as foils to ſet off the reſt, ſo in the contraction of matter to manifeſt Infinity muſt be Darkneſs, that one contrary may illuſtrate the other. Nor is the vaſt infinite ſpace a Creator, but a Genitrix, and the Word in, with, and of the Father, the Generator as the Territory makes not of it ſelf the Map, alſo the words owe themſelves to the ſpeaker or ſpeaking word.

7. Nor is the word departed, nor doth the Son depart from the Father, but is inſeparable; as the Light of a Candle abideth with the Candle, as ſaith the Son, *I am not alone, but the Father is with me*; in the Father is a Centre, in the Son is a Centre, two Principles not diviſible but inſeparable. Thus the ſecond Will opening the Principle of Light is amiable, pure and mild, alſo Omnipotent to Create all things breaking and ſhining out of the Eternal Eſſences, yet not comprehended by them, but dwelling in it ſelf.

CHAP. II. *Of the Begun Life, the Principles, and Forms, and Fall.*

1. THE ſtirring in every Life whether Senſitive or Vegetative muſt not be a ſtrange or Heterogene Power, for ſuch would blow it out rather than help it, but it muſt be the Creatures own Spirit proceeding in the Genitrix to be a Centre and Circle alſo of Life. None ſhould truſt their Souls with the Men whoſe
Home

The Threefold Life of Man.

Home is here, for the Soul stands in the Original of the Essence of all Essences in the Centre of the Eternal Band, so in the new Birth may be seen the dark and holy Worlds as that whereout the new Man is Born: Even as the Word in the Father and the Spirit which goeth forth from the power is the life of the Deity. The Eternal Will is the Creator, and the Father is the Being of the Will, and the Essences caused by the Will. There are two Wills causing two Principles in one Being, but the first is not called God but Nature or Essence, the second Will is the beginning and end, making Nature or Essence manifest.

2. The first Will being an Eternal desire to Generate the Word can be called only the desiring in the Will, which with a strong eagerness contracteth narrowness to be the manifester of wideness, which attraction is thicker than the Will, and as its darkness, and in the Egress of the desiring are the Essences, viz. a sting of sensibility which the desiring cannot endure, therefore rageth so much the more into such Enmity as is betwixt Heat and Cold, and this Impetuosity causeth Mobility, Terror and Anguish, moving upwards where being restrained it stirs Circular, whence come Multiplicity, and tho' without feeling, being meer Spirit and Forms of Nature, yet so terribly raving that it buildeth and destroyeth as Life and Death, and here is the Sulphur, Mercury and Salt of high-knowing ancient Philosophers.

3. Two Forms, sharp, cold and bitter stinging make the Wheel of the Essences, which two are in terrible Anguishes without the other Forms generated out of them; for the sharp sourness is like hard Stones, and the sting of the attracting breaketh them, which is rightly called Phur, which would hold the Will in the Darkness which cannot be captivated being incomprehensible, and is the flash of the sting. And the bitter sting dissipateth the darkness of the Astringency, as the flash ariseth from a stroke on a sharp Flint, the bitter sting extreamly sharpeneth it self consuming the darkness; even so the Fathers sharpness is a consuming Fire, being the liberty which is free from Nature as much as the Mind is above the Sences, and when the sourness hath captivated the liberty, the fourth form is generated, and the crack of the flash is the third Form making the four Anguish or Brimstone Spirit: For if the sourness sharpeneth extremely it is the proper limit of Eternal Death, the Brimstone Spirit is the Soul of the four Forms, having the Fire in it, and would enkindle Nature, and fly above it in a horrible power, as may be considered in the Devils.

4. Sul in Sulphur is the Soul, in an Herb it is the Oyl not originating in the Centre as Phur doth, but is generated after the flash, even as all the four Forms in this third Principle are by the Suns vertue in a great degree moderated and made amiable; in like manner doth the second Principle enlighten the Centre of the four Forms in the Holy Angels, making them lovely and pleasant. *Mercurius* comprizeth all the four Forms, and Sal is the greatest in corporeal things: The four Forms are the cause of all things making the Wheel of the Essences, and every Essence which are themselves innumerable is again a Centre; so that the power of God is unsearchable.

5. The Fall of the Devils was their extinguishing in themselves the Light of the Heart of God, wherefore they are shut up in the anxious four Forms. Man fell from that Light also into that of this World: Who if he enters not again into the Light of God, when this Body breaketh, he is in the first Birth of Life with the Devils; yet both would climb up above Heaven, but cannot feel or see that Principle, like as we Men without our outward Eyes cannot see God who is always present, nor the Angels who are very often with us, except we put our earnest Will into God, then we see and feel him with the Mind. So also if we go with our Will into wickedness we receive the Hellish Principle, and the Devil takes fast

hold

The Threefold Life of Man.

hold of our Heart: Whereof the Soul is so sensible, that often in desperation they destroy themselves by the Sword, Ropes or Water.

6. Tho' the Hellish Creatures have but four Forms manifest to them, yet can they turn themselves into all Forms as infinitely as Mens thoughts, except the holy Forms. The Fire is their right Life, and the four Astringency of the darkness their right Food.

7. The first Eternal Will is the Father, and Eternally generateth the Word his Son, who is the Heart of the first Will, having in him the vertue and power of the first Will, and a several Centre in it self: The Father expresseth all things by the Son, and whatever is expressed by the Spirit and Power of the Father in the word is in a Spiritual manner, for what is formed out of the Eternal is Spirit and Eternal, as Angels and Souls of Men are. And tho' the four Forms keep their own Centre, yet out of them cometh the Light, and in the Light the Love which shineth in the darkness, but the darkness comprehendeth it not. The Father is in himself the light, clear, bright Eternity, yet without a Name, for if the Eternal Liberty did not generate there would be no Father, but seeing he doth generate the Band of Nature he manifesteth himself therewith with his fiery sharpness, an angry Zealous or Jealous God and Consuming Fire, out of which presseth forth the Meekness as a sprout out of Death turning Enmity into Love.

CHAP. III. *Is concerning the Sixth and Seventh Forms.*

1. THE generating of the Love is in the sixth Form, *viz.* *Mercury* the sound, Tone or Song, as also the five Senses. The Son of God is rightly the Flame of Love who created the Angelical World out of himself, whence goeth out the Virgin of the Eternal Wisdom of God, by which God created this World out of the first Principle, and that which goeth forth with or out of the Love is the Holy Spirit of the Word, this together is the Trinity in Unity. But as in the wrath there is a striving contrary Will, here is an Embracing.

2. The sourness retaineth its strength in the sharpness of Love, but it is very soft, and the sixth Form makes Voices, Tunes and Sounds, so that the Essences hear one another, and in the Assimilation taste one another, in the breaking through of their Power feel one another, in the desirous Love smell one another, and in the Light see one another. The six Forms are the six Seals of God, what in the dark Centre is a poysonous Woe and Anguish, is in this the exalted Joy and Triumph, a satiating of the first Will which is call'd Father; for the Son is the Word, the Brightness, the Power, the Love, the Life, the Wonder of God, he is the Essence which manifesteth every Essence.

Concerning the seventh Form of the Eternal Nature. The revealed Gate of the Essence of all Essences.

3. The time of this World from the beginning to the end is the seventh Form or Seal of the Eternal Nature, wherein the six Seals disclose themselves. And natural Wisdom instead of finding the Heart of God by humble resignation, hath found the Wonders of this World by Thunders, Voices and Strife; for when after the Apostles times Men left Love and Meekness, and fell to Pomp and Pride, the Golden Candlesticks and seven Stars withdrew and were hid, and all became seven Seals. The Glassy Sea is the Angelical World. The Voices of the seven Thunders would be hid proceeding out of the stern Essences did we not put our Imagination into them, and open them in us: So that (only the Lamb excepted) none in Heaven nor Earth were worthy to open the Seals nor look thereon; we

were

were shut up by them under Death & Darkness, which only the Light in the Heart of God could open; for Man was become an abominable Beast, a Dragon with seven Heads, and ten Horns, and ten Crowns on the ten Horns; this Beast the hypocritical Woman rideth on; is this the Ass Christ humbly rode on?

4. It is hellish Pride and worldly Pomp on which the Woman of seeming Holiness rideth? she pretendeth to the Keys of Heaven, and makes Laws, Decrees and Canons, yet knoweth not the New Birth; He only that is born of God, in his inclined heart the Seals are opened. But when, and wheresoever the Lamb openeth the seventh Seal, then and there the Whore, the Beast and Dragon are cast into the Lake of Fire; then doth the good Shepherd lead his Flock into green Pastures; then they that mark, hearken, incline the heart, mind and thoughts, coming humbly with broken hearts, are met and embraced; in them Christ is born; they have him in the Baptism, Supper, and hearing of the Divine Word in all places, for the Holy Ghost satisfieth the longing of the contrite spirit.

CHAP. V. *Of the Seventh Form of Nature the Corporeity.*

1. Corporeity subsisteth in the 7th Form of Nature; and as all the other six Forms are a hunger and longing desire to each other, so are all their desires to the seventh to have a Body or Rest, and the desire of the Essences is to preserve and sustain the Body. The whole Essence of all Essences is a continued hunger of propagating from its fulness; so that when one Form attaineth the other, a third riseth, yet the two former vanish not, but all keep one in the other their own respective Powers, and so of the rest. And tho' the still Eternity is the only true Rest, yet is the seventh Form a substantial Body of Rest whereinto the six diffuse their vertues, and the same seventh Form standeth, and is the comprehensible Body of Darkness and Light.

2. The sharp Fire in the Liberty holdeth its right, and the anguish whence the Fire ariseth sinking as a death, affordeth matter and weight; as in my self I see the Fire the cause of feeling in the dead Corporeity, which else in the anguish sinketh into weight, and is burthensom as a stifling. Now what as Fire ascendeth not, or as weight sinketh not in death, doth, as anguish, remain neither uppermost nor lowermost, which as the begun anguish is the Centre of both, and not getting up nor down presseth side-ways like the lower Branches of a growing Tree.

3. The Deity longed to see the Wonders in the Eternal Nature and Innumerable Essences, yet created all for the Light, not for the Darkness; for the Tincture is awakened in the Centre in the death of the Earth, which is the life of all Gems, Minerals, Vegetatives and Animals: And in the deep the Sun having the Tincture of the Fire, is the Father and Life of all the Stars, who in the beginning proceeded from its Centre, not that they all sprang from them; for as the Sun is the Centre of the uppermost in the Liberty, so is Saturn or the Earth of the lowermost in death, yet is there no dying, but a transmutation; for neither doth this World die, but the Essences change to be what they were not, and remain as figures for ever to the glory of God's works. And if the gross Visibles were not created to the Darkness, how much less the Spirits which are out of the Eternal Mind, and therefore Eternal; like as our Mind hath diversity of innumerable thoughts, and those thoughts essentially potent when exalted, as in that of a Woman with Child, whose thoughts can magically impress foreign preternatural substances, as well as heterogene incongruous figures on the fruit of her womb.

4. When God willed the *Fiat, viz.* the creating the Eternal Essences or Powers which

The Threefold Life of Man.

which flowed into substance (which Eternal Essences before went forth without substance) then time hads its beginning. But the Holy Will still proceeded with the Powers into the love and delight in meekness, contrariwise Lucifer's direful Fall was his delight of turning back his will to domineer in the Tincture of the Fire root, his motion to which was the forms of the Genitrix before enkindling of the Light, as sour, bitter, dark, tart, stinging, envious; for in the fourth form stands Love and Anger in opposition, being the middle form of the seven, having three drawing one way, and the other three drawing the other. Lucifer therefore was drawn of both, but that the Root forms prevailed was, because he saw the Divine or Second Birth proceed out of the Centre, and himself standing in the Essences of the Nature of Eternity the great Fountain; he therefore despised the Humility whereof Love and Light are the Off-spring, and would rule over it, and so was cast out of the uppermost Life into the nethermost Death and Darkness; for he was offended to see the greatest Mysteries to stand in the greatest lowliness.

5. The attaining the Divine Light consisteth in a fixt resolution wrought in us of Humility, wherein the Love is generated: But all Laws and Devices to attain it are fabulous; and as the making costly works wherein the Artificer pleaseth only himself with things wholly unprofitable, reaching no higher than imitation of useful things, like also as there are many Spirits Aerial, Aquastrish, Terrestrial and in the Anguish, which are not out of the Eternal Well-spring, but from the beginning Will, generated by the Tincture of Heaven in Nature, which mutable at their time, leaving only their shadow to manifest the wonders of God. And from Eternity there hath been such a Government where the knowledge was only in God, but at the coming out of the Angelical World an Intellect was also in the Creatures.

The Gate into the Holy Trinity.

6. In no Creature in Heaven or this World stand the three Principles open as in Man. The first Principle or Father, tho' he standeth in the Liberty & Eternal Stilness, is not call'd Father as such, but as he is the desiring. Thus the Mind of a Man being one only Will, is desiring; yet therein out of the Eternal Will are innumerable Wills; the first Will is Master, and the other are recomprehended, leading to Light and Darkness, to Joy; and Sorrow, Meekness and Fierceness; thus it is in the Father's Nature. This twofold desiring in one substance are two Centres, that to Meekness not severed from the other is the second or Son, and is therefore call'd the Son, because generated out of the Father's Nature call'd the Word, because he is the Glance or Majesty of the Eternal Liberty, call'd a Person, because he is a Self-subsisting Essence, not the Birth of Nature, but the Life and Understanding of Nature, and call'd the Heart of the Father, because he is the Vertue and Power of the Centre of Nature, as the Heart is in the Body; and call'd the Light of the Father, because he takes his Lustre out of the sharpness of the Eternal Nature; and call'd wonderful, for by him out of the Father's Essences are all things brought to Light, the Father and Son are as Fire and Light.

7. The Holy Ghost is the third; the Breath or Noise is that which makes the Will manifest, and the Heart also. The Noise is the awakener of Life, framer of the Sences or Reason, and bringer of one Essence into another. Thus the third Person is a Self-subsisting Essence, going in triumph with the Essences the Father and manager of the Sword of Omnipotence, the destroyer of Malice and Evil, the opener of the Genitrix in the Darkness. All which is thus shewed in Man; his Body (tho' it hath the Essences) were senceless without the Spirit. Again, the Spirit is not the Understanding and Light it self, for the Light is the blossom, and originateth in the Tincture of the Fire, and the Spirit is the blower up of the Fire.

CHAP.

CHAP. V. *Of the Virgin the Wisdom of God, and of the Angelical World, and of the Holy Trinity.*

1. GOD is only One every where present, the Mind therefore asketh if the Spirit goeth out from God, whither goeth he, seeing he remaineth in the mouth of God as a Spirit in a Body, to which it is answered, he goeth forth revealing God as in the seven Lamps, and opening gradually the seven Seals; but the seven Thunders being in the dark Matrix of Fiercenels, he hideth and sealeth, not to be known till they are past, and the whole Mystery of God's Kingdom opened by the seventh Angel. And the Glassy Sea is the Water Spirit whence the *Fiat* made not only the outward Element of Water, but every thing; for in this seventh Form in great Holiness is the Father revealed in this Angelical World.

2. Thus the Father's Will maketh the cause of Nature, which is a Darkness consisting of the four first Forms to become seven, and thence infinitely the seventh, being their Body in this Earth; for the Fathers Nature in the Wrath makes this Corporeal, in which the Devil, as Prince in the Wrath, is called Prince of this World. And the same is also in the deep of the Astral Wheel. Just so is it also in the inward Holy World, which is not severed from this, but this severed by a Principle from that; for there is no Angle where the inward World is not.

3. The Angelical World of Love and humble Joy is the Sons, and at the flash two Kingdoms sever Love and Wrath; there is made the Cross with the two Centres, as Light hath another Centre than Fire, tho' not separated, and on this Cross Birth is the Heart or Son of God generated from Eternity in Eternity; at this Cross lie the Holy Children of the Virgin Image, and in the Wisdom of the Serpent are the Children of this World. The Holy Ghost goeth forth from the Father through the Son, as the Air from Fire and Light revealing in the Angelical substantiality; and this is meant by *Ternarius Sanctus*.

The highly Precious Gate for Man to consider of.

4. The Wisdom of God is an Eternal Virgin of Purity, in whom the Holy Ghost hath discovered the Image of Angels and of Man, also of the third Principle; she is the great secret Mystery, which unapprehended, goeth in the Powers and Anger of the Father, opening the Wonders in the Forms and Seals of Nature. Through her hath the Holy Ghost not only made Corporeal Existences out of both Matrixes of the substantiality, but a limit to them where the seven Forms shall go into their Ether: as after the six days Work, or six Creations they enter the seventh, being their Eternal Rest, and the time of the seventh Seal and Trumpet, yet both Mothers shall stand before the Trinity in the Eternal Figure for the glory of God's works of wonder.

5. Tho' this Virgin be incorporeal, yet is the Spirits Corporeity and Visibility, her heavenly similitude is the Beauty and Lustre of all Fruits, the Vertue of all Jewels and Vegetables; she may be as the Tincture of the Holy Element, wherein the Paradifical growing consisteth, and the seven Forms, as the holy delight of the Angels wrestle, being a fulfilling of the will of every Life; she is not circumscribed; every Divine Creature, as the Angels and holy Souls of men, hath this Virgin in the Light of their Life; in this we see the Majesty of the Deity. We comprehend not the Trinity, the Spirit of the Soul standing in the Divine Centre, seeth it but imperfectly, for the Soul is but out of one Form of Nature; as there are several sorts of Angels, yet can the Soul introduce it self into all forms, the Trinity only is perfect. God is manifest in a creaturely form in Angels, and whole Angelical

World,

The Threefold Life of Man.

World, for they are not out of the Subſtantiality (which is without underſtanding) but out of the Centre of the ſeven Forms of the Eternal Nature, out of each Form a Throne Angel, and out of each Throne his Angel, ſo was it a whole Dominion fell with *Lucifer*. And the Dominions among Men (which yet are all but Stewards) originate here, tho' a ſort of proud Clergy would rule over them.

The Diſtinction between the Subſtantiality and the Element, alſo between Paradice and Heaven.

6. The Subſtantiality is in Heaven, the Corporeity of the ſeven Spirits is call'd God's Body; alſo the Body of our Regenerate Soul, it is Chriſt's Body given us to eat in his Teſtament, comprehenſible to the Spirit of the Soul, tho' not palpable to our outward ſences, yet in it ſelf without underſtanding. And the one Element doth lead the Principle in the Subſtantiality as a movable Life, it is not the Spirit of God himſelf, but the Spirit hath this Element as a Body.

7. Heaven is call'd in the Meekneſs the Water Spirit, and is the outward incloſure or Firmament parting the Principle; and Paradice is the ſpringing up out of the Eſſences through all Forms, through the one Element, through the Subſtantiality, and through Heaven; as the flouriſhing of a rich ſpringing Roſy Garden, and therefore was *Adam* therein (that is) in that Principle, and alſo in this World.

* *The Gates of this World* [*alſo the Language of Nature.*]

8. All our knowledge of God is his own Revelation of himſelf; for the Spirit of God hath imaged the Wiſdom of God in the Wonders of this World ſo evidently, that in the Wheel of the Stars and Planets, alſo in our Orb, and every Creature, that they are an apparent ſimilitude and figure of God according to Love or Anger, generating Fire, Air, Water and Earth: That is to ſay, the extremity, impurity, mortality and groſs death of them image the Wrath; and the good property in every of them images Paradice; where tho' there be but one Element, yet in it are the four hidden, and on their enkindling and ſevering become active and comprehenſible, or palpable to the Creatures, which from Eternity was in God, yet inviſible and immaterial.

9. The Language of Nature is treated of from 84th v. to the end of this Chapter, which being alſo diſperſed in ſeveral places of the bleſſed Authors excellent Writings, it is to be wiſhed were all contracted and paraphraſed on in one diſtinct Treatiſe; not only to ſhew us the Monuments of our Ruins by the Fall, but alſo ſtir us up to preſs inward out of the ſhadow and figure, into the ſubſtance, which is the inward Power-Worlds.

CHAP. VI. *Of the World, and alſo of Paradiſe: The two Gates of high Conſideration.*

1. MAN is a Child of Eternity, but this World is an Out-birth from the Eternal Nature as its Root, and an Out-birth is corruptible, its groſneſs originates in the Anger, and the Stars are out of the Centre of Nature in all ſeven Forms, and out of each a Centre; ſo that by the wreſtlings ſo very many have proceeded, which are a certain number, tho' innumerable in our account; and their being ſo ſet a number, ſhews they muſt be reſolved into their Ether; for in every Eternal Centre is a ſpringing up without number, as is found in Man's Spirit and Soul by the Conſtellations of the Mind thoughts ariſe without number, and out of one innumerable others, which clearly prove our Eternity.

2. The Birth of the Eternal Nature is Infinite, and perpetually ſpringing up every where in all places; as if we imagine a Circle as little as an Attom, the leaſt of
P p   quantities,

quantities, and in that Circle is the whole Trinity & whole Birth of the Eternal Nature, so that Eternity is in every p ace, yet maketh no place; for it is the Out-birth that maketh place, it also maketh Beginning and End, for the Infinite Three is without Beginning and End, yet as before this Beginning there was nothing but God and that after the End of these things shall be nothing but God, so God is the α and ω, the Beginning and the End.

3. And forasmuch as the Eternity generateth nothing but what is like it, though it self be unchangeable, therefore as man is, so is Eternity, all the three Principles are in him one in another as one, yet in the Creation are three. From the Eternal Centre is made the Eternal Substantiality as a *Body* or weakness, being a sinking down, and the Spirit is a springing up, whence comes Motion, Penetration, and Multiplication; and when the Spirit did create the Substantiality into an Image, breathing the Spirit of the Trinity into it the whole Essences, even all Forms of Nature, the Power to Light and Darkness and the whole Eternity, it instantly blossom'd and became the Paradise or Angelical World.

4. In the Darkness is the Geritrix, in the Light is the Wisdom, the first imaged by Devils, the other by Angels, as a Similitude of the whole Eternal Being to speak in a creatural manner of it. And *Lucifer* imaging beyond the Meekness of the Trinity, inkindled in himself the Matrix of Fire, and that of Nature becoming Corporeal, then was the second Form of the Matrix, (*viz.*) the Meekness of the Substantiality inkindled, whence Water originated, out of which was made an Heaven to captivate the Fire, and of that Fire and Water came the Stars.

5. Then did Man, who was God's Image, form and imagine in himself the awakened Spirit of the Air, four Elements and Constellations: which though it were breathed into him, Man's Divine Spirit should have over-ruled, as the Holy Spirit of God ruleth over all, but they became his Lord, and instantly captivated him, then the Stars, Death Vanity and the Elementary Life wrought in him. And now if he would enter into God again, he must in himself be new-born in God or lost Eternally; he is now in the midst between Heaven and Hell, to which of these Spirits he yieldeth, his he is, if Man form in his Spirits the fierceness of Pride, *&c.* God loseth nothing, for the Image of God in Man withdraweth untoucht into its Principle, leaving Man to form himself into the Image of the Serpent, and the Spirit forms the Body into its Deformity [or otherwise as the Seal the Wax.]

6. The Eternal Nature doth generate it self Eternally, which this World resembleth thus, it is a high round Globe, figuring Eternity and Infinity, wherein by the seven Planets are shewn the seven Spirits of Nature, by the great Deep the Eternal Liberty, by the Sun in the midst of the seven, as a Point or Centre in a Cross the Heart of God, by the lustre God's Majesty, by the Constellations the Effects or Products of the Fountain Spirits, by the Earth the Eternal Death; for as the Earth compared with the vigorous outward upper Dominion is as Death, so the fierce Matrix is as a Death compared to God, yet is not Death, but Eternal Torment.

7. Not that it is with the Heart of God as with the Sun to be only in one circumscriptive place, but as the Centre of a Cross, signifying the Trinity in a Globular Rainbow, wherein the Red signifies the Father's Property in the glance of Fire; Yellow the Son's Lustre and Majesty; Blew the Substantiality; the dusky Brown the Kingdom of Darkness: and on such a Rainbow will Christ sit to Judge; and thus is he undivided every where and in that Man who is Born of God, is the whole undivided Heart of God, the Son of Man Christ, sitting in the circle of his Life upon the Rainbow at the right Hand of God; for that Man is Christ's Memoer, his Body, his Brother, his Flesh, his Spirit: Power, Majesty, Heaven, Paradise, Element Stars, Earth and all, is that Mans who in Christ is above Hell and Devils, though his Earthy Life be under Heaven, Stars, Elements, Hell and Devils

8. Man's

The Threefold Life of Man.

8. Man's Creation was the speaking of that into Substance which was in God, in the Virgin of his Wisdom, in Eternity, not Male and Female, which when divided was one Earthy, the other Bestial; but the new Birth restores that very Eternal Image the Eternal Virginity: wherein Christ became Man, uniting it to the fallen Man in the Mortal Virginity, for *Mary* had all the three Principles, being of the Seed of *Joachim* and *Anna*. The Soul of Christ was out of *Maries* Essences conceived in the Eternal Virgin, which Eternal Virgin came into Substantiality uniting with the Human earthy Essences.

9. The Eternal Virgin gave to Christ's Human Soul the Heavenly Body and *Mary* the Earthy, the living Word attracted *Maries* Essences or Faculties into the Eternal Virginity, and so in Nine Months there was a compleat Man in Soul, Spirit and Flesh, but the Virgin of Eternity never till then did put on Flesh, except in *Adam* before the Fall, but now the Word united to the Soul is not, though united, one and the same with the Soul but the Soul being out of the Centre of Nature, remained intirely the same Creature, and the Word being out of the Majesty penetrated it; like as a dark black piece of Iron is flaming and shining by the Fire penetrating it, but the Iron comprehendeth not, but is comprehended by the Light of the Fire: So the Deity dwelleth in the Soul, yet the Soul remaineth a Soul still, but if the flaming Iron fall into Water, it is soon as other Iron again, as it was with *Adam*.

10. *Adam* departed and Christ became Man to return us into the Angelical World, wherein Man attains the Eternal incomprehensible Flesh of Eternal Substantiality, which is hidden in the old earthy Flesh, as Gold in the Stone. This true most precious Stone of Philosophers tinctureth the old, for this is as a Son, yet a Thousand times greater than the Father, this bright Crown of Pearls is most manifest, yet most secret, who so finds it, hath such Joy as no earthy Tongue or Pen can describe.

CHAP. VII. *The Hypocritical and real Christian, the Gates of the Firmamental Heaven with Stars,* &c. *The Threefold Life of Man, and right noble Spiritual Stone.*

1. MAN's greatest Concern is to seek that which is lost, not hypocritically without our selves; for all the hearing of Heaven and the new Birth Preacred, Singing, Repetitions, Reading all Books, having the Bible without Book, Talking and Despising the Simple, requiring they be guided by Man's Art and Eloquence, and resting there, is a continuing of Men as in a dark Dungeon, and no more than casting a Stone into Water, which is taken out again as hard as before. And Mens deepest Reason, Opinions of the Pope, *Luther*, *Calvin* or *Schwenkfield*, and all Contention, Disputation, and that accounted high University Study, though the Soul fill it self therewith, only leaves the Soul in doubt, on the shaking Foundation of vain flattering Hopes, if still there be an unholy unchang'd Heart.

2. But simply with the Publican *God be merciful unto me a sinner*, gather all thy captivating Sins, and in great earnestness knock, seek, consult not thy Earthy Reason, sensual Love, and self Will, and then that Soul entreth into the Temple of Christ; instead of Disputing bring earnest Resignation, let thy Contention be such only as was *Jacob*'s Wrestling. God's Invitation and inviolable Promises are the Ground of that Faith which makes Hell tremble, produceth the new Birth, giveth the noble Stone, and then the little grain of Mustard seed growing in the Storms of Reproach and Temptation, becoming a Tree, attaineth the Angelical Garland

of Pearl; for then may the Soul say, Though this World hath my outward Body Captive, yet I have the Regenerator in my Soul that will make me free, which is as putting a Stone into Fire, which makes an effectual change on't, though Water do not, as is above mentioned.

3. Saith any one, seeing the Devil is gone into Enmity, *Why doth not God annihilate him?* A. That which is Eternal breaketh or dissolveth not like that which hath a Beginning but though the Devils were not in the Form of a Spirit from Eternity, yet their Essences were from Eternity, but the putting their Will into the stern Matrix of the Centre of Nature captivated them therein, but in their Essences remain as a Looking-glass for Angels and Souls of Men. Say also any, If the World be so dangerous for Man, *Why hath God set and continued him in it?* A. Should God reduce the third Principle into its Æther before effecting what wonders were foreseen in the Wisdom from Eternity, it cannot be; but also in time must the Forms of Nature be substantial.

4. The Infinite God being Threefold in Persons, willed to move himself according to the Property and Nature of each Person; As, 1. The Father's Property moved to create Angels &c. to bear his Image and behold his glorious Power. 2. The Son's Property moved once and never more in Eternity to become Man, by whom the glorious Majesty of the Trinity is shewn unto Angels and Men in an express Character and living Image. 3. The Holy Ghost's Nature will move it self at the Resurrection, at returning this World into its Æther, and will set the Wonders passed in time into Eternal substantiality; He is the Joy and Mover of the Creatures and of Paradise, through whom will be seen the Power and Vertue of every thing.

5. This World with Stars and Elements, shew the Eternal Centre and Being of all Forms, whereon *Adam*, who was the Image of the Trinity, doated and was captiv'd, as *Lucifer* was by the fierce Matrix. He was one, not two, the Light shone in him, and he should have propagated an Angelical Kingdom, was Lord over Fire, Air, Water and Earth, could remove Mountains, no Death was in him, Paradifical Fruit grew for him, he was a Virgin after the Form of Eternal *Sophia*, he was pure and was to place his Will on himself; for God was in him, and he in God. But seeing two Divine Forms in himself, one Paradifical within himself, the other without him, he thought to Eat of both (*viz.*) the Paradifical and the mixed of Good and Evil, while he sunk into a sleep which signifieth Death, where the Spirit of this World formed him into such a Man as we now are, and *Eve* into a Woman, and when they had eaten, the Spirit of this World captivated their Souls, their Essences were Earthy, their Flesh and Blood. Bestial, so that they begat Children in two Kingdoms; (*viz.*) of Wrath and Love, the first a Murtherer, the second Holy, for the word of Grace and Covenant had on their Fall set it self in the Light of their Life.

6. This Word was, and for ever is the only noble spiritual Philosopher's *Stone*, Christ. This *Stone* was in all the Holy Men from *Adam* downward, whereby they both were Good and did Good, but the Men of lower outside Principles or Rationists, have a counterfeit, scholastick, glistering, pleasant *Stone*, which they think is right, and they hotly persecute the true precious *Stone* to advance their own, which outside *Stone* of theirs, is only a *Stone* of the great Building of this World, for it initiateth Childhood in wantonness and bravery, requiring Covetousness and crafty Guile to support it: so they set the Paradifical Garland of Blossoming Youth on the Serpents Head, learn to contemn them as simple who have the true *Stone*, because they live as not of the World, but Childlike, and go through and out of the World weeping, yet bearing precious seed.

7. From *v.* 61. to the end, is as it were a recital of (the often treated of) the Eternal Being compar'd to Fire and Light, as Anger and Love, Strength and Meekness.

The Threefold Life of Man.

nefs, the Original Forms and Principle of Light to v. 73. The Stars are a Quint-effence or fifth Effence diſtinct from the four Elements, as the Fat in a Creature caufeth the Fountain of Life to burn, they are not only Fire and Water, but have all the Properties of hard, foft, bitter, fweet, four, dark and whatever the Earth hath, and every Star a feveral prevalent Property, according as in the Eternal Centre of Nature they ſtood open, when the Eternity mov'd it felf in the Creation.

8. The Air mixeth with all forts of Forms, therefore is unconſtant, ſometimes awakening one Form in the Centre, anon another. The whole Deep is like the Mind of a Man, which beholds fome things curforily, fome other fixedly, bringing it to fubſtance, fetting Hands and Feet to work, as the Will hath conceived and framed it; fo this Spirit of the Deep, though without Divine Underſtanding, formeth by the vigor of the Conſtellations the Spirit of our Adamical Man, alſo of all Beaſts, Fowls, Herbs, Plants, Trees, Metals, Precious Stones, Fiſhes, &c. and is the caufe of Wifdom in Arts, Polity Governments among fallen Mankind. And this is called the third Principle or awakened Life of God, not Eternal, but that in which the great Wonders are made vifible Subſtances, whoſe Figures remain as a Picture for the Glory of God and Joy of the Angels and Men, but their Effences ſhall be reduced into the Æther as it was before the Creation of the World, yet ſhall all ſtand in the Eternal Nature with its colours and figures, and there will be a ſpringing, bloſſoming and growing, yet without feeling any fire or fiercenefs, for the Effences will then be no more a Subſtance, and therefore it affordeth no fire, but the fire is an Eternal Darkneſs and gnawing, call'd the Eternal Death.

CHAP. VIII. *How by the outward World is opened the Eternal World; How a Man may feek and find himſelf; Whence is his Beginning, and what his End.*

1. AS the enlivening Spirit in the deep animates all Creatures as if they were one Body, each according to their Kind, fo the Light of Eternity within this World incomprehenfible to this Worlds Spirit, having all the Properties alſo in it, yet with no fuch inkindled Effences, is the Life of the bleſſed Inhabitants thereof. Their Fire though mighty, is yet without Pain or Confumption, burning in the foft delicate defire of dear Love and higheſt Joy; this Fire maketh Majefty, ſpringeth and bloſſometh for ever in fuch Earth as is call'd Divine Subſtantiality or Holy Ternary, ſtored with perfect Goodneſs, exempt from all kind of Evil.

2. And as the whole third Principle of Aſtral and Elementary Bodies are as one Body, fo the Infinite Holy God, Heaven, Angels, Men, Paradife with all Divine Things and Properties are but one Body, call'd God, Majefty and Eternity; wherein the Majefty is the Light, the Holy Ghoſt, the Air and Spirit. Every Angel and Man is like the total God, and the Holy Ghoſt proceeds forth in him alſo. As in a flaming piece of Iron; the Iron refembleth the Creature, its flame of Light the Deity, its Heat the Creatures Spirit, the Air proceeding from it the Holy Ghoſt: but now we live in Anguiſh, Cares, Labour, Fear, Trembling, Affliction and cloathed with fallen *Adam*'s Skin, yet alſo in the Hope of *Iſrael*.

3. And becaufe the Soul ſtands between two Eternal Principles, and the Body meerly in the Spirit of this Worlds Earthy ſtate caring little, for the Soul; therefore muſt the Body be kept under, its neceſſities only not its wanton defires anfwer'd. The Soul alfo muſt watch and pray, not pleafe it felf in its own ability, but ever humble it felf to the Divine Will and Mercy. Thefe things are irkfom to the Body and crofs to the Self will of the Soul, but the view of Eternity muſt

ſway

sway all, for the Body is an unconstant Neighbour and Death a sudden Guest. And as the danger, so the power God hath graciously given the Soul, is very great: As it is written to them he gave power (in Christ) to be the Sons or Children of God.

4. Man finds in himself more than is in the Beast, for the Beast hath no higher Will than to fill and nourish it self, and multiply according to the property of their Centre, and every Life desireth the best that is in its Mother or Centre, which shews what the best of the Centre or Mother (whence they are) is, but Man sees into the property and vanity of every thing here, and therefore, a higher Life above the Elementary Transitory Food. The Beast hath a Tincture, else the Fire of their Life would devour them, but their Fire and Tincture is but Elementary and Astral, and consequently fragil; but Man hath a desire after an Eternal Life, and shews it by his desire to perpetuate his Memory here (by his Offspring or otherwise) if he could. For tho' he enter community with the Beasts in his third Principle, yet he hath a Fire-life out of the Eternity wherein the Forms are in Anguish; and that not being the right Life, hath a Tincture of Divine substantiality of Meekness, which is the Light which quencheth the wrath of his Firesoul, wherein is the Intellect satiating the Anguish, which tincture *Lucifer* caused to disappear as a shadow, shutting himself up in Death and Fierceness.

5. Is it said why did God suffer *Lucifer* to fall? *A.* He was a Prince and Throne Angel, a Son of the first Creation or Morning, and cause of the Out-birth in the third Principle, therefore Christ called him the Prince of this World: He had also a Free-will like us Men, and we often do things contrary to God, as making Forts, Castles and sumptuous Houses for our state. So *Lucifer* would be as a Creator, which in it self was no more his Fall than *Adam*'s imagining, which caused the Tree of Temptation to grow, which therefore was severely forbidden, yet which of it self was not *Adam*'s Fall; but *Lucifer*'s Fall was when he awakened the *Matrix* of the Fire over the Meekness of God, that Fire became, and now is his Hell, which God captivated with Heaven or Water, and moved himself to the Creation as the pleasant Sun shuts up the Astringent cold, turning Ice into Water, making Fish, *&c.* to live and grow. And the cause of the Sea and unfathom'd deeps is that there the Fire was greatly enkindled; as when *Sodom*, *&c.* were a Habitation of the Devil, who would have dwelt there in his fiery fierceness, God allay'd his stoutness, bringing Water on that place.

6. The Souls dissatisfaction here shews it in a captivity, for its true Rest and Heaven was shut up in it, having in *Adam* put its desire into the Principle of this World; great is the perplexity that an Eternal Creature should be Immur'd and Married to another Principle, have another Mother and Centre, which as soon as it breaks (as dissolve it doth) leaves the Soul in indigence and darkness. This pos'd the understanding, non-pluft the wisdom of all Creatures how to help, no Prince or Throne Angel could contrive a Remedy. Then said *Jehovah* Christ, *Lo I come to do thy Will, O God*, and his own Arm wrought Salvation by becoming Man, entring Death with his Humane Soul, brake the seven Seals of the Centre of Nature, hung the old *Adam* as a Curse on the Cross, kindled again the Divine Fire in the Soul, cast away the Earthiness, and powerfully through Death introduced Life.

The highly precious Gate.

Thus the Regenerate may see that as Christ did cast away from him by Death, only the Spirit of this World, and raised himself, so shall they in his Word and Heart which is every where present, and in his Flesh and Blood, not in the corrupt Body, be raised, for the inward Body *Adam* had in Paradise is only capable of being clothed upon with the Flesh of Christ: In this new Body fixeth the new Regenerate

The Threefold Life of Man.

nerate Soul, but the old corrupt Fiesh only hangeth to the new Body, yet comprehends it not. The which old Body conceived from the Spirit of this VVorld, being at the last day raised therewith, only in a figure (in which figure all Mans works follow him) passeth into its Ether, yet remaineth in its figure. So likewise the corrupt Bodies of the wicked at the last Judgment shall be presented with their Mother the Spirit of this world, and the Souls shall hear the sentence, then shall the Bodies pass with their Mother and stand as a Figure, and their works in the figure shall follow them into the Abyss.

CHAP. IX. *Concerning the Threefold Life. Also the Inclination and whole Government of Man in this Life.*

1. MAN's whole Race is a strife 'twixt the Devil and the Soul, and the Spirit of this world and the Soul; for this worlds Spirit hath apprehension (tho not Divine) planted in its Matrix, and this world stood in the Eternal wisdom as an invisible figure before the Creation, and by Creation became a proper Principle, to the end it might bring all its wonders and works into Existence, and appear Eternally in their figure.

2. Man only being capable to exhibit this worlds wonders of Arts, and the Spirit and Life of Metals, precious Stones, Earths, Celestial Influences, &c. therefore hath the Spirit of this world longed to draw Man into it. That precious Stone of Philosophers may be found in Metals by him who understandeth this Author, in the Centre of Natures progress to the Cross of the Trinity and Glance of the Majesty, which this worlds Spirit hath a Natural longing to reveal.

3. The first Birth of things are not pleasant, as in Trees; but the Fruit is a second Birth, and what is desir'd by Man, which points us to our Noble Birth and high Descent which was Divine; for when the Kingdom of the Anger did press into the Fruits the Paradisical Principle did almost wholly withdraw. Yet though Toads, Serpents poyfonous Herbs, bitter Properties, Thistles, &c. originate in the wrathful Matrix, yet as the evil Properties explicate the inward worlds they are as good, and concur to the same end with the best; but the evil and good eaten by *Adam* being such as we now eat, was his eating of Death, because thereby the Spirit of this world captivated him, as doth both it and the Devils Kingdom rule in Man still.

Of the great strife about Man.

4. Hell saith my Anger is his Root he is therefore by Nature mine. This world pleads possession of Man in its Body, and his Community of Nutrition from it. God saith I have set my Heart upon Man and Regenerated him, he proceeded out of me I have sought and found him again, he is mine to reveal my wonders. Pursuant to this, one of three things winneth him, either, 1. His desire of Honour Glory and Power which is the Devils Will. 2. His desire of Riches, Opulence and Fulness in which he is a Beast of this World. 3. He, the somewhat sensible Sinner (but not the Swine) greatly feareth Hell and the Devil, and weakly panteth after Heaven, but the other two draw so violently, that many through desperation engulph themselves into the Abyss.

Of the Devil changing himself into an Angel of Light.

5. When the Sinner begins to be sensible of his evil and danger, the Devil willingly permits him to go to the Stone Churches, then flatters him that his diligent so doing makes him godly and devout: Where often thoughts are sown in him of Pride, Lust, &c. also of contempt of others, especially if the Preacher be a Reviler,

Reviler. If the Soul be yet afraid and would repent and pray, the Devil clouds the underſtanding, introduceth doubts, and promiſeth amendment to Morrow, he rehearſeth words, but prayeth not; for the Soul cannot reach the Centre of Nature where the Fire ſhould be ſtruck, but his words in this Worlds Spirit vaniſh into Air, or Gods Name is taken in vain.

6. But Prayer is a great (or at leaſt a true) going of the Soul to be ſpoken to of God, and brought out of the Houſe of Sin into the Houſe of God: Which when the Devil oppoſeth we are to oppoſe the more, for we have in Chriſt far greater power than he. But if the Devil covers the Heart by heaps of Sin we are not to diſpute or deſpair, but to lay them on the Devils Back, and lay up in our Hearts Gods moſt merciful Calls and earneſt Will towards us, ſhewn by the Sufferings, Wounds, Death and dear Love and Pity of Chriſt to Sinners; for there is no other Will in God but to do as the Father to the Prodigal Son, therefore to doubt of Gods gracious Intents is to ſin greatly.

The Gates of the deep Ground concerning Man.

7. The knowing what Man is in the variety of form, feature and different driving Will, hath been controverted ſince the beginning, becauſe the Gates thereof were ſunk with *Adam's* Fall, but the Spirit of the Soul of the Regenerated Man, knoweth himſelf in all the three Principles to have but one only Rule though in three Principles, the prevalence of either denominates the Man. We are as a Seed ſowen in a Field by the Luſt of Man and Woman, the Mover whereunto is that the Tincture now divided to the Male giving Life and Soul, and the ſubſtantiality now peculiar to the Female giving Spirit and Exiſtence were in Eternity one; wherein this world ſtood as a Figure, and the Tincture over-ſhadowed by the Wiſdom was received thereinto as the Body doth the Spirit, yet could not be brought into ſubſtance viſible to Angels who are in a ſubſtance unleſs God had moved the Eternity.

8. In the moving of the Trinity was moved the Centre of Nature, whereby the Tincture became ſubſtantial, and the ſubſtantiality became material, yet not divided, wherein when the *Fiat* was awakened forth came all ſorts of Beaſts, *&c.* The Tincture took ſubſtance, and the Spirit of the ſubſtance took on it a Body, the firſt had the Centre of Life, the other only an impotent Life, which may be demonſtrated by a flaming Iron; which emitteth two Spirits, *viz.* a hot one able to awaken another Fire from its own Centre, and another an airy one, which though it hath all powers of the Fire, yet not the Tincture of the Fire, but only the Spirit of the Fire, a faint Life, for in the Eternity is no Death. Hence is it that Life muſt proceed only from the Seed of the Male Tincture in the *Matrix* of the Female.

9. Every Creature Inanimate, Senſitive, *&c.* is formed according to the Tincture in the Spirit of the Species of them, as may be found by the order of the ſeveral days of the Creation; for on the firſt day God Created the Material Water which hath an impotent Life, and is a Bar to the Devils Anger Fire. And when God ſaid let there be Light, the Light of the Tincture opened it ſelf, which God ſeparated from the darkneſs, *viz.* ſhut up the fierce Fire *Lucifer* kindled, which originateth in the darkneſs, and let the Qinteſſence burn in the fat of the Water Spirit, as doth the Fire of the Life in a Beaſt.

10. The Tincture is in the Blood the Life burneth in the Tincture, and God keeps the Centre of the Fire in the darkneſs, and ſo every Life is in his own hand, for if he let the Fire into the Tincture the Spirit is in the Helliſh Fire. The Tincture was divided into a Fire Life and Light Life, the Fire Life was to be a Firmament between the Holy Meekneſs the Heart of God and the weak Air, between both which God dwelleth. The Fire Spirit of the Tincture hath Eternity for its Root,

The Threefold Life of Man.

Root, the Air Spirit hath the awakened subftantiality ruling the outward Life of Beafts, Trees, &c. having a weak Tincture.

11. Thus fee we Life ftandeth in Fire and Air, alfo the Original of Blood, fuch Creatures that have it are more noble than thofe that have it not; for fuch have a falfe Tincture proceeded from the will of the Devil as is feen in Vipers and other Venemous Reptils, for fuch lothfom ugly Bodies are figur'd in Hell, not from the divided Tincture but from the fierce dark Spiritual fubftance.

12. When the Water covering the Created Earth was feparated, and the Earth dry, the collected Water was call'd * Sea, fignifying in the Language of Nature a covering, in reproach to the Devil whofe power was drown'd. By the Water above the Firmament feparated from that below is meant the Blood wherein is the Tincture of Living Creatures, and that beneath is the Elementary Water, in which two confift two Kingdoms, 1. The Soul in the Blood in the Tincture, and becaufe the Tincture is from Eternity, therefore muft the figures remain in Eternity. And, 2. The Air Spirit in the Water which is corruptible for it had a beginning.

* *Mare.*

13. After the Earth and Elements were formed, the fiery Tincture was as a fhining Light, then God fuffered the Centre of Nature to open with its proper will out of the Effences, and the whole Principle became but one Body whereof the Sun was the Heart; and the fix other Planets the Spirits at the Centre of the Heart, the other Stars are its Effences; all juft as the Deity hath been from Eternity, whence came a true Life, Reafon, Sences and Underftanding, yet a Beftial one, and Spirit of the Air manifefting God in a figurative form, which this world fheweth, if we confider the Centre, and thence go on in the Light of the Majefty to the number three.

The Difcourfe and Figure of the Planets and Signs from the 63d v. to the end of this Chapter being it felf Summary is recommended to be perufed entirely as the Author left it.

CHAP. X. *Of the Creation of every Being; and how Man may find himſelf, and all Myſteries to, and only to the ninth Number.*

1. TO feek the Myfteries of Nature in the Stars and Elements is vain, neither *Luna* nor *Mercury* will lead you to *Sol*; but if you take the Spirit of the Tincture, following of which to *Sol* fome have been laid hold on by the Spirit of the Heavenly Tincture, and been brought into the liberty of the Majefty, where they have known the noble Stone, and ftood amazed at Mans blindnefs.

2. The number is but three, ftay at the Crofs or ten, but nine is only attainable, then take *Saturn* as a Male and Fire-Tincture, and *Luna* as the Female and Air Spirit, go thus gradually in the Wheel to *Sol*, go then on through the Suns Fire, and being through it lay hold by means of the Tincture on the Eternity which is the ninth number, bring that on the Crofs which is the tenth, the very end of nature, here handle the Stone, it is Fire-proof, free from the Wrath and Out-birth, its fplendor is in the Majefty, its Body out of the Eternal Subftantiality.

3. If now the feeker willeth the fplendor of this world, let him go from the inward into the outward *Luna* which break into a thoufand parts, giving it fuch proportion of *Sol* as its hunger defireth, and it is made bright and perfect, but we ought

ought juftly to reft fatisfied in the tenth number for this world is but, drofs and dung, therefore Chrift faith, *Seek firft the Kingdom of God, and all other things fhall be added*. All lyeth in the willing, for the will maketh the defire, the outward will muft enter into the inward, and deny it felf, as if it were dead to the outward, becaufe *Adam* turning his will to the outward, caus'd him to die to the inward, but if we turn back into the inward, we fee God, and the Eternity, and are the Similitude of what God is, and are as we were Created.

4. It is more eafie to the inward Man in the Divine Will to fee the ground of the Creation of this world than for the outward to know what the Sences inform. To create is to ccmprehend what is firft figur'd in the will, as doth a Builder frame in his will a Model of what he is to Erect. In the Creation the fix Properties ftand in every quadrat of the Circle of Time which divides the Day into Morning, Noon, Evening and Midnight.

5. On the fifth day the *Fiat* opened the Matrixes of all Similitudes, and the Wrath Kingdom preffed hard to be imaged with it, when were produced all Fowls and Fifhes, then alfo all forts of Spirits of the Fire, Air, Water and Earth went forth, fo that the whole deep even to the Conftellations is nothing but a Life and ftirring of Spirits. The Devils place is in the darkeft towards the Conftellations, and fo poor a Creature is he as not to touch any of the feven Governments.

6. The defcribing the order of Powers cannot be fufficiently feen by the orderly Wheel of the Magi, nor can it be written for Reafon to penetrate, being more fubtle, going inwards towards the Sun ; that is, upwards, downwards and fideways towards the meek fubftantiality, but the Spirit of the Soul if it look with its own Eye into the inward, and with the Eye of this world into the outward underftandeth it, and is as *Ezekiel*'s Vifion, having Eyes within and without, and the Spirit goeth right forward wherefoever it goes.

7. Now to fhew how far Man may go, and where he muft ftop, note that the Fire after the feven Spirits is the eighth and the caufe of the feventh. Now tho' Life confifts not in the Fire, yet the Fire maketh two Tinctures. 1. An inward after the Eternal Liberty, and ftill Meeknefs where fpringeth the Majefty of the Liberty. 2. An outward after the Oyl from the water of *Venus*, where fprings the outward fplendor, fo the Fire hath the eighth number, and the inward Tincture hath the ninth number, fo far and no farther ought we to go, but ftand there before the Crofs of the number three, where Angels and Men are to ftand, not reaching into the Centre of the Crofs to Create as did *Lucifer*, but caft their Minds down into the Tincture of Humility back into the ninth number, fearing God, and highly rejoicing before the tenth number with Songs of Hallelujahs to the Holy, Holy, Holy Lord God of Hofts; in this ninth is the Virgin Tincture of Wifdom, Paradife and Heavenly Subftantiality.

8. For while we keep our will in humility, tho' we fearch into the thoufandth number our will is ftill Gods will, but if we leave him, and imagine into the Wonders we are Captives, for imagination makes fubftance ; we muft go out of that again into Humility, Love, Purenefs, Mercy, &c. or we fhall not fee God ; we muft fubmiffively feek the will of God, and refign our whole felf thereinto, wherein we can do all, but in our own will and nature we muft not; we can do nothing.

CHAP. XI. *Of the true Knowledge concerning Man.*

1. THE Earth is a peculiar Centre, an Out-birth of the Eternal fubftantiality, the Matrix whereof was corrupted by the Fall of *Lucifer*, whence the
upper

The Threefold Life of Man.

upper Centre the Suns Heart drew forth from the Properties in the Earth, which longed after the upper Paradifical Fruit, of which Man only was capable to eat after an Angelical manner, and which *Adam* ftood in the *Proba* or tryal to have done till he flept, but we fee how it went with him, for that we both eat and are eaten by the Earth.

2. Of that Paradifical Earth wherein was the Heavenly Property was *Adam's* Body made; for he was to be Lord over the Earth, and to open the wonders of the Earth, therefore God gave him a palpable, yet a paradifical. (and not inftantly an Angelical) Body. Man was made an Image of the uncreated Virgin of Gods Wifdom wherein the Aftral and Elementary Powers ftood, but neither they nor the Matrix of the Earth could over-power Man, for he had receiv'd the Eternal Subftantiality.

3. It is faid God breathed into his Noftrils the Breath of Life, this was not Air, nor can it be a thing breathed in from without, for God is the fulnefs of all things. God longed after a vifible Similitude of himfelf, but his longing is only Majefty and Liberty, his breathing was from within, for Gods Holy Spirit hath awakened the Soul out of the Centre of the Fire of the Eternal Nature the fifth form where the two Kingdoms of Gods Love and Anger do part, and brought it outwards into the Tincture of the outward Spirit, into the Blood of the Heart opening it felf according to the Centre of Nature; and the Spirit of this world which reacheth into the Sun was breathed into him from without, fo became he a Living Soul ruling over Fire, Air, Water, Earth, and the Sun it felf, without Covetoufnefs, Pride, Envy, Anger, Toil, Care and Sicknefs, but was a holy pure Virgin in meer Joy and Love-fport.

4. The dividing of the Tinctures is fhewn by dividing the Crofs in the Brain-Pan, God Created Man with the whole Crofs, but now 'tis divided half to the Man, and the other half to the Woman; before *Adam's* being divided he could generate out of his will fuch a Man as himfelf, having the three Centres in him, without tearing, as neither was the Centre of the Eternal Nature whence his Soul proceeded torn, nor the Spirit of this world divided when the Spirit of God breathed it into him, nor had he Members whereof to be afhamed, his clothing was the Heavenly Tincture, his Fall was his Luft after the out-principle, and could not eat of the Word of the Lord.

5. The Male and Female Will to each other exifteth out of the two Governments of one fubftance, the Man foweth Flefh and Blood, and the Noble Tincture of the Soul out of the Fire Tincture; the Woman Spirit out of the Tincture of this World, *viz.* of *Venus* giving a foft Spirit, but Man is yielded, faln home, a Captive to the Spirit of this world, making an Earthy Elementary Child; fo that if God had not become Man our Bodies had remained Beafts & our Souls Devils, and fuch we are till Born again in Chrift, and by him turned about to fee into the tenth number again. And if this be done, when God awakens the Centre of the Eternal (which is the Souls) Fire, the Holy Ghoft fhall burn forth from the Tincture of the Soul, and the Soul be taken into the Majefty of God, and her works without lofs pafs through the Fire; for the Soul that turneth into this world when the fubftance hereof paffeth into its Ether is without God in the Hellifh Fire, wanting the Oyl of the wife Virgins, for this World neither gives it nor fells it, for it hath it not.

The great Mifery of Mans Deftruction from the Womb.

6. While the Soul is in the Seed it is only a Fire of the Tincture, and a Will of the Creature, but when it becomes a Living Creature, the Fruit is much as the Tree is, and if it be forfaken of the Holy Powers, the Will of the Soul by the Nature of the Fire formeth the Souls Spirit into the figure of horrible, cruel, crafty, poy-

Q q 2 fonous,

fonous, filthy Creatures. Alfo in the Spirit of the Seed while it is a Sulphur, *viz*. Unformed Matter, is the Spirit of this World and the Conftellation, fo that the outward Life is fallen quite under the Power of the Stars, which ftrongly inclineth fome to various Evils and Tragical Exits, others to infnaring Honours; which is done when a fixed Star having been fortified by the Sun's Vertue, is inducted by the Father of Nature, it can then powerfully imprefs its Imagination into the Seed, conveying fuch or fuch a Property into the Creatures Elementary Life in Men and Beafts.

7. Man thus making himfelf and Pofterity miferable, awakens the Wrath Kingdom in this World, where the Devil is the Great Prince: which awakening bringeth Tempefts, Wars, Peftilence, Fire, Famine, *&c.* for had not Man opened the Anger, the Devil had remained fhut up without Power to touch a Fly, or move a Leaf. 'Tis true, that fometimes the Aftral Powers make and give for a Tincture this Worlds Spirit, and then by reafon that the Spirit of the Soul hath a good Conftellation at the time of the Spirits awakening, it gives him a Friendly, lovely outfide, whereby fuch a one can give good flattering words from a falfe heart; for he dwelleth in two Kingdoms, in this World is he a Hiftory Hypocrite, and his Soul in the Anger Kingdom with the Devils.

8. But the Grace of God appeared by Chrift's becoming Man, to bring our Human Souls out of Death and the Abyfs of Anger into the Tenth Number, the Eternal Tincture, to be again the Similitude of God upon the Crofs, whence the Soul originated. And then when the Soul is turned into the Will of God in great Humility having Chrift's Body, it paffeth through Death or from Death to Life in the Death of Chrift, through the Anger of God into the Ninth Number before the Holy Trinity, and is imbraced by the Majefty.

The great open Gate of Antichrift.

9. Antichrift in Men profeffing Chrift, is a contrary will to the Divine Will, yet a Counterfeit of it: but as the Soul becomes born of God, more or lefs, in fuch proportion the renewed Will quits the Principles, and Dictates of corrupt Reafon and felf Defires cover'd by Hypocrifie, and by a fincere faithful Love rooted in the Life of Chrift, a holy Flame of felf evidencing Light arifeth, giving a diftinct difcovery of Antichrift before which it falls, and by which it is deftroy'd, for the going from Antichrift is the going from the Fire into the Light.

The highly Precious Gate, alfo the Gate of Immanuel.

10. Is it askt, *How can Chrift's Body be ours? How can we dwell in the Body of Chrift?* It is Anfwer'd, As we have *Adam's* Flefh, Soul and Spirit, which Chrift becoming Man hath, yet remaineth God; but receiv'd in the fair Virgin of Wifdom the Eternal Flefh, which *Adam's* was before dividing of the Properties, and the Property of our earthy Flefh, fo Chrift's Soul is ours, and his Body ours, and his Virgin ours, whereby we live in Chrift when we give up our felves to him, wherein alfo he liveth in us, and will at laft prefent us wholly pure with the Heavenly Flefh, Blood, Tincture and Majefty of Chrift. Thus alfo he liveth in us, and we are his Members, Temple and Body.

11. Where one faith, *Here is Chrift*, and another *There*, it is, becaufe they have loft the Key, for the Body and Blood of Chrift is in the Eternity, and not fhut up by fpace or place, but as the Sun fhineth from Eaft to Weft, and whofe Light fills the World, how much more doth Chrift fill every part of his Incarnation? And when we defire his Flefh and Blood, we receive it, and are fed by it; for as the Father gives Being, and upholdeth all, fo the Son gives Vertue and Light. The Congregation of Chrift is in every Nation where Men turn from their Sins to God, be they *Greeks, Turks, Afians, Africans*, &c. God refpects not Perfons nor Opinions, but feeks the Heart; thofe who call on the only true God in plain Simplicity are

in

The Threefold Life of Man.

in Chrift, but the Tyrannous, Proud, Covetous, Malicious, Blood-thirfty Antichrift, with their endlefs Contentions and Difputations offend the Heathens, whofe Life and Cuftoms are far more Innocent and Pious, and when Antichrift's Lyes have ftifled him, broken his Murthering Sword, and laid him in the Pit, then fhall Chrift feed his Lambs, and the Turk be of the Fold of the Lambs.

12. The whole World is full of God; the inward holy Life dwelleth in God, and the inward dark Abyfs ftandeth in God's Wrath, the ftrife is, which may Image us into it felf in this outward Life, here God fets Light and Darknefs before us, and all the teaching here is to warn of the fevere Property of the Fire; for every thing hath Free-will with an Inclination to its Property; therefore we muft either embrace the true Good, or the certain Evil. Young Children are our School-mafters, with all our Cunning we are but Fools to them, who firft play with themfelves, and after one with another, this the Devil grudg'd us, and made us fall out at our Play, and fo we quarrel till we go to fleep, and then others Act over again the fame quarrels, and all is about a defiled Garment which yet is not ours, while we fhould obediently fearch for a new fair Garment: when amongft the Rofes, Lillies and Flowers, we fhall in our own Country fing the Song, How the Driver (who did fet us at variance) is captivated.

CHAP. XII. *Of the true Chriftian Life and Converfation. What Man is to do,* &c.

Confidering well the 34 firft Verfes of this 12th Chapter, it may be comprifed moftly in thefe words. *He hath fhewed thee, O Man, what is good, and what doth the Lord thy God require of thee, but to do juftly, to love Mercy, and to walk humbly with thy God?*

The Way we muft walk through this World into the Kingdom of God.

We muft, it we will fo walk, Crucifie Self, Repent, Convert from Evil, hourly pafs out of Death into Life, we muft not take pleafure in our felves, but fo humble our felves before the clear Countenance of the Trinity, (before whom we always ftand) and look on Jefus who always fitteth on the Rainbow in us: I fay, we are fo to converfe without Self-pleafing, that our ways may pleafe God, the heavenly Hoafts and Man.

The reft of this fweet Chapter is of various and copious Rules and Monitions, yet fo confpicuous, that the perufal is rather to be recommended than the particulars extracted.

Only this afferteth, That a Self-defence againft outward Force or War, having only a defire of Self-defence, is not againft God; for he whofe Houfe is on Fire may quench it. (v. 42.)

CHAP. XIII. *Of Chrift's Precious Teftaments the Lord's Supper and Baptifm.*

1. VVHEN Chrift's Apoftles and Difciples met together, after fervent Exhortation of one another, They took, brake, divided amongft them, and did eat Bread in commemoration of Chrift's giving his Body for us on the Crofs, as himfelf had commanded. So alfo took they the Cup in their hand, faying one to another, Take this Cup and drink the Blood of our Lord which he shed

shed on the Cross for Remission of our Sins, to shew forth his Death till he come again to Judgment, and bring us into himself. This was the true great Paschal Lamb instituted by Christ after they had eaten the Passover.

2. He gave them and they did eat and drink his Flesh and Blood, not his earthy and mortal Flesh and Blood to be chewed with their earthy Teeth and swallow'd; for that Body of his was not divided amongst them, but he gave them his Immortal holy Body and Blood, new and unknown to the earthy Man, yet which did hang in, or was United to the outward on the Cross; this holy Body became as a Body to their Souls, making them his Members.

3. As the Eternal Virginity, Substantiality and Wisdom wherein was the promised Word, gave it self into the perished Tincture became a new Man at the Incarnation in the Virgin *Mary*; so the new Body of Christ which was cover'd or veiled by the outward Mortal Body, and cannot be comprehended by the Mortal, but is he that cometh down from Heaven, gives it self under Bread and Wine into the Tincture of the Souls of those who go out from themselves into his Will; thus was in Christ two Kingdoms, a Heavenly and an Earthy, the new Man born of God, wherever he is, receiveth this heavenly Flesh and Blood, or holy Humanity, for it is every where, and had the predominance in *Adam*, till he went back into the Lust of the outward earthy Principle, wherein the Devil hath entrance to us poor Captives, so that often the Soul turns its Will to the outward, wherefore God by his Testament reneweth the Soul by this new Body. How careful therefore should the Soul be, that it go not back as did *Adam*. For the Soul of Man hungereth and thirsteth after this Food, being the word intended, when Christ said *Eat, This is my Body*, and without this Substance, God is not known; it being the Manifestation of the Deity. Yet doth the outward Humane Nature remain in Heaven palpably and apprehensibly seen by Men in that Form it was in here when upon Earth, and in that Body is seen nothing but the Majesty, Clarity and Brightness which filleth the Angelical World.

4. Now wherever the Majesty is, there is the Substantiality, which is the Body of the Word, yet without Image; for the Creature only is an Image or Formation, like as the substantial Earth is come, though in the Deep is only Air, Water and Fire; whereof the Sun (though but one) is the cause.

5. We receive not in the Supper another Creature with a new Soul, but we receive on our Soul the Body of Christ which is already the Eternal Creature, whose Flesh and Blood filleth Heaven: and which is such a Body to the Soul, as can at the End of the World go with the Soul through the Fire of the Anger of God without feeling, changing the Fire by the allay of Meekness into a meer Love-desire, a brightness of the Majesty; Thus are we in God the Children of God. *Allelujah*.

Concerning the Testament of Baptism.

6. A Child hath by the Masculine Seed the Fires Tincture or that of the Soul, and by the Feminine hath the Lights or Waters Tincture, or that of the Spirit, but by *Adam*'s Fall both were corrupted; so that the Fires Tincture or Soul was captivated by God's Eternal Wrath; and the Water or Spirits Tincture was captivated by the Spirit of this great outward World, and both had remained the Devil's Captives, had not the Word of the Lord taken our Soul and Spirit, and been made Flesh. Therefore he instituted Baptism for little Children, being an Office managed by the Holy Ghost, in whose Vertue the Soul's Water is made a Water of Life, for the Water belongs to the Spirits Tincture, and so the Spirit of the Soul receiveth the Vertue wrought by the Holy Ghost's Office, which is the great Mystery. Even as the Vertue convey'd to the hunger of the Soul's Fire, is most immediately from the Vertue in the Flesh and Blood of the Son, the second Person of the Trinity.

The Magia *cut of the Wonders.*

7. Where there is but one only Will, there is no breaker nor Enmity, but it draweth into it self, and goeth out of it self in the same one free Will; but where there are two Wills, there is separation and contrariety; for one Will goeth inward, and the other outward; and if it be in one thing or body, that Kingdom hath intestine opposition: Whence comes a third Will mixed of the two first: Hence spring many needing a Judge, but if they all be strong Wills, they constitute severally every one a Judge, and the flown out Will hates that whence it sprung, because it hath got a contrary Will, and it self proceeds to its highest number: But seeing it can get no higher, nor attain rest; therefore at that place of inquiry the Prophet is born, who sheweth the cause why the out-flown Will, instead of going to the Crown-number, hath awakened the *Turba* or disturbance, which shall have an end by rising of a new Kingdom, whereof the Prophet is the Mouth; which new Kingdom being generated out of the breaking, causeth the Pride, Covetousness and Envy of the strayed Wills, like evil Twigs to be broken and wither: And whereas they call themselves Children of the good Root, the Prophet tells them they are Murtherous Wolves; and if the *Turba* be grown up with it, it breaketh the multiplicity.

8. Now when the Father pours Oyl into the Wounds, the Oyl it self becomes Poison, which should have been a Remedy; for the strayed Will hath made an Oyl by his own Wit and Art wherewith it feeds and actuates its earthy sensual desires; so that the true Oyl is death to this Evil Will of the multiplicity, for it calleth it self the Good Tree, so there is no Remedy but it must be its own destroyer, and the apostated Children are given to the *Turba* to be devoured one of another. They boast themselves to know much, but do it not, but retaining the History, deny the Power, as their Father the Devil, who knoweth as much as they, doth it not.

9. But the Mother of the Genitrix finding her Children become strange to her, falling into lamentation and anguish, doth conceive and bring forth a young Son; on him she puts a garment of childish simplicity, and he became a Lilly Twig of Purity; he shall break the *Turba*, and doing the Divine Will, remain in the house for ever; whence the other by following the Devil revolted, feigning to themselves good words, blessing themselves for hearing and seeing what they hear and see, and taking the Covenant of God into the mouth while they hate to be reformed, and dwell in falshood.

CHAP. IX. *Of the Broad and Narrow Ways.*

1. THE Broad Way leading to the Abyss of Wrath, is what we strongly incline to, being as to the inward or first Principle (the Soul's Original understood of the four Anguishes) in the way of craft, cruelty, pride, revenge, desire of Rule and Pomp: And as to the outward, the way of ease, pleasure, voluptuousness, with a swinish appetite to get and keep all.

2. Our Temporary Nature is captive to the Bestial Properties, whereto it is severally formed by the Spirit of this World, according as the Wheel of the Outward Nature stood at the instant of the formation: But if Men remain guided only thereby, it giveth the Body to the Earth, and the Soul to Hell. Yet so broad is the Evil Way, that the Travellers therein may, as with full Sail, traverse it, tho' by constitution they be adapted to desire of deep search after knowledge, skilful inspection into secret Mysteries, many practical and speculative Arts and parts of Wisdom

dom by quick Aſtral Reaſon. Others, tho' in the ſame broad Road, may have excellent skill in diſputes of Antient and Modern Religious Controverſies and Traditions in Doctrine and Diſcipline, they may be prudent exemplars in Manners, great Proficients in Philoſophy, profound Caſuiſts in Theology, with ſo good progreſs as if they were Pillars in God's Houſe, and all this adorned with a blameleſs Converſation to human obſervation.

3. But all this deſtitute and excluſive of a changed Will, but retaining unmortified affections and deſires, having an unregenerate Heart, a Soul dead to any Life of Reſignation and Sacrifice, but is ſtill immutably ſtubborn; is therefore as concerning the Faith reprobate, for the right Faith is the right Will, which (diveſted of its ſelf-luſts) enters into the living Word, whereas the other is without God in the World, tho' flattering himſelf all his life long with the merits of Jeſus Chriſt is ſhare in them, his Predeſtination from Eternity, his aſſurance never to fall away, whereas he was never riſen with Chriſt, but lies drowned with, and under the deſires of the preſent Evil World, and lives wholly a ſtranger to the dying of Chriſt, to the emptying of the corrupt ſelf-will; for the Pearl is in That man's account too dear, nor will he buy Oyl.

Of the Company and Aſſiſtance of the Holy Angels.

4. As Men fearing God readily help each other in their miſery; ſo do the Holy Angels powerfully aſſiſt Men; for they affect the company of vertuous, humble, chaſt men, themſelves being very pure, chaſt, modeſt, humble, friendly, and know no deceit or iniquity; they have alſo great delight among little Infants, and ſometimes manifeſt themſelves to them, and play with them, if they be the Children of God; for they do nothing but what is innate in them, both the Angels and the Children. They have alſo great joy for one poor Soul delivered from the Snares of the Devil, and are at hand ready to deliver ſuch in their greateſt extremities, having an over ballance of Power to that of the Evil Angels, elſe what Ruins would the Devils make in the buſie execution of their Office in the *Turba magna* of terrible Storms? *&c.* as far as the fierce Wrath is therein enkindled, were they not curb'd and drove away by the miniſtration of the Heavenly Hoſts of the holy and mighty Angels ſent out by the Almighty gracious *Jehovah.*

5. There is therefore no cauſe at all of deſpair, tho' the whole World ſeem to be againſt us. Nor are Prayers to be made to them, for they accept not that honour, but direct us to God. Whatever befals us, is to purifie us as Gold; for God aims to have fair lovely Children, and of underſtanding, to diſcover the Deceits of the Old Serpent.

God ſets Heaven and Hell before us, therefore muſt the Soul have Underſtanding to chuſe, and Faith to fight, for it muſt be a continual Warriour. If we make our ſelves fierce, falſe, covetous, proud Devils, we are ſo; but if we image in our Souls humble, meek ſubmiſſiveneſs, with a love to follow the Lord we enter into the Holy Principle, and are in the Paradiſical and Angelical Regiment. Let all therefore be warned according to what they form their Spirits, which is commended to ſeaſonable and moſt ſerious and continued conſideration.

CHAP. XV. *Of the mixed World, its wicked exerciſe, being a Glaſs wherein every one may try out of what Spirit themſelves are.*

1. MOſt juſt and neceſſary is it to reprehend practical Impieties, Immoralities and Debauchery, eſpecially among ſuch profeſſing goodneſs; the
which

The Threefold Life of Man.

which unchriftian Converfation is chargeable on high and low, Prieft and People, old and young, who all are yet apt to account this a Golden Time, and blefs themfelves in it, tho' it is a time of lamentation, being the opening of the laft Seal, and of pouring out the Vial of God's Wrath, bringing to light the Wonders of Hell, particularly the Pride and Oppreffion derived from thofe fent to the Univerfity, enflaving the People in their Underftandings by Conftitutions, Orders, Statutes, &c. and in their Bodies and Eftates by wrefting from them their fweat, and the fruit of their labours wherewith thefe pamper themfelves; a practice not grounded in Nature, but is hellifh, for there one Form vexeth and plagueth another, fo that among thefe the Dog is more happy than the poor of the people.

2. And this hath another confequent Evil, in that it induceth, and in a fort inforceth the poor to imitate them, and to live by deceit, doing that alfo fwinifhly, which the other do in pride and bravery: All which is convinced of great madnefs, confidering the fhortnefs and uncertainty of the prefent time, the great ftrict folemn Judgment day, and the Eternity of the Life to come, on the brink whereof we ftand, ready to enter unconceivable happinefs by the narrow way, or intolerable mifery and fhame by the broad way. Yet this Chapter concludes that a fincere Chriftian doth not here wholly know himfelf, feeing comparatively nothing but his vices, for his Sanctity Chrift hideth under his Crofs.

CHAP. XVI. *Of praying and fafting, what praying its power, ufe, benefit and preparation to God's Kingdom is.*

1. THE earneft reftlefs hunger and thirft of Man's Spirit after the meek reft of Divine Love, from the Property of the driver, being fo impetuous, that the Morning calleth to the Evening, the Night to the Day, and one Day to another panting, when will the refrefhment come? Sheweth whence Man came, and how greatly he is ftrayed, having no place of reft till he be driven back to his ftill Eternal Mother (the Eternal Nature) for here the driver taketh him by the very throat; & he lieth as one among the flain in a great Battle, who dares not lift up his head for fear of the cruel overflowing Conquerors, or as one furrounded with malicious Foes, who all ftrike at him to murther him; or as one fallen into a deep Pit, hoping for help only from above, or as one fallen into a deep Sea fwimming, yet feeing no fhoar, fighteth for help from Heaven.

2. So is it with Man's Soul, for if the Soul fearch its own flefh, blood, marrow and bones, they are Enemies incompaffing and captivating it; the Spirit of this World fuppreffeth it, and would, like a Sea, drown it, by pampering the Beftial Life; the Devil alfo, as a cruel proud Enemy, draweth it into the fierce aking Abyfs, ftriking at it with hellifh anguifh and defpair.

3. Then, if it will be faved, its Will muft depart from the outward, and from its own thoughts and mind into God's mercy; for the Word that made Man's Soul became Man, and his holy Humanity the flefh of the Eternal Word his food, his blood alfo the Water of Eternal Life is as a pure new Body, and this Word was a meek, pure, defirous Love, and then the Holy Ghoft leads it out of Prifon from the Battle of the driver, cooling its flames, and the Soul becomes an humble Child.

4. When the whole man refolves into a Will of leaving every Evil, and feeking God with the whole heart, he is received as *Daniel*, when he began to fet himfelf to pray, and chaften himfelf, the command came forth. But the Life is from within, as when Chrift raifed *Lazarus* by a power from within from the Centre

of the Soul, as so also shall we be raised at last; for the Word with the three Principles dwells in us. And all Souls are as it were one Soul, being all propagated of one Soul, therefore will they all hear the Voice of the Human Soul of Christ, and arise with their Bodies.

5. So when we pray, it is not to a God afar off, for God heareth in the Centre of the Soul of the repenting sinner, pressing out of the anguish of the first Principle, and out of the Spirit of this World into the holy second Principle, which is also in the Soul; for when we pray aright, the Word which became Man, having the Holy Ghost in it, goeth from the Father, and meeteth the pouring out Soul; for the Body is not worthy, but the new Body of the flesh of Christ (when the Soul attains it) is the Temple of the Holy Ghost. Then comes the Soul to God as the Prodigal Son, with an humble, submissive, obedient Will, from the Swine: He knocks at his evil heart, and breaks open the doors, and the Father saith, *This my Son was lost, and is found, was dead, and is alive*.

The latter part of this Chapter is not extracted, being a brief Exposition of the Lord's Prayer, according to the Language of Nature, which is little known.

CHAP. XVII. *Concerning God's Blessing in this World.*

1. THE Soul finds it self in such an Earthy Garment, causing shame, and is so choaked by the Devils smoky Pit, which represents God a cruel severe Judge, that stands at a catch to damn it, or decreed its eternal perdition before the present World was; that the Soul must needs be under total despair, or great doubt (at least) of falling short of the Light of God; for such is the Effect of shame and guilt. Therefore the Soul by this misunderstanding starts back, seeking some satisfaction from the Spirit of this World, and support for the outward Life only (or chiefly) to be had by its own distrustful carking and toiling in his own contrivances and subtle reason; a consequent of the Curse; whence so many potent delusions spring, for he thus falls home to the Earthy Life for meat, clothing and habitation.

2. And this is contrary to the Life Man should have led; for as God dwelleth in the Earth, yet the Earth apprehendeth him not; so Man should with the Soul have eaten the Divine Word of God's Love, tho' the Body had been of the Matrix of the Earth, yet not captivated in it, but eating of the Blessing of God. The Body was taken out of the Centre of the Fire and Waters Tincture, the Soul out of the second Principle, why then should the Body captivate the Soul?

3. The Outward Life consists in three parts, one in the dominion of the Stars, another in the one Element divided into four and the other the dominion of God. So that the Man who trusteth in God, and not in his Reason, the Spirit of God is with him, blessing what he is, hath and doth: For seeing the Soul hath the Body of God, how can God's Spirit forsake the outward Body, which must open its Wonders; God wants none, and all are alike profitable to him, the politick and the weak; for with the outwardly wise he ruleth, and with the outwardly simple he tilleth, buildeth, &c. and this Worlds outward Spirit gives degrees to men here; so according as the Soul is indued with Divine Power, such are the degrees in Heaven, yet all in one Love; but God's Children are in this an that World as Good Herbs and sweet Flowers, which yield their several Vertues in harmony to the Apothecary, and the wicked are as poisonous Weeds, Thorns and Thistles, who separate themselves and their Off-spring into an evil Self-will and Property.

4. Cove-

The Threefold Life of Man.

4. Covetousness is madness, driving Man (Devil like) to Torment, others about a handful of Earth or a Stone, of which the World hath enough, and plague himself, to get the Good of that he must speedily leave, and the gnawing guilt which will never leave him. This Man still runneth after that Care and Sorrow, which runneth after him, whereas every one, it content, hath a sufficient Portion from the Spirit of this World; and of Care and Sorrow also, as saith the Lord, *Sufficient for the day is the Evil thereof.* But Man's mad Will is all to advance Pride; whereas the Kingdom of God is Love and Humility, and if Man suffers not himself to be captivated) Heaven and Earth is his by God's free Donation, so not only Heaven, but the Sun, Stars, Elements, Earth, Sea and &c. is Man's by Natural Propriety. To trust therefore in God, is to build sure in Heaven and Earth.

CHAP. XVIII. *Of Death and Dying. How Man is when he Dieth, and how it is with him in Death.*

1. THE Life consisteth in three Parts; 1. The Inward which is God's Eternal hidden Mystery in the Fire, whence Life existeth. 2. The Middle or Eternal Image of God, wherein God seeth himself as a Man doth himself in a Glass. 3. The Spirit of the great World which this Eternal Image got in the Creation as a Glass to see it self in; so the out-principle figures the inward, and the inward Image hath so gazed on the outward, as that it hath received the outward, which must break off again, which because it is bound to the Eternal Centre of Nature, therefore is the breaking in Death so very painful.

2. The outward consisteth in the Sun's Tincture and its Dominion are the Planets and Stars, each of which still drive on to its Limits, and when it comes again to its place where it stood in the Creation, all whereof it was Lord ceaseth, for there it commenceth a new Age, whence many a young Child in the Womb dieth; for its Lord is at its Period. And to hit the Point of our limited End, it is required to know exactly the Number and Period of the Sign which is our Leader.

3. How hardly can the Living Man express how it is with one that is Dead, which himself hath not experimented? A Dead Man's sence is ceased with extinguishing his Fire, his Elementary Spirit evaporateth, his Blood and Water pass into Water and Earth, also therewith his Essences, thus his Beginning finds End. But because the corruptible hath an Eternal Root, therefore the Eternal worketh in the Fragile, and because the outward Imageth the Eternal, it should bring its Wonders and Similitudes into the Eternal, whence it is originated.

4. The Souls Will worketh in the Centre or Eternal Root, the Astral Spirit works in the Body, adhering so to the Soul, that the Soul often lusteth to do what the Starry Spirit doth; and such Souls who get no higher fall into Covetousness, Pride, Envy and Anger, whence if they convert not in those very works, must the Soul Eternally dwell, doing the Devils Will, hating God, loving Folly, which was here and is there their only Treasure: but only in the time of the Body, hath the Souls Will-ability to withdraw thence, and turn into the Meekness and the Holy Will, where, with the Water of Eternal Life the Fire is quenched, and the Soul hath Ability through Jesus Christ to draw by a renewed Will out from the Evil Lusts, but those Souls, who at deceasing of the Body, even then enter into the Will of God having little of the Heavenly Substantiality, do lye in rest in great Humility in the Delight of Paradise, or the one Element, but not in the Majesty, in hope of farther increase of Heavenly Light at Christ's great appearing.

5. But

5. But the Zealous Souls who here did put on the Body of God, and were Obedient under the Crofs in Righteoufnefs and Truth, their Works in their ftrong Will follow them; fo great is their Glory, Power, Might and Majefty, as no Tongue can exprefs, they are God's Children, his Wonder, Power, Strength, Vertue, Love, Praife and Glory, all whatfoever the Will defireth, is there in full Perfection and Eternal Power. God's Kingdom confifts in Power to conceive of which muft be brought a Heavenly Mind, to fuch God's Spirit will fhew the Heavenly Subftance; for it is much eafier for the enlightened, to fee the Heavenly Subftance, than the Earthy.

6. The Soul dwelleth not in the outward Spirit, but is thereby hindred from exercife of its Natural Principle which is the Eternal, fo is it that Antichrift puts Holinefs in that which comes in at Peoples Ears in Sermons, which often coming from an Hypocritical Ground, covereth the Soul that it enters not into it felf, and bring the outward into Obedience of the inward, by forfaking Sin and Hypocrifie: but reft in a conjectural Knowledge as of Matter without Spirit. 'Tis true, if an Evil Man fpeaks God's Words, he that is of God hearing, hears God's Word, but the wrathful or otherwife Evil Spirit in Man, is not appeafed or amended by its like, for he is not thereby awakened.

Forty

Forty Questions
OF THE
SOUL,

Answered by

Jacob Behmen.

Quest. 1. **WW**^{*Hence the Soul exifted from the Beginning of the World?*}

Answ. To underftand the Subftance of all Subftances, confider outward Fire, which burneth out of a harfh, aftringent Matter. The Fire is a fharp defiring, which in great Anguifh entreth into it felf, and grafpeth after the Liberty, and carcheth it, and fo flameth. And though in the Eternal, is no fuch Fire to be underftood as fhineth in the outward, yet it is fo in the inward in the harfh, defiring. The outward remaineth a Darknefs, and within it felf, in the Will of the Eternal Liberty it is a Light, fhining in the ftill Eternity. In Fire are ten Forms, *Ten Forms of* or diftinct manner of Differences all generated in the Will, being the Eternal Wills *Fire.* Propriety, therefore it is Gods, and the Liberty which hath the Will, is God himfelf.

The firft Form of Fire, is the Eternal Liberty which hath the Will, and is in it *The Liberty.* felf the Will.

The fecond Form is, That it is defirous. *Defire.*

The third Form, is a fharp drawing, where originateth the Eternal Enmity, and *Attraction.* Oppofite Will.

The fourth Form, is the Flafh of Lightning, caufed by the Liberty, and is the *Flafh.* caufe of the Anguifh fource.

The fifth Form, is the Eternal Nature, in which ftandeth two Kingdoms, viz. *Eter. Nature.* One, an Image of God, the pure Virgin Wifdom, the caufe of the Firmament, Elements and Stars: and the other a Similitude of the fevere fierce Wrath, according to which God calleth himfelf a confuming Fire.

The fixth Form, The two Principles, one whereof, is the caufe of the other, *Fire and* the Fire-life is the caufe of the Light-life, and the Light-life the Lord of the Fire- *Light.* life : one is Life, the other is Food of the Life.

The feventh Form is, one *Magia* going always out of the other, and is the others *Magia.* Looking glafs. In Fire and Water, Life confifteth. The firft caufe of Life is Fire. The fecond is Light. The third is Spirit : Every thing confifteth in an inward and outward Subftance. The

Turba.   The eighth Form is the *Turba*, which breaketh the comprized Life again, and sheweth such things to the Beginning, as were not from Eternity, but came to be in the comprized time: but the *Turba*, must be understood in a twofold Form. A fierce wrathful Fire, in a corruptible Body: the Spirit without a Body, must be swallowed up in the Eternal Wrath-fire. But the other is a Light and Love-fire, and the Spirit which hath a Body, *(viz.)* An incorruptible Body, hidden Man, old [or first] Adamical Man, Christ's Flesh, remaineth Eternally in God's Body, such a one, is no more in it self, but hath died to its own Will, and the Love-will satiateth or filleth the Fire of the Original, and then liveth Eternally.

Tincture.   The ninth Form, is the Virgin Tincture, the Love, Meekness, Humility an unsearchable, incorruptible Life, a Fire and yet no Fire, it burneth but consumeth not, it is the Life of Angels and Holy Souls.

Holy Ternary.   The tenth Form, is the entrance into the Holy Ternary, in which Angels and Holy Souls become corporized in the Heavenly Substantiality. Although their Number belongeth to the place between the 5th and 6th Numbers.

To Answer yet further to this first Question. It is said, That though the Child knoweth its Father and Mother well, yet knoweth not the time and place of its Begetting. If we say, Angels and Souls have been from Eternity, the Propagation of Souls, will not admit it.

It is therefore summarily answered, That the Soul originateth out of God from Eternity without Ground or Number, and endureth in its Eternity: but the beginning to the moving of the Creature, which is done in God, should not be mention'd: only the Number Three, hath delighted to have Children like it self and out of it self, and so hath revealed it self in Angels and in the Soul of *Adam*, and passed or transmigrated it self into an Image, as a Tree doth into the Fruit, for that is the right manner of Eternity.

     Q. 2. *What the Soul is in the Essence, Substance, Nature and Property?*

     A. 1. Its Essences are out of the Centre of Nature, all the three Principles lye therein, and is as a branch out of the Holy Trinity.
     2. It's Substance, is out of the heavenly Substantiality.
     3. Its Will is free, to sink down and account it self nothing, and sprout only as a branch out of God's Tree: Or otherwise, to climb up in its own Will, into the Fire.
     4. Its Nature, is the Centre it self, with the seven Spirits to propagate with.

The Soul is a total Similitude of the Trinity, or of all Devils.   5. It is a total Substance, out of all Substances, and Similitude of the Trinity, if it be in God: if not, is a Similitude of all Devils. Its Property, was in the first Soul created of both Mothers, on which followed the Command and Tryal, it should not have lusted after Evil and Good, but only have eaten Paradifical Fruit, but all Properties lye in it, it may awaken and let in what it will.

     Q. 3. *How the Soul is Created to the Image of God?*

     A. The pleasure of the Trinity was to have a total Similitude. That longing awakened the Astringent *Fiat*. That Desire hath drawn out of All into One, a Similitude of Heaven, this World and the Anger-World. And as there is no Thing higher than the Soul, so nothing can annihilate it, being a Child of the Substance of all Substances.

     Q. 4. *What the Breathing in of the Soul is, and when it is done?*

                                                                          A. 1.

Forty Questions of the Soul Answered.

A. 1. Every Spirit without a Body, being unknown to it self, desireth one for its Food and Habitation, and the third Principle, being created before the Soul as a Looking-glass of the Deity, and generated materially out of the Eternal Wonders, desired a material Similitude on the Soul, and there did the outward *Fiat* Form an Image, out of the Earth's Matrix, a mixture consisting of Fire and Water.

2. The *Fiat* of the Heavenly *Matrix*, which did Create before the Earthy, longed after the Soul, and out of the Centre of the Word, went forth the *Fiat* of the Word, so was the third Principle created in the second. The Virgin Wisdom, clothed the Souls Spirit, with Divine Flesh; and the Heavenly Tincture, made Heavenly Blood in the Water.

3. Thus the inward Man, stood in Heaven, his glance in the Inward Eye, was Majesty, and understood the Language of God, and the Angels, viz. That of Nature. And tho' he stood in the outward, also yet knew not the outward by experience.

4. Into this twofold Body Created on the sixth hour of the sixth day, was the Royal Soul breathed in, by the Holy Spirit into the Holy Man like an awakening of the Deity, and the outward Spirit of the Stars and Elements breathed its Life, through the Nostrils into the outward Heart, also the quality of the fierce wrath pressed in, with the original of the Soul; so that the Soul could not continue to be Gods Image, otherwise than in humble obedience: Else could he not overpower two Principles, the angry and outward, which was generated out of the Anger. And the Temptation was for Forty days, signified by *The Souls need of Humility.*

1. *Moses* on the Mount Forty days, when *Israel* stood not, but made a Calf.
2. The Spies Forty days searching the Land.
3. *Israel's* being Forty years in the Wilderness.
4. *Elias* Fasting Forty days.
5. Chrifts being Forty days Tempted in the Wilderness.
6. And being Forty hours in the Grave.
7. Chrifts being Forty days on Earth before his Ascention.
8. *Israel's* Forty Journeys in the Wilderness.
9. *Goliah's* Forty days Challenge.
10. *Esau* lived Forty years, then took two Evil Wives which grieved *Isaac* and *Rebekah* all the days of their Lives.

Q. 5. *How the Soul is peculiarly form'd and fashioned, or framed?*

A. 1. A Twig is like the Tree, a Child like the Mother. The Soul is like a round Globe ☉ ⊙ ♓ the right Arm of the Cross, signifieth the second Principle, the Spirit. The Left Arm signifieth the first Principle, its Original, Might and Power; the upper part signifies its sprouting through Anguish, in the Fire: The lower part, its sinking, the Water the Humility, into Gods Majesty, and be dead to its own will.

2. The Soul in its first Principle hath the form of an Eye, yet twofold wherein the Cross standeth, unless it let the Devil into the Will, viz. Pride and Covetousness; if so, it loseth the Cross.

3. In the second Principle, it is a Spirit, and a total intire Image, such a one as the outward Man is.

4. And in the third Principle, it is a Looking-glass of the whole world, the Potentiality of Heaven and Earth, and all Properties of Creatures lye in it.

Q. 6. *What the Ability or Potentiality of the Soul is.*

A. The

318   *Forty Questions of the Soul Answered.*

1. The Souls Will can transform the Body.

A. The first power of the Soul, is, That if the will go strongly forward, it is Faith : And so, can form another Image in the Spirit, out of the Centre of Nature : It can give the Body another form, being Lord of the outward, but that transmutation is not permanent ; because *Adam* did let in the *Turba*, and this kind of power is call'd Nigromancy; for the Body is Sulphur, the Spirit of the Soul hath the Tincture. But the Devil readily mixeth therein ; for it is the Abysses Wonder, whereof he is Lord.

2. It can reform, or deform the Spirit to Good or Evil.

2. The second power of the Souls will is, that the earnest will which otherwise is called faith, can put the Spirit into another form : If the Spirit were an Angel, the will can make it a stubborn Devil: Also if it be Devilish, it can, by sinking down in Humility under the Cross, cast it self again into Gods Spirit.

3. It penetrateth the Bones of others.

3. The third power of the Souls will or Spirit is, that it hath power to enter into another Mans Marrow and Bones, and, if he be wicked, can introduce the *Turba*, into one who is not armed by Gods Spirit, as do Sorcerers, &c.

4. If in God it can pour the Turba on the ungodly.

4. The fourth power of the Souls will is, that it hath power (if it be Gods Child) to lead Captive the *Turba*, and pour it out on the House of the ungodly: As *Moses* on *Pharaoh*, and *Elias* did the Fire : It can throw down Mountains, break Rocks, as far as the place is capable of the *Turba*, having made the Anger stirring.

5. It can search Nature and work Wonders.

5. The fifth power is, that it can search out all wonders or works in Nature, Arts, Sciences, &c. So *Moses* commanded the Sea, *Joshua* the Sun. And (if it be in God) it can over-power the Devil: Also can heal the Sick, raise the Dead : But not unless Gods Spirit stir it up, having lost the exercise of its power by the Fall, yet the Soul in its original is greatly powerful : But only in that Principle into which it looketh, or in which it standeth is its might.

Q. 7. *Whether the Soul be Corporeal or not Corporeal ?*

A. The Soul is a Fire-Globe, with a Fire-Eye, and a Light-Eye. The Tincture is a Spirit, existing from the Fire and Light: And is its Meekness, out of which cometh Water, which the Fire draweth to it self, to allay its fierce quality ; turning that Water (of Life) into Sulphur, according to the seven Spirits of Nature: And that Mystery, changeth it self into red, from the Fire, and into white, from the Tincture, the glance is from both ; so that the Life seeth it self, out of

The pure Soul is not corporeal. The Tincture is its Body which only can comprize Gods Body, the Heavenly Flesh given in the Supper.

which Reason and Thoughts exist. The Blood is the House of the Soul. The Tincture is its Body. The pure Soul is not Corporeal, but there groweth a Body in the Tincture, not palpable or comprehensible to the outward, but a Power Body, Gods Body, Christs Heavenly Flesh; which he gives us in his Supper: A Body the *Turba* cannot touch, unfadeable, comprized in nothing, but in the noble precious Tincture: Which being perished in *Adam*, therefore God became Man, and brought the Divine Image again into the Souls Tincture, and we must now be Born again in Christ if we will see God.

Q. 8. *In what manner the Soul cometh into Man, or into the Body ?*

A. This Question is understood of propagation ; the Creation of the first Soul being shewn before. 'Tis answered, That *Adam*, when fallen, could not generate but in an Earthy way, slept, and God took the Rib and half cross in *Adam*, and fram'd a Woman ; also gave the Woman a Branch, out of *Adam's* Souls Spirit, that she might not generate Devils. So, the Man hath the Fires Tincture, and the Woman the Lights Tincture, and (seeing it could not be otherwise) they propagate, after the manner of all Beasts, the Man soweth Soul, the Woman Spirit.

Forty Questions of the Soul Answered.

rit. So then, the Soul cometh not into the Body from without, but the three *By propagati-* Principles are each its own Work-master. The one striketh Fire, making the *on: The Man* Centre of Nature; the second Tincture and Fire, and the third the great Earthy *soweth Soul,* Mystery: All done in the Mixture of the Seed, as a Twig or Branch out of a Tree. *the Woman*
Spirit. The
Q. 9. *In what manner the Soul uniteth it self with the Body?* *Elements the*
third Princi-
A. It is above explained, that all the three Principles are one in another. The *ple or Earthy* Soul hath its seat in the Blood of the Heart. The outward Water and Blood *Mystery.* naturally captivateth the inward, but not the Light of the Majesty, nor Lights Tincture: Save only by the imagination; therefore, often is a Child, more blessed than one that is old: Though many are not Born Holy, yea though from good Seed, because often some potent wrathful Constellation, insinuateth it self: But God knoweth who are his.

Q. 10. *Whether the Soul be* ex traduce *by production, or every time new breathed in by God.*

It is propagated, as a sprout cometh of a Grain set, with this difference, that *Answered a-* the three Principles, wrestle which may have it, which often introduceth a won- *bove.* derful *Turba* while it is yet a Seed. And where the Parents are both captivated by the Devil, it is rare, that of a black Raven should come a white one: But the Child can *(if it convert)* enter into the Word of the Lord; for God casteth away no Soul. But O Parents, procure good Souls for your Children. For, where the Parents have Christs Flesh in their Souls, of the good Tree cometh good Fruit: But the *Turba* can, by their acting according to selfish Reason, get entrance into such Children also.

Q. 11. *How, and in what place the Souls seat in Man is?*

A. It dwelleth in the three Principles, but the Heart is its original, it is the in- *It is the in-* ward Fire in the inward Blood, and in the Tincture is the Spirit, which like a *ward Fire in* Brimstone light, moveth on the concavity of the Heart, and distributeth it self in- *the inward* to every Member, and carrieth its dominion into the Head. And if the Soul sink *Blood of the* it self down into God, the outward must suffer it self to be subdued. The out- *Heart. The* ward Death reacheth not the Soul; one Principle it seizeth on, but not on the *Spirit is in* substance of that neither, no Fire or Sword can touch or kill the Soul; but the *the Tincture.* Imagination that is its Poyson, thence it proceeded, therein it ever dwelleth.

Q. 12. *How the Souls Enlightning is?*

A. The Soul hath two Eyes, with the right it looketh forward, into the Eternal Liberty, into Gods Light: With the other, backward, into the desiring, into the Looking-glass, and *(if not restrained)* imagineth, into the glance of the Looking glass, into Pride, Covetousness, and Self, This Eye, must by the right Eye, be drawn backwards, let the left Eye draw Wonders to it, but not Matter: Let it *By dying to* seek Earthy Food, but not go into it. For from this, the right Eye, must ever *Matter and* in this Life time, account it self, and be really dead; and then the Soul layeth *self, and by* hold on liberty, and becometh enlightened. The noble Image, which is subtiler *laying hold on* and purer than any thing, standeth in Heavenly Flesh and Blood, in the Fire of *the liberty of* the Majesty, and in the Heart of that Image, sitteth the Holy Spirit, who teach- *God it be-* eth, that my self am Gods Servant, my Children, my Estate, my Work are all *comes enligh-*
his, *tened.*

his, and when he calleth me into my Native Countrey, may give my labour to whom he will, this is a converfing with God in Love and Humility, a going out from felf into the Majefty, Power and Clarity, a giving up of darknefs, a receiving of Eternal Light and Triumph.

Q. 13. *How the Souls feeding on the Word of God is?*

A. The Soul hath a Mouth, as well as the Body, and groweth by eating: It is not only Gods Similitude, but Child, and when it entreth into the Majeftick Light, it continually longeth, panteth and draweth into its defire, the Virtue and Power of God, which is his Body, Chrifts Heavenly Flefh, the Bread of God, *John* 6. 27. Chrifts Teftaments are nothing elfe, we eat not Spirit without Body; for the Soul is Spirit before hand, it would have Body. And this inward is fubftance (confifting in its own Principle in Power) is Magical, not as a thought, but Effential and Subftantial.

Q. 14. *Whether fuch new Soul be without Sin?*

A. 1. So great was *Adam*'s heavy Fall, as let in the Spirit of this World, the *Turba*, and a monftrous Image, making the Soul a vehement hunger: That had not the word (inftantly) fet it felf in the middle, Man had remain'd Eternally broken off from God, and if the Soul do not convert its right Eye into the word again, and fo acquire a new Body, Born of God, its precious Image muft remain hidden and loft: However, it is half Earthy, having the * *Turba* in it. How then can a clean Soul be generated? It cannot.

* Viz. The Fire-Spirit. It comes not pure, but if the Parents be Vertuous it is Baptized with their Spirit.

2. It is finful in the Mothers Womb; thence came Circumcifion. Yet if the Child die in the Mothers Womb, if the Parents be vertuous and in God, it is Baptized with the Father and Mothers Spirit, the Holy Spirit dwelling in them. But the Child of wicked Parents, dying in the Womb, falleth home to the *Turba*, remaining as a Brimftone Flame, or *Ignis Fatuus*, in the Myftery, between Heaven and Hell, till the Judgment of God, gather in its Harveft, and give every thing its own repofitory; but in Eternity it reacheth not to God.

3. *Babel* faith, Jews, Turks, &c. not having Baptifm are rejected of God. But bleffednefs lyeth not in the outward word only, but in the Power and Virtue. They may vehemently prefs into Gods Love, by their Teaching, Life and Death; for God and Chrift are every where.

Q. 15. *How Sin cometh into the Soul, feeing it is Gods Work and Creature?*

A. Sin maketh not it felf, but the will maketh it, and becaufe Children (even of good Parents) come not pure and clean; as the Soul is drawn of the Word of the Lord, fo is it (mightily) of the *Turba*, efpecially in Youth, when the Earthy Tree, flicketh full of green, fprouting, driving Effences and Poyfon. That which ftandeth in equal Ballance, by putting more weight into one end, finketh down, be it to good or evil.

Q. 16. *How the Soul, both in the Adamical, as alfo in the new or regenerate Body, is held in fuch Union together.*

A. 1. There is no full Union betwixt the inward and outward, for the *Turba* is in the very Seeds, which tho' the Spirit doth fubdue the deeds of the Body, Yet the *Turba* fo caufeth it to imagine, that the fincere Soul is afhamed and offended

Forty Questions of the Soul Answered.

ded at it, and groaneth to have it Banished; for the outward devoureth the inward, if the inward continue not in strife. *They are not in Union, for*

2. Yet the three Principles are one in another. The Soul is the Jewel, the Spirit is the finder of the Jewel, the Earthy Spirit is the seeker, the Earthy Body is the Mystery; so three seekers belong to the Soul. *the sincere Soul is ashamed at the*

3. We undervalue not the outward Life, it shews Gods Wonders, but, let Men go with the inward into the outward; for the' the outward be a Beast, yet the Wonders, which have discovered themselves in a comprehensible substance, belong with their figures, not their substance, to the inward. *Imaginations the Turba insinuateth into the Body.*

4. The inward understanding Spirit, is Lord of the outward: But if it let the outward be Lord, that Man is a Beast, and if it let the Fire-spirit, *viz.* the *Turba*, be Lord, that Man is a Devil: But the outward Life is Water to that Fire, else how would many a Man become a Devil, if the outward Life did not hinder it, as is to be seen in the Gall, which is a Fire Poyson, but mixed with Water it allays the fierce Pomp of the Fire, from going aloft above the Meekness of God as *Lucifer* did.

Q. 17. *Whence, and wherefore is there a contrariety, of the Flesh and Spirit?*

A. Water is a death to Fire, but the contrariety is not totally such in Man; because the Light ever causeth the Fire; but rather such as between God and Hell; for the Anger Fire sharpeneth the Divine hiddenness of Gods Eternal Majesty, for it generateth the high Light in the free Liberty, and thus the other, or second World, cometh to be, out of the first. The Soul is the Centre of Nature: The Spirit is the precious Image, tho' not sever'd, as Fire and Light are not sever'd, the Fire is fierce, yet the cause of the Meek Light, and in the Light is the Life. *The contrariety is that the inward would be Lord as it ought to be,*

The contrariety is, that the inward Spirit hath Gods Body, out of the meek substantiality, the outward Spirit hath the great Wonders, which lye in the *Arcanum* of the Souls sternness; therefore the Love-spirit hindereth, that the fierce wrath destroyeth not the Soul by inflaming it. The contrariety is, that the inward Spirit would be Lord, and subdue; and the outward would be Lord, saying it hath the Mystery, of which it hath but a Looking-glass. *and the outward would, be Lord tho it ought not.*

Seek not the Mystery in the outward Spirit; for there is but a Glimpse; but go into the Cross, and from the Cross, back into the fourth Form, there is Sun and Moon one in another: Bring it into Anguish, into Death. Drive on that Magick Body so far till it be again, what it was before the Centre in the will, and then it is Magical and hungry after Nature, it is a seeking in the Eternal seeking, and would fain have a Body, therefore give him for a Body, *Sol, viz.* the Soul, and then it will suddenly make it a Body, according to the Soul, for the will sprouteth in Paradise, with very fair Heavenly Fruit, without spot or blemish. *Verse 14. Lapis Philosophorum.*

The inward Spirit would have God; the outward would have Bread, which is also good in its place. But beware thou let not the outward Spirit be Lord.

Q. 18. *How the Soul departs from the Body in the death of a Man?*

A. There is need of the Eyes of all the three Principles, to take Death Captive, to see this sharp question. The beginning, which is Magical, having found the limit, casteth away the seeking, the Looking-glass, the Earthy Life: And lets the Body depart, without complaint; for there is no woe done to the Soul, but the *Turba* or Fire life, the Matter or Earthy Life ceaseth. The Soul dwelleth in the will which hath a glance or lustre burning in it, and the Fire becometh impotent

v. 21, 23, 24.

Purgatory.

tent and a darkness: unless the Spirit hath Heavenly Substantiality: if so, it is swallow'd up in the *Magia*, hath the same meek Body, for a Sulphur, and Eternally burneth in the Love-fire.

Thus, Sickness unto Death is, that the *Turba* hath kindled it self, and destroyeth the introduced Medium. The Life's Fire being withdrawn, the Body goeth into its Æther: when, if the Soul's Fire hath not in its Spirit, God's Body, (*viz.*) nothing of the Power of Humility, to sink down in it self through Death, into Life, it is a dark Fire, in great horror in the first four Forms of Nature. The stern Astringency, Bitterness, Anguish and Fire without flaming. The Covetous one hath Frost, the Envious one Bitterness, the false Deceitful one Anguish, the Wrathful one, Fire. Hence consider the last Judgment, to be such, as at which the Devils do tremble.

Q. 19. *How the Soul is Mortal, or who it is Immortal?*

No Dying, but only a Will of Dying.

A. The Soul is from the Eternal and continueth Eternally, it came out of God's Mouth, and at Death, goeth into God's Mouth again. But the wicked Soul, hath lost its Image, yet Immortal; for the Eternal Nature dieth not. also if the Anger Fire should die, God's Majesty would extinguish, which can never be. The wicked Soul, hath introduced a Substance into the Will, thence comes wo, it is a Dying, yet only a Will of Dying: an Anguish, ever thinking, if I had not done this or that, I might have attained God's Salvation, which Evil things done, make Eternal Despair. No Soul Dieth, be it in God, or in Hell: but its Substance or Doings stand Eternally, to the Glory of God's Wonders.

Q. 20. *How the Soul comes, or returns to God again?*

A. Answer'd in the foregoing Answer.

Q. 21. *Whither the Soul goeth when it Departeth, &c. be it saved or not saved?*

A. 1. It goeth not out at the Mouth, for it came not in at the Mouth, but the *Turba* having broken the Earthy Life, goes as a Conqueror unapprehended by Wood or Stone through the Anger of God and Death and then is in God's Body, in Christ's Flesh and Blood, seeth God's Majesty and the Angels face to face in the unsearchable World without end or limit, 'tis swift as a Thought, is magical, its words and deeds done here are its House.

The Heavenly Body of the Soul.

2. The Heavenly Body of the Soul is from the pure Element (out of which the four are come) that gives Flesh the Tincture, blood. Its external substantiality is Paradise, where spring all bright heavenly Fruits which the Soul may eat, they are as pure as a Thought, yet substantial with colours, Power and palpable to be handled by the Soul, Juicy, full of the Water of Life.

3. Only those who are gone out of their own Will into God's in this Life, have Christ's Flesh on them, but most go so out as by Faith hang by a thread: and are in the still rest, waiting for the last Judgment Day sunk down in Humility through Death, yet a Cliff or Gulph is betwixt them, and the Holy Souls in Christ's Flesh and Blood, but are in the same Principle, yet under the Altar.

4. The wicked are in the innermost, which is also the outermost Darkness, and can appear again in the starry Spirit, seeking rest: make terrors in Houses till that be consumed, and then their Power lyeth in Darkness, waiting the last Judgment: when the Holy shall be seen by the Wicked.

5. If any conceit a place where they sit one among the other that is quite contrary

Forty Questions of the Soul Answered.

trary to the *Magia*, every one is where it will be, and where ever it is, it is in God or in Darkness, but this Deep is our Æther and Kingdom.

6. A Soul may, if it desire it, go into the upper Angelical World, where God's Angels will lovingly entertain it, and they have pure Works with them, they also delight to be with us.

Q. 22. *What every Soul departed doth, whether it rejoyceth or no, till the Day of the last Judgment?*

A. 1. They all abound with great inward Joy, and wait to put on their bright, fair, holy new Body out of the old: their Joy and Hope is different, as Labourers Expectations are; who at the end of the Week, receive every one, according to their degrees of Labour and Diligence.

2. Those who have put on Christ's Body here are as one, who having overcome his Enemies in a Fight, represents the Victory before his King, who receives him with great Joy and Honour.

3. The Expectation of the wicked Soul is, as an imprison'd Malefactor, still listening when any thing stirs, and the Executioner comes; all their passed wickednesses stand before them, in such different Aggravations as they had here.

Q. 23. *Whether the wicked Souls, without difference in so long a time before the Day of Judgment, find any Mitigation or Ease?*

A. 1. The Souls of the wicked have no Mitigation; their greatest Mitigation, is the climbing up of their Minds, to do still the wickednesses they did here, and the terror of the last Judgment, continually seizeth on them.

2. In this Life, the Soul is in the Angle of the Ballance: and may go into Love or Anger, but, when the Ballance breaketh, it is past recovery; for who can break Eternity?

3. But here, God's Spirit in his Prophets teacheth the Cross, and the Devil teacheth Pleasures, take which you will, and be taken in it Eternally: the Cross leadeth to Love, and Pleasure to the Anger Kingdom.

Q. 24. *Whether mens Wishes profit them any thing, or sensibly come where they are, or no?*

A. 1. The Prayers of the Righteous pierce into Heaven, not into Hell; out of Hell is no recalling Prayer, for such returns to you again, and continueth in its own Principle.

2. But where such leave much falshood behind them, for which torment is wished them, that cometh where they are. But let all beware they sow not into Hell; that they reap it not.

3. Some Souls, hang as by a thread, 'twixt Faith and Doubting, where Fire and Light part, whose weak Faith is detained by their *Turba*: some a tedious time, yet the Anger cannot devour their little Faith; but they sink down at last, through Anguish, into the meek Kingdom.

4. To such, may come a total, hearty, zealous Prayer, of a faithful Brother; for, the Prayer of such, can open the Gates of the Deep, a whole Principle; and take hold of that, which is capable of it. For the weak Soul, layeth hold on its loving Brother's Divine earnest Will and Might: and sinks down out of Anguish through Death, and attains God's Kingdom: But cannot help it to Glorification; for that shines out of the Souls own Substance.

A zealous Prayer of a faithful Brother may help the weak faith of one hanging between Faith and Doubting.

5. The Popish Juglings for Money, by * Masses is gross Deceit; for the Prayer of the Covetous, entreth only into his Chest. But Christ's Holy Congregation, where all is done in true earnestness, hath great Power.

*Masses,viz. Souls Meals.

Q. 25. *What the Hand of God and Bosom of Abraham are?*

A. It is the All-Substantial, or All-Being, every-where-presence, of God, in the Messiah Christ, (viz.) in its own Principle, as is sufficiently explained before.

Q. 26. *Whether the Souls of the Deceased take Care about Men, their Children, Friends and Goods, and know, see, like or dislike their Purposes and Undertakings.*

Three Conditions of Departed Sou's. 1. Those not yet in Heaven, who by Earthy Concerns appear in the starry Spirit. 2. Such as are free of all wherein is the Turba, and appear to reveal good and profound Arts. 3. Such as are in Abrahams Bosom in Christ's heavenly Substantiality, those none can stir.

A. There are three distinct sorts of Souls, or in three several Conditions.
1. Such as have not yet attained Heaven: but have Humane Matters on them, searching the cause of their detention, and many of them appear in Human Form, in the Starry Spirit: take care about Wills, &c. Sometimes their earthy Business sticks to them, taking care of their Children and Friends: but when the Starry-spirit is consumed, they have no more feeling Knowledge, only see it in the *Magia*; for in care is the *Turba*, which they are sunk through. But a living Man, hath Power to reach into Heaven: as King *Saul* did to *Samuel*.
2. Such as are sunk down farther, but are yet in one place of the Principle, with the other, these meddle with no business wherein the *Turba* sticketh: but rejoyce, when living vertuous Souls send their Works to them, and are so friendly as to appear to Men magically in their sleep, instruct them in good, and often reveal Arts, which lye deep in the Abyss of the Soul. For now the Soul is free, and in the *Arcanum* of God. Even so do the Damned Souls, magically teach the wicked great Master-Pieces of Evil and Mischief: This the Devil doth by Human Souls; himself being too rough, and terrifying the *Magia*.
3. Such, as-are in *Abraham*'s Bosom, in Christ's heavenly substantiality, those none can stir, unless they will themselves: nor do they, but to serve God's Honour, nor Pray they for us, our Blessedness lyeth in our entring into God, who will receive a converting Sinner; they rejoyce that God's Kingdom is coming into us. But Wonders have been wrought by the Livings Faiths, laying hold of the Deceased Saints Faith.

Q. 27. *Whether the Souls in Death know or understand this or that Art or Business in which they were Skilled when they were in the Body?*

A. They know the deepest founded Arts but awaken them not, because they are in the *Turba*. But the highly enlighten'd Souls have Skill in heavenly Matters, and all that lyeth in the Mystery, especially those who have been conversant in the Mystery here, and every one in those he hath most delighted here, but all in an humble Paradisical simple Childrens life.

Q. 28. *Whether they have any more Skill or Knowledge of Divine, Angelical and Earthy things, and also of Devillish things: and can have more certain Experience of them than they had in the Body.*

A. Of Divine and Angelical Skill, they have much more; but it is various; for the Souls (without a Body) are under God's Altar, till the last Judgment Day, and stir up no Wonders. But the highly enlightened Souls, that have God's Body, have overflowing Skill. Yet take no care about devilish things; it belongs to the Angels, to strive with the Devil, and defend Men.

Forty Questions of the Soul Answered.

Q. 29. *What the Souls Rest, Awakening and Clarification are?*

A. This is sufficiently Explain'd before.

Q. 30. *What the difference, of the Living, and Dead, resurrection of the Flesh, and of the Soul, is?*

A. God shall move all the three Principles, Fire, Light and Looking-glass. The Judge Christ, shall sit upon the Omnipotence of Eternity, and the Spirit of God will then go forth in two Principles, in the Anger, viz. in the Fire, as the severe Wrath of the Fire-life, and in the Light of the Love, as a flame of the Divine Majesty: and in the Spirit of this World, as a Wonder of Life, then will the Dead, and those who shall be then alive be call'd: and those who have the Noble Image will shew it, and those who have lost it, will shew the Bestial Image, they have got.
The Earth must deliver up the Phur, or Body. The Water, the Essences: The Air all the Words it hath received into it, or served to make. See the last Chapter of the three Principles.

Q. 31. *What manner of New Glorified Bodies the Souls will have?*

This is sufficiently declared before. They will have fair bright Works of Faith: as every one, is indued with the Power of Love and Purity, but very different; for the Works of many, will (almost all) remain in the Fire, and themselves hardly escape; for that as one Star excelleth another, so they: and every one, will receive God's lustre, as his vertue or power is capable of the Light; for after this Life there will be no bettering, but every one remains, as he entred in.

Q. 32. *What other Form, State and Condition, Joy and Glory, will there be, to Souls, in that other Life?*

A. 1. Paradice was in us, but *Adam's* lusting after the outward Spirit, drew *Paradisical* him and us into it, and lost the Substance, whereof this Worlds Fruits, Colours, &c. *Eating.* is a dead, dark shadow; but our restitution thereinto, will be Eternal Joy, in the spring of all Flowers, Trees, Herbs, Fruits, &c. which shall be Angelical as our Heavenly Bodies: no need of Teeth and Entrails, we eat in the Mouth, all is Power and Vertue.

2. The Kingdom consisteth not in Eating and Drinking; but there are Divine *Praises.* Songs of Praise, as Children, in a Ring, on a Mount.

3. We shall all know each other, by our new Names, which in the Language of *Knowledge of* Nature is understood: but the *Turba* being left in the Fire; none is concerned for *one another.* his Relations, as Parents, Children, Friends who are in Hell.

4. We are all there but one Sex, the first Image, Heavenly Virgins, full of Modesty and Purity. And shall there speak the great Mysteries of the Divine *Magia*, *All in Paradise are* and the Song in Reproach and Scorn of the Driver, *Rev.* 15. 3. *Masculine Virgins.*

Q. 33. *What kind of Matter our Bodies shall have in the other Life?*

A. 1. Christ saith, None goeth to Heaven, but the Son of Man which is in Heaven, *The heavenly* John 3. 13. He spake not only of his Deity, but the Son of Man, the Word that be- *Flesh and* came Flesh: in which Flesh and Blood, we must live Eternally, if we will be in *Blood.* God. *Adam* had the Virgin of God's Wisdom, but when he fell, was divided and
the

Forty Questions of the Soul Answered.

the Woman framed, and he had the bestial deformity, whereof we are ashamed.

2. But Christ is become Man, in that Virgin Image of God's Wisdom: is become Flesh, in the Water of Eternal Life, which Virgin and Water, when *Adam* fell, withdrew, and stood in its own Principle. Christ became Man, in a pure Vessel, (*i.e.*) in the first Image, for the sake of the Soul he assum'd from *Mary*, and the outward Man hung to him. And when we are new born, we put on Christ, and are new born out of Christ's Flesh and Blood.

3. The converting Sinner, becomes God's Child in Christ, and in that very Body (consisting of heavenly Flesh and Blood, which yet is real, substantial and visible, to be felt and handled by our heavenly Hands) shall we have Heaven. Thus, shall we have Christ's and God's Body which filleth Heaven; for our substantiality is out of the Eternal, and must Eternally be in the same, and not in gross bestial Flesh.

Q. 34. *What is the lamentable horrible miserable Estate of the Damned?*

A. This is sufficiently answered above. God's Anger is their Habitation, their Blasphemy and Abominations are their boast, their whole Life is one continual fear, horrour, anguish, despair, and a gnawing Worm. Fruits grow to them out of their Principle outwardly fair, but within is fierce wrath: all their cursed Practises on Earth follow them thither, and that would they do there.

Q. 35. *What the Enochian Life is: and how long it lasteth?*

What and where Enoch is.

A. The Father of *Enoch* is *Jared*, significant in the Language of Nature. *Enoch* begat *Methuselah*, who attained the greatest Age. After which, *Enoch* was taken up, with both Bodies: The outward was swallowed up, and is in the Mystery, and the inward is a heavenly Mystery; so he liveth in two Mysteries in Paradise, but hath still the *Turba* in the Mystery, and in the heavenly Mystery hath God's Body. Paradise is still upon Earth, at hand, not vanished, but as it were swallowed up by the Curse, yet lyeth as a Mystery uncorrupted.

Enoch is not gone out of this World, he is God's Preacher, and after the *Turba* hath overcome the World he must be silent, till the six Seals and Angels of the *Turba* have poured out their Vials: then cometh *Enoch* again, and reproveth the World; after which the World becometh fat and their *Turba* also, *Methuselah* dieth, and the Deluge of Fire (by *Elias*) cometh. O ye Elect, desire not to live after *Enoch's* taking up, but while he Preacheth is the Golden Time.

Q. 36. *What the Soul of the Messiah or Christ is?*

The restoration of the heavenly Virgin Image.

A. 1. Christ's Soul is Human, conceived in *Mary*, in a twofold Virgin. The outward Mortal Life in *Mary*, was no pure Virgin; no Daughter of *Eve* is so, nor was *Eve*, more than half a Virgin, *Adam* was the other half; for *Adam's* Fall divided the Tinctures, which were one total entire Virgin before, in pure Love and Chastity: both Tinctures (of Fire and Light) being in a mixture, with Power to generate a Spirit out of the Fires Tincture. but the Earthy life captivating him, he imagined into *Eve*. Where was then his Modesty? His Imagination became bestial. Of great love to the lost Image, and that it might become One again, did the Word, which spake forth the Soul at first, become incarnate.

2. So, to the Soul of *Mary*, the Heavenly Virgin of God's Wisdom is put on: but in the Soul's Principle, not in the Earthy Flesh. And in that very Virgin, hath the word, assumed the Seed of the Woman, the Soul's Seed, as also the first Images Seed,

Forty Questions of the Soul Answered. 327

Seed, which had stood (so long time) in the Mystery, broken off which he * made * Or regene-
again, one whole, intire Image; by remixing the Water of Eternal Life, with the rated.
Soul's Spirit's Water; for the Word took hold of the Soul's Tincture, and the Holy
Spirit, of the Spirit's Tincture, and both became one Soul.

3. Yet did the Creature remain distinct from God's Spirit, but God's Spirit cohabited therein. And out of God's Tincture and Water, and *Maries* Tincture and Water, came one Flesh and Blood. Thus was he *Maries* true Natural Son, with Soul and Body, and also God's true Son by Eternal Generation standing in the Majesty of the Sacred Trinity, and in the Body of *Mary*, equally, alike, at Once.

Q. 37. *What the Spirit of Christ is, which was Obedient, and which he commended into his Fathers Hands?*

A. 1. This is that great Jewel, that Pearl, *Matth.* 13.46. The Philosopher's Stone
and shining Sun, not so noble. The Heavenly and Earthy Mystery is in it: Nothing *Christ's Spi-*
in this World is like it, but the mean Simplicity, which standeth still and awaken- *rit.*
eth not the *Turba*: in such a Spirit is this Jewel hid, as the Gold in the Stone.

2. The Soul is the Original of Life, as a Fire of God, which should be turned into God's Eternal Will: in the Magick seeking of which Will, the Soul is originated, and wherein lyeth the Deity, with all the three Principles.

3. And out of the Soul's Fire, the Light is generated; by blowing it self up, by which it is its own Life, and in the Lights Meeknefs is the Noble Tincture; with two Forms, one red, of the Fire; the other thin, of the Water, which generate the Life. And in the *Exit*, or going forth of that Power and Vertue which is free from the Fire, is the Light of Life, or true Spirit, wherein, is the Virgin the Image *The Christians*
of God. In this Spirit, lye the Thoughts and Understanding, and if it casteth away *renewed Spi-*
its own Soul's Fire, Pomp and Wit, it attains God's Image, God's Body. For it is *rit.*
so subtil, that it Uniteth it self with God, for it can and may enter into God. And, because this Spirit, originateth out of the Fire-life, and the Fire-life, in the Abyfs, standeth in the quality of the Anger of God; therefore, Christ commended not this his Spirit, into the fiery Life, but, into his Father's hands, (*viz.*) into his Lovedefire, wherewith he reacheth after our Spirits, when we enter into God.

4. Thus is shewed, what Christ's Spirit is, and what our Spirit is (*viz.*) not the Soul it self, but its Life's Spirit. In the Trinity, the Son hath the Spirit proceeding out of his Heart and Mouth, the Heart is the flame of Love, which meekneth the Father's Anger: so is it in Man, and no otherwife, in one Syllable.

Q. 38. *What are to be done at the End of the World?*

A. Future things, are to be answered, only in a Magical manner, or by way of Similitude; becaufe the future Wonders, are all feen in the *Turba*. And concerning this Queftion, there is enough fpoken in the Anfwers of the former Queftions.

Q. 39. *What and where Paradife is, with its Inhabitants?*

A. It is explained in the Enochian Life, that Paradife is not altered: only withdrawn from our fource or quality: if our Eyes were opened, we fhould fee it. Nay, God is with us, only we have loft the Quality and Fruit of Paradife; as the Devil hath loft God. For *Adam* would eat of the Earthy Fruit, whereby he got an Earthy Life, and fecluded himfelf the Garden, where heavenly Fruit groweth.

T t   Q. 40.

Q. 40. *Whether Paradise is alterable, and what shall be afterwards?*

The Paradisi-cal World.

A. 1. As little as God is alterable, so little is Paradise. When the outward Dominion shall pass away, then shall, in the place of this World, be pure Paradise: an Earth of heavenly substantiality. No Night, Heat, Frost, Old-Age, Sickness, Fear, Sorrow, Death nor Superiour but Christ, in one Communion with the Angels: then will the Tabernacle of God be with Men.

2. This Earth, will be a Christalline Sea, where God's lustre will be the Light. It will be a Holy Priestly Life, all speaking of God's Wisdom, and Infinite Wonders: all Fruits will grow to us, according to our wish: it will be a Life of meer Love and Delight; for to this end, hath God manifested himself, in the created Images of Angels and Men, that he might rejoyce himself, in his Life's Essences, Eternally. *Hallelujah.*

This was the Author's Fourth Book, Written *Anno* 1620.

THE FIFTH BOOK

Of the AUTHOR

Jacob Behmen

Confisting of Three PARTS, Viz.

First, *The Incarnation, or becoming Man of Jesus Christ.*

The second Part is, *Of Christs Suffering, Dying, Death and Resurrection.*

The third Part is, *Of the Tree of Christian Faith.*

1. TO the right knowing Christs Incarnation, the Knowledge how *Adam* was, and whereof made, much importeth.

2. *Adam*, was made out of all the three Principles. God the Fathers Property, compared to Fire. The Sons Property, compared to Light: The Spirits Property, to the Wind or Air, the out-birth proceeding from both. God, according to the first Principle, is not called God, but a consuming Fire.

3. The Father is the Eternal Will, the Son the Eternal Meekness and the Impregnator, the Spirit the Eternal Life.

4. The Trinity, Created the one holy Element called Centre of Nature, Divine substantiality, the substantiality of the Light, Paradise, the Mother of a giving Power, Meekness and Substance to all Forms. *The Trinity made the one Holy Element:*

5. Out of this one holy Element, were made Angels and Men. Only Man was made, not only of the one holy Element, but as to the out-birth of the four Elements also; over which he was to rule both Stars, Elements and Creatures, by his Power given him out of that one holy Element. *Out of it An-gels. Man not only out of it but out of the four Elements.*

6. *Adam's* Body was Paradisical, Holy, and of Power to penetrate Stone or Earth, Immortal, yet real Flesh and Blood, but Holy and Heavenly: He was both a Masculine and Feminine Virgin, and was to propagate Magically (for both the Tinctures were in him) and to eat only Paradisical Food, which needed neither Guts nor Bestial Draught, &c. *Male and Female Tinctures were in A-dam.*

7. But *Adam* did not continue so; for the four Elements gaining Power over the one holy potent Element, by which they were to have been governed; he slept; *The four over which he was*

to Rule over-powering the one, the Tinctures were divided.

Tt 2 for

for he was not able to continue in the state wherein he was created; so, God divided the Tinctures, and form'd of the Feminine a Woman. giving her the half Cross in the head, and to them the Members of distinction and propagation, yet still in Paradise.

8. And *Eve* being tempted by the Serpent (tho' the Law of God was explained to her by her Husband) fell, and drew him also.

The Eternal Virgin reincorporated.

9. But God had incorporated the Virgin of Wisdom in them, which (viz.) the Eternal Virginity in the Covenant of Promise, hath lain shut up in the Virgin *Mary*, and in all *Adam*'s Children, in every Man's Light of Life; wanting only this, that the Soul's Spirit give it self up thereinto, and in that Soul-Spirit, God becometh generated again.

CHAP. VIII.

Ver. 37.

1. FOR, Christ is not become Man in the Virgin *Mary* only, so that the Divine Substantiality did sit bolted up therein; no, the Divine Substantiality in the Water of Eternal Life, entred into, and became flesh and blood. It made Heavenly Tincture, and Divine *Magia*.

2. So that we may say, when with our imagination we enter into God, that we enter into God's flesh and blood; for the Word became Man, and God is the Word.

3. This takes not away the Creature of Christ: We liken the Creature of Christ, which is indeed a Body, to the Sun, which enlighteneth the whole Deep; one Power and Lustre receiveth the other. The Deep with its Lustre is hidden, but yet hath the power of the Sun in it.

4. So Christ's Substantiality filleth Heaven and Paradise, and swalloweth up the Earthiness also, where it is received and obeyed.

5. Thus Christ brought back what *Adam* lost, and much more; for the Word is every where become Man.

See the Extracts of the latter part of the 18th Chapter of the Three Principles.

The 2d Part being of Christ's Suffering, Dying, Death and Resurrection.

CHAP. I.

Q. IS it said, Was it not sufficient that God became Man, why must he also die? Could God no other way save Man? What pleasure takes he in Death and Dying? If God had by his Sons Death paid a Ransom for us, why must we also die?

CHAP. V. *Ver. 54. to the end.*

Ans. 1. MAN had lost the Divine Substantiality and Angelical Property, and imagined into the Out-birth, (viz.) into the Earthy part, was departed from the Divine Light into the Light of this World; and captivated in the fierce Wrath of God, which the Devil had kindled, (viz.) the four first Forms, according to which God calleth himself a consuming fire.

2. The

The Incarnation of Jesus Christ.

2. The corrupted Out-birth also had put a Body on him, which it destroyed and swallowed up again, in its essential fire.

3. But being the Soul was breathed into Man out of the Holy Spirit of God, out of the Eternal, and so is an Angel.

4. Therefore hath the Power of the Holy Light-World, the Heart of God, resumed the same, entring into the Human Essence, which lay in the Anguish Chamber, surrounded with Death, and took to himself a Soul out of our Essence, and our Mortal Life, and introduced the Soul through Death, through the earnest severe Fire of God the Father, into the holy, meek, Light-World; and so destroyed Death by bringing in Divine Substantiality into the fierce Wrath of the Father, the Centre of the Anguish-Chamber, the Fire World in the Soul. Christ being the right Centre of the Holy Trinity, is, with the out-gone Holy Spirit, the flaming Majesty the Light-World.

5. And whosoever will possess the Light-World, and be an Angel, must enter in through the same path; bear old *Adams* Cross; go forth through the harsh, astringent, stern and malignant, corrupted, Adamical Man, and slay him, and be born anew out of the Anxious Wheel.

6. But seeing we were not able to do this, Christ gave himself into the Centre of the fierce Wrath in the Soul; brake and extinguished it with his Love. So that now, when we go out of our selves, to the death of sin, we come into the death of Christ, the path he hath prepared for us, and leads to his Resurrection, whereby we ascend into his Arms, the unshut Light-World, which is also *Abraham's* bosom, the Paradise wherein we were created, our true, dear, native Country.

7. It consisteth not in this, that we think it enough to pourtray and represent what Christ hath done and suffered for us, and tell of a Faith in that, but that we daily and hourly fight and slay the Evil *Adam*; as to his will and doings with resigned and resolved earnestness, and then we enter into Christ's Death, in our living Bodies, & put on his Life in us, & become impregnated with the Kingdom of Heaven: Get on us Christ's Thorny Crown, and still be accounted one that is not worthy to live on the Earth; through all which we must faithfully proceed on, knowing we must either be Angels or Devils.

8. In this Death, nothing dieth to or in us, but only the Earthy Evil dead *Adam*, whose will and life we have here continually destroyed. This Enemy departeth from us, into the Essential Fire; into the four Elements, and into the Mystery; and must at the end be tryed through the Fire of God, and then our Bodies and Works, must be given us again, through that Fire, whatever the Earthy Mystery had swallowed up. But not such an Evil one, for the Fire of God devoureth the Evil, but such a one as we here in anxiety have sought, a Divine Spiritual Substance like the Wonders and Wisdom of God.

9. Hypocritical Reason saith, Christ hath done all for us, we cannot. It is right, Christ hath done what we cannot do; he hath broken Death, and restored a new Life, and is in Heaven. But 'tis not knowing, but doing; the Devils know, but what availeth that we know if we remain without, and enter not into Christ in the way and passage he hath made for us, doing good for evil in truth and simplicity?

CHAP. VII. *Ver.* 75.

1. IT is not enough to cry, Lord, give me a strong Faith in the Merits of thy Son, he hath satisfied for my sins: But I must enter into Christ's suffering and dying

The Incarnation of Jesus Christ.

dying, and be born a second time out of his Death; become a Member in and with him: Constantly crucifie the old *Adam*: Always hang on Christ's Cross: Become an obedient child. Tho' I plainly walk this way, yet I have so evil a ghest in me, that I still work too much evil, must therefore continually strive and fight, till I vanquish.

2. Christ indeed hath in and for us broken Death, and made way, but what doth that comfort me, unless I enter in that very way and path as a Pilgrim or Stranger here?

CHAP. IX.

Christ's Sufferings, &c. 1. Men content them to participate of in the Lord's Supper, v. 29. But his Divine Flesh and Blood is that, which the wicked cannot participate of, (that is) Sacramentally.

2. They receive the four Elements in the Anger of God, because they discern not the Lord's Body, which is every where present in Heaven and Earth, and is fed upon by the Heavenly Soul, not as a sign, as others dream, not Spirit without Substance, but the Substance of the Spirit, Christ's Flesh which filleth the Light-World, which the Word that became Man brought with it into the Virgin *Mary*, and there became opened in its Flesh and Blood the assumed Human Essence.

3. Yet was it at that very time, while Christ lay in the Virgins Womb, in Heaven, in the one Element in all places. It came not into *Mary* from many miles off, but the Centre which *Adam* in God's Anger had shut up in death, the Word of the Deity did unlock and bring in the Divine Substantiality, not entring in, but unshutting, ingenerating, and in this World exgenerating, God and Man, one person heavenly Substantiality and Virginity, one only Man in Heaven and in this World.

See the latter part of the 18th Chapter of the three Principles.

The third part being of the Tree of Christian Faith.

CHAP. I.

WHat *Faith is?* 1. It is not our forcing the mind to belief of Articles which are the work of our Reason.

2. But true Faith is one Spirit with God, working in and with God, is the might of God, dwells in the liberty in God's Will, inclined to his Love and Mercy, is free from the fierce Wrath and Torment in Nature; is not comprehended; subsisteth in Eternity as a nothing, and yet is all.

3. But if it becometh apprehended, then it is entred into Reason, as into a Prison, where it works the wonders in the Fire of Nature; but in the Liberty, the wonders of God, and so is the Companionness or Play-fellow of *Sophia*, the Wisdom of God.

CHAP.

CHAP. II.

WHY *Faith and Doubting dwell together?* 1. Tho' Faith is God's Image, (*viz.*) the defiring, feeing and mind, an Eternal Figure; yet in the time of the Body, it may change it felf into the Anguifh Fountain.

2. For Faith in its original is only a Will, which Will is a Seed, and that Seed muft the Soul (being a Fire-fpirit) fow, into the Liberty of God, and fo will a Tree grow, on which the Soul feedeth, to allay and meeken its Fire, and becometh powerful, and giveth ftill its vertue to the Root of this Tree, which groweth in the Spirit of God, even into the wonders of the Majefty of God, and fpringeth in the Paradife of God. *Ver. 4.*

3. There is a continual vehement ftrife in Man, while he is in the Tabernacle of this Earthy Life, unlefs he fo earneftly fink down in himfelf, that he introduce the Lifes-fire into the Liberty of God, and then is dead as to reafon, and liveth to God; which is an highly precious life, and rarely found; for it is like the firft Image that God created. The mortal only hangeth to it, but this right Life is in another Principle and World [and is the firft, right, Paradifical Human Life.] *Self-refignation reduceth the Lifes fire into Liberty. Ver. 8.*

4. That Earthy Human Life into which *Adam* fell, originateth in the Mothers Womb, moving chiefly in Fire, Air, Water and Earth, or Flefh tinctur'd, inform'd and made rational, by the conftellations to pleafure or difpleafure, being no more but a Beftial life, reafon looketh no higher.

5. Yet Man's great panting after a higher and Eternal Life, is a Magick feeking, a Myftery implanted at his Creation; it lieth in Reafon, but Reafon, nor the Spirit of this World comprehendeth it not. It is a fecret Spring opening in another Principle, hidden in the Anguifh, held captive by the Spirit of this World, which the outward Lifes Reafon hath might to fupprefs; fo that it is ftifled, cometh not to the light, generateth not, abideth hidden; and when the Body breaketh, the Will hath not wherewith to open the Myftery, which Myftery is God's Kingdom, but the Fire or Souls Spirit abideth in Eternal Darknefs.

6. The Myftery being God's Kingdom, giveth a longing defire, ftanding hidden in the Soul, incomprehenfible to Nature, and hath its Root in the Souls Fire. This Will is no parting or renting from the Soul, but becometh one Spirit with God, and fo is the Soul's Garment, and the Soul, in that Will and Spirit is become environ'd and hidden in God, tho' it dwelleth in the Body.

7. This is the right earneft Faith, a Child of God, and dwelleth in another World. It is not an Hiftorical Will, Reafon knoweth, there is in it felf a defire after God, and yet holdeth that very defire captive, from entring into the Life of God, in the lufts of the flefh, in the Sidereal *Magia*, faying, To morrow thou fhalt go forth to God, introducing Self-ability of finding, and is furrounded with Opinion and Conjecture, keeping from the Liberty of God. *Ver. 23. Holdeth the Truth in unrighteoufnefs.*

8. But the Will, that finketh it felf out from Reafon into Obedience and Love to God, is an obedient humble Child, and accepted; for it is pure, and God's fimilitude. And feeing God is free in himfelf, from the Evil, fo muft the Will, and then, tho' God be no accepter of perfons (nor will let fin into himfelf) yet he will accept the humble, free, obedient Will; for what comes to him into his Liberty he will not caft off.

CHAP.

CHAP. III. *Whence comes Good and Evil, Joy and Sorrow, Love and Anger, Life and Death?*

1. THO' from the Eternal Substance all proceedeth, Good and Evil &c. yet we cannot say, that Evil and Death come from God; in God is no Evil nor Death, nor in Eternity doth any Evil go into him. The Eternity manifesteth it self by similitudes.

2. In the Eternal Nature is the *Magia* of Life; where one Form desireth and awakeneth the other, whence the Essences of multiplicity exist, and out of which, the wonders [the Created Beings] are generated, and out of the same Fire of Nature the fierce Wrath proceedeth.

3. In God's Will is a desiring, which causeth the *Magia*, out of which existeth the multiplicity; yet the multiplicity it self is not God's willing, which is free from all substance; but in the desiring or longing of the Will, Nature generateth it self, with all Forms, (*viz.*) out of the Eternal *Magia*.

4. What Spirit soever, imagineth, with the Will into Nature, is the Child of Nature, and one Life with Nature; but, whosoever goeth forth, from the Reason of Nature, with its will and longing, into the Free Will of God, and therein abideth, is one Spirit in and with God, and is God's Child, and the Nature Spirit is God's wonder [or Creature.]

CHAP. IV. *How to attain the Liberty of God. How God's Image is destroyed. The State of the Wicked after the dying of the Body.*

1. WHere our will and heart is, there is also our Treasure. Is our will in God's Will? then have we the great Mystery, out of which this World as a similitude is generated, and have both the eternal and corruptible; yea, we bring the wonders of our corruptible works, into the eternal.

2. But if we turn our desiring from the Eternal, into the Earthy Mystery, our will is captivated, and hangeth only to the Looking-glass, and attaineth not the Liberty of God.

3. And when the Body dieth, the Soul retaineth the Image of those things in its Will-Spirit, wherewith it is become infected, be it Pride, Covetousness, Malice, or any other abominations; for the wicked Will having captivated and destroyed the Noble Image, and lost the Liberty, is the Root of its own Image, and draweth the Mystery to it self. VVhere, on the other part, the right VVill is regenerated in Christ, and entreth into the Liberty; for in the VVill, through Faith, we attain the Noble Virgin Image that *Adam* lost.

CHAP. V. *Why the Wicked convert not. What the most smarting thing in Conversion is,* &c.

1. THE wicked multitude, have the Noble Jewel hidden in them in the Divine Principle, and can, very well, go forth with their VVill-Spirit into the VVill of God; but, the self-honouring life-pleasing them so well, that they
obstinately

The Incarnation of Jesus Christ.

obstinately let the fierce wrath hold them. Gods Spirit desireth the Soul, setting it's *Magia* towards it, the Soul needs only to open the Door and it goeth voluntarily in.

2. But the most smarting bitter thing in Conversion is, to break the Will-spirit from the Earthy substance, and its Treasure [the beloved Lusts and Self] and from falshood; by sincere, earnest turning about of the Will into Gods Love, which is the Divine Mystery, that Gods Spirit may blow up the Divine sparkle. And this must be, or he is but a Bestial Man, a Jugler, and near to the Devil. And after this time, there is no remedy more; for the Souls Fire is naked, and cannot be quenched with Gods Meeknefs, but a Gulph or Principle is between them.

3. Man is the Image of God, and so standeth in a threefold Life, the first is the Souls Life, existing chiefly in seven Forms according to the Spirit of Nature. The second is, in the Image generated out of the Eternal Nature, out of the Souls Fire, standing in the Light: The meek. pure, amiable Spirit. The first the Fire, is the cause of the second the Light. Thus are two Worlds, one in another, one not comprehending the other: But at Death, divides into two Principles of Anger and Love.

4. As we in *Adam* went out of the Meek Spirit into the outward Life of fiercenefs. God became Man, to lead us through the Anguish Fire, through Death, into the Light and Love-life.

5. The Prince Christ breaking the Bar or Fort of Death, and so destroy'd the Devils Kingdom: for the Light of God, and the Water of Meeknefs, is his Death.

6. The third Life is the outward Created Life, from the Sun, Stars and Elements. Man should have used the outward, as a Looking-glafs to the Eternal, and Gods Honour: But he did put his Will-spirit into the outward Principle, by wicked Lust longing after the Earthy Life, and so went out of Paradife, which sprouteth through Death into the second Principle, and went into Death, and destroy'd his Noble Image. This we Inherit from *Adam*; but from the second *Adam*, the Regeneration, by which we must enter (through his Incarnation) with him into Death, and through Death, [or Annihilation] sprout into the Paradifical World, into the Eternal Subftantiality of the Liberty of God.

CHAP. VI. *What Luft can do. How we are fallen in* Adam *and helped again in Christ; and yet that it is not easie to be a Right Christian.*

1. DEstruction came, and still cometh out of Luft. The outward Spirit of Man, which is a similitude of the inward, by Lusting after it, infected the inward; which (not feeling present death) gave room to the outward, who then became Host of the House and so the fair Image disappeared, for it fell among Adam's *Soul* Murtherers, the sern Spirits of the Lives original (of which *Cain* was afraid) *opened the* then came the good Samaritan, Christ, who became Man. *Fires Essen-*

2. As *Adams* Soul had opened the Fires Essences and let in the Earthy; so Gods *ces.* Heart, opened the Lights Essences, and compassed the Soul with Heavenly Flesh; *Christ opening* wherewith, when the Soul became impregnated, it went with its will into the *the Lights Ef-* Paradife Life. Hence came Chrifts Temptation, to try whether he could eat of *fences feed and* the Word of the Lord, and would enter through Death into Gods Life, which *clothed the* was fulfilled on the Crofs, where Chrifts Soul went through the Fire of the fierce *foul with hea-*
U u *wrath, vently Flesh.*

The Incarnation of Jesus Christ.

wrath, through the stern source, through Death, and sprouted forth again into the Holy Paradise. We must die unto our Earthy willing, and continually become Regenerated into the new World.

3. The right will must couragiously Fight against the corrupt will, sinking down from Earthy Reason into Christs Death; so that it will hazard the Earthy Life upon it: And he that thus sinketh down, passeth through Gods fierce wrath, through all the holding Cords of the Devil, into the Paradise of God, into the Life of Christ. And the more the noble Pearl Tree is sought, the more strongly it groweth, and suffereth it self not to be suppressed, tho' it cost the outward Life, which must but hang to us as it did to Christ.

CHAP. VII. *To what end this World was Created?*

1. THE two Eternal Mysteries. Mans strife about the Image. And where the Tree of Faith beareth Fruit.

2. The inward World desires a Similitude of it self, which the Angelical World (standing only in the light) could not be: This therefore, standing in a twofold Genitrix of Love and Anger, and Man being in a threefold Life from the Fire, Light and Out-birth clearly represents: Who was Created, to manifest the same Mystery, and bring the Wonders into Forms according to the Eternal Mystery.

Man was more fully a Similitude of the inward World than the Angels.

3. The Noble Image [the true Paradisical Man] is strove for; 1. By the stern Fire life. 2. By the Divine Life. 3. By the outward Life, and thus being drawn of three: There is great need of Fighting, Hope, Faith, Humble Prayer and Patience that the Tree may grow, which the outward Man nor Reason knoweth not, but is very well known to the Noble Image. The Cross, Scorn, Tribulation and Persecution attend him every hour; for he is unknown to his Brethren, all suppose his own Folly plagueth him; but great will his Harvest be.

CHAP. VIII. *In what manner God forgiveth Sins; and how Man becometh a Child of God?*

1. MAN is not to bring his Conscience into the History, and hope for pardon in the manner of an Earthy Judicatory, and yet remain wicked: He must be a Son, it is else, as if a Servant should comfort himself, that his Lord would give him his Estate; not considering he is not his Son: Whereas whosoever is Born of God in Christ, is a partaker of Crists Sufferings. Dying and Resurrection; for a continual Battel must be, till the Reason and Will of the corrupt Flesh be subjected.

Strong Earthy Reason makes strong Resistance to Gods Spirit.

2. And if the Earthy Reason be strong, it goeth often sadly, and there is requir'd, not only strict Sobriety, but Watching Fasting and Prayer to tame it; that Gods Spirit may find place to generate some fair little Branches out of the Tree of Faith, which under the Cross, Anguish and Tribulation, may bear Fruit with Patience.

These three Parts or Books were the Authors fifth Book.

THE
Great Six Points.

The First POINT.

CHAP. I. *Of the first sprout of Life out of the first Principle, whereby we may distinguish the Divine Being from Nature.*

1. TEXT. 1. The first or Abyssal Will without and beyond Nature, is like an Eye or Looking-glass; yet retains Nature.
2. This Will is the cause of the Desiring. The Desiring is the cause of the Essences. The Essences are the cause of every Life; for Life lyeth in them, as a hidden Fire which burneth not.
3. In the Will all the Forms of Nature from Eternity (tho' but as a nothing in respect of Nature) yet are truely, and entally or really, but not essentially in the Will.
4. The Eternal Will which comprizeth the Eye, wherein standeth the Seeing or Wisdom, is the Father.
5. The Eternal Wisdom comprizing a Centre out of the Abyss, is the Form, Heart and Son.
6. The entring Eternally into it self to the Centre, is the Spirit; for it is the finder, and then goeth forth, manifesting the Wisdom of the Father and Son.

2. TEXT. 1. Thus the Abyssal being of the Trinity generateth to it self a Centre of Rest, *viz.* the Eternal Word or Heart, wherein is understood a threefold Spirit. where the one is ever the cause of the other, and is not measurable, fathomable, divisible nor circumscriptive, dwelling in it self as a substance, equally, alike, and at once, filling all things, but hidden to the things, not dwelling in the things; for it self hath a substance in it self, after the manner of Eternity.

2. The first Eternal Principle is Magical, and like a hidden Fire, is Eternally known in its Colours, in the figure, in the Wisdom of God, as in a Looking-glass: The opening of which Mystery, openeth the three Principles according to the Trinity.

3. The Magical Centre of the first Principle is Fire, which (as also the second) is as a Spirit, without palpable substance, therefore the longing is to generate the third. where the Spirit of the Principles might manifest it self by Similitude. In this desiring; Powers, Colours and Virtues come to be.

4. And for as much as every desiring is attractive, The first Principle impregnateth it self with Nature, and the second with Light. And this meek Fire of the Majesty of the second being set opposite to the Fire of the first quenching its wrath, puts it into an Essential Substance thereby, and the first giveth the second power, strength and might being together an Eternal Band; that without the one the other could not be.

5. What

The Great Six Points.

5. *What the first Principle is wholly and alone in it self.* The first Will willeth to be free from the darkness, and by defiring cannot attain it; for the defiring is a stern attraction. So that out of the thin rare liberty where nothing is, a darkness comes. And the greater the defiring, the greater will be the attraction: The drawing giveth sting, and the attracted giveth hardness, from the defiring comes the feeling, thence also comes the third form, *viz.* the Anguish, which is as it were the Centre where Life and Will originate.

6. Hence it is the Will would flee, but is withheld by the harshress, so that it becomes whirling as a Wheel, and the greater the Anguish the greater the whirling, and the greater the bitter sting of the Essences and Multiplicity. But in the whirling the Essences become a mixed will where lye innumerable multiplicity of Existencies or Beings, justly called the Eternal Mind.

7. The first will which is called Father, and is in it self the Liberty, desireth Nature, and Nature groaneth after the liberty from the Anguish. The conception of which in the Imagination, causeth a shriek of joy, and when it attaineth the liberty the shriek becomes a flash in the meekness, breaking the sting of Death, and passeth into the Kingdom of Joy, and so into the Love, for the meekness draweth the Joy into it, and that is the Water of Eternal Life.

8. And when the Fire drinketh the Water of Eternal Life, it giveth forth the Light of the Majesty, where dwell the Father and the Son. And the Holy Spirit is the Life of it, opening the meek substantiality, *viz.* Colours, Wonders and Vertues: That is called the Divine Wisdom, the House of the Holy Trinity, and in its Colours and Vertues, the Spirit hath all the Angelical Quires.

9. The second substance of the shriek is an Inimicitious Quality, exciting a panting to be loosed from the quality of Anguish. Whence in the Fathers Will ariseth pity, compassion and mercifulness.

10. Hence also cometh the Gall into Creatures, which tho' it be a Poyson, is the cause of Life, *viz.* of Mobility, for Death is the Root of Life, as may be seen in Christs Death, and also in our own.

11. ⎧ The Souls Fire uniteth with the Eternal Nature.
⎨ The right Souls Spirit is one Spirit with God.
⎩ The Images Corporeity is of the Substance wherein the Faithful shall live Eternally.

CHAP. II. *What the Principle is, or what they all three are.* Further of the First Point.

1. When Life findeth it self where none is, that is a Principle. Fire is a Property, so is Light; for tho' it be caused by the Fire, it is not the Fires Property, and the wrathful Anguish is the cause of both.

2. But the Will to the Anguish, called Father, a Man cannot search out. We only fathom how the Anguish gains the highest Perfection in the Holy Trinity, and manifesteth it self in the three Principles. What Essence is, and how it originateth; because thence spring the Senses and Thoughts, and the Wonder of all Beings.

3. The third Principle of the Stars and Elements, manifesteth the other two. And that which in moving attained the fierce wrath, became the Globe of the Earth. Thence is it, that out of it, while the Centre of Nature is in it, and it freed from Death, the pure Child of the Eternal substance may be extracted, as in Gold. Tho' by defect of attaining the Eternal Fire, Life is not so brought out of Death, save only in Man, and what is beyond Man belongs to God, and we wait the Renovation in the end of time.

The Great Six Points.

4. *Of the Substance and Property of the three Principles.* The first Principle standing in the Fire of the Will: The second in the Will to the Light, the one giving its desire into the other, yet are not mixt, each retaineth its Property, yet dwelleth in the other. The third hath the Properties of both, yet is neither. It is an awakener, manifester and similitude of the Eternal, yet is not the Eternal, but is become a substance in the Eternal desire.

5. The Creation was an awakening of the Power and Form which was in the Eternal Will, and because it was in the beginning comprized in the Eternal, therefore must the substance in this World, together with the figure go into the Eternal.

6. But whatsoever became comprized in the desire out of the beginning recedes into its Ether, becoming what it was when it was no substance. So this Worlds substance being a coagulated Vapour, returns into the *Magia* or Mystery whereof it served a while to be a manifester.

7. For nothing attains the liberty of Eternity, that subsisteth not in the Will-fire of the Eternal, in which the Light can bring its lustre and dwell, and that it be as subtle as the Lights substantiality.

8. Mans Soul may (if it will) become generated out of the fierce wrath into Renovation by forsaking the Earthy, renew what he hath generated out of the Eternal, which else remaineth in the quality of Torment. For whatever is not like to the Love fire, Light and Water, cannot subsist in the liberty, but remains in an opposite Will, in the dark Torment it awakened in it self.

9. The right Man out of the new Birth, is these Worlds, the Eternal Light World shineth through all whatsoever is thin, rare or transparent, and thereby capable of it, which can no more be hinder'd than the Sun can be, that it should not shine.

10. The Properties of the first Principle sprout, making Sulphur, Mercurius and Sal.

11. The second Principle sprouteth in it self, making Love a Friendly, Vertuous, Pious, Humble, Patient Will to stoop and bear with evil in others, ever hidden to the old Man lashing it forward as a lazy Ass, denies him the worldly Jollity it lusteth after, and makes him a Servant· it withstandeth the evil Influences of the Stars, and the fierce Devil and Malicious Men so far as they are holy and capable of it, which their possessing the second Principle enables them to be.

12. The third Principle hath its sprouting, but it is in Warring, the cold against the heat, and every thing against its contrary. The cold gives substance, the heat Spirit, the Light Meekness And then the Fire consumes all both Evil and Good.

13. Seeing therefore Man hath the two inward Principles in strife, let him beware; which he makes Lord, for that will be his Lord Eternally, when Death hath broken the Ballance.

CHAP. III. The Second Point.

1. IN the Light World which is Gods Kingdom is rightly known no more but one Principle, into which the four Properties give up their Will, being chang'd into a desire of Love in Meekness· That which in the Light World is well doing, triumphing Joy and Pleasant Songs, is in the dark a stinging Enmity, Horror and Trembling.

2. Therefore, is the anxious evil the Light-worlds Original, and all is Gods, but the Light only call'd Gods Kingdom, the other his fierce Wrath, which
Kingdom

Kingdom hath the Conſtellations of the greateſt and moſt ſevere eager might.

3. That which melodiouſly ringeth in the Light, rumbleth and thumpeth in the dark. The cauſe of the ringing in Metals is that in the moving of the All-ſubſtantial God in the Creation, the Metalline Tincture became ſhut up in the hardneſs.

4. In the dark World are many ſorts of Spirits or Helliſh Worms, according to their Conſtelations and Properties, without underſtanding or woe; for it is their Life as in this are unreaſonable and hurtful Beaſts, Toads, Serpents, &c. for all Properties would be Creaturely.

5. The Principles are not at ſtrife but in a conſtant league. But Death and Anguiſh is the cauſe of Fire, and Fire is the cauſe of all Life. To the Abyſs it gives ſting and fierceneſs; elſe there would be no Mobility. To the Light-world Eſſence, elſe there would be no production but an Eternal *Arcanum*. To this World it gives Eſſence and ſpringing, ſo is it the cauſe of all things.

6. The Anguiſh of the dark World caus'd by Fire panteth after the liberty, and the liberty longeth after manifeſtation, thus is the Harmony between the Principles; but in the Eſſences is ſtrife, elſe all things would be nothing.

7. God Created Creatures in each Principle, therein ſhould they continue, but when they introduce into themſelves another, that makes the Enmity; as did the Devil introduce Pride and the fierce Wrath of the firſt Principle. And Man into this World, where he hath neceſſity and ſtrife to make him go out again, which if he with Divine Might doth at any time, the Spirit of this World, will drive on the Children of this World to hate, plague and kill them, whereto the Devil helpeth to drive them from among his Slaves.

8. Man therefore is highly concerned to know, that being in this World as a Priſoner, he ſhould not enter into the Earthy Malady, but conſtantly go hence into the Light-world: But if he preſs not thereinto with earneſtneſs, he (like an Ape) only imitates or plays Jugling Tricks, for which the Devil derides him, for thereby he gives his Body to this World, and his Soul to the dark Abyſs.

9. Thus is ſeen, that the Creatures of each Principle deſire not thoſe of the other, nor can they ſee each other, there being a Gulph between them.

CHAP. IV. *Of the Original of Contrariety in the ſpringing of Life.* The Third Point.

1. WHere is one only will there is no ſtrife, but where many are is contrariety, unleſs one rule over the reſt, there then doth multiplicity harmonize, for the harſh Anguiſh and bitter Properties are at Civil Hoſtility, and Fire is the Incendiary ſetting them all into great Anguiſh, Exaſperating the reſpective Enmities, till Light be produced and crowned King: There it ruleth lovingly, and rewards them with Meekneſs, which appeaſeth and well-pleaſeth them all.

Thus is multiplicity reduced to an united will, called the mind; which by Imagination can create evil and good.

2. The Mind inkindling it ſelf, inkindleth the whole Body and Spirit, be it in Wrath or Love. As is the Matter, ſuch is the Flame, be it Brimſtone or ſweet Oyl, and ſuch is the favour.

3. In the Souls Fire ſtands the Light of Life, and in the Light of Life the Noble Image. When therefore the Souls Fire in the fierce quality introduceth Earthy Matter into it, the Noble Image withdraws: The conſequence of our hard and heavy Fall, bringing on us ſo great danger and miſery. 4. There-

The Great Six Points.

4. Therefore hath Christ taught us Patience, Meekness and Love, for we are captives in God's fierce Wrath between Anger and Love, so that if the Will-Spirit before the dissolution of the Body hath attained God's Love as a sparkle, somewhat may be done, but not without such irksom tedioufness to break the dark fierceness which would extinguish it, and that is *Purgatory*, and how great Enmity, Terror and Anguish the Life is in, before it can in the sparkle sink down into the Liberty of God, he well findeth, who so nakedly with (as it were only) a glimmering Twilight, departeth this World.

5. It is therefore of absolute necessity that we take the Cross by entring into Humility, Patience, and the Meek Life, therewith to break the will of the Dark fierce Centre, and this World's Voluptuousness, nor by wrong to excite Rage in thy Brother, for that hindereth the Kingdom of God; but thy meek self denial will further it, that by beholding that Spirit in thee, thy Brother may be convinced and judge himself, seeing thy valuing more God's Love than temporal goods; knowing thy self to be only a stranger. But if the Evil-doer will not convert, his Evil in the Anger of God gnaweth him, to cause him to return: If yet he hardeneth himself in wickedness, he becomes a total Evil Tree, devouring his own abominations, growing for his dark God *Lucifer*.

The above is the Contents of the latter part of the fourth Point, but the first part of the fourth Point contains, viz.

CHAP. V. *How the Holy Tree of Eternal Life sprouteth through All the three Principles, yet not comprehended.*

1. THE Divine Power and Light dwelleth in it self every where in Nature, yet not toucht by any thing that is not of its Property, not comprehended: but as the Sun shineth in all the Elements, yet not laid hold on by any, and what the Sun doth in the third Principle, the Light of God doth in the Forms of the Eternal Nature, attoneing the Schism and Enmity of them: that Light shineth through the Darkness, but not comprehended by it.

2. The three Principles comprehend not one the other, unless the Will by falling into Death give up its Essences into the Light.

3. The Devil is the poorest of Creatures. The Sun is not profitable to him; he cannot stir a leaf nor pile of Grass, unless the anger be in it; his Will neither goeth, no can go into the Light's Property. He goeth not readily, but hateth every thing that sprouteth in, and uniteth with the Sun's Power.

CHAP. VI. *The outward manifestation of the inward three Worlds. How God is in all things. How all the World might be a meer Sun. What Man is. And wherein God beholdeth himself.*
Further of the 4th. Point.

1. THE Earthy Tincture hath no communion with the Heavenly, though the outward proceedeth out of the inward, and yet the Tincture of the precious Metals hath communion with the Heavenly.

2. The Dark World hath the first Centre, the Light the second; whence behold our danger; for if we cast our selves into the Earthy seeking, that captivateth us; the Dark Abyss is our Lord, and the Sun our Temporal God.   3. The

3. The three Worlds are not sever'd, for the Eternal Abyssal substance, may not sever it self. The outward is the place which comprehends not the inward, but is comprehended by it, what the inward giveth forth out of it self; that it also possesseth, and cometh not into a place, but was there *before-hand*.

4. Thus God dwelleth in all things, but no more comprehended than the face is by the Looking-glass, or the Sun by the Water, tho' the outward hungreth after the inward, and can receive the inward into it, but the inward cannot receive the outward; for it dwelleth not in the outward, but in it self; nor is the inward remote from the outward, as the Sun from the Water, but as the Water hath the Suns Property in it, else could not catch the Suns lustre. And this World would all be a meer Sun, if God would kindle and manifest it, for every thing animate and inanimate, and all the four Elements receive the Suns glance.

5. If Man, who is all the three Worlds, standeth in them in equal harmony, without introducing the one World into the other, saving that he by the Light-World rule the Dark and Outward Worlds, then is he God's similitude, and the Outward World must catch the Light, as the Water doth the Suns planet. But if the Water be mixt with Earth, it receives not the Suns Light: No more can the Human Spirit the Light of God, unless it remain pure, and then that Man's Life is such a Looking glass, as wherein God beholds and finds himself, as also in the Angels, and Beauties of Heaven; for in the Dark World is no Looking glass capable of the Light. But if the Water be mixt with Earth, it must sink down from the Earths dark fierceness, wherein it was captive, before it be capable of seeing the Light.

6. So what Man imagineth after, it receiveth, if he hath filled himself with the Earthy hunger, he must be new born; that he may with Christ break the Earthy Darkness, and with Authority introduce the clear, pure Looking-glass of the Deity.

CHAP. VII. *How a Life passeth out of Joy into Misery.*
The fifth Point.

1. Life is like a terrible flash, but when it receiveth the Light, it passeth into meekness and joy; but because it sprung from its Mother the Dark World, it hath power either to retire thither, or proceed forward by the Fires Anguish, to kindle the Light. Its perdition is therefore evident, it inclineth to the multiplicity to be its own Lord, but yieldeth not to the Liberty beyond Nature, for if it did, then would the Liberty kindle the Love-fire, and become a light, (*viz.*) a clear Looking-glass of God's Majesty. In that manner as the second Principle hath kindled it self from Eternity; for entring into the Liberty, it arrives at that which was before Nature, and was the cause of Nature.

2. The Soul hath three Eyes or Looking glasses in the time of this World, and seeth with that only to which it turneth it self, tho' by right of Nature it hath but one, *viz.* the fourth Form of the Dark World, (*viz.*) Fire, and into which it goeth with its will, of that it receiveth its spiritual substance.

3. And if it go into the Dark World, or Outward World, the Light World is hidden and as dead, as Fire is in Wood. Here should Man prove himself, what World is Lord in him. If wrath, envy, deceit, pride, avarice, bestial unchastity, *&c.* be his desire, he may make, Register, accompt and inventory that, certainly he is not a Man, but a Dog, Goat, Beast, Serpent or Toad. And when the four Elements forsake him, his Souls Image is form'd by the Hellish *Fiat*, into that Property of theirs that most strongly drew his delight.

The Great Six Points.

4. Yet he that hourly striveth against the Evil Properties, and though he be damped by the Evil, his constant desire to repentance, sheweth God's fire glimmereth in him; and when the outward Body with its damp breaketh, and can no more hinder the glimmering week, then the Divine Fire kindleth, and figureth him after the Image of the strongest Property he here introduced into his desire. But if he continue not his serious desire, he may desperately perish.

5. But he whose desire is so potent, that he can subdue his Evil Nature, and pass into humble Patience, contemn the glistering of the World, do good for evil, and can yield himself and all his to do and suffer misery for God's sake. In that Man the Divine Power floweth up, the Noble Image dwelleth, and Jesus is born.

6. The Devil knoweth him not, only is inraged and irritateth incarnate Devils, and Men Beasts to plague him, This Man is the surest, never dieth, but the outward Kingdom that was a hinderance to him falleth from him; and as he tasted what God is, and bare the heavenly substance here, so now much more, and is eternally perfected.

CHAP. VIII. Further of the 5th Point. *The True Human Essence or Substance is not Earthy, nor out of the Dark World, but out of the Substance of God.*

1. THE right substantial Man is of the Light World; there is a Gulph of Death 'twixt that and the Dark World, and Outward World, yet is it shut up in the Outward World. Christ is come to save what is lost, and will suffer it self to be helped, unless it be a totally Devilish fruit of evil Parents. But while there is any small Tinder of Divine stirring, the Child is capable by Baptism, to have the Light glimmering in that part given *Adam* out of the Angelical World, not that Earthy part be introduced, and so far as the Divine Power stirreth, is the Child baptized after life in the womb, by the Holy Ghost.

2. *Obj.* What can the Child do to it, that the Parents are wicked? *Answ.* The Evil Man is shut up in Body and Soul, why not in the Seed? Must God turn the seed of Thistles into Wheat, and throw Pearls to Swine? The Sun maketh nor desireth any Weed, but giveth to all Vegetables Life, but the Soil produceth the Evil. Many times the wicked Parents cause Curses to stick to their wicked Conforts, and should not their wills be done to them?

3. And being both wicked, what can an Evil Beast beget but an Evil Beast, baptized in God's fierce Wrath? So also it receiveth the Lord's Supper without distinguishing the Lord's Body, and put it and its own will, into the Earthy, as a common thing, prophanely offering it up to God, it brings fruit to perdition.

4. For the Spirit of every Life appropriates its like to it self; for one Property receiveth not another; what the Soul willeth, the thing received willeth the same, for it is all Magical. So the Devil was an Angel, but when he willed Evil, his heavenly substance became poison. Yet is it not the Deities will that we perish, but his Angers will and our will.

CHAP. IX. *Of the Life of Darkness; wherein the Devils dwell; of what kind it is.* The Sixth Point.

1. THE Life of Darkness is a fierce, false, inimicitious, stinging Essence; having many Forms, each would murther the other. Nothing can cease the contrariety; for the opposing it is as the blowing up of fire, only God's

Light can make it soft, meek, sweet and joyful: But that cannot be, for it is an Eternal Terror to the Darkness. And if the Kingdom of Darkness should be enkindled with the Light, the Light would have no Root, no Fire, no Omnipotency; thus all must serve to God's Glory.

2. The Life of the Darkness is a fainted poison Life, like an Eternal dying Property. It is also manifest that every Life existeth in poison, which poison the Light both withstandeth, and causeth that the poison faileth not.

3. The Dark Life is especially in seven Properties, with the Principle of the Centre of Nature. The Light Life is also in seven Properties of the right of Nature: So that what in the one giveth sadness, that in the other giveth joy.

4. What the malicious, arrogant and wicked men do in this World, that the Devils do in the Dark Worlds Property. And what the poisonous Evil Creatures do in this World, that do the other Creatures (who also have Spiritual Bodies) in the Dark World. The whole Dark Worlds Dominion is principally in the first four Forms of Nature, and from the fierce contrary Qualities are the Eternal Wonders manifested and brought to substance; which substance parteth into three Fountains not rent one from the other, but giving each to the other, as Fire, Light and Matter whereout Fire burneth.

2. In Man is the substance of all substances, carrying the Properties of Heaven and Hell in him; which soever he awakeneth, of that is the Soul capable. Nor is it necessary to search farther.

3. But Man having broke himself off from the first Image and Order, must learn how to be regenerated, by introducing the Meekness and Light to rule over his false and fierce Property, and then the Law that pursued him ceaseth, because the Law of Love and Meekness sets him free.

4. Whatever departeth from its first will, is pursued by the Law to restrain its wandering; but when ever it is return'd to its right State, and first Image and Order, or by Death of the Outward Body is totally confirm'd in the erroneous will, the Law and Strife ceaseth.

CHAP. X. Further of the sixth Point. *Of the four Elements of the Devil.*

THE four Elements of the Devil are, Pride, Covetousness, Envy, Anger.

Gods four Elements are,	*The Outward Worlds four Elements are,*	*The Devils four Elements are;*
Humility,	Air,	Pride,
Meekness,	Earth,	Covetousness,
Patience,	Water,	Envy,
Love.	Fire.	Anger.

The discourse of the four Elements of the Dark World being both very plain, and the Subject of several of this Authors other Writings, The Extracts of it is forborn.

A Brief Exposition of the Small Six Points.

The first Point. *Of the Blood and Water of the Soul.*

1. THE Soul is a Magick Fire, its Form is generated in the Light, and though it self be no Substance, yet it hath a Substance and Preservation which is its Flesh, Blood and Water; for the Tincture of Fire and Light in the Water makes Blood, which is the Life of the Wisdom, having in it all the Forms of Nature, and all colours, being another or second Magick Fire.

2. According to the Light it is Divine Vertue, and according to the Fire it is a sharpness of Transmutation, and driveth up every thing to its highest pitch or degree.

3. The Flesh and Blood of the Soul is the Divine Substantiality consisting in the highest Mystery, and at the Death of the outward Body it retireth to the same: and the outward Mystery goeth home to the inward. And because each Magick fire hath its Clarity or Darkness;therefore a final Day of Separation is appointed.

The second Point. *Of Election and Reprobation.*

1. God alone is all, whose Infinite Abyssal Substance parteth into three Distinctions (one in the other, (yet the o e is not the other) (viz.) The Fire world, Dark-world and Light-world. From the Desire comes the Centre of Nature, and from that Centre, the first three Forms who have no pain in them, but the Fire causeth Pain.

2. In the Fire is the Life, tending to Light and Darkness: which of them the Desire filleth it self with, in that it burneth, be it Heaven or Hell. If it give it self to self Property, it burneth in the Fire of dark Anguish, but if to the Universal Will in Resignation, it's Fire burneth in the Light, driving up no Substance, but is in the Liberty of God.

3. God's Predestination is not in the first Essence, that is only a Mystery. But Predestination passeth upon the introduced Substance be it the Wrath or Love; for the Life is regenerated into one of them. And in which of them the Will kindleth it self, on that passeth the Election or Reprobation. Hence is it that God causeth us to be Taught, so doth the Devil, each of them willeth that Man's will should converse and kindle it self in his Fire. [See the Book of *Predestination.*]

The third Point. *What Sin is, and how it is Sin.*

1. Two contrary Wills are an Enmity. God is purely One without Source, and though every Source be in him, yet not manifested; for the Good so subjecteth the Evil, that it may be only a cause or Root of Light and Life.

2. The Good or Light is as a Nothing, into which when a Something entreth there must be a Spring to preserve that Something. The Something is dark, and the Qualities are manifold. And Covetousness filleth the one, wherein God dwelleth with multiplicity.

3. Though an unfathomable dwelleth not in a fathomable, yet God dwelleth in the highest or preciousest Life of Man, therefore must the Will of Life tend

The Small Six Points.

and subject it self to the One, in, before and above every Creature; for it is pregnant with that it lusteth after, and no Fire-source subsisteth in the free Fire, or Fire of the Liberty: therefore can none Unite to God, till they are emptied of their own Will; till then God and Man are at Enmity. Hence stands the immutable Law, That Man depart from Self, or be separated from the One.

Matth. 12.30.   4. Thus Sin is manifest, to be a Will departing from God, by awakening of and burning in the Root of Self-lust, maketh it self a sole Lord, a contrary opposite Will. So Christ saith, *He that gathereth not with me, scattereth.*.

5. This estranged Heterogene Will must be slain, and the Multiplicity corrupt with the Body: and the departure of the Will again from Self, to the One the Good, is the Regeneration, for the Will of the Soul is Fire, having been captivated in the Earthy Desire, hath wrestled and got into the One, whence it sprang originally, finding it true that Man's Will is nothing, God's Will is all things, whereinto when Man gets, all things are also its own.

The fourth Point. *How Christ will deliver up the Kingdom to his Father.*

1. In the Creation, the Father moved himself with the Dark and Fire-world, also in the Light or Heart wherein God became Man, and the Love of the Light, wherewith the Father did rule in the Son, and the Love overcame the Father's angry Property. Then did the Son rule in such as clave to God.

2. But in the End, the Holy Ghost moveth himself in both the Fathers and Sons Properties, and driveth on Eternally the Rule in both Properties, and proceeding from the Father and Son, is the alone Revealer of the Wonders. Thus is the Eternal Rule deliver'd up to the Father, who is All, which Rule he driveth on by the Spirit.

The fifth Point. *What the Magia and Magick Ground is.*

What it is not.   1. The *Magia* is not the Majesty, but the Desire in the Majesty. Not the Divine Power, but the Desire of the Power. Not the Omnipotency, but the Driveress in or into the Might. It is not a Fire, but the potence to the burning Fire.

What it is.   2. It hath the *Fiat* in it, and is the greatest Substance in the Deity; drawing Abyss into Byss. It is such a Will as driveth it self forth through the Desire into Substance. It Self is a Spirit and Substance is its Body. It is the Mystery of the Trinity. The Mother to Nature, and the Understanding is the Mother proceeding forth out of Nature. The Understanding leadeth it (which is its Mother) into its own Love-fire. It self is without Understanding, yet it is the Comprehension of all things.

What it doth.   3. What the Will modelleth, the *Magia* makes to be Substance, serving those that love God with Divine Substance, making Divine Flesh. By the *Magia* are all things wrought in their various Properties, Good and Evil, serving God's Children to bring them to God's Kingdom, and Negromancers to the Devil's King om It is from Eternity and its Profundity is inexpressible. It is the School-Mistress of Philosophy, the Book of all Learning, from the Plowman to the most Sublime. It is the best Theology. To reproach it, is to reproach God. It is the Acting and Performance in the Will-spirit.

The sixth Point. *Of the Mystery, What it is?*

1. The Mystery is the Imaging Power remaining in the Desire of the Magick Will, as it becomes in the Tincture, is by the *Magia* substantiated.

The Great Mystery.   2. The great Mystery is the hiddenness of the Deity, the Substance of all Substances:

A Brief Summary of the Earthy and Heavenly Mysteries.

stances: whence issue all Mysteries, each representing that which was his immediate Producer. The greatest Wonder of Eternity, the Reflexion of the Wisdom. And all existeth as it hath been foreknown from Eternity; but every thing according to the Property of the Looking-glass, even all the Forms of Nature, Light or Darkness, Love or Wrath.

3. The *Magus*, if arm'd sutably to what he would produce, may do what he will, else he will be captivated by the Spirits thereof.

A Brief Summary of the Earthy and Heavenly Mysteries Contracted and Comprised in Nine Texts.

THE Abyss is an Eternal Nothing, but a seeking: Which seeking is meerly a Will, and a giving of Somewhat, and that Somewhat, is the Eternal *Magia*.   1. *Text.*

1. The Will or seeking in the Abyss, is a Spirit like a Thought, and being gone out, findeth its Mother the Seeking. So the Seeking is a *Magia*, and the Will a *Magus*.   2. *Text.*

2. The Seeking is Inoperative, but the Will a Life without Original. So may be considered Nature and the Spirit of Nature, to have been from Eternity.

Thus the Will ruleth the Seeking, for the Seeking hath a moving, desiring Life without Understanding, and the Will doth therewith what it will; therefore we apprehend the Eternal Will-spirit to be God, and the Eternal Seeking to be Nature, the Eternal Will-spirit is the knowing of the Abyss, and the life of the Seeking, an Eternal knowing of the willing.   3. *Text.*

1. The Will is no Substance but Lord in it, which Substance desireth Substance. The desiring is a strong Magical attracting of Substance, and an Eternal proceeding Life.   4. *Text.*

2. And because this Magical Impregnation hath no Substance, it self is a Voice or Word in the Original of the Spirit, in which Word is a Will, and the Life of the Original going into Nature, opening the unintelligent Life of the *Magia*, which is the Mystery of Substance, the Abyssal Wonder, where infinity of Lives are generated.

3. Of this the Threefold Spirit is Master, of whom the Word is the Heart: And the Spirit of the Word in the first Will (*viz.*) God, openeth the Essential Life (*viz.*) Nature.

4. In the desiring of the Spirit Life, the Divine Substance or Heart of God is generated from Eternity to Eternity.

Thus apprehend we both, what God and Nature are, and both, in an Abyssal Endurance from Eternity in Eternity.

1. The two Eternal Substances are not sundered, but the Spirit life in it self is turn'd inward, and the Nature-life turn'd forward, like a Globe the Nature-life worketh to the Fire, the Spirit life to the Light and Glory.   5. *Text.*

2. In the one the consuming fierceness, in the other the generating of Water; their commixture, gives a light, blew or azure; or like a Cherubin or Ruby and Chrystal, &c.

3. Thus

A Brief Summary of the Earthy and Heavenly Mysteries.

3. Thus we may see that the Will can create a Source, out of the Magick Substance or great Mystery : especially in the Fires Property, which before the awakening lay hidden, as did the Devils; for in the Eternal Nature lyeth the *Turba*, though unawakable, unless the Creature in the fierceness do it.

4. Also we see when the Eternal Nature awaked it self with the creating, the Wrath also awakened, in some Creatures more evidently, as in poisonous Herbs, evil Trees and venomous Creatures; as Toads, Serpents, &c. which the Eternal Nature loatheth, and willeth to forsake, spewing it out, that the Malignity may stand in its own anguishing Mystery.

§. *Text.*

1. The desire every Will hath of Purity without *Turba* from without (though it hath the *Turba* in it self) is the cause of loathing, and that the stronger ruleth and oppresseth the weaker till it become Monarchy, which Nature must acknowledge to be in its Essence. Yet was not commanded in the Beginning by the highest Good.

2. And whereas the seeking in the beginning, was by one parting it self into many : So the Multiplicity seeketh the one again, and findeth it when a Lord shall be generated governing the whole World through man Offices which shall be in the hour of the Worlds Creation the sixth day in the Afternoon, when the purity shall drive out the *Turba* for a time, till the beginning pass into the end, and then is the Mystery shew'd in various Figures.

7. *Text.*

1. Seeing from the Eternal Nature all evil and good have proceeded ; by that it appears the one Property hath lusted and magically produced the other ; for Gods Spirit hath not predestinated the evil.

2. And in the four Colours lye the great secresie, viz. Blue, Red, Green and Yellow ; the White is Gods Colour, which only subsisteth in the Fire. The Black is only a Vail.

3. So in Languages, are first that of Nature, then Hebrew, Greek, Latine, and the fifth the Spirit of God, the Opener of all Alphabets. But the multiplicity of Speeches or Languages sprout and grow all against or contrary to the Tree.

8. *Text.*

1. From what hath been written resulteth the Original of two Religions, out of which *Babel* and Antichrist are generated. In Heathens, Jews and Christians. The Heathen going forward out of themselves and their own seeking, into the *Magia* of Multiplicity, for outward Rule and Kingdoms, tho' Gods free will rebuke them, the *Magus* of the Multiplicity not comprehending the will of the Unity, is an Idol, and a Malignant Devourer ; for the will hath its Treasure in the Multiplicity, becaufe by *Lucifer's* Apostasie the *Magia* of Nature is eager after falshood.

2. Hence spring Covetousness and Wars. But those that went away from the seeking of Perdition, into the Light of Nature, tho' they knew not God, yet liv'd in purity ; the Spirit of the Liberty led those Children of the Free-will into the Mystery, as may be seen by the Wisdom left behind them.

3. Thus also the Jews and Christians, whose wills were poyson'd by their Covetous *Magia*, while their Hands only are about the works of Gods Law, do Crown the Whore, Generate Antichrist, and Build *Babel*.

9. *Text.*

1. As there are two *Magia's*, that of the Unity, and that of the Multiplicity : So there are two *Magi* in Man, viz. The Spirit of God, and that of Reason, into which the Devil insinuates.

2. Hereby may Man most clearly try himself to which of these is his longing.

But

Of the Divine Vision or Contemplation.

But Man, being Magical, hath might, by sincere earnestness to subdue his Starry Spirit, by a temperate, sober and quiet Life, with continual giving up to the will of God, and going out of the Influxes to evil Lusts and Passions; which is effected not without great Toil, fiery Tryals, continual Sacrifice of the Fleshly Will, and working in the Will of God. To which the Lord help us.

Of the Divine Vision or Contemplation.

CHAP. I. Reason, *Because it seeth not God with the outward Eyes, and observeth the Good and Vertuous, go often afflicted to the Grave, saith there is no God.*

Answer. Reason is a Natural Life, and hath a Natural Will, yet proceedeth out of the Supernatural.

1. It willeth evil, and judgeth it self for it, fearing a Judgment which it seeth not, this is the reproof of the unseen and unapprehended God.
2. When it suffereth wrong, it hopeth for Rest in that which Created it.
3. Thus God reproving the evil in the Conscience, draweth the Sufferer by suffering to hate it self, and the Natural Will, and return, that it may attain the Supernatural Life, out of which it is gone forth.

Argument 2. 1. *Seeing God is the beginning of all things why is opposition permitted, and not the Good only to be in all?*
Answer. Contraries manifest contraries; for were a thing only one, without separability, it would have no Motion, Knowledge or Skill; for one only thing hath nothing in it to make more than one only thing perceptible.

2. And had not God, who is one only substance and Will, brought himself forth out of the Eternal Wisdom in the Temperature into Divisibility, and that the same Life stood in strife, how would his hidden Will be reveal'd to himself?
3. The strife is in the departed sever'd wil's, going into infinite variety, from one only Unity or Root. The Mind, as a Tree or Fountain, is not broken, but intire; but the Exit of the Thoughts or Senses is it only that divides into evil or good, as Twigs or drops.

Argument 3. *What good ariseth from this, that with the good there must be an evil?*
Answer. The evil opposite will, causeth the good to press again after its Original.

1. God, so far as he is called God, can Will nothing but himself, and what he willeth floweth out from him, as his Copy or Counterportraiture, which is divided and compressed into substance.
2. So also if Mans Mind did not flow forth, it would have no Senses nor Thoughts, nor know it self, nor ought else.
3. Now if in the Centres of the Thoughts, representing the Mind, there were only one will, and no will contrary, how would the Wonders of the
Divine

Of the Divine Vision or Contemplation.

Divine Wisdom be figur'd; for the Mind is an Image of the Divine Revelation.

4. From the strife of Contraries exist Substances; thence also the will is caused to link down from tormenting Anguish into the Eternal Rest, its Original, whence Exist Faith and Hope. That Nature being unvoluntarily over-laden, may be freed from Vanity into a clear Chrystalline Nature; and then it will appear that Nature was subjected, because the Eternal Power might introduce it self into Forms and Perception by Separation.

5. Wisdom must be manifest through Folly, and Eternal Stability be known in Mortality; for the Mortal is only a Play, Scene or Object of the right Life, and the wise breaketh the folly, dying to it, and giveth its will to God, tho' it be not deliver'd till it come to the Grave, nor is the Mortal Body of the wise to be regarded, for he that Buildeth on the Flesh shall of the Flesh Inherit Perdition.

CHAP. II. Argument I. *Seeing the Mind and Senses, or Thoughts is a beginning Natural Life subject to Corruption, how may the Supersensual Divine Life be in this Life?*

ANswer, Tho' Mans Life is a Form of the Divine Will, and its Imaged Word, yet by the Devil and Temporal Nature it is poysoned in its Earthy Image: Now in three Principles. The first according to its true Original in the Exit of Divine Knowledge, which in the beginning was a Temperature or sensible working of the Divine Power, a Paradise. But the fierce wrath of the Devil drove it into Dissimilitude and Inequality, wherein the Multiplicity strove against the Unity. When this was done the Wisdom of God, *viz.* his substantial Will or second Principle disappear'd.

1. The Eternal Abyssal Will of the Life or cause of the Motion of the holy substance had perverted it self to Earthiness, Gods Kingdom became (as to it) extinguished, and the third Principle (*viz.* that of the Constellations and four Elements) took place, making the Thoughts and Senses Earthy, and the Body Gross and Bestial, and the Life to seek rest in Mortality, and to be its own God; who by this domineering became foolish. And when this fragil Kingdom breaketh (as a Vapour) the Life continueth as a Contrariety, and becometh an unquenchable painful Fire in the dark Property.

2. But the great Love of God, instantly after the Apostacy, came, and still cometh to help, breathing it self again into the disappear'd Divine Property, and into all the three Properties of the Humane, even to the Thoughts and Senses, breaking the will of self and of the Devil, and hath brought the holy Life through Death into a Paradisical sprouting; making Death and the Devil a reproach, and shewing how the Eternal one can rule mightily over the Multiplicity, and give an open Grace Gate for us poor Men to enter the Life of Christ.

Rom.5.12,18. 3. We are therefore to come with our captivated will out of the Prison of Earth and Self, and solely sink down into this Incorporated Grace, which pressed from one, *viz.* the first Man upon all, and with the resign'd will sink down into the Hyperbyssal, Supersensual, Unsearchable Eternal one, into the ground out of which Life first sprung, and then it reacheth the Temperature and true Rest.

Argument. *How can a Man do that, (viz. that last above written) being the Scripture saith, The first Man is made to a Natural Life to rule the Creatures, therefore must the Life go into the Earthy Properties.*

Answer

Of the Divine Vision or Contemplation.

Answer 1. The Humane Life is set in a reflex Image of the Divine Will, in and with which God willeth, and the Earthy Creatures are set in a representation of the Humane.

2. And though Mans Life was set in Nature, yet it was in the Temperature. Without Christ we can do nothing, but if Man sink into the Incorporated Grace of God, and in Divine Hope rest from self-will, and work, and resign its will to work only what God speaketh, it is beyond Nature: And the Abyss God himself speaketh through him and manifesteth himself in and with him, thus new-born in Christ, who now ruleth over the outward Reason Life.

3. Till this be done Man is no Child of Heaven, but his will an Apostate just as the Devil and his Body, an evil Beast, and gathereth not with Gods Incorporated Grace, but scattereth.

4. As an Herb without Sap is burnt by the Sun, while the Herb that hath Sap is warn'd. So if Mans Essence hath not *Ens* from Gods Love and Meeknefs, it impreffeth it felf into a fierce, wrathful, fiery sharpnefs, and the Mind is totally rough, covetous, envious and stinging

5. Yet if the fiery Life eat of the Divine Love, it is no more receiving as the Fires Property is, but giving and working good in all, as the Property of the Light, for having eaten of the Bread which cometh down from Heaven, it is quickned by it.

The Sun in a hard Stone (where the Water is coagulated) cannot work, as in Metals, Herbs and Trees, becaufe his Light and Vertue penetrateth not, fo is it in this.

CHAP. III. *How Nature reprefenteth and maketh vifible the Divine Eternal and Abyffal Knowledge.*

1. THE Word is the Efflux of the Divine Will and Knowledge; as the Thoughts and Senfes are of the Mind, yet the Mind remaineth totally but one. So the Word was, is and ever will be the Eternal Beginning, flowing out, and revelation of the Eternal one.

2. And the Wifdom is the Eternal out-flown Beginning, and caufe of all Powers, Colours, Vertues and Properties.

3. Their Powers are again an Efflux into the various Self properties, whence come the Multiplicity of Wills, thence the Creaturely Life of the Eternal fpringeth, *viz.* Angels and Souls.

4. Not that Nature and Creature is here, but the Spirit of God fporteth himfelf in forming Similitudes of the Powers of the Wifdom; as doth the Mind with reflex Images, which are the Thoughts; and every Property hath its own Separator, as hath the Eternal Unity; whereby the Efflux of the Unity becomes perceptible in Infinite Multiplicity.

5. For the Efflux fharpeneth it felf fuperlatively by the Magnetick longing of the receiving Powers, in the fiery kind wherein the Eternal One becomes Majeftick and Light. And the inkindling through Fire makes it a Kingdom of Joy. The vifible World with its Hofts, is the out-flown word of Fire, Light and Darknefs feparated by the Officer of Nature, who hath imprinted each Body according to its own Property,

Of the Divine Vision or Contemplation.

Of the Twofold Life in the Representation of the Divine Will.

1. An Eternal.   2. A Temporal.

1. The Eternal is the sensible Life in the Eternal Fire and Light, a spark of the out-flown or out-breathed will of God, bound to will nothing but the out-breathed will of God, a Separator and Instrument of Gods Omnipotent Glory, wherewith he will rule all things, having therefore given it Divine Understanding.

2. The Temporal and Mortal Existence, is the Efflux of the Separator of all Powers call'd the Soul of the World, making the visible Creatures such a Similitude, as wherein the Spiritual World of Fire, Light and Darkness beholdeth it self; hidden in and working through the Elementary World. But the Visible possesseth not the Invisible so as to be chang'd thereinto, but is only an Instrument whereby the Inward Powers Image themselves, as in Herbs, Trees, Metals, &c.

Of the Threefold Spirit in the Growing Powers.

1. The outward Spirit is the gross Brimstone, Salt and Mercury, which coagulating it self in the four Elements, and by drawing the Spiritual Separator to it, the Signature is instantly perform'd.

2. The second Spirit or Quintessence hath a Centre of its own, viz. a Root of the four Elements, being the Meek Joy of the painful Brimstone and Salt Spirit, nourished from within of the Light of Nature, and from without of the subtle Power of the Spirit of the World, which fifth Essence, is the right cause of all Vegetation, and such a Joy of Nature as the Sun to the Elements.

3. The third's the Tincture, of which see Chap. 12. of the three Principles. The Tincture is that wherein all Powers lye in equality, a Spiritual Fire and Light in one substance, a Paradise, the Mansion of Divine Power, and of the Eternal Soul, known to the Creature only in the Regeneration, and to no ungodly one, for such drive on a false will.

4. It is not Elementary, but issueth through the gross Elementary Spirit, even into Taste and Smell. But the Elements are a cause of the motion of the Tincture; the sharpness of the Smell is Elementary, but the vertue in the Smell is the Tincture which in Medicines Cureth ; for it imprinteth it self in such Balsams.

5. As the voice to the Fig-tree, Be thou withered, did not that Miracle, but the Power whence the voice proceeded. As neither is the Confession of a thing Faith, but that Intellectual Power is Faith out of which the Confession proceedeth wherewith Gods Spirit Co-worketh.

6. Thus all whatsoever, whether evil or good, represent in their several Properties the hidden Spirit of the Separator of all things; and the Elementary is the Efflux of the Tincture, and Spiritual World, for the visible, moveable, material World is the substance of the invisible, immoveable, spiritual World.

7. So the desire of the Efflux out of the darkness is become sharp, stern and gross, and hath coagulated it self into Matter, even unto the drossy Earth. So out of the Light cometh the Noble Tincture of Love, Mildness, Softness, Sweetness. Yet in hard Bodies as of precious Stones, Metals, Trees, &c. is a high Tincture, as we see the greatest sweetness in Marrow.

8. God, distinct from his moving manifestation, is the greatest meekness, but in his motion is called a God in Trinity, for here the Divine will maketh it self an Object, viz. the Wisdom through which the Original of all things descended.

9. Now all things in the World that are soft, meek, rare or transparent, as Air and Water is without pain, and according to the unity of Eternity.

10. And

Of the Divine Vision or Contemplation.

10. And hard impressing Bodies, as Wood, Metals, Stone, Bone, Fire, Earth, &c. originate from the divine Inclusion, from the Efflux introducing the Self-will of Nature, as a noble Jewel and Sparkle of the Divine Motion of Divine Power, caused by the Effluence of Divine Desire.

11. Thus the Tincture hideth it self in the hardness, but In transparency is alike equal to all things; as in Water and Air. But the dry Water is the pearly Matter, where centreth the subtile potent Unity.

12. Therefore seek not the grand Secret in soft, without the fiery Kind.

For as Rare and Transparent is next the Unity, so the fiery Hardness is a dry Unity and Temperament, and the noblest Concret of divine powerful Manifestation, because where the Will is rent, rests no great Might; for there the Tincture is volatile, whereby a Cure is attempted by the Salt or Soul only, without the Spirit, which unites not the Life's Enmity, but kindles its Contrariety.

But unite the Properties in the Love, so have ye the Pearl of the whole World.

CHAP. IV. *Of the Will of God flowing OUT, and in the perceptibility IN again into the ONE.*

John 1.11, &c. *He came into* [or unto] *his own, &c.* In which words lyeth the Divine Manifestation, viz. the hidden Power or speaking Word of the Unity, out-flown into his own the Creaturely Word, or averted Will of Flesh and Blood; which Self-power received not the Efflux of Divine Grace, but would be its own Self-lord, for it cannot inherit the Filiation.

But that Will which turneth it self about and coingenerateth with the Unity, hath Power to become the Child of God. For it is like or equal to all things which God willeth and worketh.

Hujus Argumenti hic scripsit Huc Autor & Nil amplius.

A Brief Explanation of the Knowledge of God, and of all things, also of the true and false Light.

1. THE hidden God out-breathing his distinguishable Power, made his speaking Word substantial, by creating the Body, Soul and Spirit of Man, who is an Abstract of all the three Principles, and an Image of the speaking and spoken word.

2. Whence so great knowledge of all things is in Him, as to know the composition and dissolution of Nature; for every Creature can see into its Mother, those of the Elements into the out-spoken word.

3. So Man, after the manner as the out-breathing of the Eternal Will introduceth it self into the manifold Properties of Love and Anger, Good and Evil, and can frame it self into the multiplicity of Properties, those into the desire, and that into substance, forming its Self-will out of the great Mystery.

4. So, if in this out-speaking there were no Divine Free Will, the speaking would be under compulsion, void of longing delight, and be finite and inchoative, which it is not. But a breathing of the Abyss and Eternal Stilness a distributing it self into Powers, and in them a several Self-will existeth, whence originateth Nature, and the creaturely Life, with their various centers, impressions, magnetick desires, perception and bodies, according to the manner of the third Principle of Divine manifestation, producing bodies evil and good, manifold Earths, Salts, Stones, Minerals, in which the three Principles are mixt, where every Centre breatheth it self, yet all originate out of the Eternal One.

1 Centre. 5. The first Centre is the out-breathing of the Abyss, God bringing himself into Trinity.

2 Centre. The second Centre is called the Wisdom of God, through which the Eternal Word breatheth it self into Infinity of multiplicity, and that into longing delight, the delight into desire, the desire into Nature and Strife, and Strife into Fire. And through the dying of the Self-hood through Fire into the Light. The which Light is a second Principle, and true great Mystery. And the Fire is the first, (*viz.*) the Eternal Nature.

6. The first giveth Soul: the second Spirit, and this Lights Power through the Fire is the Mother of the Eternal Spirits, Angels and Souls of Men. Also the hidden Spiritual Angelical Power word, the Mother of the outward World.

3 Centre. The third Centre is the *Verbum fiat*, the natural Word of God, the separator and maker of all Creatures in the inward and outward World. The same speaker hath out of the Fire, the Light and the Darkness, made it self material, moving and perceptible, out of which existed the third Principle, the Visible World, the life and substance whereof is come out of the Eternal Nature the Fire, and out of the great Mystery the Light, also out of the Darkness, which is the separation of Fire and Light, Love and Enmity, Good and Evil, Joy and Pain.

7. There are two sorts of Fire, and two sorts of Light, *viz.* according to the dark impression a cold Fire, and a false Light, originating in the stern might and imagination, desiring a Self-will dominion.

The second Fire, is a hot Fire and true Light, originating in the Eternal One, in the substance of Divine Geniture, and that Light shineth in the Darkness, and illustrateth it; standing in a perceptible Life. The Life of Man is in it, and he is the Light of the World. 8. Therefore

Of the Knowledge of God, &c.

8. Therefore should Man lift up the Eyes of his understanding, wherein God's Light desireth to shine into him, and not be like a Beast which hath a temporary Light in a finite Separator, in which Man's palpable Body is.

9. For his Spiritual Body is the true substantial word of Divine Property, in which God speaketh and imageth himself; into which, if Man giveth not up his own will, he is more hurtful to himself than the rude Earth, which yieldeth to be made what its Separator will.

10. But from the Devil False Will, a false Light hath raised a false Separator, in which the Stars and Elements have dominion.

11. In this Man finding no quietness, seeks his first Native Countrey; for the true Man finds himself oppressed with a monstrous Separator environed with Enemies, as a Rose in a bush of Thorns.

12. Yet all his seeking brings not any true Life, unless Grace become awakened, to do which Man must sink down into a willing of nothing but Grace, that it may overcome and mortifie him as the Sun doth the night.

13. In that true Light the Man may see himself, and the separation of every thing and work magically and divinely, if he see the breathing, in its inward ground, according to the manner of speaking, how out of one all proceed, and one Centre out of another.

14. Reason lighted at this Sun, is the true house of Knowledge, else but a Constellation of the Visible World; all other seeking out of the resignation to the Divine Love, Grace and Will, is a shadow; for it cannot know how God hath through his Word made himself perceptible, findable, creatural and formal.

15. He is the Bottom and Bottomless, and to the Creature in its ability as a nothing, yet through all Nature and Creature is the somewhat wherewith he makes himself visible both according to Time and Eternity.

All things, even the four Elements, exist from the Divine Imagination.

Signature.

Signatura Rerum.

CHAP. I. *Of the Signature, what it is, and that it lies exactly in the Mind of Man.*

1. Every thing spoken, or taught of God without knowledge of the Signature is dumb; for it is not sufficient to my understanding that I hear and read what another teacheth and writeth of God, unless his Similitude and Signature by entring into mine own, imprinteth it really and fundamentally, for so only hath he the Hammer that strikes my Bell.

2. Hence we know, all Human Properties have one only Root; for one like tone catcheth and moveth another, either in good or evil, and doth assimilate into one Form, one Will, one Spirit and Understanding.

3. The Signature is no Spirit, but the receptacle: As a prepared Lute is dumb till toucht by the Spirit of the Will, and what strings he toucheth sound according to their property.

4. The Signature lies so well compos'd in Man, that he wants only the true Spirit of the high might of Eternity to strike his Instrument, if that be quickened in Man, and doth act the Mind, so speaketh the Mouth.

5. Man hath the Forms of the three Worlds in him, being the compleat Image of God; and there are three Masters contest for his Form in his Incarnation, but the predominant only tunes his Instrument, and the other two lie hid; and as soon as he is born, his innate genuine Form appears by his words and conversation: And so great is the difference in the procreation, that one Brother or Sister doth not as the other.

6. Yet one *Fiat* doth not alwaies keep the dominion; for sometimes an Evil Man, is by a *contra* tune, (*viz*.) the meek, loving Spirit of a Good Man, moved to cease his iniquity and repent, his hidden Lute or Form being played upon. Contrariwise, in a Good man is stirr'd up the Form of Anger by the Wrath-Spirit of a wicked man: So is the will broken by the coming of a stronger will: As the bitter sour quality of the fruit, is by the potent influence of the Sun made pleasant. And as a good Herb receiving a *contra* Essence from a bad Soil, cannot sufficiently shew its real genuine vertue; but if replanted into a good Soil, its vertue and smell is recovered. Thus a wild Beast, being over-aw'd and tam'd, hath another property, unless its innate Form be stirr'd up. Also we see the inward gives external Character of Good or Evil in Man, Beasts and Vegetables. The Form and Sound in Animals, the smell and tast in Herbs and Flowers, &c. shewing, to what it is good and profitable.

7. And because by the desire sound and voice all Creatures shew the inward Spirit, Man may know both them, himself, and the Essence of all Essences; wherein lieth the greatest understanding. The Signature is the Language of Nature; for every thing sheweth its Mother giving will to the Form.

CHAP.

CHAP. II. *Of the Combate in all Beings. Of Antipathy and Sympathy. And of the Corruption and Cure of each thing.*

1. THE oppofition of one Being to another caufeth pains and ficknefs, yet if this were not, Nature would not be revealed, but be an Eternal Stilnefs; for the *contra* Will makes the motion and feeking. The Cure is, when the Will findeth its affimilate, and therein its fatisfaction and higheft joy and reft. As every pallate defireth to taft its like.

2. Man's Life confifteth in a threefold Effence : (1.) The Eternal Nature, the Fire's Property. (2.) The Light, the Divine Effentiality. (3.) The outward World.

3. The fatisfaction of the Will is the Liberty, which if it feek outwards, it attracteth Darknefs, but if it enter inwards, the Luftre of the Liberty fhineth, and fatiateth the Anguifh, extinguifhing the Wrath.

4. No joy can arife from the ftill nothing; for we fee that from the poifonful Gall arifeth joy and forrow, becaufe therein is the twofold Will, one to the Fire the original of Nature, the other to the Light, which is the Cure and Liberty of the Will, and if obtained, maketh triumphant joy.

5. The Properties lie in the Effence, as a well tun'd Inftrument with many ftrings, which ftand ftill, and the Spirit, (*viz.*) the Egrefs is the real life; he may play as he pleafeth to Evil or Good, to Love or Anger. The Properties are one in another as one, but fever themfelves being different; and when they enter one the other, comes Enmity and a flagrat. As when the Sun ftirreth up the Fires Form in the Salnitre, that Ethereal blaze penetrateth the cold Salt Spirit, and difmayeth it; whofe inftant flight caufeth the Thunder-claps, by opening the aftringent Chamber, whence follows a cool Wind with Hail and Rain.

CHAP. III. *Of the Grand Myftery of all Beings.*

1. Without Nature God is a Myftery, an Abyffal Eye of Eternity, and the fame Eye is a Will to manifeftation. (1.) To Nature. (2.) To Vertue, Power and Joy.

2. The defire is egreffive, and the Egrefs is the Spirit of the Will, a moving forming the infinitenefs of the Myftery, and this Signature or Form is the Eternal Wifdom of the Deity.

3. Here is underftood the Trinity, but how the Will arifeth in the Abyfs, which is called Father, we muft not know, but diftinguifh the Deity from Nature, namely, how the Deity manifefteth it felf with the Eternal Generation.

4. God is a pure Spirit, and the Eternal Nature is his Corporeal Effence. The external Birth is a fimilitude of the dark Fire and light World, and each Property fees its Mother. The Soul fees the inward Eternal Nature : The Spirit of the Soul fees the Angelical and Light World : The Sidereal Spirit fees the Birth and Property of the Stars and Elements.

5. The Effence of this World confifts of Sulphur, Mercury, and Sal. *Sul* is the free *Lubet* of the Eternal Abyfs, in the Internal *Sull* is God, and *Phur* is Nature, (*viz.*) the Eternal Nature, a hard attraction the caufe of Fire, and *Sul* the caufe of the Luftre in the Fire, but the Light rifeth not in the Sulphur alone; but in Mercury is the dividing made, and its true real body is Sal.

6. The

6. The Aftringency makes grofs Stones, &c. Mercury and the *Lubet* Metals. And of the freeing from the wrath by the light and meeknefs comes the precious Stones, Gold, &c. for all things confift in thefe three Forms, Sulphur, Mercury and Sal, as well the inward heavenly Quires, as the very Plants and Stones, all ftand according to its firft fude, boiling or vegetation.

CHAP. IV. *The Birth of the Stars, &c.*

1. THere are feven Forms in Nature, which yet principally confift in three; *viz.* Aftringency, Compunction and Anguifh; according to which there are feven Planets, and no more, and feven Metals fixt. The Temporal Spirits hungereth a Temporal Body; and the Eternal Spirits hunger an Eternal Body; both in each other, but diftinct, as Time and Eternity.

2. In Saturns Property the *Lubet* makes Lead, and according to the Water, Salt; according to Saturns mortal Property, Earth, Stones,&c. according to the Liberty in Saturn,Gold, which he keeps fhut up. See *verfe* the 27th to the 34th.

3. There is in Man, (1.) The Divine Golden Man. (2.) The inward holy Body from Fire and Light, like pure Silver, if not corrupted. (3.) The Elemental Man like Jupiter. (4.) The Mercurial growing Paradifical Man. (5.) The Martial Soul-like Man. (6.) The Venerine, according to the outward defi (7.) The Solar, a feer of the Wonders of God.

4. Mercury in the internal was as the Word by which God created.

5. Mars, his impreffion is Anguifh caufing the Love-will to feparate from him, which is called God, but the Anguifh is God's Anger or Wrath of the Eternal Nature.

6. Venus Metal is Copper, receiving its roughnefs from Saturn, its rednefs from Mars, tho' Mars his Metal be Iron. But Sol may tincture Mars and Venus into Gold; for Venus longeth after Sol her Mother, her Joy; whence fhe hath a peculiar fmiling twinkling Afpect.

7. The Sun is a figure in the outward World of the heart of God, each thing longeth after the Sun in Sulphur, being the univerfal Tincture; and what the firft defire with Saturns impreffion makes evil, the Sun reftores to be good; caufing a pleafant temperature blooming and growing in all Creatures.

CHAP. V. *Of the Sulphurian Death, and how the Body is revived, &c.*

1. MAN was created good according to, and out of the three Worlds. But the inward *Lubet* generated in the Centre, (*viz.*) the fire (wherein ftands the Life) by Luft enkindled the Divine Meeknefs, wherein Joy confifteth, turning from Eternal Liberty to Time, from the one pure Element into the four Elements.

2. Then did the Precious Gold of Heavenly Corporality which tinctur'd the outward Body, difappear, then alfo the dominion of Time deftroyed its own contrived Spirit, and fo the Body paffed away and died.

3. The only Remedy is, that Gods Love, Defire, Effentiality and Divine Water, enter again into, and quench the Souls Wrath-Fire For Mans Salvation confifts in his full unfeigned defire after God, fo rifeth the Meeknefs, and Love tinctureth Death and Darknefs in the four Elements, and fever from the New Man, who and the Heavenly Body remaineth only in it felf. So is it done in the tranfmutation

Signatura Rerum.
tion of Metals; See Verse the 12th, and to the End of the Chapter. *De Lapide Philosophorum.*

CHAP. VI. *Of the generating Difference and Vegetation caus'd by Water and Oyl.*

1. ALL life and growth consist in the Lubet and the Desire. The Lubet is out of the Liberty, so God hath the free Lubet, needeth nothing; Himself (as far as he is called God) is all. But the Desire is a hunger: stirring up the Lubet to manifestation; so the Lubet is the hungers Food and Essence.
2. The free Lubet or Esse c giveth an Oyl, and the Desire giveth a life to the Oyl; The Oyl is a Light the Desire giveth the Fires Property, so that it shineth. In the Desire ariseth the Natural Spirit, in the Lubet the Supernatural, which yet is belonging to Nature: not spontaneously, but from its meek resignation to the Desires Property.
3. But a twofold Property ariseth out of one Spirit, thus, a fiery, according to the Property of the Desire, and a joyful lucid according to the Liberty.
4. The fiery giveth in its water Essence, a sharpness or saltness and from the fiery in its anguish, Brimstone; whence are Stones Earth and Me als.
5. The Oleous Property gives Meekness (*viz.*) Vegetation, what the raging Mercury spoils, the Lubet of the Love-oyl heals; thus Good and Evil are in each Life; the Evil comes when the Hunger Spirit too much impresseth its own Form, so that it cannot receive the free Lubet to appease its Hunger. Whereas Nature's Property should be sincerely inclined to God's Love Ens, that it become not a dark raging poisonful Hunger, but a Love-desire, which is called God's Nature; for the hungry fiery desire is God's Anger, in the outward 'tis Fire, but in the inward where it doth energize in the free Lubet, it is the Divine Desire, whence joyfulness proceedeth.
6. All sharpness of taste is Salt, all smell proceeds of Sulphur: and Mercury distinguisheth all Motion in tast, smell and power.
7. In the strongest poisonful Mercury lyes the highest Tincture, but not in its own Property, but in an Oyl from the Light, which is its Food. If this be sever'd from him, it is a mighty potent inkindler, a lifter up of all sick, fainting, weak, obscured lives; for in this Oyl is the joyful Life, a hunger after Life. So in a Toad, Viper, Adder, *&c.* lyes the highest Tincture, if the oily Substance be reduced from the wrath of Mercury.

CHAP. VII. *How Adam and Lucifer were Corrupted through Imagination, &c.*

1. WHEN *Adam* was Created, the Light of his Life shone in the pure Oyl of Divine Essentiality: but, by his Fall, Mortal Water penetrated, so that his Mercury became a cold Poison, which was before, an Exaltation to joyfulness. So came darkness into his Oyl, and he died to the Divine Light, drawn thereto by the Property of the Serpent; for, in the Serpent the wrath Kingdom and outward also, was manifest, whose subtilty *Eve* desired.
2. For as much as the Serpent is not out of the Eternal Ground (as Angels and the

Signatura Rerum.

the Souls of Men) but out of the Beginning where Fire and Light sever, *Eve* should not have gone with her desire out of Eternity into time, and be a Selfist, but with a desire resign'd to God, to the quiet, still, meek Liberty; for each Hunger maketh it self an Essence, according to the Property of the Hunger.

3. The Devil went with his desire into himself, into the Property of the Centre, forsook the Eternal Lubet of Love, and became a Poisonful Mercury, or as an anxious Fire as Wood burnt to a Coal, a dark glowing without Oyl or Water in it, whence springeth a stinging Envy in his Lifes Forms, where one Form hates the other in his aspiring Pride. Out of the strife of which Properties, when God said, Let all sorts of Beasts come forth, each according to his Kind or Property, then came out of the divided Evil Properties, Vipers, Serpents, Toads, *&c.* Not that the Devil made them, but that there, where God and the World sever, the inward Wrath (according to which God is called a Consuming Fire) manifested it self in External figures of the inward wrath Kingdom.

4. And because *Adam* died to God, and lived to Death, it was necessary God should regenerate him, from the Essence of time, the Mortal Oyl which God had Cursed (*viz.*) withdrawn from, to the Essence of Eternity, the Living Oyl which God's Love desire penetrateth. So doth the Womans Seed break the Serpent's Head, deprive the Wrath of its might, put it into Divine Joyfulness, the dead Soul ariseth: the Anger was Master, but in the Light is become a Servant.

From the 24th Verse exclusive to the End of the Chapter is *de Lapide Philosophorum.*

CHAP. VIII. *Of the Seething and Growth in the Earth, and the Separation of the several Kinds of Creatures.*

1. ALL things consist of a sulphurous Property. The visible as the likeness of the Eternal proceed in Generation according to the right of Eternity in the Limit of Measure, Weight and space of Time which is as a dead Instrument of Eternity. Now for accomplishing all, God hath substituted the Soul of the great World his Officer, and over him the understanding, wherewith he ruleth the Officer, shewing him the Severation, Degrees and Process; for Sulphur contains all, Mercury enliveneth, and Salt impresseth, and fixeth, that it fall not to Ashes.

Mercury by boyling in Sulphur, produceth two Forms, *viz.* One Oleous, from the Liberty of the Divine Power, the other Mortal from the dissolution of the Salnitral flagrat. Mercury is the Officers Faber, which in the Oily Property doth pullulate, willing always to fly from the Anguish as his Death: not to be captivated thereby, from which strife proceedeth Growth: in the Mortal Property it is the Life of Death, Hell and the Anger of God, but in the oleous good Property is a Heavenly Light.

3. And because the Essence of Eternity is hid in the anxious Mercury; these and the other Writings of this Author teach, how to bring the desire out of the poisonful Mercury into the inclosed Essence of Eternity, and reassume that for a Body, and therewith Tincture the Essence of time, and reunite the inward and outward World to have only one Will, *viz.* A Love Hunger; so that no Will to Evil can arise any more. And may be attained, like as we see Eternity Travelling through time with longing to be free from Vanity which when the Hunger of Mercury obtains, it becomes joyful, is pregnant, making the free Lubet Corporeal in him; whence come good Herbs, Metals, Silver, Gold, Pearls, *&c.* all according to the prevalency of one of the seven Forms of Nature, and the Boiling or Sude in each place.

CHAP. IX. Of the Signature, *Shewing how the Internal doth sign the External.*

1. THE Kingdom of God confifts in Power and the outward vifible World is a Figure or Signature of the Spiritual and Eternal Powers, both the inward and outward are efpecially in feven Properties or Forms, each the caufe of the other, none is firft or laft of them.

2. That of the feven which is Superior in any Creature or thing chiefly figneth that Body and the other Forms adhere to it.

3. But the Artift with the true Mercury by fubjecting the Superior and exalting an Inferior Property, may caufe the Spirit to obtain another Will, giving other taft, odour, colour, found and fhape than before; viz. Life and Good, or Death and Evil prevailing.

4. The Properties are Labourers in the Heavenly, Earthy and dark impreffion alfo. So the inward Mercury is the Eternal fpeaking Word both in the Holy Light World in the outward, and in the oppofite perverfe World.

5. That where *Saturn* is moft potent is of colour greyifh, black or grey, or whitifh Buds in Vegetables of touch hard, of taft fharp or falt, the Eye of a dark blew, a lean, long Body or Stalk. If it (as ufually it doth) awaken *Mars* it curbs the heighth, and is crooked, knotty bufhy as in Oak fhrubs.

6. Where *Venus* is next *Saturn* not hindred by *Mars*, the Sude in that Saturnin P.
Sulphur makes a tall great Man, Beaft, Tree or Herb.

7. If *Jupiter* be ftronger in *Saturn* than *Venus*, and both than *Mars*, it makes an excellent fair, vertuous, potent Body of good tafte, its Eyes whitifh blue.

8. But if *Mercury* be betwixt *Venus* and *Jupiter*, and *Mars* weakeft, then is this Property in *Saturn* graduated in the higheft Power and Vertue in word and work. If it be in Vegetables they are long, of middle-fized ftalk, of curious form, fair, white or blue Bloffoms, which if the Sum influenceth incline to yellow; and if *Mars* hinder not, be it in Man or other Creature, is Soveraign Univerfal Vertue, exempted from falfe Influences, but is rarely found, being near to Paradife.

9. But if *Mars* be next *Saturn* fuperiour to *Venus* and *Jupiter*, and *Mercury* caft an oppofite Afpect, all is poyfon'd, and the Creature prone to evil, which if the Moon alfo Influenceth, Witchcraft is manifeft.

10. If a Bloffom be reddifh ftreak'd with white, *Venus* is there; but if only reddifh with dark ftreaks, a rough Skin on the Stalk or Leaf, a loathfom tafte, it obfcureth Life; for there lodgeth the Bafilisk. It is Peftilential, but if the Artift extracteth the Mercurial Poyfon, and feedeth *Mars* with *Jupiter* and *Venus*, it becomes a Love fire in *Sol* and an Antidote.

11. This Property makes the Voice or Sound grofs, dull, yet inclining to be fhrill by reafon of *Mars*, falfe and flattering, the Vifage hath red Pimples or Streams in blinking, rouling or unfteady Eyes.

12. But if *Mars* be next *Saturn*, and *Jupiter* under it, *Mercury* weak, *Venus* oppofite, it produceth good hot Herbs; for hot Difeafes, rough and pricky, yet the ftalk is fine and thin, the Flower brownifh.

13. *Saturn* alone, hurteth in *Mars*-like Difeafes; for it awakeneth *Mercury* in the cold Property.

14. Nor may the undigefted hot *Mars* be ufed in which *Mercury* is inflamed, but both be firft fublimed into Joy.

15. An Herb in the aforefaid Property grows not high, is rough in fuch degree

as *Mars* hath strength in it, and to be used only externally, but the fine subtle part is expulsive, and near to Mans Life, being then most potent.

16. But if *Mercury* be next *Saturn*, and next him the Moon, and *Venus* and *Jupiter* beneath and weak, then all is Earthy at best, let *Mars* be where he will; but if *Mars* be too near, is also poysonous, unless *Venus* opposeth; by whose Power it hath a greenish Colour.

17. If *Venus* be next *Saturn*, and the Moon not oppos'd by *Mars*, and *Jupiter* be powerful, then in that Constellation all is pleasant, the Herb slender, single and soft, the Blossoms white, unless *Mercury* by *Sol* and *Mars* intermix yellow and red.

18. There are three Salts in Vegetables chiefly Medicineable which the Spirit of the Sun makes operative.

1. Salt of *Jupiter* of pleasant Smell and Taste inwardly from the liberty of the Divine Essence, and Externally of the Sun and *Venus*.

2. Salt of *Mars* is fiery, bitter and austere.

3. Salt of *Mercury* is anxious and raging, inclined to heat and cold assimilating it self to each Property, where it is in *Jupiter*'s Salt, it causeth potent Joy.

19. In *Mars*'s Salt it makes Pangs and Stitches, and Woe. In *Saturn*'s Salt, Swellings, Anguish and Death, if not oppos'd by *Jupiter* and *Venus*, for they two oppose and temper *Mars* and *Mercury*, yet by *Mars* and *Mercury* is the Life in *Jupiter*. *Venus* and *Sol*, where would else be a stilness, thus is the worst as profitable as the best.

20. And when the Physician hath reconciled *Mars* and *Mercury* with *Venus* and *Jupiter*, that they all obtain one will, the Sun of Life will revive and correct the nauseat of the Disease into a pleasant *Jupiter*: This is only applicable to the Vegetative or Sensitive Soul of the Elementary Body.

21. The rational Soul hath its Diseases, springing from care and distress till it lead to heaviness and Death, cured by removing the causes of that care, *&c*.

22. So Sin hath poysoned the Mental Soul by Inflaming his Eternal *Mercury*, which with the sting of his *Mars*, burns in the horrible impression of his *Saturn*; his *Venus* is Imprison'd, his Intellectual *Jupiter* Infatuated, his Sun quenched, his Moon dark.

23. To Cure this he must with *Venus* the Love of God, and *Jupiter* the Divine Understanding, quench and apprease the flaming *Mercury*, and raging *Mars*: So is the Soul Tinctured with Love, his Sun then shineth, and *Jupiter* rejoiceth; for Divine Love begetteth a Divine Will so Tinctured as able to die to self-will, which Death doth attain the nothing wherein is no *Turba* to touch or hurt the Soul, who now doth neither see, know nor live, but according to the resignation.

24. Here doth Christ break the Serpents Head, and God become all in all.

25. It is possible to live without sickness but very difficult to bring the inward into the outward as the Sun illustrateth Water because the opposite will hath introduced wrath in the outward Body, it must die and putrifie, and enter again into the nothing, into the beginning of the Creation out of which it departed with *Adam*.

CHAP. X. *Of the Inward and Outward Cure of Man.*

1. TO Cure Man God brought not a strange thing into him, nor did cast away the Humanity, but with the like of that which was corrupted introduced a Di-

a Divine Property into him. In Man was the expressed Word or Eternal *Mercury* inspoken; which was the Soul with the Properties of all the three Worlds; Fire, Light and Love.

2. *Adam* should have put his defire into the humble, meek, light and love, but he made in himfelf the hunger after evil and good, and fo could not Tincture his Fire-world and outward World with Love.

3. To reftore Mans right Image God introduced the holy *Mercury* in the fiery Love-flame, with fuch a defire of Divine *Effentiality* as makes Divine Corporality; which reinkindled the Light of the Eternal Sun in the Humane Property, fo that the Humane *Jupiter* of Divine Underftanding might again appear.

4. So is the outward Cure done, Mans *Mercury* was inkindled, a *Mercury* muft Cure it, but that muft firft it felf be inkindled in *Venus* and *Jupiter*, which alfo gives it the Suns Property. Not with dark cold *Saturn*, unlefs firft fweetly appeas'd with *Venus* and *Jupiter*, fo will the Sun fhine in *Saturn*, and Death be chang'd into Life,

5. The Knowledge how God reftores the Univerfal, is learnt by ftudy of the procefs of Chrift from his firft Incarnation to his Afcention. The Effence of *Venus* fhut up in Death, muft be Baptiz'd in the Water of the Eternal Effence: By which the Imprifon'd Incentive (as Fire falling into Tinder) gloweth. Then muft the outward Food be withdrawn, and the hungry Defire be tempted, whether it will go into God, and be fed with *Manna*, (let the Effence of time by refignation be fubject to that of Eternity, and fo poffefs the Elected Throne whence *Lucifer* fell) or defire the Earthy Kingdom of Good and Evil, for outward Dominion: If its will remain in Gods Love-fire, the Water is turn'd to Wine, fo is the outward Cure alfo done.

NB.

6. But before the Univerfal Reftoration be manifeft, all the feven Properties muft be Chryftalized. each Form by a peculiar procefs forfaking their will in the wrath, and come into the Loves Property wherein is no *Turba*, all which Chrift did in the Humanity before the Body was glorified.

7. When therefore the Frozen Mouth in *Saturn* of all the Properties is opened, and that Food given to their hunger wherein is no *Turba*, the flagrat of Joy in Love, difmayeth the wrath (and is as a Tranfmutation, but not fixt) the Angelical Properties appear in view.

8. In Chrifts Temptation the fpeaking *Mercury* in the Light, was given to the expreffed *Mercury* of the Fires Property; becaufe *Adam*'s Fires Property had que:ched the Lights Property. Chrift was tempted to depart out of the Refignation into a defire of felfifh Propriety of worldly Avarice and Dominion, to the Knowledge and Kingdom of Good and Evil, where pain and wrath is manifeft, but in the Refignation is facred Love, and no Breath of Anger; as in the Light of the Fire is no pain of Fire manifeft. 29.

9. The Mother and Womb of all Beings is Sulphur: *Mercury* is her Life, *Mars* her Senfe, *Venus* her Love, *Jupiter* her Underftanding, *Luna* her Corporeal Effence, *Saturn* her Husband. 56.

10. In the Philofophick work the Artift raifeth in the firft Kingdom the dead Apoftate Child fhut up in *Saturn*, opening by degrees Paradife again by Gods permiffion. 67.

In the fecond Kingdom *Luna* Corporally feeds; where the outward *Mercury* hath not laboured. So Chrift fed the 5000.

11. In the third Kingdom, *Jupiter*, Chrift made Babes wife; fo the Artift feeth the new Life rife up, the four Elements appear with all Colours.

13 In the fourth Kingdom of the Mercurial Orb, Chrift reftor'd the Deaf, Dumb and Lepers; fo the Artift fees how Heaven fevers it felf from the Earth,

and

and again finks into it, Coloureth and Purifieth the Matter, appearing in Antimony.

14. In the fifth Kingdom Chrift ejected the Devils; fo the Artift will fee how *Jupiter* in *Mercury*, drives up a black twink'ing fiery Vapour out of the Matter ſticking like Soot, a hunger of the Poyfon in *Mercury*, the Devils Property.

15. In the fixth Kingdom Chrift in *Virus* loved his, and humbly waſhed his Diſciples Feet, gave himſelf up to be mock'd, beaten and crucified; fo the Artift will fee (as foon as the material Devil, the dark fiery ſteam is gone) the Virgin very Glorious, which the Artift will be apt to think is the Philoſophick Child, but in the tryal finds it to be a Woman, not the Virgin with the Tincture of Fire and Light; for now *Saturn*, *Mars* and *Mercury* oppoſe, but *Jupiter* and *Luna* hold with *Venus*, but when the Power of wrath cometh, *Luna* changeth her will, *viz*. Colour, and cryeth with the common people (fignified by her) Crucifige.

CHAP. XI. *The Proceſs of Chriſts Suffering, Death and Reſurrection Symbolized in the Philoſophick Work.*

THIS whole Chapter confiſting of eighty verfes, being a profound purfuit, eſpecially of the ſixth Kingdom, and the Eſſence and alteration in the Symbolical Philoſophick proceſs to the Suffering, &c. of Chrift, even from the almoſt Triumphant Glory of the Philoſophick Virgins Child, to his ſeeming Nonexiſtence, and again a meaſure of reſtoration to Royalty, is not thought fit to be Abridged, but its entire Contexture left to farther Contemplation; to which the Reader is referred.

CHAP. XII. *How the Seventh Kingdom, viz. the Sun is reviv'd.*

1. WHEN Chrift died the Natural Death, it was for that *Adam* had brought his Humane and Senfitive Life, the out-ſpoken Word, into another Form and Sound than the ſpeaking Word or *Fiat* had ſpoken it, *v.z.* into a Selfiſh will, by which death of Chrift, the true Humane Life fell again into the place whence *Adam* brought it, where Gods Ruling Spirit was the alone Life of it in all the three Principles, not to be longer to the Aſtrum of the four Elements, but in the pure Divine Element.

2. Chrift was the Death of Death, bringing Life thence into Eternal Liberty. And whatſoever Jeſus hath done through Chrift, in his and my Humanity, he yet now to day doth in me.

3. The Proceſs is the Curfe, being deſcended into the ſeven Forms, of which the Life confiſteth; therefore as Chrift was a Death to the Human Self-hood, yet the Humanity was not deſtroyed. So the ſeven muſt in the Philoſophick Work be by Death brought to one Will and Defire in the Eternal *Sol*, from Strife to Love, yet remain in ſeven, as heated Iron, though ſhining as Light, is yet Iron.

4. Let the Artift confider how he may give Death to Death with the pure Life, and how to awaken the diſappear'd captivated Life which is Heavenly; ſo that it may again receive the Fire-ſoul, and it worketh of it ſelf.

5. And ſeeing it is not poſſible to bring the Earth to Heaven, the Heaven muſt be brought into the Earth, (*viz*.) The Soul muſt be overcome, and eat of Heaven will ſhe nil ſhe, till ſhe entreth with her Defire into the Heavenly Eſſence; for the dear Love life diſmayeth the Murtherer, and ſhineth in the Love-fire. So the

ſeven

Signatura Rerum.

seven Forms become unanimous, proceeding to the Universal, the Fundamental Knowledge whereof is apprehended only by such as enter into the Resignation of Christ, and to such, the way is Facile and Childlike.

CHAP. XIII. *Of the Enmity of the Spirit and of the Body, and of their Cure.*

1. THERE is a Vegetative Life consisting in the four Elements, a sensitive in the seven Forms of Nature, a ratiocinative in the Constellation, but the understanding proceeds from God arising out of the Eternal Nature, from the Oyl of the one Element, the free Lubet in the speaking *Mercury*.   NB.

2. The Enmity originateth in the Mercurial Life, which consists in Sulphur hungring after Matter: which austere hunger impresseth to Coldness or a cold Fire, (*viz.*) hardness, density and darkness, wherein it strives for Life, and in that Life is the heat inkindled devouring the cold of its Substance, begetting Light, when also the Fire-spirit dyeth; for the Life of the one is the Death of the other. So the cold fire continually without intermission by dying, becomes Life to the hot fire, and the hot fire by its strong hunger draweth, devoureth and liveth by its Mother the cold, out of the impression whereof it had its Ens, which it letteth free into the Lubet of the Nothing: Thus the Fire is in the Light of the Lubet a Joy, and in the Darkness an akeing Wo, yet without the one, the other could not be, as is demonstrated.

3. Man's desire was in the Beginning in the Liberty of God in resignation to his Love-will, but by Self-will awaken'd in Nature, Heat, Cold, Astringency, Bitterness, Anguish, Torture.

4. The only Cure must be a full and free resigning the Self-will into the first will, by dying to the erring will, and thereby become that to which God at first created him. Then will the pure Body of the Element (in which the Love-life of God's Spirit inkindleth in the Soul the resign'd will) make the disappear'd Body spring from the same pure Element, become the Mansion of the Soul, in a Paradifical budding or blooming Renovation.

5. The most high gave every Property at first a fixt Perfection, but the Curse brought the *Turba*. And now seeing God hath given us Power to become his Children, and rule over the World: Why not then over the Curse in the Earth, so as to open and set free the captivated Paradifical Powers.

CHAP. XIV. *How the three Principles interchange generating Good and Evil, yet all remain as at first to manifest the Glory of God.*

1. THE first Eternal Creatures Angels and Man, and unfixt Products of Time Vegetables and Animals are all one thing, differing according as the Properties impressed on them.

2. The Impression is call'd Nature, and is the Mother and Manifestation of the Mystery; what hath been in the Eternal Will in both Centres according to Fire and Light, also according to Darkness and Essence in the Motion of the desire to a manifest Mystery out of Eternity into a time, which consisted in Sulphur, Mercury and Salt.

3. These

3. These Powers introduce themselves into Evil and Good by the seven especial Properties, when they are not in due Weight and Measure but by the prevalency of some, the rest are captivated.

4. Whatsoever exceeds or departs from the first order to which its Mother brought it forth, cannot go back and re enter with its depravity into the first Root and good state unless it die; So, and so only can stand again there, whence first it proceeded before it became Corporeal.

5. The lower Hemisphear is the first Principle, * Kingdom of Darkness. The upper part the Salniter. The Cross above the Circle the Kingdom of Glory. The Form of Separation between the Living and Dead Essentiality is the fifth Form, the Love-desire, or Love flame.

6. Sulphur is the Mother of the Creatures, arising out of the Darkness, Fire and Light; on the dark part it is Astringent. Bitter, Anxious; but on the part resembling the Deity, 'tis Fire, Light and Water. The Fire divides it self into Death, (viz.) Water, and into Life (viz.) Oyl, wherein the true life of all Creatures in the external World consists.

7. Mercury is the Wheel of Motion in the Sulphur, on the dark part is a sting, and severs in the Fire in its Mother Sulphur into a twofold Water; in the Death of Fire, into a Living-light Water producing Silver in Brimstone in the seventh Property of Nature; but in the Fire its Water is quick-silver, and in the dark Anguish 'tis rust and smoak in it, it is also Poison.

8. Salniter is the Comprisor of all Properties, Mother of all Salts in the Creatures, in those which grow in the Love desire, 'tis potent and pleasant, in the Evil it's Eternal horror; ever aspiring above the Humility of Love. Whence is the Will of Pride, and of all Devils. It giveth weight, in Austereness, Earth, Sand and Stones, in the Water in Sulphur and Mercury, Flesh, in the Oleous and Love Property, a sweet Spiritual Essence, pleasant smell, in the Fire and Light, the one Element, in the lustre, it gives the precious Tincture, in the Salnitral flagrat, is the sude of growth and pullulation, it also holds Sulphur and Mercury from severing from each other, yet in the Salnitral flagrat they pass into the four Elements.

9. The Properties are as so many hungry Desires, eating of their several likenesses: the hunger of Time eateth of Time, and that of Eternity, of Eternity: but Man's Original, being from two Principles may by dying to the dark Self-hood bring his hunger into God's Kingdom, and feast with the five Divine Senses on the Divine Mercury. Yet so great was our Fall, that the outward Man apprehends this only by Imagination, though the inward Man penetrateth it, as the Sun doth Water, which yet remaineth Water.

CHAP. XV. *How in the Will of the great Mystery a Good and Evil Will ariseth, and the one introduceth it self into the other.*

1. THE great Mystery was from Eternity, whence the one Element which also was from Eternity proceeded, in the Motion whereof, the free Lubet of Eternity proceeded, as a Spirit, which Spirit is Gods.

2. And in or from the desire to Nature the Properties proceeded, having their Root in the great Mystery; as Air out of Fire uncontroulably and incorruptibly.

3. In the desire of Essence in the one Element arose the four Elements with manifold Wills, whence variety and contrariety came, as Heat and Cold, Fire and Water,

Signatura Rerum.

ter, &c. each a Death to the other, all things under that Dominion are in a continual strife, dying and Enmity, no other way to be remedied but by the Death of the Multiplicity of Wills, and Resignation of all Self Wills and Lust to the one Will *(viz.)* the one Element, the right of Eternity, a dying to Self-fulness and Lust, which like a disobedient Child striveth against its Mother, and is its own Enemy and Destroyer unless Mortified in the Death of the Lord Jesus.

4. The resign'd Will is not at all careful, save only to bring its desire into its Eternal Mother, and united with her, be it self a Nothing, this the Self-will calls foolishness, but the resign'd Will doth (as a potent Champion) continually bruise the Serpents head.

5. The Elemental and Sydereal Man is only the Instrument wherewith Man's Soul laboureth in the resigned Will; for thereto it was Created, but the Soul in *Adam* makes it Lord and Master.

6. The resigned Will hath no rest in this Cottage, but is still in Combat, and the good Angels defend him from Satan's fiery Darts. (v.25.) The Doctrines of Christ's Satisfaction, which teach not also the Death to Self in Man, and resigning of the Will in Obedience as a new-born Child, are flattery and words from without, not in the Speaking Voice of God, Christ's Dove which teacheth the bearing Fruit in Patience, budding forth always as a fair Flower out of the Earth.

7. The knowing Doctor and Disputant attaineth not as such, what the humble Herdsman by dying to his false Will doth; for a Christian is the most simple and plain Man upon Earth, having nothing of his own to lose, all being given up already, nor any thing to seek for himself, but for the Lord; being dead to himself, what he possesseth as an ownhood, is only as a Steward, Servant or Distributer.

8. But all arrogated Authority which is introduced to self-hood and extraduced it self quite from God, is Sacrilegious. The self-will generates it a Form according to the prevalency impressing most vigorously in the enmity of his innate depraved Nature, both inward and outward. But the resigned Will is formed by the Model of Eternity as an Instrument of Musick into the Love-harmony, where is no *Turba*, but the end of Nature, Rest; whence first it sprung a meer ravishing delight of all the Senses, where God is all in all.

CHAP. XVI. *Of the Eternal Signature and Heavenly Joy, and why were produced Good and Evil.*

1. WHAT God is in his Eternal uninchoative Generation, that is also the Creation, not in Omnipotence, but, like an Apple *(which is not the Tree)* to manifest the Glory which was in the Eternal Mystery. As one only Air melodiseth variously in several Pipes and Organs, sounding also in each Note, in some pleasant, in other harsh: Thus in Eternity is one only Spirit the Manifester of all the Works of God.

2. The seven Superior Stars, and all the lesser, as so many Kingdoms, figure the Angelical Principalities, and most Inferior Existences as one Clockwork.

3. Let none therefore blame the Creator, as if he made it Evil; for the Creatures departure from the equal accord, makes that Evil which was very Good, as did *Lucifer*, who leaving the Harmony, brought him to the cold dark Fire, out of which is the hot Fires Generation. In the Holy he is Holy, so Angels and Men praise him in the might of Love, and Devils praise him in the might of Wrath; God's Wrath is * his Joy, not as if he lived in impotency, but in Fiery Might, as a   * *The Devil.*

A a a   Potent

Potent King in the dark Principle in trembling Anguish. So in the Divine Angelical Creatures is a trembling Joyfulness, in the Holy Light and Fire of Love.

4. Thus is all a Fire in their severed Properties, the one the Poison and Death to the other; yet if there were no Wrath, there would be no Love: as no Fire, no Light.

5. God, is himself all, but called God only according to the Light of Love, but in the Darkness a consuming Fire.

6. The Creature when departed out of the first Harmony, becomes an Enemy to the Being of all Beings. Even Hell and Nature in the Wrath Property is the Devils Enemy; for that he would be Lord in that wherein he was not created.

7. Every Spirit of Angels and Man was created out of the two Eternal Principles, of Love and Anger, Light and Darkness in equal weight, and may take to it self a Lubet either of Good or Evil, and what Property the Will-spirit of the Creature awakeneth, by that it is ruled; for dying to the one, it liveth to the other.

8. He is elected that dyeth to Sin in Christ's Death, and by Divine earnest Desire breaking the Sinful Will, so persevereth as by the new birth to rise in Christ's Resurrection. Christ calleth to gather, as the Hen her Chickens, but *they would not*, 'tis not said, *they could not*. He that blameth God, despiseth his Mercy introduced by him into the Humanity, and bringeth Judgment on his own Soul and Body.

Gods Election of Grace
CALLED
Predeſtination.

CHAP. I. *What the Only God is, or the Sole Will what it is?*

1. THE Abyſſal Will is the Father. The conceiv'd innate Will of the Abyſs the Son.   *v.* 14, 15, 16.
2. The Exit of the Abyſs through the conceived *Ens*, the Holy Spirit.
3. The Lord our God is One only God, that neither willeth nor can will Evil, for if he did, there were a Rent in him, and ſome cauſe of Contrariety, as far as he is called God : * but hath (as the Sun) one only Will, to give out himſelf in Life and Power to all things, and is without ground, place or time; take away Nature and Creature, and all is God : forego the out-ſpoken Word, and you find the ſpeaking Word.   *v.* 67.   * 56.   *Where and how to find God.*
4. The neareſt way to find God, is for Man (who is his Image) to ſink down from all imprinted Images, Diſputes and Strife, depart from Self-will, and Deſire: and demerſe it ſelf ſolely into the ſingle Love of God, which he (in Chriſt) hath, after Man's Fall, firſt introduced into the Humanity.
5. Let Man go forth from all Images, when he will underſtand the Eternal ſpeaking Word; but when he would know whence Evil and Good proceeded, and God's calling himſelf an angry Jealous God, let him look towards the Eternal Nature to the out-ſpoken and formed Word, and then to Nature, the Beginning Temporal Nature, wherein lyeth the Creation of this World.   *v.* { 75, 77, 78.

CHAP. II. *Of the Original of Gods ſpeaking Word, &c.*

1. CReaturely Reaſon thinketh, God from Eternity by Predeſtinate purpoſe reſolved his Wrath on ſome ſhould reveal his Majeſty : and on others his Love and Mercy, as Fire doth Light. If ſo, then there muſt have been Thoughts, Conſultation and Cauſe of it. But he is only one, nor can only one thing be at ſtrife in it ſelf, whence Conſultation ſhould ariſe to decide it.
2. Every thing ſpringing from a Beginning leſs Ground, hath nothing before it can deſtroy it, unleſs it bring it ſelf into a Heterogene Will, incongruous to that whence it ſprung, and ſo ſeparate it ſelf from the total intireneſs (as did the Devils and Soul of Man) break it ſelf into a peculiar, off from the intire Will, and Divine Unigeniture.

3. *The

*41.   3. * The Powers to the Production of the Word are God, and the Magnetical Attraction, Science or Root, in the beginning of Nature. That attraction of the Desire revealeth God's Majesty in the Power to Joy and Glory, which is the Root of Darkness coming to the kindling of the Fire, according to which God calleth himself an angry God, and consuming Fire. Wherein also the Divisibility, Death and Dying, and gross creaturely life existeth.

*37.   4. * Men that say God willeth Evil, do accompt him a Devil; for the willing Evil is a Devil: they should distinguish God from Nature.

God never willed nor can will Evil.   5. In Nature, as Metals, &c. having in them Evil and Good, one thing is set against another, not to be at Enmity, but that the *Mysterium Magnum* should enter into distinction, and be at an exulting Joy in the Eternal one.

6. The Eternal Will, *Jehovah*, manifesteth its Word through Nature, but taketh not Nature into him: but the Word taketh Nature to it, in the Science or Root.

v. 105.   7. * God is called God only according to the Light, in the Love-fire and Temperature: not in the Divisibility.

CHAP. III. *Of the Seven Forms and Creation.*

1. THE First Form of the Beginning to Nature, is Astringency, Father of Sal. The second Form, is perceptibility, the Wo, &c. Father of the Mercurial Life.

The third Form, is Anguish, Father of Sulphur, arising from the strife of the other two.

The first ariseth from the Fathers, The second from the Sons, The third from the Spirits Property. The first, the Ground of Strength and Might; The second, of Distinction, Speech and the five Senses; The third of every Life of Light, Love-fire, and consuming fire, of Joy and Sorrow.

The fourth Form, is the kindling of the Fire, where Light and Darkness sever, here is the Shrieks, Terror, Poison Life, Torment, Hell resulting from the first Three: The Trembling is at the great Meekness, as when you pour water into the fire, here riseth the flash, at this parting riseth the Light out of the Temperature. The Tincture goeth hence, the Power of Fire and Light, Virgin *Sophia*. From v. 41 to 56. lye high Mysteries.

The fifth Form, is the true Love-fire which severs it self from the painful Fire into the Light, having all the Properties of the three first in joyfulness, drawing into it the Tincture of Fire and Light, Virgin *Sophia*. This is the power of the Speaking Word, the Water-spirit which flows into a Fountain of Eternal Life, *John* 4. 14. Spiritual Blood, Divine Substantiality, Heavenly Corporeity, of which Christ saith, he came from Heaven, and at the same instant was in Heaven, *Joh.* 3.13. The Food of the fiery Soul, Angels, &c.

The sixth Form the Sound, Spiritual Senses all in the Temperature in which *Adam* was, but Lust would tast the multiplicity of Properties and leave the Temperature, and so the Properties departed each from other, as heat, cold, dry, moist, hard, soft, harsh, astringent, sweet, bitter and sour, which God did forbid; thence followed bestial Desires, heat, cold, bitter, stinging rushed in; thence were brought in Poison, *Turba magna*, and Chamber of Death.

The seventh Form, is where the Sound makes it self audible, for the fifth Form is wholly Spiritual. *Luna* and *Saturn* the beginning and end. Thus the seven Spiritual Properties and Powers bring themselves into creaturely formation, by the strife of the seven outward Properties; for in the Temperature no Creature can be.

Gods Election of Grace call'd Predestination. 371

be generated, for it is the only One God, but in the Exit the Wonders and Creature-Images may spring forth and exist.

CHAP. IV. *Of the Original of the Creation.*

1. ALL Eternal Creatures have their Root in the Speaking Word. The Temporary have theirs from the out-spoken Word.

2. The first Principle in the fiery Root (which is the Centre of Nature) ariseth not in the Trinity, but where the Power of Distinction puts it self into Nature, to perceive and move: which first Principle in the Darkness, is a cold aking fire, according to which God calls himself an angry jealous (or zealous) God. *God according to the first Principle, is called Angry, Jealous or Zealous.*

3. The second Principle is, where the Divine Root in the Fire parteth it self into the Light, and introduceth it self into Nature to Manifestation of Divine Joyfulness, according to which God calls himself a loving Merciful God, that willeth nor can will Evil.

4. The third Principle is in the seven Days Work, in which the seven Properties of Nature brought themselves into Substance, which Substance is Holy, Pure, Good. The one Element called the Eternal Heaven, City of God, Paradise. *In the second Principle, Merciful and Loving.*

5. The Being of all Beings, the Holy Spiritual World is the Expressing Word of God, which bringeth it self into Substance in Love and Anger, so that in the Impression of Darkness is understood Evil, and yet in God is not Evil, but in the Creatures Self-hood, and yet there also is Good, as far as the Creature standeth in the Temperature. *v. 20. v. 39, &c.*

6. The Angels were made in the seven Properties, which drew themselves into three Hierarchies, according to the three first Properties or Principles. *Three Hierarchies of Angels.*

7. The first Hierarchy standeth in the Father's Property, in the fire of Strength: the Tincture of the Substance of Nature.

8. The second, consists in the Light-fires Tincture, the Son's Property in the Eternal Nature, and is the Holiest.

9. The third, in the Self-hood of Nature playeth in the Properties, as the four Elements do in the starry Powers, into this, *Lucifer* hath given up himself, with his Root into Lust of Phantasie: and hath left the Temperature; introducing false evil Magick. *Lucifer gave himself into the third Principle.*

10. Their Will is meer Pride, also Covetousness, from the Astringency and multitude of Properties, a stinging Envy, from the Fire, a despairing from the Anguish.

11. The Angels were created, before the time of the third Principle. The Devil lifting up himself was in the Power of the first Principle, so came his mighty Kingdom of Phantasie; which caused the Mother of Nature, the Wrath of God, in which Compression came Earth and Stones, not that the Devil caused that, but caused the cause of that, in the lump whereof they would do juggling feats, but that is also withdrawn; so that he is the poorest of Creatures. *v. 82.*

Obj. Though the Angels fell, God might have re-infused his Love into them.

12. *Answ.* The Devils whilst Angels (Eternal Creatures) stood in their free will, in the Temperature, to what they would incline themselves, that they would be, and so establish and confirm themselves. If he had after sate in the Holy Power of Light, he would accract only the source of Torment and Poison: as if a Toad were put on a heap of Sugar.

13. But as the Sun, for Days and Months shines on, warms and pierceth a Thistle, which yet the more strongly grows to be such; so the Devil would be and no otherwise but is in God as Night is in the Day, shut up in the Centre of Nature not manifested.

CHAP.

CHAP. V. *Of the Original of Man.*

THE Original of every Creature may be found by their Being and Food; for every one reprefents its Root, and will feed of its Mother, there being in the expreſs word,

v. 64.   1. The Property of the dark wrathful Nature, whence came venemous evil Beaſts and Worms, which would dwell in dark holes from the Sun.

2. There are ſome from the Kingdom of Phantaſie, the *Spiritus Mundi*, as Apes, *&c.* that play tricks, and hunt, vex and worry others.

3. There are quiet, good, friendly, tame Creatures, the Model of the Angelical World, yet evil Properties mix among the tame.

v. 85.   The Creatures of time are of the four Elements; but the Body of Man is out of the Temperature, whence came the four Elements, Earth, Stone, *&c,* out of the quinteſſence, wherein Heat, Cold, *&c.* ſtood in equal ballance and weight.

v. 95.   So that being deeper (that is, greater) than the Creatures, was to rule in and over them: Not that Man's Beſtial Properties, were then creaturely or manifeſt, but the *Ens* of all Beings lay in the Human *Ens.*

v. 112.   *Adam* did eat Paradiſical Fruit in the Temperature, not to be ſwallowed down into a Carkaſs for the Worms; but the Centres of diſtinction and ſeparation were

v. 116.   in the mouth. He was naked, yet clothed with glorious Paradiſe, and was totally a Chriſtalline Image, a Maſculine Virgin, yet with both Tinctures in the Temperature; had he ſtood, Man's propagation had been Magical. As the Sun penetrateth Glaſs or Chriſtal, without breaking it. But God well ſeeing Man would not ſtand, ordained him a Saviour and Regenerator before the foundation of the World.

CHAP. VI. *Of Man's Fall, and of his Wife.*

1. GOD (having made Man) ſaith, *Gen.* 1.31. *All was very good,* and yet *Gen.* 2.18. ſaith, *It is not good for Man to be alone*; and therefore made the Woman out of him.

Q. *Why was not the Woman made at firſt, as the Female was of all other Creatures?*

A. 2. Becauſe perfect Love is not in one only Tincture; Man could not ſtand eternally but in two; and thoſe the Fathers and Sons Properties; he had both, and ſo was the Image of the one only God (undivided) Fire and Light.

3. But when the Lights and Waters Tincture, his Paradiſical Roſe Garden, wherein he lived himſelf, was ſevered from him into a Wife, he could not in the Image he afterwards came to be, ſtand eternally.

Q. 4. *Why did God divide him into two Images? he foreſaw what would be before the Creation; and therefore it muſt be his predeſtinate purpoſe that he ſhould be, what he came to be by his Fall.*

Illuſtr. 1.   A. God's fore-knowledge, and his fore-ordination are not the ſame thing.

Illuſtr. 2.   God created no Devil; had it been Divine predeterminate purpoſe that ſuch ſhould be, he had been created ſo.

Illuſtr. 3.   The only Will of God gave it ſelf into an Angelical figure, but the fiery Science or Root, according to the Property of the Dark World, preſſed forth, and begot it ſelf into a predeſtinate purpoſe.

Election call'd Predestination.

So when the Light became creaturely, the dark, cold, painful, Fire pressed the *Illustr.* 4.
Image of Phantasie into the Will; which Will did generate contrary to the temperature, and so was thrust out from God.

No one should dare to say, a Will is given it *ab extra*; but the Will to Evil and *Illustr.* 5.
Good existeth within the Creature.

God generateth (as far as he is called God) nothing evil and opposite to himself, *Illustr.* 6.
but heat and cold come from one Root; the Enmity riseth in the place of distinction.

The Science of the Soul which could frame it self to evil, could also frame it *Illustr.* 7.
self to good; for God is no way the cause of Man's Fall, or of the Devils, but the division or variety, of the manifested Word being drawn into Properties, and the influence of the Dark World drew Man from the temperature.

Now this Divisibility of the manifested Word of God, is not called God; but *Illustr.* 8.
God (as far as he is called God) willeth only good, yet may be said to will evil and good; in the good Angels he willeth good, and in the evil Angels he willeth evil; and whatsoever hath separated it self to evil, willeth evil. *Vide* from v. 70. to the end of the 6th Chapter.

The fiery Science of *Eve's* Soul imagined into the crafty subtilty of the Serpent, *Illustr.* 9.
and desired to know evil and good, which first she gazed on, and then admired, then tryed, did eat, and finding she fell not presently down dead, gave to *Adam*, who had plunged himself in it when he stood in the Image of God, but yet had not eaten it into the body till that very time.

CHAP. VII.

1. v. 118. Q. **A**LL are dead in Adam, *therefore some are predestinated to Life, others reprobated, and how can the Child help it if God will not have it?*

v. 132. Q. *What can the Child help it, that it becomes a Thistle Child?*

v. 133. Q. *And are not men at coming into the World excluded by Reprobation?*

A. 2. That evil Parents introduce pride, falshood, malice, covetousness, cruel *Illustr.* 10.
cursings, laid on them (by cause given) and so the *Ens* of a Serpent, Dog, Wolf, Goat, Swine, Toad, Fox, Lion, or other Beast, is formed in the Child, that is its Reprobation.

And how can the Love of God help it, that *Adam* left the Temperature, and *Illustr.* 11.
turned his Free Will into the Tree of Evil and Good?

And now from the Fountain of the Actual Sins of the Parents and Ancestors *Illustr.* 12.
come Thistle Children, and there lieth the hardening.

CHAP. VIII.

v. 115. **E**Very Child is generated out of the Properties of the Seed of the Parents, and like them, tho' often the Constellations alter in the Configuration, with Authority and Power. It is objected, How can the Child help it? It is answered:

The Child and the Parents are one Tree. When did the Sun alter a branch *Illustr.* 13.
on a sour Crab-tree, so that it became sweet? and should God go quite contrary

Illustr. 14.
to the predestinate purpose of his out-spoken or expressed word for a Thistles sake? v. 177.

The Will to partition existeth in the *Ens* to the Creature, and the Will to the Holy Life existeth out of God in Christ. See *chap.* 10. v. 110, 129. to 135, 145, 151, 153. also *chap.* 11, 130. to the end. And *chap.* 13. *per tot.* especially the 15th v. to the 40th. After all which followeth an excellent Appendix of Repentance. And lastly the *Clavis*.

See more concerning Free Will, *&c.* in the *Mysterium Magnum*, Chap. 26.

This being the Author's 16th Book, was written *Anno* 1623.

BAPTISM

BAPTISM
AND THE
Lord's Supper.
The firſt Part being of Baptiſm.

CHAP. I. *Firſt Book of Baptiſm.*

1. THAT Chriſt's communication of himſelf to the Soul by his Teſtaments, is not in an Image-like way, as the reaſon of one part of men judgeth, nor are the Teſtaments only Signs and Symbols to keep what he hath done for us in lively remembrance, as others diſpute.

2. But the Inward World being Paradiſe, (whence ſprung the Outward World) Chriſt filleth, and ruleth viſibly, and the Outward inviſibly, and penetrateth the faithful Soul, as Fire doth Iron, or the Sun doth the Plant, which it nouriſheth and matureth till it becomes wholly ſolar, and the Fruit ripe and tender; yet is not the Sun rent, or any part broken off, but the power of the Sun dwelleth in the Plant.

CHAP. II.

1. MAN's Fall was the breaking its deſire from the Love and Meekneſs of God, into its own, which became a wrathful fiery Soul, whence the Eternal Darkneſs exiſted; ſo that it wanted for remedy the Spiritual Oyl and Water, wherein Divine Love and Meekneſs might flow into it again, and make all a Love flame.

2. To this flowing in again, there muſt be a Medium, Subject or Antitype, whereby the Human Faith might receive Divine Vertue, and kindle the Light; which Medium was the Circumciſion and Sacrifices, Baptiſm and the Supper; for God did ſet in the Human Heavenly Being, periſhed in *Adam*, his new Grace Covenant.

3. So that the holy Sacrificers before the Flood, did ſee the Soul ſacrificed in the Fire of God's Wrath, and through that in-ſpoken Covenant changed into a Love-fire, the faſe will being burnt and dying, and a new-born Child of Meekneſs in the Light, was apparent, as Light ſevereth from Smoke, and how the Soul, through Chriſt's death, would give up it ſelf, and be changed into an Angel. But this was not common Fire.

4. But when Mens vanity prevailed with the Souls falſe Fire, over the holy Fire, the

Baptism and the Lord's Supper.

the Floud, (the Type of Baptism and God's Meekness) overthrew them; to shew what the holy Water of Eternal Life would do. And then was renewed the Covenant with *Abraham* and *Isaac*, by Circumcision on that same Member, to shew the unclean bestial Birth should be cut off from the Virginity *Adam* had, and should have stood in.

CHAP. III.

1. ALL the three Worlds Properties (or three Principles in Man) needed Baptism; *viz.* The first, which is the Eternal Nature, whence sprung the true Eternal Soul. Secondly, The heavenly *Ens*, which was vanished in *Adam*, that holy Lights Power, the true Eternal Spirit. Thirdly, The Outward Worlds substance, the Astral Soul with its Body out of the *Limus* of the Earth, standing in the four Elements; and therefore the great holy Fire of Love manifested in the Humanity of Christ, must baptize this our threefold Humanity, that each Principle might be baptized with its like; *viz.*

2. The Fathers holy Fire. The Sons holy Light. The holy Spirits Life.

3. The first is the found to continual Repentance, a concussion and trembling with Fire, wherein is seen the bitterness of sin and sufferings, and death of Jesus Christ. And when the Self-will is shaken through Repentance, then the holy Oyl of Love penetrateth, and by the anointing of Love healeth those wounds.

4. And the Holy Ghost manageth the Office, baptizing with a new Life.

5. But Man's third Principle, the right Adamical Man out of the four Elements, is baptized with the Outward Worlds substance, the Water.

6. By the aforesaid Adamical Man, is meant the *Spiritus Mundi*, *viz.* the right Astral Soul, which at the last day shall come again and be tryed.

7. Note; Man hath an immortal Soul, and a mortal Soul. (*viz.*) the Astral, but it was Christ's heavenly Blood that fell with the other, which made the Earth tremble.

8. He that is himself baptized with the holy Anointing, hath Faith, which may enable him to baptize; else he effecteth nothing, but is as the Font-stone; but to the believing Parents Child, the work is not wholly powerless, for the sake of the unworthy hand; for if Parents have put on the Anointing, why not their Children whom they generate out of the Property of their Seed?

CHAP. II. *The Lord's Supper.* Part II.

1. THE Soul is the Fathers Fire. The holy Love-fire of the Divine *Ens*, heavenly Flesh and Power in the Light, being Christ's substance, tinctureth the Soul with the Tincture of supernatural glance and life.

2. As sweet Oyl put into common dark Fire ariseth into a Light; so is Christ received by the mouth of Faith, become the Light of the World by kindling again the vanished heavenly *Ens* of *Adam*, and shining in the unlocked Paradisical ground, which is the City of God, where the Holy Ghost dwelleth in Man, of which Christ saith, *Joh.* 6. 56. *He that eateth my flesh, and drinketh my blood, continueth in me, and I in him,* which is a real and substantial eating and drinking Christ's heavenly Flesh and Blood.

The Soul's mouth eateth and drinketh Christ's Flesh and Blood *as truly as the Plant the Sun's Virtue, or the heated Iron the Fire.*

3. The

The Lords Supper.

3. The Holy Flesh and Blood is taken into the Soul, which cometh freely as the Sun doth into Water which retaineth its heat and light; or as Fire penetrateth Iron, and gives it heat and light.
4. Also 'tis the whole Christ, as they did eat the whole Paschal Lamb.
5. The Bread and Wine is the Medium in which the Heavenly Humanity of Christ meets the unlocked awakened Word of Promise and Grace Covenant, which is hid in Man.
6. By the Bread and Wine said here to be the Medium, is not meant the gross Elements of Bread and Wine, but the Tincture [or Quintessence] whence cometh or groweth Bread and Wine. *Chap.* 3. *ver.* 24.

CHAP. III. *How the Disciples of Christ did Eat and Drink Christs Flesh and Blood?*

1. NOT the palpable Fleshly Humanity, but the Spiritual Humanity the Virtue and Power of his Body and Blood, his own *Mumia* in which was the Divine and Humane Power, which is a true Humane Substance of Flesh and Blood, a Spiritual Flesh out of which the visible Image groweth, not only by Faith in remembrance of his Sufferings, Death, *&c.* as is ignorantly said, but really, Chrifts Paradifical Humanity presseth into their Souls, as a sparkle of Fire falleth into Tinder, and turneth the whole Tinder into Fire and Light.
2. The Divine Flesh and Blood of Christ, cannot be receiv'd but by a Mouth fit to receive it.
3. The Mortal Flesh comprehendeth it, no more, than the gross Stone doth the Tincture of fine Gold that is in it.
4. A Man cannot say I am Christ, because Christ dwelleth and worketh in me; no more than the Herb can say, I am the Sun, because the Sun worketh in it.

Christs Paradifical Humanity presseth as Fire into Tinder.

CHAP. IV. *What the Wicked partake of, and how a Man should prepare, that he may be Worthy?*

1. HE that receives this without Repentance (that is) turning from Sin receiveth, as *Judas*, his own Judgment and Condemnation; for his wicked Will desireth not to die in Chrifts Death, but only to arise and live with his Sins in Chrifts Resurrection, yet in the Spirit of *Lucifer* he treadeth on the Death of Christ, and participateth indeed on Chrifts Anguish, Death, and going into Hell, but in the Spirit of the Devil, without rising to newness of Life: Better it were he did not touch or meddle with it.
2. They talk of Absolution and Pardon of Sin, but leave it not, and so Sathan, as he did to *Judas* after the Sop, entreth. These Crucifie Christ.
3. But they that rightly prepare, die to Sin, resign themselves to God, have the Spirit of Christ erecting his Kingly Office and Pallace in their Hearts, a living Conqueror over Death and Hell, these rightly receive Chrifts Flesh and Blood.

CHAP. V. *Of the Disputes, &c. about Chrifts Teftaments.*

1. ONE Party fay, the Bread and Wine is fubftantially changed into Chrifts Flefh and Blood, and fo will receive Chrift into the Beftial and Mortal Man.

2. Another Party fay, it is only a Sign that the Body of Chrift was broken and died for us, and deny the fubftantial participation.

The right A-damical Humanity is eaten and drunk by the Soul.

3. The third Party fay Chrift is participated with and under the Bread and Wine, that is, Chrifts Flefh and Blood, is eaten and drunk with and under the Bread and Wine, but yet know nothing of the right Adamical Humanity, and deny the fubftantial Inhabiting of Chrift.

4. For they will not know how the participation is wrought, but rely barely on the dead Letter; hence come fuch Contentions that are really Spiritual Murther, and in the end come to outward Murther: Every one for the Idol of his own Opinion, but the Kingdom of God is inwardly within thee, the outward imputed Grace, without the Innate Filial Grace, is falfe.

5. Let the Sufferings and Death of Chrift be fulfilled in us, and we fhall be the Children of Chrift, and not the Children of Images.

This was the Authors 21d Book.

𝔐𝔶𝔰𝔱𝔢𝔯𝔦𝔲𝔪

Mysterium Magnum.

PART I.

The First Part contains the nine first Chapters of *Genesis*, and thirty fourth Chapter of the Book, whence these Extracts are; called the *Great Mystery*. *Exposition of* Genesis.

CHAP. I. *What God manifested is, and of the Trinity.*

1. GOD is the One, the Will of the Abyss, the Will of the Wisdom. The Wisdom is his Delight and Manifestation, he begetteth himself, from Eternity to Eternity, in which Eternal Generation are, 1. The Will. 2. The Mind of the Will. 3. The Egress from the Will and Mind.

2. The Will is the Father, the Mind is the Wills Heart and Seat, the Egress is the Spirit and Power of the Will and Mind: The *Lubet*, Motion, Life and Eye of the Deity: A speaking Word.

3. God is no where, far from, or near unto any thing, Infinitely more deep than any thought can reach, comprehended only by himself.

CHAP. II. *Of the Word or Heart of God.*

1. THE Word is in the Will a nothing, but with the Conception in the *Lubet* of the Will, is an Eternal Generation. This Eternal speaking Word, maketh a Mystery call'd the Centre of the Eternal Nature, out of the Powers, Colours and Virtue whereof, as out of a great Eternal Mystery, was formed by Coagulation, the Spiritual World: Which two, are as Soul and Body.

2. And tho' the speaking Word rule through, and over all, yet cannot be comprehended, by either; but in the inward World conceiveth it self, into a Spiritual Essence, as one only Element, wherein the four lye hidden, but when the Word moved the one Element, the hidden Properties did manifest themselves, as there are four Elements.

CHAP.

CHAP. III. *How out of the Eternal Good, an Evil is come to be ; the Original of the Dark World.*

WE cannot say that Eternal Light or Eternal Darkness is Created ; for they are not comprehended in time, but Concomitant in their Generation : But not in the Word of the Deity, but Originate in the desire of the speaking Word. For the free *Lubet*, wherein is the Wisdom, could not have sensible perceivance, of its own Vertue, Smell, Taste and Colours, if it brought not it self, into a desire like a hunger, and so bring it self, from Abyss into Byss, by over-shadowing Attraction : And remains a Property, *viz.* a darkness. For where a Property is, there is a something, yielding obscurity : Unless something else, *viz.* a Lustre, fill it, and then 'tis Light, yet remaineth a Darkness in the Property. And this is the Eternal Original of the Darkness: So that we are to understand,

1. The free *Lubet*, the wisdom, which is no Property, but is one with God.
2. The desire of the free *Lubet*, which in the hunger or coagulation comprehends the free *Lubet*, and maketh it self out of the free *Lubet*.

For the desire is the Fathers Property. And the free *Lubet*, the wisdom, is the Sons Property : Tho' God, here, until the Manifestation through the Fire in the Light, is not called Father or Son, but set down thus, to shew to what Person in the Deity, Nature, and to what the Power in Nature, is to be ascribed. The desire proceeding from the will of the Abyss, is the first form, and it is the *Fiat*. The free *Lubet* is God who governeth the *Fiat*, the Centre of Nature: And both together, are the Eternal Word, and in the desire are the seven Properties of Nature.

The profound distinct Discourse of them, taketh up the remainder of this Chapter, and the fourth, fifth and sixth CHAPTERS.

CHAP. VII. *Of the Holy Trinity and Divine Essence.*

THE Eternal and Temporal Nature, especially consists in the dark world, in the four first Forms ; Astringent, Bitter, Anguish and Fire : But the Powers in all are understood in the Light, or Love-desire, or Love-fire.
1. For the first ground is the one.
2. The free *Lubet*, *viz.* the Wisdom.
3. The Love desire, wherein the free *Lubet* exacuateth it self, through Nature into a Kingdom of Joy.
4. The Oyly Spirit, wherein the *Lubet* amasseth it self in the Meekness and co-amasseth the Lustre, the Power whereof is the true holy Tincture.
5. The watry Spirit, begotten by the devoration of the Fire, *viz.* its death : Which also it must have again for its Life; else neither Fire nor Light could subsist, so there is an Eternal giving and receiving.

(*a*) *cb.* 4, 5. The (*a*) 8th Chapter of the Creation and Dominion of Angels ; and the (*b*)
(*b*)*ch.*13,&c. 9th Chapter of the Fall of *Lucifer* ; and the (*c*) 10th of the Creation of Heaven
(*c*) *ch.* 18,19. and the outward World ; and the (*d*) 11th of the Mystery of the Creation. Are
(*d*)*cb.* 19,20. all clearly, deeply and largely treated of in the *Aurora*, *viz. Aurora*.

CHAP.

Myſterium Magnum. Part I.

CHAP. XII. *Of the Six Days Work.*

1. Though there is no Night in the Deep above the Moon, yet in the length of ſix Days and Nights was all Created, which hath this ſubtle acute meaning, *viz.* ſix of the Properties of Nature only, belong to the active Dominion, to good and evil: The ſeventh is the Eſſence, Houſe, Body or Reſt, wherein all the other work.

2. The Planetick Orb (which is the Figure of the ſix Properties of the Spiritual World) belongeth to the *punctum* of *Sol.* But *Saturn* doth not proceed from the Sun.

3. The Firſt Day. With the Word when God ſaid let there be Light, the holy Power which was amaſſed in the wrath, (*viz.* the confuſion cauſed by *Lucifer*) moved it ſelf and became Light, by which the Devils ſtrength wholly withdrew, and the Light, *viz.* that of Nature was wholly uſeleſs to him, and the Darkneſs being ſevered remained in the wraths Property both in the Earth and the whole Deep. (1.)

4. Of the Second Day. As the Moon ruleth the firſt Hour, ſo is this the moſt External or Inferiour Heaven next the Earth, and the Laboratory of the other ſix Properties. See more of the Second Day in the 20th Chapter of the *Aurora,* p. 254. (2.)

5. Of the Third Day of the Creation: *Mars* rules the firſt Hour on *Tueſday*, on this third Day, God moved the third Property of Nature, *viz.* the Sulphurous, in which the Saltiſh and Mercurial were alſo mutually unfolded and feverized; by the Salnitral flagrat, from the poyſonful *Mars*; for they felt the Light, and became hungry till they were coagulated. (3)

6. In which Joy, aroſe, unto pullulation and growth, or vegetation; for when the Light ſpringeth up in the water ſource, *Mars* ſpringeth up for great Joy in the *Sulphur*, ſo came Graſs and Trees: The Inward Nature made it ſelf External, and yet remained alſo Internal. Yet therewith did the Properties of the dark world preſs in alſo, whence came poyſonous Roots and Weeds.

CHAP. XIII. *Of the Creation of the Fourth Day.*

1. Mercurius hath the firſt Hour, giving a ſenſitive feeling Life. In the third is only an inſenſitive Life, but now in the Fire is a painful, and in the Oleous a meek joyful Life. (4.)

2. This Light of Nature hath a Fiery, Airy, Oily, and Watry Property, yet no Intellective Life, but only Properties to Life.

3. The Intellectual Life, is the ſpirated word from the free *Lubet*, whence comes a Sulphur Salnitri, that is, a Magical Aſtrum, in manner of Mans Mind; which hath thence its real Original.

4. The whole Aſtrum, is a breathed Voice or Tone of the Powers: An Eccho out of Gods Love and Anger, the Dark and Light World: Out of this have the four Elements their Original, and they ſpeak forth a Corporeal Eſſence, and the Stars breathe a Spiritual, both which rule in the viſible World, as Soul and Body.

5. And from the four Aſtrums is procreated the Soul of the outward World, as an enduring great Mind or Myſtery.

6. And

6. And in this Office hath God raised up a King, or as a God of Nature the Sun, with the other six Planets, his Counsellors or Assistants. First the Nature-God, the Sun, receiveth its Lustre from the Tincture of the inward Fire and Light-world. Next *Venus* giveth Body to all the seven Metals.

CHAP. XIV. *Of the Creation of the Fifth Day.*

(5.) 1. *Jupiter* rules the first Hour of that day. The superior Astrum actuated the four Astrums in the four Elements (all from the motion of the holy Eternal speaking Word) into Forms, according to the Properties of the Astrum in the Spiritual Body: And thence were Creatures in the Astrum of every of the four Elements produced; Birds, in the Astrum of the Air, Fishes, in that of the Water, Beasts, in that of the Earth, and Spirits, in the Astrum of the Fire.

2. The two Sexes the Male and its Female arise one from the Tincture of the Fire, the other of the Water, as of Fire and Light.

CHAP. XV. *Of the Sixth Days Work of the Creation.*

(6.) Vide Chapter 11. of the *Aurora*, p. 254.

CHAP. XVI. *Of the difference of the Heavenly and Earthy Man.*

1. THE Image of God Created unto Eternal Life in Paradise, cannot be the gross Property of Earthy Bestial Flesh; for the Properties of the inward holy Body and outward, were in *Adam* compos'd in equal Harmony, and gave up their desires to the Soul in which the Divine Light shone as in the holy Heaven; The Properties were all Tinctur'd with the sweet Love delight. For the inward holy Man, of the pure Element, penetrated and swallowed up the outward, as Light doth Darkness, which when extinguished the darkness is manifested.

2. But the Earthy Bestial and Corruptible Body, made so by the Lust of *Adam*, is not the Man; for what the Soul is in the Spirit, the same is the true Humane Body in the Essence: As the Souls Mansion, and as Iron is made Lustrous when through heated in the Fire. Neither Heat, Cold, Sickness, *&c.* could annoy him, his Body was as Gold that endureth the Fire, or as a Tincture penetrating all things, and gives way to nothing: So, neither was Man subject to any thing but his God alone who dwelt in him.

3. Nor are here two but one only Man, in the Likeness of God. See more of this in the 11. Chap. of the *Aurora*, in the 10th Chap. of the Three Principles, and that of the Incarnation, and that of Predestination, Chap. 5.

(7.) 4. Of the Creation of the seventh Day. God Created all things in six Days out of the seven Properties, and brought them all into the seventh as into one Body, which is a Mystery of all the other, whence they came, and in which they work as a Spirit in a Body. The seventh Property standeth still, as a senseless Life; but the seventh and the first Properties mutually belong to one another as one Property.

CHAP.

CHAP. XVII. *Of Paradise.*

1. THE Garden of *Eden* was a place on Earth where Man was tempted; but Paradise was the Seventh Days Property, the Essentiality of the second Principle, which penetrated the four Elements, as Eternity doth Time, as the Sun the Fruit: as the Day swallows up the Night, or as the Fire illustrateth the heated Iron. Yet was no more apprehended by the outward Elements (though then in their best Purity) than the Terrestrial doth the Celestial. The Internal was to rule over the External; the Heaven, was the Husband to the Earth, before the Curse.

2. And whereas *Moses* distinguisheth the Tree of Knowledge of Good and Evil, from the Tree of Life.

3. By the Tree of Knowledge of Good and Evil, is understood,
(1.) The Holy Power of God in the Tree: which was the Middlemost Kingdom.
(2.) Paradise, the Outermost, through which the Middlemost penetrated, and manifested it self: This was the Knowledge of the Good, which *Adam* should as little have known (in its Original) as the Evil; for he should have kept a Child-like Mind resign'd to God.
(3.) The Dark World, which also was manifest in the Vanity, as now the Earthy Essence of the outward Worlds Fruit.

4. Because *Adam* should have eaten with the inward Heavenly Mouth, not with the outward Earthy Desire, he had such Fruit growing for him, which the inward Mouth could enjoy. The outward Mouth did also eat it, but not into the Worms Carcass.

5. The Celestial swallowed up the Terrestrial; and changed it again into that, whence it proceeded; for now was *Adam* in God's Power Kingdom, with both Tinctures before his *Eve*: and the Divine World was Predominant, so, that the three Principles stood in equal Harmony and Will, with pleasing Taft, ravishing Melody, sweetest Odours, smiling, meek, friendly Aspect, of highest Love-desire.

6. But, as *Lucifer* elevated himself, into the first Principle, totally extinguishing the Light; so *Adam*, lusted into the outward or Vanity hanging to the third Principle: But left his Light, should be totally extinct also, and drawn into the first Principle, and become a Devil, God well knowing the Devil would tempt him.

7. The High and Holy Name Jesus, with deepest Love interposed, and gave himself to regenerate this Hierarchy, and Purge it, through the Fire, with highest Love, to overcome the Wrath, and change it again into Divine Joy; the Holy Heaven. And this is what St. *Paul* saith, *Man was Elected in Christ Jesus, before the Foundation of the World.*

8. Is it asked, *Why did God suffer this Plant to grow?* It is answered, *Adam's* earnest Desire became a Hunger, and caused that the *Fiat* drew out such a Plant. For *Adam* was then a potent Spark of God's Might and Omnipotence. For now, that he hath broke himself off from the Universal Being, and become subject to Vanity, if Faith as a Grain of Mustard-seed can remove Mountains, what could he not then do, who was subject to nothing but God?

9. And the Tree of Good and Evil being thus distinguished, the Tree of Life is also manifest, to be one Tree with the other, but only in the Holy Divine Principle: viz. In the second, in due Temperature with the first and third.

CHAP. XVIII. *Of the Paradisical Life, State or Dominion, how it should have been if* Adam *had not fallen,* &c.

1. HAD God created *Adam*, to the earthy, corruptible, naked, sick, toylsom Life, he had not brought him into Paradise.
2. If God had willed him the bestial Copulation, he would first have created both Sexes, as he did other earthy Creatures.
3. But every Creature brings its Cloathing from its Dam, Man only cometh in deepest Poverty, the most forlorn and shiftless, with the Worms Carcass, and bestial Members for Propagation; whereof the poor Soul is always ashamed.
4. But *Adam*, was a Man and Woman, yet neither, distinct; but a Virgin full of Modesty, Chastity and Purity. Such was he before his *Eve*, as shall arise and Eternally possess Paradise, a Virgin, and as the Angels.
5. Two fixt and stedfast Essences were in *Adam*; A Spiritual Body from the inward Heaven, which was God's Temple: and the outward Heaven, a *Limus* extracted out of the good part of the Earth, which was tne Mansion of the inward; and at the Last Judgment shall be sever'd from the Curse and Corruption. These two were espoused into one, wherein was the most Holy Tincture of Fire and Light: and had ardent Love to each other; the inward loved the outward, as its Manifestation and Sensation: and the outward loved the inward, as its sweet Spouse and Joy.
6. And the Magical Power of Impregnation, stood in the fiery Love-Desire. No Winter, Sleep, Sickness, nor need of the Sun had he, before his *Eve*: only he stood in the Temptation, Forty days in Paradise, where had he been stedfast. God had confirmed him to Eternity. He was drawn of all the three Principles, and though they did Equiponderate, and were of equal Measure; yet the Devil was very busie in the first Principle, which *Adam* desired not to prove, as *Lucifer* had done.

The following Instances are as so many Figures to point at the time Adam stood in the Proba.
Esau *lived Forty years, then took two Evil Wives.*
Israel *Forty years in the Wilderness.*
Forty days searching the Land of Canaan:
Moses *Forty days on the Mount.*
Goliah's *Forty days Challenging the Host of* Israel.
Elias *Fasted Forty days.*
Christ Forty days Tempted.
And Forty hours in the Grave.
And Forty days after his Resurrection.

7. But his Lust was to taste Evil and Good, then came the severe Command, *Thou shalt not Eat,* &c. which tho' he did not with his Mouth, yet his desire to it made his Heavenly Tincture to disappear, and his fair Image fell into a swound, and his clear, pure, steddy Eyes and Sight were darkned, by the impress of the Vanity: So that now, he could not Magically propagate himself; then God said, *It is not good that he should be alone, I will make a help meet for him.*

CHAP. XIX. *Of the Building of the Woman, and how Man was Ordained to the outward Natural Life.*

1. THE Woman was taken out of *Adam*'s Essence, in Body and Soul: The Rib betokeneth Mans dissolution; in the place of it, entred *Longinus*'s Spear, when Christ was Crucified, to Tincture and Heal the breach with Heavenly

Mysterium Magnum.   Part I.

ly Blood : His sleep was the real Type of Christs rest in the Grave, his breaking or bruising was of the breaking or bruising Christs Body on the Cross, from the sixth hour to the ninth ; so long was the *Fiat* in *Adam's* sleep, separating the Woman, in which space, the Female Person was compleatly finished, so long Christ stood as in *Adam's* thirst, and then said, It is finished, that is, had redeemed the Virgin Image, from the divided Sex of Male and Female.

2. *Eve* was the right Magical Child, as to the right Life then manifested ; which after disappeared : So, that after the eating the Apple, God said the Seed of the Woman shall, *&c.* Her disappeared Heavenly Matrix, should like the dry Rod of *Aaron* Bud again, tho' now the Holy part was shut up.

3. The Woman had the fifth Property of the Eternal Nature, the Centre of the Angelical World, the Sons Property, and was *Adam's* dearest Rose Garden, and the Man kept in his *Limbus*, the Divine Fire-world, the Fathers Property. She received from *Adam's* Flesh and Bones, only the Rib and the half cross in the Head ; but now, was the Bestial Worms Carcass, Bowels and Members for Propagation, Mans shame hung on them. Nor was there any strange, alien thing, from without them that formed his *Eve*, as was in the Creating *Adam* and all other Creatures ; but only their own very propriate, the *verbum fiat* in them ; for God hath left in all Creatures a power to their own Multiplication and Making.

Ver. 26.
Ver. 28.

CHAP. XX. *Of the Lamentable and Miserable Fall and Corruption of Man.*

1. WHEN *Adam* saw *Eve*, the fiery Tincture of his Soul, impressed his desire into her Tincture of Light, and tho' they were both yet in the Garden of *Eden* and in Paradise, *Adam's* desire had imprinted it self, into the Magical Image, as a Mother doth on a Child in her Womb ; therefore the Woman had Earthy Lust, so soon : As to this day, most of that Sex, coming to any years, selfish Will or Lust is predominant, appearing in glittering Pride, contrary to Virgin Modesty, Chastity and Humility.

2. The Devil then in the Serpent, laid himself on the Tree of Temptation ; for the Serpent was more subtle than all the Beasts of the Field ; because *Lucifer*, falling from his Divine Hierarchy, and infecting the Essence of the expressed word in the *Fiat*, according to the dark Worlds Property, his desire drew the thorny subtilty out of the Centre of Nature, which as to one part was the Serpents *Ens*.

3. Tho also in the Serpent, is found. (by the wise) excellent Art and Vertue ; for the Devils Poyson being taken out, there is Divine Power, in a fiery hunger in him : As is also in the Earth, where may be found the *Arcanum* of the World.

4. The Devil by the Serpent insinuated to *Eve*, as if God had with-held some great thing from them, and that if she would eat, she should as God, know good and evil, which was true : For the Essences of that Tree were Discordant, but said not, that Heat and Cold, Sickness and Death would force into her. But that by the Serpents eating thereof, he had attained so great prudence.

5. *Eve* liked well to be a Goddess, and so fell from the Divine Harmony, from the resignation in God, and united with the Devils Desire.

6. Then the Holy Spirit departed, and the Heavenly *Limus* in the Flesh disappeared or died : As the extinguishing a Candle which enlightened a dark Room.

7. VVhile Man stood resigned in God, all the Properties were in Harmony, equal

qual weight and measure, as time is in Eternity, or in God. But when Mans own will began effectually to work, the whole Magical *Astrum* wrought also, contrariety and enmity in the outward *Astrum*, and four Elements.

8. The Properties of all good and evil Beasts, did awake and become domineering in him; yea, of a Fox, Bear, Wolf, Lion, Dog Bull, Cock, Cat, Horse, Toad and Serpent. Also, that *Astrum* which is most predominant at the time of Conception, hath its desire in the Seed; and also Figures the outward Person, and the poor Soul becomes Married to such a Beast, unless a Man be Born anew, forsake this Bestial Property, and come as a Child into the Kingdom of God pointed at by Circumcision and Baptism.

9. How great was that Horror and Anguish now in Man? When in Astonishment they crept behind the Trees in the Garden from the dread of Gods awakened Anger, making their Love-fire tremble; on Knowledge of their new-gotten Bestial Properties: Even so did the *Limus* of the Earth, whence *Adam*'s outward Essence was extracted, tremble and shake when the Lord Jesus on the Cross, with his great Love, in his Heavenly Blood, did overcome Gods Anger; which was effectually working in it.

CHAP. XXI. *Of the Impression, and Original of the Bestial Man, and beginning of Sickness and Mortality.*

1. THAT only which stands in the Temperature, hath no Destroyer, but subsisteth Eternally; for opposite Essences, weaken and destroy each other. Yet, if the captive Essence of the Heavenly Property, may be redeemed from the curse and wrath of Nature, it comes into the Temperature; and awakens the Heavenly Worlds Essence, in a living Body (if such there be in that Body) and expelleth evil.

2. So great a sway, the outward Beastly Man hath over the hidden, inward, heavenly Man, that it holds it, as Gold shut up in the gross Oar, unable to shew it self, but lyes as dead; it must therefore be Born anew, and fed with the second Principle, or remain ever uncapable, of the Kingdom of God. It must re-obtain Divine Essence, and die to the Beast; and Regeneration to its first Estate is brought to pass in Christ.

3. The Scope of this Author is,
(1.) To search out the Image of God.
1. How it was Created.
2. How Corrupted.
3. How it shall be restored.
(2.) What is the New-birth out of Christ.
1. What is the Inward and Immortal Man.
2. What the Outward and Mortal. That, being known how it was corrupted, it may come again into its first Estate.

CHAP. XXII. *Of the Original of Actual Sin,* &c.

1. EVery word of Man proceeds from an Eternal *Ens*, either of Love or Anger. A word conceived becometh substance when 'tis sounded, and then must have a place of Rest, either in its like in another, or it will return to its Mother; the Fountain or Mind whence it is.

2. Doth

Mysterium Magnum. Part I.

2. Doth a wicked Man Curse? Eccho a word of Love against him; let not his Curse enter, infect and take Root, but will return and heap Coals of Fire on the Reviler; for the enkindled Spirit layeth hold of the Inventers very outward Body.

3. Sin, at first, and ever since, is Born of a strange *Ens*; when the will, leaving the pure simplicity in which it was Created, entreth into the Serpents Craft and Poison. But tho' the will to good, may have evil adhere to it, yet, if it hath not consented to the evil, but rejects it, that the sinful desire cannot come into Essence, that good will hath not hereby wrought evil, but the holy Word judgeth the false.

4. The Serpents *Ens*, was a Virgin of Heavenly Beauty, but *Lucifer* introduced thereinto the dark Worlds Property; yet hath the Serpent (according to the right of Eternity) both Tinctures. The Pearl is in it, but hidden; because of the Worlds false Magick, that the holy Virgin *Ens* might not be introduced into an ungodly Serpentine one. It were good the Artist knew this.

5. The Children of God are the Temple of the Holy Ghost who dwelleth in them; without this, there is no true knowing or will, but strife by the Craft of the Serpent about confused verbal wranglings, as did the Jews carry *Moses* words in their Mouths, but mixed them with the crafty Serpents *Ens*, and so it must be still, that the word in Gods Children may be stirr'd and whetted, and the Truth struggle to the Light. Therefore must the Body die, it cannot Inherit the Kingdom.

See more of the Original of Sin in this Book of Extracts of *Aurora*, and in the sixth Chapter of the Book of Predestination. And mentioned also in the 15th of the Forty Questions.

CHAP. XXIII. *How God recalled* Adam *and his* Eve, *and ordained the Saviour?*

1. After *Adam* and *Eve* had eaten of the Tree of Knowledge of Good and Evil; seeing their gross bestial flesh, hard bones, and deformed Worms carkass, shewed it self in their tender delicate body, their shame drove them behind the Trees; for God's rebuke awaked in them, as it had done in *Lucifer*; and they, as revolted Rebels, were in great shame, before God, and all the holy Angels; and scorn'd by the Devils. Into this shame and scorn did Christ enter, which caus'd the bloody sweat, his being contemned, crowned with Thorns, his mixt draught of Gall and Vinegar; this made the Earth tremble.

2. They dreaded now the Lord's voice, for the *Turba* of the Dark World awakened its sad knell. In the cool of the day, that is, when *Adam*'s Eternal day, in the Temperature, was awakened into cold and heat.

3. But in the Lord's voice, was the holy Light-world, Christ the second Principle; who in deepest Love espoused it self again, to the disappeared heavenly *Ens*: And the holy Word, re-entring into the vital Light, did reincorporate it self in the Woman's seed, which in time did move its self in *Mary*'s seed, quickening the disappear'd heavenly Virginity, by introducing the holy living *Ens*.

4. This ingrafted Word, was inspoken into *Eves* Matrix, as a limit of a certain Covenant, which was all along propagated in *Eves* seed, from Man to Man, in the heavenly part, as a glimmering incentive of the Divine holy Lights fire, until the awakening of it in *Mary*, where the Covenant was fulfilled, by the most holy name Jesus, signified by the holy Fire, in the Jewish Sacrifices, kept from prophane strange Fire. 2. This

Mysterium Magnum. Part I.

5. This bruised or brake the Serpents head; that is, did infuse, inspire, recal, inhost the right Virgin Purity with the precious holy name Jesus, who introduced the living heavenly *Ens* into the disappeared captiv'd *Ens*, and mortified the Serpents desire in flesh and blood.

6. For the Child of the Man and Woman is a Bastard, nor shall inherit; but the chast Virgins Child, born out of the death of the brutal and bestial Man and Woman, with both Tinctures of peculiar Love : He is the Heir who dieth not, and at the Resurrection, shall take on it the pure *Limus* of the Earth, *viz.* the third Principle as a Garment.

CHAP. XXIV. *The Cause of the Curse, and of the Body of Sickness.*

1. THE Curse was, that the holy Element, Tincture or *Ens*, which had budded and bare fruit through the Earth, holding captive the Property of the four Elements, hid withdrew, kept it self secret, and became a mystery to Man in his awakened vanity; who remained, with a half Serpentine desire of Earthy hunger; half dead, between Time and Eternity, chain'd till he should return to Earth whence he was (as to one part) extracted; and be sown into the Earth; but, as a fixt Metal is not destroyed, but the Artist brings thence excellent Gold; so the fixt part of the Human Body, waits only for the Divine Artist to raise it; which because it must be tryed by Fire, such as the *Ens* is, such shall be the enkindled Fire.

2. All wicked Serpentine works, shall, as Quick silver, evaporate. But if Man's Human Soul, hath impressed into the mortal part of the *Limus* of the Earth, by Divine Desire and Faith, a Divine *Ens*, it lieth, as precious Gold shut up in Lead or Dross, as a glimmering Incentive, waiting till the great Artist release it, to burn and shine.

3. Our gracious God, not only gave his holy living Word, for cure of all, whose minds (casting away abominations) immerse themselves thereinto; but knowing Man would not stand, caus'd all Medicinal Herbs, for hunger and health, to grow for him. Thus Man hath his Cure, the Devil hath not.

4. God created Man naked; whatever is in the World is his, but it is common; but the hunger for Propriety, Power and Domination is of the Serpent.

5. Therefore must we become as little Children, and so rule over the bestial Man : So great is the Enmity God hath put between the two feeds in Man; who now is according to the outward Man, a Beast, & according to the inward, an Angel or Devil.

CHAP. XXV. *How God drove* Adam *out of Paradise, and laid the Cherub before the Garden.*

v. 18. 1. LUcifer's Fall, tainted the *Limus* of the Earth, before it was brought into compaction. *Adam's* outward Body was taken out of the *Limus* of the Earth : Him God set to be Judge, by his Word; having the Judicial Sword, against the Devil's enkindled wickedness, *(v.* 17.)

2. Also, God seeing *Adam's* first Body should fall to ruine, brought him and *Eve* into Paradise, that afterward they and their Children, might, by Regeneration re-enter thither, in the Spirit of Christ, through the Fire-Sword.

3. When Man dieth, if the Soul be captivated in God's Anger, and be not a Virgin Child, it cannot pass the Sword, *v.* 5. 4. This

Mysterium Magnum. Part I.

4. This Sword is alſo in Man ; the Virgin-bud forceth through in the anxiety of true Repentance: Then riſeth the Morning Star, in the occluſe or ſhut up Gate of the true Womans ſeed, v. 13.

5. Yet at death if the Soul hath taken in much of the Serpents craft or luſt, it ſtands under God's Anger, till the Conſumption of the introduced vanity, which to many, is Purgatory enough.

6. For, the Fire-Soul muſt be as pure, as the clear refined Gold, to be the Huſband of the Noble Virgin *Sophia*, the Lights Tincture; to ſpeak which needs an Angels Tongue.

7. Before the Foundation of the World, God choſe this *Limus*, out of which he would make Man in Chriſt Jeſus. For, the *Ens* thereof, had ſomewhat of falſe luſt, by reaſon of the Devils introduced deſire; therefore a time of the Judgment of Severation, was then founded, and a new *Limus* out of the tainted one.

CHAP. XXVI. *Of the Propagation of Man in this World, and of* Cain *the Murtherer of his Brother.*

THIS Chapter treating copiouſly of Free Will and Predeſtination, the Extract of it is forborn, and it's referr'd to the Extracts of the Book of Election.

CHAP. XXVII. *Of* Abel*'s and* Cain*'s Sacrifices.*

1. THE Souls Free-will (originating from the Abyſs) is thin or ſubtile, and muſt amaſs or conceive it ſelf into ſomething, wherein to work. As Gods Free-will, conceived or maſſed it ſelf with the inward Spiritual World, and works through it and that Worlds Free-will, amaſſed the outward World, and works through it.

2. And becauſe that which the Soul had amaſſed, was diſtempered with Sin, ſacrificing came. In the inkindling whereof, by Magical and Love-fire, not ordinary Fire, the Free-will of the Soul, and of the Heavenly part of the Body, did immaſs into a ſubſtance: As a Figure of the New-birth in Chriſt, and by conſuming the Beſtial Man, did preſs in before the Holineſs of God. For here the *Lubet* of God did meet the Inſpired Free-will of the Heavenly Humanity. Here is the ſinful Man conſumed by Gods Anger-fire, and cut off by the flaming Fire-Sword of the Cherub, and the Serpents Head bruiſed.

3. The Souls Free-will which was Inſpired wholly pure into Man, is in the Covenant in Jeſus attoned, and again Tinctured by Gods Love-fire; as Braſs or Iron is tinged and changed to Gold. For the Earthy part, wherein lay the Curſe, being conſumed, the Eſſence became Spiritual: Even ſo the Soul by Sorrow and Repentance introduceth it ſelf into a Divine deſire, which is called Faith.

4. Alſo the words of the Prayer of *Abel* and *Iſrael* became amaſſed into an Incorruptible Eſſence. And this deſire of Faith or Eſſence, in the Spirit of Chriſt, in all Gods Children, is that, whereby they bring to nought the works of the Devil.

5. But *Cain*'s Offering is the Type of Verbal, Titular Chriſtendom: Who relye only on the Offering; and teach, that Chriſts Teſtaments abſolve from Sin, tho' themſelves remain Impenitent, Domineering Murtherers.

CHAP.

Mysterium Magnum. Part I.

CHAP. XXVIII. *Of* Cain'*s Murthering his Brother* Abel.

1. THE cause of that was (as still it is) a strife, about Religion. The Devil envied Man, who was to succeed in the Throne, whence he was become Apostate. But the Death of *Abel*'s outward Body, is a Figure, that the Bestial Man must be devour'd, that out of Death may spring forth Eternal Life, till then, must be maintain'd a resolute Conflict. And *Abel* as to the Heavenly part is a Figure of Christ.

2. And *Cain* in the Wrath, is a Figure of the Enmity and Darkness in the Eternal Nature, but outwardly a Figure of the Pharisees, who Crucified the Lord: And of all Persecutors to the end of the World.

CHAP. XXIX. *How the Adamical Tree hath put forth it self into Branches and Pullulation.*

1. THE seventeen first verses is a profound Tract, how from *Adam*, &c. sprung evil and good, *ver.* 18. *Cain* in the Language of Nature signifieth a Source out of the Centre of the fiery Desire and Self-will, out of the fiery might of the Soul, *viz.* out of the first Principle.

2. *Habel* in the Language of Nature signifieth an out-breathed Angel, *viz.* from the second Principle, and as a Type of Christ went out Childless, for Christ was to generate a new Humane Tree.

3. Therefore was it, that *Adam* generated *Seth*, which in the Language of Nature, signifying a forth-running or leap, where the Love-will riseth out of the Fire-will. From him went the Line of the Covenant.

4. *Cain* begat *Hanock*, and Built a City which he called also *Hanock*, signifying an outward selfish Dominion. *Hanock* begat *Irad*, signifying a Potentate or *Tyrant*. *Irad* begat *Mehujael*, signifying an assuming of the outward and inward Centre of Nature, an Earthy God, that would possess Riches and Domination; out of this Name came *Babel*. *Mahujael* begat *Methusael*, signifying that mine is the Divine Might. I am the Ordnance of God, which indeed was true, but only according to the first Principle. *Methusael* begat *Lamech*, signifying the sending of the Angel over the fleshly Life.

5. *Lamech* took two Wives, *viz.* a Twofold Essence and Will. *Ada* signifying that fain would be honest, and *Zilla* signifying fleshly Joy and Pleasure. *Ada* bare *Jabal* a plain Man, of him were such as kept Cattle; but the other was *Jubal* signifying Temporal Joy, *viz.* the Harp and Organ. *Zilla* bare *Tubal Cain*, it hath an excellent understanding; shewing how the Sulphurous Mercurial Wheel, opens it self in the Generation of Metals; and his Sisters Name was *Naema*; here lyeth the precious Pearl, a Heavenly Property, a Virgin of Purity; by the dying of the outward Man, *Naema* becomes manifest. And *Lamech* said, *I have slain a Man to my Wound, and a young Man to my Hurt.* The Man was *Abel*, the young Man was Christ.

6. *Cain* was to be Avenged sevenfold, if any of the evil Spirits should kill him, vengeance should be on such Spirit, by all the seven Properties of the dark World; and the mark God set on him, was the mark of the Covenant. But *Lamech* was the seventh from *Adam*, and spake Prophetically, of what should befal his Posterity

Mysterium Magnum. Part II.

rity; viz. should lose the unity, and fall into the seventy Languages; so that the ten Forms of Fire, should open themselves in every of the seven Properties of Nature, is seventy, and thereto belong the seven unchangeable Forms of the Eternal Nature is seventy seven.

CHAP. XXX. *Of the Line of the Covenant.*

1. THE Covenant, was to the Line of *Seth* as to the outward, that they should be Preachers of it: But it was as well to the Line of *Cain* in the Spirit; even as Sin passed on the Line of *Seth* as on others, for the Covenant was made to *Adam*, and to the Virgin Image thereby to be restored.

2. The evil Beast of the Godless Form, God Predestinated to Condemnation, but the Covenant is in the Life, whose Free will soever resigneth to it, in every such Christ riseth, and the strange Beast dieth.

3. *Seth* signifieth in the Language of *Nature* a forth-breathing Spring out of the Life through the first Centre of the Soul. *Seth* begat *Enos*, which signifies a Divine *Lubet*, The fifth was *Kenan* signifying a forth-going re-conceived *Lubet* or desire of Divine Contemplation. The sixth was *Mahalaleel* signifying an Angelical Form of an Angelical Kingdom.

4. The seventh was *Jared* signifying a Priest or Prince of the Spiritual Kingdom, as *Irad* was of the worldly Dominion. The Office of *Jared* is Twofold, outwardly 'tis *Moses*, and inwardly Christ, as *Lamech* had two Wives. And *Jared* begat *Enoch* signifying the out breathed Breath of the Divine Good Pleasure. The seven Generations have these Figures.

5. (1.) *Adams* purity before the Fall, and *Abel* to whom the Fall hung, and his being Murthered point out Christ, who should bring us through Death into the pure Life.

(2.) *Seth*'s time continued to the Deluge.
(3.) *Enos* time goes under *Seth*'s and till *Abraham*.
(4.) *Canaan*'s time goes under *Seth* and *Enos*, and until Christ in the Flesh.
(5.) *Mahalaleel* goes during Christ in the Flesh, and the time of the Apostles of Christ.
(6.) *Jared* began after the death of the Apostles, and ruled inwardly in Christs Children, and outwardly the Cherub with the Sword bare rule. This sixth time is known and yet hidden, and passed under Antichrist as in a Mystery.

6. True Christians wage no War; for they having broken the Sword of the Cherub are dead, and risen with Christ, and live not to External Might, his Kingdom not being of this World. This sixth time continues till Translated *Enoch* appears in Spirit, and *Elias* Sword comes, then falls the outward *Jared Babel*. (v. 41.)

7. And God will restore the Spirits of the Letters.

CHAP. XXXI. *Of* Enoch's *Wonderful Line.*

1. ENoch begat *Methusalah* of the highest Age signifying a forth proceeding Voice. *Methusalah* begat *Lamech* as the *Lamech* in *Cain*'s Line had two Wives or Wills, so this begat *Noah* signifying the end and the beginning.

2. *Noah* had three Branches, *Sem* signifying an out-breathing Divine Lubet, *Ham* signifying a strong breathing out of the Centre of Nature. *Japhet* signifying

Mysterium Magnum. Part I.

an Appendix of *Sem*, viz. a Natural Wonder. *Sem* is a Type of the Light World, *Japhet* of the Fire World, *Ham* an Image of the Out-birth.

Gen. 6. 1.

3. The Sons of God looked on the Daughters of Men, &c. viz. those in whom Gods Spirit manifested it self looked according to the Lusts of the Flesh. And Giants, viz. Tyrants were Born, viz. Men whose Pride would receive no rebuke.

* v. 5, 6.

Therefore came the Deluge, and after the three Families were sever'd. * It repented God that he had made Man, and grieved him, &c. viz. according to the Creation of the formed Word, not the Eternal speaking Word.

CHAP. XXXII. *Of the Covenant of God with* Noah.

1. That *Ham* was admitted, sheweth an open Gate to all Men; and that the Election passeth, when the Souls Free-will goeth out of good into evil.
(1.) The Mystery of the three Sons of *Noah*;
(2.) The three Stories of the Ark;
(3.) The three Men that appeared to *Abraham*;
(4) Especially Christ, *Moses* and *Elias* at the Transfiguration, denote the Trinity and three Principles. The seven pair of clean Beasts, shew the seven Properties of the Natural Life; of the unclean, but one pair, represents only, the Property of the Dark World.

2. The Raining just Forty days, points at *Adams* time of *Proba*, in which he introduced the *Turba*.

3. Gods Promising respite 120 years, and bringing the Deluge in 100, points out, that God will shorten time, in the Conclusion of all Beings. The Ark being rested, at the end of Forty days, *Noah* sends out a Raven, signifying the Earthy Man, which flew to and fro, but return'd not to the Ark.

4 After seven days, he sent forth a Dove signifying the Children of God, who finding no rest in this World, return to the Ark. After seven days more, he sent forth a second Dove, who return'd in the Evening with an Olive Leaf, the Unction. After other seven days, he let fly the third Dove, which denotes Antichrist, flying out of the Ark, but will no more forsake the World, to return to the Ark.

CHAP. XXXIII. *Of the beginning of the second Monarchy; and of the Covenant of God with* Noah, &c.

1. I Have set my Bow in the Clouds, &c. The Rainbow, is a Token of Gods Covenant, a representation to Man of all t' e three Principles, out of which he was Created, viz. the red and dark brown, betoken the first Principle, viz. the dark, Fire-world, the Kingdom of Gods Anger. The white and yellow shew the second Principle, the Majestick Colour, the holy World, Gods Love. The green and blue, is the third Principles Colour, the blue from the *Chaos*, the green from the Salt peter, where in the flagrat, the Sulphur and Mercury do sever, and produce various Colours, which betoken the inward World's hidden in the four Elements.

2. The Rainbow also, betokens Christ the Judge, who shall then appear in all the three Principles, viz. in the first or fiery, into which the *Turba* in all Beings shall be swallowed up. In the second, or that of the Light to defend all his in Love and Meekness, from the Flames of Fire. In the third or Kingdom of Nature,

ture, in his Assumed Humanity; all the formed Word, shall be manifest before him according to good and evil.

3. Also the Rainbow, is a reflex contra-glance of the Sun, and in it the *Chaos* (or hidden World) out of which the four Elements, with the hidden Humanity shews it self. And if the Sun be in a good Aspect, it may with the Astrum, produce a wonderful Birth both in Animals and Vegetables. For there the *Chaos* doth open it self, which *Saturn* hungrily attracts: The Sun enkindles *Mars*, and so makes *Mercury* quick and active; which *Saturn* amasseth, and the *Fiat* of the outward World becomes a flying Life. And *Saturn* may take the distilling Dew into it self, which after falls on the Water, and by some Fishes being eaten up, may coagulate in them, and become precious Pearls. For the Paradifical Property, doth open it self, all along in the *Chaos*, if it be not hindered by evil malignant Aspects. For the *Chaos* is the Root of Nature, and yieldeth it self nothing but a good Property, but by an evil Constellation, may be changed into evil; as a good Man, may by evil Company.

CHAP. XXXIV. *How* Noah *Cursed* Ham, *and the Mysteries concerning the three Sons,* &c.

1. Noah's Drunkenness, sheweth, how *Adam* by Lusting after this Worlds Property, was overcome therewith; and introduced the Bestial Lusts; standing in nakedness and shame, then did the Monster of false Lusts (whereof *Ham* was the Figure) mock the precious Image, by introducing the shame. *Gen.* 9. 20, 21, 22.

2. *Sem* did Typifie the fair Image of God in the Light, the Sons Property, who stood in the Covenant. *Japhet*, did Typifie the Soul, the Fathers Property.

3. The Garment to cover the shame, is the new Heavenly Virgin Humanity, in the Covenant, the precious *Sophia*, which should open it self out of the Angelical World. This Garment, *Sem* alone did not lay over the shame; but *Japhet*, the poor Soul, must help, by resignation.

4. They went backward, by Repentance; for if Christ must lay the Garment to cover us the Soul must not dispute, but resign its will and go back.

5. *Ham* must be a Servant of Servants; the mocking Spirit must never rule, but always be kept under. Of *Ham* came the Beastly Sodomites, and Brutish Canaanites, whom *Joshua* destroy'd.

6. *Japhet*, were the Gentiles, who walked according to the Light of Nature which is Tenant to the Light of Grace, for so they lived in *Sem*'s Tents.

7. Thus was the Tree of the second Monarchy, in the same three Properties as the first was.

The Second Part.

CHAP. XXXV. *How the Humane Tree by the Children of* Noah *hath spread it self,* &c.

1. THE long Lives before the Flood were because the Divine Powers of the formed Word were then undivided: But when the Language of Nature was

Mysterium Magnum. Part II.

was divided at *Babel*, the ſtem of Nature was faint and enfeebled. Seventy ſeven is the whole number of the Divine Manifeſtation, ſeventy two are *Babel*, the five are holy.

2. The Sons of *Japhet* are recorded to be ſeven. *Japhet* noteth the firſt Principle, out of which riſeth Nature, viz. The firſt ſeven Properties of Nature, and the ſeven free Arts.

3. After which, from two of *Japhets* Sons are named ſeven to ſpring; whoſe Names ſignifie the Kingdom of Humane Rule. In the fourteenth are the Prophetical and Apocalyptical Number, and in them lye couched the Angelical will; for in the wiſe Heathen the inward holy Kingdom beheld it ſelf, they ſaw by the Light of Nature the reſtitution of all things, and they ſhall when the covering is taken off dwell in the Tents of *Sem*.

4. *Ham* had *Cuſh*, and of him came *Nimrod* the Hunter. Man was fallen under the wrath in Nature, and the wild Nature, muſt be awed by a more mighty Hunter than it ſelf, and be caught, torn and deſtroyed: But 'tis lamentable, that tame Beaſts which are none of his Game, ſhould be devoured: But they alſo are outwardly but Beaſts before God, and have the Hunters hide on them. *Ham*'s Children and Grand Children are numbred twenty nine, himſelf makes thirty, for *Ham* ſold the Righteous One for thirty pieces. And in the thirtieth year Chriſt ſeparated himſelf to his Office.

Gen. 10. 24.
v. 26.

5. *Sem* is ſaid to be the Father of all the Children of *Eber*; which *Eber*, was the third degree after *Sem*, but the mark of the Covenant was that chiefly intended. *Eber* had two Sons *Peleg* and *Jocktan*, in theſe two were the Seed of *Adam* and Chriſt divided, as after in *Iſaac* and *Iſhmael*, *Jacob* and *Eſau*. *Jocktan* had fourteen Names, hinting the Humane Kingdom.

Ch. 11. *v.* 11.

6. *Peleg* had but one, which he begat at thirty years of Age. The one pointing at Chriſt the only Son the thirty at the number of thirty years, at which Age Chriſt manifeſted himſelf in his Office. And the Spirit namet.i five that came out of *Sem*'s Loins, and ſaith he begat more, but nameth them not, pointing at the five head Speeches, from the high Name of God. The Spirits of the Letters, in the Alphabet are from the one Spirit, in the Language of Nature. The Vowels, the holy Name J E O V A into which the Ancient Wiſemen, skilful in this Tongue, put in (H) which was done with great underſtanding; for by that the Divine *Lubet* doth breathe forth it ſelf. All five fold themſelves up into three; A, O, V; Father, Son, Holy Ghoſt, The Triangle ſignifying the three Properties; the V the Spirit, in the H. The other Letters in the Alphabet without the Vowels, come of the word * Tetragrammaton, or of four Letters. The twenty four Letters by the Builders of *Babel* were taken ſeverally after all the three Principles $\frac{2\ 4}{7\ 2}$ to make up the ſeventy two Languages.

* Teteg-yeſμιατω.

CHAP. XXXVI. *Of* Babel, *and the Myſtery of the Speeches ſprung thence, and the Recovery therefrom.*

1. Moſes faith, *Nimrod* (Grandſon of *Ham*) began his Kingdom at *Babel*, not that *Ham*'s Children only did thus, but *Sems* and *Japhets*, joyned as one People, to build a Tower, to get up to God by, and make them a great Name.

2. This Tower, is the Type of the fallen ſelfiſh Man, having loſt the right underſtanding of God, elevated its own fancy. And now the Spirit of the mental Tongue of the five Vowels; the Language of Nature (by which *Adam* gave Names,
being

Mysterium Magnum. Part II.

being departed: they conceived the senfual, divided, confufed Tongues, whereof, as alfo, of the dark World, this Tower was a Figure; where is underftood the Beaft, the Animal, Ham-like Man; and the Whore, the Self-will, revolted from God, by which the poor Captive Soul lies bound under Vanity, till the corner ftone (the Rock of offence) bruife the divided fenfual Tongues.

3. All Rabbies of all Nations, who run, devoid of God's Spirit are Builders here, and though they all deftroy each other, yet are of one Spirit, and * worfhip *Maozim*, the God of Forces. * *Dan.* 11.

4. Now, to become one again, muft the divifion be kill'd, by giving up the Will into the one *JEHOVAH* or *JESUS*, and know only what God willeth to know in us. The Spirit of the five Vowels, and the one is in us * the Letter killeth, the Spirit giveth life. Like as the Divine Sun worketh in and through us as it pleafeth him, fo muft we diffufe our Virtue and Will, with all Simplicity and Purity. * 1 *Cor.* 3. 6.
* For, the living Word is therefore become Man, that the literal Image might die, and the firft Man be regenerated in Chrift's Spirit, who, once Born, then the Image-Teachers rather hinder, than help; by fetting up their imagination into the Temple of Chrift. * *v.* 66.

5. *Babel* muft fall, not be pieced and patcht; for fo, the Whore is only trimmed, not made a Virgin, for fhe is judged, the Zeal of the Lord doth it.

6. The Spirit of the Lord, forms into the Word of the Mouth Truth, Faith, Love, Patience, &c. of the Serpent, come Lies, ftinging Envy, Pride, Covetoufnefs, &c. by which let every Man prove himfelf. For fpeech and underftanding come not from the Stars and Elements, for then other Creatures could alfo fpeak, but from the formed Word of God, it is the Name of God, which Man muft not abufe, on pain of Eternal Punifhments.

7. This incorporated Word, Man hath, out of all the three Principles, with Power to form a Subftance, out of which Principle he will; and therefore muft follow at laft, a reaping in of every thing, into its own receptacle.

CHAP. XXXVII. *Of the Line of* Abraham, *and of the Heathenifh Gods.*

1. FROM *Noah* (exclufive) to *Abram* (inclufive) are Ten Names, in the Line of the Covenant; viz. *Sem, Arphaxad, Salah, Eber, Peleg, Regu, Serug, Nahor, Terah, Abram;* in whom is underftood, the ten Forms of Fire: the feven firft of which are formed in the feven Forms of Nature. The 8th is the Fire of the Eternal Nature which at the end fhall purge the Floor: the Ninth is the heavenly Tincture of the Fire and Light, and the Tenth is the Love-fire, viz. The Holy Trinity in the Majefty.

2. Out of the ten Properties of the Names in the Line of the Covenant the Oracle, the Divine Voice was manifeft in *Abraham;* and therefore he muft go from his own Kindred, he fhould not fee God in his own Country (viz.) not in the Earthy Man. He fhould have a great Name (viz.) in the Perfon of Chrift; for *Abram* had no Dominion here, but was a Stranger: and Chrift faith his Kingdom is not of this World.

3. And whereas God bid *Abram*, look Eaftward, Weft, North and South, and all that Land fhould be his, and his Seeds for ever: 'tis ftill fo, *Abraham* and his Seed have it, in the Eternal, not in the External Kingdom, in the Holy Paradifical Principle (though the Turk hath it in the four Elements) in the Holy Spiritual part fhall Eternally hold it, when the Earth fhall be cryftallized like a glafsy Sea.

4. The

Mysterium Magnum. Part II.

4. The three Sons of *Terah*, were *Nahor*, *Haran* and *Abraham*, a Type of the three Principles, to be opened in the Holy flaming Line of the Covenant.

5. The Oracles of the Heathenish gods, originate from the inward dark Fire-World, and the outward Astral and Elemental World. They knew the Stars and Elements rul'd the outward Life; whence they found the Soul of the World, like a Horologe, did shew the rearing up and dissolving of Nations, Kingdoms and Men.

6. From this Soul the Horologe of Nature, through the sence of the *Astrum*, which their Faith (that they powerfully brought thereinto) did move and stir up, had they Answers from their Images and Idols: and not wholly by the Devil, as Men ignorantly say, who themselves worship the Image God *Maozim* and *Mammon*.

CHAP. XXXVIII. *Of the Beginning of the Heathenish War, of* Abraham's *rescuing* Lot, *and of* Melchisedeck.

1. THE Gentiles and Children of *Ham* at *Sodom*, when the Powers of the formed Word, the Properties of Nature, did divide themselves into Enmity and Selfishness, the Centre of the Nature of the Dark World domineered in Man, fallen from the Kingdom of God's Love and Humility, unto the outward Stars and Elements, and became half Devil and half Beast, would be great, destroy by War and possess: though they had the whole Earth before them. But Pride, Covetousness, Envy and Anger are the Roots of War in which the Devil and all wicked Creatures live.

2. But God, as far as he is called God, *viz.* according to the second Principle, desireth nothing Destructive: but according to the first, is a Zealous God, a consuming Fire; so that when Nations kindle that wrath, God did bid *Israel* smite them; else the Fire of his Anger would have kindled it self in them, and made them as at *Sodom*.

3. God's Anger was set on Fire in *Adam*, and passed on all Men, and the gross bestial Property, the Serpents *Ens* and enkindled Anger, was in *Abraham* and his Childrens own Property, as in the Children of *Ham*, except the Line of Christ, which was in God's Power, and stood in them, as Heaven doth in this World, also in Hell, or as the Day doth in the Night, yet not confounded. So in the angers Property, *Abraham* and his Family smote the Heathen, and rescued *Lot*, so also have the Children of the Saints waged War.

4. But such who would be call'd Christians, do wage War not as Christians, but as Heathens; for the Christian is dead with Christ, to Wrath and the four Elements, and new born in Christ's Spirit of Love and Patience, he is not of this World, liveth not to himself, but to God, his Conversation is in Heaven. Nor did *Abraham* desire ought he took, the Goods he restored to the King of *Sodom*.

5. *Melchisedeck* the Royal Priest, was the real figure of Christ, who blessed *Abraham*, left the *Turba*, after his fighting, should return on him. To him, *Abraham* gave Tithes, (*viz.*) the 10th Property of the Human fiery Tongue of the Soul. And the Priest gave his Bread, and Wine, and Blessing thereinto, (*viz.*) Love-fire, Tincture of the Light, Heavenly Substantiality, that the Soul's fiery Tincture, might again become a compleat Image of God, with Male and Female Property, Heavenly Corporiety, by the King of *Salem*. *viz.* of Salvation.

CHAP.

Mysterium Magnum. Part II. 397

CHAP. XXXIX. *God's Covenant with* Abraham, *his Faith, and Sacrifice.*

1. *A*brabam's Faith, was his receiving the Speaking Word of God, (*viz.*) in the Promise into his Human Ens: His Desire, *viz.* the aim of the Covenant or formed Word, and both these were formed into one Power, and real Spiritual Substance. For Faith is the taking hold of God's Will, and Uniting it to ours. *Gen. 15. from v. 1. to v. 17.*

2. The Offerings were of three sorts of Beasts: a Heifer, a She-Goat, and a Ram, each three years old, betokens the whole outward threefold Man, of Salt, Mercury and Sulphur. The dividing them, the twofold *Limus* of the Earth, (*viz.*) The gross Property out of the Dark World; the other, the *Limus* out of the Heavenly Worlds Property, which lyes in one Compaction in the Earth, whence Man was created. The Turtle Dove, the poor Soul, captivated in the bestial Property. The young Pigeon, the inward disappeared Humanity. Their not being divided shews, nothing shall be taken from the Soul, nor from the inward Man of the Heavenly *Limus*. The Fowls which *Abraham* drove away, the Essence of the wrathful Property of God's Anger in Man, which hungreth after the Humanity, and would devour the same. *Abraham's* deep Sleep, the Death of Christ. The horror the Wrath of God. The darkness, the dark World, into which the Word should enter and resign its Will. The enkindled Fire passing between the pieces, the Holy Love-fire, tincturing all into a pure Gold. The Servitude in *Egypt*, that Christ in his Members should be only a Pilgrim, and that we are here in the Kingdom of the Heathen, where God's Children must be embroiled in Servitude with them: to which the Potent do compel the Poor, whereto he must be subject, else he resisteth the Kingdom of Nature (*viz.*) the formed Word. But if the Worldly Rulers, rule only according to their Will and Lusts, they will find, that God will Judge them.

CHAP. XL. *Of* Hagar *and* Ismael.

1. THE scope of this, toucheth that of Predestination. For as much as *Ismael* and *Esau* are erroneously taken, to be of Eternal reprobation: we are to know, that *Ismael* represenceth the Father's Property, and Kingdom of Nature in *Adam*: *Isaac*, the Sons Property, and Kingdom of Grace in the second *Adam*.

2. *Babel* (indeed blindly) teacheth, that God hath ordained a certain Number and Company to Damnation, and the rest to Salvation; but if so. Nature must needs be limited, confin'd and determin'd, when to bring forth a Child of God, or of Wrath, and nothing would be in the Human Property free: yea, God himself, must confine, and shut up his unchargeable, one Infinite Will, into a Beginning and Limit, which opens a Gate to horrid Prophaneness; makes void God's Holy Laws and Rules; renders needless the offers of Grace, and bars up the Door of Repentance

3. Yet the Holy Name of God (thus taken in Vain) is from Eternity free, and offers it self to all poor Sinners. Thus the Angel met *Hagar*, and blessed *Ismael* then in her Womb, who figur'd the Runagate Adamical self Will; for God inwardly calls all wicked Men, not only in the Womb, but all the time of their lives, as the Sun shines all the Day.

4. So

398 *Mysterium Magnum.* Part II.

4. So God calls the Turks and Heathens, figur'd by *Cain, Ham, Ismael* and *Esau*, who are in the Kingdom of Nature, as *Ismael* in *Hagars* Womb; they went not to *Isaac* but to *Abraham*, nor these to Christ's Person, but to God, and he heareth them in Christ. They, and painted Christendom, are as the two Sons: one promis'd but did it not, the other said he would not, but went and did it; so may they attain the Adoption, though the letter Christians grumble at the returning Prodigal, who is neverthelefs embraced by the Father.

CHAP. XLI. *Of the Seal of the Covenant of Circumcision, and of Baptism.*

1. GOD ratified his Covenant with *Abraham* by the Seal Circumcision; shewing, what *Ens* was Blessed; also what must, and what (in Man) must not, inherit (viz.) not the grofs Earthy Man, conceived in the beftial Luft of Man and Woman.

2. That Copulation, is only born with, by Divine Patience and Permission; Man having loft the Magical Birth of Paradice, and therefore, was every Male circumcifed on that Monftrous Member. The beftial Seed of Man and Woman, being the Seed of their own Will, shall not put on the Covenant and Blessing, but he,* who is not Born of the Will of Man, nor of the Flesh, but of God.

* *John* 2. 13.

3. The Earthy Members, die in the Spiritual Birth, through Chrift's Death. Externally 'tis cut off, in the Temporal Death; and 'tis Buried in the Eternal Death, in the Nothing, and a new Angelical Form shall arife.

4. The Males were only Circumcifed, for *Adam* had both the Tinctures, and was a Mafculine Virgin. It was to be on the eighth Day becaufe fix Days are the Man in Nature, the Seventh is the Day of Reft, which he had brought into difquietness; by reafon that the feventh Property, the Heavenly Nature died in him, therefore God gave him of Grace another Day (viz.) the Eighth, which is Chrift. *Ismael* was the firft Man (though a Mocker) thus taken into Covenant; for Chrift came, for *Ismael's* fake alfo, though the Doctrine of fome damn Children from the Womb.

5. Baptifm is for both Sexes, on all Days; shewing the need all have, and Chrift's Univerfal offer of God's Mercy: alfo pointing out Chrift's Humanity, who was both Circumcifed and Baptized, and the Firft born from the Dead. But the *Ens* of Faith, by the Spirit was the Fire-baptifm, for both Jews and Chriftians.

CHAP. XLII. *Of the three Men who appeared to* Abraham *in the Plain of* Mamre, &c.

1. THE three Men, fignified the Trinity, in higheft Humility. In the heat of the Day, when the Humanity was enflam'd, with higheft Rage, under God's Indignation. Appear'd to *Abraham* (viz.) to *Adam's* Children in the Souls Tent. *Abraham* bow'd himfelf (viz.) in his Faiths *Ens*. The three Meafures of Meal, the three Principles or three Worlds in Man: and kneaded, the Heavenly Humanity muft be mixed with ours. The tender Calf, the *Limus* of the Earth, which is as a Beaft before God.

Gen. 18.

2. The Lord asked for *Sarah*, he said, she is *in the Tent* (viz.) covered with earthinefs; that is, fees not who is with me. *Sarah* laughed, and fearing lyed, the Figure of *Eve*.

CHAP.

CHAP. XLIII. *Of the Ruin of* Sodom *and* Gomorrah, *how foretold to* Abraham.

1. GOD faith, *I am come down, to see if the Sin of* Sodom *be so great, as the cry of* Gen. 18. *it, which is come up,* viz. God, according to the Property of the Anger, seeth in the Devils and falſe Souls; but his Love-eye, feeth not into the Apoſtate Souls.

2. Reaſon knows not what God is, nor where he dwells. God is every Eſſence, and dwelleth through every Eſſence, but poſſeſſeth no Locality, nor doth need ſpace for Habitation.

3. But as far as he is called God, is no Eſſence, but through all things, and giveth himſelf in an Energetical way, but worketh not from without into it, but from within out of it, to his Manifeſtation.

4. The cry going up, and God's coming down, is thus;

5. Inward, is above: outward, is below; the Angelical World, is ſaid to be above, and the formed outward, below; as when a Fire is kindled, the light is above, the ſubſtance [or matter] below.

6. For the being within, without the ſubſtance, is the being above.

7. * *Abraham's* Praying for *Sodom,* ſhews *Abraham* to be a figure of Chriſt, with- * Gen. 18. holding the ſevere Righteouſneſs from falling on Man; but there were only three capable of Mercy.

8. And whereas there * went but two Angels towards *Sodom (viz.)* not the Per- * ch. 19. v. 1. ſon of Chriſt, but God's Truth and Righteouſneſs. The Truth brought out *Lot,* and the Righteouſneſs remained in *Sodom.*

9. *Lot* knew them, and bowed, humbling himſelf before the Lord, but they at firſt denied to go in with him; becauſe his Wife (by whom the earthy Matrix is ſignified) could not go through the Judgment.

10. The Men bid *Lot* call all his together, but his Sons that were to Marry his Daughters would not; for the wrath in them was ſo ſtrong, as to withhold though the Truth drew them, as it did alſo *Lots* Wife, by which ſhe was tranſmuted, as a terrible Example, till the laſt Judgment.

CHAP. XLIV. *Of* Lot's *Departure out of* Sodom, *and the terrible overthrow of that whole Region.*

1. THE Angels took *Lot*, his Wife and Daughters by the Hand; they were in- Gen. 19. 15. wardly taken by the hand of Faith in the Covenant. So were the Men of *Sodom*, taken by the hand of their Eſſence, and brought into Judgment and Execution.

2. The Sun was Externally riſen, ſo was Internally the Sun of God's Truth, the Sun of the Covenant, on *Lot* : and the ſcorching Sun of God's Anger, on *Sodom.* This figure concerns *Babel.*

3. *Lot* obtain'd the ſaving of *Zoar* (and himſelf in it) as oftentimes God's Chil- (v. 17. to 23.) dren do with-hold great Plagues from falling on People. The Angel ſaith, *I can do nothing till thou come thither.* God's Anger becomes impotent as it were, where the Sons of Love are preſent. It rained Brimſtone and Fire from the Lord, &c.

4. It was not the Helliſh Fire, which at the End ſhall purge the Floor; if ſo, the

Mysterium Magnum. Part II.

the four Elements had been changed; for that inward Fire consumes Earth, Stones and Elements; but this Fire, was generated in *Turba Magna*, an Egest or Thunderclap: And though it be no palpable Matter, yet is a spiritual Substance, in which *Mercurius* doth enkindle, and there the flagrat doth fix it self into a Substance.

5. The first Principle did behold the third with a darting flash, or aspect. As if the inward dark spiritual World should move it self; the outward with the four Elements would forthwith be swallow'd up.

6. *Lot's* Wife was apprehended in the *Proba*, and remain'd in the Salt Spirit; for that, Covetousness was most predominant in her.

7. *Lot's* Daughters, caus'd him to drink Wine, and lay with him; that they might receive the Holy Seed: which is not so as reason censureth, but that *Ammon* and *Moab* might spring from one Root in Affinity with *Abraham's* Line.

CHAP. XLV. *How God defended* Abraham *and* Sarah.

1. *A*Braham's continual Travels, figureth Christianity; which goeth from place to place, as a Stranger, without any continuing abode.

2. His being still protected, sheweth the particular care of God, still, as then, over every one of his Children.

3. His being faint and timorous, when he came to *Pharoah* and *Abimelech*, shews we are not to go in our Strength; *Abraham's* Will of self, looking only on it self, was dismay'd; yet in him was the great Might over all Powers: but it belonged not to the Human Ownhood, neither doth Christ in his Children belong to the Human Ownhood, but to the humble resign'd Will.

4. So in *Abraham* and in all Christians, are a twofold Will, one of this World, always standing in fear, the other according to the second Principle, the Kingdom of Heaven; the poor captive Soul's Will, which immerseth its self into God's Mercy in Hope.

CHAP. XLVI. *Of* Isaac's *Birth, and casting out* Ismael *and* Hagar, *and what it means.*

1. *L*OT being out, and *Sodom* destroyed, *Abraham* removed, shewing, that. where Christ's Kingdom is corrupt, he will depart.

2. He lived under King *Abimelech*, (*viz.* the Man of ingenious reason. At *Gerar* (*viz.*) the austere Life of Nature.

3. In this removal, *Abraham* followed his reason: Reason-light is the winnowing cross of God's Children; this brought his Fear, also his Reproof, from *Abimelech*, whom he should have Taught.

4. God's Children are in themselves weak, as all others, yet not to be rejected; for the Cross always stands by them; as *Abimelech* by *Abraham*, *Ismael* by *Isaac*, *Hagar* by *Sarah*.

5. *Sarah* ejects her, and she wanders in the Wilderness; of brokenness of Heart; then gave her Self and Son to die; but the Angel comforts her. That is, in the Figure.

6. When Christ is Born in the Convert, the new-born Will rejecteth its own evil Nature, the Mocker; then doth the poor forsaken Nature, wander and give up it self to Death, till the Angel comes and comforts it, that is, some faithful upright Man,

Mysterium Magnum. Part II.

Man, or some beam of Light from Christ in the Heart, to give Living Water; for of this Child must come a Nation, Christ must be Born, as a fair blossom out of the wild Earth.

7. These precious Figures have remained speechless to the World; because of Man's Vanity, but now *the Mystery of the Kingdom of God shall be finished, and *the Child of Perdition be revealed. Man's unworthiness causeth Truth to be hidden, wherefore it was Christ preach'd in Parables.   *Rev. 10:7. *2 Thess. 3.

8. Also we must know, whoever will understand the Old Testament, must set before him the two Types; externally, *Adam* the earthy Man: and internally, Christ: and change both these into one, and so he may apprehend *Moses* and the Prophets.

CHAP. XLVII. Of the Covenant of Abimelech and Abraham, and what it points at.

1: **B**Eershebah, a bruising to Death, is the same Fountain which the Angel shewed Hagar; which *Abraham* (viz.) Christ digged, and there afterwards preached the Eternal God. The Covenant between *Abimelech* and *Abraham* is the Covenant of Christ, with the Humanity, where he sware, not to destroy the Humanity, as he said, he was *not come to condemn the World. Abimelech* (viz.) the Soul, out of the Father's Property: *Picholl* the outward Nature, the third Principle, Field-Captain or Officer of the Soul: *Abraham* is Christ, in the Humanity. Now *Abimelech's* restoring *Abraham's* Wife, saying he knew not, &c. signifieth, That the Soul of *Adam* knew not Christ, in the Tincture of Heavenly *Venus*; therefore went into Self-lust; but when God shewed it to the Soul, the Soul said, I knew not that God's Wife was the Holy Tincture, the Heavenly Matrix, was in me.   *Gen. 21. 22. to 34.   *Joh. 3.17.*

2. But now, I restore whatever I have taken of the Divine Worlds Property, it is thy Wife; then all the Women of *Abimelech* and his Servants, *Eves* Daughters, were healed.

3. Christ here sweareth, not to shew any unkindness to the Human Property, nor to the Children, nor to the Grandchildren or Nephews (viz.) those springing out of the wild Property, where often a wicked Husband or Wife are joyned to a godly one, and so those Children spring from the wild Property. 'Tis said, Thou shalt do according to the kindness that I have done unto thee (viz.) in restoring thy Wife thy Image shalt thou do to me, and to the Land (viz.) the outward Man, wherein thou (viz.) Christ, sojournest, art a Stranger. Which Christ Sweareth, * *As I live, saith,* &c. Then *Abraham*, Christ, reproved *Abimelech*, the Soul, that the Soul's Servants, the Essences of Nature had taken away the Well, the Essence from the Heavenly Corporality (viz.) Christ's Body, in *Adam*; for Christ's Holy Fountain sprung up in the fiery Essence of the Soul: which being taken to Self-Power, the Heavenly Image disappeared. And *Abimelech*, the Soul, answered, I knew not till this Day (viz.) that the Devil had deceived me.   *Ezek. 33.11.*

4. Then *Abraham* (viz.) Christ, took Sheep, his Children the Jews, and Oxen the Gentiles, and gave them to the Father (of whose Property the Soul is) by an everlasting Covenant. And set seven Ewe Lambs apart (viz.) the seven Properties of the Natural Humanity of Christ, manifested in us. A part viz. a distinct Person.

5. We poor Jews and Gentiles may not say we are Christ, but his House: he is a *part with the Divine Property. But in right resignation when Man's Will is Dead to Self, Christ only liveth in it; such Eternally witness, that Christ digged the Well. At *Beersheba*, the place of Contrition, Christ planted Trees, Heavenly   *By himself.*

venly Branches: Preached, &c. and remained there a long time (viz.) all the time of the Natural Life.

CHAP. XLVIII. *Of* Abraham's *Offering up* Isaac.

1. Abraham is represented in *Adams* stead: *Isaac* in Christs Humanity: The Voice is God the Fathers; so is Christ Offered by *Adam's* Children the Jews, to the Fathers Fire. Thy Son whom thou lovest, viz. thy will brought into Self-love, in the devoration of which in Gods Wrath-fire, the true Man Created in *Adam*, must be form'd and preserv'd as Gold or Silver in the Crucible, where Copper and all Impurities evaporate. On Mount *Moriah*, which God, not we, chuseth.

1 Cor. 5. 15.
2. Christ wholly resigns up our Humane Will of self to his Father, in his Death for all, and in all Men: As when the stock of a Tree dyeth, the Branches die also, and as the Tree reneweth its Youth (as the Rod of *Aaron* did) it introduceth new Life into its Branches. *Abraham* rose early, teaching immediate obedience.
* Gen. 22. 3. * And girt his Ass, the Bestial Man, with power. Took with him two young
* (v. 4.) Men; one the Soul from the first Principle, the other the Spirit of the outward Life. Clave the Wood; as *Adam* clave Gods Love and Anger. * On the third day; pointing at *Adam's* sleep to the Angelical World, and the time of Christs Resurrection. Afar off; the Final Offering of Christ, above two Thousand years. The two young Men to tarry with the Ass, till Christ is Offered and come again.
* (v. 6.) *Abraham* took the * Knife, and Fire, Gods Anger and Death. * *Isaac* said, Here
* (v. 7, 8.) is the Wood, the Sins of all Men; and the Fire, Gods Wrath; but where is the Lamb? *Abraham's* Ens of Faith saw the Lamb. *Abraham* bound *Isaac*, so was Christ, and so must our self-wills be bound, and resign'd to God in entire earnestness. The Angel calleth hurt not Nature, as he had done to *Hagar* at *Beersheba*. He saw a Ram hung, &c. shews death kills not the true Man, but the pushing Beast, hung in the Devils Thickets of Thorny Cares and Vanity. Next follows the Blessing, increase and prevalency. And *Abraham* return'd with his Son and two young Men to *Beersheba*, into the toil and labour of this World; so God exerciseth his people not always in operation of the Spiritual Figures, but in weakness and infirmities, in the Kingdom of Nature: And sometimes again under the Cross, and so they grow as in a Field, sometimes Storms, sometimes Sunshine.

3. *Nabor Abraham's* Br other, had eight Sons by *Milcah* of whom came great Nations. the Assyrians, who tho' they sprung not from the *Ens* of Faith in the Line of Christ, the Blessing of *Abraham* passed on them.

CHAP. XLIX. *Of* Sarah's *Death, and* Abraham's *Hereditary Sepulchre.*

1. While *Abraham* lived he was a Stranger, no continuing abode had he.; but when his *Sarah* died he would have a certain Possession of a peculiar and Hereditary Sepulchre, for his Wife, himself and Children; which he would not have to be given him, but bought it of the Sons of *Heth* and *Ephron*, for four hundred Sheckles of Silver, viz. the Cave of *Machpelah*. The inward Figure of which is, That,

2. When

Mysterium Magnum. Part II.

2. When *Isaac*, *viz.* Christ, is come, the twofold Body returns back to its original Mother, the Eternal and Temporal Nature. When the Saints die to self the outward Life: The resigned Life will no longer stand in a strange Serpentine one, it cannot of due right take the first true Field, but it must be purchased. Thus *Abraham* in the Figure of Christ, doth, of the Sons of *Heth*, who stand in the Fathers Figure. And that Christs Ransom is signified by four hundred Sheckles, hath this meaning. The first is the true Magical Fire, the second is the Light, the third the holy found of the Mental Tongue, the fourth the conceived *Ens* of the other Properties, forming the holy Life: This is the pure Silver.

3. And whereas the Children of *Heth* would freely have given it, yet at last took Money for it: So hath God the Father freely given the Kingdom of Grace to Christ in our Humanity, but Christ would have it for a Natural Right.

4. By *Canaan*, understand the holy Chrystalline World or Earth, which shall be manifest.

5. By the twofold Cave or Pit of *Machpelah* is signified, Man hath a twofold Humanity; one out of the Divine *Ens* and Heavenly Essence, the other out of time this Worlds substance, both which should be put into an Eternal Sepulchre, and lye in its original Mother, leaving the one will in Death; so that God might alone live, rule and will in the Soul, and Mans Life be only his Instrument. For the Soul hath turn'd it self aside from the only Eternal Word, into self-hood. This Distemper and unlikeness, must be buried and put again into a twofold Cave, and thence come into the Temperature, the Essence whence the Body and Soul did arise.

CHAP. L. *Of* Abraham's *sending his Servant for a Wife for* Isaac.

1. *A*Braham, is herein the Figure of God the Father, *Isaac*, in that of Christ, Abraham's Servant, in that of Nature. The *Canaanites*, in that of the introduced Serpents *Ens*, the Bestial Man, which shall not Inherit. Here God makes his Servant, Nature, by whom he governeth, Essentially bind it self, that it will not introduce the Serpents *Ens*, the dark Worlds Bestial Canaanitish Property for Gods Childrens Yoke-fellow, but Nature must take substance out of *Abraham's* true Humane Essence, in pure Love of the Heavenly Matrix, that so the New Birth might be holy in its Virginity as to the inward Man. *Gen.* 24. 1, 3.

2. * Nature saith, How if, *&c.* *viz.* the right Humane *Ens* will not follow me? * And God said, Beware, *&c.* *viz.* go not according to thy Reason; but an Angel shall go before thee, *viz.* the Divine Will; for self-will and reason must not Lord it, but Nature must be a Servant; do as it is commanded, and commit it to God to bring on the Eternal Marriage. But if the Humane Will will not follow, the Messenger hath discharged his Office: The Rain ascends not up again without Fruit, Nature must declare that God hath given Christ all his Goods; and now desireth Man to be his Wife. * And the Servant sware, *&c.* *viz.* When God put his Holy Word with the formed Wisdom into the Natural *Ens* of *Mary*, then the Humane Nature sware Obedience. *Gen.* 24. v. 5. *v.* 6. *v.* 9.

3. And the Servant took ten Camels, (and went to the City of *Nahor* in *Mesopotamia*) *viz.* the ten Forms of the three Principles, to the Natural and Supernatural Life, *viz.* seven Forms of the Centre of Nature, and three Forms of the three *Gen.* 24. v. 10.

'*Mysterium Magnum.* Part II.

three distinctions of the Principles; which are they whereby God causeth all things; and the Goods of the Lord are the formed Wisdom of the great Wonders and Powers.

v. 11. 4. And the Servant caused the Camels to kneel by the Well near the City, at Evening. At, or in the last time or days of the World. The will of the Fathers Nature, the Mystery of the Nature of the three Principles, the Carriers of the formed Word, hath laid it self down by the Well-spring of God, the Divine Fountain.

v. 53. 5. The Silver and Golden Jewels, Bracelets and Ear-rings given to *Rebekah*, signifie the Heavenly Humanity of Jesus Christ, which is not given wholly into the power of the Fire-soul in this Life; lest it become haughty as *Lucifer* and *Adam*, but Virgin *Sophia* meant by *Rebekah*, remaineth with her Bridegroom Christ, in the second Principle.

* *v.* 54. 6. The Spices signifie the Holy Spirit. * *Then they sate down to eat,* viz. the Mar-
* *v* 61. to 67. riage Feast, the Joy whereof none but the Children of Christ know. * *And when Rebekah saw Isaac, &c.* When the disappear'd Humanity discovers Christ in it self, it falleth into deepest Humility, and is ashamed, vailing its Face before Gods Holiness and Clarity, that it hath lain so long Captive in the Bestial Man, but Christ taketh it into his Arms and leadeth it into his Mothers Tent, into the Heavenly Worlds Essence. And then was *Isaac* comforted for his Mother, for the disappeared Matrix, which was lost in *Adam*, now re-obtain'd in Virgin-like Chastity for his Spouse.

CHAP. LI. *Of* Abraham's *taking* Keturah *to Wife, and of his Six Sons and Death.*

1. A*Braham* was old when he had *Isaac*, to shew Christ was to be in the old Age of the World, and *Sarah* was old, that so the Divine *Ens* might have the preheminence over the Humane, and she must have but one, for so is Christ, and all are Branches in the one Tree, viz. Christ in all.

2. But *Abraham* by *Keturah* had six Sons signifying the six Properties of the formed Nature, the operation of the six days: *Isaac*, viz. Christ is the seventh, the Sabbath. Of these six sprang six Nations, to them he gave gifts of his Goods, tho' not the Inheritance, yet had the free Gift of Grace. So every Man hath Christ as the free Gift of Grace in him, none predestinated to destruction, for by those six are signified all *Adam*'s Children.

3. In the right Adamical Man, out of which the Earth had its Original is the Covenant of the Free gift, but the own-self-made-gross-earthy *Adam*, who by Lust made himself a Beast is not capable of the Gift in the Covenant, but the right Man (as a Tincture in gross Lead mortifieth the Saturnine will, and changeth it into Gold) swalloweth up the gross Man, viz. the dark Worlds Property.

4. The Jews, Christians and Heathens have all this Gift, and Christ is the only available obedience; all Men therefore who give up themselves in obedience to God are received in Christs obedience, for Names are not accepted.

5. My believing that Christ was Born, Died and Rose for me makes me not a Christian, but I must put on Christ, enter into his Obedience and Sacrifice, arise in him and Live in him.

6. When *Abraham* had brought his Lifes Forms into right order he resigned up himself into Mortification, tired with the Life of self, rested in God.

CHAP.

Mysterium Magnum. Part II.

CHAP. LII. *The History of* Isaac, *Birth of* Esau *and* Jacob.

1. After *Abraham*'s Death, God blessed *Isaac*, and he lived by the Well *Labai-roi, viz.* the Well of Living and Seeing, his Soul dwelt by the Fountain of Divine Love. The desire of the Soul, is the *Fiat*, which takes the holy Love Tincture into it self, and makes it Essential; as the Metalline *Ens* gives its desire into the Suns Tincture; that out of them both the fair and precious Gold is generated: So doth the Deity inhabit in the Soul, and co-worketh, but is not comprehended. *Gen.* 25. v. 11.

2. The Souls Magical Fire, by the Divine Love desire is inkindled into a shining Lustre, so doth the Souls Magical Fire become the Bridegroom to the precious *Sophia* but the Mortal Soul; from the Stars or four Elements attains it not in this Life, but that Soul that cometh from the Centre of the Eternal Nature, out of the Divine *Lubet* through the Word, whereby the Divine longing formeth the Wisdom into Substance. This Soul is that which is betrothed to *Sophia*.

3. *Ishmael* had twelve Sons, six of the Inward, and six of the Outward Nature of the Humane Property: They were afterward Potent, Renowned Nations. Whereas *Isaac* and his Children were as Pilgrims; shewing, Chrifts Dominion is not of this World; and yet the Kingdoms of this World shall fall before Him.

4. *Esau* and *Jacob*'s strife in the Womb, shews, that when Christ first manifests himself in the Adamical Nature, the strife of the two Kingdoms begins. The Serpent stingeth the New Birth (Christ) on the Heel, (a woful Distress) but Christ assaults the Head: And tho' *Esau* be First-born, *Jacob* comes soon after and deprives him, and makes *Esau* (the Kingdom of Nature) his Servant. * And, in that *Esau* came forth First, and was Red, and all over Rough: The Red betokeneth the Fathers Nature in the Fire, (the Rough the Earthy Bestial Nature.) * *Gen.* 25. 24; 25, 26.

CHAP. LIII. *How* Esau *contemn'd his Birthright, and sold it for a Mess of Pottage.*

1. There is in this a Twofold Figure; for Outwardly, it is the Figure of the Earthy Man, who carelesly and profanely gives away the Heavenly Substance, to satiate its Lustful Will, and fill its Carnal Belly: But Inwardly, *Esau* had the Souls Centre, *viz. Adam*'s Nature, for a natural due Right, which was Faint, and wearied by the Driver; This would *Jacob*, (who betokened the Power of the other *Adam* (Christ) have him [This Day] *viz.* from That day forward, wholly to give up and Resign. And would give him the Divine *Ens*. And in This Inward Understanding, *Abraham* was the Field, *Ishmael* the Root, and *Isaac* the Fruit: Also now, *Isaac* the Field, *Esau* the Root, and *Jacob* the Fruit. And we see the Blossom and Fruit hath far a more subtle, pure Property, than the Stalk and Root (by influence of the Solar Rays.)

2. The meaning of this Figure is, that the evil Adamical Mans Will, must be resigned up. It is Rejected, and availeth not in the Kingdom of God.

Not that the Person of *Esau* was intended (as *Babel* ignorantly teacheth) to be by Gods Soveraignty Reprobated and Hated.

CHAP.

CHAP. LIV. *How* Isaac, *by reason of the Famine, went down to Abimelech at* Gerar, *&c.*

1. HEre is shewed *the Kingdom of Grace and Nature*. *The Famine*, shews *Adams* Temptation, wherein he should have fed on the Word of God, and not gone into the *strange Kingdom of the Stars and Elements*; where he Denied his Wife, *viz.* the Heavenly Genitress in him, and brought his Lust into the Bestial Property.

2. And that *Isaac* grew so Great there that *Abimelech* was afraid of him, shews Gods Blessing on the Kingdom of Christ.

3. The Servants of King *Abimelech's* stopping the Wells, digged by the Servants of *Isaac*, sheweth, that *Abraham* and *Isaac* having digged in the *Ens* of their *Faith*, the *Knowledge* of the *Messiah*, the same is obscured and stopped up by the Earthy Reason. * And then they digged and said, we have found Water; and *Isaac* call'd it *Sheba*, (hinting at *Saba*, the *Saboth*, (Christ) call'd also *Beer-sheba*, *viz.* the *Contrition or Breaking* ; where the *Saboth* through Death, brings forth the Fountain of Life.

* *Gen.* 26. 32, 33.

5. That *Esau* lived Forty years, and then took two Evil Women to Wife; points at *Adam's* Forty days in the *Proba*; and then took two Evil Wives, *viz.* one of the Bestial Property of the four Elements; the other the Astral, which were a vexation and grief of Heart to *Isaac* and *Rebekah* all their Life. Thus as the whole *Old Testament*, is a *Figure* of the *New*, so is the *New* of the *Future Eternal World*.

CHAP. LV. *Of* Isaac's *Blessing* Jacob *unknowingly when he was Old, and ready to Die.*

The Gates of the Great Mystery of the whole Bible.

Gen. 27.

1. REason from this Figure conjectureth,
  (1.) That *Rebekah* lov'd *Jacob* more than *Esau*.
  (2.) That it was from Gods Predestinate Purpose; because *Esau* was not worthy of it.

2. But rightly to interpret it : The Patriarch *Isaac* is the Figure of God the Father ; *Esau*, of the depraved Humane Nature ; *Jacob*, of the New Birth in the Humanity of Christ ; *Rebekah* of the Virgin *Mary*.

3. The Fathers Blessing would bring it self into *Adam*, but his Heavenly *Ens* was extinct ; and the Kingdom of Nature so Poyson'd, that it must be Dissolv'd ; for *Adam's* Fiery Tincture (by being awakened in the wrath) became an Earthy Image ; and mortified the Heavenly ; so that the Kingdom of Nature was (in its own power) uncapable of the Fathers Blessing ; and could not be remedied only by a Blessing ; the Blessing must become a Substance ; the Fathers Blessing woud it self on the Adamical Female Lights Tincture ; and from the power Thereof, did assume the Souls Nature ; and then bruise the fiery Serpents Head, and transmute the Souls fiery Will into a Love-fire or Meekness, *viz.* the power of the Light.

4. *Esau* was Hairy or Rugged ; signifying the gross Bestial Property ; and Christ did

did put on our Hairy Beaſt-like Skin, to make us capable of the Bleſſing, and deſtroy our Death of the Beſtial Property. Even as *Jacob* could not get the Bleſſing, without having the hairy Garment on.

5. *Iſaac's* feeling *Eſau's* hairy Garment on *Jacob*, ſignified the Fathers reaching into the Eſſence of Chriſt, whether it were the firſt Image 'Created in *Adam*; whence was Chriſts Agony and Bloody Sweat.

6. And as *Iſaac* found outwardly *Eſau's* Skin, but inwardly heard *Jacob's* Voice, yet Bleſſed him inſtead of *Eſau*: So had Chriſt our Rugged, Humane Property, yet God ſaid, *This is my Beloved Son*, &c. and Bleſſed our Humanity.

7. The Bleſſing given *Jacob* denotes, that the New Man in Chriſt ſhould take away the Scepter and Might from the Devil, and Man of Sin, and be Lord over his Brethren (the Adamical Nature) in Fleſh and Blood.

8. The Corn and Wine, and Dew of Heaven ſhew God bleſſed our Humanity in Chriſt, with the Earth and Reſurrection.

9. *Eſau's* bringing his Veniſon, and *Iſaac's* Aſtoniſhment, ſhew, that Gods holy People would have the Will of their Reaſon be done. Their Miſery is, that *v.* 35. Reaſon entreth into its Dominion, which knoweth not the ways of God.

10. *Eſau* was Bleſſed alſo with the Dew of Heaven and Fatneſs of the Earth; ſhould live by his Sword; and when he ſhould have the Dominion ſhould break the Yoke.

11. But *Iſaac* doth not ſay, *Live thou by thy Sword*; but *Thou wilt Live ſo*, &c. wherein he Propheſieth that the corrupt Nature would be a Tyrant and Murtherer; and doth not juſtifie the uſe of outward Weapons and Violence, but that he (through his Anger) ſhould ſerve the Anger of God; and ſo his hating *Jacob* noteth what the Great Ones of the World ſhould do, for the Devil rageth, that the Kingdom of Chriſt ſhould take away his Throne.

CHAP. LVI. *Of* Jacob'*s Leaving his Parents for fear of* Eſau, *and of his Viſion of the Ladder.*

1. *Jacob* having the Bleſſing and Unction, ſoon departed from his Fathers Houſe and left all to *Eſau*; ſo did Chriſt (of whom this is a Figure) after he had anointed our Humanity, fled with it out of our Adamical Houſe, to the firſt Paradiſical Houſe. So muſt the Chriſtian *fly the Depraved Nature*; begin the *Pilgrimage*; leave the *Temporal Honour and Goods to* Eſau.

When *Jacob* had left the Riches of the World, he ſaw the Ladder (which was Chriſt) leading to the *Eternal Kingdom*; and by It, the *Angelical World* deſcendeth, uniting Heaven to the World in Man, while the World Hate, Reproach and Perſecute them: An Example of which Mocking, are *Eſau's* two Iſhmaelitiſh Wives.

2. God ſaid, *In thy Seed ſhall all Nations be bleſſed;* * ſhewing that Chriſt hath Gen. 28. 14. truly taken on him our Humanity, (the Adamical Soul) in which the Divine * *See the Ex-* Ens hath unfolded the higheſt Love in the Name Jeſus; and overcome the Wrath *tracts of the* of the Eternal Nature in our Souls, (which is from the Fathers Property in the *Book of the* Anger) and chang'd it into Love and Divine Joy; not through a ſtrange Divine *Incarnation.* Seed only, but in, and through *Adam's* Soul and Body (deſtroy'd Hell) which was reveal'd in Paradiſe.

3. *Jacob's* Fear when he awaked, Typified Chriſts Agony in the Garden.

CHAP. LVII. *How* Jacob *kept* Laban's *Sheep Fourteen Years for his Two Daughters,* &c.

1. *R*Achel is here the Figure of the Noble *Sophia,* (the Bride of Christ) whom the Soul having once seen with great Joy, earnestly desireth and serveth (as *Jacob* seven years) willingly for: But at the Wedding the other Sister *Leah,* signifying the Cross of Christ is laid by him, that the Soul may not sport it self in the Garden of Roses, but be in Trouble; Tried and Humbled: Her tender Eyes signifie tenderness of Heart.

2. And then the Virgin *Sophia* is given to it, but what That Joy is, They only know, who have been Guests to this Wedding; which Joy afterwards passeth away, and the Noble *Sophia* is as it were Barren. Mean while *Leah* under the Cross of Christ, beareth Fruit with Patience and Labour.

3. And as *Rachel* said, *Give me Children, or else I die,* so saith *Sophia,* Work (in my Love-desire) Divine Fruit, else I will depart; which the Soul (in its own power) cannot; but doth Therefore Pray earnestly; Then is *Joseph* the Prince of *Egypt, viz.* the House of Flesh and Blood, where dwells the Heathenish *Pharaoh* (the Bestial Spirit) but over It (and Reason also) is the humble, chast, modest *Joseph,* made Ruler.

4. But the Children of *Leah, Reuben,* &c. bare the Figure of Lust, Glory, &c. The rest of this Chap. is referr'd to 77. of the *Myst. Mag.* and *Gen.* 49.

CHAP. LVIII. *Of* Jacob's *serving* Laban, *and of his Wives, and Children, and Wages.*

1. *J*Acob was in a servile condition twenty years, till he had begat the Twelve Stocks of the Twelve Tribes. So is a Christian Born under the servile Yoke of the domineering self Adamical will: And their being Begotten in Servitude, shews Gods Children are but strange Guests here, but shall go out with great Riches. *Leah's* being despised for her blear Ears, shews the same.

2. The inward Figure is, *Adam* went out of Paradise and serv'd the Kingdom of this World; yet as he was going out, God shewed him the entrance in again, *viz.* by the Womans Seed, (as is signified by *Jacob's* Ladder) mean time the Kingdom of the Stars, &c. vexeth *Adam,* with heat, cold, sickness and misery. *Jacob's* getting great Riches by peeling Rods, &c. shews how *Adam's* Children should by subtle working in Nature acquire to themselves for a Propriety the Wonders in Nature which they shall carry away as an Eternal Propriety, so did the Destroyer of the Serpent with Divine subtilty put on Humanity, and took away the outward Kingdoms Power.

3. The ring-streaked, speckled and grizled denotes the half Earthy, and again the new-born heavenly Nature.

4. The Kingdom of Nature lay in *Adam* in the Temperature; all the Properties were of equal weight, but when the will of the Soul went into the separation it was thereby captivated till the Divine subtilty draws the Kingdom of Nature to it self, and re-easneth with the Wonders in its new Man again into Paradise.

5. But *Jacob's* peeling the Rods justifieth not subtilty of deceit, but only is a Figure representing the Spiritual subtilty.

6. And

Mysterium Magnum. Part II.

6. And as *Laban* disappointed *Jacob* by changing his Wages ten times, so goes it with the Child of God here, whose expectation of Gods Blessing is often frustrate, but yet his Faiths desire draweth to him Christ the Eternal Wages, and in him the out-spoken Word the Kingdom of Nature, wherein lye the Wonders and Being of Man which is kept to the great separation, when every one shall reap what he hath here sown.

7. *Jacob* had *Dinah* by *Leah*, who was the Figure of *Eve*, who fell by her Curiosity.

8. When *Rachel* had Born *Joseph*, whose great chastity and fear of God shews Gods Blessing had stirred up the Tinctures of the Kingdom of Nature, then doth *Jacob* call for and receive his Wages, for *Joseph* (that is) Christ, was Born, who should feed him, and give the Eternal Succor, by bringing his Father and Brethren into his Lords Countrey.

CHAP. LIX. *Of* Jacob's *departure from* Laban, *&c.*

1. *Laban*'s Children said *Jacob* hath gotten all our Fathers Goods, and *Laban*'s Countenance was changed; pointing us, that when Christs Spirit in Man hath won the rule of the Humane Nature, then the Serpent in the wrath of Nature enviously opposeth the poor Soul, pressing for worldly Honour and Pleasure. But then God saith to the Soul, as here to *Jacob*, Return into thy Fathers Countrey, viz. into the Eternal Word out of which it proceeded, which it doth and flyeth, as did *Jacob*.

2. And as *Laban*, so do the wicked World pursue, but God aweth them. Thus also is Christ Figured, who put himself in Mans servile Yoke, took *Adam*'s Daughter, viz. the Humane Nature in Flesh and Blood, and in the end carried to his Fathers Countrey his acquired Goods, which *Laban* nor his Company, viz. the Devil nor his, could not rob him of.

3. *Laban*'s Gods stoln by *Rachel*, might well be the Images or Statues of those of his Ancestors deceased, his Love of whom made them patterns for his Instruction.

4. *Rachel*'s stealing them, hath an inward and an outward Figure. First Christ took the *Rachel* our Humane Nature, which had taken to it self the Idol wills, and broke those Idols. Outwardly, it points that as *Jacob* left *Laban*, so did *Israel* *Egypt*, but brought their fleshly Idol desires with them, which in time swery'd them from the true God.

5. But *Laban*'s pursuing, noteth those of Natures Kingdom persecuting them that leave *Babel*'s Worship and Pageantry, refusing to be conducted on their way by the Worlds Mirth, Tabrets and Solemnity; for Christ being Born in them, their Mind leaveth *Adam*'s servile House of Images, and Gods Host of Angels are appointed his Guardians.

CHAP. LX. *Of* Esau's *going to meet* Jacob *with Four Hundred Men.* Jacob's *Present and Wrestling, &c.*

1. *Esau*'s coming with four hundred Men signifieth the Kingdom of Nature in the Anger of God, which was the first born, and in the four Elements, at which *Jacob* was astonished, so was Christ at Mount *Olivet*.

Mysterium Magnum. Part II.

2. *Jacob's* dividing the Herds into two companies points at Chrifts twofold Humanity, viz. the Heavenly and Earthy, that when thefe Warriours fhould fmite the Earthy, the other which came down from Heaven fhould efcape.

3. *Jacob's* Prefents are Chrifts Prayers.

4. His humbling himfelf, faying, I came over with my Staff only, but am now two Bands; fo did Chrift in the Garden; whofe two Bands were the Heavenly Humanity perifh'd in *Adam*, and that of the *Limus* of the Earth; with both which *Jacob*, viz. Chrift was to return to his firft Paradifical Countrey and Angelical Kindred.

5. Sent five hundred and eighty Cattel, viz. Chrift fent our Lufts to the Anger of God.

6. *Jacob* alfo fent his two Wives, viz. Chrift fent the twofold Spirit of Man, viz. the Soul and the *Spiritus Mundi*, viz. the inward Eternal Soul, and the outward Soul.

7. Two Handmaids, viz. the twofold Humanity of the Body.

8. The Eleven Children, viz. the Eleven Apoftles.

9. And paffed over the Brook *Jabeck*, viz. *Kidron*.

10. *Jacob's* Twelfth Son lay yet unborn, fo now was Chrifts Twelfth Apoftle not chofen in the room of *Judas*.

11. *Jacob* ftaid alone, and there wreftled a Man with him, viz. the great love of God in the Name Jefus, did wreftle with Gods Righteoufnefs and Truth which was on Mount *Sinai*.

12. All Night of the darknefs of Gods Anger.

13. The Ham of his Thigh was difplaced, viz. the Adamical Humanity was difplaced, but not broken, to die Eternally. He halted, viz. being Lame to the Pride, Vanity, Malice, Lafcivioufnefs, &c. of this World.

14. The Man faid, Let me go, for the day, viz. the Eternal day dawneth: But *Jacob*, viz. Chrift faid, I will not let thee go until thou blefs me, viz. the Humanity.

15. And the Man faid, What is thy Name? He faid, *Jacob*. Then the Man faid, Thou fha't no more have a felf name, but *Ifrael*, viz. a Tree of Life, or Chriftian, viz. a fprout on the Vine Chrift.

16. Ard *Jacob* asked what is thy Name? But Chrift faid why askeft thou, (that is) I am no ftranger, thy Name and mine fhall be one. But God without Nature and Creature is the Eternal one and Eternal good, the Abyfs and Profundity, no place is found for him, no Creature can Name him; for all Names ftand in the formed Word: But God is the Beginninglefs Root of all Power, the Vegetables know not how the Sun bleffeth them.

17 Man hath lamentably loft the five Vowels, the Holy Ghofts Language, for the whole New Teftament is couched up in the Old.

18. When God bleffed *Jacob* he called the place *Penuel* (that is) where God is manifeft in the Soul.

19. And when he was departed thence, the Sun, viz. of Righteoufnefs, arofe in him, and he halted his felf-will was lame in its ability.

20. And the Children of *Ifrael* eat not of that Sinew to this day; for they underftood that Myftery, and Inftituted this Memorial, viz. the difplacing of their Beftial Wills; which if the prefent Jews and Chriftians well underftood they would not hunt after Covetoufnefs and Luft, yet under Chrifts Purple Mantle.

CHAP.

CHAP. LXI. *Of* Jacob *and* Esau *meeting all Heart-burning turned to Joy,* &c.

1. **B**Lind Reason should learn the meaning of Gods Decree, *Rom.* 9. 13. and *Mal.* 1. 2, 3. for, here was *Esau* the Type of the corrupted *Adam*, and *Jacob* of Christ, who came to help *Adam*, and were of one Seed, to shew Christ must become Flesh. And *Jacob* appeased *Esau* by his Humility, as did Christ by his great Love in our Humanity in our Anger-soul, appease the Anger of God, when he gave up his Heavenly Blood, with the Tincture of Love into the Anger of God ; for then was the Anger in the dark World turn'd into a Love-fire.

2. *Jacob* seeing *Esau* coming with four hundred Men, divided his Children to *Leah*, and to *Rachel*, and to both the Handmaids, and passed before them, and bowed seven times, *&c.*   *Gen.* 33. 1, 2, 3.

3. When Christ in our Humanity entred his Sufferings. Gods Anger in the four Elements met him. Then Christ divided the Heavenly Worlds substance which he brought from God, signified by *Rachel* from the Natural Humanity, from *Adam* (or *Spiritus Mundi*) Typed by blear ey'd *Leah*, wherein yet the destroyer of the Serpent was Born, as *Judah* of *Leah* while *Rachel* was Barren, till Christs Spirit made her fruitful.

4. And as *Jacob* set the Handmaids foremost. so did Christ first cause the Earthy to pass through the sharpness of Death, next *Leah* the Body out of the *Limus* of the Earth follow'd.

5. And after her, *Rachel*, the Heavenly *Limus*, with the Prince *Joseph*, the Divine Worlds substance.

6 *Jacob* bowed seven times in this Humility, appeasing *Esau*, so did Jesus through all the seven forms of Natures Life.

7. As *Jacob* yielded up his Riches and Life to *Esau*, to do what he would with him, so did Christ to Gods Anger.

8. *Esau* ran to meet him, fell on his Neck, wept and kissed him, so when the Essence of Gods Anger in Man, tasted the sweet Love in the Name and Blood of Jesus, it was transmuted into Compassion.

9. And *Esau* beheld the Women and Children, and said, whose are these? *&c.* Man, while held in the Anger and Darkness, was not known to the holy Image, but Love made him known.   *Gen.* 33. 5, 6, 7.

10. Their order of coming to *Esau* shews how poor *Eve's* Children were brought through Christs Suffering and Death, into the Countenance of God, first the Body of Sin through Death, then the Body out of the *Limus* of the Earth, which in the Resurrection is esteemed strange. therefore Typed by a Handmaid. And lastly, the fair Image Created in *Adam*.

11. *Jacob's* Presents signifie the Children purchased by Christ, and given to the Father, so shall Christ deliver up the Kingdom to the Father.

12. Yet is *Esau's* Compassion, and weeping on *Jacob* the Type of repenting Sinners sorrow.

13. *Esau* said , Let us go together ; *Jacob* saith, The Children are tender, *&c.* I will follow softly, *&c.* When Christ in his Sufferings had appeas'd his Fathers Anger in the Kingdom of Nature, the appeas'd Anger would instantly take the

Note. *The Blessed Author taking occasion at Mans false Inference, from Gods saying, Esau have I hated, &c. to conclude Gods predetermining Men to Damnation, doth fundamentally discuss that great Mystery from the 22d to the 68th verse of this Chapter,*   *Gen.* 33. 12, 13, 14.

Mysterium Magnum. Part II.

Chapter, so convincingly, and yet as plainly as so profound a subject will admit. But because it is treated of in a select Volume, *Vide p. 369, [call'd Predestination] beginning * p. 369. &c. of this of this. I refer this place thither. Book of Extracts.* the Journey, viz. in the Life of Man. But the Love said, Man is too tender, and may fall (by Temptation) in one day I will follow slowly with them, to the end of the World.

14. *Esau* would have left some of his Men with *Jacob*, but *Jacob* said, what needeth it? viz. God the Father said, Let me leave some Laws of my severe Righteousness, but Christ saith, Let me with my redeemed Children only find Grace in thy sight; for they cannot fulfil thy Laws.

CHAP. LXII. *Of* Dinah *Deflour'd,* all the Males of Sichem *slain by* Simeon *and* Levi.

1. *Jacob* had Twelve Sons, six of them were of *Leah*, and *Judah* (of whom came the Humanity of Christ) was one of the six.

2. Then bare *Leah Dinah*, which Daughter of Fleshly Love went after the Daughters of the Land a gadding, lively prefiguring *Christendom* who instead of continuing in the humble simplicity of *Jacob's* Tents at *Succoth*, and remaining a Stranger to the Customs and Behaviour of the proud wanton Daughters of the Land, mixeth with the Heathenish Wisemen in Fleshly Lust, and bringeth forth a Bastard, half Christian, and half Heathen, compos'd of the Profession of Christ, and the Heathenish Notions, viz. Philosophy, Schools, Colledges, Heathenish Festivals, &c.

3. And as *Simeon* and *Levi*, after the Men of *Shechem* had Circumcised themselves, yet Murthered not only guilty *Hemor*, but all the Males, tho' Innocent, so hath Christendom dealt by many Nations, who having conformed to some of their Opinions, yet are causlesly kill'd by the Antitype of *Simeon* and *Levi*. Therefore are the Potent Countries of the East departed from these Murtherous Pretenders to Religion, to the Doctrine of Reason.

CHAP. LXIII. *How* Jacob *leaves* Sichem. Rachel *bare* Benjamin, Isaac *died.*

1. After *Simeon* and *Levi* had Murthered the Males of *Sichem*, *Jacob* by command of God removed to *Bethel*, after he had first taken away from his people their Idols and Ear rings, and buried them under an Oak. And at *Sichem* built an Altar. Which hath this Figure, That when the Spiritual Whoredom of the Jews and Christians had drawn on them Wars and Miseries, God commanded his people to withdraw and erect an Altar of Humility and Fear in their Hearts.

2. Then are their Idolatries, Wars and Pride buried in Gods Anger, in his hungry wrath, viz. under an Oak which hath a Magnetick, Tenacious, Attractive Property, making a hardness and blackness, there will their Sins and Blasphemies lye buried, till the Earth can no longer cover them. But the fear of the Lord will fall on the pursuers of those that so depart, and Build Gods Altar in them.

3. God appear'd to *Jacob* in *Bethel*, which *Bethel* signifies a condescention of the Deity in the Humanity.

4. And they went from *Bethel*, and it was a Field breadth from *Ephrath* where *Rachel* brought forth *Benjamin*, but in hard labour, so as she died.

5. *Alsm*

5. *Adam* was gone a Field breadth from Gods Altar, *viz.* out of the Spiritual World into the Earthy, where with the Death of the old Man the new must be Born.

6. So also, when Christ had consummated his Passion, and *Judas* had perished, *Matthias* was chosen an Apostle.

7. After this, *Reuben* defiled *Bilhah Rachel's* Maid, his Fathers Concubine. This Concubine representeth the Stone Churches in which God generateth his Children, but the Adamical Man playeth the Hypocrite in them ; for none that is dead can awaken another that is dead, nor can one that is Blind shew the way to another that is B'ind, but both will fall into the Pit, their Ministers having lost the true Divine Power. *Reuben* was given to fleshly Lust and Self-love, and in that regard rejected of God.

8. Yet those places, though no more holy than other places hurt no Man, being at first well intended, yet their Ministers who Officiate for Honour and Profit without the Divine Unction are Adulterers, and as profitable to the Church as a fifth Wheel to a Waggon.

9. *Jacob's* returning to his Father, and *Isaac's* Death at *Hebron*, where he was a Stranger, shews Gods Children to be all Strangers here, and must all go to their Fathers Country, *viz.* the Angelical World.

CHAP. LXIV. Esau's *Genealogy, his own Name and Posterity; and of* Joseph.

1. ESau's Children and Childrens Children being set down with so great obser- *Gen.* 35. vation, is not without its Figure. We must know we may not condemn him to Hell, but that he and his Posterity bare the Image of the Earthy Glory, Might and Power.

2. From his own Name *Esau*, the *sau* being cut off, *viz.* the Swinish-Beastial-Property, there remains the *E* the Angelical Property.

3. And the Spirit calls him *Edom*, which *dom* in the * High Tongue signifies * *Hebrew* Red, as Tinctured by the Blood of Jesus. But of his Children more is said in ano- *Montanus*. ther place, *viz.* of this Authors Writings.

The remainder of Chap. 64. follows, beginning the Third Part.

Mysterium Magnum.

The Third Part.

CHAP. LXIV. *Of* Joseph Jacob's *Son*.

1. Jacob had cast his Natural Love on *Rachel* (being Fair) but she was unfruit- *Gen.* 37. 8. ful till their Age had wither'd fleshly Love. A Child they desired, prayed for

Mysterium Magnum. Part III.

for and obtain'd, which reprefented the pure and right Adamical Humanity in its Primitive Chaftity and fear of God; as the firft *Adam* in Innocency.

2. For in *Leah*, viz. in the fimplicity and lowlinefs arofe the Line of Chrift. A Chriftian fhould ftand at once in Chrifts Image, and in *Adam*'s; fuch was *Jofeph*, therefore *Jacob* moft lov'd him, fprung from his chaft Love to *Rachel*, wherein Chrift had imprinted and revealed himfelf, in this copious Figure of Regeneration.

3. Thence was it *Jofeph* difcover'd all falfhood of his Brethren to his Father, as did Chrift reprove the World for fin.

4. *Jofeph*'s Natural Brethren, in the Type of Chriftendom became his Enemies.

5. His Vifion, that he fhould be a Prince over his Father and Brethren, points at the new Man, undergoing all hatred, Reproach and Perfecution.

6. Sometimes God raifeth up fome honeft pious Ruler, like *Reuben* (the eldeft Brother) to reftrain their Cruelty; yet not fo wholly to oppofe, but divert them, that he may deliver; willing them to throw him into a Pit.

7. *Jofeph* was fold for twenty pieces of Silver, and Chrift for thirty, to fhew the Humanity of Chrift is higher and more perfect than the Humanity of others: For he was not from the Seed of Man, but fprung from the natural Property of the Lights Tincture, which affum'd the Fires Property, viz. the Adamical Soul.

8. A Chriftian is fold into the hands of Men to fuffer; but Chrift not only fuffered in the hands of Men, but gave himfelf up alfo to the wrath of God, thence came the Sweating Blood.

9. The whole acts of *Jofeph* paint out how *Adam*'s Children come to be Chriftians, by being put (by the procefs of Chrift) into the Figure, and be made an Image of Chrift.

10. Alfo how God in the procefs of Chrift, fets Chrift at the Right Hand of God: As *Jofeph*, after he had been brought through the procefs of Chrift, was fet at the Right Hand of *Pharaoh*.

CHAP. LXV. *Of* Judah *and* Thamar, *and how they Figure Chrift and* Adam.

1. THE Figure of *Judah* and *Thamar* interrupts the Hiftory of *Jofeph*, for his reprefents the demeanour of the true Chriftian. Theirs a Chriftians growth out of *Adam*'s Image.

* *Gen.* 38. 1, to 10.

2. * *Judah* Figur'd here the old and new *Adam*, *Thamar* the Earthy, and alfo the new Eve.

3. *Judah* went away from his Brethren; and faw a Canaanitifh Woman, &c. fo did *Adam* go in his Luft, from his Fathers Houfe into the four Elements.

4. *Judah* begot three Sons, the firft he called *Er*, viz. felf-will, fignifying the firft World before the Deluge. The fecond the Mother call'd *Onan*; the World next after the Flood *Onan*, *O no*, my Lord drown me no more. The third fhe call'd *Silah*, a recomprehenfion, viz the time of the Law of Nature offering righteoufnefs to Man, and laying open of Sin which reached till Chrift.

5. *Judah* gave this firft Son a Wife call'd *Thamar*, the incorporated Covenant in the Seed of the Woman, but they look'd only on the outward *Eve*, and committed Whoredom with her, but the inward *Eve* was fruitlefs. Therefore God flew *Er* the old World, and bid the new Mary *Thamar*, and raife up Seed to his Brother, viz. in the Covenant; but the fecond Son brought this Seed into Vanity as did *Nimrod*.

Mysterium Magnum. Part III.

rod, then the Lord flew him also, *viz* Sodom and Gomorrah, and the *Canaanites* whom *Ifrael* drove out. * Then said *Judah* to *Tamar* remain a Widdow till my * Gen. 38.11 third Son *Shelah* be grown up.

6. But the Woman was not given to the Law, but *Judah* Gods Word and Power must raise up this Womans Seed which was fulfilled in *Mary*.

7. * The Pledges given were his Ring, Bracelet and Staff. The Ring is the Soul, * v. 18, 19. the Bracelet the outward Spirit, or *Spiritus Mundi*, the Staff the Body. Then she put on again her Widows Apparel, to do Gods Children after Christ is conceiv'd in great Joy in them, that the noble Seed be not known, they do after this Union ever again into the State of Mourning as of a forsaken Widow.

8. And as *Judith* committed and intended Whoredom, so did the Jewish Priests in their curly and Sacrifices which God bore with, but mixed himself only with the Faith in the Body, Soul and Spirit of Man.

9. Tho' the precious Line of the Covenant preffed in *Perez* through *Judah's* Whoredom, yet it shews Mans Misery that even the Children of God in their corrupt Nature in their Wedlock, have nothing chaft and pure in the sight of God, but is Beftial and a Whoredom.

10. How then should we pray that Chrift would enter with his Heavenly Virgin Seed, and change it into the Paradifical Image again?

11. Such a Figure we fee also in *David* with *Bathsheba*, under whofe Murther and Adultery God set the Line of the Covenant in the middle. And after again in *Solomon* who had so many Wives and Concubines and joyned himself to Idolatrous Women: To shew Chrift should set himself in the midst amongst the Heathen, and tear away their Idolatry, and convert their Hearts to himself.

12. * Of the Twins, the first put forth his Hand and the Midwife tyed a red * Gen. 38.27. Thread on it, but he pulled back his Hand, and the other came out first. First 28, 29, 30. the Humane Nature according to *Adam's* right and self-will puts forth, about this Humanity of Chrift, the red Thread, with shedding of Blood is bound, then muft it return again into the Word, then cometh the inward new Man first. Thus is modellized Chrifts breach through Hell, Death and Wrath of the first Principle.

CHAP. LXVI. *How* Joseph *was sold to* Potiphar. *And of his Chastity and Fear of God.*

1. Potiphar having bought *Joseph*, set him over his whole Houfe; fo muft the Gen. 39. 7, 8, Chriftian let the Government be Chrifts, then shall his twenty pieces of 9, 10. Silver become thirty pieces, *viz* the Adamical Humanity be exalted.

2. The Wife of *Joseph's* Mafter caft her Eyes on *Joseph*, *viz* The Whorifh Eye (the Beftial Luft in the Prifon of Flefh and Blood, wherein is the Serpents fting) affaulteth the new regenerate Child, who muft converfe in this World with fuch impure Lufts; for which caufe the Body muft die and rot, and this Beftial Spirit be deftroy'd; for in it the Devil draweth the Noble Virgin Child, the chaft *Joseph*; who faith, I will not lye with thee, nor be near thee, thou art the Wife of the Spirit of this World.

3. *Joseph* was alone, and she caught him, and he fled and left his Garment, *&c.* Gen. 39. 11, The Soul is alone, the Spirit of God not ftirring in it, and then doth the Devil (by 12, 13, 14, 15. the Whorifh Woman) ftorm the Soul in the Lifes Effence to defile the precious Virgin Child, for the Serpent would copulate with the Soul, but the chaft Divine Child flies *viz* hides it felf in its own Principle, that it comes not near this Whore in Flefh and Blood, thus ftrongly the Divine Purity fhields it felf.

G g g 4. Gods

4. Gods Children have no danger greater than worldly Exaltation, for that is the Throne of Pride, Lust, Cruelty, Wrath, and of the Prince of this World, which is not resisted but by giving up self, as did *Joseph* and *Daniel*.

5. Then his Master put him in Prison, &c. This figureth the final Tryal of the Child of God, who is resigned wholly to God, and dead to himself, and his own will. (As a Prisoner condemn'd expecting Death, knoweth not how to get comfort from any Creature.) But liveth in the unsearchable will, standing again in the first Image is a similitude and spark of the One and the All.

6. It is better not to know than to will according to self, for the will of that which knoweth not, passeth away with the creaturely Life, but the will to self rendeth it self off from the intire will into restless inquietude ; which is the Source and Torment of all the Damned, the strife of the will bringing Enmity.

7. But God is the will of the intirely resigned Man, in him Sin ceaseth, and tho' Gods will of Anger stir in him to bring down Fire as *Elias*, yet all is right; for God doth it by him as an Instrument. Night is turn'd into day, the Curse and Malice of the World into Paradise, as did *Joseph*'s Prison, and *Daniel*'s Den lift them up.

CHAP. LXVII. *Of* Joseph's *Expounding the Dreams of* Pharaoh's *Butler and Baker.*

1. THE Art of Astronomy according to Astrology may Interpret. But *Joseph* got by resignation into the total ; and in it the Divine Eye which sees the ground of all.

2. Every Man hath the Image of his Constellation in himself, and when time comes for kindling the Magick Image to work, the Astral Spirit seeth what Figure it self hath in the Elements : But the Elements affording only a Bestial Figure, the Astral Spirit hath only a Bestial appearance. So a Beast dreameth according to Fancy, as doth a Bestial Animal Man. But there is great difference betwixt the false wicked Soul, which daily willeth and figureth Bestial things, and the pious Divine Soul wherein Gods Spirit is manifest.

3. But the right Visions are, when Mans will resteth in God ; then it seeth with Gods Eyes, for then the Astral Spirit cannot model it self into the fancy.

CHAP. LXVIII. Pharoah *Dreaming saw seven Fat Kine,* &c.

Gen. 41. 1, to 8.

1. THese Dreams were shewn *Pharaoh* out of the Centre of Nature, therefore the Natural Magicians who saw only into the working of Nature in the Constellation understood them not ; but *Joseph* being a Divine *Magus* understood them.

2. The *Egyptian* Art Magick was common, but being abus'd to Witchcraft, was suppress by the Divine *Magia* in the Kingdom of Christ. And it was well, that thereby the Heathens Faith in their Idols, which tho' they had their ground in Nature, were above their Sphere, worshipt for Gods, Might be rooted out of Mens Hearts.

3. But Titular Christendom is surcharg'd with such *Magi* as have only an empty babling of supernatural Magick without natural understanding of God or Nature, but make Images of Faith and Opinions about Religion, being really dumb Idols.

4. Therefore

Mysterium Magnum. Part III.

4. Therefore as it was necessary that the Natural Magick should be discontinued where the Faith of Christ was manifest; so is it now more necessary that the Natural Magi k were again restored, that Titular Christendoms Idols might through the formed Word in Nature, also by new Regeneration be suppressed; not to take up Heathen Idols again, but to shew by the formed Word in Love and Anger with its re-expression, the Essence of all Essences.

5. The seven Fat-Kine and good Ears of Corn, denote the seven Properties of the Eternal Nature in the good and holy Ground, the Lean Kine and Blasted Ears the seven Properties in the Wrath.

The seven Fat and Well-favoured Kine and full Ears, Figure what God made Man at first; and the seven Lean and Blasted, shew what Man made himself to be, * *Gen.*41.14, 15, 16.

And *Joseph* Figureth Mans Restoration by his Deliverance and Advancement.

CHAP. LXIX. *How the Famine driveth* Joseph'*s Brethren to him, and how he shew'd himself to them.*

1. THE 41 of *G n.* Figureth excellently the real Christian, who by Persecution is in Chrifts process: And how he not only forgiveth, but is graciously bountiful to his Persecutors. Also how Sin brings Anxiety on them. And Gods severity against Sin, that the Sinner may dread it and leave it. *Gen.* 42.

2. By *Benjamin* the youngest Brother, is signified the Adamical Humanity, *viz.* that Image of the Heavenly Worlds substance which faded in *Adam.*

3. The particular parts of this 42. Chap are so manifest, that the inlightened Soul, tho' it runs may read its Tendency, Figure or Language.

CHAP. LXX. Jacob'*s Sons went into* Egypt *the second time, and did eat at* Joseph'*s Table, yet knew him not.*

1. THIS 43. Chap. sheweth how the outward Nature bringeth all its Lifes Essences, very timorously, into Christs Death, yet in the end is made willing to enter into the dying of self: As *Jacob* having lost *Joseph* and *Simeon*, is content to give up *Benjamin* also; and this Death it willingly tasts on Divine confidence that it bringeth the will of God with it. *Gen.* 43.

2 This Chapter shews how the Forms of Life, by reason of an evil Conscience tremble before God, as *Jacob*'s Sons before *Joseph.*

3. It shews how God entertains the Soul by feeding him at his Table tho' in a strange Form, then lets him go in Peace, yet afterwards comes with a terrible Tryal; as *Joseph* did them, with his Cup in *Benjamin*'s Sack; which Cup signifieth the Lords Testament.

I restrain my Extracts to this brevity; because the total of the Excellent Discourse on this Chapter is so evident an Exposition, as if written by the Sun-Beams.

CHAP. LXXI. Of Joseph's Cup being put into Benjamin's Sack.

1. *Joseph's* Brethren stand here in the Figure of the truly converted Christian. *Joseph* of the Wrath of God in Nature. The Cup in that of Christ's Sufferings. Thus, *Joseph's* Brethren, viz. The Christian is by the Wrath of God in the fleshly Evil Nature, the Evil World and the Devil accused to have stoln the Silver Cup of Christ's Sufferings, who though Innocent, do give themselves up to suffer Bonds, Servitude, Shame and Death. Christ saith, He came not to send Peace on Earth; but Strife, &c.

2. Those of our own Family in Flesh and Blood, must be Enemies, as a Tree groweth in heat, and Cold, and Storms, so in Strife groweth the Tree of Pearl.

3. The Cup's being uppermost in the Sack, denotes Gods Peoples Sufferings to be uppermost *(viz.)*, on all *(viz.)* continually.

From the 10th Verse to the 37th, is a most profound convincing Discourse of the use of Strife.

Gen. 44. 7, 8, 9, 10. 4. Joseph's Brethren answered the Steward, him with whom the Cup is found let him be put to Death, and we will be my Lords Servants. Shewing, 1. How ready the Man who received some Grace is to justifie himself. They would not be thought Thieves, though they had stoln even *Joseph* himself. 2. How confident they are in their justification, He that did it should die, and they all would be his Servants.

5. The Christian presently thinks he should be exempt from Sufferings, and all wrong him. But his guilt standeth open before God's Righteousness, who requireth Man to be in the imitation and process of Christ in his Sufferings and Death; Therefore hath the Christian no Excuse when God causeth him to be laid hold on in Anger by his Steward the Children of this World as a Thief, Novellist, Enthusiast Heretick which though imputed to them wrongfully from the World, yet is he guilty of all Adamical Sins, and suffereth in Christ's Process justly, what Christ suffered innocently.

Gen. 44. 11, 12, 13. 6. And they hasted and searched every Mans Sack, beginning at the Eldest, and the Cup was found in *Benjamin's* Sack, and they rent their Cloaths and returned. When *Adam* sinned, the Law fetched him back into the City, viz. The Earth out of which the Body proceeded, there did Righteousness search all the Natural Properties, beginning at the first Form of Nature, but the Cup of *Joseph*, viz. of Christ, was found only in *Benjamin's* (viz.) in the youngest Brother's Sack (viz.) the Youngest, the Word of the inspoken or inspired Grace.

v. 14, 15, 16, 17. 7. And *Judah* went with his Brethren, and they fell down before *Joseph*, &c. The Law having brought Man back, cannot answer, but yields. But God would not have future *Israel* to be his Servant, the first Forms, viz. in outward Worship only, but *Benjamin* the inward heavenly Worlds Substance.

8. *Judah* who was Surety for *Benjamin*, his Pleading so hard that he durst not go home without him, let he bring his Fathers grey hairs, &c. Shews, That if the Adamical Man should go into Paradice without Christ's Life and Substance, the Life's Nature would not be manifest, viz. would not live in the Kingdom of Heaven.

CHAP.

CHAP. LXXII. *How* Joseph *manifested himself before his Brethren.*

1. BEcaufe the Law could not bring Man back into Paradife, the great *Joseph* (of *Gen.* 45. 1, meer Compaffion, feeing Mans Mifery) could no longer withhold, but 2, 3. cried, Let every one go forth (*viz.*) When Jefus would manifeft his higheft Mercy, the Law, Ceremonies and Mans Ability, and will muft depart.

2. Then *Joseph* wept aloud, fo that the Egyptians (*Pharaoh's* People) heard him, (*viz.*) the Weeping and Compaffion of Jefus founded to the Heathen and Nations, and he faid, *I am Joseph your Brother ; Doth my Father yet live?* (*viz.*) I am Jefus in thee : is the Father's Nature(*viz.* a Breath of the Divine Life)yet in the Soul ? And they could not anfwer him ; nor can the Soul, for the Soul's own will is terrified to Death, there is a gnawing guilt making him Dumb.

3. Then faith *Joseph*, Come near, be not careful, nor think that I am angry that you fold me ; for God fent me to preferve you alive (*viz.*) I am no more angry that I have been fold into thy Death ; for it was, that I might nourifh thee.

4. There will yet be five years of Famine (*viz.*) the Divine hunger will yet remain in thy five Senfes.

5. Make hafte, let my Father and all his Children and Cattle come to me, *&c. Gen.* 45. 11, (*viz.*) thy Nature, thy whole Life, Converfations, all thy Thoughts, thy Temporal Eftate. 12,13,14,15.

6. Your Eyes, as alfo the Eyes of my Brother *Benjamin*, fee that it is I, that fpeak to you (*viz.*) your inward Eyes, and the Eyes of the new Man ; for they fee through the outward Sences as the Sun pierceth through Glafs, and yet it remaineth Glafs ftill.

7. And *Joseph* fell about *Benjamin's* Neck, and wept, and kiffed them all (*viz.*) when Chrift in the inward heavenly Subftance which faded in *Adam* is manifefted : Jefus, with his weeping love (Gods great fweetnefs) kiffeth the creaturely Souls Effences: whereby it re-obtaineth its life, and fpeaketh with God in Chrift Jefus.

8. And when the report came to *Pharaoh* it pleas'd him well. And he commanded Chariots fhould be fent to fetch *Jacob*, and all his into *Egypt* (*viz.*) when Chrift's Voice foundeth in the Soul, the report thereof preffeth into the Fathers Property of Fire, which is therewith pleafed, and Chariots are fent (*viz.*) the Spirit in the Word, which bring it to Paradife.

9. And he fent a prefent for his Father, (*viz.*) his Flefh and Blood, wherewith the Soul feafteth.

10. The five fuits to *Benjamin*, the five Wounds.

11. The thirty Pieces of Silver given him, the Gifts of Chrift, wherewith the Chriftian muft Trade.

12. The ten Affes loaden with the choice things of *Egypt*, the ten Commandments in the Law of Nature.

13. The ten Affes loaden with Corn; the ten Forms of the foulifh and natural Fire life.

14. The Food to fpend on the Way the Word of God, which the poor old *Adam* muft eat, that he may live.

15. He commands they fall not out by the Way, but walk in love and peace to Paradife.

16. And they came to their Father, and told him of the great Glory of *Joseph*, his Prefent and his Words ; but *Jacob* believed them not, but when he faw the Chariots, his Spirit revived, (*viz.*) when Chrifts Apoftles were loaden with his Prefents,

Mysterium Magnum. Part III.

sents, which they carried to their Relations (*viz.*) those who were in the Kingdom of Nature; they believed not those exceeding great things, till the Chariots of the Holy Ghost came and then they revive and live, and say it is enough, I will go into repentance that I may see my Saviour before I die.

CHAP. LXXIII. *How* Jacob, *and his Children, and all his,* &c. *went into* Egypt.

1. Jacob is the Figure of the new Man, having received the Present, (*i.e.*) the earnest of Christs love and the Chariots of *Joseph* viz the Holy Ghost; goeth to *Egypt* (*i.e.*) into Repentance with all his Children (*i.e.*) his Powers, and coming to *Beersheba*, the founding Voice of his heart, sacrificeth (*viz.*) his Soul.

2. The Powers proceeding out of his own Loins are 66. the mystical number of the Beast; and himself *Joseph* and *Joseph*'s two Sons make 70 the Number of *Babel*.

3. This going forth, is an Image of the last Exit or true Christians departure out of *Babel*, in the end of the Reign of the Beast and Whore. The signal Star with the Chariot of *Joseph*, are already appear'd.

Gen. 46. 28, 29, 30.
4. *Israel* sends *Judah* before him to *Joseph* (*viz.*) the incorporated Covenant of God in Man to *Joseph* and *Goshen*, the rest in Christ.

5. And when the heavenly *Joseph* meeteth *Jacob*, the old Adamical Man, he falleth about his Neck, *viz.* his desire and longing, and filleth it with Tears, shed in his Sufferings leading to Victory and Eternal Joy. Then saith the Natural Man, now would I willingly die (*viz.*) give up all my right and willing of Vanity now, that the new Man in Christ is manifest in me

Gen. 46. 31, 32, 33, 34.
6. *Joseph* saith, *I will go up and tell* Pharaoh, *&c.* Christ (*viz.*) The word of Love and Grace, which is come from the Father into our Humanity, speaketh the word of the Natural Human Life, into the Eternal Word of the Father; which is here called telling the King. That is, reconciled the Rent made, by the natural speaking of Self and Vanity in the Human Word of the Father's Anger, with and again unto his Love and Kingdom of Joy.

7. They were Herdsmen, and such were an Abomination to *Pharaoh* and the Egyptians, (*viz.*) to Gods Majesty and Holy Power. The Animal Soul in the Spirit of this World, hath awaked many hundred Beasts (*viz.*) Lusts, which it must be conversant with and rule.

8. They were placed apart in *Goshen* (*viz.*) in the outward Nature, yet in the Blessing, and should dwell near God, but a Principle is the Distinction, as time and Eternity.

9. And *Joseph* willed them to say to *Pharaoh*, Thy Servants are Herdsmen; so must all say as well Potentates as Beggars, Priests, *&c.* We cannot stand and subsist before thee, O Holy God; we are but Herdsmen, even from our Youth (*viz.*) from *Adam* till now, we keep and manage our bestial Property. Let thy servants find Grace in thy sight to dwell before thee in this *Goshen*.

CHAP. LXXIV. Jacob *and five of* Joseph*'s Brethren set before* Pharaoh. Egypt *Sold for Corn.*

Gen. 47. 1, 2, 3, 4, 5, 6.
1. Pharaoh standeth here in the Figure of the Eternal Father, *Jacob* of old *Adam* *Joseph*'s five youngest Brethren of the five Sences in the Properties of Life.

So

Mysterium Magnum. Part III.

So should we humble our selves before God, thy Servants are but Herdsmen, &c. Then saith the Eternal Father to Christ, Is this thy Father *Adam* ? are these thy Brethren according to the Humanity ? The Kingdom of Heaven and of Nature standeth open : If any of them be Expert, set them over my Cattle, viz. into the Apostolick Office, to feed my Flock.

2. *Jacob* blesseth *(viz.* thanketh*) Pharaoh,* and acknowledgeth his own Evil and anxiety in the cares and disquietness of this Life.

3. The Famine in *Egypt* and *Canaan,* figureth the poor fallen Man in Body and Soul, wither'd by Gods Anger : *Joseph's* Corn, the Divine Word of Grace : The Money, the creaturely word of the Human Life : The Beasts given when the Money was spent, the Image-like Property in Man's Life. Thus the fallen Man bringeth the heavenly *Joseph* his imaginary, fictitious, formal and customary Prayers, meant by the Money. But when anguish of Conscience withereth up the Hope drawn from such cold Prayer, the Famine prevaileth, and forceth to bring the Beasts and Cattle, viz earthy Desires, Self-wit and Subtlety. *Gen.* 47. 13, 14, 15, 16, 17.

4. They gave themselves and their Land to *Pharaoh,* &c. This figureth the real, earnest resignation, of Body, Soul, and whole Interest to God, to receive Food from Christ. *v.* 18, 19.

5. So whole *Egypt* became *Pharaoh's,* but the Land of the Priests he bought not, &c. *v.* 20, 21, 22.

6. In *Adam* all Men became untrusty, but Christ hath bought the whole Nature, and given us to God again, but the Priests Fields were left to them for a Possession (viz.) the incorporated Word of Grace, the Temple of Christ, the City of God, which no Man can Sell, Pawn or Engage by Oaths, for it belongeth to the Eternal one ; this inward Man, God willeth Man should keep.

7. Four parts shall be yours, but the fifth shall be *Pharaoh's, (viz.)* This Seed shall cherish the four Elements of the Body, and four Properties of the Souls Firelife, but the fifth, (viz.) The Love-fire in the Light, is the Lords, herein is the Soul an Angel, and Gods Kingdom of Divine Joy is in us. *v.* 23, 24, 25, 26.

8. The Priests Field, the heavenly Worlds Substance, Christ buyeth not with his Blood as the averted Soul was bought ; for that never received the *Turba* in it ; but in the Fall disappeared, and the Soul was blind concerning it ; into this was the Word inspoken again in Paradise, and is filled with Christs Flesh and Blood. It is in the Soul, through the Soul and of the Soul, but hath another Principle, as Light hath than Fire, from which Fire and Light proceeds Air, and a dewy Water which again nourisheth the Fire.

9. The History of the Five Books of *Moses* is this, in the Figure. The Exit out of *Canaan,* and return into *Canaan,* shews, how Man went out of Paradise to be a Bondslave of Gods Anger, and there be afflicted, persecuted and tormented : and how the right Adamical Man should, with great Hosts and Armies and much purchased Goods (got in the Divine Operation) enter again into the Promised Land.

CHAP. LXXV. *How* Jacob *blesseth the two Sons of* Joseph, *and preferreth the Youngest,* &c.

1. Joseph brought *Manasseh* in his left Hand towards *Jacob's* right Hand, and *Ephraim* (his youngest) in his right Hand towards *Jacob's* left Hand. These two signifie the inward Man : the Eldest, the fiery Soul : the Youngest, the Spirit of the Soul, the Power of the Light, the second Principle, That with its Love it might be set.

Mysterium Magnum. Part III.

set before God's left Hand (viz.) his Anger, and break the Serpents Head. The Soul he setteth before his right Hand, to receive the Blessing, but that could not be. *Israel* stretched his right Hand and put upon *Ephraim*'s Head, God would not give the Government to the first Birth (viz.) to the fiery Soul seeing it had turned away its will from God; but laid his Hand of Omnipotency on the Image of the Light, so was the second Birth uppermost in the Dominion.

Gen. 48, 17.   2. *Jacob* gave *Joseph* (above his Brethren) a piece of Ground which he got from the *Amorites* by his Sword and by his Bow, which signifieth, Christendom got by the Sword of the Spirit of Christ.

CHAP. LXXVI.

THIS Chapter (though excellent) is with part of the 77th referr'd to the Abridgment the Author himself makes of all the Twelve in the close of the 77th Chapter.

CHAP. LXXVII.

1. Ruben beareth the Image or Figure of the first World, who was fickle though in the greatest Dominion.
2. *Simeon* beginneth with *Noah*, and hath *Levi*, viz. *Sem* with him: but *Simeon* was the Sword of *Ham* and *Japhet*.
3. *Levi* beginneth with *Moses*, whose Sword cuts very sharply.
4. *Judah* beginneth under the Prophets, and is manifest in the Incarnation of Christ.
5. *Zebulon* cohabiteth (in and) with the Kingdom of Christ, representing Christendom, who sits pleasantly; for she is a new Love.
6. *Issichar* was the time of Christendoms being settled in Rest and Dominion, yet must bear the Cross of Christ, and was about 300 years after Christ.
7. *Dan* began the Potency of Christendom, when they set up Kings. Emperors, Popes and Pompous consecrated Places. The Adder and Serpent sate in Judicature, cloak'd under Christ's Name. Then saith the Spirit of Christ, I wait for thy Salvation, O Lord; now is Truth bitten in the heels.
8. *Gad* beginneth the time of Universities and Schools, when with might of Arms, Men set up Antichrist in Christ's Chair by babling Disputes; so bring in Tradition and Canons, making the Tail to be the Head 800 years since.
9. *Asher* began the time of flattering Antichrist for fat Bread, about 600 years ago and nearer.
10. *Naphtaly* beginneth the searching deep Disputes about God's Council and Predestination, that Men might cover themselves with a Mantle of plausible Maxims, acute Logick, this hath continued to this time.
11. *Joseph* beginneth Christ's remanifestation, he Ejecteth the Adder, and *Joseph*'s Brethren must now be ashamed of their Unfaithfulness and Selling him, for now their subtilty, craft, &c. and *Babylon* is fallen, and become the Habitation of Abominable Beasts; but *Joseph* flourisheth.
12. *Benjamin* beginneth with *Joseph*'s Evening to divide the Spoil of the first Christendom, he is the first and last time, he beginneth to devour Antichrist as a Wolf, yet is but a Wolf.

So

Mysterium Magnum. Part III.

So Jacob, having finished all these Sayings, drew up his Feet on the Bed and departed. Shewing, that when God will recall the unfolded Nature in the strife of time into himself, strife shall cease, and be drawn into the Temperature.

CHAP. LXXVIII. Jacob's *Burial in* Canaan *accompanied with all the Children of* Israel, *and many of the* Egyptians.

1. SHEWS Christ's powerful Exit hence to Paradise: and that when Christ will bring home his Bride, he will have many of the Heathen with him also.
2. Their Weeping and Mourning shew (in the *Magi*) Eternal Joy.
3. *Joseph's* Brethrens fear, and falling down before him, and *Joseph's* weeping and gracious Answer, not only of Pardon, but to provide for them and theirs: is a mighty comfort to *Joseph's* Brethren (*viz.*) to the Repenting Sinner, under Anguish, for his first committed Sins: who faith, they shall not only be Pardoned, but turn'd into the best.
4. *Joseph's* Desire of an Oath, to carry his Bones out of *Egypt* to his Fathers, signifies God's Oath in Paradise, that Christ would come again to his Brethren, and stay forever with them. *Amen.*

Gen. 50. 15, 16,17,18, 19,20, 21.

This was the Author's Eighteenth Book.

FINIS.

Hhh Some

Some Brief Remarks concerning the Life and Conversation of the Blessed Jacob Behmen, Collected out of the Relations published concerning him.

Jacob Behmen was Born in the year 1575. at a Town in the upper *Lusatia* named *Old Seidenburg* distant from *Gorlitts* about a Mile and a half, his Parents were of the poorer sort, yet of sober and honest demeanour. His Education and Breeding was suitable to their Wealth; his first Imployment being the care of the common Cattel amongst the rest of the Youths of the Town: But when grown Elder, he was placed at School, where he learned to read and write; and was from thence put an Apprentice to a Shoemaker in *Gorlitts*, with whom having served his Time in the year 1594, he Married one *Katherine* the Daughter of *John Hunshman* a Citizen of *Gorlitts*; by her he had four Sons, living in the state of Matrimony thirty years: His Sons he did in his Life time place to several honest Trades. He fell sick in *Silesia* of a hot burning Ague, but was at his desire brought to *Gorlitts*, and there died the 18th of *November*, 1624. being in the 50th year of his Age, and was Buried in the Church-yard. A Hieroglyphical Monument was Erected over his Grave by a Friend, which had remained but a while, but was razed and embezelled by the rude Hands of the envious: As to his Personage, I may truly say it was not such as was Amiable among the Children of Men, yet so hath God in his Providence frequently disposed his Gifts, and made Stewards thereof, such as in Mans Eye could not by the Symmetry of Face, and composure of Behaviour, take upon trust the meanest Office.

He was Lean, and of small Stature; he had a low Forehead, his Temples prominent, somewhat Hawk-nosed, his Eyes Grey and very Azure, his Beard thin and short, his Voice low, a pleasing Speech, Modest in his Behaviour, and Humble in his Conversation. Concerning his second Birth, and what was in order thereto remarkable, we find many things therein observable and strange, which may peradventure bring some distaste to Persons not versed in the general Providence of God, who believe that he hath confined his Mercy and Bounty to their Ministrations, and like wilful Children, are peevish if their Father use Indulgence to any but themselves, or out of his usual order.

Whilst he was a Herd Boy, in the heat of mid-day retiring from his Play-fellows to a little stony Crag, hard by, called the Lands Crown, where the natural Situation of the Rock had made a seeming Inclosure of some part of the Mountain, finding an entrance into it, he went in, and saw there a great wooden Vessel full of Money, at which sight, being in a sudden Astonishment, he did in haste retire, not moving his Hand thereinto, and came and related his Fortune to the rest of the Boys, who coming up along with him, sought often, and with much diligence an entrance, but never found any; tho' some years after, a Forreign Artist, as *Jacob* himself related, skill'd in the finding out such Magick Treasures, took away the same, and thereby much inricht himself, yet perished by an Infamous Death, that Treasure being Lodged there, and it seems laid covered with a Curse to the Finder and Taker away.

Our Saviour had tendred him the World and the Glory thereof, which was a

fair

Extracts of the Life of Jacob Behmen.

fair offer, had the condition been any thing tolerable, tho' I assuredly believe few obtain it at less rate.

When he had been an Apprentice some short time, his Master and Mistress being abroad, there came a Stranger to the Shop, of a reverent and grave Countenance, yet in mean Apparel, and taking up a pair of Shoes, desired to buy the same; the Boy being scarce got higher than the keeping of the Shop would not presume to set a Rate for the same, but told him his Master and Mistress were not within, and himself durst not Adventure the Sale of any thing without their order.

But the Stranger being very importunate, he offered them at a price, which if he got, he was certain would save himself harmless in the parting from them; supposing also thereby to be rid of the importunate Chapman, but the old Man paid down the Money, took the Shoes, and departed from the Shop a little way, where standing still, with a loud and an earnest voice, he called, *Jacob, Jacob,* come forth: The Boy within hearing the Voice, came forth in much afrightment, at first amazed at the Strangers familiar compellation of him, by his Christian Name, but recollecting himself he went to him; the Man with a severe but friendly Countenance fixing his Eyes upon him (which were bright and sparkling) took him by his Right Hand, and said to him, Jacob *thou art little, but shalt be great, and become another Man, such a one as at whom the World shall wonder. Therefore be Pious, fear God, and reverence his Word ; read diligently the Holy Scriptures, wherein you have Comfort and Instruction ; for thou must indure much Misery, and Poverty, and suffer Persecution, but be couragious and persevering, for God loves, and is gracious unto thee ;* and therewithal pressing his Hand, he lookt with a bright sparkling Eye fixed in his Face, and departed.

This Prediction took deep impression in *Jacob*'s Mind, made him bethink himself and grow serious in his Actions, keep his Thoughts moving in consideration of the caution he had received from that Man of such uncouth demeanour, so that from thence forward, he did much more frequent the publick hearing of the Word, and profited well therein, in the outward Reformation of his Life, and seriously considering with himself that Speech of our Saviour, *Luke* 11. 13. *My Father which is in Heaven will give the Spirit to him that asketh him.* He was thereby throughly awakened in himself, and put forward to desire that promised Comforter, and continuing in that earnestness, he was at last, as is his own Expression, environ'd with a Divine Light for seven days together, and stood in the highest Contemplation and Kingdom of Joys; and this hapned to him while he was with his Master in the Country about the Affairs of his Vocation.

When the Vision and Revelation was pass'd by him, he grew more and more accurately attentive to his Duty to God and his Neighbour, frequented the Church carefully, read the Scriptures, and lived in all Observance to outward Ministrations. Scurrilous and Blasphemous words he would rebuke, even in his own Master, who was somewhat Intemperate of his Tongue, and from day to day continuing upon his Watch, he endeavoured after the Christian Growth, becoming by his contrariety of Manners, a Scorn and Derision to the World; and at the last his own Master being not able to bear a Reprover so near Home in that Relation, set him at Liberty, with free permission to seek his Livelihood as him best liked.

After this about the year 1600. in the Twenty fifth year of his Age, he was a second time surrounded by the Divine Light, and replenished with the Heavenly Knowledge; insomuch as going abroad into the Fields, to a Green before *Ney's* Gate, at *Gorlitts*, he there sat down, and viewing the Herbs and Grass of the Field, in his Inward Light he saw into their Essences, Use and Properties, which was discovered to him by their Lineaments, Figures, and Signatures.

Extracts of the Life of Jacob Behmen.

In like manner did he behold the whole Creation, and from that Fountain of Revelation wrote his Book *De Signatura Rerum*.

In the unfolding these Mysteries, before his Understanding he had an over-measure of Joy, yet returned home and took care of his Family, and lived in great peace and silence, scarce intimating to any these wonderful things that had befaln him, till in the year 1610, being a third time taken into this Light, left the Mysteries reveal'd unto him should pass through him as a stream he took Pen and Ink in hand, and rather for a Memorial, than intending any Publication, he writ the first Book of his call'd *Aurora*, or the Morning Redness.

The Book being found about him by a Man of great Quality with whom he convers'd, was received with that desire that he immediately disjoyned it, and caused it to be copyed out in a few hours. Thus, contrary to the Authors intention, it became publick, and after a while, fell into the hands of one *Gregory Richter*, the Superintendant of *Gorlitts*, who making use (as is usual) of his Pulpit, and the Liberty granted him of speaking without a Gainsayer, to revile what and whom he pleased, he endeavoured to stir up the Magistracy to exercise their Jurisdiction in rooting out this supposed Church Weed.

And this he did with so much vehemency and pretence of Godly Zeal, that the Senate took some notice of it, and convened *Jacob Behmen* before them, seizing his Book, and admonishing him to imploy his Mind in the Affairs of his Trade, and for the future leave off the writing any more Books, wherein he saw was so much offence.

This occasion brought this Man first into publick notice, for, at the hearing of the Business, such was the Unchristian Heat and Distemper of the Minister, and so much the meekness of *Jacob Behmen*, that it gave great advantage to his repute, and credit to that inward School, from whence he came out so well taught.

For afterwards this very Book which the Senate had seized on, was by themselves presented to the Electoral Court Marshal at *Dresden*, when he came to *Gorlitts*, and was afterward by him sent to *Amsterdam*, from whence I believe the first Impression, came forth.

Upon the command of the Senate, he abstained from writing seven years, at the end of which a new Motion from on high seizing upon him, and taking captive these rational Humane Prohibitions that held him bound, he again writes; out of what Principle, and how moved, his own words can best express.

Art (saith he) hath not written here, neither was there any time to consider how to set it punctually down, according to the right understanding of the Letters, but all was ordered according to the direction of the Spirit, which often went in haste; so that in many words Letters may be wanting, and in some places a Capital Letter for a word; so that the Penmans Hand, by reason he was not accustomed to it, did often shake; and tho' I could have written in a more accurate, fair, and plain manner, yet the reason was this, that the burning Fire did often force forward with speed, and the Hand and Pen must hasten directly after it, for it cometh and goeth as a sudden Shower: And further he saith, I can write nothing of my self, but as a Child which neither knoweth nor understandeth any thing, which neither hath ever been Learnt, but only that which the Lord vouchsafeth to know in me according to the measure as himself manifests in me.

For I never desired to know any thing of the Divine Mystery, much less understood I the way to seek and find it; I knew nothing of it, as it is the condition of poor Laymen in their Simplicity.

I sought only after the Heart of Jesus Christ, that I might hide my self therein from the wrathful Anger of God, and the violent assaults of the Devil; and I besought

Extracts of the Life of Jacob Behmen.

sought the Lord earnestly for his Holy Spirit and his Grace, that he would please to Bless and Guide me in him, and take that away from me which did turn me from him; and I resign'd my self wholly to him, that I might not live to my own will, but his; and that he only might lead and direct me, to the end I might be his Child in his Son Jesus.

In this my earnest and christian seeking and desire (and wherein I suffered many a shrewd repulse, but at last resolved rather to put my self in hazard than give over and leave off) The Gate was opened to me, that in one quarter of an Hour I saw and knew more than if I had been many years together at an University, at which I did exceedingly admire, and thereupon turn'd my praise to God for it.

For I saw and knew the Being of all Beings, the Byss and the Abyss, and the Eternal Generation of the Holy Trinity, the Descent and Original of the World, and of all Creatures through the Divine Wisdom; I knew and saw in my self all the three Worlds, namely, 1. The Divine Angelical Paradisical; 2. And the Dark World the Original of the Nature to the Fire; 3. And thirdly, The External and Visible World, being of a Procreation or Extern Birth, from both the Internal and Spiritual Worlds; and I saw and knew the whole working Essence, in the Evil and in the Good, and the Mutual Original, and Existence of each of them; and likewise how the fruitful Bearing Womb of Eternity brought forth. *Ep. Paul 1 Cor. 2. 10; τὰ βάθη τοῦ Θεȣ̃. The Depths of God.*

So that I did not only greatly wonder at it, but did also exceedingly rejoice, and presently it came powerfully into my Mind, to set the same down in Writing, for a Memorial for my self, (albeit) I could very hardly apprehend the same, in my External Man, and express it with the Pen. Yet however I must begin to labour in these great Mysteries, as a Child that goes to School; I saw it as in a great deep in the Internal.

For I had a through view of the Universe, as in a Chaos, wherein all things are couched, and wrapt up, but it was impossible for me to explicate the same.

Yet it opened it self in me, from time to time, as in a young Plant; albeit the same was with me, for the space of Twelve years, and it was as it were breeding, and I found a powerful instigation within me, before I could bring it forth into External form of Writing; and whatever I could apprehend with the External Principle of my Mind, the same I wrote down.

But however afterward the Sun did shine on me a good while, but not constantly, for the Sun did hide it self, and then I knew not, nor well understood my own labour. So that Man must acknowledge that his Knowledge is not his own, but from God, who manifests the Ideas of Wisdom, to the Soul of Man in what measure he pleaseth.

In the Guidance of this Light, and from this Principle, he wrote these following Works.

1. He wrote the first Book called *Aurora*. 1612.
2. Of the Three Principles. 1619.
3. Of the Threefold Life of Man. 1620.
4. Answers to the Forty Questions of the Soul.
5. { Of the Incarnation of Jesus Christ. Of the Suffering, Death and Resurrection of Christ. Of the Tree of Faith.
6. Of the Six Points Great and Small.
7. Of the Heavenly and Earthly Mystery.
8. Of the last times to *P. K.*
9. *Signatura Rerum.* 1621.
10. A Consolatory Book of the four Complexions.
11. An Apology to *Balthasar Tilken*, in two parts.
12. Considerations upon *Isaias Stiefel's* Book.

13. Of

Extracts of the Life of Jacob Behmen.

13. Of true Repentance. 1622.
14. Of true Refignation.
15. A Book of Regeneration.
16. A Book of Predeftination and Election of God. 1623.
17. A Compendium of Repentance.
18. *Myfterium Magnum*, or an Expofition upon *Genefis*.
19. A Table of the Principles, or a Key of his Writings. 1624.
20. Of the Super-fenfual Life.
21. Of the Divine Vifion. ( )
22. Of the Two Teftaments of Chrift, Baptifm and the Supper.
23. A Dialogue between the Enlightned and Uninlightned Soul.
24. An Apology for the Book of true Repentance, againft a Pamphlet of the Primate of *Gorlitts*, *Gregory Richter*.

25. A Book of 177 Theofophick Queftions ( )
26. An Epitome of the *Myfterium Magnum*.
27. The Holy Weeks, or the Prayer-Book ( )
28. A Table of the Divine Manifeftation, or an Expofition of the Threefold Werld.
29. Of the Errors of the Sects of *Ezekiel Meeths*, or an Apology to *Efaias Stefel*.
30. A Book of the laft Judgment.
31. Certain Letters to divers Perfons, at divers times, with certain Keys for fome hidden words.

The Books which the Author finifhed not are marked with this fign ( ).

The publication of his firft Book called *Aurora*, or the Morning Rednefs, brought from all parts great refort to him of Learned Men, and fuch as were experienced in the knowledge of Nature with whom much converfing he got the ufe of thofe Greek and Latine words that are frequent in his Works, himfelf often complaining of the Barrennefs of his Mother Tongue to bring forth into fignificant Expreffion that Notion that lay clear and orderly in his Mind, and frequently wifhed that he had in his Youth made himfelf mafter of fome other Language from whence he might perhaps have commanded a Word or Phrafe of great ufe, and conveniency, to the unfolding what he had to propofe.
Of thofe Learned Men that converfed with him in greateft familiarity, was one *Balthazar Walter*, this Gentleman was a *Silefian* by Birth, by Profeffion a Phyfician, and had in the fearch of the Ancient Magick Learning, Travell'd through *Egypt*, *Syria*, and the *Araby's*, and there found fuch fmall remainders of it, that he returned empty and unfatisfied into his own Country, where hearing of this Man, he repaired to him, and having obtained Acquaintance with him rejoyced, that at laft he had found at home in a poor Cottage that for which he had Travelled fo far, and mift of fatisfaction ; then he went to the feveral Univerfities in *Germany*, and did there collect fuch queftions concerning the Soul as were thought and accounted impoffible to be refolved fundamentally and convincingly, of which he made a Catalogue, being in number forty, and fent them to him, from whom he received Anfwers to his fatisfaction. (which Anfwers are publick in many Languages) from whence, and from frequent Difcourfes with him, he was fo fatisfied that he ftaid there three Months, and profeffed that he had received more folid Anfwers to his curious Scruples, than he had found amongft the beft Wits of thofe more promifing Climates, and for the future defifted from following Rivulets, fince God had opened a Fountain at his own Door.

King Charles *the Firft his Opinion of* Jacob Behmen.

The Tranflator of the faid Anfwers into Englifh gives us the following Relation, That when that Book was firft printed he endeavoured by a Friend to prefent one of them to His Majefty King *Charles* that then was, who vouchfafed the perufal of it: About a Month after was defired to fay what he thought of the Book, who anfwered that the publifher in Englifh feemed to fay of the Author, that he was

no

Extracts of the Life of Jacob Behmen.

no Scholar, and if he were not, he'd believe that the Holy Ghost was now in Men, but if he were a Scholar, it was one of the best Inventions that ever he read. I need not add the Censure of any other Person.

It is a strange thing to see how Nature, Reason and Humane Wit have busied themselves to understand and comprehend this Divine Wisdom, how many have been distracted in the search of it, and forced back in their bold attempts, into foolish Infatuations, Madness and stupid Brutisms.

Others through Ignorance or Malice, or both, have mistaken the true Sons of Wisdom, traducing them as being agitated by a power Diabolical, Wicked and Detestable, or else as Impostors and Deceivers of the worst sort. Thus the Pharisees concerning our Saviour, Say we not well thou art a Samaritan and hast a Devil? So loth is Humane Reason to submit to, or conceive a possibility of that perfect Wisdom and Power, that is brought forth through Self-denial and Death, to the Glory of him that is the Father of it.

Such like measure received *Jacob Behmen* in his day, for the appearing of that unusual Knowledge, and deep Revelation of Mysteries, in a Vessel so contemptible to the Magnificent Mind of Man, brought hard Censures upon him, from the stupid World; which appeared one time most especially; the manner thus.

Sitting by himself in his House, one knock'd at his Door, to which he repairing, when he had opened it, a Person of a mean Stature, of a sharp and stern look, saluted him courteously, congratulating to him that great and wonderful Knowledge he had received, and humbly made known to him, that he heard that he was Blest with a singular Spirit, the like whereof had not lately appeared among the Children of Men; that it was a Humane and Friendly Duty, lying upon every Man, to impart the good things vouchsafed him, to his needy Neighbour, and himself was now a needy Petitioner, that he would yield some of that Spirit to him; in which request if he pleased to gratifie him, he would in such things wherein he abounded, give a fitting recompence, making a Covert tender of some Moneys, to satisfie his Necessities, to whom *Jacob Behmen* replyed with thanks, That he did count himself unworthy of the esteem of having these greater Gifts, and Arts, as was by him imagined, and found only in himself, an intire Love to his Neighbour, and simple perseverance in the upright Belief, and Faith in God, and for any other Indowments beyond these, he neither had them, nor esteemed them; much less (as his words seemed to intimate) enjoyed the Society of any Familiar Spirit.

But (saith he) if there be in you that desire of obtaining the Spirit of God, you must as I have done, do earnest Repentance, and pray the Father from whom all good Gifts do come, and he will give it, and it will lead you into all Truth.

This foolish Man contemning this plain Instruction, became somewhat uncivilly importunate, and began with words of Magick Conjuration, to force the supposed Familiar Spirit from *Jacob Behmen*, at which his Boldness and Folly, *Jacob Behmen* being not a little moved in Spirit, took him by the right Hand, and look'd him sternly in the Face, intending an Imprecation; at which this Exorcist trembling, and amazed, asked forgiveness, whereupon *Jacob Behmen* remitted his Zeal, dehorting him earnestly from that Simonian and Diabolical practice, permitting him in hopes of future amendment, to depart in peace.

Doctor *C. Weisner* in a Letter to his Friend gives the following Account of his Acquaintance with *Jacob Behmen*, and of the Troubles that befel him at *Gorlitts*.

To answer your friendly Request, in attesting what I know for Truth concerning

Extracts of the Life of Jacob Behmen.

ing the Blessed Man *Jacob Behmen*, I am no less willing, than in the Duty of a Christian obliged.

My Acquaintance with him began about *July* 1618. at *Lauben*, by means of two common Friends to us both, the one a Tradesman by Name *Liberius Schnoller*, the other was one *Solomon Schroter*, a young Minister, his Wifes Brother, both Studious of his Writings, and such as had by real Experiment found the Truth of what he affirms about those extraordinary Illuminations God usually imparts to Souls that in a way of Humility and Obedience do with Ardent and unwearied Prayers desire his Spirit.

The occasion of our first converse came from a prejudicate Mind I had against him, being Tutor to the Sons of Mr. *Balthasar Tilcken* then his Enemy, whence expressing in too harsh Language, (which God forgive me) my dislike of the Man and his Tenets; these Friends upon his coming to *Lauben*, desired my Company with him to an amicable Conference about my Dissatisfactions, wherein his solid Answers and Mildness in bearing with that disputing, caviling frowardness the Schools had infected me with, struck so deep into my Conscience, as I could not longer resist the Spirit and Power of Christ in his Discourses, but yielded up my self Truth's Prisoner; for which I ever Praise God.

But as for what passed 'twixt him and his Antagonist *Gregory Richter*, Minister of *Gorlitz*, and Superintendent of that Country, as 'twas first related to me by a Friend, and after confirmed by Divers Persons of Credit, I shall now give you a Relation.

This Minister had lent a young Baker a Doller to buy a little Meal, to make Cakes against the Holy-days, out of which he brought him a pretty big one for a Thank offering, and having within a Fortnight sold off his Batch, restores him presently his Money with Thanks, not imagining an expectation of any further Interest for so short a Loan; but this it seems satisfied not, the Minister in high Rage pronounced against him God's Anger and terrible Curse, which so terrified the young Baker, that he fell into deep perplexity and despair of his Salvation, in that he had inraged the Minister, and had such a Curse or Anathema from him, so that for several days he went up and down Sighing in great Perplexity, nor would say what hurt him: till at last upon the Desire of his Wife, her Uncle *Jacob Behmen* discoursed him so Friendly, that he confessed what it was that lay so heavy upon him, who understanding the Cause of his Distemper, spake comfortably to him, and repair'd to the enraged Preacher, and offer'd to him with all Submission, that if the Young Man through Ignorance had in any thing offended him, he should have the utmost Satisfaction he desired, and upon these terms intreats his favour to the perplexed Soul.

But the Minister turning his Choler upon the Intercessor, demands angrily, What he had to do to trouble him? bids him get him gone about his own Business, or he would send him away with a Vengeance. So seeing no hopes to appease him, he bid God keep his Worship, and departed; but ere he was got out of the Door, the Preacher was yet more enraged at his mild Salute, throws his Slipper at him, calling him Wicked Raskal, and disdaining a Good Night from his Mouth; the Humble Man nothing moved, takes up his Slipper and lays it again at his Feet, intreats him not to be Angry, that he knew not in what he had wronged him, Prays God to have him in his keeping, and so parts.

The Superintendant's Choler ceased not boyling: but the next Sunday he rails bitterly in the Pulpit against *Jacob Behmen* even by Name, thundring against the Senate for tolerating such a pernicious Heretick and sworn Enemy of the Ministerial Function, who not content to write Blasphemous Books, and pervert Souls, durst

Extracts of the Life of Jacob Behmen.

durst presume to come and disturb him in his own House, that if they longer suffered and did not expel him their Territories, they would move God in his Wrath, to sink their City, as he did those withstanders of *Moses* and *Aaron*, the rebellious *Corah*, *Dathan* and *Abiram* with their Complices.

The innocent Man was present, and with much Patience heard himself most bitterly railed at and reviled, and afterward stayed in the Church till the People were departed, and as the Superintendant was going forth, he followed him, and expressed his Grief to hear himself so publickly, and as he thought causelesly defamed, and requested that rather than proceed in that way of publick reproach, he would, before his Chaplain that then was with him, let him know his Offence, and it should be amended. The Minister would at first give no Answer to his Suit, at length upon much importunity, turning to him with a stern Visage, cries, *Get thee behind me Sathan, Avant thou turbulent, unquiet Spirit to thy Abyss of Hell; Doest thou still persist without all respect to my Function to Molest and Disgrace me?* to which surly repulse, the true-spirited Christian gave this Modest Reply.

Yea, Reverend Sir, I know well, and much honour your Function, I desire not to lay any Aspersion upon it or your Self, only intreat you (for your own and your Functions honour, which engages you not to trample upon a Submissive Offender, much less innocent) to tell me candidly where my Fault lyes: And further, turning to the Chaplain, said, *Courteous Sir, I pray be pleased to intercede for me with our Minister, that he would, laying aside this violent Passion, tell me ingenuously wherein I have offended him, that I may, by the best Satisfaction I can, appease his Wrath; that he may cease incensing the Magistrates against me*: But no Submission would allay his Rage, but in heat he sends his Servant for the Town Serjeant to lay hold of him, and carry him away to Prison; but his Chaplain modestly excusing the poor Man, dissuaded him from it, and bid him go home to his House.

The next Morning the Magistrates meeting in the Council-House, cite *Jacob Behmen* to appear before them, they Examined him as to his Life and Conversation, in which they could not find any thing blameable; They asked him what Injury he had offered the Minister, that made him with such vehemency to exclaim against him, but he constantly affirmed that he was utterly ignorant of any Just cause of Offence he had given him, and humbly prayed the Complainant might be sent for to declare the Grounds of his Accusation; they esteeming this a Just Motion, sent two Men of Quality of the Town to him, to desire him either to come and personally make known his Grievances to the Court, or at least inform them of the Matter by those they had sent to him for that purpose; But he again falling into Passion at this Demand, said, he had nothing to do with the Council-House, what he had to say, he would speak from the Pulpit, and what he did there dictate, they must obey without Contradiction; and without more ado disable this wicked Heretick from further opposing the Ministerial Function, by Banishing him their City, else the Curse of *Corah*, *Dathan* and *Abiram*, would light upon them all.

With this the poor Senate, a little terrified, fearing the Preacher's Anger, and his Power in the Duke of *Saxony's* Court, fall to fresh Consultations, and concluded to Banish their innocent Fellow-Citizen out of the City, but several of the Council would not consent thereto, but rose and went their way: The Sentence of Banishment was to be executed presently, and the City Officers ordered to perform it.

It being so ordered, he humbly craved he might go home to his House and settle his small Affairs there, and take his Family with him, or at least take leave of them, but it could not be admitted, he must according to the Sentence immediately depart; To which he answered, that seeing it would be no better, he with all willing Submission obeyed their Decree, and forthwith departed the Town.

Extracts of the Life of Jacob Behmen.

But the Council meeting again the next Morning, and reconciling their Difference, repeal'd their Sentence and send to seek out their innocent Exile, and at length found him, and brought him back with Honour into the City; yet still tir'd with the Preachers inceffant Clamours, they at length send for him again, and intreat him, that in love to the Cities quiet, he would seek himself a Habitation elsewhere; which if he would please to do, they should hold themselves oblig'd to him for it, as an acceptable Service. In compliance with this Friendly Request of theirs, he removed to *Dresden*.

I have observed, that if any Member of the Church, should have a Doctrine, or Exhortation, made known to him, or have his Mind furnished with other Notions than what he learned from his Pastor, it is Felony in Divinity, and if they cannot find an old Heretick in their black Calendar, that will challenge the Opinions, an Indictment that they are *Ignoti cujusdam*, will by them be esteemed good in Law, whereon to bring him to Trial and Judgment.

What a Presumption is it, to believe that the Wisdom and fulness of God can ever be pent up in a Synodical Canon? How over-weening are we to limit the successive Manifestations, to a present Rule, and Light, persecuting all that comes not forth in its length and breadth?

It would be exceeding unnatural, for a Parent to desire the perpetual Infancy of his Child. And yet how frequent is it, that if any get the start of their Brethren in growing up towards the stature of a Perfect Man in Christ, they become the Objects of Hatred, Calumny and Persecution.

Concerning the Proceedings at *Dresden*, we have the Relation thereof from Persons worthy of belief, and without exception.

Jacob Behmen was cited to appear before his Highness the Prince Elector of *Saxony*, where were Assembled Six Doctors of Divinity (besides Mathematicians) as Dr. *Hoben*, Dr. *Mey'ner*, Dr. *Baldwin*, Dr. *Gerhard*, Dr. *Leysern*, and these (in the presence of his Highness the Prince Elector) examined him concerning his Writings, and the high Mysteries therein, as also of many profound Queries in Divinity, Philosophy, and the Mathematicks, they propounded unto him; to all which he answered and replied, with such meekness of Spirit, such depth of Knowledge, and fulness of Matter, that none of these Doctors and Professors returned one word of dislike or contradiction.

The Prince his Highness much admired him, and required to know the result of their Judgments, in what they had heard, but the Doctors desired to be excused, and intreated his Highness that he would have Patience, till the Spirit of the Man should be more plainly cleared to them; for in many particulars they did not understand him; nevertheless they hoped that hereafter he would make it more clear unto them, and then they would tender their Judgments, but as yet they could not.

Then *Jacob Behmen* propounded some Questions to them, to which they returned Answers with much Modesty; and as it were amazed that they should (so much beyond their Expectation) hear from a Man of that mean Quality and Education such Mysterious Depths as were beyond the Fathom of their Comprehension.

Then he conferred with them touching most of the Errors of those times; pointing as it were with the Finger, at the Originals of them severally; declaring unto them the naked Truth, and the great difference betwixt it, and some erroneous Supposals.

To

Extracts of the Life of Jacob Behmen.

To the Astrologers also (for there were two present) having discours'd something of their Science, he said, *Thus far is the knowledge of your Art right and good, grounded in the Mystery of Nature, but what is over and above* (instancing in several particulars) *are Heathenish Additions, through their Ignorance and Blindness, which we ought not to follow or imitate.*

Then his Highness the Prince Elector, being very much satisfied in his Answers, took him apart from the Company, and discoursed with him a good space concerning several Points of Difficulty, wherein being well satisfied, he admitted him into his favour, and courteously dismissed him his Attendance at that time.

After this, Dr. *Meisner* and Dr. *Gerhard* meeting at *Wittenberg*, began to discourse of *Jacob Behmen*, expressing how greatly they admired at the continued Harmony of Scriptures produced by him at his Examination, and that they would not for all the World have served his Enemies Malice in censuring him, for says Dr. *Meisner*, Who knows but God may have designed him for some extraordinary Work, and how can we with Justice pass Judgment against that we understand not, for surely he seems to be a Man of wonderful high Gifts of the Spirit, though we cannot at present from any certain ground, approve or disapprove many things he holds forth?

After this, it pleased God the Hearts of many Learned Men and Preachers were turned to a Studying, themselves, and teaching of others those Doctrines of the Regeneration, and the means of attaining it, they had formerly in a blind Zeal exclaimed against as Heretical, whereupon they ceased from Preaching up Disputes and Controversies in Religion, many of those being no ways determinable, but by a beam of Divine Light arising out of the Principle of the New Birth, which though it clears up that Man's Judgment that is possessed with it, yet can it not always make its way to the dispelling those Clouds of Ignorance that remain upon the Souls of others, whence they Judged all Contests about those Difficulties (being most Pregnant Mothers of Pride, and Contention) as baneful to Divine Charity, and the Common Peace of Mankind.

But for resolution of all Doubts, referr'd Men to an earnest Endeavour after the recovery of the Life of Christ, the only Fountain of all true Light and right Understanding in Divine things.

Thus was that excellent Light, shining in this heavenly Man's Soul, by the cross Design of an Adversary, lifted up into its Candlestick, and brought upon a Publick Stage to give Light to Many; for by these Questionings, the Man's worth came to be taken notice of, and his Writings sought after, and studied not only by mean People, but many Great and Worthy Men, and some who in their Hearts were Infidels to all Religion, in catching only at the Bait of his mysterious Philosophy, were drawn into the true Faith of God, and Universal Charity.

His Superscription, and Motto in most of his Epistles, were these Ten words; *Our Salvation in the Life of Jesu Christ in us.*

In his Seal, he had Engraven a Hand out-stretch'd from Heaven, with a Twig of Three blown Lillies.

It is a Custom in *Germany*, and I have seen some *Germans* (whom the War had compell'd for Relief to come into *England*) to carry a little Paper Book in their Pockets, into which their Friends do write some remarkable Sentence, and Subscribe their Names, and this Book is called *Album Amicorum*; into such as these our Author wrote these following Verses:

Extracts of the Life of Jacob Behmen.

Text. **Meine Zeit ist wie Ewigkeit,
Und Ewigkeit wie die Zeit,
Der ist befreyt vom allem Streit.**

Englished,

*Unto that Man whose time and ever
Is all the same and all together:
His Battel's done, his Strife is ended,
His Soul is safe, his Life's amended.*

Or,

*To him who wisely doth not sever
This fleeting Time, and State for ever.
And to this Maxim frames his Life,
Is freed from anxious Care and Strife.*

On Sunday, November 18. 1624. early in the Morning he called his Son, and asked him, If he heard the Excellent Musick? he replied, *No: Open,* saith he, *the Door, that it may be the better heard*; afterward he asked, *What the Clock had struck,* and was told, it had struck two; He said, *It is not yet my time, three Hours hence is my time;* In the mean while he spake these words.

O thou strong God of Hosts, deliver me according to thy Will. O thou Crucified Lord Jesus, Have mercy upon me, and receive me into thy Kingdom.

When it was near about Six, he took leave of his Wife and Son, Blessed them, and said, *Now I go hence into Paradise*; and bidding his Son turn him, he fetch'd a deep Sigh and Departed.

Thus have you had a short Account of the Journey of this Blessed Man on Earth, with his last Farewel. And it is well worthy of Remark, that although he was indued with such rare and singular Gifts, he sought not to make himself the Head of some Church, and separate a People into some peculiarity of outward Form, and Discipline: But sought earnestly, to promote in himself and others that Universal Love, Uprightness and Serviceableness we owe to the whole Creation.

The Seven Spirits of God, or Powers, or Forms, in Nature.

    1   2   3   4   5   *The Seven*
Binding, Attraction, Anguish, Fire, Light,   *Fountain Spi-*
  6   7   *rits.*
Sound, Body, are the Seven Spirits Might.

        OF the Ten Forms of Fire know the Skill,   *The Ten Forms*
1.   The *Liberty* both hath and is the Will.   *of Fire.*
2, 3. Next's *Strong Desire*. Third's, sharp *Drawing Might*
4. Makes An opposing Will. Fourth, *flash of Light*
5. Brings *Anguish*. And in the Fifth Form doth Lye
    Tn' *Eternal Nature* or *Great Mystery*.
6. Sixth, The two Principles of *Fire* and *Light*.
7. The Seventh *Magia* with reflecting Sight.
8. The Eighth the *Turba* Ends the outward Life.
9. Ninth *Virgin Tincture* Pacifying Strife.
10. The Tenth, makes holy *Flesh* and holy *Earth*,
    Of *Angels*, and Blest Souls, the holy Birth.

        1   2   3
Figur'd by *Sem*, *Arphaxad*, *Selah*, and
    4   5   6
Eber, *Peleg*, *Regu*, next whom do stand
    7   8   9
Serug, *Nahor*, with *Terah*, and the Blest
   10
Abram, whose Seed Sanctifies all the Rest.

    THREE, and but three Principles Comprehend,   *The Three*
        Eternal Things, and those that have an End.   *Principles.*
1. The *First*, such Darkness as doth Light Desire,
    Which till it Gain, is a fierce Anguish Fire.
2. The *Second*, A Meek, Yielding, Loving Light;
    Majestick, Potent, Sacred, Sweet, and Bright.
3. The *Third*, Resulting as from Fire and Light,
    Brings Good from Evil, Day from Pitchy Night;
    Impregnates fully with Redundant Bliss
    Each Great, or Little thing that Blessed is:
    Did in Six Days the whole Creation hatch,
    Still Swaddles, Feeds and over it doth watch.

ERRATA.

PAge 30. Line 47. *wants a Comma at Creature*, p. 77. l. 4. *place the Parenthesis at Bodies*, p. 79. Penult. for *eachs* read *each*, p. 102. l. 2. for *It is* r. *Is it*, p. 181. l. 38. for *Rod* r. *Root*, p. 277. l. 10. *place the Parenthesis at through*, p. 322. Q. 19. for *who* r. *how*, p. 396. for *Enkinded* r. *Enkindled*.

The

The General Heads of the following Treatise.

                                                              Page

Considerations by way of Inquiry and Search into the Subject Matter and Scope of the Writings of the Divinely Instructed Jacob Behmen.   1

The 177 Theosophick Questions of Jacob Behmen Answered, shewing their Scope and Design.   41

Meditations and Contemplations on some of the preceding Questions and Answers.   219

Extracts of the Works of Jacob Behmen, beginning with his Book called Aurora.   241

The Three Principles of the Divine Essence.   260

The Threefold Life in Man.   288

The Forty Questions of the Soul.   315

The Incarnation of Jesus Christ.   320

The Six Great Points.   337

And Six Smaller Points.   345

A Brief Summary of the Earthy and Heavenly Mysteries Contracted and Comprized in Nine Texts.   347

Of the Divine Vision or Contemplation.   349

A Brief Explanation of the Knowledge of God, and of all things, also of the True and False Light.   354

Signatura Rerum.   356

Gods Election of Grace, call'd Predestination.   369

Baptism and the Lords Supper.   375

Mysterium Magnum.   379

Extracts of the Life of Jacob Behmen.   425

A Brief TABLE.

A.
Of the Abyss of all things. Page 42
Of Abraham and his Seed, and of the Line of the Covenant. 395
How Abraham's Travails figureth Christianity. 400
Of Abraham's rescuing Lot. 396
Of the Covenant made betwixt Abraham and Abimelech. 401
Of Abraham's Offering up Isaac; Sarah's Death, and the rest of the History of Abraham, what it all points at. 402 to 404
Of Abraham's Bosom what it is. 324
Of Adam's Eyes being opened. 102
Of Adam and Eves Shame. 103
Of Adam and Eves Death. 104
Out of what the Angels were made. 44. 59
Of the Work of the Angels. 44. 244
Of their Dominions, Thrones and Principalities. 57. 221. 246. 294
Of Antichrist, what it is. 178. 306
Of the Antichristian Church. 279
Of the Archeus, Separator, or Workman. 73. 233. 263

B.
Abel, what it is. 180. 394
Of Baptism. 132. 373. 358.
The Beast in the Apocalypse, what it is. 180. 395
What the Ruin of the Beast is. 182
Of God's Blessing in this World. 312

Of the Water and Blood, what they are. Page 168. 172
Of the Flesh and Blood of Christ really enjoyed, what it is. 168. 172
Of the Bread and Wine in the Sacrament. 168. 173

C.
Of Cain's Murthering his Brother Abel. 109. 390
Of Cain's Despair of Grace. 111
Whether Cain was Damned in respect of his Sin. 111
Of the Mark set on Cain what it was. 112
Of the Kingdom of Cain. 279
Of the Chaos whence it proceeded. 62. 63
Of the Cherub with the naked Sword before Paradise, what it was. 107
Of Childrens Baptism. 281. 308
Of Christ, what he is. 31. 32. 105
Of his Incarnation. 32. 275. 329
Of his heavenly Humanity, and how participated of by us 35. 105. 306.
Of the Uniting the Deity and Humanity in his becoming Man. 129
Why he conversed 30 Years on Earth, before he entred on his Office. 131
How it is that he increased in favour with God and Man. 131
Why he was Baptiz'd of John. 132
Why he was Tempted 40 Days. 133

How

A Brief TABLE.

How he was in Heaven, and also on Earth. 134
Why he Taught in Parables. 134
Why he did not describe his Gospel in Writing. 135
Why the High Priest and Scripture-Learned persecuted him. 135. 139
His Process through his Suffering, and why it was so. 136. 142. 283. 330. 332.
Why must he Die on a wooden Cross. 140
Of the two Murtherers Crucified with Christ, what they figure. 140. 283
Why must his Side be opened with a Spear. 141
Why did the Earth tremble when he hung on the Cross. 142
What did the darkness signifie that came over all Nature. 143
Of Christs Dying, Descending, &c. from 143. to 158. and 283
Of the true Christian. 170 176. 297
Of the Titulary Christian. 171. 176 297. 310.
Of the True Christian Church. 279
Circumcision what it signifies. 116. 376. 398
Conversion what it is. 324
{ Contrariety whence it sprung. 340
{ What use it is of. 349 357
Of the Covenant with Noah. 391
Of the Covenant with Abraham. 116. 397
Of the Line of the Covenant. 391
{ Of the Mortal Creatures, from whence they sprung and Exist. 64. 72. 233. 242
Of their Differences. 73. 235

The End why they were Created. 74. 235
Of the Creation. 19. 234. 252. 303. 371. 381.
What was before the Creation. 43
Of the inward and outward Cure. 363
{ Of Gods Curse what it is. 275
{ The Cause thereof. 388

D.

OF the two Principles of Darkness and Light. 1
Of the Temporal Darkness, whence it is, 65. 227
How the Devil came to be, and what he is. 45
Of Death and Dying. 191. 192. 277. 313. 321. 358.
Of the Divine Nature. 260
Of the Divine Being in Nature. 241. 380
The Divine Being and Nature distinguished. 337. 341
Dinah deflowered, what it figureth. 412

E.

WHat the Earth was before the Curse. 87. 106
What the Earth is since the Curse. 106
Of the Constitution and Form of the Earth. 253
Egypt. The bringing the Children of Israel out thence, what figure it bears. 121
Of Election and Reprobation, what they are. 345
What the four Elements are, and whence proceeded. 62. 224. 263.
Of Enoch's Wonderful Line. 391
Of the Enochian Life what it is, and

A Brief TABLE.

Page.

and where hath Enoch *remained.* 113. 326
The History of Esau, *what it figureth.* 405 to 413
⎰ *Of the Eternal Nature or Originality.* 286
⎱ *Of the infinite Productions thereof.* 261
⎰ *Of the Knowledge of the Eternal through the Corruptible.* 272
Of Evil, fierceness and anger, whence they proceeded. 2.223.247.334 380.

F.

TRue *Faith what it is.* 332
Of the Fathers Property. 243
Of the Firmament in the midst of the Waters. 66. 228 254
Of the Flesh and Blood of Christ, how the Disciples did Eat and Drink it. 377
Of the Flesh and Spirit, the contrariety betwixt them. 321
Of the forbidden Fruit, what it was. 99
Of the Forms of Nature. 292
How God Forgiveth Sins. 336

G.

IN *what Grace the old World was Saved without Law.* 110
Of God distinct from Nature and Creature. 42.369.379
Of Gods Love and Anger. 42
Of Gods being All in All. 201
Of Gods working in Hell. 54.55.220
Of the Word or Heart of God. 379
Of Gods Voice when the day grew cool. 104
Of Good and Evil, whence they proceeded. 334.366.380.

H.

Page.

OF *the Human Tree.* 390.393
Of the Hand of God, what it is that Christ commended his Soul into. 144
Of Heaven, what it is, where it is, and how. 56.158.213.221.252
Of Hell, its beginning, continuance, and place. 47.51.55.213.219. 220.263.
Of the Heathenish Gods, whence they sprung. 396
Of Hagar *and* Ishmael, *what their History figureth.* 397 to 400
Of the shedding forth the Holy Ghost after Christs Ascension, what it benefits us. 163

J.

⎰ **T**HE *History of* Jacob *and* Esau, *what it figureth.* 405
⎱ *The Vision of* Jacob's *Ladder.* 407
⎰ *The rest of the History of* Jacob. to 423
Of Jehovah. 19
The Image of God in Man, what it is. 78. 238. 245. 273. 316
The History of Joseph *what it figureth, from* 413 to 423.
Concerning John Baptist *what he was.* 125
Of Isaac's *Birth and casting out* Ishmael *what it figureth* 400.405.
Of Judah *and* Thamar. 414
Of the last Judgment, what it is, and how effected. 195. 285

K.

THE *Kingdom of Christ how it is assumed or taken by him.* 183
How Christ will deliver the Kingdom to the Father. 346

Kkk L.

A Brief TABLE.

L.
              Page
Concerning Lamech, Cain's
  Succeſſor.   112
Of the Language of Nature,
                      295. 395
Of the Language ſpoke by the Apo-
  ſtles at Pentecoſt.   162
What the Law is.   122
How the Divine Life may be ma-
  nifeſted in this Life.   350
Of the Life of Darkneſs what it is.
                            343
Of the Principles of Light and
  Darkneſs.   1
Of the true and falſe Light. 354
Of the Temporal Light and Dark-
  neſs.   65. 227
{ Lot's Wife becoming a Pillar of
    Salt, what it figureth. 118
  Of his departure out of Sodom.
                            399
  Of his Daughters Lying with
    him.   118
  What each ſignifies.
Luſt, what it can do.   335
{ Lucifer what moved him to de-
    part from God.   44, 45
  Of his doleful Fall. 250. 359
  Of his Office in Hell. 47. 219
  Of his place at preſent. 257

M.
OF Mans Eſtate before the
  Fall. 21.82 84.85.86.274
By what Degrees Man fell.   26.
274. 359. 372. 385
What Mans Eſtate is by the Fall.
  28. 83. 274. 290. 335. 342.
  373. 388
Of Mans Recovery. 30. 38.
  39. 40. 170

              Page
Mans miſtaken way towards a
  ſuppoſed Happineſs.   37
Of Mans Immortal Life.   77.
  81. 237
Of Mans Mortal Life.   77.
  81. 237. 255.
The Difference of the Heavenly
  and Earthy Man.   382
Mans Body whence derived. 75.
  237. 255. 264.
Of Mans Birth and Propagation.
                            271
Why but one Man Created in the
  Beginning.   81
Of the Government of Man over
  the Creatures.   92
Why the firſt Man born of a Wo-
  man was a Murtherer.   106
How Man may find himſelf and
  all Myſteries.   303. 342
Of Mans deep Ground and Know-
  ledge.   46. 299. 304. 343.
  358. 372.
Of Mans Threefold Life. 288. 301
Of the Male and Female kind
  whence proceeded.   67. 229.
Magia, what it is and doth. 346
Of Natural Magick what it is. 417
Concerning the Metals.   358
Of the Mind.   273
Of the ſtrife between Michael and
  the Dragon, what it is.   45
{ Moſes, what doth his being
    drawn out of the River ſigni-
    fie.   119
  Why the Lord appeared to him in
    a Flaming Buſh.   119
  From what power he did his
    Works of Wonder.   120
  Why muſt he remain forty days
    on the Mount.   122

                            The

A Brief TABLE

The Great Mystery what it is. 346. 357.

N.

How the outward Nature representeth the Divine. 351
Why must there be a strife in Nature. 223. 357
What doth Noah's Flood figure. 115
What doth his being Drunk figure. 115

O.

The Office of a Shepherd or Pastor in the Spirit of Christ what it is. 165
The Office of the Keys. 167
Of a Teacher of the Letter without the Spirit of Christ. 166

P.

Paradise, what it is, and where. 79. 264. 295. 327. 328. 383. 384.
Of Pentecost, or the shedding forth of the Holy Ghost. 159. 160. 161. 284.
Pharaoh's Dream what it figured. 416
Of true Prayer what it is. 311
Of Predestination. 369. 397
Of the Three Principles of the Divine Essence. 11. to 18. 260. 262. 338.
Why the High-Priest, &c. persecuted Christ. 135. 139. 145.
Of the Prophets and Prophesying. 123
Of a Virgin Propagation. 24. 88

Q.

Of the Qualities Good and Bad what they are. 241

R.

Reason what it is, and whence proceeded. 349
Regeneration what it is, and how effected. 186. 277. 286
Of true Repentance. 282
Reprobation what it is. 345
Resurrection of the Dead how effected. 198. 325

S.

Of the Sabbath. 234
Of the Saviour. 387
Of Cain and Abel's Sacrifices. 108. 389
Why did Cain Murther his Brother for the Sacrifice sake. 109
Of the Sacrifices under the Law. 123
Of the Seed of the Woman, and of its treading upon the Serpent. 104. 275
Of Seed or Sperm what it is, its various kinds, growth and increase. 69. 70. 71. 230. 231
The Serpent on the Tree of Knowledge, &c. what it was. 98
The beginning of Sickness and Mortality. 386
Sin, what it is, and whence proceeded. 99. 100. 101. 102. 320. 345. 386.
What was the Sin of the Old World. 113
Signature, what it is. 356
Of the Eternal Signature. 367
How the Internal doth impress the External. 361
Of Sodom and Gomorrah their destruction, and what it figures. 117. 399
The Soul of Man, whence existed. 315

Its

A Brief TABLE

	Page		Page

Its Essence. 316
Its Imbreathing. 76. 264. 310
Its Form and power. 317. 318
Its Union with the Body. 318. 320
Its Inlightning and Food. 320
Its Life and Actions till the last Judgment. 194. 322. 323. 324
Of the Eternal State of the Good and Bad. 210. 214. 277. 325. 326. 334
Of the Soul and Spirit of Christ. 326
A description of the seven Fountain Spirits. 3. to 11. 247. 249. 370
Of the Spirit of this World, its Principles and Office. 68. 230. 286. 352. 357. 360.
Of the Stars from whence proceeded. 257. 358
Their Use and Benefit. 63. 225. 257. 298.
Their various Properties. 258
Of the Noble Spiritual Stone of the Philosophers. 298. 303. 321
Of the Lords Supper. 376

T.

OF Adam's Temptation, what it was. 266. 267
The Testaments of Christs, what they are. 168. 281. 307
How enjoyed. 170. 281
Of the outward Institution. 172
Of the Disputes about them. 378
What the wicked partake of by unworthy Receiving. 377
Of the Tincture what it is, and its manifold degrees. 72. 232. 268. 273. 341. 345. 352.
Of the Tree of Life. 90
Of the Tree of Knowledge of Good and Evil. 90. 91. 99.
Why forbidden to Man. 92

What the Trees in Paradise were. 89.
The Turba, what it is. 348

V.

HOW Vegetation is caused. 255. 359
Of the Divine Virgin the Wisdom of God. 88. 89. 294
Of the Virgin Mary. 126. 130
Why she must be Espoused to Joseph. 127
Of the Understanding. 273

W.

WArs, whence they arise. 348. 396.
Of the Water above the Firmament. 66
And of the Water beneath the Firmament. 228
Of the Will of God flowing out. 353. 369
The Whore in the Apocalypse, what she is. 180
Of the Will of Man. 353. 367
Of the Creating of the Woman. 269. 384
Of the Literal and Living Word. 164.
Out of what this visible World is Created, and what it is. 60. 222. 296.
To what end it was Created. 336
Whence proceeded the Evil or Contrariety in the Essence of this World. 61
How must it pass away, and what shall remain thereof. 199
Of the Wrath of God, what it is, why poured forth, and its duration. 52. 53. 220.

FINIS.

www.ingramcontent.com/pod-product-compliance
Lightning Source LLC
Chambersburg PA
CBHW032006300426
44117CB00008B/916